CROSSROADS AND BOUNDARIES

THE ANNUAL OF
THE AMERICAN SCHOOLS OF ORIENTAL RESEARCH

Volume 65

Series Editor
Joseph A. Greene

CROSSROADS AND BOUNDARIES:

THE ARCHAEOLOGY OF PAST AND PRESENT IN THE MALLOURA VALLEY, CYPRUS

edited by

Michael K. Toumazou, P. Nick Kardulias,
and Derek B. Counts

American Schools of Oriental Research • Boston, MA

ANNUAL OF THE AMERICAN SCHOOLS OF ORIENTAL RESEARCH
VOLUME 65

ISBN: 978-0-89757-086-2

Library of Congress Cataloging-in-Publication Data

Crossroads and boundaries : the archaeology of past and present in the
    Malloura Valley, Cyprus / edited by Michael K. Toumazou, P. Nick
    Kardulias, and Derek B. Counts.
       p. cm. -- (The annual of the American Schools of Oriental Research ; v 65)
    Includes bibliographical references and index.
    ISBN 978-0-89757-086-2 (alk. paper)
    1. Malloura Valley (Cyprus)--Antiquities, Roman. 2. Malloura Valley
        (Cyprus)--Antiquities, Byzantine. 3. Bamboulari tis Koukouninas Site
        (Cyprus) 4. Excavations (Archaeology)--Cyprus--Malloura Valley. I.
        Toumazou, Michael K. II. Kardulias, P. Nick. III. Counts, Derek B.
    DS54.95.M36C76 2011
    939'.37--dc23
                              2011041092

Printed in the United States of America on acid-free paper

Dedicated to all Athienites, in Cyprus and abroad, that support our work, in any way, through their friendship, generosity, and hospitality.

~

Αφιερώνεται σε όλους τους Αθηενίτες, της Κύπρου και του εξωτερικού, που άοκνα στηρίζουν το έργο μας με την φιλία, γενναιοδωρία, και φιλοξενία τους.

Contents

Illustrations

Figures

Tables

Acknowledgments

Any research endeavor that has extended over two decades as has the Athienou Archaeological Project (AAP) will have accumulated a long list of organizations and individuals that have made its efforts possible. Our project is no exception. Indeed, we have benefited enormously from a vast array of contributors, at the institutional and community levels on Cyprus and in the academic sphere in the United States and beyond. Since 1990, we have worked under permits granted by the Department of Antiquities of Cyprus and are grateful to the successive Directors Vassos Karageorghis, Athanasios Papageorgiou, Mihalis Louloupis, Demos Christou, Sophocles Hadjisavvas, Pavlos Flourentzos, and Maria Hadjicosti; personnel at the Larnaka District Museum, particularly Andreas Savva, have been most helpful in facilitating access to our material; the Cyprus Museum Conservation Department, particularly Andreas Georgiades, saw to the conservation of coins and other metal artifacts. The Cyprus American Archaeological Research Institute (Stuart Swiny, Nancy Serwint, Robert Merrillees, and Thomas Davis, Directors; Vathoula Moustoukki, Executive Assistant) provided excellent research facilities and a 'home' away from Athienou, and continues to organize, with the Department of Antiquities, annual workshops where the results of our investigations are presented to the broader public.

A number of organizations have provided funds to subsidize our work over the past 20 years. Davidson College, AAP's sponsor, was the main source of funding. In addition to Davidson, Kenyon College, The Ohio State University, the University of Wisconsin-Milwaukee, and the College of Wooster made travel and research support of senior staff possible through various internal grant programs. We are particularly thankful to Davidson's Grants and Contracts office for its assistance in fundraising.

Support staff at Davidson College and at the other institutions have helped make sure that the project runs smoothly; Diane Stirling (Davidson College) has done yeoman's work in this respect for the last two decades since the project's inception. A grant from the Dumbarton Oaks Foundation supported the 1991 field season. Since 1995, we have received generous support from the National Science Foundation – Research Experience for Undergraduates Sites program that, altogether, supported nine field seasons (SBR-942165 [1995]; SBR-9619760 [1997]; SBR 9732407 [1998]; SES-9820549 [1999–2002]; SES-0354003 [2004–2007]). Donations from private individuals were especially important in the early years of the project. Various expatriate natives of Athienou in the United States and Australia were instrumental in funding the initial phases of the field investigations. In particular, we wish to thank Nikos Mouyiaris; without his generous contribution the project would not even have started. Special thanks are also due to Duffy and Lalita Cofer for their generous support of the project.

From the outset, we have been the beneficiaries of extraordinary support from the people of Athienou. We wish to thank the Athienou municipal councils and mayors (Kostas Sakkalos, Panayiotis Koumi, Gavriel Kazazis, and Spyros Papouis) who provided housing and laboratory space, vehicles and fuel, as well countless other logistical accommodations and favors. We are most grateful to the successive presidents and board members of the Athienou Cooperative [Bank] (Vasos Papaioannou and Marios Karakokkinos, general managers) for facilitating financial transactions, paying for weekend field trips and other needs, and providing subvention funds to aid the publication of this book. We also wish to thank the successive presidents and members of the Athienou school councils for kindly providing educational facilities and equipment for our field school lectures. Our financial burdens have been greatly lessened thanks to generous assistance from the Athienou Cattle-owners Association, Zorbas Bakeries (Andreas Zorbas, owner), and the Hadjiyannakou Brothers Farm (Loukas Hadjiyannakou, owner) for unlimited supplies of halloumi cheese, bread, and eggs, respectively. We are greatly indebted to Dr. Niki Hari for free medical care to scores of AAP staff and students, Kostas and Ellada Lambaski for free use of their Athienou home as AAP headquarters ('the Palace'), and Euthymios Georgiou for provision of scaffolding for site photography. In addition, many individuals have opened their homes to us and also offered sage advice and aid in innumerable ways; among these friends of the project are Kostas and Maria Hadjiyannakou, Kostas and Georgia Sakkalos, Christos and Evangelia Hadjiyannakou, and Lenia and Savvas Koursaris. We would be remiss if we did not acknowledge Giorgos Koursaris for leading Toumazou to Malloura for the first time, as well as mayor Kostas Sakkalos and Christos Hadjiyannakou for persuading him that such an undertaking was 'imperative'! And what *would* AAP do without the resourcefulness and boundless assistance of Nikolaos Kantzilaris (aka MacGyver) and Eleni Kalapoda? The exceptional level of support, hospitality, and good cheer that the people of Athienou have offered us in the past 20 years has enriched both our research and our personal lives and we stand deeply indebted to all. This book is dedicated to them.

In the preparation of the manuscript we have received advice and assistance from several quarters. Joseph Greene, series editor, has ably guided our efforts and two anonymous reviewers provided both practical and insightful comments that have improved the volume; the individual contributors are responsible for any errors that may remain. We thank Susanne Wilhelm for her expertise, professionalism, and patience in the final preparation of the manuscript. We are also grateful for permission from colleagues and various institutions to reproduce certain images: Musée du Louvre (fig. 4.1), Gilles Grivaud and Francesca C. Romanelli (fig. 5.1), Bank of Cyprus Cultural Foundation (fig. 5.2), Metropolitan Museum of Art (figs. 10.1 and 11.4), Cyprus Museum (figs. 12.4, 12.12, and 12.14), University of Cambridge (fig. 12.3), Bildarchiv Preussischer Kulturbesitz (fig. 12.5), and Marfin Popular Bank Cultural Foundation (fig. 26.2). Finally, we thank Katie Iselin for assistance in proofreading the manuscript and preparing keywords for the index, Stephanie Bosch for proofreading and preparation of correction files, Billie Jean Collins (Lockwood Press) for preparation of the final index, Julia Gaviria for copyediting the text, and the following people for preparing specialized maps for individual chapters: Jim Johnson (fig. 24.3), David Massey (map 1, map 2, figs. 7.2–7.4, and figs. 22.1–22.6), Adam Prins (figs. 6.1, 7.4, and 26.1), and Ioannis Panayides and Zomenia Zomeni of the Geological Survey Department (Republic of Cyprus) (figs. 2.1 and 2.3).

Last, but certainly not least, we wish to express our gratitude to the hundreds of students (Americans, mostly, and Cypriots) and many colleagues (Americans, Cypriots, Greeks, French, Dutch, Canadian, Italian, and Swiss) who have participated in the field work and undertook analytical studies since the beginning of the project. Their efforts are reflected in the pages that follow. While it is not possible in this space to name all of the individuals who have been part of AAP (although we do maintain a list of annual staff on our webpage), we wish to recognize the 1990 field crew of Erin Casey, Derek Counts, Alec Macalister, Joseph Parvis, Walter Payne, and Diane Stirling, under the direction of Michael K. Toumazou. We also wish to thank Richard Yerkes, AAP Associate Director 1991–1997, for his continued contribution to the project.

Introduction

Michael K. Toumazou, P. Nick Kardulias, and Derek B. Counts

As the mythical birthplace of Aphrodite, the main source of copper in the ancient eastern Mediterranean, the home of Zeno, who founded the Stoic school of philosophy, the location of Saint Paul's first mission, the setting for Shakespeare's *Othello*, and now a political flashpoint in the 21st century, Cyprus has played an important role at the interface between Europe, Asia, and Africa. Cyprus is the third largest island in the Mediterranean, with a diverse landscape that people have inhabited for more than 10,000 years. Over that great span of time, the residents have demonstrated tremendous resilience to the many environmental and cultural changes that have characterized the region. They have exploited the island's rich resource base (including major copper sources, fertile land, and mild climate) and its strategic location at the crossroads of the Mediterranean, with easy access to Anatolia (Turkey) to the north, the Levant to the east, Egypt to the south, and the Aegean to the west. As a way station and bridge between three continents, Cyprus actively participated in the age of internationalism of the 14th and 13th centuries BC, which witnessed the expansion of trade networks from the Aegean to the east and carried a wave of Mycenaean material culture to the island. Following the collapse of the Mycenaean palatial economy at the end of the Late Bronze Age (primarily 12th century BC), the island saw the permanent establishment of its first Greek-speaking population, followed several centuries later by Phoenician colonists from Tyre. Subsequently, the island was brought within the sphere of influence of Assyrians, Egyptians, Persians, Greeks, Romans, Byzantines, Arabs, Franks, Venetians, Turks, and British. During this extended process of connecting with other societies, the Cypriots have adopted a flexible approach of selectively accepting those outside influences that suit them best and rejecting others, thus contributing to the distinct character of the island and its material culture. From antiquity to the present, the Cypriots have simultaneously balanced the benefits of being at the confluence of numerous trade routes with the need to set and maintain political, religious, and social borders.

The region of modern Athienou, the focus of our project, is situated in central-eastern Cyprus on the southern edge of the agriculturally rich Mesaoria plain. This location offers an equidistant (and fairly unimpeded) line of communication and travel to three of the island's largest modern/*ancient* urban centers (Nicosia/*Ledra*, Famagusta/*Salamis*, and Larnaka/*Kition*), as well as numerous other important settlements in the region (e.g., Dhali/*Idalion* and Politiko/*Tamassos*). The area witnessed the earliest organized archaeological work on the island, including the efforts of the infamous Luigi Palma di Cesnola (1878), a contemporary of Heinrich Schliemann and one of the 19th-century romantic antiquarians who defined the new field of classical archaeology. Cesnola, who served as a Union colonel during the Civil War and later as American, Greek, and Russian consul to Cyprus, primarily explored tombs and sanctuary sites to the north and east of Athienou — an area identified with the ancient Golgoi mentioned in classical texts (e.g., Catullus, Theokritos, Ovid, Pausanias; see Counts, Ch. 4) that inspired the search for antiquities by various investigators. Cesnola later became the first director of the Metropolitan Museum of Art in New York; his collection of statues from Golgoi formed the core of the museum's holdings. Somewhat earlier, a French mission under the leadership of Melchior de Vogüé explored several sites across the island, including Golgoi; it was the mission's architect, Edmond Duthoit, who initially explored a religious sanctuary at Malloura to the southwest of Athienou in the 1860s, from which the team retrieved scores of statues now in the Musée du Louvre in Paris. Despite the efforts of authorities on the island, the area was ignored by archaeologists for nearly 80 years. In the intervening time, looting of sites by locals was common. Prior to the Greek coup and subsequent Turkish invasion of 1974, important excavations in the late 1960s and early 1970s at Athienou were carried out by teams from Greece (Bakalakis 1988) and Israel (Dothan and Ben-Tor 1983). It is interesting to note that these two projects represent the first excavations by Greeks and Israelis outside of their respective national boundaries.

Since 1990, the Athienou Archaeological Project (AAP) has examined the Malloura Valley on the edge of the central Mesaoria plain near the modern town of Athienou. Excavation at the site of Malloura has concentrated on the late Cypro-Geometric–Roman sanctuary initially investigated by the French team under Duthoit (rediscovered by AAP in 1991) and the adjacent settlement and cemeteries. In conjunction with the excavation, locational survey has revealed the presence of other sites that range in date from the Aceramic Neolithic (ca. 8200–5500 BC) through Iron Age, Roman, late medieval, and modern periods that bear evidence of human exploitation of valley resources (Toumazou et al. 1998). From the outset, the project's research agenda has focused on how inhabitants of this rural area balanced local and external forces as expressed in economic, ritual, and political behavior (Counts 2008; Kardulias 2007). In addition, the ceramic evidence from the excavation and survey has revealed the presence of both imported and locally or regionally produced wares, reflecting the integration of domestic and political economy over time.

The work of AAP covers the full range of archaeological investigation. The central focus since 1990 has been excavation at Athienou-*Malloura*, a large site in the center of the valley. The earliest component of the site is a rural sanctuary dating to the late Cypro-Geometric through Early Roman periods (ca. eighth century BC to first century AD) that has yielded thousands of pieces of limestone and terracotta sculpture in addition to coins, lamps,

worked bone, and ceramic vessels. The majority of these objects were deposited in the sanctuary as pious acts of devotion; as such, they bear witness to a strong tradition of votive religion characteristic of sanctuaries throughout Cyprus and the Mediterranean in antiquity. The project has also excavated a series of tombs of the same time period about 300 m north of the sanctuary. Ancient residents cut the burial chambers into bedrock and interred successive generations of deceased with mortuary vases and jewelry. Finally, east of the sanctuary, excavation has uncovered the remains of a substantial village that dates from the Early Roman period to the 19th century, with a hiatus in occupation between ca. AD 700 and 1200. In addition, systematic archaeological survey has placed these results in the broader context of the region; teams walked over most of the valley in designated swaths and identified 30 sites, including flint quarries mined in the Aceramic Neolithic for material to make stone tools, Roman farmsteads, medieval lookout posts on hilltops, and hamlets abandoned in the past century.

These two primary field techniques (i.e., excavation and survey) have yielded a wealth of information that requires a range of analytical methods to examine. Many of the chapters in the volume are the preliminary reports of specialists who explore the nature of culture change in a Mediterranean context. Section I situates the investigations conducted by AAP within the broader disciplines of classical archaeology, anthropology, art history, and classics, among others. The individual chapters in this section provide the context for other contributions, lay out our research agenda, and give the environmental and historical background of the project area. Chapter 1 explores the project's primary research questions and outlines many of the guiding theoretical principles that have informed our work, including issues of urban vs. rural, boundaries and the negotiation of social identity, and comparative regional analyses. Yerkes (Ch. 2) discusses the terrain and climate of the Malloura region, with emphasis on what natural resources the area offered people in the past. In Chapter 3, Gordon, Kardulias, and Toumazou describe the historical background of the Athienou region through a discussion of broad developments in Cypriot history and their manifestations in a local context. Chapter 4 surveys previous archaeological work in the Athienou environs, beginning with the earliest activity in the second half of the 19th century until the present day. In Chapter 5, Counts and Parvis present a carto-historical sketch of regional settlement patterns focusing on the Malloura Valley and the area around Athienou between the 16th and 19th centuries AD.

Section II includes two chapters that detail the nature and extent of archaeological fieldwork conducted in the Malloura Valley, in addition to summarizing the results from that work. Toumazou and Counts (Ch. 6) present an overview of excavations to date, outlining the project's methodological approach and innovative techniques, followed by a trench-by-trench account of site occupation and use as revealed in the architecture and finds. Kardulias and Yerkes (Ch. 7) use data from the surface survey to reconstruct the occupational sequence in the Malloura Valley over time, showing how settlement has waxed and waned due to external and internal forces. Each of these chapters recounts the major results of the respective fieldwork and, most importantly, brings our results up to date. By reconstructing the physical and cultural landscape of the Malloura Valley, these chapters provide a backdrop for the subsequent specialized articles that approach a wide range of data through a variety of theoretical and methodological frameworks.

Section III presents data and preliminary results from the specialized study of various artifact assemblages found through excavation and survey. Topics include a discussion of flaked stone tools, which represent the oldest technology in the valley (Kardulias and Yerkes, Ch. 8); the use of ceramics as evidence for chronology and cult activity in the sanctuary (Fourrier, Ch. 9); the role of terracotta figurines in ritual activity (Averett, Ch. 10); the iconography and typology of sculpted images as indices of artistic connectivity and social boundaries (Counts, Ch. 11); iconography related to the Greek god Pan as witnessed in limestone sculptures from the sanctuary (Cofer, Ch. 12); the study of inscriptions and what these may indicate

in terms of linguistic affiliation and ethnicity (Cova, Ch. 13); Hellenistic and Roman lamps from the tombs (Gordon, Ch. 14); the use of pottery to reconstruct trade patterns as well as to inform us about the varied aspects of social life (Moore and Gregory, Ch. 15); consideration of the evidence for flax production in the Malloura Valley during the Venetian period (DeMasi, Ch. 16); and analysis of millstones in the context of agricultural production (Spigelman, Ch. 17).

The fourth section contains three chapters on bioarchaeological material. In Chapter 18, Reese discusses the faunal remains from Malloura, with a focus on local context and broader, islandwide trends. Harper and Tung (Ch. 19) present information on the multigenerational use of the ancient tombs to build a population profile. Harper (Ch. 20) offers an analysis of remains from a Venetian cemetery and presents the evidence for craft activity in late Medieval Malloura.

Section V foregrounds the practice of archaeology; the chapters represent a selection of the innovative methods used to enhance the interpretation and presentation of archaeological data. Sarris (Ch. 21) describes the results of geophysical prospection in the Malloura Valley, highlighting what geophysical methods reveal about subsurface features and how such techniques can help target excavation. Chapters 22 (Kardulias and Massey) and 23 (Blackwell and Johnson) employ Geographic Information Systems (GIS) to study spatial relationships; Kardulias and Massey examine the distribution of sites to understand settlement dynamics, that is, where and why people established villages, farmsteads, and ritual sites in the valley since antiquity, while Blackwell and Johnson consider artifact distributions and sacred space to chart ritual activity during the final, Hellenistic–Roman phase of the sanctuary. Beeston (Ch. 24) examines chemical traces in the soil that reflect the intensity of human activity over time and in different archaeological contexts (ritual, settlement, industrial, funerary).

The final section showcases archaeology as a link between past and present. Breuker and Breuker (Ch. 25) discuss site preservation from the perspective of assessment and conservation and detail efforts by the project to protect the remains at Malloura. Yerkes (Ch. 26) employs ethnoarchaeology to estimate the size of the ancient population in the Malloura Valley through a detailed study of an abandoned modern village and to explore an aspect of ancient agriculture by examining threshing sledge flints. Finally, in the last chapter of this section, the editors (Ch. 27) recount the mutually beneficial interaction between the modern community of Athienou and the project; conversations with colleagues who work in both the Old World and the New World have reinforced for us the unique synergy that characterizes the AAP.

The book concludes with a synthetic statement from the editors about how the individual research avenues we pursue can result in a nuanced portrayal of the past that emphasizes both what is unique to the area and how the Athienou region is an example of general patterns that persist over time. This concluding statement emphasizes again that AAP is fully interdisciplinary and benefits from the perspectives of classical archaeologists, anthropologists, ceramicists, philologists, art historians, numismatists, osteologists, chemists, geophysicists, architects, and conservators.

The present volume is a comprehensive overview of AAP to date. The chapters are designed to disseminate data while also providing preliminary results and observations related to our work. These studies do not represent the final word; in fact, their primary goal is to initiate scholarly discourse both within our own team of investigators and with our colleagues in Cyprus and around the Mediterranean. The final publication of AAP will take the form of a series of individual monographs that cover results from both excavation and survey, broadly defined by the loci themselves (sanctuary, tombs, settlement, etc.). This volume's individual studies reveal a continuous effort by residents of the valley to establish and maintain a distinct social identity through their various subsistence, religious, political, and mortuary pursuits. Collectively, they illuminate the rich mosaic of life in this region and, by implication, elsewhere in the Mediterranean. The central theme here is that culture acts as a repository of information on how to live in a certain area. Since flexibility is necessary to survive fluctuations in the environment or political regime, culture is an open-ended system that is constantly evolving; archaeology and related disciplines are the means to understand this process of social evolution. The people of central Cyprus, both past and present, have left traces of this fluid system on the surface and beneath it in the form of houses, religious structures, resting places for the dead, and the many objects they used. The contributors to this volume use a variety of techniques to record and interpret the sometimes faint but nonetheless indelible marks of human action on the Cypriot landscape.

REFERENCES

Bakalakis, G.
1988   *Ανασκαφή στο Λόφο Γιόρκους ΒΑ της Αθηαίνου, Κύπρος.* Athens: Αρχαιολογική Εταιρεία Αθηνών.

Cesnola, L. P. di
1878   *Cyprus: Its Ancient Cities, Tombs, and Temples.* New York: Harper and Bros. Reprint 1991.

Counts, D. B.
2008   Master of the Lion: Representation and Hybridity in Cypriote Sanctuaries. *American Journal of Archaeology* 112: 3–27.

Dothan, T., and Ben-Tor, A.
1983   *Excavations at Athienou, Cyprus. 1971–1972.* Jerusalem: Institute of Archaeology, Hebrew University of Jerusalem.

Kardulias, P. N.
2007   Negotiation and Incorporation on the Margins of World-Systems: Examples from Cyprus and North America. *Journal of World-Systems Research* 13(1): 55–82.

Toumazou, M. K.; Yerkes, R. W.; and Kardulias, P. N.
1998   Athienou Archaeological Project: Investigations in the Malloura Valley, Cyprus, 1990–95. *Journal of Field Archaeology* 25: 163–82.

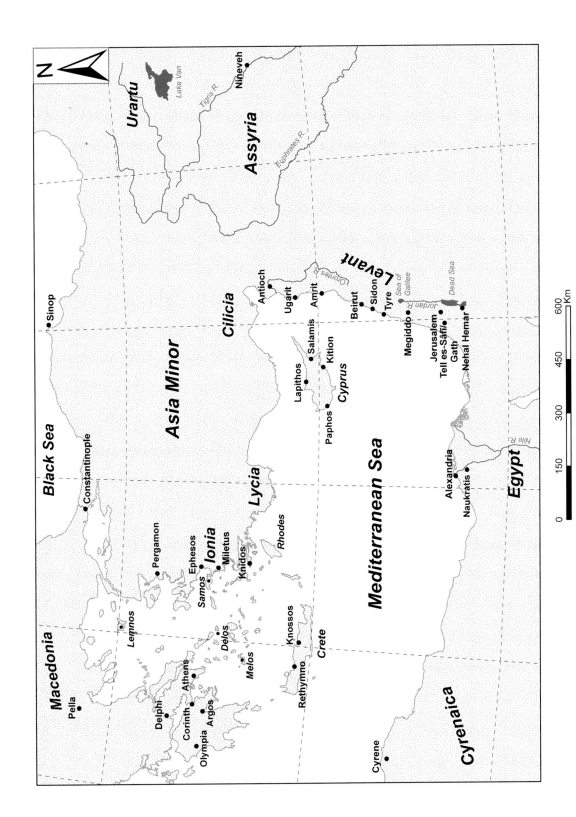

MAP 1   *The eastern Mediterranean region.*

xxi

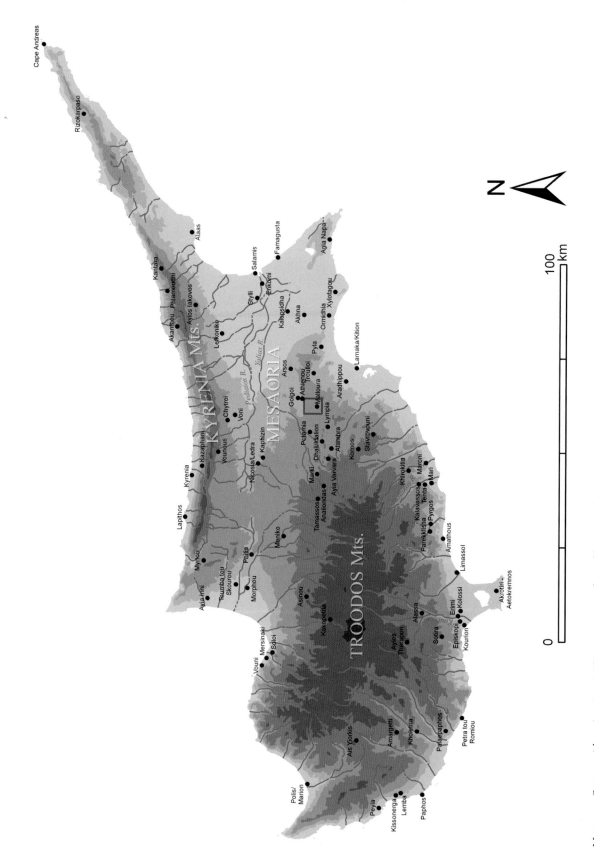

MAP 2   *Cyprus with major sites; AAP project area indicated by rectangle.*

Chronological Chart

Akrotiri Phase	/10,000–9500/ BC
Aceramic Neolithic	/9500–5800/5500 BC
Ceramic Neolithic	4900/4500–3900/3700 BC
Chalcolithic	3900/3700–2500/2300 BC
Early Cypriote (EC) I–III	2500/2300–1950 BC
Middle Cypriote (MC) I–III	1950–1650 BC
Late Cypriote (LC) I–III	1650–1050 BC
Cypro-Geometric	1050–750 BC
CG I	1050–950 BC
CG II	950–900 BC
CG III	900–750 BC
Cypro-Archaic	750–480 BC
CA I	750–600 BC
CA II	600–480 BC
Cypro-Classical	480–310 BC
CC I	480–400 BC
CC II	400–310 BC
Hellenistic	310–30 BC
I	310–150 BC
II	150–30 BC
Roman	30 BC–AD 330
Byzantine	AD 330–1191
Early	AD 330–647
Arab Conflict	AD 647–965
Late	AD 965–1191
Frankish	AD 1191–1489
Venetian	AD 1489–1571
Ottoman	AD 1571–1878
British	AD 1878–1960
Republic of Cyprus	AD 1960–
Greek Coup/ Turkish Invasion-Occupation	AD 1974–

Chronological Note: The chart presented here reflects recent and, in some cases, standard chronological phases for the major periods in Cypriot history. For the prehistoric periods (before CG I), we have adopted the chronology presented in J. S. Smith, *Views from Phlamoudhi, Cyprus*, AASOR 63 (Boston, 2008). Gordon et al. (Ch. 3, this volume) provide a useful chronological overview with special reference to the Malloura Valley.

Chapter 1

Research by Design

An Integrated Approach to Culture Contact in the Malloura Valley

by P. Nick Kardulias, Derek B. Counts, and Michael K. Toumazou

> Besides the natural advantages arising from its size, fertility, and wealth, Cyprus derived from its position, within a day's sail of the coast of Syria, great importance in the remote ages when civilization had only begun to dawn in Greece, but had already advanced to a high degree in Assyria and Egypt. In later times this position between the East and the West gives its history a chequered character of war and conquest. (Cesnola 1878: 1)

Despite his reputation as an unscrupulous anti-quarian collector, with this quote, Cesnola captures a central truth about Cyprus and its relationship with other cultures in the eastern Mediterranean. Many places claim the status of a crossroads, but few have the geographic credentials and chronological longevity to support such an assertion. Geologically, Cyprus sits near the juncture of the Eurasian and African tectonic plates but has been separated from the neighboring Asian mainland since at least the Miocene epoch (see Yerkes, Ch. 2). Its connections to the outside world, then, have been mediated by an insularity that prevented regular, unimpeded contacts with the Levant and Asia Minor (especially in early prehistoric periods); at the same time, its proximity to major landmasses made travel to it more common in later prehistoric and historic times. As a result, Cyprus has existed as a contact point between great empires to the north, east, west, and south. As an example of the selective adoption of outside cultural traits, the people of Cyprus took on many Hellenic traits, at least in terms of borrowing elements of material culture and language (Karageorghis 1990: 36–41), beginning in the Late Bronze Age, despite its greater distance from the Aegean Greek world compared to Asia Minor. This important fact tells us something critical about the people of the island; mainly, that since antiquity they have borrowed, modified, and rejected outside ideas, customs, and artifacts on the basis of what might work best in a Cypriot context. One can argue that this hybrid culture and the willingness to mix and match elements from different traditions are what characterize Cypriot culture since antiquity; the ancient sites exhibit elements of the Greek west to be sure, but forms of artistic and religious expression, as well as development of crafts, also exhibit Phoenician, Egyptian, and southern Levantine influence (Counts 2008). Foreign objects, ideas, and practices passed through a Cypriot filter that removed, modified, or reassigned many elements. The result is a uniquely Cypriot way of life. This book tracks this process of amalgamation through the presentation of research in the Malloura Valley adjacent to the town of Athienou, which lies near the center of the island. What our various lines of research reveal is a notable effort by the people of this region to create a balance in their lives by blending adherence to tradition with a flexibility that encourages innovation under certain conditions. This chapter lays out the primary goals of our project, its guiding principles, the educational component, and concludes with a discussion of the region's relationship to Cyprus as a whole and to this part of the Mediterranean.

Guiding Principles, Research Questions, and Perspectives

The Athienou Archaeological Project (AAP) originated in 1989 when Michael Toumazou traveled to Cyprus to identify a site for excavation. During a visit to Athienou (his mother's hometown), Giorgos Koursaris showed him the area of Malloura, less than 5 km southwest of town, where farmers had found ancient artifacts and where there were a number of looted tombs. While disposed to excavating a prehistoric site, Toumazou was convinced by the visit of the need to investigate the site because the intensive agricultural activity in the valley threatened the remains. The mayor at the time, Kostas Sakkalos, promised any help that the municipality could offer, and Nikos Mouyiaris, a native of Athienou living in New York, provided funds to subsidize the initial seasons of work. The alliance that was borne of that initial agreement has provided great benefits to both the project and the town and is an example of the positive things that accrue to archaeologists and the communities in which they work when they operate on the basis of mutual respect and interest (see Kardulias et al., Ch. 27). It is indicative of the Cypriot spirit of *philotimo* that the arrangement was based on verbal promises, not a formal written agreement. This formative episode highlights the primary principle in our work: a

respect not only for the past that archaeologists reveal but also for the contemporary residents of the area where we undertake our work. At its best, archaeology is simultaneously an academic discipline and a way to communicate to the lay public a deeper appreciation of the past. At the same time, archaeologists learn to acknowledge and value the detailed knowledge of physical environments and social networks that local populations possess. In many ways, this situation comes to inform, and in some cases transform, our views of the world and our place in it.

Research never happens in a vacuum. From the outset, our field investigations have occurred in the context of several perspectives that generated a series of research questions. Among these approaches are regional studies, cultural ecology, and world-systems analysis; these three actually share the goal of demonstrating the integration of various facets of human activity. Regional studies start with the premise that individual sites exist within a complex physical and cultural landscape and that study of individual sites, while important and necessary, is not sufficient to understand fully how people operate in the world. The focus is "on the landscape as a dynamic, integrated phenomenon, the understanding of which requires consideration of the interplay between natural and cultural forces through time" (Kardulias 1994: xxi). Regions have fairly distinct geographic boundaries in the form of coasts, rivers, and mountains. The features of the topography that distinguish various regions include particular types of bedrock, soil, terrain (e.g., hillslope vs. plain), and mineral deposits; the proximity and abundance of potable water is another important element, which is tied to the structure of the drainage basin. The prevailing ecological conditions in demarcated regions provide the foundation for different human subsistence strategies; of particular importance in the Mediterranean basin are the conditions suitable for agriculture and pastoralism. Thus, forms of cultural expression vary between different regions, but similarities in regional conditions can lead to similar social, political, and economic regimes in diverse areas (Braudel 1966: 18–24). Landscape archaeology has emerged in the past two decades as another way to think about regions. This approach examines the cultural and ideational dimensions of the spaces that people inhabit as well as the physical terrain (Rossignol and Wandsnider 1992; Ashmore and Knapp 1999; Athanassopoulos and Wandsnider 2004).

Archaeology has had a long tradition of studying regions, at least implicitly. When scholars described various Mediterranean cultures, they often linked aspects of the physical environment to boundaries of ancient polities, as with the Egyptian culture of the Nile Valley, Attica under Athens, and the Iron Age kingdoms of Cyprus. This geopolitical approach focuses on spatial and cultural heartlands where the defining characteristics of the area are most fully expressed, but it also considers the contact zones or frontiers between regions that may fluctuate over time. To study how regions retain cohesion over time, archaeologists conduct excavation and locational survey, and combine their work with insights from geomorphology, ethnography, and other disciplines (see below and Kardulias and Yerkes, Ch. 7). While this volume focuses on the region around Athienou and the Malloura Valley, we also view the project area as a microcosm of the larger Mediterranean area. Houston (1964: 2–7; also discussed in King 1997: 6–9) identified six characteristics of the Mediterranean setting. First, across the basin there is a climate with hot, dry summers and wet, cool winters. Second is the dual role of the sea, which affects weather patterns and provides relatively easy passage between various points. Third, the land is largely defined by mountains and complex topography, with significant seismic activity in certain zones. Fourth, there is a widespread vegetational regime that includes olive trees, Aleppo pine, vines, and figs. Fifth, the Mediterranean has a long tradition of urban social life. Sixth, there are some general similarities in how people of the basin perceive and assess the natural resources that the environment offers. Our project area exhibits clearly all these traits, and thus what we learn in this region of central Cyprus has implications for other parts of the Mediterranean basin.

Cultural ecology explores the relationship between geography and humans as not only integrated but also interactive (Netting 1977). Culture is viewed as an active, flexible system that provides an avenue for adapting to particular environments. The ecological approach argues that the natural environment sets the basic parameters for human action; within those limits, people are presented with a range of options among which they must choose as part of the process of adaptation. In so doing, people form their culture from the ground up. Ideological elements reinforce certain behaviors that practice has demonstrated to be valuable. The ecological approach also stresses the interconnected nature of culture; that is, all aspects of human social behavior are deeply linked, with a common purpose of adaptation to prevailing environmental conditions. As Fagan (1994: 432) notes in describing this approach, "The adaptation of any population is achieved primarily by effective subsistence strategies and technological artifices, but social organization and religious beliefs are important in ensuring cooperative exploitation of the environment as well as technological cooperation. Religious life provided an integrating force in many societies." For example, supernatural beliefs provide important sanctions against environmentally detrimental practices. In viewing religion as functional as well as spiritual, we can see its pragmatic role in the structure of social life. We argue that a functional approach is not necessarily static, as was the case with early versions of this perspective (e.g., Malinowski 1922). Rather, we view cultures as evolving, dynamic systems (more spiral in operation than circular and unchanging), but with a certain level of regularity that makes social life possible. This ecological approach has led us to examine the interplay among the social, economic, and religious dimensions at Athienou-*Malloura* as expressed in the artifacts, architecture, and alterations of the physical landscape. The ecological perspective also corresponds strongly with the regional approach in its ability to see one system embedded in another.

The focus on ecology and regions corresponds well with the third element of our approach, an emphasis on the multiple dimensions of the relationship between urban and rural settlements in a region. The specific problem that guides the project's research agenda is the degree to which rural areas were assimilated into regional and inter-regional economic, political, social, and religious networks of exchange. Our focus on regions is essential to such considerations because it is only by comparison to events in other parts of Cyprus and elsewhere in the eastern Mediterranean that past and present human activity in the area of Athienou can be understood. As Knapp and Blake (2005: 2–3) have suggested, such detailed, localized analyses are necessary to construct a larger framework for studying interactions within and across regions in the Mediterranean. While the Athienou region, and in fact Cyprus as a whole, has often been viewed as marginal in the evolution of western civilization, the project area can, nonetheless, be seen as a laboratory for the study of culture change. We also see the need to study rural areas to balance the over-emphasis on urban centers in most examinations of ancient and medieval Mediterranean culture. Among the specific approaches informing this part of our work are world-systems theory, postcolonial theory, and the use of stylistic and typological variation as chronological and functional indicators to build a local culture history in the context of larger social, cultural, religious, and economic systems. The interactions of cores and peripheries are of particular interest. As defined in the early work of Wallerstein (1974) and Frank (1967), cores possess complex political structures (stratified class systems with large bureaucracies) and, by means of superior technology, exercise control over the major facilities of production, transportation, and communication. Political organization in peripheral areas is at the pre-state or incipient state level and is relatively weak compared with that in cores. Core states incorporate peripheral areas into the capitalist world economy because these peripheral regions often contain important natural resources. Through political and economic control of the system, Wallerstein contends, core states exploited the labor and material resources of peripheral areas and received a disproportionately large share of the surplus or benefits. He argues further that European nation-states, through colonization, competed among themselves for control or access to peripheral areas to increase profits. Interposed between cores and peripheries are semi-peripheries,

which often act as intermediaries between the two extremes of the system. Over the past three decades, various scholars have significantly augmented the original world-systems formulation to address a series of issues in an effort to adapt the approach to ancient and medieval times. Among the archaeologists who have used and refined world-systems concepts are Alexander (1999), Algaze (1993), Blanton and Feinman (1984), Kepecs (Kepecs and Kohl 2003), Kohl (1989), Pailes and Whitecotton (1975), Schortman and Urban (1987, 1992), and the Sherratts (Sherratt and Sherratt 1991; Sherratt 1993, 1997, 2003, 2006). Various prehistorians have offered approaches that deal with other aspects of interaction (e.g., the peer-polity approach [Renfrew and Cherry 1986]) or combine aspects of several models to handle issues of scale (Parkinson and Galaty 2007). Of equal importance is the extensive work that sociologists, historians, and political scientists have undertaken in building more rigorous world-systems concepts and applying them to the pre-capitalist past. Hall (1986) was among the first to amend the approach to incorporation. He noted that incorporation into a world economy is a matter of degree and that non-state peripheral societies play a more active role than generally believed. This aspect is particularly true for various periods in antiquity when complete domination of a peripheral zone was technologically and politically impossible. As a result, incorporation was less encompassing in antiquity, making the potential for resistance and adherence to tradition in the face of culture contact(s) as likely as adoption and change. Furthermore, some scholars note that people on the periphery can at times negotiate effectively because they control access to a key resource. Chase-Dunn and Hall (1997) argue there are two kinds of core/periphery relationships. What they call core/periphery differentiation involves groups of varying sociopolitical complexity that engage in active interchange. Core/periphery hierarchy refers to the situation in which one or more groups dominate others in the system. They argue this distinction is necessary because exploitation does not necessarily characterize all interactions between cores and peripheries, a point that we emphasize for various periods on Cyprus.

A concept that is central to our interpretation of the data we collect is that of negotiation, by which we mean the multiple ways in which people adapt to circumstances by making conscious choices to accept, reject, resist, or modify social practices, material goods, and ideas that they encounter through both inter-societal and intra-societal contacts. Negotiation is one of the ways that people demonstrate their ability to adapt to changing circumstances, and provides a way to build theory from the ground up. We view the social arena as flexible, with people having the ability to select from an array of options that may be more or less limited at different times. We do not make an assessment of the morality or even the practicality of these choices, only that people make decisions. Often, people do not envision the long-term consequences of these actions, so that an action taken to enhance themselves may have unforeseen negative consequences. Of course, under some circumstances, the options open to people are very limited, but some action is still taken. This process can be particularly important in peripheral areas where people can engage selectively in "trade, ceremonial exchange, intermarriage, adoption of outside religious and political ideologies, etc. with representatives of expanding states" (Kardulias 2007: 55).

The great French historian Fernand Braudel (1966) introduced several concepts that are directly relevant to our work on how central and marginal areas interact. Building on his predecessors in the Annales school, Braudel espoused the study of long-term history, or the *longue durée*, that emphasized general trends over individual events. Braudel believed that the study of the past requires collaboration between historians and other social scientists to provide a deeper understanding of the various structures in which people are enmeshed and how these change over time. This type of generalizing interdisciplinary approach is at the core of our research. Another aspect of the Braudelian perspective relevant to the present work is the concern with how social interaction occurs between regions. In discussing the nature of life on islands, he noted that people must balance tradition against change:

Whether large or small, these islands of all sizes and shapes make up a coherent human environment in so far as similar pressures are exerted upon them, making them both far ahead and far behind the general history of the sea; pressures that may divide them, often brutally, between the two opposite poles of archaism and innovation.... This archaic character of the islands (Sardinia and others), their strange capacity of preserving for centuries antique forms of civilization and mixtures of folklore has been so often remarked upon that there is no need to describe it at length....

"Isolation" is a relative phenomenon. That the sea surrounds the islands and cuts them off from the rest of the world more effectively than any other environment is certainly true whenever they are really situated outside the normal sea routes. But when they are integrated into shipping routes, and for one reason or another (often external and quite gratuitous reasons) become one of the links in a chain, they are on the contrary actively involved in the dealings of the outside world, less cut off from them than some inaccessible mountain areas. (Braudel 1966: 149–50)

What Braudel says in this passage relates very well to Cyprus. In fact, the complexities of "island archaeology" and Cyprus's position within the network of Mediterranean exchange from western Asia to the Aegean remain a central focus of scholarly debate. Broodbank (2000: 32–33) has described islands as "tricky, changing places ... seldom absolutely isolated from the rest of the world nor fully integrated in it." Others have questioned the utility of studying the Mediterranean as a coherent analytical unit (Horden and Purcell 2000; Harris 2005). Obviously, there is significant variation across the breadth of this large area, but at the same time there are certain patterns that are evident in terms of things such as agricultural practices that affect social, political, and religious organization (see Butzer 1996). The evolution of Cypriot culture over the millennia exhibits both a conservative streak and the ability to adopt outside elements when necessary or advantageous. Yet, as a unit of study, the material culture of ancient Cyprus rarely seems insular but always remains unmistakably distinct.

Our investigations have provided new data on the long-term history of rural settlements in central Cyprus that can be compared with nearby larger urban centers in the interior (e.g., Idalion, Tamassos, Golgoi), as well as centers on the coast (e.g., Salamis, Kition, Amathous, Paphos). It has been suggested that marginal areas are less stable than population centers, and that responses to cultural and environmental changes in the hinterlands are more dramatic. If this is the case, then a clearer picture of the rich and diverse archaeological record of Cyprus may emerge when viewed from the periphery. As a hinterland, the region reflects the dynamic relationship between urban centers and rural regions, as seen elsewhere on Cyprus (Rautman 2003: 210–11). While conventional wisdom holds that cultural influences flowed outward from cities to the countryside, our work demonstrates the very active role that rural areas played in forging the structure of ancient and modern societies (Toumazou et al. 1998; Kardulias 2007). In many parts of the world, it was not until quite recently that urban dwellers formed a majority of a region's population. On Cyprus, and in the Mediterranean region as a whole, the urban bias of standard archaeological work has downplayed the vibrant, innovative nature of village life. Our work challenges the standard model of traditional societies as bound to custom for custom's sake, unwilling or unable to change, locked in the past in such a way that they are out of step with the rapid pace of life in the modern world. Instead, the archaeological, historical, and ethnographic evidence clearly indicates that the people of central Cyprus have adapted to local environmental changes and to shifting political tides by taking advantage of opportunities as they arose. By applying the careful field methods of prehistoric archaeology to historic levels and looted tombs, we have contributed significantly in altering the way classical archaeology is done and maximized the retrieval of information. In brief, excavation has brought to light evidence of the religious, domestic, and mortuary practices of past Malloura residents. On the one hand, the work of AAP has revealed a continuous effort by residents of the valley to establish and maintain a distinct social identity through their various subsistence, religious, mortuary, and political pursuits. On the other hand, the particular emphasis on regional studies has shown how hinterlands are able to reflect the dynamic relationship between urban centers and rural regions.

Because of our position in a rural hinterland, our research contributes to the development of theory by more clearly defining peripheries. Peripheries exhibit variation. In general, peripheries tend to have decentralized political and economic systems, especially when compared with core regions. Furthermore, there are several types of peripheries. One type is an extraction zone that supplies raw materials to core states, something that we see in the earliest occupation of the Malloura Valley. In such places, indigenous populations perform most of the labor required to procure raw materials and can be identified by the presence of quarry pits, but with minimal evidence of processing (e.g., metal quarries with initial processing of ores into ingots, but not finished products). Second, a fully incorporated periphery will have evidence of foreign installations that indicate the incursion of a core state, complete with administrative structures and central storage facilities. A third type is the contested periphery between competing cores (Allen 1996; Cline 2000). In such areas, there may be fortified outposts facing each other in strategic locations; barrier walls may also be present. Cyprus as a whole and the Malloura Valley in particular are exemplars of contested peripheries.

The discussion of core–periphery interaction provides an avenue for exploring the political, economic, and religious structures of Cyprus in the past and present. The value of the world-systems perspective is its insistence on the nature of interaction. For example, Chase-Dunn and Hall (1997: 52–55) suggest there are four types of networks with flexible boundaries in world-systems: (1) a network of information or cultural flows; (2) a network of luxury or prestige goods flows; (3) a network of political/military interaction; and (4) a network of bulk goods flows. Mundane materials, which often constitute the majority of bulk goods, are typically nested in the information and prestige nets, yet distinct from the military net. Ancient societies were bounded by these flexible overlapping networks, so that the exchange of information and to a slightly lesser extent of prestige goods, for example, extended well beyond the scope of the political/military component. In this way one can envision the development of a cultural substrate in a region in the form of religious beliefs represented by the materials at a sanctuary (see Fourrier, Ch. 9; Averett, Ch. 10, Counts, Ch. 11; Cofer, Ch. 12; Cova, Ch. 13) or the exchange of preciosities that extended to the edges of and beyond the boundaries of the early states of Bronze Age Cyprus or the Iron Age city-kingdoms. Since the movement of bulk goods was often limited by the means of transport, these moved over the shortest distances, with some notable exceptions, such as copper ingots (Knapp and Cherry 1994; Stos-Gale et al. 1997). These networks expanded and contracted in concert with the level of societal complexity. This point is particularly important in relation to periods of transition that scholars are exploring, among them the Middle to Late Bronze Age (e.g., Fall et al. 2008), and the period after the Bronze Age to the development of the city-kingdoms, as well as to conditions during the height of these various periods (Keswani and Knapp 2003). On the one hand, the lack of evidence for occupation of the Malloura Valley during the second millennium BC limits what we can say about the Bronze Age in our project area; perhaps what we have is an instance of exploitation of certain resources (chert, limestone, grazing for herds) by residents from Bronze Age sites that surround the valley (e.g., Athienou-*Pamboulari tis Koukounninas*; Dothan and Ben-Tor 1983). On the other hand, our project, and specifically the excavation of the sanctuary (see Toumazou and Counts, Ch. 6), can speak directly to the important question of conditions during the period of the Cypriot city-kingdoms. Rupp's (1987) hypothetical (and controversial [e.g., Iacovou 2004]) reconstruction of the boundaries of these Iron Age states is important in this respect in that it "foregrounds the importance of considering the distribution of sanctuaries in light of the sociopolitical control of those spaces. In the case of the Cypriot Mesaoria, it is interesting to observe that several city-kingdoms may have been vying for con-

trol of the resources available in this agriculturally rich plain (Kition, Idalion, Tamassos, Salamis…)" (Counts 2004: 175). We could extend this discussion to consider the status of ancient Golgoi (see Counts, Ch. 4), just north and east of the project zone. Our investigations have established an important network of exchange between Golgoi and Malloura evidenced, for example, by ceramics (see Fourier, Ch. 9) and sculpture (Counts, Ch. 11; Cofer, Ch. 12). The proximity of the Malloura sanctuary to Golgoi and Idalion, and to a lesser extent Kition, may indicate it was on the border between several competing primary and secondary urban centers, and that the visitors to the ritual site negotiated their political as well as religious statuses (Counts 2008; see also Counts, Ch. 11; Harper and Tung, Ch. 19). The fluctuation or pulsation of the societal networks that Chase-Dunn and Hall describe is one way to think about the oscillation of political boundaries over time. What they note is that the different networks are not all equal in extent, and this may be a valuable way to model activity in the first millennium BC, that is, the information network that includes religious expression encompassed larger areas than the political network of these early states.

The Educational Component

Archaeologists regularly confront the issue of relevance. How does research affect the discipline and, more broadly, the general public? From the outset of our investigation, we have had an educational mission with several components. AAP represents a multidisciplinary undertaking combining field training in archaeological methods (excavation and survey) with analyses of natural and cultural contexts of ritual and secular use of the ancient and modern landscape. The multiple forces that shape human behavior find expression in the material remains our excavations, survey, and ethnographic work uncover. This materialist approach is balanced with attempts to determine the meanings of individual artifacts, features, and so forth. To undertake this ambitious research agenda, AAP staff members include classically and anthropologically trained archaeologists (with specializations in Cypriot ceramics, statuary, environmental studies, lithics, ethnoarchaeology, and other areas), geophysicists, physical anthropologists, and historians. The directors of the project reflect well this approach, coming from three different academic departments: classics (Toumazou), art history (Counts), and anthropology (Kardulias). Furthermore, through the work of specialists from other fields and sub-disciplines, we have been able to expand the questions we ask of the material, not only to open new avenues for our own research but also to provide models for colleagues confronting similar data sets. In this manner, both humanistic and scientific perspectives play roles in interpretation. The results of this interdisciplinary collaboration are presented in the succeeding chapters.

Student training has always been a central goal of the AAP. Field and laboratory instruction in archaeological methods and techniques, regional archaeological survey, computer-assisted topographic and site mapping, GIS, archaeological documentation, artifact processing and analysis, physico-chemical analysis, and computer database management occurs under the direct supervision of the Principal Investigators, senior staff, other specialists, and graduate-student associates. To provide the students with the necessary archaeological and cultural contexts, there is regular classroom instruction through evening lectures and seminars led by senior AAP staff members and other resident or visiting specialists. This classroom instruction is followed by field trips to major archaeological/historical sites discussed in the seminars (e.g., Amathous, Idalion, Khirokitia, Kition, Kourion, Paphos) and to medieval churches and monasteries, to mosques and fortresses, as well as to the main museums on the island (e.g., at Nicosia, Larnaka, Limassol, Paphos). The trips are led by the program directors and, when possible, include site lectures by the excavators themselves. Students make short oral presentations on an aspect or component of selected sites. These trips reinforce the topics covered in the lectures and seminars and provide the basis for comparisons with our work in the Malloura Valley.

The centerpiece of our educational program is the independent research project that each student plans and carries out under the direct supervision of the project faculty. Students are assigned one or more faculty advisors who consult with them on the design and organization, feasibility, and significance of their independent research. The projects are related to the ongoing archaeological investigations at Malloura and the surrounding valley. The students select their topics and submit an outline of their proposed research, including a problem statement, preliminary bibliography, description of the methods of analysis, and significance of the research. These projects have resulted in a number of undergraduate honors theses, presentations at professional conferences, and publications. Thus, the students contribute to the process of analysis by untangling some of the individual knots that obscure our vision of the complex picture that was life in ancient and medieval Cyprus. As they train their powers of observation and hone their analytical skills, students begin the transition to professional status.

We define our educational mission broadly. Not only do we engage our students in the investigation of the past; we also impart what we discover to the local community (see Kardulias et al., Ch. 27). Elementary-school children from Athienou visit the site of Malloura for guided tours of the remains. Their teachers have incorporated this information into various class assignments (essays, posters, etc.) through which the students associate archaeological materials with local history. These activities reflect our desire to build historical sequences from the ground up by seeing what the remains tell us. To transmit information to the community as a whole, each year the project director (Toumazou) presents, in Greek, an illustrated lecture open to the entire town. Through such efforts, a deeper understanding and appreciation of the ancient site have seeped into the local consciousness, as expressed in the formation of a cultural organization for the preservation of local history and traditions and the construction of a large municipal building in which substantial space has been set aside for a museum and laboratory. Furthermore, several Cypriot high school and university students have participated in the field and laboratory work, thus broadening the educational scope.

We also need to say a word here about the relationship between the members of our project and the people of Athienou. In many regards we have enjoyed an exceptional level of acceptance and support from both current residents and expatriate Athienites. We examine the nature and reasons for these important linkages in Chapter 27. Some might ask how this level of support has influenced the conclusions we reach in various studies. The answer is that we have enjoyed complete academic freedom to present information at conferences and publications. On their part, the people of Athienou have used some of the information we have uncovered to present their narrative of local history in which they can be part of the larger conversation about the Cypriot past. In many ways, the two routes lead to similar conclusions. Our work has revealed a long-standing pattern in which local, regional, and national identities emerge through a process of molding and reformulating various aspects of social life to meet the challenges of political, economic, and religious forces. One recent important manifestation of this process centers in part on the "Cyprus Problem" of how to deal with the effects of two groups with competing interests and claims over territory and associated resources in the context of a globalized world in which local interests at times clash with the strategic concerns of other nations. Our work contributes to an understanding of this problem by showing that it is not new, and that Cypriots, both in the northern and the southern parts of the island, have negotiated a

modus vivendi that reflects their ability and willingness to work in the interstices of larger political and other structures. Our reconstructions of past events privilege this idiom of negotiation because we do not believe that all approaches deal equally well with the variety of data we have generated through our various studies.

CONCLUSION

What our study of the Athienou region reveals is the ebb and flow of cultural traditions over eight millennia that have created the landscape, both cultural and natural, we witness today. To tease out the details of this process of long-term human utilization of a local environment, we have had recourse to a number of field techniques to extract a body of data about the past residents. Our theoretical approaches give us the means to make sense of the information we collect, both in terms of our immediate area and in the context of Cyprus and the Mediterranean as a whole. While a worthwhile task, the study gains greater relevance when information is communicated to the broader academic public, and to the people who are the descendants of those who inhabited the sites, made the artifacts, and buried their dead in the Malloura Valley. The other chapters in this book provide the details about how we gathered the data and what specifically we have learned in a process that will continue with future research.

REFERENCES

Alexander, R.
1999   The Emerging World-System and Colonial Yucatan: The Archaeology of Core-Periphery Integration, 1780–1847. Pp. 103–24 in *World-Systems Theory in Practice: Leadership, Production, and Exchange*, ed. P. N. Kardulias. Lanham, MD: Rowman and Littlefield.

Algaze, G.
1993   *The Uruk World System: The Dynamics of Early Mesopotamian Civilization.* Chicago: University of Chicago.

Allen, M.
1996   Contested Peripheries: Philistia in the Neo-Assyrian World-System. Unpublished Ph.D. dissertation, University of California at Los Angeles.

Ashmore, W., and Knapp, A. B. (eds.)
1999   *Archaeologies of Landscape: Contemporary Perspectives.* Malden, MA: Blackwell.

Athanassopoulos, E. F., and Wandsnider, L. (eds.)
2004   *Mediterranean Archaeological Landscapes: Current Issues.* Philadelphia: University of

Pennsylvania Museum of Archaeology and Anthropology.

Blanton, R., and Feinman, G.
1984   The Mesoamerican World System. *American Anthropologist* 86: 673–82.

Braudel, F.
1966   *The Mediterranean and the Mediterranean World in the Age of Philip II.* Vol. 1. Second edition. Trans. S. Reynolds, from the French. London: Harper and Row.

Broodbank, C.
2000   *An Island Archaeology of the Early Cyclades.* Cambridge: Cambridge University.

Butzer, K. W.
1996   Ecology in the Long View: Settlement Histories, Agrosystemic Strategies, and Ecological Performance. *Journal of Field Archaeology* 21: 141–50.

Cesnola, L. P. di.
1878   *Cyprus: Its Ancient Cities, Tombs, and Temples.* New York: Harper and Bros. Reprint 1991.

Chase-Dunn, C., and Hall, T. D.
1997   *Rise and Demise: Comparing World-Systems.* Boulder: Westview.

Cline, E.
2000   "Contested Peripheries" in World Systems Theory: Megiddo and the Jezreel Valley as a Test Case. *Journal of World Systems Research* 6(1): 7–16.

Counts, D. B.
2004   Art and Religion in the Cypriote Mesaoria: The View from Athienou-*Malloura. Cahier du Centre d'Études Chypriotes* 34:173–90.
2008   Master of the Lion: Representation and Hybridity in Cypriote Sanctuaries. *American Journal of Archaeology* 112: 3–27.

Dothan, T., and Ben-Tor, A.
1983   *Excavations at Athienou, Cyprus. 1971–1972.* Jerusalem: Institute of Archaeology, Hebrew University of Jerusalem.

Fagan, B. M.
1994   *In the Beginning: An Introduction to Archaeology.* Eighth edition. New York: Harper Collins.

Fall, P. L.; Falconer, S. E.; Horowitz, M.; Hunt, J.; Metzger, M. C.; and Ryter, D.
2008   Bronze Age Settlement and Landscape of Politiko-*Troullia*, 2005–2007. *Report of the Department of Antiquities, Cyprus*: 183–208.

Frank, A. G.
1967   *Capitalism and Underdevelopment in Latin America: Historical Studies of Chile and Brazil.* New York: Monthly Review.

Hall, T. D.
1986   Incorporation in the World-System: Toward a Critique. *American Sociological Review* 51: 390–402.

Harris, W. V.
2005   *Rethinking the Mediterranean.* Oxford: Oxford University.

Horden, P., and Purcell, N.
2000   *The Corrupting Sea: A Study of Mediterranean History.* Oxford: Blackwell.

Houston, J. M.
1964   *The Western Mediterranean World. An Introduction to Its Regional Landscapes.* London: Longmans.

Iacovou, M.
2004   Mapping the Ancient Kingdoms of Cyprus: Cartography and Classical Scholarship During the Enlightenment. Pp. 263–85 in *Eastern Mediterranean Cartographies,* eds. G. Tolias and D. Loupis. Tetradia Ergasias 25–26. Athens: Institute for Neohellenic Research.

Kardulias, P. N.
1994   Preface. Pp. xix–xxvi in *Beyond the Site: Regional Studies in the Aegean Area*, ed. P. N. Kardulias. Lanham, MD: University Press of America.
2007   Negotiation and Incorporation on the Margins of World-Systems: Examples from Cyprus and North America. *Journal of World-Systems Research* 13(1): 55–82.

Kepecs, S., and Kohl, P. L.
2003   Conceptualizing Macroregional Interaction: World-Systems Theory and the Archaeological Record. Pp. 14–20 in *The Postclassic*

Mesoamerican World, eds. M. E. Smith and F. F. Berdan. Salt Lake City: University of Utah.

Keswani, P. S., and Knapp, A. B.
2003   Bronze Age Boundaries and Social Exchange in North-West Cyprus. *Oxford Journal of Archaeology* 22(3) 213–23.

King, R.
1997   Introduction: An Essay on Mediterraneanism. Pp. 1–11 in *The Mediterranean: Environment and Society*, eds. R. King, L. Proudfoot, and B. Smith. London: Arnold.

Knapp, A. B., and Blake, E.
2005   Prehistory in the Mediterranean: The Connecting and Corrupting Sea. Pp. 1–23 in *The Archaeology of Mediterranean Prehistory*, eds. E. Blake and A. B. Knapp. Malden, MA: Blackwell.

Knapp, A. B., and Cherry, J. F.
1994   *Provenience Studies and Bronze Age Cyprus: Production, Exchange and Politico-Economic Change.* Madison, WI: Prehistory.

Kohl, P. L.
1989   The Use and Abuse of World-Systems Theory: The Case of the "Pristine" West Asian State. Pp. 218–40 in *Archaeological Thought in America*, ed. C. C. Lamberg-Karlovsky. New York: Cambridge University.

Malinowski, B.
1922   *Argonauts of the Western Pacific.* London: George Routledge and Sons.

Netting, R. McC.
1977   *Cultural Ecology.* Menlo Park, CA: Cummings.

Pailes, R. A., and Whitecotton, J. W.
1975   The Greater Southwest and Mesoamerican "World" System. Pp. 105–21 in *The Frontier: Comparative Studies*, Vol. 2., eds. W. W. Savage and S. I. Thompson. Norman, OK: University of Oklahoma.

Parkinson, W. A., and Galaty, M. L.
2007   Secondary States in Perspective: An Integrated Approach to State Formation in the Prehistoric Aegean. *American Anthropologist* 109(1): 113–29.

Karageorghis, V.
1990   The Late Bronze Age (Late Cypriote) c. 1600 – c. 1050 BC. Pp. 22–46 in *Footprints in Cyprus*, ed. D. Hunt. Revised edition. London: Trigraph.

Rautman, M.
2003   *A Cypriot Village of Late Antiquity. Kalavasos-Kopetra in the Vasilikos Valley.* Journal of Roman Archaeology Supplementary Series 52. Portsmouth, RI: Journal of Roman Archaeology.

Renfrew, C., and Cherry, J. F. (eds.)
1986   *Peer Polity Interaction and Socio-Political Change.* Cambridge: Cambridge University.

Rossignol, J., and Wandsnider, L. (eds.)
1992   *Space, Time, and Archaeological Landscapes.* New York: Plenum.

Rupp, D. W.
1987   Vive le Roi: The Emergence of the State in Iron Age Cyprus. Pp. 147–61 in *Western Cyprus: Connections*, ed. D. W. Rupp. Göteborg: Åström.

Schortman, E., and Urban, P.
1987   Modeling Interregional Interaction in Prehistory. *Advances in Archaeological Method and Theory* 11: 37–95.

Schortman, E., and Urban, P. (eds.)
1992   *Resources, Power, and Interregional Interaction.* New York: Plenum.

Sherratt, A.
1993   What Would a Bronze-Age World System Look Like? Relations between Temperate Europe and the Mediterranean in Later Prehistory. *Journal of European Archaeology* 1(2): 1–57.
1997   *Economy and Society in Prehistoric Europe: Changing Perspectives.* Edinburgh: Edinburgh University.
2003   The Horse and the Wheel: The Dialectics of Change in the Circum-Pontic Region and Adjacent Areas, 4500–1500 BC. Pp. 233–52 in *Prehistoric Steppe Adaptation and the Horse*, eds. M. Levine, C. Renfrew, and K.

Boyle. Cambridge: McDonald Institute for Archaeological Research.

2006 The Trans-Eurasian Exchange: The Prehistory of Chinese Relations with the West. Pp. 30–61 in *Contact and Exchange in the Ancient World*, ed. V. H. Mair. Honolulu: University of Hawai'i.

Sherratt, A., and Sherratt, S.
1991 From Luxuries to Commodities: The Nature of Mediterranean Bronze Age Trading Systems. Pp. 351–86 in *Bronze Age Trade in the Mediterranean*, ed. N. H. Gale. Studies in Mediterranean Archaeology 90. Jonsered: Åström.

Stos-Gale, Z. A.; Maliotis, G.; Gale, N. H.; and Annetts, N.
1997 Lead Isotope Characteristics of the Cyprus Copper Ore Deposits Applied to Provenance Studies of Copper Oxhide Ingots. *Archaeometry* 39 (1): 83–123.

Toumazou, M. K.; Yerkes, R. W.; and Kardulias, P. N.
1998 Athienou Archaeological Project: Investigations in the Malloura Valley, Cyprus, 1990–95. *Journal of Field Archaeology* 25: 163–82.

Wallerstein, I.
1974 *The Modern World-System I: Capitalist Agriculture and the Origins of the European World-Economy in the Sixteenth Century*. New York: Academic.

Chapter 2

Environmental Context of the Athienou Archaeological Project

by Richard W. Yerkes

GEOLOGY AND GEOGRAPHY OF CYPRUS

Cyprus has an area of 9,251 km² (3,572 square miles), making it the third largest island in the Mediterranean. It is the only large island in the eastern (Levantine) basin of the sea, with a maximum length of 240 km and a maximum width of 100 km (see map 1 on p. xxi). The island has a relatively low population density. Its area is about the same as Puerto Rico's, but the Caribbean island has more than five times as many people (Solsten 1993). Cyprus lies only about 70 km south of Turkey and 100 km west of Syria, but since the Miocene epoch (ca. 22–5 million years ago, see fig. 2.1), it has never been physically connected to the Asian or European continents by a land bridge. The island is surrounded by a narrow continental shelf (1–2 km wide) extending out to deep-sea troughs ranging from 500 m to more than 1,500 m deep that isolate it from the mainland (Gifford 1978; Constantinou 1982). Because of this isolation, and the absence of any indigenous ancestors of domesticated species, zooarchaeologists have concluded that during the Aceramic Neolithic (9500–5800/5500 BC), several wild species (cattle, pig, fallow deer, sheep, goat, dog, cat, fox) were

imported to the island. The lack of significant morphological modifications in the bones of the hoofed animals suggests they were part of a Near Eastern predomestic husbandry that developed during the late PPNB and quickly diffused throughout the eastern Mediterranean. The wild species must have been transported across the Mediterranean Sea to Cyprus (Vigne et al. 2000; Croft 2003; Horowitz et al. 2004; Colledge and Conolly 2007).

Cyprus has a long association with the cult of Aphrodite. It is said that she emerged from the foam near Petra tou Romiou on the southwest coast of the island (Keshishian 1954; Robertson 1987). Geologists tell us the island of Cyprus also emerged from the sea in the area where the major African and Eurasian tectonic plates meet (Gifford 1978; Swiny 1982; Poole and Robertson 1991; Knapp et al. 1994). Earthquakes spawned by this tectonic activity have spread havoc in the ancient and modern settlements of Cyprus (Swiny 1982; Soren and James 1988; Thomsen 1995; Butzer and Harris 2007).

During most of the Paleocene–Oligocene (65.5–22 million years ago) and Miocene (22–5 million years ago, see fig. 2.1) periods, there were two Cypriot islands, the southwestern Troodos igneous massif and the sedimentary northern Kyrenia or Pentadaktylos mountain range (fig. 2.2). The Troodos mountain island rose during the late Oligocene (ca. 29 million years ago, see fig. 2.1). Its structure resembles midocean ridges, with extrusive and intrusive volcanic rock distributed in a concentric circle around an ultramafic core (Allerton and Vine 1991). The bow-shaped Kyrenia island was thrust up during the Miocene (ca. 19 million years ago) as the southernmost fold in the Tauro-Dinaric tectonic belt. There are thrust plates of crystalline limestones (Triassic–Lower Cretaceous, 250–135 million years ago) in the core of the Kyrenia range, covered by foothills of folded Oligocene age (35 million years ago) flysch (figs. 2.1, 2.2; Gifford 1978; Poole and Robertson 1991; Knapp et al. 1994; also see Geological Survey of Cyprus: http://www. moa.gov.cy/moa/gsd/gsd.nsf/dmlSediments_en/ dmlSediments_en?OpenDocument).

During the Paleocene-Oligocene and Miocene periods, these two islands in the Tethys Sea were separated by a basin of marine sediments that were lithified, deformed, and then uplifted during the Plio–Pleistocene transition (ca. 2 million years ago), when Cyprus assumed its present horned shape. The area between the mountains became the Mesaoria, or central lowlands, which consists of flysch in the north and Paleocene–Oligocene marine limestones, marls, and gypsum in the south. Both are covered with alluvium along the courses of the major streams.

VEGETATION

Today, nearly half the island of Cyprus is under cultivation (46.8%), and about 21% of the arable land is irrigated. Groves of olive and carob trees are found over most of the plains and hillsides. Vineyards and fruit trees are common in the mountain valleys, and cereals (mainly barley and wheat), vegetables, and fruits are grown in the lowlands. Almost all the important ancient and modern agricultural crops (wheat, lentils, peas, pistachio nuts, almonds, sugar cane, cotton, carob, potatoes, citrus, and other fruits and vegetables) have been introduced to Cyprus. In fact, of the nearly 1,800 species of flowering plants found on

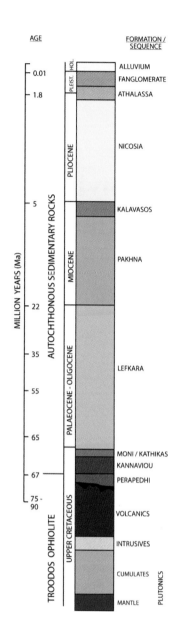

FIG. 2.1　*Stratigraphic column of geological sediments in Cyprus (© Geological Survey Department, Cyprus).*

Cyprus today, only 128 are known to be endemic (Meikle 1977; 1985; Swiny 1982; Hansen 1991; Miller 1992: 46; Republic of Cyprus 1994: 80). While wild olive (*Olea europaea,* ssp. *olesaster*), fig (*Ficus carica*), grape (*Vinus vinifera* ssp. *sylvestris*), and barley (*Hordeum spontaneum*) are present on Cyprus, cultivation of these plants seems to have been introduced as part of a Neolithic "package" of

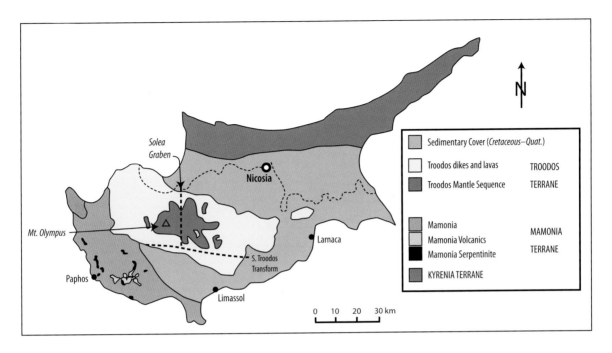

FIG. 2.2   *Map showing the three major tectonic units or terranes of Cyprus (adapted from Borradaile and Lucas 2003).*

cereals (that included barley) and a later horticultural complex of olives, grapes, and figs (Zohary and Hopf 2000).

Only a few wild barley remains have been recovered from archaeological contexts at Kissonerga-*Mylouthkia* and Parekklisha-*Shillourokambos* on Cyprus, and while some have suggested there could have been local domestication of cereals (Willcox 2002, 2003), most agree that domesticated cereals (einkorn, emmer, hulled barley), along with lentils and peas, were brought to Cyprus by Neolithic colonizers (Zohary and Hopf 2000; Peltenburg et al. 2001; Murray 2003; Charles 2007; Colledge and Conolly 2007). Charred olive stones were found at the Ceramic Neolithic site of Dhali-*Agridhi* on Cyprus and possibly at the site of Cape Andreas-*Kastros* (Colledge and Conolly 2007). While it is difficult to distinguish the stones of wild olives from cultivated olives, Zohary and Hopf (2000: 149) believe that the olives from Neolithic contexts on Cyprus were wild. Charred fig pips were also recovered at Dhali-*Agridhi* and Cape Andreas-*Kastros*, and grape pits were identified in the floral samples from Dhali-*Agridhi* (Colledge and Conolly 2007). Zohary and Hopf (2000: 149, 163–64) believe

they also came from wild species and that the cultivation of olives, figs, and grapes spread from the Levant to Cyprus during the Bronze Age.

The large numbers of introduced plant species make it difficult to reconstruct the "natural" vegetation of Cyprus (Christodoulou 1959: 225–30; Meikle 1977, 1985). Nonetheless, a few general observations about the vegetation patterns can be made. Cyprus is located at the intersection of three major floral zones, the Euro-Siberian, Mediterranean, and Irano-Turanian (Meikle 1977, 1985); but the distribution of the flora of the island is influenced by local elevation, relief, and rainfall (Christodoulou 1959: 45; Gifford 1978: 13). Euro-Siberian species common in lands with a wetter and cooler climate are limited to the higher mountain areas of Cyprus. They include pine, oak, cypress, and cedar forests, and open fields above the treeline that resemble the mountain fields of Europe. The mesic Mediterranean species found in the countries ringing the Mediterranean Sea are found on the *terra rossa* soils of Cyprus and in the littoral zones and lower parts of the upland areas. The drier Irano-Turanian species, which are also found in the Asian steppes of the Syrian desert, the

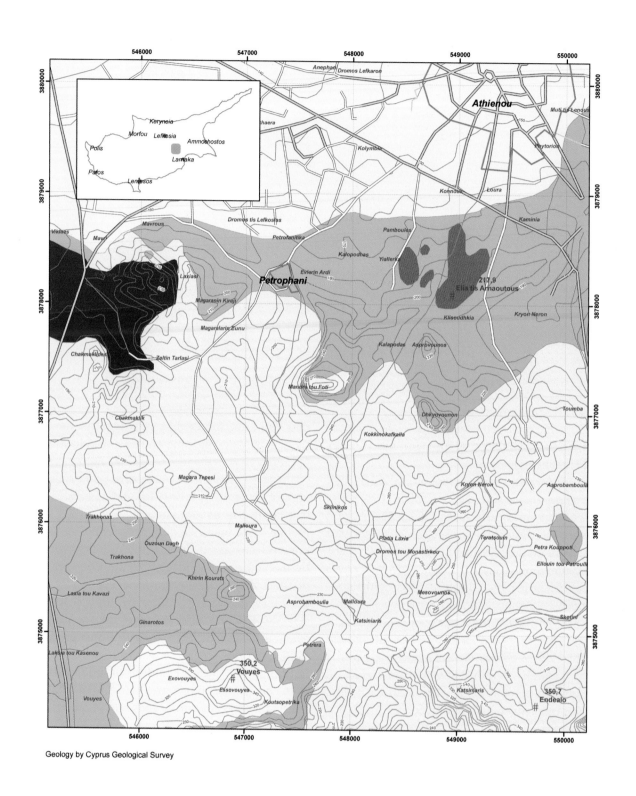

Geology by Cyprus Geological Survey

FIG 2.3 *Geological map of the Malloura Valley and surrounding area prepared for AAP by the Cyprus Geological Survey. See fig. 2.1 for color-coded key to formations (© Geological Survey Department, Cyprus).*

Gobi desert, and Anatolia, are found on the gray and white steppe soils in the lowlands of Cyprus (Christodoulou 1959: 45).

Government reforestation programs have increased the stands of trees, and today more than 18% of the island is covered by forests (Republic of Cyprus 1999: 71). Most of the forests in the Troodos and Kyrenia mountains consist of Aleppo pine (*Pinus brutia*) and Troodos pine (*Pinus nigra*), Cyprian oak (*Quercus alnifolia*), and wild cypress (*Cupressus sempervirens*). Only a single stand of the native Cyprus cedar (*Cedrus brevifolia*) remains in the Paphos forest of the western Troodos. These valuable trees were logged nearly to extinction in antiquity (Christodoulou 1959: 50–51; Gifford 1978: 14; but see Butzer and Harris 2007). The mesic parts of the island had a native vegetation of maquis (xerophyllous evergreen shrubs and bushes), primarily Shinia (*Pinus lenticus*)-dominated maquis or Cistus maquis (*C. creticus* or *C. villosus*).

THE MALLOURA VALLEY

The Malloura Valley is located in central Cyprus (35°01' north latitude and 33°30' east longitude) just south of the Mesaoria and about halfway between Nicosia and Larnaka (see map 2 on p. xxii). The valley is within the area of chalk hills composed of marine sediments (Lefkara and Pakhna formations, Paleocene–Oligocene and Miocene in age, ca. 67–5 million years ago) that lie along the flanks of the Troodos (figs. 2.1., 2.3; Gass 1960; Koucky and Bullard 1974). The uplifted sedimentary deposits in the chalk hills form a series of cuestas, or asymmetric ridges, with a gentle northerly dip slope and a steep south-facing scarp. There are some irregularities caused by gentle folding and the presence of a remnant of the old igneous land surface (pillow lavas of the Petrophani inlier) in the northern portion of the project area (fig. 2.3; Gass 1960).

The valley is drained by a network of intermittent streams that flow north and west to join the Haji Dere, which flows east and north to join the Yalias River. The river once flowed eastward across the Mesaoria toward Famagusta Bay, but its waters are now impounded behind the Kouklia and Akheritou reservoirs. Most of the project area lies north of the scarp that forms the drainage divide between the Yalias River system and the incised streams that flow southeast across the Larnaka lowlands into Larnaka Bay. This scarp of uplifted Paleocene–Oligocene to Middle Miocene sedimentary rock extends westward and southwestward from the dome of pillow lavas at Trouli to the eastern edge of the Troodos foothills south of Lympia. The gradient of the north-flowing streams is not steep, and they are not as deeply incised as the south-flowing torrents. The more vigorous south-flowing streams have cut all the way back to the steep southern slopes of the scarp. The extreme example of this vigorous headward elongation of the south-flowing streams can be seen just to the west of the project area where the Tremithos River has breached the scarp, captured part of the Yalias flowage, and now drains the northeastern slopes of the Troodos (Christodoulou 1959: 16; Koucky and Bullard 1974; Gifford 1985). The incised south-flowing streams give the southern portion of the AAP project area a barren, dissected "badlands" appearance that contrasts with the gently rolling hills in the areas where the streams flow northward.

The highest elevations in the project area are atop the Essovouyes (354 m above sea level [ASL]) and Exovouyes (336 m ASL) mesas in the south. These flat hills are composed of Pliocene fragmental limestones, marls, sands, and calcareous siltstones of the Nicosia Formation (fig. 2.3; Gass 1960). Today they are outposts for the National Guard of the Republic of Cyprus. The elevation at the base of the mesas (vouyes) is about 280 m ASL sloping down to about 160 m ASL at the northern edge of the project area. The hills on the southwest and northeast crests of the anticline that runs through the Malloura Valley range from 220 m to 280 m ASL. Traveling south from Turkish Cypriote village of Petrophani (Turkish Esendagh) to the Malloura site across the ridges near the Petrophani inlier, one has the illusion of going downhill; but the highest elevation in the village of Petrophani is 195 m ASL, while the lowest elevation in the Malloura settlement is 205 m ASL, 10 m above the crest of the hill at Petrophani.

CLIMATE AND SOILS

Cyprus has a Mediterranean climate, with strong seasonal contrasts. Hot and dry summers last from mid-May to September and are separated from the rainy winters (November to mid-March) by pleasant, but short, autumn and spring seasons. While the island was never linked to the mainland, its climate is certainly influenced by the nearby continents. In summer, a shallow trough of low pressure that extends from the continental depression over southwest Asia brings high temperatures and clear skies. In the winter, fluctuations in the paths of the storm tracks that pass between Europe, Africa, and Asia can result in different amounts of rainfall and snowfall from year to year. The storm tracks that bring most of the winter precipitation to Cyprus are the ones that cross the Mediterranean Sea from the northwestern continental anticyclone of Europe and flow south to the low-pressure belt of North Africa or flow east toward Asia (Bar-Yosef and Meadow 1995: 43–44; Republic of Cyprus 2008: 15).

The annual precipitation mirrors the topography of the island, with the highest rainfall (more than 1,100 mm annually) on the peaks of the Troodos Mountains (elevation 1,950 m ASL), and the lowest precipitation (300 mm annually) in the western Mesaoria (elevation about 100 m ASL; see Butzer and Harris 2007: 1939). The boundary between irrigation farming and dry farming in the Near East and North Africa follows the 400 mm annual precipitation isohyet (Walton 1969: 8; Gifford 1978: 10). Since agriculture in Cyprus depends on the autumn and winter rainfall, which can be quite variable from year to year, dry farming in regions where annual rainfall is below 400 mm is risky. Most of the streams in Cyprus are not well-suited to free-flow irrigation systems, so underground water resources need to be tapped in these regions of lower rainfall (Christodoulou 1959: 39; Gifford 1978: 12).

The Malloura Valley is in one of the hottest and driest parts of Cyprus. The summer temperatures average about 32° C, while mean winter temperatures range between 16° and 20° C. Annual rainfall in the project area is about 380 mm, with most of

it falling between October and April. The streams only flow between November and May. Dry farming is risky here, and unlike the Mesaoria, there is little underground water in the chalk hills. Only one spring is recorded in the project area. It is located about halfway between the sites of Athienou-*Malloura* and Petrophani, in the break in the western ridgeline north of Chakmaklik and south of the Petrophani inlier where the main stream in the valley turns west to join the Haji Dere.

Subsurface waters flowing through the permeable alluvium of the streambeds would have been vital to the farmers in the Malloura Valley. Today there are ten wells located along the main watercourse within the limits of the project area, and an ancient well was found in EU 3 (see fig. 6.1 in Toumazou and Counts, Ch. 6, where the wells are indicated with the symbol: O; also see Toumazou et al. 1998: 176). This well, which was located adjacent to a large house that dates to the Venetian period (AD 1489–1571), was 8.5 m deep, with the upper 1.2 m lined with stones and the lower 7.3 m cut into bedrock. Two cisterns were discovered associated with the Hellenistic–Roman rock-cut chamber tombs at Mağara Tepeşi, as well as an aquifer constructed sometime after the disuse of Tomb 27 (see Toumazou and Counts, Ch. 6). There are also many wells located near the village of Petrophani.

Since the project area is located some distance away from the Yalias and Tremithos rivers, the underground water resources in this region would be limited in their volume and extent. While the cultivable land here is quite abundant, the water supply is not (Christodoulou 1959: 39). The lack of rainfall and limited subsurface waters may have discouraged prehistoric groups from establishing farming settlements in the Malloura Valley. In later times, settlements may have been restricted to locations where subsurface water was abundant enough to be tapped effectively by hand-dug wells. By the beginning of the Ottoman period in AD 1571 (if not earlier), water management strategies included the digging of chains of wells (*quanat*) to carry water farther away from the local aquifers in the alluvium (Gifford 1978; also see fig. 6.1 in Toumazou and Counts, Ch. 6).

Drought

Droughts and water shortages are serious problems for the people of Cyprus, and the government has invested more than 200 million Cypriot pounds (more than $400 million) in water projects from the founding of the Republic in 1960 to 2003. The dams, pipelines, and irrigation projects allow 90% of the modern population to have clean drinking water flowing from their household taps year round and for 28,000 ha of farmland to be irrigated (Republic of Cyprus 1994: 89–95). Before these water development projects were completed, the effects of drought and water shortages were much more severe (Meikle 1977: 3–4). The drought in the summer of 2008 was very severe, and fresh water had to be imported from Greece (Kambas 2008). A terrible drought and famine early in the fourth century AD is said to have caused the island to be abandoned for 36 years. The medieval Cypriot historian Leontios Makhairás wrote that the drought did not end and the people did not return until Constantine's mother Saint Helena built the churches at Stavrovouni (Mountain of the Cross, west of Larnaka) and at Tokhni, where she landed when she came to Cyprus with her holy relics from Jerusalem (Runciman 1982: 136; Chrysos 1993; Thomsen 1995: 30). Nevertheless, no evidence corroborating a fourth-century drought has been found from the limited excavations of the late Roman/Early Byzantine settlement at Malloura (see below; also see Butzer and Harris 2007). Marginal areas like the Malloura Valley would have been particularly vulnerable during times of drought and water shortages. Settlements here may have been limited to periods when the climate was more favorable.

Soils, Stratigraphy, and Ancient Landscapes

The Malloura Valley is filled with alluvium and colluvium overlying limestones, marls, and chalks. The valley soils consist of gray and buff-colored

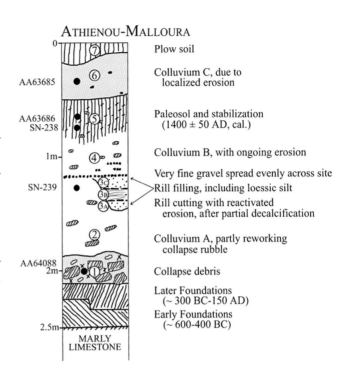

FIG. 2.4 *Composite stratigraphic profile and interpretation for Athienou-*Malloura *based on investigations by Butzer and Harris (after Butzer and Harris 2007). AA numbers indicate University of Arizona AMS samples, SN numbers refer to samples with insufficient organic matter for dating.*

rendzinas, which are usually chalky and sticky. These are good soils but not quite as productive as the fertile Mesaoria soils to the north, which have been renowned since antiquity (Christodoulou 1959: 44). Insights on the effects of land-use intensification and climate change on the landscape of the Malloura Valley were presented in a recent survey of the geoarchaeology and environmental history of Cyprus by Butzer and Harris (2007: 1948–49). In their article, they discussed the composite stratigraphic profile from the Athienou-*Malloura* site (fig. 2.4).

Butzer and Harris (2007) remarked that the stratigraphy of Malloura can be used to reconstruct ancient patterns of land use and environmental change. Stable landscapes existed while the rural sanctuaries were in use from ca. 600 BC to AD 150. This stability gave way to more degraded conditions during the Roman period and later when an Early Byzantine hamlet was established. This was followed by perhaps a millennium of slope stabiliza-tion and soil formation after the Byzantine hamlet was abandoned and when Athienou-*Malloura* was resettled during the Venetian period. This was followed by a brief interval of soil erosion during Ottoman times. However, Butzer and Harris be-lieve that a combination of land-use intensification and climatic anomalies caused the instability and erosion. Human actions were not the sole cause of the landscape degradation.

ANCIENT USE OF THE CHERT, CHALK, AND LIMESTONE OF THE MALLOURA VALLEY

Beds of tan, brown, and green chert are found in the Chalk and Chert Member of the Middle Lefkara Formation (Lapithos Group), which lies along the axis of an anticline running north-west/southeast across the Malloura Valley. At the western valley margin, on the ridge known as Chakmaklik (hill of flint, see fig. 2.3), chert was ex-tracted from outcrops and processed at a series of lithic workshops (see Kardulias and Yerkes, Ch. 8). Use of this chert source may have begun in prehis-toric times, and it seems to have continued into the early 20th century, when chert was still collected from Chakmaklik and used to fashion chipped-stone blades for threshing sledges, or *dhoukanes* (Pearlman 1984: 216; Yerkes and Kardulias 1994; Kardulias and Yerkes 1996; Whittaker 1996, 2000; Yerkes 2000; also see Yerkes, Ch. 26).

The chalk hills of central Cyprus are well-known as a source of stone for sculptures (see Counts, Ch. 11). Joan Connelly (1988: 2–3, pl. 53; see also Gass 1960: 33–36) observed that the sculptures found at Archaic to Hellenistic sites along the margins of the Mesaoria were all carved from soft chalk or limestone of the Lapithos Group. The well-bedded, white flaggy chalks of the Upper Lefkara Formation of the Lapithos Group and the fine-grained, mas-sive, cream-colored foraminiferal chalks of the Middle Lefkara Formation are known as "the stone of Athienou" because they are so common in this area (Gass 1960: 35; Hermary 1981: 10). Reyes (1994: 36–37) suggests that the practice of dedicating votive sculptures made of this soft chalk or lime-stone began early in the Archaic period in central

Cyprus at sanctuaries such as Arsos, Golgoi, Voni, Tamassos, Potamia, Idalion, and Akhna, and then spread to other parts of the island. This can be seen at Amathous on the southern coast of Cyprus where Hermary (1981: 10) found that Upper Lefkara chalks were used for the majority of the sculptures.

The Malloura Valley lies within this limestone-rich region, but while no ancient quarries were found within our project area, limestone quarries east of Athienou in the area now occupied by Turkish forces were probably used in antiquity (see Counts, Ch. 11). Several ancient quarries have also been identified at Idalion and Lympia and farther to the east near Xylofagou (Gass 1960: 35; Vermeule 1979; Connelly 1988). A modern quarry for Upper Lefkara chalk is located 3.5 km south of the sanctuary at Athienou-*Malloura* along the Nicosia–Larnaka road at Kalalakkos (shown on sheet 40/III of the 1:5000 topographical series for Cyprus), but there is no clear evidence that it was used in ancient times. Connelly (1988: 2 n. 3) noted that it was a common practice to quarry stone for votive sculpture close to the sanctuaries where they were dedicated, and while a detailed analysis of the lithology of the stone used for the statues in the sanctuary at Athienou-*Malloura* has not been conducted, this seems to have been the case.

Hard, compact limestone from the Lapithos Group (Gass 1960: 29–36) and the secondary sur-face limestone that caps many of the mesas and *pamboulas* (low hills) in the AAP project area do not seem to have been used for sculpture, but they were sources of building material. In fact, Gaber (1995: 33) noted that the limestone used in the in-ner facing of the Iron Age fortifications at Idalion came from the "region of Athienou."

The secondary surface limestone on the *pam-boulas* consists of a variably cemented, incoherent but compact carbonate-rich *havara* deposit that is capped by a hard limestone crust, or *kafkalla* (Gass 1960: 59). It formed by evaporation that concentrated calcium carbonates in the soil or subsoil through capillary action. At a stone-cutting workshop (Site 18) in the southeast corner of the project area, secondary limestone was quarried and used to make rectangular stone washing basins or animal troughs. A trough made of this material was found near the southern doorway to a large late-medieval building in EU 2 at Athienou-*Malloura* (Toumazou 1991; Toumazou et al. 1998). *Kafkalla, havara,* or any rock that happened to outcrop nearby was used by the ancient inhabitants of the Malloura Valley for building foundations (the upper portions of the walls were made of sun-dried rectangular mudbrick). This has been the practice in rural Cyprus until quite recently when concrete buildings came into vogue (Christodoulou 1959: 64; Allen 1989: 426).

Other Mineral Resources

The only other mineral resources in the Malloura Valley were deposits of gypsum and umber (a brown hydrated ferric oxide containing manganese oxide and clay that can be used as a dark brown pigment; see Gass 1960: 28, 102–3). Laminated gypsum, which is known as *marmara,* or Cypriot marble, was used as building material in the Venetian and Ottoman periods at Malloura and Petrophani, and it continued to be used for flooring and decorative stonework into the 20th century (e.g., in the modern town of Athienou). Outcrops of laminated gypsum are found in the upper Pakhna Formation along the margins of the Malloura Valley (Gass 1960: 103). Earlier in the 20th century, umber was quarried from a deposit on the northern end of Chakmaklik. There are no known deposits of copper, gold, or silver in the Malloura Valley, but these minerals were mined 10 km to the east at Troulloi, and 15 km to the west at Ayia Varvara, Mathiati, and Sha (Gass 1960: 92–102; Koucky and Steinberg 1989).

Environmental Overview

Cyprus has been described as a crossroads between the Near East, Africa, and Europe. The Pleistocene fauna of the island, with its pygmy hippopotami and dwarf elephants and giant rodents, was quite different from anything on the mainland, and the island seemed remote and insular to foraging societies (Davis 1985; Croft 1991; Reese 1995; Swiny 1995). However, the fertile soils and diverse vegetation of the island were abundant and attractive to Neolithic colonists. The island's mineral deposits were coveted later by complex societies, but the wild and domestic plants and animals they introduced transformed the landscape. The anthropogenic vegetation of Cyprus may have deep roots, and since the Neolithic period, the inhabitants of the island have had to adjust to the changing social and economic landscapes they helped to create.

Acknowledgments

The author would like to thank Senior Geological Officer Ioannis Panayides and Geological Officer Zomenia Zomeni of the Geological Survey Department (Republic of Cyprus) for preparing the stratigraphic column of geological sediments in Cyprus (fig. 2.1) and the geological map of the Malloura Valley and surrounding area (fig. 2.3).

References

Allen, P. S.
1989   Dhali: A Traditional Community in Transition. Pp. 425–46 in *American Expedition to Idalion, Cyprus 1973–1980,* eds. L. E. Stager and A. M. Walker. Oriental Institute Communications 24. Chicago: Oriental Institute of the University of Chicago.

Allerton, S., and Vine, F. J.
1991   Spreading Evolution of the Troodos Ophiolite, Cyprus. *Geology* 19: 637–40.

Bar-Yosef, O., and Meadow, R. H.
1995   The Origins of Agriculture in the Near East. Pp. 39–94 in *Last Hunters–First Farmers: New Perspectives on the Prehistoric Transition to Agriculture,* eds. T. D. Price and A. B. Gebauer. Santa Fe: SAR.

Borradaile, G. J., and Lucas, K.
2003   Tectonics of the Akamas and Mamonia Ophiolites, Western Cyprus: Magnetic Petrofabrics and Paleomagnetism. *Journal of Structural Geology* 25: 2053–76.

Butzer, K. W., and Harris, S. E.
2007   Geoarchaeological Approaches to the Environmental History of Cyprus: Explication and Critical Evaluation. *Journal of Archaeological Science* 34: 1932–52.

Charles, M.
2007   East of Eden? A Consideration of Neolithic Crop Spectra in the Eastern Fertile Crescent and Beyond. Pp. 37–51 in *The Origins and Spread of Domestic Plants in Southwest Asia and Europe*, eds. S. Colledge and J. Conolly. Walnut Creek, CA: Left Coast.

Christodoulou, D.
1959   *The Evolution of the Rural Land Use Pattern in Cyprus*. The World Land Use Survey, Regional Monograph 2. Cornwall: Geographical Publications.

Chrysos, E.
1993   Cyprus in Early Byzantine Times. Pp. 3–14 in *The Sweet Land of Cyprus, Papers Given at the Twenty-Fifth Jubilee Symposium of Byzantine Studies, Birmingham, March, 1991*, eds. A. Bryer and G. S. Georghallides. Nicosia: Cyprus Research Centre.

Colledge, S., and Conolly, J.
2007   A Review and Synthesis of the Evidence for the Origins of Farming on Cyprus and Crete. Pp. 53–74 in *The Origins and Spread of Domestic Plants in Southwest Asia and Europe*, eds. S. Colledge and J. Conolly. Walnut Creek, CA: Left Coast.

Connelly, J. B.
1988   *Votive Sculpture of Hellenistic Cyprus*. Nicosia and New York: Department of Antiquities of Cyprus and New York University.

Constantinou, G.
1982   Geological Features and Ancient Exploitation of the Cupiferous Sulfide Orebodies of Cyprus. Pp. 13–24 in *Early Metallurgy in Cyprus, 4000–500 BC*, eds. J. D. Muhly, R. Maddin, and V. Karageorghis. Nicosia: Pierides Foundation.

Croft, P.
1991   Man and Beast in Chalcolithic Cyprus. *Bulletin of the American Schools of Oriental Research* 282/3: 63–79.
2003   The Animal Bones. Pp. 49–58 in *The Colonisation and Settlement of Cyprus: Investigations at Kissonerga-Mylouthkia, 1976–1996*, ed. E. Peltenburg. Studies in Mediterranean Archaeology 70:4, Lemba Archaeological Project, Cyprus 3.1. Sävedalen, Sweden: Åström.

Davis, S.
1985   Tiny Elephants and Giant Mice. *New Scientist* 105(1437): 25–27.

Gaber, P.
1995   The History of Idalion: A History of Interaction. Pp. 32–9 in *Visitors, Immigrants, and Invaders in Cyprus*, ed. P. W. Wallace. Albany: Institute of Cypriot Studies, SUNY Albany.

Gass, I. G.
1960   *The Geology and Mineral Resources of the Dhali Area*. Memoir 4. Nicosia: Geological Survey Department, Cyprus.

Gifford, J. A.
1978   Paleogeography of Archaeological Sites of the Larnaca Lowlands, Southeastern Cyprus. Unpublished Ph.D. dissertation, Center for Ancient Studies, University of Minnesota, Minneapolis.
1985   Paleogeography of Ancient Harbour Sites of the Larnaca Lowlands, Southeastern Cyprus. Pp. 45–48 in *Harbor Archaeology*, ed. A. Raban. British Archaeological Reports, International Series 257. Oxford: Oxbow.

Hansen, J.
1991   Palaeoethnobotany in Cyprus: Recent Research. Pp. 225–36 in *New Light on Early Farming: Recent Developments in Palaeoethnobotany*, ed. J. Renfrew. Edinburgh: University.

Hermary, A.
1981   *Amathonte. Testimonia 2: Les sculptures découvertes avant 1975*. Paris: A. D. P. F.

Horowitz, L. K.; Tchernov, E.; and Hongo, H.
2004   The Domestic Status of the Early Neolithic

Fauna of Cyprus: A View from the Mainland. Pp. 35–48 in *Neolithic Revolution: New Perspectives on Southwest Asia in Light of Recent Discoveries on Cyprus*, eds. E. J. Peltenburg and A. Wasse. Oxford: Oxbow.

Kambas, M.
2008   Greek Water Sent to Drought-Hit Cyprus. Reuters online news, http://www.reuters.com/article/latestCrisis/idUSL30377566.

Kardulias, P. N., and Yerkes, R. W.
1996   Microwear and Metric Analysis of Threshing Sledge Flints from Greece and Cyprus. *Journal of Archaeological Science* 23: 657–66.

Keshishian, K. K.
1954   *Romantic Cyprus.* Sixth edition. Nicosia: K. K. Keshishian.

Knapp, A. B.; Held, S. O.; and Manning, S. W.
1994   The Prehistory of Cyprus: Problems and Prospects. *Journal of World Prehistory* 8: 377–453.

Koucky, F. L., and Bullard, R. G.
1974   The Geology of Idalion. Pp. 11–25 in *American Expedition to Idalion, Cyprus, First Preliminary Report, Seasons 1971/72*, eds. L. E. Stager, A. Walker, and G. E. Wright. Bulletin of the American Schools of Oriental Research, Supplement 18. Cambridge: American Schools of Oriental Research.

Koucky, F. L., and Steinberg, A.
1989   Ancient Mining and Mineral Dressing on Cyprus. Pp. 275–327 in *American Expedition to Idalion, Cyprus 1973–1980*, eds. L. E. Stager and A. M. Walker. Oriental Institute Communications 24. Chicago: Oriental Institute of the University of Chicago.

Meikle, R. D.
1977   *Flora of Cyprus, Volume One.* Kew: Royal Botanic Gardens.
1985   *Flora of Cyprus, Volume Two.* Kew: Royal Botanic Gardens.

Miller, N. F.
1992   The Origins of Plant Cultivation in the Near East. Pp. 39–58 in *The Origins of Agriculture: An International Perspective*, eds. C. W. Cowan and P. J. Watson. Washington, D.C.: Smithsonian Institution.

Murray, M. A.
2003   The Plant Remains. Pp. 59–71 in *The Colonisation and Settlement of Cyprus: Investigations at Kissonerga-Mylouthkia, 1976–1996*, ed. E. Peltenburg. Studies in Mediterranean Archaeology 70:4, Lemba Archaeological Project, Cyprus 3.1. Sävedalen, Sweden: Åström.

Pearlman, D. A.
1984   Threshing Sledges in the East Mediterranean: Ethnoarchaeology with Chert Knappers and Dhoukanes in Cyprus. M.A. thesis, University of Minnesota.

Peltenburg, E.; Colledge, S.; Croft, P.; Jackson, A.; McCartney, C.; and Murray, M. A.
2001   Neolithic Dispersals from the Levantine Corridor: A Mediterranean Perspective. *Levant* 33: 35–64.

Poole, A. J., and Robertson, A. H. F.
1991   Quaternary Uplift and Sea-Level Change at an Active Plate Boundary, Cyprus. *Journal of the Geological Society, London* 148: 909–21.

Reese, D. S.
1995   *The Pleistocene Vertebrate Sites and Fauna of Cyprus.* Cyprus Geological Survey Department Bulletin 9. Nicosia: Republic of Cyprus, Ministry of Agriculture, Natural Resources and Environment.

Republic of Cyprus
1994   *Cyprus.* Nicosia: Press and Information Office, Republic of Cyprus.
1999   *Cyprus.* Nicosia: Press and Information Office, Republic of Cyprus.
2008   *The Republic of Cyprus. An Overview.* Nicosia: Press and Information Office, Republic of Cyprus.

Reyes, A. T.
1994   *Archaic Cyprus: A Study of the Textual and Archaeological Evidence.* Oxford: Clarendon.

Robertson, I. (ed.)
1987   *The Blue Guide to Cyprus.* Second edition. New York: W. W. Norton.

Runciman, S.
1982   The Byzantine Period. Pp. 134–62 in *Foot-prints in Cyprus*, ed. D. Hunt. London: Trigraph.

Solsten, E. (ed.)
1993   *Cyprus: A Country Study.* Fourth edition. Area Handbook Series. Washington, D.C.: U.S. Information Service.

Soren, D., and James, J.
1988   *Kourion: The Search for a Lost Roman City.* New York: Anchor.

Swiny, S.
1982   The Environment. Pp. 1–5 in *An Archaeological Guide to the Ancient Kourion Area and the Akrotiri Peninsula*, ed. H. W. Swiny. Nicosia: Department of Antiquities, Republic of Cyprus.
1995   Giants, Dwarfs, Saints or Humans, Who First Reached Cyprus? Pp. 1–19 in *Visitors, Immigrants, and Invaders in Cyprus,* ed. P. W. Wallace. Albany: Institute of Cypriot Studies, SUNY Albany.

Thomsen, O.
1995   Written Sources. Pp. 26–40 in *Ancient Akamas I: Settlement and Environment,* ed. J. Fejfer. Aarhus: Aarhus University.

Toumazou, M. K.
1991   Excavations at Athienou Malloura. *Annual Report of the Department of Antiquities, Republic of Cyprus* (1991): 54–55.

Toumazou, M. K.; Yerkes, R. W.; and Kardulias, P. N.
1998   Athienou Archaeological Project: Investigations in the Malloura Valley, Cyprus, 1990–1995. *Journal of Field Archaeology* 25: 163–82.

Vermeule, C. C.
1979   An Imperial Commemorative Monument Never Finished: A Possible Memorial of Trajan's Eastern Conquests at Salamis on Cyprus. Pp. 189–93 in *Studies Presented in Memory of Porphyrios Dikaios*, ed. V. Karageorghis. Nicosia: Lions Club of Nicosia and Zavallis.

Vigne, J.-D.; Carrère, I.; Saliége, J. F.; Person, A.; Bocherens, H.; Guilaine, J.; and Briois, J. F.
2000   Predomestic Cattle, Sheep, Goat, and Pig during the Late 9th and the 8th Millennium cal. BC on Cyprus: Preliminary Results of Shillourokambos (Parekklisha, Limassol). Pp. 83–106 in *Archaeozoology of the Near East IV: Proceedings of the 4th International Symposium on the Archaeology of Southwestern Asia and Adjacent Areas*, eds. H. Buitenhaus, M. Mashkour, and F. Poplin. Gronigen: Center for Archaeological Research.

Walton, K.
1969   *The Arid Zones.* Chicago: Aldine.

Whittaker, J.
1996   Athkiajas. A Cypriote Flintknapper and the Threshing Sledge Industry. *Lithic Technology* 21(2): 108–20.
2000   Alonia and Dhoukanes: The Ethnoarchaeology of Threshing in Cyprus. *Near Eastern Archaeology* 63(2): 62–69.

Willcox, G.
2002   Geographical Variation in Major Cereal Components and Evidence for Independent Domestication Events in Western Asia. Pp. 133–40 in *The Dawn of Farming in the Near East*, eds. R. T. J. Cappers and S. Bottema. Berlin: Ex Oriente.
2003   The Origins of Cypriote Farming. Pp. 231–38 in *Le néolithique de Chypre: Actes du colloque international organisé par le Département des antiquités de Chypre et l'Ecole française d'Athènes, Nicosie, 17–19 mai 2001*, eds. J. Guilaine and A. Le Brun. Athens: Ecole française d'Athènes.

Yerkes, R. W.
2000   Ethnoarchaeology in Central Cyprus: Interdisciplinary Studies of Ancient Population and Agriculture by the Athienou Archaeological Project. *Near Eastern Archaeology* 63(1): 20–34.

Yerkes, R. W., and Kardulias, P. N.
1994   Microwear Analysis of Threshing Sledge Flints from Cyprus and Greece: Implications for the Study of Ancient Agriculture. *Helinium* 34(2): 281–93.

Zohary, D., and Hopf, M.
2000   *Domestication of Plants in the Old World.* Third edition. Oxford: Oxford University.

Chapter 3

The Historical Background

Regional Chronology and Local History

by Jody M. Gordon, P. Nick Kardulias, and Michael K. Toumazou

As noted in the introduction, there is a constant interplay between centers and peripheries in particular periods and over time. In order to explore this relationship below in the individual chapters, we present here an overview of Cypriot prehistory and history with summary statements about what was occurring in the Malloura Valley in the various periods. The chronology we utilize (see the chronological chart on p. xxiii) is adapted from several sources, and while there are debates over certain aspects of dating, we will not engage those issues in the present work.

PREHISTORIC PERIODS

Akrotiri Phase (10,000 BC)

For many years, scholars argued that humans did not occupy Cyprus prior to the Neolithic, despite its proximity to the Asian mainland, because the people of the Palaeolithic and Epipalaeolithic lacked the necessary navigational skills and technology to negotiate the open waters of the eastern Mediterranean (Simmons 2001: 1; Steel 2004: 23–24). Furthermore, the foraging lifestyle of these hunters and gatherers required extensive

territory, at an average population density of one person/km², to support a sufficiently large population that could sustain itself. The evidence for such early inhabitants was meager, consisting of sporadic discoveries of stone tools that seemed to be Palaeolithic in character. The excavation of Aetokremnos on the tip of the Akrotiri peninsula on the south coast between 1987 and 1990 (with some additional work in 2009) altered this perspective. Simmons (1999) found the remains of several hundred pygmy hippopotami in association with an Epipalaeolithic stone tool assemblage, which places humans on Cyprus at ca. 10,000 BC. We know that people were retrieving obsidian from Melos in the Aegean from at least the terminal Palaeolithic (ca. 11,500 BC; Renfrew and Aspinall 1990), and the recent discovery of Acheulian-style tools on Crete indicates human presence there perhaps as early as the late Lower Palaeolithic (Strasser et al. 2010). The occupation on Cyprus was limited in extent and duration. The Epipalaeolithic foragers may have contributed to the extinction of the hippopotami, but beyond this their impact on the island environment seems to have been minimal and their stay short-lived. Akrotiri-*Aetokremnos* is the only site demonstrably assigned to this phase, and there is no indication of human occupation in the Malloura Valley at this time.

Neolithic (9500–3900 BC)

Aceramic Phase (9500–5800 BC)

After a hiatus of over a thousand years, the next group of human immigrants arrived in the form of farming communities that transported the whole suite of Near Eastern domesticates, including wheat, barley, lentils, cattle, sheep, pigs, and goats (Hansen 2001; Vigne 2001), from the neighboring mainland. These people effectively transplanted the agricultural regime of Pre-Pottery Neolithic B (PPNB) southwest Asia to Cyprus, but simultaneously developed and maintained an idiosyncratic culture, a process that has remained a hallmark of Cyprus ever since. For example, in addition to the domesticated food sources, it appears that the people also imported fallow deer, which they then hunted as an important part of their diet. The revolutionary development of food production altered not only subsistence, but also settlement size and form; architecture; ecological relationships between people, plants, and animals; tool technology; religion; and social organization and kinship (Redman 1978; Swiny 2001; Bar-Yosef 2001; Renfrew and Bahn 2004: 275–316).

During the Aceramic period, divided by some into an early phase that is also called Cypro-PPNB (and some even suggest the presence of a yet earlier Cypro-PPNA [McCartney et al. 2007]) and a later phase that is also referred to as the Khirokitia Culture after a key site, a number of farming communities developed both along the north coast and the southern river valleys. These settlements exhibited a number of common features. Peltenburg (1990: 2) notes the similarities in location on hill flanks or summits, and the construction of round buildings with stone foundations and mudbrick or pisé superstructures. The structures vary in size, but generally have hearths, benches, and windows, and occasionally central supports; the roofs were typically flat. Intramural burial was common. These settlements seem to have been self-contained units, although some trade and social exchanges probably occurred. Among the key sites for this period are Kalavasos-*Tenta*, Khirokitia-*Vouni*, Kholetria-*Ortos*, Kissonerga-*Mylouthkia*, and Parekklisha-*Shillourokambos*.

As its name implies, this period did not have pottery. Instead, the people carved stone bowls, some with great artistic flair, for carrying, and probably cooking and serving as well. They used flaked stone extensively for various tools. Exotic trade goods, such as carnelian and obsidian, appear in small quantities at most sites, but the early settlement at *Shillourokambos* has a substantial quantity of obsidian that was brought from the mainland. In general, it seems that the people attempted to meet the needs for basic technology by exploiting local resources when possible.

Ceramic Phase (4900–3900 BC)

Pottery was introduced to the island in the later Neolithic period, referred to as the Sotira culture (5000–3900 BC). There has been a long-standing debate about the origins of this culture, with some suggesting that it represents a new wave of immigrants from the Asian mainland (for a discussion of the issue, see Knapp 1994: 408–9). The numbers of sites increased by about a factor of two over the Aceramic Neolithic and are distributed more broadly across the island, with the major exceptions of the Troodos region and the Mesaoria. Architecture was subrectangular in outline, and occasionally semi-subterranean (Peltenburg 1990: 5–6). In terms of subsistence, the presence of large grinding slabs indicates the importance of grains or nuts in the diet. Goats, sheep, and pigs were common domesticated animals. The presence of substantial quantities of deer bone reflects a significant reliance on this wild species. Knapp (1994: 407) describes the people of this period as "egalitarian farmers, herders, and deer hunters" living in nucleated settlements on high spots on the landscape. The presence of beads and pendants of picrolite at various sites indicates the existence of an exchange network linking various parts of the island (Peltenburg 1990: 6–8). Pottery developed from a monochrome form to the distinctive Red-on-White form.

It is in the Aceramic Neolithic period that we have the first traces of human presence in the Malloura Valley. What we have found is evidence for the exploitation of chert outcrops in the hills on the west side of the valley (Kardulias and Yerkes, Ch. 8). These locations (Sites 9, 11, and 28) would have been ideal quarries for the prehistoric occupants of the region because the material is exposed on the surface as bedrock, and large angular chunks could be removed with minimal effort. The material was then reduced to more portable pieces (Kardulias and Yerkes, Ch. 8) and then taken to some other area for further refinement and use. Our best estimate is that as early as the Aceramic Neolithic, residents of Dhali-*Agridhi* were among those who visited the quarries to extract usable stone and transported it out of the valley. However, there were no permanent human residents in the valley during the Neolithic, a pattern that would recur in other periods for various reasons.

Chalcolithic (3900–2500 BC)

A significant expansion in the number of settlements to about 100 marks this period in which there was also substantial enhancement in various technologies, including an expanded range of ceramics and the introduction of metallurgy. Originally named the Erimi Culture after an important site near the south coast (see Steel 2004: 11–15 for a detailed discussion of the problems of using particular site names to designate periods), the people of this period settled extensively on the western side of the island and elsewhere in hamlets with "curvilinear architecture…[and] communal storage" (Knapp 1994: 410). Characteristic artifacts include Red Polished pottery, and cruciform pendants and beads of picrolite. Some burials of the period contained stone vessels, ceramic drinking cups, and various metal implements, suggesting the emergence of social differentiation. Major sites include Erimi, Lemba, Kissonerga, and Souskiou.

From this time on through to the end of the Bronze Age and slightly beyond, the Malloura Valley remained culturally quiescent. We have no

evidence of human presence in the valley during the Chalcolithic or Bronze Age (see below).

Bronze Age (2500–1050 BC)

As in Greece, Anatolia, the Levant, and elsewhere in the eastern Mediterranean, the second half of the third to the end of the first millennium BC on Cyprus witnessed a major cultural efflorescence. It is clear that Cyprus and the Aegean lagged behind Egypt and Mesopotamia in the development of social complexity, but as a consequence it is likely that the Near Eastern world-system stimulated development in trade, and offered a model and catalyst for nascent elites as they strove to enhance their wealth and status (Sherratt 2001). Beginning in the Early Cypriot period, there is a fairly consistent increase in both the number and extent of settlements due to innovations such as the plow, which permitted the cultivation of areas with heavy soils, and the secondary products revolution (Sherratt 1981) that paved the way for more intensive exploitation of animals through their use for traction, milk, and wool, in addition to meat. The surpluses generated by these innovations subsidized economic specialization and eventually the development of political elites (Knapp 1994: 422–23, 2008: 76–77, 132–33, 165–73; Peltenburg 1996). The demand for bronze from Egypt, the Near East, and later the Aegean, and even areas as far as the central Mediterranean, spurred the development of metallurgy more fully than had been the case in the Chalcolithic.

Settlement numbers increased fairly steadily throughout the Bronze Age, from over 200 in the Early Cypriot period to over 300 by the Late Cypriot phase. Site hierarchies accompanied this development, as groups of sites became more tightly integrated than had been the case previously. By the Late Cypriot period, a number of major centers had developed at Enkomi-*Ayios Iakovos*, Kition-*Kathari*, Hala Sultan Tekke-*Vyzakia*, Kalavasos-*Ayios Demetrios*, Maroni-*Vournes*, Morphou-*Toumba tou Skourou*, and Myrtou-*Pigadhes* (Knapp 1994: 422–25; Karageorghis 2002: 57–68). Many of these sites provide evidence of contact with Egypt, the Levant, and Anatolia but also Minoan

Crete and the Mycenaean world (Karageorghis 2002: 11–17; Sherratt 2010). In addition to pottery, faience, and other products, a key import may have been the Minoan script, modified to fit Cypriot needs in a process of linguistic negotiation that probably modified the original to meet Cypriot needs (Karageorghis 2002: 17–21; see discussion of negotiation as general principle in Ch. 1, p. 9).

Despite all of this activity, the Malloura Valley contains no evidence of a Chalcolithic or Bronze Age human presence. Our survey retrieved no sherds or other material belonging to these periods (Kardulias and Yerkes, Ch. 7). Compounding this conundrum is the fact that the phases, especially the Bronze Age, are well represented in the surrounding area. For example, for the Middle Bronze (Cypriot) Age, the settlement of Alambra (Coleman 1996) is ca. 12 km to the southwest and Kalopsidha 25 km to the east (Åström 1966). On the northern outskirts of Athienou is the important Late Bronze Age metal-processing site of Athienou-*Pamboulari tis Koukounninas* (Dothan and Ben-Tor 1983). Less than 10 km west of Malloura, Dhali has a significant Late Bronze Age component, and there is a cluster of smaller sites near Potamia and Ayios Sozomenos north of Dhali. On, or near, the coast to the south and east, there are important sites at Hala Sultan Tekke, Kition, and Pyla-*Kokkinokremnos*. We have suggested that the Malloura Valley had no permanent residents in these periods, but could have been exploited for its fertile soil as an agricultural zone.

Historic Periods

Cypro-Geometric Period (1050–750 bc)

During the Cypro-Geometric period, Cypriot civilization underwent several formative political and cultural developments. Unlike other eastern Mediterranean civilizations that experienced social collapse at the end of the Bronze Age, Geometric Cyprus seems to have been relatively prosperous and retained many of its external trading connections (Coldstream 1990: 50; Sherratt 2003: 47–51; Iacovou 2006: 34–35).

The key political development was the formation of the city-kingdoms. Although the chronology

and causes are debated, later epigraphic evidence proves that the kingdoms existed by the Cypro-Archaic period (Iacovou 2006: 47–48). Thus, most scholars cite archaeological evidence as well as Greco-Roman historical sources stressing the kingdoms' Greek cultural antiquity to suggest their pre-Archaic date (Gjerstad 1944: 122–23; Vanschoonwinkel 1994; Steel 1993; Iacovou 2008; cf. Rupp 1987, 1998). Although little is known about how such foundations actually occurred, Iacovou (2006: 36) suggests that new sites could appear in various ways. Some cities (e.g., Salamis, Kition, Kourion, Palaepaphos, and Lapithos) were formed near previous Late Bronze Age settlements and often continued their cultural traditions, while in other places entirely new urban foundations appeared (e.g., Amathous, Chytroi, Tamassos, and Soloi). It should be emphasized that the resettlement of Kition was unique, because Phoenician immigrants gradually altered local cultural and political practices (Smith 2009: 10–12). This introduced a new ethnic and linguistic group into the Cypriot population whose influence would be chronologically and culturally extensive (Markoe 2000: 170–71; Karageorghis 2002: 140–49).

Because of the lack of historical sources, archaeological evidence provides the best insight into Cypro-Geometric innovations. The most convincing data for kingdom formation probably come from Kourion and Salamis. A small golden jeweled scepter surmounted by two falcons that is arguably of Late Bronze Age or Early Geometric date and may have come from the Kourion region (Goring 1995) has been viewed by some scholars as a royal object (Rupp 1987; Coldstream 1990: 50). The most impressive evidence, however, comes from "Royal" Tomb 79 at Salamis, which has been dated to the eighth century bc (Coldstream 1990: 59–64; Karageorghis 2002: 158–68). Overall, the ostentatious architecture, funerary ritual with horse sacrifices, and opulent furniture with eastern and Egyptian motifs indicate that a highly organized social structure, probably kingship, existed at late Geometric Salamis.

In addition to shedding light on the city-kingdoms' genesis, Cypro-Geometric archaeology also indicates the different cultural groups that were present in Cyprus (Iacovou 2006: *passim*). It appears that Greek speakers, who first appeared on the island in the Bronze Age, remained the foremost cultural group. Tomb architecture, weapons, ceramics and figurines all betray Aegean influences; the chief evidence comes from the 11th-century-BC cemetery at Palaepaphos-*Skales* (Karageorghis 2002: 121–34). Here, a bronze *obelos*, or skewer, was unearthed, which was inscribed in Minoan-derived Cypro-syllabic characters spelling out the word "o-pe-le-ta-u." When translated, it was shown that this was simply the genitive/possessive form of the proper name *Opheltes* in the Arcado-Cypriot dialect (Cova, Ch.13). This is the earliest direct evidence for the presence of Greek speakers in Cyprus (Iacovou 2006: 38).

Besides the Greek element, the archaeological evidence illustrates the presence, starting in the ninth century BC, of Phoenicians at Kition, while several undecipherable Cypro-syllabic inscriptions may indicate that some Cypriots continued to speak an indigenous language (Reyes 1994: 13–17; Iacovou 2006: 42–43; Cova, Ch. 13). Despite these differing ethnic and linguistic backgrounds, Cypriot ceramics and material culture seem to have become relatively homogeneous, indicating a degree of insular harmony and interaction (Iacovou 2006: 44). Finally, although connections with mainland Greece may have been less intensive, the presence of ceramics imported from Syria and Phoenicia as well as eastern iconography at Salamis and especially at Kition in the form of the Stele of Sargon II, indicates continued links with Near Eastern cultures (Karageorghis 1982: 122; Radner 2010: 431). During the Cypro-Geometric, then, it seems that the Cypriot kingdoms, perhaps shielded by their insularity and aided by regional political instability, were able to maintain contacts with mainland cultures while retaining a degree of political independence.

Following the lack of prehistoric activity, the Cypro-Geometric is the first phase of a cultural resurgence in the Malloura Valley. The evidence consists of 46 Cypro-Geometric III potsherds excavated in EU 94 of the Malloura sanctuary (Site 1; see Toumazou and Counts, Ch. 6; Fourrier, Ch. 9). These sherds may indicate the beginning of ritual activity at what would become a major religious center in the valley. Besides this deposit, Malloura's cultural resurgence is not evident from the survey data that show the valley did not have a nucleated settlement (Kardulias and Yerkes, Ch. 7). Given the presence of Malloura between the kingdom centers of Idalion and Kition, it is probable that the agricultural potential of this fertile valley was tapped by one of these kingdoms.

Cypro-Archaic Period (750–480 BC)

If one considers the opulent remains from Salamis' "Royal Tombs," it is fair to say that the Cypro-Archaic era began with a cultural efflorescence. The kingdoms continued to prosper, while Cypriot art entered a creative period stimulated by an expansion of religious sites.

Cypro-Archaic prosperity also attracted the attention of several reinvigorated empires, including the Assyrians, possibly the Egyptians, and the Persians (Reyes 1994). Thus, according to epigraphic and historical evidence, the Cypriot kings were forced to pay tribute to each of these empires in turn (Tatton-Brown 1990: 65). As there is little proof of foreign occupation, however, Cyprus' insularity and geographical position on imperial borders must have allowed Cypriots some autonomy (Reyes 1994: 69–84; Stylianou 2000; Zournatzi 2005: 64–65; Radner 2010). Hence, both kings and artisans were free to choose which foreign influences to adopt in their politics and artistic productions, respectively. The result was the creation of a society and material culture that was uniquely Cypriot, combining local, eastern, Egyptian, and Greek traditions (Reyes 1994: 3–4).

The royal cultural traditions first attested at late Geometric Salamis continued during the Cypro-Archaic as evidenced by the "Royal Tombs" of Tamassos (Buchholz and Untiedt 1996). These tombs are on a smaller scale, yet they are more ornately decorated. Narrow *dromoi* lead down to rock-cut burial chambers that were carved to resemble wooden architecture and whose entrances were flanked by pilasters with Aeolic capitals. One of the tombs was also guarded by apotropaic or regal limestone sculptures of lions and sphinxes (Solomidou-Ieronymidou 2001). These features may illustrate the builder's attempt to show off his political power and his appreciation of various artistic styles. For example, the "wood-style" tomb carving is characteristic of Anatolian traditions, whereas the Aeolic capitals were popular in Phoenician contexts, and the sphinxes seem influenced by Egypt.

Another Cypro-Archaic phenomenon was the widespread appearance of religious sanctuaries. Indeed, sanctuaries had been previously established at Palaepaphos, Kition, and Enkomi, but it was only in the Cypro-Archaic period that the number of sanctuaries increased (Karageorghis 1982: 139–42, 2002: 191–93; Ulbrich 2008: 6–8).

Cypro-Archaic sanctuaries are significant for both their architectural appearance and their sculptural decoration (Karageorghis 1982: 144–51, 2002: 183–90, 200–211; Tatton-Brown 1990: 72; Ulbrich 2008: 199–252; 65–102). A sanctuary generally consisted of an open-air court surrounded by a *peribolos* (precinct wall). Within this wall, in the *temenos*, there would be one or more small buildings that would surround the focal point of the sanctuary, the sacrificial altar. Here, food offerings would typically be offered to the god or goddess (Toumazou and Counts, Ch. 6).

More spectacular than a sanctuary's architecture, however, were the near life-size votive sculptures of divinities and worshippers dedicated within the *temenos* (Connelly 1989: 213–17). The best example of this practice comes from the site of Ayia Irini, where hundreds of terracotta and limestone sculptures were discovered (Ulbrich 2008: 378). Cypro-Archaic limestone statuary in particular has often been regarded as one of the most unique creations of the ancient Cypriot psyche. This is because the statues display the confluence of artistic influences available to Cypriot sculptors. Some votives appear modeled on Greek *kouroi/korai*, while others reflect Near Eastern and Egyptian models. Finally, there are votaries that wear garments and assume poses that can only be described as "Cypriot" (Counts, Ch. 11).

A major cache of Cypro-Archaic votive statuary has been excavated from the "Persian Siege Ramp" at Palaepaphos (Tatton-Brown 1990: 71; Ulbrich 2008: 405–6). It was here that the last major historical event of the Cypro-Archaic period

occurred, when in 499 BC several Greek-Cypriot cities, as well as Phoenician Kition, joined the revolt of the Greek cities of Asia Minor against Persian rule (Herodotus 5.16). Unfortunately for the Cypriots, the Persians invaded Cyprus and gradually regained control by sacking several cities. Thus, even as the cities of mainland Greece were soon to defeat the Persians at the battles of Marathon in 490 BC and Salamis in 480 BC, the Greek Cypriots would remain within the Persian empire for another 150 years.

The Cypro-Archaic II period marks the first major phase of cultural development in the Malloura Valley with the establishment of a formalized religious sanctuary and a number of tombs. Although much of the sanctuary's architecture lies buried below later debris, several structures can be stratigraphically associated with Cypro-Archaic ceramics (Toumazou and Counts, Ch. 6; Fourrier, Ch. 9). These remains include two rectangular structures, both of which have hearths. In addition, a great many fragments of votive terracotta and limestone sculptures have been recovered, which can be dated stylistically to the Cypro-Archaic period. Because many sculptures display iconography associated with a variety of male divinities such as Herakles, Zeus Ammon/Baal-Hammon, Apollo, or Pan, it is now assumed that the site was dedicated to a male deity. On the whole, this period seems to represent the sanctuary's *floruit* and it is assumed that its appearance resembled other better-preserved examples.

According to survey and excavation data, Cypro-Archaic cemeteries were initiated in the region of Mağara Tepeşi (Site 2), as well as in the northeast section of Malloura (Site 1). The presence of cemeteries indicates that a settlement must have been established somewhere in the valley. Nevertheless, the survey did not locate evidence for this settlement nor any other habitations in Malloura's immediate vicinity (Toumazou and Counts, Ch. 6; Kardulias and Yerkes, Ch. 7).

Cypro-Classical Period (480–310 BC)

Cypro-Classical history focuses on the role of Cypriots, many of who were both Persian imperial subjects and Greek-speaking, within the conflict between Persia and Greece. Since historians recorded the conflict's main events, it is possible to present a brief overview of its effect on Cyprus.

Following their defeat in the Ionian Revolt, the Cypriots, who were accomplished sailors, were pressed into the Persian navy and forced to help attack Greece in 490 and 480 BC. Although the Greeks halted the Persian western advance, they were unable to strike eastward for twenty years until the Athenian admiral Kimon attempted to rid Cyprus of Persian rule in 460 BC. Kimon besieged Phoenician Kition (which probably had a Persian garrison), yet his attack came to naught after his sudden death (Thucydides 1.112; Diodorus Siculus 12.2.2–4). By this time, Phoenician Kition may have been locally powerful, as it seems to have soon gained political control over the kingdom of Idalion (Hadjicosti 1997: 57–60).

Cyprus next became embroiled in Greco-Persian hostilities with the accession of the King of Salamis, Evagoras I, in 411 BC. In the span of twenty years, this philhellenic ruler rebuilt Salamis, struck coinage using the Greek alphabet, made connections with Athens, and, most importantly, briefly brought all the other Cypriot city-kingdoms under his control (Diodorus Siculus 15 and 16; Isocrates *Evagoras*). Nevertheless, Evagoras' rise to power, which was partly aided by specific Persian and Greek foreign policy stances as well as infighting amongst the Cypriot kingdoms, was not enough to end Persian supremacy (Maier 1994, 312–17). In 386 BC, Evagoras' Athenian allies recognized Persian authority over Cyprus, which allowed for a Persian invasion of Salamis in 380 BC. Evagoras retained power over Salamis, but lost control of the other kingdoms and was soon assassinated.

Cyprus would have to wait until the coming of Alexander the Great in the late 330s BC to finally escape Persian interference. The Greek kings of Cyprus, along with Poumiathon of Kition, who now controlled Idalion and Tamassos, aided Alexander at the siege of Tyre, and after the defeat of Darius, they became Alexander's vassals (Plutarch, *Alexander* 24.2; Arrian, *Anabasis* 2.20.3). While Alexander trekked across Asia, the Cypriots were once again allowed some autonomy. Yet because of Cyprus' strategic position and its port facilities, this idyll was soon disrupted by the political chaos that ensued at Alexander's death. Cyprus became a military battleground between the armies of Alexander's generals, Ptolemy and Antigonus Monophthalmus (Diodorus Siculus 19.59.1–5). Ptolemy gained the advantage and secured Cyprus, then destroyed its last powerful kings, Poumiathon, Nikokles, and Nikokreon (Diodorus Siculus 20.21). Though Antigonus' son Demetrius briefly wrested Cyprus from Ptolemaic control following the battle of Salamis in 306 BC (Diodorus Siculus 20.46.4–53.4; Plutarch *Demetrius* 15.1–17.5), by the 290s BC the island was a secure province of the Ptolemaic empire (Plutarch, *Demetrius* 35.3).

Cypro-Classical culture continues many of the trends of earlier periods with the chief exception that mainland Greek stylistic influences seem to have profoundly affected Cypriot aesthetics (Karageorghis 1982: 158; Tatton-Brown 1990: 92). Such a situation is not surprising, given the frequent contacts between Athens and Greek Cypriot rulers. Thus, imported Athenian ceramics are found at many sites, and statuary, especially grave reliefs, clearly imitate Attic prototypes (Vermeule 1976). Simultaneously, however, many Cypriot artistic traditions continued, and large numbers of mostly limestone votive sculptures were still displayed at sanctuaries throughout the island. As mentioned, the Greek alphabetic script begins to appear alongside Cypro-syllabic, or even Phoenician, especially on royal coinage, which mainly displays images of Greek divinities. Large royal palaces, such as the massive palace of Vouni, were built according to local architectural designs (Tatton-Brown 1990: 88–89; Maier 1985: 36–37).

If long-term cultural developments began at Malloura during the Cypro-Archaic period, then these were consolidated in the Cypro-Classical era. Since pottery as well as limestone and terracotta sculptures discovered at the sanctuary can be dated to Cypro-Classical times, the sanctuary appears to have thrived (Toumazou and Counts, Ch. 6; Fourrier, Ch. 9). More specifically, perhaps Malloura was controlled by Kition, which had taken over the nearby kingdoms of Idalion and Tamassos (Maier 1985: 34 and n. 13). Such a situation might help to explain the stratigraphic evidence for a general reorganization of the sanctuary during the late fourth century BC. Perhaps the renovation reflects altered conditions that faced interior dependencies, including Malloura and Idalion (Hadjicosti 1997: 60), after Ptolemaic forces destroyed Kition (Diodorus Siculus 19.79; Calvet 1993: 123).

Although there is still no evidence for a nucleated settlement in the Malloura Valley during the Cypro-Classical period, survey evidence has revealed several sites with scatters of Classical coarsewares (Toumazou and Counts, Ch. 6; Kardulias and Yerkes, Ch. 7). The most intriguing specimen is from Site 27, located on the east slope of a hill overlooking the Kryon Neron Valley, which is both within reach of the sanctuary as well as an earlier series of tombs.

Hellenistic Period (310–30 BC)

The history of Hellenistic Cyprus is tied to its position as a possession of the Greco-Egyptian Ptolemaic empire (Mehl 2000: 620). With Ptolemy's victory over Demetrius in 294 BC, the empire coveted Cyprus because of its economic and strategic value (Hauben 1987: 214 ff.; Tatton-Brown 1990: 99). Cyprus was once again forced to submit to the authority of external rulers. The Ptolemies were not only politically and economically successful, but they were also culturally Greek. Taken together, these factors may have helped to maintain the peace and prosperity that seem to have characterized Hellenistic Cyprus.

Indeed, it is often peace and prosperity that is cited for the lack of information about Hellenistic Cyprus within historical works, and so our information primarily comes from epigraphic and archaeological sources (Hill 1940: 185). According to inscriptions, Cyprus was administered by a Ptolemaic general or *strategos* (Bagnall 1976: 38–49). The *strategos*, based in the new capital city of Nea Paphos, was not only a civilian and military leader but also the island's chief priest. Below the *strategos* were a host of military officers and administrative officials who monitored Cyprus' defense, finances, and resources (Bagnall 1976: 49–53).

Garrisons of mercenaries from all over the eastern Mediterranean were stationed in Cypriot cities, most of which retained their urban status (Bagnall 1976: 53–57; 263–66). Within the cities themselves, Cypriots seem to have been able to participate in local governments, and most cities had an assembly, or *boulé*, and cultural institutions such as gymnasia (Bagnall 1976: 52–73). Though it seems that few Cypriots participated in the Ptolemaic government, many belonged to the League of Cypriot Cities, the *Koinon Kyprion*, which was dedicated to promoting the royal cult of the Ptolemies (Karageorghis 1982: 73). Through it they were able to show their allegiance to the Ptolemaic rulers whom they hardly ever saw.

The political and economic decline of Ptolemaic Cyprus during the first century BC is directly related to the failing fortunes of the Ptolemaic dynasty. Following the death of Ptolemy VIII in 116 BC, the kingdom was wracked by civil wars, which led to the loss of Ptolemaic possessions in Cyrenaica and eventually resulted in Cyprus' conversion into a separate kingdom (Hölbl 2001: 222). It was this kingdom, ruled by Ptolemy, King of Cyprus, an uncle of the last Alexandrian Queen, Cleopatra VII, that was annexed by the expansionist Roman republic in 58 BC (Plutarch, *Cato Minor* 34.2–35.2; 36.1–37.2). For a brief period, the island was joined to Cilicia and was administered by the famous orator Cicero. Then Mark Antony temporarily returned Cyprus to Cleopatra VII during his civil war against Octavian (Cassius Dio 49.41.1–4). With Octavian's victories over Antony and Cleopatra VII in 31–30 BC, Cyprus became a secure part of the Roman world-system.

In regard to cultural developments, Cyprus entered the more cosmopolitan Greek environment that characterized the eastern Mediterranean during the Hellenistic age (Tatton-Brown 1990: 106). This change was probably due to a variety of factors, including the Greek identity of many Cypriots, the similar background of their rulers, the arrival of an array of Hellenic mercenaries, and the Ptolemaic desire to spread their imperial artistic ideology to their possessions. Some types of material culture, such as coinage and the funerary architecture of the Tombs of the Kings at Paphos, soon completely resembled that produced in Alexandria (Wright 1992: 536). Furthermore, both the Phoenician alphabet and Cypro-syllabic script either completely fell out of use or were eliminated by Ptolemaic decree (Iacovou 2006: 56–57). Other artistic forms, however, like votive sculpture, carried on established traditions, amalgamated now with Ptolemaic fashions (Connelly 1988: 111–13).

Following the regional disruptions caused by the struggles among Alexander's successors, it seems that prosperity returned to the Malloura Valley once the Ptolemies restored order. Very early in the Hellenistic period, the third major cultural phase begins in the sanctuary (Toumazou and Counts, Ch. 6). First, a large-scale *peribolos* wall was built of rubble and fragments of earlier votive statues that were presumably broken in late Cypro-Classical times. Within the *temenos*, finds of statue bases and worked limestone fragments indicate that new votive statues must have been erected. The most significant discovery, however, is a mudbrick platform that may have functioned as an altar. Both votive statuary and animal remains were found in its immediate vicinity. Evidently, the Hellenistic era was another cultural high point for the Malloura sanctuary.

Outside of the sanctuary, a new set of chamber tombs (T. 25–28) were created at Mağara Tepeşi. These tombs contained primarily Roman material, yet the discovery of many Hellenistic coins, lamps, and ceramics indicates 5. that they may have been constructed earlier (Gordon, Ch. 14). Despite these signs of habitation, survey data still provide no evidence for a nucleated settlement in the valley at this time (Toumazou and Counts, Ch. 6; Kardulias and Yerkes, Ch. 7).

Roman–Early Byzantine Period (30 BC–AD 647)

Octavian's victory over Antony and Cleopatra resulted in Cyprus' incorporation into the Roman empire. Cyprus now entered into one of history's great world-systems and its fate became linked to imperial fortunes. The Roman and Early Byzantine eras were also marked by peace, prosperity, and good government, as Cyprus, an island in a Roman lake, lost its strategic importance.

Cyprus' irrelevance, however, did permit a degree of local autonomy the like of which Cypriots had not experienced since Persian times.

Several Roman and Byzantine writers wrote about Cyprus, but most were more interested in the island's myths, geography, and hagiography than Cypriot involvement in political developments (Mitford 1980: 1297). Even so, a narrative of key events can be established. In 22 BC Octavian entrusted Cyprus to the Roman Senate and this initiated the primary form of Roman proconsular administration (Cassius Dio 54.4.1). Epigraphic evidence also illustrates that the proconsul was assisted by a small staff and one cohort of troops (Mitford 1980: 1298–1308; 1341–45). Evidently, the Cypriots were loyal and it seems that they did their best to honor the emperor, again through the League of Cypriot Cities (Karageorghis 1982: 180–81). In exchange, the emperor granted earthquake damage relief and support for building projects.

An important event of AD 45 was the missionary journey to Cyprus of St. Paul, accompanied by St. Barnabas, a native of Salamis, and Mark the Evangelist (Acts 13:4–13). Though Christianity would take several centuries to be fully established, Paul's apostolic journey, his first, introduced the new faith, with Barnabas becoming a founding bishop. The next major recorded event is the Jewish insurrection of AD 116 (Cassius Dio 68.32.1–2). This appears to have been a large-scale disturbance in which thousands were killed. Besides several damaging earthquakes, few events are recorded until the late third century AD, when the administration of the island was transferred to the Diocese of the East by Diocletian (Hill 1940: 230; Mehl 2000: 856).

Following the transfer of the imperial seat to Constantinople, Cypriot history becomes entwined with that of the Christian Byzantine empire (Chrysos 1993: 3–5). By the mid-fourth century AD, the Cypriot administrative capital was transferred to Salamis, which was renamed Constantia, and Cyprus had become a Christian land (Michaelides 1990: 128). During this time, Cypriot culture and politics were linked to that of the early Orthodox Church and it seems that Cypriot bishops were formidable individuals, both at home and at the major ecumenical councils. While originally under the jurisdiction of the Jerusalem and then Antioch patriarchates, the Church of Cyprus was granted autocephaly (self governance), with the right to elect its own Archbishop by a decree of the Byzantine emperor Zeno in AD 487 (Hill 1940: 275–78). The Early Byzantine period in Cyprus comes to an end by AD 647–649, when the war-weary Byzantines were unable to defend the island against the raids of the Arab Muslim governor of Syria, Muawiya (Runciman 1990: 147–48; Gregory 2005: 171).

The archaeological remains from Roman and Early Byzantine Cyprus offer a valuable insight into cultural developments. Roman Cyprus was evidently incredibly wealthy, judging by the marble-clad architectural remains of theaters, amphitheaters, fora, temples, and porticoes. Even more spectacular are the remains of villas decorated with exquisite mosaics and imported marble statuary. The majority of these remains have been uncovered at coastal cities, like Salamis, and major sanctuaries, like that of Apollo Hylates at Kourion (Michaelides 1990: 130–34). Thus, as vast amounts of imported ceramics illustrate, Cyprus remained a prosperous trading hub, closely connected to maritime commerce. Despite the links to *Romanitas*, the remains of coins, inscriptions, statuary, and architecture all indicate that some uniquely Cypriot cultural characteristics, such as the preservation of religious traditions that were local variants on pan-Mediterranean norms, endured throughout Roman times (Gordon 2008).

With the adoption of Christianity in the Early Byzantine period, Cypriots began to construct monumental Christian basilicas. Many such basilicas decorated with mosaics and imported marble columns have been uncovered not only at major urban centers (e.g., Salamis/Constantia, Nea Paphos) but also in rural areas (e.g., Kalavasos-*Kopetra*) (Runciman 1990: 149–51; Papageorghiou 1993; Rautman 2003). In general, the remains of these ornate and imposing structures confirm that peace and prosperity were preserved and that the Greek language and Christianity remained the dominant cultural forces at least until the Christian/Arab conflict (Chrysos 1993: 3–7).

The evidence from both excavation and survey suggests that the Roman and Early Byzantine periods were the most prosperous pre-modern eras in the history of the Malloura Valley (Toumazou and Counts, Ch. 6). At this time, ritual activity continued at the Malloura sanctuary, and the tombs at Maǧara Tepeşi were enlarged and filled with dozens of bodies, ceramics, and luxury offerings such as gold jewelry. Excavations in EU 3 and EU 5 have both revealed the remnants of the valley's first recognizable settlement, which lasted from Early Roman times until the Arab raids. The discovery of a stone cross in EU 6 even suggests that the settlement had its own basilica. According to the evidence from survey, the settlement could have been as large as 7 ha and may have had a population of around 500–600 people. Survey data also point to a marked increase of sites throughout the valley, as well as an increase in imported pottery from both the western and eastern Mediterranean (Kardulias and Yerkes, Ch.7; Moore and Gregory, Ch. 15). Site 16 even yielded a coin of the Byzantine emperor Phocas (AD 602–610). Hence, Roman and Early Byzantine Malloura seems to have reaped the benefits of imperial inclusion, which increased its connectivity to the coast and its markets for agricultural exports.

The Christian-Arab Conflict and the Late Byzantine Period (AD 647–1191)

If there ever was a "dark age" of Cypriot history, it was the second half of the first millennium, when references to Cyprus become only a footnote to Byzantine imperial histories (Hill 1940: 257; Runciman 1990: 154). Nevertheless, it is clear that the Roman/Early Byzantine period's political tranquility and economic interconnections were disrupted as Cypriots found themselves poised between the cross and the crescent.

From ca. 647 to 965 Cyprus was governed through a political settlement, referred to as the "Condominium." Throughout the seventh century, the Byzantine empire was intermittently at war with the Muslim Umayyad dynasty. However, in the 680s, the Byzantine emperor Justinian II and the Umayyad Caliph Abd al-Malik made a pact to neutralize Cyprus. Basically, it was agreed that neither empire would militarize the island, it would be mutually defended, and all revenues would be divided (Runciman 1990: 149). So it seems that both empires used Cyprus as a convenient place to build and provision ships, buy local silk (a new lucrative export), collect taxes, and exile heretical dissidents. In short, Cypriot Christians and Arabs seem to have co-existed in relative harmony, while their co-religionists frequently fought each other in coastal waters.

This comparatively successful political experiment ceased at the end of the millennium, when the island was reincorporated into the Byzantine empire and forced to reorient its economic and cultural connections in response to the advent of Western Crusaders (Gregory 2005: 240). Although Cypriots were once again full subjects of a Christian empire, this did not better their situation. In fact, the evidence suggests that taxation was harsh and that Cyprus was often used as a base for rogue governors who wished to revolt. Such governors not only gouged the people but also jousted with the archbishops, who had become leaders of the people and who protested on their behalf (Runciman 1990: 162–63).

Provincial revolts were possible by the late 11th century, as Byzantine Anatolia had recently been overrun by the Seljuk Turks (Gregory 2005: 255–56). These conquests helped to initiate the Western Crusading movement, which saw the Catholic Pope call on his lay supporters to raise armies to wrest the holy land from Muslim control. The first Crusaders arrived in the east in 1097, and by 1099 Jerusalem had been captured. This brief removal of the Muslim threat in the Levant was at first a boon for Cyprus, since it opened new trading routes (Savvides 1995: 7–9). Yet further infighting amongst Byzantine emperors and Cypriot dukes, along with Arab and Ottoman Turk attacks on the empire, resulted in Cyprus being repeatedly raided by both Muslim and Christian armies. Eventually, Byzantine control became so degraded that Isaac Comnenos was able to proclaim himself King of Cyprus (Gregory 2005: 273). Isaac's reign proved to be short-lived, however; Richard I of England, *Coeur de Lion*, took the cross in 1191 and arrived in Limassol, where he and several other Latin dukes, including Guy de Lusignan, achieved the conquest of Cyprus (Runciman 1990: 173–74).

The most important cultural monuments of the Late Byzantine period are the painted churches located in the Troodos Mountains (Stylianou and Stylianou 1985). As the Orthodox faith played a major role in preserving Cyprus' Greek identity, it is not surprising that such religious artworks were produced. The two most famous churches are St. Nikolas of the Roof at Kakopetria and Panagia Phorviotissa at Asinou, both of which are painted with some of the best-preserved Late Byzantine images of saints, Christ, and Mary (Solomidou-Ieronomidou 1999a: 30–35, 1999b: 36–41). Finally, besides building churches, several new urban centers were Byzantine foundations, including Famagusta, Limassol, and, most importantly, the subsequent capital, Nicosia (Hill 1940: 261 ff; Runciman 1990: 166).

Both survey and excavation data gleaned from Malloura have shown that the "Condominium" and Late Byzantine eras were cultural low points. By this time, the sanctuary at Malloura was only a memory and, more importantly, the thriving Roman and Early Byzantine settlement seems to have been abandoned during one of the early Arab raids (Toumazou and Counts, Ch. 6). This decline is also supported by the survey evidence, from which Byzantine ceramics represent less than 5% of the total (Moore and Gregory, Ch. 15). Hence, it seems that the valley may have even been abandoned during these difficult times as people fled to port cities seeking a livelihood or even to the mountains for security when external attacks were under way.

Frankish Period (AD 1191–1489)

With Richard the Lionheart's conquest, Cyprus was swept into the politics and culture of the Western Crusading movement. For nearly 300 years, Cyprus would be ruled by a dynasty of Frankish monarchs who seem to have been more interested in hunting than serving the island's population. As a result, most Cypriots were forced into serfdom, and as the administration became less effective, political and economic power played into the hands of the maritime masters of the east, the Genoese, and especially the Venetians.

Cyprus became a Frankish dominion when Richard I used the island as a bargaining piece to convince Guy de Lusignan, an opportunistic knight from Poitou in France, to give up his claims to the Kingdom of Jerusalem (Riley-Smith 1995: 40–41). Making the best of a bad situation, Guy took Cyprus as his personal kingdom and invited any Crusading nobles who had lost their lands to Muslims to become his vassals. So, until the late 15th century, Cyprus was ruled by a French Catholic royal house that promoted both the French language and the Latin Church at the expense of the Greek language and Orthodox religion. Cyprus was administered from the inland capital of Nicosia according to the tenets of medieval feudalism (Hunt 1990a: 187–88). The agricultural wealth of vast parcels of land and the labor of the Greek serfs tied to them was divided amongst vassals sworn to defend the Lusignan realm. In addition, various Latin religious orders were welcomed to Cyprus and granted tithes, while the Orthodox clergy were tolerated but found solace mainly in monasteries (Hunt 1990a: 191, 194).

The high point of Lusignan success coincided with the loss of the last Frankish strongholds on the Syrian mainland by the early 14th century. Under kings like Peter I, Cyprus' position as the last Christian bastion in the east made it a lucrative entrepôt for the powerful yet predatory Italian trading states of Genoa and Venice (Housley 1995: 187–91; Coureas 1995: 107–24). Unfortunately for the Lusignans, these Italian connections, combined with the attacks of the Egyptian Mamelukes, would weaken their hold on Cyprus (Hunt 1990a: 202–3; Edbury 1993: 1–23). The changing of the guard occurred when the last king, James II (the Bastard), died and left the kingdom to his Venetian wife, Caterina Cornaro, in 1473. By this point, the Byzantine empire had ceased to exist due to the capture of Constantinople by the Ottoman Turks, and so, with the Ottomans threatening their eastern trade routes, Queen Caterina's Venetian countrymen convinced her to yield Cyprus to the Republic of Venice, bringing an end to Frankish rule.

Even if the historical sources tend to present the Lusignans as lethargic rulers, it is impossible to say that they were not energetic builders. In Nicosia, Famagusta, and Bellapais, the Latin Church's glory was commemorated in stone with cathedrals designed in the most opulent French Gothic styles (Papageorghiou 1995: 275–78). Equally impressive are the reconditioned Byzantine castles of the Kyrenia/Pentedactylos mountain range, Kantara, Buffavento, and especially St. Hilarion, which remain classic examples of Crusader fortifications (Hunt 1990a: 190–91). Yet the power of Greek Orthodox religious art remained indomitable throughout the *Frankokratia,* and amazing frescoes that maintained Byzantine traditions were executed in churches at Kalopanayiotis, Moutoullas, and Pelendri (Papageorghiou 1995: 279).

When compared to the abandoned landscape of Late Byzantine times, it seems that a renaissance of sorts occurred at Frankish Malloura. In fact, it is almost certain that a new settlement was founded near the valley's seasonal streams. Support for this view comes primarily from survey evidence, yet it can also be corroborated, for the first time, by other evidence. Specifically, along with millstones, significant amounts of clearly identifiable medieval glazed pottery (*sgraffito*) dating to the 14th century have been discovered (Kardulias and Yerkes, Ch. 7; Moore and Gregory, Ch. 15; Spigelman, Ch. 17). Furthermore, documents from the time of James II indicate that the Malloura region was granted as a fief to Mutio de Costanzo of Naples and, interestingly, a town at Malloura begins to appear on many subsequent cartographic representations of the island (Counts and Parvis, Ch. 5). Based on this evidence, it is possible that Malloura's feudal landholder initiated a small agricultural settlement in order to begin processing the valley's agricultural goods so they could be exported via Italian merchants to overseas markets. If this was the case, the developments at Malloura may be crucial to our understanding of the nature of Italian infiltration into Cypriot affairs during the Late Frankish period.

Venetian Period (AD 1489–1571)

In keeping with its historical fate, from the 15th to 19th centuries Cyprus continued to be a bone of contention between whichever states held the balance of military power in the eastern

Mediterranean. Cyprus first fell to the Venetians, but within a century it was conquered by the Ottoman Turks who had become the largest regional empire.

When the Venetian state inherited Cyprus from Caterina Cornaro in 1489, the *Signoria* set out to convert the island into an outpost that could defend against the Ottoman threat and generate new sources of income. A provincial administration based in Nicosia was created consisting of a series of officials, including the "three rectors," who oversaw Cyprus' finances and justice (Hill 1940: 767–71). Military defense was entrusted to the "Captain of Cyprus." If the administration ran smoothly, which it often did not, large profits could be made both through a salt tax and the export of grain or cotton.

Under Venetian administration some Frankish aristocrats were permitted to keep their estates and some laws were maintained. Yet many traditional privileges were granted to parvenu Venetian nobles, and Italian became the *lingua franca* of justice and commerce (Hunt 1990a: 215–16). Greek peasant life continued to be difficult because taxes were harsh and people had to provide corvée labor and serve in the army. However, some Cypriots bought their way out of serfdom and gained some degree of personal liberty (Hill 1940: 780).

The Venetians prepared the defenses of Cyprus by rebuilding the fortifications of Famagusta, Kyrenia, and Nicosia, but these undermanned and underfunded bastions proved ineffective when faced with an increasingly powerful Ottoman empire (Hunt 1940: 844–64). The reckoning for this neglect occurred during the years 1570–71, when the Beylerbey of Damascus, Lala Mustafa Pasha, was sent to conquer the island. Nicosia was quick to fall and the final stroke was delivered at the siege of Famagusta. After holding out for nearly a year against incredible odds, the commander, Marco Antonio Bragadino, submitted to the Pasha's demands only to be publicly humiliated and suffer a violent death. Thus, in August 1571, the *Serenissima Repubblica* gave way to Ottoman rule in Cyprus.

The Venetian era has proven to be one of the high points of settlement in the Malloura Valley. According to excavation, survey, as well as cartographic evidence, Malloura's embryonic Frankish settlement was expanded and its industrial potential realized. Excavation disclosed the remains of a lavish domestic dwelling in EU 3, while a cemetery containing 57 skeletons was revealed in EU 6 (Toumazou and Counts, Ch. 6; Harper, Ch. 20). The presence of typical glazed *sgraffito* ceramics dates both units to the Venetian period. More impressive, however, is the large structure unearthed in EU 2, which can be dated to the 15th and 16th centuries. Briefly, the building's eastern section is divided into a series of closely-spaced compartments lined with gypsum and presumably covered with wood planks. It likely represents an agroindustrial architectural design. The two best interpretations are that it served either as a flax-processing establishment (DeMasi, Ch. 16) or as a granary (Spigelman, Ch. 17).

The regional survey also encountered much higher numbers of Venetian ceramics than those from previous periods, especially at Sites 20 and 6, the latter of which also contains lime kiln fragments (Kardulias and Yerkes, Ch. 7; Moore and Gregory, Ch. 15). Besides ceramics, Venetian-style millstones were also recovered on the survey. These were probably employed for grinding grain in water-powered mills located near the local streambeds (Spigelman, Ch. 17). All these data suggest that Venetian Malloura was a prosperous community, a fact reinforced by the settlement's continued representation on Venetian maps (Counts and Parvis, Ch. 5).

Ottoman Period (AD 1571–1878)

The siege of Famagusta ushered in 300 years of largely ineffective Ottoman rule in Cyprus (Luke 1969: 2–3). The primary reason for this poor administration was that, once again, Cyprus had become an insignificant province within an imperial heartland. The Sublime Porte seems to have been relatively uninterested in Cypriot affairs, which resulted in an uneven provincial policy (Hunt 1990b: 226). First, the Porte was often indecisive about who should administer Cyprus and from where. Generally, a Pasha of three tails led an administration based in Nicosia, but sometimes officials in Anatolia or even the Grand Vizier in

Istanbul were in charge. A second problem was that the officials sent to the island were typically incompetent, underpaid, or both. Incompetent officials bred corruption, while underpaid officials led to the practice of tax farming. This resulted in the periodic rise of Turkish *aghas* who terrorized both Greek and Turkish populations and who frequently revolted, causing great social disruptions (Given 2000: 213).

Ottoman rule also introduced a new ethnic, linguistic, and religious element into the Cypriot population, the Turks (Luke 1969: 18–22; Hunt 1990b: 226–27). Indeed, many Turkish immigrants settled in Ottoman Cyprus either as traders, farmers, soldiers, or *agha*-landholders. Although they never achieved a demographic majority, the Turks founded villages, mosques, and *tekkes* (monasteries) and gradually created a new Turkish Cypriot culture. Because many Frankish and Venetian buildings were reused during this period, few Ottoman building projects were initiated. Nevertheless, the *Boyuk Khan* (Traveler's Inn) in Nicosia and *Hala Sultan Tekke* in Larnaka offer a faint glimpse into the refined nature of Ottoman architecture (Hunt 1990b: 251–53).

Life was often difficult for non-Muslims in the Ottoman empire. Collectively known as *rayah* (cattle), non-Muslim subjects were politically categorized according to their *millet* or religious denomination (McCarthy 1997: 127–29). The advent of this system in Cyprus made the leader of the Greek Orthodox community, the archbishop, the primary spokesman (or ethnarch) for the island's majority (Given 2000: 212). The archbishop even had the right to appeal directly to the Sultan himself. For most of the *Tourkokratia*, Greeks and Turks lived together in relative harmony, and both groups were free from the hardships of Frankish serfdom (Hunt 1990b: 232–33; Quataert 2005: 174–79). Some Greeks, such as the *dragoman*, or "Pasha's interpreter," could even rise to prominent positions in the local Ottoman administration. This situation changed, however, in 1821 when the Greeks of the Peloponnese began an ultimately successful revolt against Ottoman rule (Hunt 1990b: 244–48). To prevent Cypriot collusion, the Ottoman governor preemptively hanged Archbishop Kyprianos and

then proceeded to slaughter nearly 500 prominent Greek-Cypriot clerical and civil leaders. Hence, Cyprus' position as an Ottoman province was secured while the fortunes of the Greek population were greatly weakened. Nevertheless, Greek culture and especially the Orthodox religion continued to thrive as attested by the maintenance of medieval churches and the continued development of icon painting.

The Ottoman period also saw the rediscovery of Cyprus' ancient past through the burgeoning Western European pursuit of antiquarian treasure hunting (Balandier 2001). Among such antiquarians were Melchior de Vogüé, Robert Hamilton Lang, and, most notably, Luigi Palma di Cesnola. These individuals scoured the island for ceramic, metallic, and especially sculptural artifacts that could be displayed as "Western" heritage in the imperialist museums of France, Britain, or America or could be sold to wealthy private collectors (Morris 1994: 17; 25). In fact, it was at this time that a great number of Cyprus' most impressive antiquities, including the Chatsworth Head, the "Apollo" of Malloura, and the Amathous Sarcophagus were removed from the island (Bouquillon et al. 2006; Hermary 1989: 315–17; Karageorghis 2000: 201–4). The removal of such items was possible partly because of lax Ottoman laws concerning the removal of antiquities and also because of the rising power of foreign consuls vis-à-vis the Ottoman administration (Karageorghis 2000: 4). It is not surprising that de Vogüé's expedition was supported by Napoleon III, while both Lang and Cesnola were of consular rank (Balandier 2001: 5–6).

The end of Ottoman rule was once again related to Cyprus' changing position in geopolitical affairs. By the late 19th century, the Ottoman imperial structure had ossified and many of its provinces were poorly administered, in open revolt, or harassed by imperialistic European powers. Britain in particular was convinced that supporting the Ottoman empire against Russia might check Russian designs on the seaways linking England to its colonial jewel, British India (Holland and Markides 2006: 164–65). Therefore, the British negotiated with both the Ottomans and the Russians so that the Russians gained some Ottoman land, the Ottomans halted further Russian advances, and the British kept the Russians away from the Suez Canal (Hunt 1990c: 256–60; McCarthy 1997: 198). The British occupation of Cyprus, which was granted by the Ottomans in 1878, was key to this strategy, as it provided a base from which Anatolia or, more importantly, the Suez could be defended. After 300 years, then, Cyprus became a British colonial outpost and was to remain so until recent times.

If one travels to Malloura today, there are few visible reminders of the vigorous culture of earlier times. Because of a new set of challenging geopolitical realities, the valley is completely devoid of settlement and is utilized exclusively for agricultural purposes. Indeed, the site's situation within the United Nations' "Buffer Zone," which separates the military factions embroiled in the "Cyprus problem," forces AAP team members to come to grips with how socio-political differences and macro-historical developments can affect regional settlement patterns both in antiquity and the present.

As AAP's research has revealed, the decline in settlement in the Malloura Valley actually began in the Ottoman period. Evidence in the form of later architectural modifications and Ottoman-era clay pipes from the Venetian building in EU 2 shows that this industrial structure was eventually abandoned and probably frequented by squatters (Toumazou and Counts, Ch. 6). The survey data also reveal a drop-off in the number of new sites, indicating that population numbers may have dwindled even as new mini-settlements sprung up at Petrophani and Palio-Chanouta (Kardulias and Yerkes, Ch. 7). Archival census data further shows that a handful of Greeks inhabited Malloura by the time of the Greek War of Independence, and cartographic examples show Malloura labeled as "ruins" in Kitchener's survey in 1882 (Counts and Parvis, Ch. 5). It was these "ruins" that would be investigated by Edmont Duthoit, Melchior de Vogüé's architect, in 1862 (Toumazou and Counts, Ch. 6).

It is impossible to say what ultimately led to Malloura's abandonment in the 19th century, but a decline in population certainly reflects island-wide trends beginning in the latter part of the 18th century, due to poor administration, excessive taxation, plague epidemic, bad crops, and earthquakes. Yet some specific factors for the case of Malloura may be suggested. First, if Malloura was engaged in a specialized industry such as flax processing and its markets were removed following the Ottoman conquest, then this could have led to a localized economic collapse. Second, the low population figures for Malloura during the Greek War of Independence may suggest that many inhabitants were killed or fled to larger cities for protection. Third, the inhabitants of Malloura may have moved to the nearby town of Athienou in order to find work, as Athienou was situated on the main thoroughfare between the trading cities of Nicosia and Larnaka (Counts and Parvis, Ch. 5). Because several factors probably played a role in Malloura's decline, it is best to seek the cause not in isolated events but as the result of a gradual series of systemic incidents that led to regional political and economic reorientation.

Summary

This chapter's goal has been to provide a historical backdrop for AAP's diachronic research in the Malloura Valley. The cultural developments revealed by archaeology did not take place in a vacuum. Instead, the evidence suggests that Malloura could be insulated from greater geopolitical changes, as in the Archaic and Roman periods, or directly affected by them, as during the Ptolemaic conquest or the Arab raids. Ultimately, Malloura's disposition as either a crossroads or bounded space was intimately related to Cyprus' precarious position between east and west, and between political centers and peripheries.

References

Åström, P.
1966   *Excavations at Kalopsidha and Ayios Iakovos in Cyprus.* Studies in Mediterranean Archaeology 2. Lund: Åström.

Bagnall, R.
1976   *The Administration of the Ptolemaic Possessions Outside Egypt.* Leiden: Brill.

Balandier, C.
2001   Cyprus, a New Archaeological Frontier in the XIX Century. Pp. 3–12 in *Cyprus in the 19th Century A.D.: Fact, Fancy and Fiction,* ed. V. Tatton-Brown. Oxford: Oxbow.

Bar-Yosef, O.
2001   The World Around Cyprus: From EpiPaleolithic Foragers to the Collapse of the PPNB Civilization. Pp. 129–64 in *The Earliest Prehistory of Cyprus. From Colonization to Exploitation,* ed. S. Swiny. American Schools of Oriental Research Archaeological Reports 5. Boston, MA: American Schools of Oriental Research.

Bouquillon, A.; Descamps, S.; Hermary, A.; and Mille, B.
2006   Une nouvelle étude de l'Apollon Chatsworth. *Revue archéologique* 42(2): 227–61.

Buchholz, H. G., and Untiedt, K.
1996   *Tamassos. Ein Antikes Königreich auf Zypern.* Jonsered: Åström.

Calvet, Y.
1993   Kition, Travaux de la Mission Française. Pp. 107–38 in *Kinyras: L'Archéologie française à Chypre.* Travaux de la maison de l'orient 22. Paris: Boccard.

Chrysos, E.
1993   Cyprus in Early Byzantine Times. Pp. 3–14 in *The Sweet Land of Cyprus: Papers Given at the Twenty-Fifth Jubilee Spring Symposium of Byzantine Studies, March 1991,* ed. A. A. M. Bryer and G. S. Georghallides. Nicosia: Cyprus Research Centre.

Coldstream, N.
1990   Early Iron Age (Cypro-Geometric): The Rise of the Ancient Kingdoms c. 1100–700 BC. Pp. 47–64 in *Footprints in Cyprus: An Illustrated History,* revised edition, ed. D. Hunt. London: Trigraph.

Coleman, J. E.
1996   *Alambra: A Middle Bronze Age Settlement in Cyprus: Archaeological Investigations by Cornell University.* Jonsered: Åström.

Connelly, J.
1988   *Votive Sculpture of Hellenistic Cyprus.* Nicosia: Department of Antiquities of Cyprus.
1989   Standing Before One's God: Votive Sculpture and the Cypriot Religious Tradition. *The Biblical Archaeologist* 52(4): 210–18.

Coureas, N.
1995   Cyprus and the Naval Leagues, 1333–1358. Pp. 107–24 in *Cyprus and the Crusades: Papers given at the International Conference 'Cyprus and the Crusades', Nicosia, 6–9 September 1994,* eds. N. Coureas and J. Riley-Smith. Nicosia: Cyprus Research Centre.

Dothan, T., and Ben-Tor, A.
1983   *Excavations at Athienou, Cyprus, 1971–1972.* Qedem 16. Jerusalem: Hebrew University.

Edbury, P.
1993   *The Lusignan Kingdom of Cyprus and its Muslim Neighbours.* Nicosia: Bank of Cyprus Cultural Foundation.

Given, M.
2000   Agriculture, Settlement and Landscape in Ottoman Cyprus. *Levant* 32: 209–30.

Gjerstad, E.
1944   The Colonization of Cyprus in Greek Legend. *Opuscula Archaeologica* 3: 107–23.

Gordon, J. M.
2008   Roman Cyprus: A Study of the Effect of "Permanent Island Features" on Imperial Agendas and Local Identities. Paper presented at the

Annual Meeting of the American Schools of Oriental Research, Boston.

Goring, E.
1995   The Kourion Sceptre: Some Facts and Factoids. Pp. 103–10 in *Klados: Essays in Honour of J. N. Coldstream*, ed. C. Morris. Bulletin of the Institute of Classical Studies Supplement 63. London: Institute of Classical Studies, University of London.

Gregory, T. E.
2005   *A History of Byzantium.* Oxford: Blackwell.

Hadjicosti, M.
1997   The Kingdom of Idalion in the Light of New Evidence. *Bulletin of the American Schools of Oriental Research* 308: 49–63.

Hansen, J.
2001   Aceramic Neolithic Plant Remains in Cyprus: Clues to their Origins? Pp. 119–28 in *The Earliest Prehistory of Cyprus. From Colonization to Exploitation,* ed. S. Swiny. American Schools of Oriental Research Archaeological Reports 5. Boston, MA: American Schools of Oriental Research.

Hauben, H.
1987   Cyprus and the Ptolemaic Navy. *Report of the Department of Antiquities, Cyprus*: 231–26.

Hermary, A.
1989   *Catalogue des Antiquités de Chypre: Sculptures.* Paris: Ministère de la culture, de la communication, des grands travaux et du Bicentenaire, Editions de la Réunion des musées nationaux.

Hill, G. F.
1940   *A History of Cyprus.* Cambridge: Cambridge.

Hölbl, G.
2001   *A History of the Ptolemaic Empire.* Trans. T. Saavedra. London: Routledge.

Holland, R., and Markides, D.
2006   *The British and the Hellenes: Struggles for Mastery in the Eastern Mediterranean 1850–1960.* Oxford: Oxford University.

Housley, N.
1995   Cyprus and the Crusades, 1291–1571. Pp. 187–206 in *Cyprus and the Crusades: Papers given at the International Conference 'Cyprus and the Crusades', Nicosia, 6–9 September 1994,* eds. N. Coureas and J. Riley-Smith. Nicosia: Cyprus Research Centre.

Hunt, D.
1990a   The Frankish Period 1191–1571. Pp. 175–226 in *Footprints in Cyprus: An Illustrated History*, revised edition, ed. D. Hunt. London: Trigraph.
1990b   The Turkish Period 1571–1878. Pp. 226–54 in *Footprints in Cyprus: An Illustrated History*, revised edition, ed. D. Hunt. London: Trigraph.
1990c   The British Period 1878–1960. Pp. 255–79 in *Footprints in Cyprus: An Illustrated History*, revised edition, ed. D. Hunt. London: Trigraph.

Iacovou, M.
2006   'Greeks,' 'Phoenicians' and 'Eteocypriots'. Ethnic Identities in the Cypriote Kingdoms. Pp. 27–59 in *"Sweet Land. . ." Lectures on the History and Culture of Cyprus*, eds. J. Chrysostomides, and C. Dendrinos. Surrey: Porphyrogenitus.
2008   Cultural and Political Configurations in Iron Age Cyprus: The Sequel to a Protohistoric Episode. *American Journal of Archaeology* 112: 625–59.

Karageorghis, V.
1982   *Cyprus from the Stone Age to the Romans.* London: Thames and Hudson.
2000   *Ancient Art from Cyprus: The Cesnola Collection.* New York: Metropolitan Museum of Art.
2002   *Early Cyprus: Crossroads of the Mediterranean.* Los Angeles: The J. Paul Getty Museum.

Knapp, A. B.
1994   The Prehistory of Cyprus: Problems and Prospects. *Journal of World Prehistory* 8(4): 377–453.

Luke, H.

1969   *Cyprus under the Turks 1571–1978: A Record based on the Archives of the English Consulate in Cyprus under the Levant Company and After*. London: Hurst.

Maier, F. G.

1985   Factoids in Ancient History: The Case of Fifth-Century Cyprus. *Journal of Hellenic Studies* 105: 32–39.

1994   Cyprus and Phoenicia. Pp. 297–336 in *Volume VI: The Fourth Century B.C. The Cambridge Ancient History*, second edition, ed. D. Lewis, J. Boardman, S. Hornblower and M. Ostwald. Cambridge: Cambridge University.

Markoe, G.

2000   *The Phoenicians*. London: British Museum.

McCarthy, J.

1997   *The Ottoman Turks: An Introductory History to 1923*. London: Longman.

McCartney, C.; Manning, S. W.; Sewell, D.; and Stewart, S. T.

2007   The EENC 2006 Field Season: Excavations at Agia Varvara-*Asprokremnos* and Survey of the Local Early Holocene Landscape. *Report of the Department of Antiquities, Cyprus*: 27–44.

Mehl, A.

2000   Ελληνιστική Κύπρος. Pp. 619–761 in *Ιστορία της Κύπρου, Vol.II Αρχαία Κύπρος Part 2*, ed. Th. Papadopoullos. Nicosia: Archbishop Makarios III Cultural Foundation.

Michaelides, D.

1990   The Roman Period. Pp. 110–35 in *Footprints in Cyprus: An Illustrated History*, revised edition, ed. D. Hunt. London: Trigraph.

Mitford, T.

1980   Roman Cyprus. Pp. 1275–1382 in *Aufstieg und Niedergang der römischen Welt* II.7.2. Berlin: de Gruyter.

Morris, I.

1994   Archaeologies of Greece. Pp. 3–47 in *Classical Greece: Ancient Histories and Modern Archaeologies*, ed. I. Morris. Cambridge: Cambridge University.

Papageorghiou, A.

1993   Cities and Countryside at the End of Antiquity. Pp. 27–51 in *The Sweet Land of Cyprus: Papers Given at the Twenty-Fifth Jubilee Spring Symposium of Byzantine Studies, March 1991*, eds. A. A. M. Bryer and G. S. Georghallides. Nicosia: Cyprus Research Centre.

1995   Crusader Influence on the Byzantine Art of Cyprus. Pp. 275–94 *Cyprus and the Crusades: Papers given at the International Conference 'Cyprus and the Crusades', Nicosia, 6–9 September 1994*, eds. N. Coureas and J. Riley-Smith. Nicosia: Cyprus Research Centre.

Peltenburg, E. J.

1990   Palaeolithic to Late Bronze Ages. Pp. 1–21 in *Footprints in Cyprus*, ed. D. Hunt. London: Trigraph.

1996   From Isolation to State Formation in Cyprus, c. 3500–1500 B.C. Pp. 17–44 in *The Development of the Cypriot Economy: From the Prehistoric Period to the Present Day*, eds. V. Karageorghis, and D. Michaelides. Nicosia: University of Cyprus and Bank of Cyprus.

Quataert, D.

2005   *The Ottoman Empire 1700–1922*, second edition. Cambridge: Cambridge.

Radner, K.

2010   The Stele of Sargon II of Assyria at Kition: A Focus for an Emerging Cypriot Identity. Pp. 429–49 in *Interkulturalität in der Alten Welt: Vorderasien, Hellas, Ägypten und die vielfältigen Ebenen des Kontakts*, eds. R. Rollinger, B. Gufler, M. Lang, and I. Madreiter. Philippika 43. Wiesbaden: Harrassowitz.

Rautman, M.

2003   *A Cypriot Village of Late Antiquity: Kalavasos-Kopetra in the Vasilikos Valley*. Portsmouth, RI: Journal of Roman Archaeology.

Redman, C. L.

1978   *The Rise of Civilization*. San Francisco: W. H. Freeman.

Renfrew, C., and Aspinall, A.

1990   Aegean Obsidian and Franchthi Cave. Pp 257–70 in *Les industries lithiques taillées* de Franchthi (Argolide, Grèce). Tome II: Les industries du Mésolithique et du Néolithique Initial, by C. Perlès. Bloomington: Indiana.

Renfrew, C., and Bahn, P.
2004 Archaeology: Theories, Methods, and Practice. Fourth edition. London: Thames and Hudson.

Reyes, A. T.
1994 Archaic Cyprus: A Study of the Textual and Archaeological Evidence. Oxford: Clarendon.

Riley-Smith, J.
1995 The Crusading Heritage of Guy and Aimery of Lusignan. Pp. 31–45 in Cyprus and the Crusades: Papers given at the International Conference 'Cyprus and the Crusades', Nicosia, 6–9 September 1994, eds. N. Coureas and J. Riley-Smith. Nicosia: Cyprus Research Centre.

Runciman, S.
1990 The Byzantine Period. Pp.136–74 in Footprints in Cyprus: An Illustrated History, revised edition, ed. D. Hunt. London: Trigraph.

Rupp, D.
1987 Vive le Roi: The Emergence of the State in Iron Age Cyprus. Pp. 147–61 in Western Cyprus Connections. Studies in Mediterranean Archaeology 77, ed. D. Rupp. Göteborg: Åström.
1998 The Seven Kings of the Country of Ia', a District of Ia-ad-na-na: Achaean Bluebloods, Cypriot Parvenus or Both? Pp. 209–22 in Stephanos: Studies in Honor of Brunilde Sismondo Ridgway, eds. K. Hartswick and M. Sturgeon. University Museum Mongraph 100. Philadelphia: University of Pennsylvania Museum of Archaeology and Anthropology.

Savvides, A.
1995 The Consolidation of Power in Cyprus on the Eve of the First Crusade and the First Decades of the Empire's Relations with the Crusaders. Pp. 3–18 in Cyprus and the Crusades: Papers given at the International Conference 'Cyprus and the Crusades', Nicosia, 6–9 September 1994, eds. N. Coureas and J. Riley-Smith. Nicosia: Cyprus Research Centre.

Sherratt, A.
1981 Plough and Pastoralism: Aspects of the Secondary Products Revolution. Pp. 261–305 in Patterns of the Past: Studies in Honour of David Clarke, eds. I. Hodder, G. Isaac, and N. Hammond. Cambridge: Cambridge.

Sherratt, S.
2001 Potemkin Palaces and Route-Based Economies. Pp. 214–38 in Economy and Politics in the Mycenaean Palace States. Proceedings of a Conference Held on 1–3 July 1999 in the Faculty of Classics, Cambridge, eds. S. Voutsaki and J. Killen. Cambridge Philological Society Supplementary Volume 27. Cambridge: Cambridge Philological Society.
2003 The Mediterranean Economy: 'Globalization' at the End of the Second Millennium B.C.E. Pp. 37–62 in Symbiosis, Symbolism, and the Power of the Past: Canaan, Ancient Israel, and Their Neighbors from the Late Bronze Age Through Roman Palaestina, eds. W. G. Dever and S. Gitin. Winona Lake, IN.: Eisenbrauns.
2010 The Aegean and the Wider World: Some Thoughts on a World-Systems Perspective. Pp. 81–106 in Archaic State Interaction: The Eastern Mediterranean in the Bronze Age, eds. W. Parkinson and M. Galaty. Santa Fe: School of Advanced Research.

Simmons, A. H.
1999 Faunal Extinction in an Island Society: Pygmy Hippopotamus Hunters of Cyprus. New York: Kluwer Academic/Plenum.
2001 The First Humans and Last Pygmy Hippopotami of Cyprus. Pp. 1–18 in The Earliest Prehistory of Cyprus. From Colonization to Exploitation, ed. S. Swiny. American Schools of Oriental Research Archaeological Reports 5. Boston, MA: American Schools of Oriental Research.

Smith, J.
2009 Art and Society in Cyprus from the Bronze Age into the Iron Age. Cambridge: Cambridge University.

Solomidou-Ieronymidou, M.
1999a Agios Nikolaos tis Stegis (St. Nicholas of the Roof), Kakopetria. Pp. 30–35 in *World Heritage Sites in Cyprus*. Nicosia: Cyprus National Commission for UNESCO.
1999b Panagia Phorviotissa (Asinou), Nikitari. Pp. 36–41 in *World Heritage Sites in Cyprus*. Nicosia: Cyprus National Commission for UNESCO.
2001 The Discovery of Six Unique Cypro-Archaic Statues at Tamassos. *Report of the Department of Antiquities, Cyprus*: 165–86.

Steel, L.
1993 The Establishment of the City Kingdoms in Iron Age Cyprus: An Archaeological Commentary. *Report of the Department of Antiquities Cyprus*: 147–56.
2004 *Cyprus before History: From the Earliest Settlers to the End of the Bronze Age*. London: Duckworth.

Strasser, T. F; Panagopoulou, E.; Runnels, C. N.; Murray, P. M.; Thompson, N.; Karkana, P.; McCoy, F. W.; Wegmann, K. W.
2010 Stone Age Seafaring in the Mediterranean: Evidence from the Plakias Region for Lower Palaeolithic and Mesolithic Habitation of Crete. *Hesperia* 79: 145–90.

Stylianou, P.
2000 Τα Αρχαία Βασίλεια. Pp. 465–618 in *Ιστορία της Κύπρου Vol.II Αρχαία Κύπρος Part 2*, ed. Th. Papadopoullos. Nicosia: Archbishop Makarios III Cultural Foundation.

Stylianou, A., and Stylianou, J.
1985 *The Painted Churches of Cyprus: Treasures of Byzantine Art*. London: Trigraph.

Swiny. S. (ed.)
2001 *The Earliest Prehistory of Cyprus: From Colonization to Exploitation*. American Schools of Oriental Research Archaeological Reports 5. Boston, MA: American Schools of Oriental Research.

Tatton-Brown, V.
1990 The Archaic Period 750 – 475 B.C. Pp. 65–83 in *Footprints in Cyprus: An Illustrated History*, revised edition, ed. D. Hunt. London: Trigraph.

Ulbrich, A.
2008 Kypris : *Heiligtümer und Kulte weiblicher Gottheiten auf Zypern in der kyproarchaischen und kyproklassischen Epoche (Königszeit)*. Alter Orient und Altes Testament 44. Münster: Ugarit-Verlag.

Vanschoonwinkel, J.
1994 La presence grecque à Chypre au XIe siècle av. J.-C. Pp. 109–32 in *Cyprus in the 11th Century B.C.*, ed. V. Karageorghis. Nicosia: A. G. Leventis Foundation.

Vermeule, C.
1976 *Greek and Roman Cyprus: Art from Classical Through Late Antique Times*. Cambridge, MA: Copy Quik Corporation.

Vigne, J.-D.
2001 Large Mammals of Early Aceramic Neolithic Cyprus: Preliminary Results from Parekklisha *Shillourokambos*. Pp. 55–60 in *The Earliest Prehistory of Cyprus. From Colonization to Exploitation*, ed. S. Swiny. American Schools of Oriental Research Archaeological Reports 5. Boston, MA: American Schools of Oriental Research.

Wright, G.F.
1992 *Ancient Building in Cyprus*. Leiden: Brill.

Zournatzi, A.
2005 *Persian Rule in Cyprus: Sources, Problems, Perspectives*. ΜΕΛΕΤΗΜΑΤΑ 44. Athens: National Hellenic Research Foundation.

Chapter 4

A History of Archaeological Activity
in the Athienou Region

by Derek B. Counts

It is perhaps safe to suggest that, aside from landholding records and simple designations on early maps of Cyprus (see Counts and Parvis, Ch. 5), the region of Athienou-*Malloura* received little or no attention from the scholarly world until March 1862. At that time, the French architect Edmond Duthoit discovered through local informants and excavated a site southwest of Athienou, which he referred to as "Malloura" (fig. 4.1) (Foucart-Borville 1985; pls. 1–3 reproduce sketches made by Duthoit of sculptures he had discovered, with several preserving the label Μάλλουρα beneath them; Toumazou et al. 1992; 1998). While it is likely that chance discoveries and surface finds gathered by locals made their way into an emerging market for antiquities in the mid- to late 19th century, the arrival of the French at Athienou represents the earliest documented case of organized exploration in the region. Duthoit was part of the French *Mission de Phénicie* under the direction of Ernest Renan (Hermary 1990: 9). After the death of his sister, Renan transferred direction of the expedition in Cyprus to Melchior de Vogüé, under whom Duthoit and the English epigrapher William-Henry Waddington served (Masson 1971: 307–10; Foucart-Borville 1985: 24–25;

Hermary 1988). Duthoit's work was unfortunately left unpublished (Vogüé had apparently planned a comprehensive volume prior to his death); consequently, there are no plans or maps that help identify the exact location of Duthoit's Malloura. This situation is somewhat remedied by the preservation of numerous letters written by Duthoit and Vogüé that illuminate the nature and extent of the discoveries (Duthoit's letters to Vogüé that discuss archaeological work in the Athienou environs have been published by Foucart-Borville [1985]; two of Vogüé's [1862a–b] letters to Renan were published in the *Revue archéologique*).

In a letter dated February 8, 1862, Duthoit writes that the purpose of the mission to Cyprus was: "recueillir les éléments propres à faire connaître les Phéniciens, tout ce qui concerne leur histoire, leurs arts, leurs mœurs, etc." (collect the elements appropriate to make known the Phoenicians, everything about their history, their arts, their habits, etc.). This mission statement reflects the contemporary perception that Cypriot art represented a by-product of Phoenician artistic influence (Foucart-Borville 1985: 14). Accordingly, the French mission traveled between villages throughout the island conducting small-scale excavations, in ad-

FIG. 4.1 *Edmond Duthoit's sketches of sculptures discovered by the Mission Vogüé, listing provenience (including Malloura). Photo courtesy of the Département des antiquités orientales, Musée du Louvre.*

dition to procuring antiquities from local residents. For example, a well-preserved late-seventh-/early-sixth-century BC statue with head and torso in the Louvre is said to have been purchased in Athienou (Hermary 1989: 44; inv. no. AM 3444).

In 1862, Vogüé and Waddington traveled to Beirut and left Duthoit behind in Cyprus to conduct investigations alone. The nature of his excavations and the specifics of discoveries in the region of Athienou (fig. 4.2), most notably at the sites of Ayios Photios in the vicinity of Golgoi and Malloura, are illuminated by the various correspondences of Duthoit and Vogüé (Counts 1998: 51–56). In a letter dated March 24, 1862, Duthoit writes:

> La manière dont se découvrent tous ces fragments est singulière. A Agios-Photis (aujourd'hui Agios Photios) j'ai trouvé en même temps l'une sur l'autre quinze à vingt têtes, plus loin des pieds et des jambes, tous ensemble à l'état de gisement, plus loin des troncs et des bustes, les mains et les bras étaient dans un autre trou; le fait singulier se reproduit à Malloura. (Foucart-Borville 1985: 25)

The manner in which all of those fragments are being discovered is unusual. At Agios-Photis [today Agios Photios] I found together one on top of the other fifteen to twenty heads, a bit further feet and legs, all together as a deposit, and further again torsos and busts, the hands and arms were in another trench; this unusual fact is reproduced at Malloura.

Vogüé himself repeated the account of Duthoit's discovery of an ancient deposit of sculptures at Malloura in a letter addressed to Renan:

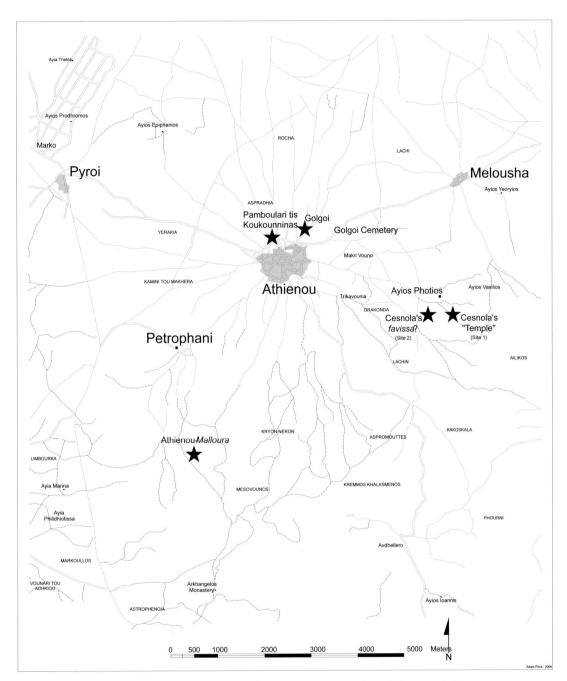

Fig. 4.2   *Map of Athienou region showing archaeological sites mentioned in text (drawing: A. Prins, 2009).*

Trois ont été fouillés et complétement déblayés: l'un à Agios Photis, près de Golgoi; l'autre à Arsos, situé à une heure plus loin; un troisième à Malloura, dans la région de Dali. Le premier et le dernier nous ont donné plus d'un millier de fragments, parmi lesquels j'ai fait choix

d'une centaine de têtes, qui toutes, malgré leur mauvais état de conservation, ont un intérêt particulier... Tous ces morceaux sont sculptés dans cette pierre blanche et friable. (Vogüé 1862b: 245)

Three have been excavated and completely cleared: the one at Agios Photis, near Golgoi; the other at Arsos, situated one hour from there; a third one at Malloura, in the region of Dali. The first one and the last one have given to us more than a thousand fragments, among them I chose a hundred heads, all of which, despite their bad state of preservation, have a particular interest.... All those fragments are sculpted in this white and fragile stone.

Finally, a letter written by Duthoit roughly two months after the excavations in May 1862 summarizes his activities:

> Pendant l'absence de M. de Vogüé, et d'après ses ordres, j'ai fait fouiller sur l'emplacement supposé de Golgos, à Dali (Idalium), à Malloura, et à Agios Photis, puis à Arsos. Ces fouilles ne nous ont donné que faibles résultats, si l'on en juge du mérite des objets trouvés. Si, au contraire, les oeuvres d'art se jugeaient à leur poids, la récolte serait forte belle: 150 à 200 têtes, dont quelques-unes intactes et d'un très beau style archaïque. (Foucart-Borville 1985: 33)

> During the absence of M. de Vogüé, and following his orders, I excavated on the spot that was supposed to be the site of Golgos [Golgoi], at Dali (Idalium), at Malloura, and at Agios Photis, and then at Arsos. Those excavations gave us only poor results, if they are judged on the value of the objects found. On the contrary, if the works of art were judged on their weight, the harvest would be really nice: 150 to 200 heads, from which some are intact and are in a very nice archaic style.

Having focused his activities at Malloura and Ayios Photios in the initial season of work, Duthoit returned in 1865 and excavated an additional site to the northeast of Athienou, which he called "Golgoi" (Hermary 1989: 17–19; Beer 1992: 79). The exact location of this third site is unknown, but Duthoit noted "fondements de blocage mal fait," which may suggest that the site corresponds

to the temple excavated by Cesnola less than a decade later (Cesnola 1878: 117–18; Foucart-Borville 1985: 25). At any rate, we can assume a connection to the ancient city of Golgoi, which is attested in various literary sources as early as the third century BC (e.g., Theokritos, *Idyll* 15.100) and well into the Roman (Pausanias 8.5.2) and later (Stephanus Byzantius, s.v. "Golgoi") periods, as well as on a Roman-period stele signed by an artist with the name "Golgios" (Savage 1881; Myres 1914: 238–39, inv. no. 1381). The ancient toponym had been identified with the remains north and east of Athienou by the learned Greek philologist Athanasios Sakellarios in the mid-19th century. Sakellarios argued for a linguistic connection between the ancient name "Golgoi" and the locale Giorkous, the name given to him by locals when he visited in 1851 (Sakellarios 1855: 187; Masson 1961; 1971). As noted above, the region had not been subjected to any organized exploration prior to Duthoit's arrival. Apparently, Sakellarios observed only some surface remains, including large portions of the city wall and an eastern gate, later excavated by Bakalakis.

The total number of statues excavated from the three areas is unknown. The letters reveal that Duthoit secured eight carts and 24 mules to transport a select number of statues, but apparently this number was "rien d'entier" (Foucart-Borville 1985: 27). Although it is impossible to determine how many sculptural fragments were actually removed by Duthoit's excavations, at least some of the discarded statuary may have been reburied in close vicinity to the sanctuaries at Malloura and Ayios Photios. Judging from the preponderance of well-preserved heads in the Louvre, these discarded fragments may have been "pieds," "jambes," "mains," and "bras" deemed unsuitable to 19th-century French artistic taste. Indeed, evidence of this earlier French activity is suggested by numerous, large caches of sculptural fragments recovered by AAP from disturbed contexts such as looter's pits, although it is admittedly difficult to distinguish this 19th-century activity from later, 20th-century looting that ravaged the site.

Duthoit's excavations were among the first in a sporadic and complex archaeological history for

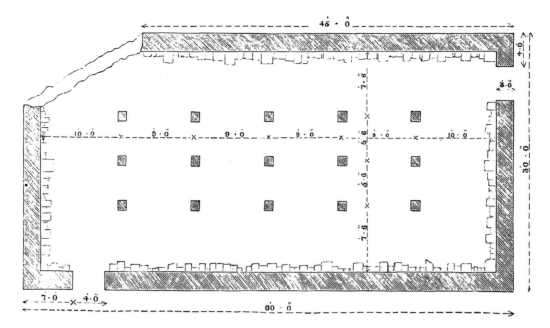

Plan of Temple of Golgoi.

FIG. 4.3   *Cesnola's 'temple' near Ayios Photios (after Cesnola 1878: 139).*

the region of Athienou. Less than ten years later, the American Consul to Cyprus in Larnaka, Luigi Palma di Cesnola, conducted excavations near Athienou. Beginning in 1870, Cesnola concentrated his efforts on the numerous tombs northeast of the modern village, as well as sanctuary site(s) in the area of ancient Golgoi, near the small chapel of Ayios Photios (see fig. 4.2 for locations). The murky dealings of Cesnola are well-known to students of Cypriot archaeology (Cesnola 1878, foreword by Swiny; McFadden 1971; Marangou 2000). The credibility of the accounts of his diggings throughout Cyprus and, most notably, at the sites of Golgoi and Ayios Photios has been the subject of debate since their completion (James 1888: 150). The situation is partly remedied by several contemporary accounts and documents produced by antiquarians and visitors (e.g., R. H. Lang, G. Colonna-Ceccaldi, J. Doell) that partially restored the various lacunae in Cesnola's own reporting (Masson 1961: 276–77). In particular, scholars have questioned the exact findspots of the Cesnola sculptures, although it seems clear that the majority were found in an area near the small chapel of Ayios Photios at two principal locations: a limestone "temple," attributed by

Cesnola to Aphrodite, and a second site to the west of the temple structure, possibly a *favissa* (ancient deposit of discarded material from religious sites) (Cesnola 1878: 128; Masson 1961; 1971; Connelly 1988: 75–78; Beer 1992: 79). While Cesnola had originally suggested that he had excavated a single site near Ayios-Photios, the criticisms of Colonna-Ceccaldi and Lang, who had visited the site during excavations, required some reaction (although short of a redaction) in Cesnola's later accounts (see especially the discussion in Masson 1961: 277–78). Nevertheless, a two-site hypothesis remains the scholarly consensus, solidified by Masson's (1961; 1971) important historiographical work on the region.

The first site included a "temple" (fig. 4.3) oriented north–south and measuring roughly 9 × 18 m. The interior contained 15 regularly aligned stone bases, presumably to support wooden columns for a roof, because Cesnola also reports finding two stone capitals and carbonized wood within the enclosed area of the structure (Cesnola 1878: 139–40, 150). Openings were observed off-center along the northern and eastern walls (Cesnola 1878: 139–45). According to Cesnola, 72 variously-shaped statue bases were discovered, along with a large cache of 228 limestone votive sculptures (Cesnola 1878: 140–46). The sculptures suggest that the temple was in use from the Cypro-Archaic to Late Hellenistic period; an ash layer noted by Cesnola (1878: 150) signals the final destruction of the site, perhaps in the Early Roman period. Cesnola's second site, likely a *favissa*, was located roughly 200 m west of the temple and contained an equally impressive number of sculptures.

As Masson (1961: 276–78) prudently suggests, Cesnola's original identification of the site as representative of a single temple is surely incorrect, but equally troubling is his association of the cult with Aphrodite. The assemblage of predominantly male votaries and divine images corresponds well to the worship of a male divinity in Cyprus (for a discussion of male divinities in Cyprus, see Counts 2008: 19–23). Still, the presence of some female images, both human and divine (e.g., the famous Aphrodite with Eros said to be from the temple; Karageorghis 2000: 212–13), suggests the later addition of a female divine cult, a pattern noticed elsewhere across the Mesaoria in the late Cypro-Classical–Hellenistic period (see Counts and Toumazou 2003: 241–44). The heart of the Cesnola collection, which includes the largest and best-preserved collection of Cypro-Archaic–Hellenistic limestone sculptures from Cyprus, is now housed in the Metropolitan Museum of Art in New York; other finds resulting from Cesnola's activities are found in Boston and several other museums in the United States (e.g., Kelsey in Ann Arbor, Ringling in Sarasota, Semitic Museum at Harvard University), Paris, London, Istanbul, Berlin, and Athens (Cesnola 1885; Myres 1914; Karageorghis 2000; see also discussion in Counts 2001: 134–35).

After Cesnola, archaeological pursuits in the region for the next century took the form of systematic looting. The abundant material recorded from Athienou, as well as the town's proximity to Larnaka, encouraged looting operations in the area. Looting appears to have been particularly rampant in the 1920s and 1930s when adverse economic conditions forced villagers to seek more profitable enterprises (M. K. Toumazou, personal communication). During this period (and continuing to the present), the only sanctioned excavations in the area took the form of salvage operations conducted by the Department of Antiquities.

Prior to the Turkish invasion and occupation of the island in 1974, which effectively barred access to the archaeological remains north and east of the village, two foreign projects, from Greece and Israel, conducted scientific excavations at the outskirts of Athienou. An extensive settlement centered on a knoll less than one kilometer northeast of Athienou along the road to Ayia was excavated by Giorgos Bakalakis of the University of Thessaloniki from 1969 to 1972 (Bakalakis 1988). Bakalakis revealed archaeological remains ranging from the Late Bronze Age to the Early Christian periods, most notably impressive remains associated with the Cypro-Classical period, which include fortification walls and associated defensive towers, an acropolis, and various production and storage facilities. He identified three principal phases at the site: Phase III, intermittent habitation and use throughout the Roman and Early Christian periods, including partial rehabilitation of the Phase II remains; Phase II, the Classical city with walls, various domestic/industrial structures, and a water reservoir, destroyed at the end of the fourth century BC, perhaps by Demetrios Poliorketes; and Phase I, a long, initial period of occupation with some architecture and ceramics of the later Cypro-Archaic period and scatters of ceramic material from the Late Bronze Age and Early Iron Age (Bakalakis 1988: 142–60). Despite a paucity of aboveground remains and modest material record associated with Bakalakis's earliest attested habitation at Golgoi (sometime before the beginning of the Iron Age), the author (1988: 153–55) suggests that the settlement's development may be linked to a shift (or expansion) in population from the Late Bronze Age site of Athienou-*Pamboulari tis Koukounninas*, excavated by the Israelis, after that site's final abandonment, sometime after the 12th century BC.

At the same time Bakalakis was investigating ancient Golgoi to the northeast of Athienou, a team from the Institute of Archaeology at the Hebrew University in Jerusalem, under the direction of two preeminent Israeli archaeologists (Trude Dothan, Amnon Ben-Tor), began full-scale excavations

FIG. 4.4 *Aerial view of Athienou-*Pamboulari tis Koukounninas *excavations from the north (Photo courtesy of the Athienou Municipality).*

200 meters north of the modern town at the site of *Pamboulari tis Koukounninas* (fig. 4.4). Digging at the site took place in 1971 and 1972, with the final publication following more than a decade later (Dothan and Ben-Tor 1983). Prior to the Israeli team, the Department of Antiquities conducted a survey of the area by Porphyrios Dikaios and Chrysostomos Paraskeva, which collected fragments from large pithoi, votive vessels, and metal slag (Karageorghis 1959: 354; Megaw 1959: 18; Dothan and Ben-Tor 1983: 1–3).

The total area investigated at Pamboulari by the Israelis covered about 2,500 m², situated on a low hill rising approximately 2 m above its surroundings; the excavated strata that exposed the occupation levels reached a depth of about 1 m (Dothan and Ben-Tor 1983: 3). The excavators identified four occupational phases from the 16th to the 12th centuries: Stratum IV, dated to the early 16th century BC, was not represented by preserved architecture but mostly understood from material deposited in pits and sealed within the floor of

Stratum III; Stratum III, the principal phase of the site, is dated to the 16th to 13th centuries BC and includes complex architectural design for a large public building with a central court and flanking rooms to the north and east, a large amount of copper slag, imported (Mycenaean IIIB and Late Minoan III) and locally made (White Painted, Red on Black, Composite, Red Painted, Black Slip, and Bi-chrome) pottery, an impressive votive(?) cache of more than 2,000 intact juglets, an ivory rhyton, a cylinder seal of local manufacture, and imported objects from Egypt including scarabs and a bronze ring with hieroglyphs; Stratum II, dated to the 13th and 12th centuries BC, represents the continuation of Stratum III, with some minor additions, and featured both imported (Mycenaean IIIC) and local pottery; and Stratum I, dated from the 11th and 10th centuries BC, corresponds to the abandonment of the site (without an associated destruction layer) and subsequent, small-scale use into the Iron Age, perhaps as late as the eighth or seventh century BC (Dothan and Ben-Tor 1983: 3–24, 139–40). The site has been interpreted as a multifunctional facility encompassing both metallurgical industry and cultic installations (see especially Dothan 1981: 93; Dothan and Ben-Tor 1983: 139–40; Knapp 1986: 83–84; 2008: 233–35; Webb 1999: 28). Dothan (1981: 93) characterizes the site as a "station on the trade route leading from the mining areas to the large marketing centers on the east coast of the island." This reconstruction of the site's use and function mirrors sanctuaries at the coastal sites of Kition and Enkomi where evidence for metalworking was discovered (Knapp 2008: 235). Athienou's position in the central eastern Mesaoria may suggest that the site benefited from the traffic of raw materials and general trade between Enkomi and Kition and the interior sources of copper in the foothills of the Troodos Mountains. Dothan (1981: 91) notes the lack of an associated settlement; however, the presence of a contemporary cemetery in the area suggests its presence, perhaps even under the modern village (Catling 1963: 145, 155 [site no. 15]).

Since 1974, work has halted at all locations within the U.N.-controlled buffer zone and Turkish occupied areas to the north and east of the village. Although nominally in the U.N.-controlled buffer zone, the acropolis of Golgoi is now occupied by the Turkish army, serving as a lookout point with a gun emplacement. Pamboulari, however, remains accessible from the northern end of Athienou and has now been properly protected with a gated fence mounted within a low concrete wall. Since 1990, archaeological activity in the area has been renewed by AAP through its survey and archaeological excavation of the Malloura Valley, and also by numerous salvage excavations in and around Athienou completed by the project under the authority of the Director of the Department of Antiquities and by the Department of Antiquities itself. Further information has been accumulated from interviews with patrons and friends of the project, local informants, the examination of local, registered collections, archival work, and pedestrian survey of some accessible areas in the immediate environs. Thanks in part to the project's work, the region of Athienou has reemerged as an important link between the island's rich past and the theoretical, methodological, and historical debates current in Cypriot archaeology.

Acknowledgments

The author's translations have attempted to preserve the nuance of the original texts, despite some resultant infelicities. The author would like to thank Annie Caubet, former Conservateur général chargé du Départment des Antiquités Orientales of the Louvre, for providing access to departmental files that contained copies of sketches by Duthoit and for permission to reproduce fig. 4.1. Thanks are also due to Adam Prins, who produced the useful map (fig. 4.2). Michael Toumazou provided valuable assistance concerning the history of previous archaeological work in the area, as well as with the translation and interpretation of Bakalakis's findings at Golgoi. John Oswald and Sarah Harris completed useful background research on the archaeological activities of the late 1960s and early 1970s, while Stavroulla Georgiou and Sabine Fourrier graciously commented on the English translations of Duthoit's and Vogüé's letters.

References

Bakalakis, G.
1988   Ανασκαφή στο Λόφο Γιόρκους ΒΑ της Αθηαίνου, Κύπρος. Athens: Αρχαιολογική Εταιρεία Αθηνών.

Beer, C.
1992   Ethnic Diversity and Financial Differentiation in Cypriote Sanctuaries. Pp. 73–84 in Economics of Cult in the Ancient Greek World: Proceedings of the Uppsala Symposium 1990, eds. T. Linders and B. Alroth. Uppsala: S. Academiae Ubsaliensis.

Catling, H. C.
1963   Patterns of Settlement in Bronze Age Cyprus. Opuscula Atheniensia 4: 129–69.

Cesnola, L. P. di
1878   *Cyprus: Its Ancient Cities, Tombs, and Temples.* New York: Harper. Reprint 1991.
1885   *A Descriptive Atlas of the Cesnola Collection of Cypriote Antiquities in the Metropolitan Museum of Art, New York.* Boston: James R. Osgood.

Connelly, J. B.
1988   *Votive Sculpture of Hellenistic Cyprus.* Nicosia: Department of Antiquities of Cyprus.

Counts, D. B.
1998   Contributions to the Study of Cypriote Sculpture: Limestone Votives from Athienou-*Malloura.* Unpublished Ph. D. dissertation, Brown University.
2001   Prolegomena to the Study of Cypriote Sculpture. *Cahier du Centre d'Etudes Chypriotes* 31: 129–81.
2008   Master of the Lion: Representation and Hybridity in Cypriote Sanctuaries. *American Journal of Archaeology* 112: 3–27.

Counts, D. B., and Toumazou, M. K.
2003   Artemis at Athienou-*Malloura. Cahier du Centre d'Etudes Chypriotes* 33: 237–51.

Dothan, T.
1981   The High Place of Athienou in Cyprus. Pp. 963–68 in *From Temples and High Places in Biblical Times*, ed. A. Brian. Jerusalem: The Nelson Glueck School of Biblical Archaeology of the Hebrew Union College.

Dothan, T., and Ben-Tor, A.
1983   *Excavations at Athienou, Cyprus. 1971–1972.* Jerusalem: Institute of Archaeology, Hebrew University of Jerusalem.

Foucart-Borville, J.
1985   La correspondence chypriote d'Edmond Duthoit (1862 et 1865). *Cahier du Centre d'Etudes Chypriotes* 4: 3–60.

Hermary, A.
1988   Nouvelles découvertes sur la Mission Vogüé de 1862. *Cahier du Centre d'Etudes Chypriotes* 12: 15–20.
1989   *Musée du Louvre, Département des antiquités orientales: Catalogue des antiquités de Chypre. Sculptures.* Paris: Editions de la Réunion des Musées Nationaux.
1990   Historie des études sur la sculpture chypriote. *Cahier du Centre d'Etudes Chypriotes* 14: 7–28.

James, M. R.
1888   Excavations in Cyprus, 1887–1888. The First Season's Work: Preliminary Narrative. *Journal of Hellenic Studies* 9: 149–58.

Karageorghis, V.
1959   Chronique des fouilles et découvertes archéologiques à Chypre en 1958. *Bulletin de Correspondance Hellénique* 83: 336–61.
2000   *Ancient Art from Cyprus: The Cesnola Collection of the Metropolitan Museum of Art.* New York: Metropolitan Museum of Art and Abrams.

Knapp, A. B.
1986   *Copper Production and Divine Protection: Archaeology, Ideology and Social Complexity on Bronze Age Cyprus.* Göteborg: Åström.
2008   *Prehistoric and Protohistoric Cyprus: Identity, Insularity, and Connectivity.* Oxford: Oxford University.

Marangou, A.
2000   *The Consul Luigi Palma di Cesnola 1832–1904: Life and Deeds.* Nicosia: Cultural Centre, Popular Bank Group.

Masson, O.
1961   *Inscriptions chypriotes syllabiques.* Paris: de Boccard.
1971   KYPRIAKA IX: Recherches sur les antiquités de Golgoi. *Bulletin de Correspondance Hellénique* 95: 305–34.

McFadden, E.
1971   *The Glitter and the Gold.* New York: Dial.

Megaw, A. H. S.
1959   *Annual Report of the Department of Antiquities, Cyprus for the Year 1958.* Nicosia: Cyprus Government Printing Office.

Myres, J. L.

1914   *Handbook of the Cesnola Collection of Antiquities from Cyprus, Metropolitan Museum of Art, New York*. New York: The Metropolitan Museum of Art.

Sakellarios, A. A.

1855   *Ta Kypriaka, etoi, Pragmateia peri geographias archaiologias, statistikes, historias, mythologias kai dialektou tes Kyprou*. Athens: I. Angelopoulou.

Savage, A. D.

1881   A Greek Inscription Concerning Golgoi. *The American Journal of Philology* 2: 223–24.

Toumazou, M. K.; Kardulias, P. N.; Yerkes, R.

1992   Excavation and Survey in the Malloura Valley, Central Cyprus: The 1991 Season. *Old World Archaeology Newsletter* 15: 18–23.

1998   Athienou Archaeological Project: Investigations in the Malloura Valley, Cyprus, 1990–1995. *Journal of Field Archaeology* 25: 163–82.

Vogüé, M. de.

1862a   Letter to M. Renan. *Revue archéologique* 5: 345–47.

1862b   Letter to M. Renan. *Revue archéologique* 6: 244–49.

Webb, J.

1999   *Ritual Architecture, Iconography and Practice in the Late Cypriot Bronze Age*. Studies in Mediterranean Archaeology Pocket-book 75. Jonsered: Åström.

Chapter 5

Mapping Malloura

A Carto-Historical Survey
from the Early Modern Period to the Present

by Derek B. Counts and Joseph A. Parvis

The Malloura Valley (map 2 on p. xxii) lies in central eastern Cyprus at the southern edge of the Mesaoria, the fertile plain that connects the great Troodos Massif to the west and the Kyrenia range to the north. The center of the valley is ca. 2 km south of the now deserted Turkish Cypriot village of Petrophani (Turkish Esendagh) and ca. 4 km southwest of Athienou, roughly halfway between the modern cities of Larnaka and Nicosia. In antiquity the Malloura Valley was centrally located in close vicinity to Kition to the south and Idalion to the west, both of which had significant prehistoric components and served as urban centers for Iron Age city-kingdoms; the Late Bronze Age–Iron Age settlement (and later Cypro-Classical–Roman city) of Athienou-*Golgoi* is located less than 5 km to the northeast, just north of modern Athienou. Moreover, Chytroi, Tamassos, and Salamis (all centers of Iron Age city-kingdoms) are slightly farther to the north, west, and east, respectively, yet close enough to permit frequent interaction. During the first half of the first millennium BC, the surrounding region skirting the eastern Mesaoria witnessed the establishment of many smaller, secondary sites (e.g., Pyla, Arsos, Lefkoniko, Voni, Potamia), which

all preserve remains of sacred precincts datable to the Cypro-Archaic and Cypro-Classical periods. Significantly, it is at this very moment when the valley sees its first permanent use evidenced by the rural sanctuary of Athienou-*Malloura* (see Toumazou and Counts, Ch. 6; Fourrier, Ch. 9). This chapter considers local settlement patterns in the Malloura Valley and its immediate environs, as well as broader regional systems of exchange in Cyprus, from the 16th through 20th centuries using maps and textual information from travelers' accounts, administrative archives, and local histories.

THE NAME *MALLOURA*

There is no evidence that the toponym *Μάλλουρα* (*μαλλός* [*ὁ*], lock of wool, wool) derives from any ancient testimony; the name does not occur in ancient literary sources, nor is it found within the epigraphic record of Cyprus. Nevertheless, it is possible that the word preserves some trace of the ancient name, since the etymological history of many site names in Cyprus reveals a similar phenomenon (e.g., Tamassos, Asinou, Alassa, Dhali). In his *Historical Toponymy of Cyprus* (s.v. "Malloura"), Goodwin (1984: 1052) traces the etymology to an ancient Arcado-Cypriot root, suggesting that an earlier toponym is possibly preserved. The connection of this toponym with the project area currently under investigation by the Athienou Archaeological Project is supported by local traditions that have always assigned the name "Malloura" to this particular spot, as well as by its early mention during the Frankish period and it appearance on 16th-century Venetian maps. The conservatism of place-names in Cyprus is strong (Neumann 2000); thus, it is perhaps not surprising that the toponym "Malloura" survived on maps after 300 years of Ottoman rule, even though the fields located in the valley were owned by Turkish Cypriot farmers from Petrophani (who likely referred to it by an otherwise unattested name in Turkish). While we do not know exactly when the toponym Malloura is attached to our project area (or whether or not this happens earlier than its first appearance in the Medieval period), the name is quite common on the island. The *Gazetteer* of Cyprus (Christodoulou and Konstantinidis 1987: 773) records a total of four separate locations with the toponym "Malloura" within the Larnaka District (three associated with the Athienou/Petrophani region and one locale in the area of Xylofagou), as well as several variant forms across the island, such as "Malloures," "Mallouris," and "Mallouri." In our project area, two separate locales are identified with Malloura: the valley currently under investigation by AAP and a location to the south where the church (and former monastery) of Archangelos is located. This does betray a certain level of confusion and/or repetition, leaving open the possibility for sites and names to have been conflated or even shifted over time.

The earliest known reference to Malloura comes from Frankish-period documents of the mid-15th century AD (Grivaud 1998: 160). Florio Bustron, in *Chronique de l'île de Chypre*, records a list of land grants made by King James II of Cyprus ("the Bastard," who ruled Cyprus ca. AD 1463–1473) to a sea captain from Naples, Mutio de Costanzo. Here, Malloura is mentioned with four other towns (San Demeti [Ayios Dometios?], Ara, Chiendinari, Glaugia) and "li casali che teniva in

duario dama Annes de Verni" (Mas Latrie 1886: 418). According to Peter Edbury (personal communication, July 2009), the authority of René Mas Latrie's marginalia, which dates the grant to AD 1464–1468, is unclear. Nevertheless, the association of Malloura with the activities of James II in the mid-15th century AD is consistent with stratified deposits from Athienou-*Malloura*, which suggest the medieval phase of the settlement at Malloura (after some abandonment during the Arab raids) was founded during Frankish rule (see Toumazou and Counts, Ch. 6).

CYPRUS, "MALLURA/MALURA," AND THE VENETIAN CARTOGRAPHIC TRADITION (AD 1489–1571)

The earliest cartographic reference to Malloura comes from a 1542 map of Cyprus signed by Leonidas Attar, a Cyprus-born cartographer and surveyor (fig. 5.1) (Romanelli and Grivaud 2006: 18–30). The map, which is part of the rich cartographic collections of the Civico Museo Correr in Venice, was drawn in pen, ink, and watercolor on two attached pages. The site is labeled "Mallura" and is located south of settlements labeled "S. Zorsi" (perhaps modern Petrophani; see Grivaud 1998: 162–64; on Petrophani, see Yerkes, Ch. 26) and "Piroi," north of a "Damitia" and to the west of "Atirnu" (modern Athienou). The cartographic symbols, which include churches, houses, one- and two-tower settlements, and fortified cities, employed by Attar to denote settlements across the island are of some interest. For example, the symbol for "Mallura" features two towers with a central gate suggestive of a settlement larger than surrounding towns such as "Atirnu" and "Dali" (modern Dhali), which receive symbols with only a single tower. Romanelli and Grivaud (2006: 47–8) sensibly argue that such relative designations regarding settlement size and population are not without suspicion; nevertheless, such a hierarchy of settlements in the region does corroborate Malloura's relative importance on a later map by Giovanni Francesco Comocio in 1574. For its time, Attar's map represents an impressive record of 721 toponyms (including 656 named vil-

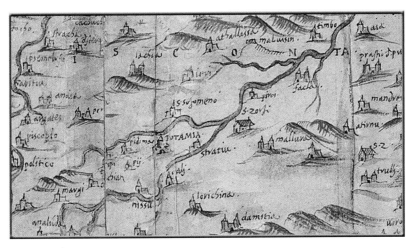

Fig. 5.1   *Detail of the map of Cyprus by Leonidas Attar, 1542, now in the Civico Museo Correr, Venice (after Romanelli and Grivaud 2006).*

lages) derived from both Frankish and Venetian documents; earlier maps by Francesco Bustron (in 1533) and Matheo Pagano (in 1538) listed far fewer villages with 400 and 273, respectively (Romanelli and Grivaud 2006: 47–9). Unfortunately, the 1542 map had little to no impact on Venetian or Mediterranean topography; it was apparently removed from circulation by Cosmo Da Mosto, who had commissioned the map and subsequently deposited it into his family archives in the fall of 1543 (Romanelli and Grivaud 2006: 57–60). Had historical circumstance run a different course, Attar's mapping of Cyprus would have likely been influential; while derivative on some levels, the number and accuracy of place-names and the overall shape of the island as surveyed by Attar represented significant improvements over his predecessors.

With Attar's map out of circulation and presumably unavailable to later Venetian mapmakers, a loose sheet map engraved by the Italian Jacomo Franco in Venice and produced in 1570 occupies a place of singular importance for the history of Cypriot cartography (fig. 5.2). Franco's map significantly breaks with earlier forms, incorporating an improved shape for the island (Hadjipaschalis and Iacovou 1989: 22; see also Stylianou and Stylianou 1970: 149–51). Malloura is indicated, this time as "Malura," and placed directly southwest of Athienou (now labeled "Atirna"). The settlement is positioned

roughly halfway between the towns "Dali" (to the west) and "Atirna" (to the east), with the settlements of "S. Zorsi" and "Damalia" (which had also been listed by Attar) to the north and south, respectively (Stylianou and Stylianou 1970: fig. 1; 1980: figs. 64, 66b). A village illustrated between "Malura" and "Atirna", without a toponym, indicates another, smaller settlement slightly north and east of Malloura, in the area of Kaphounda (the remnants of which were noted by Kitchener and are still recognizable today). It is interesting to note that this "nameless" town continues to appear on later maps that follow Franco. The addition of "Malura" and many other new locales reflects an amplified list of known villages and towns (notwithstanding Attar's heroic, yet forgotten, attempts three decades earlier); for example, Franco's map provides a total of 564 toponyms compared to the 273 listed on the 1538 map by the Venetian cartographer Pagano (Hadjipaschalis and Iacovou 1989: 22). Grivaud (1998: 455–61) conveniently records Venetian inventories of adult freedmen (*francomates*) in the region, which offer important evidence for the relative size of the various settlements in the area: Malloura (81 *francomates*), Athienou (60), S. Zorsi/Petrophani (1), Damidia (31), Lympia (88), Louroujina (186), Potamia (66), and Dhali (158). Malloura thus appears to have been a relatively important settlement during the 16th century, which accords well with the extensive settlement and

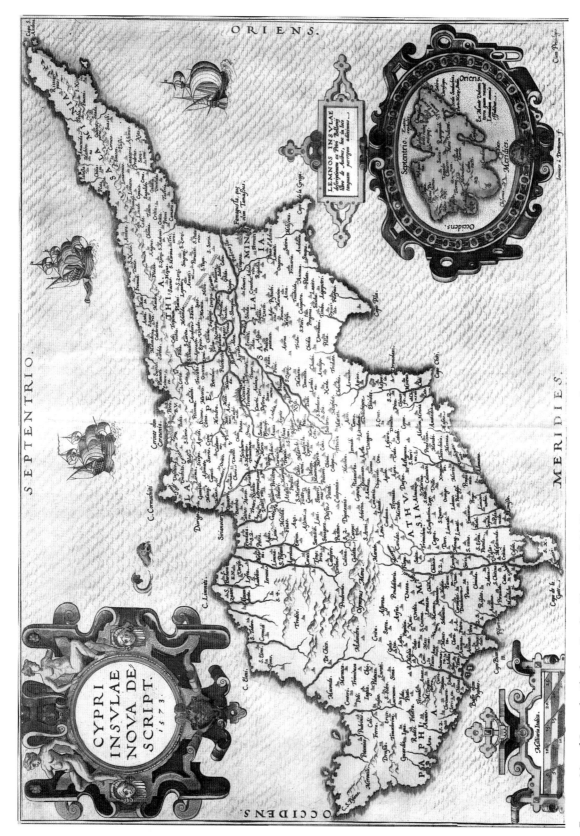

FIG. 5.2   *Map of Cyprus by Abraham Ortelius,* Theatrum Orbis Terrarum, *1573, a reprint of Jacomo Franco's 1570 map (© Bank of Cyprus Cultural Foundation, Nicosia).*

industrial activity evidenced by the excavations of AAP (for Venetian-period Malloura, see Toumazou and Counts, Ch. 6; De Masi, Ch. 16; Spigelman, Ch. 17; Harper, Ch. 20; and Beeston, Ch. 24).

Franco's map appears to be the result of a new or improved survey of the island, undertaken by the Venetians shortly before the Ottoman invasion of 1570, and reflects the preeminence of Venetian cartography in Cyprus while the island was under its control from AD 1489 to 1571. In fact, the map would serve, at least indirectly (see Hadjipaschalis and Iacovou 1989: 22), as the prototype for many other mapmakers in the succeeding centuries, most notably the well-known Dutch cartographer Abraham Ortelius who included it in his atlas (*Theatrum Orbis Terrarum*) for the year 1573 (Stylianou and Stylianou 1970: 151–54; 1980: 59–63; Hadjipaschalis and Iacovou 1989: 22–23, 58–59). The feudal estates and villages in the area of "Malura" on Franco's map correspond well to the written evidence from the late Frankish and early Venetian period, which lists them as fiefs held by various nobles. At that time, the settlement at "Malura" must have been substantial; its designation and prominence on the map are equivalent to that of "Dali" and "Atirna", which eventually emerged as agro-industrial regional centers in the modern era (Stylianou and Stylianou 1980: fig. 66b). An additional clue regarding the relative importance of the "Malura" settlement in the late Venetian/early Ottoman period comes from a copper-plate map of Cyprus prepared by the Venetian cartographer Comocio, now in the Civico Museo Correr in Venice (for Comocio and a discussion of an earlier map of the island by him [but not the one in the Correr], see Hadjipaschalis and Iacovou 1989: 21, 52–53). The map is dated 1574 and is a derivative of the 1538 Pagano map (for Comocio and Pagano, see Stylianou and Stylianou 1970: 148–51). What is most extraordinary, however, is that despite its rather simplified form (with less than 50 total toponyms indicated), the settlement of "Malura" appears alone in the region occupying the space between "Nicossia" and "Larnaca," with both Dhali and Athienou absent. Comocio's map suggests that the Malloura Valley was especially prominent along the principal route between the southern

coastal port at Larnaka and the fortified capital of Venetian Nicosia during this period; significantly, this same north–south route would prompt the emergence of Athienou as a regional center for trade and exchange in the Ottoman and British periods. In fact, a similar positioning of "Malura" is seen again, as late as 1687, on a map contained in Antonio Maria Graziani's *The History of the War of Cyprus*. While the shape of the island reflects the updated mapping established by Franco and Ortelius, the scarcity of sites and prominence of "Malura" on Graziani's rendering follow the tradition of Comocio (Hadjipaschalis and Iacovou 1989: 118–19). On Graziani's map, as on Comocio's, the site dominates the central eastern part of the island along the Larnaka–Nicosia route (again, Dhali and Athienou are conspicuously absent).

CYPRUS UNDER OTTOMAN RULE (AD 1571–1878)

Building on the Venetian tradition, but especially the map of Ortelius (and Franco), a host of sumptuously illustrated maps date from the first two centuries of Ottoman rule in Cyprus; unfortunately, they provide little additional evidence to determine any changes in toponymic designations and settlement patterns in the research area. In fact, the maps are often just simple, yet extravagantly illuminated copies (and copies of copies). Perhaps the most influential of these is a double folio map by Willem Blaeu first published in 1635 and based entirely on Ortelius's 1573 version. Although it was a direct copy, it was greatly enhanced with artistic effect and considered the best copper-plate map of the island at the time (Hadjipaschalis and Iacovou 1989: 104–5). Other notable copies include a map of the island published by Jodocus Hondius in Gerard Mercator's *Atlas* in 1606 (Hadjipaschalis and Iacovou 1989: 216–17), one published by Olfert Dapper in 1688 (Hadjipaschalis and Iacovou 1989: 122–23), a double folio map by Vincenzo Maria Coronelli that appeared in 1689 (Hadjipaschalis and Iacovou 1989: 126–27), and a lavishly colored map that appeared ca. 1705 by Gerard Valk and Petrus Schenk (Hadjipaschalis and Iacovou 1989: 138–39). As late as the second half of the 18th century, variations of Ortelius's map of 1573 remained standard, and there were apparently no new surveys conducted. As Hadjipaschalis and Iacovou note (1989: 23), the Ottoman administrators of the island apparently did not commission such a survey throughout the 300 years of their control over the island. As a result, the settlements mapped earlier in the region of the Malloura Valley remain fixed. This period is also relatively barren of other textual sources; thus, inference about the demographic patterns of these centuries must be constructed based on the patterns visible in the late 18th and 19th centuries (on sources, see Given 2000, 2004). Although there are several new maps of the island produced by 18th-century travelers, extensive reworking of the inland settlement data is not conducted until the work of L. de Mas Latrie (1862) in the 1850s and the mapping begun by Kitchener in 1878. A relatively new interest in documenting roads and lines of communication, characteristic of 19th-century maps, represents a significant trend away from tradition. For example, the Larnaka–Nicosia route that connected the port to the capital city is included on most maps. Likewise, the village of Athienou, located midway along the route, consistently appears on these same maps, most notably on a hydrographical mapping by a British navy captain, Thomas Graves, in 1849. Graves's new map was among the most influential in the 19th century, as witnessed on several derivatives printed by A. Sakellarios, W. J. Conybeare and J. S. Howson, and Mas Latrie (Mas Latrie 1862; Stylianou and Stylianou 1980: 150–53). This emphasis on roads is suggestive. The increase of interest in inland communications by the western European mapmakers and chroniclers fits with the greater involvement by Europeans in the economy of the eastern Mediterranean that accompanied the development of the modern world system (Wallerstein 1974; see also comments in Kardulias et al., Ch. 1).

By the mid-18th century, various sources attest to the importance of Larnaka as a regional and international trade hub. The city was used as a provisioning stop by many of the ships traveling in the eastern Mediterranean. A wealthy and active foreign consular community at Larnaka also contributed to the growth in trade moving through the

port (see, e.g., the interesting accounts of Heyman in Van Egmont and Heyman 1759: 293–94; Light 1818: 240–42). In the mid-18th century, Heyman noted that the consuls were engaged in a network of moneylending and trade, in which the interest from the peasants was paid in marketable agricultural goods (Van Egmont and Heyman 1759: 292–95). Light, who visited in 1814, noted that this trade, centered on the consuls, also was carried out by a multitude of local traders (Light 1818: 239–42). In this situation, it is hardly surprising that the western Europeans became increasingly interested in the communication and transport routes to the interior of the island. As early as 1769, Mariti (1792: 38) attests to Athienou as an important point on the road, where travelers would halt, as it was the home village of the famed *muleteers*, who dominated the intertown transport of the area (see also the comments in Cesnola 1878: 106–9). Mas Latrie (1879: 44), who conducted research in the mid-19th century, writes, "Le gros village d'Athiénou, situé à mi-chemin entre Nicosie et Larnaca, est le rendez-vous des *kéradjis* qui louent leurs soins et leurs mullets pour les transports et les voyages dans l'intérieur d'île. L'abondance des grains et l'industrie des habitants, tous grecs, y entretient quelque aisance" (The large village of Athienou, situated halfway between Nicosia and Larnaka, is the meeting place of the *muleteers* who rent out themselves and their mules for transport and journeys in the interior of the island. The abundance of grains and the industry of the inhabitants, all Greeks, allow them to maintain a comfortable livelihood). Christodoulou (1959: 97), who discusses communication routes within the island, also notes the significance of Athienou's location and primacy of the *muleteers* from Athienou for the internal movement of goods and people throughout the island during the 19th and early 20th centuries. He writes: "There was a break in the journey between Nicosia and Larnaca and muleteers could put up visitors for the night. The muleteers' quarters were at the north of the present village. They maintained an office in Nicosia and they undertook the transport of visitors to any part of the island…. This professional group of muleteers were famed for reliability and honesty." There is little doubt that the settlements in and around Athienou, including those in the Malloura Valley, benefited from this flourish of activity and commerce.

The frequent inclusion of Athienou and the Larnaka–Nicosia route on 19th-century maps attests to the importance (at least to the western Europeans) of the route and the *muleteer* village. Tax records prepared by the archbishopric in the early 19th century, and a tax list compiled for the Ottoman governor in the mid-19th century, suggest that this dynamic may well have correlated with settlement patterns. Although the limited data do not allow any conclusions as to demographic trends in the area, they do reveal a varied pattern of settlement during the first half of the 19th century. According to the documents, Athienou is by far the largest village in the area, with between 130 and 150 taxable inhabitants. Louroujina, Lympia, and Potamia, although larger than others, all probably had less than half the population of Athienou. British census figures from 1881 suggest similar developments among settlements in the region: the population of Athienou is recorded as 1,192; Louroujina (598), Lympia (356), and Potamia (184) are all relatively smaller (Grivaud 1998: 454–61). Other villages located in the immediate Athienou environs are also significantly smaller, such as Petrophani (18), Melousha (82), Arsos (185), Tremithousa (139), and Troulloi (165); the only other village of comparable size in the area is Dhali, with a recorded population of 867 (Grivaud 1998: 454–61).

The Ottoman period marks the end of recorded settlement activity in the Malloura Valley, which is perhaps symptomatic of the general depopulation and abandonment of settlements on the island during this period (Given 2000: 212–13). In 1825, three Greek inhabitants at Malloura are subject to taxation (*djizya*) under the Ottomans. By the British census of 1881, the settlement of Malloura is apparently abandoned, although there is no reason to doubt that its relatively fertile lands did continue to be exploited (Grivaud 1998: 160). Prior to their abandonment, most of the smaller surrounding villages, including Malloura, must have had only a handful of taxable inhabitants, who surely utilized their location along the route to trade local prod-

ucts and engage in business transactions. Although a more detailed study is necessary to determine the relationship between regional trade patterns and differentiated pattern of settlement, this preliminary evidence at least suggests that this dynamic may have been important in late Ottoman-period settlement in the area.

Cyprus Under British Rule (AD 1878–1960)

More than 300 years after Attar, the toponym *Malloura* is preserved on an 1882 map by the British lieutenant Herbert Horatio Kitchener (fig. 5.3) with the parenthetical label "Ruins" beneath (Kitchener 1885; Hadjipaschalis and Iacovou 1989: 180–81; Shirley 2001). On June 4, 1878, control of Cyprus was transferred from the Ottoman Turks to Britain. It was at this moment that the British realized the pressing need for a new, scientific mapping of the island — a project commenced under the direction of Kitchener, who had assumed the role as the first British Director of Lands and Surveys. The results, which served as the basis for the modern cartography of Cyprus, represented the first triangulated survey of the island. The designation of Malloura as ruins corresponds well with the British census figures of the prior year that suggest the site's abandonment. As noted above, Athienou appears to be an important mercantile center, with other secondary settlements in the region, such as Petrophani, Louroujina, Melousha, Tremithousa, Arsos and Troulloi, remaining in a rather dependent status.

The published letters of the French members of the Mission Vogüé (see Counts, Ch. 4) would appear to be the only other direct reference to the toponym "Malloura" in the 19th century. By the time of the British census of 1881, Malloura must have been abandoned. In the 20th century, aside from the much later archaeological publications of French scholars (e.g., Masson and Hermary), Malloura was mentioned in Gunnis's *Historic Cyprus* in 1936. Here the author mentions a site near Petrophani called "Malloura" where there exists "a temple" and "fragment of [its] floor," as well as a church that was "erected, as was so often the case, on the site of the heathen temple; a num-

FIG. 5.3   Detail of H. H. Kitchener's map of Cyprus, 1882 (after Kitchener 1885).

ber of broken and defaced limestone statues have been built into its walls" (Gunnis 1936: 380). The paucity of aboveground remains in the Malloura Valley today, in addition to the uniqueness of this reference, might suggest that Gunnis has wrongly attributed the name *Malloura* to another site. It is likely, in fact, that Gunnis was referring to the nearby church of Archangelos (which was also indicated on Kitchener's map of the area), located to the south of our site in a locale also named "Malloura;" nevertheless, it must be noted that the description of "broken and defaced limestone statues" built into the walls of the church is not evidenced at Archangelos. Hermary, however, suggests that Gunnis was referring to another site of Malloura in the vicinity of Louroujina. Confusion on the part of Gunnis is certainly possible since, as Hermary has also pointed out, Gunnis conflates the excavations of R. Hamilton Lang with those of Edmond Duthoit, the French architect who excavated ancient deposits in the Malloura Valley (Hermary 1988: 19). Goodwin (1984: 1052) apparently relied heavily on Gunnis's account, as he repeats much of this information regarding the extant remains at Malloura (and the claim that Lang worked at Malloura, which is likely not true). While Gunnis's source for his reference is unknown, Duthoit had almost certainly been shown the site by local farmers, since it is clear from his letters that he was in contact with the local population. Although our excavations at Athienou-*Malloura* have revealed some traces of a church (or churches), including two fragmentary stone crosses, neither of these is likely to have been visible in the 1930s when Gunnis was on the island — an inference seemingly confirmed by local elderly Athienites, who cannot recall aboveground architecture of the sort Gunnis describes in the immediate vicinity of Athienou-*Malloura*.

Concluding Remarks: Stasis and Movement, Maps and Human Settlement

This brief introduction to the cartographic and historical sources relative to the Malloura Valley has provided some preliminary information about settlement patterns and possible socioeconomic forces relative to them. Nevertheless, there is a tendency, in maps and other historical sources, to oversimplify and fix the complicated and fluid pattern of settlement and land use in rural areas (consider, for example, the debates concerning the borders of the ancient Cypriot city-kingdoms; see the discussion in Iacovou 2004, with bibliography). Places are marked as either inhabited or not. In fact, settlement has been less fixed than this presentation would indicate. Historical research on the rural dynamic in the Ottoman empire, as well as archaeological survey and ethnohistorical evidence, indicates that, in many areas, there existed isolated field buildings and even small village-like groupings of buildings that served as temporary areas of residence during periods in the agricultural cycle. It seems clear that temporary settlements were a common feature of the settlement pattern and were even given separate tax designations (as *mezra'a*) in Ottoman times. The line between "village" and temporary habitation area was thus fluid, and many such areas grew to be permanent settlements, while other villages were only used seasonally.

Such a pattern might be suggested for the settlement(s) associated with the Malloura Valley from the 16th to 19th centuries. Although most travelers describe the inland areas as barren, both Mariti (1792) and Light (1818) describe an uncultivated landscape that was occasionally punctuated by more verdant, cultivated areas, accompanied by rough field buildings. Indeed, local Athienites remember that as recently as 50 years ago, before the switch to extensive grain cultivation, it was common to live in the fields temporarily to harvest and tend crops. Traditionally rich agricultural areas, such as Malloura, probably were not completely abandoned but continued to be used seasonally, even after they disappeared from textual or cartographic sources (on seasonal settlements and land use, see especially the comments in Given 2000: 217–18). Thus, while the type of carto-historical research discussed here provides an idea of the general demographic dynamics in an area, archaeological excavation and survey are best suited to determine the patterns accompanying these general trends.

Acknowledgments

The authors would like to thank Peter Edbury for valuable references to Frankish-period Malloura, as well as Michael K. Toumazou for assistance with various topographical quandaries related to the Athienou and its environs. We especially thank G. Grivaud and F. Romanelli, who generously offered permission to reproduce a detail of the Attar map from their important 2006 publication.

References

Cesnola, L. P. di
1878   *Cyprus: Its Ancient Cities, Tombs, and Temples.* New York: Harper and Bros. Reprint 1991.

Christodoulou, D.
1959   *The Evolution of the Rural Land Use Pattern in Cyprus.* The World Land Use Survey, Regional Monograph 2. Cornwall: Geographical Publications.

Christodoulou, M., and Konstantinidis, K.
1987   *A Complete Gazetteer of Cyprus.* Nicosia: Republic of Cyprus.

Given, M.
2000   Agriculture, Settlement and Landscape in Ottoman Cyprus. *Levant* 32: 209–30.
2004   *The Archaeology of the Colonized.* London: Routledge.

Goodwin, J. C.
1984   *An Historical Toponymy of Cyprus.* Nicosia: n. p.

Gunnis, R.
1936   *Historic Cyprus.* London: Methuen.

Grivaud, G.
1998   *Villages désertés à Chypre.* Nicosia: Archbishop Makarios III Foundation.

Hadjipaschalis, A., and Iacovou, M.
1989   *The Bank of Cyprus Cultural Foundation Collections I: Maps and Atlases.* Nicosia: Bank of Cyprus Cultural Foundation.

Hermary, A.
1988   Nouvelles découvertes sur la Mission Vogüé de 1862. *Cahier du Centre d'Études Chypriotes* 12: 15–20.

Iacovou, M.
2004   Mapping the Ancient Kingdoms of Cyprus: Cartography and Classical Scholarship During the Enlightenment. Pp. 263–85 in *Eastern Mediterranean Cartographies,* eds. G. Tolias and D. Loupis. Athens: Institute for Neohellenic Research.

Kitchener, H. H.
1885   *A Trigonometrical Survey of the Island of Cyprus.* London: E. Stanford.

Light, H.
1818   *Travels in Egypt, Nubia, Holy Land, Mount Libanon, and Cyprus in the Year 1814.* London: Rodwell and Martin.

Mariti, G.
1792   *Travels Through Cyprus, Syria, and Palestine: With a General History of the Levant.* Italian Trans. Dublin: P. Bryne.

Mas Latrie, L. de
1862   *Notice sur la construction d'une carte de l'île de Chypre.* Paris: A. Lainé and J. Harvard.
1879   *L'île de Chypre: Sa situation présente et ses souvenirs du moyen-age.* Paris: Firmin-Didot.
1886   *Chronique de l'île de Chypre par Florio Bustron.* Collection de documents inédits sur l'histoire de France. Mélanges historiques 5. Paris.

Neumann, G.
2000   Ἐπίμετρον. Τοπωνύμια τῆς Ἀρχαίας Κύπρου, Pp. 1077–1109 in *History of Cyprus,* ed. T. Papadopoulos. Nicosia: Archbishop Makarios III Foundation.

Romanelli, F. C., and Grivaud, G.
2006   *Cyprus 1542: The Great Map of the Island by Leonida Attar.* Nicosia: The Bank of Cyprus Cultural Foundation.

Shirley, R.
2001   *Kitchener's Survey of Cyprus, 1878–1883: The First Full Triangulated Survey and Mapping*

of the Island. Nicosia: The Bank of Cyprus Cultural Foundation.

Stylianou, A., and Stylianou, J.
1970   An Important Venetian Map of Cyprus in the Map-Room of the British Museum, London. *Kypriakai Spoudai* 34: 145–58.
1980   *The History of the Cartography of Cyprus.* Nicosia: Cyprus Research Centre.

Van Egmont, J., and Heyman, J.
1759   *Travels Through Part of Europe, Asia Minor, the Islands of the Archipelago, Syria, Palestine, Egypt, Mount Sinai &c.* London: L. Davis and C. Reymers.

Wallerstein, I.
1974   *The Modern World-System I: Capitalist Agriculture and the Origins of the European World-Economy in the Sixteenth Century.* New York: Academic.

Chapter 6

Excavations at Malloura (1990–2010)

Context, Methods, and Results

by Michael K. Toumazou and Derek B. Counts

Since its inception in 1990, the Athienou Archaeological Project (AAP) has conducted 15 seasons of field excavations in the Malloura Valley. Complemented by the results of both systematic pedestrian survey (Kardulias and Yerkes, Ch. 7) and geophysical prospection (Sarris, Ch. 21), our excavations have documented a built environment in the valley that extends from (at least) the Cypro-Archaic period well into the modern age. The ambitious scope of the project's research agenda, which seeks to document the long-term history, settlement, and use of a specific region (see especially Kardulias et al., Ch. 1), is somewhat unique on Cyprus, as is the project's choice to investigate with relative equity the various occupational components of a single area regardless of their date or function. Religious, domestic, industrial, and funerary architecture have all been unearthed, representing a complex mosaic of Malloura's use and occupation over two and a half millennia — eighth century BC to 19th century AD. After some brief comments regarding the historical context of the project's work, this chapter describes the methods of excavation, recovery, and documentation employed by AAP, in addition to offering a brief overview of the *in-situ* remains discovered by the project.

A Historical Perspective on the Excavations at Malloura: Some Preliminary Observations

To place the excavations at Malloura in a slightly larger context, we offer here a brief sketch of the history and extent of archaeological fieldwork in Cyprus, from the initiation of systematic exploration in the 19th century to the rapid pace of scientific investigation in the 21st century. A full explication of the island's rich tradition of both antiquarian and archaeological investigations can be found in other fora (*e.g.*, Karageorghis 1987; Goring 1988; Tatton-Brown 2001; Pilides 2008); likewise, this chapter does not offer a detailed inventory of ongoing projects. Rather, we feel that a brief, if not idiosyncratic, survey of previous work helps situate our project at Malloura within its historical context, while also foregrounding the importance of our innovative methods and comprehensive approach to documenting the material remains of the valley.

The Age of Discovery in the 19th Century AD

As early as the Venetian period (AD 1489–1571), and no doubt stretching back into ancient times, the antiquities of Cyprus (especially those found in tombs) were being collected from sites throughout the island (Hermary 1990: 7–8; Bernhard-Walcher 1999: 46–50). But it was the 19th century AD (especially the second half) that witnessed the first substantial archaeological investigations, primarily in the form of European antiquarians overseeing the excavation of sites and the collection of artifacts (see, e.g., Goring 1988; Tatton-Brown 2001). This period is especially noteworthy since it represents work conducted by some of the great personalities in early Cypriot archaeology: L. Mas Latrie, A. Sakellarios, L. Ross, M. de Vogüé and E. Duthoit, L. Palma di Cesnola, T. B. Sandwith, R. H. Lang, and M. Ohnefalsch-Richter, among others.

A diverse range of factors motivated this early work (Ulbrich 2001 provides an excellent commentary). Mas Latrie (1862) traveled to the island in the mid-19th century in an effort to produce a revised map of ancient settlements (see Counts and Parvis, Ch. 5). As noted elsewhere in this volume (Counts, Ch. 4), the mission of de Vogüé, which was initiated as part of E. Renan's *Mission de Phénicie*, sought to collect elements of Phoenician material culture (Foucart-Borville 1985: 14; Hermary 1988; 1990: 9). In other cases, antiquarian pursuits were tied more directly to a desire by foreign museums, which financed operations, to expand their holdings (e.g., Ross, Lang, Ohnefalsch-Richter, Murray). Ohnefalsch-Richter (1893: 2–28) inventoried 72 "ancient places of worship," some excavated, others identified (by himself or others) on the basis of inscriptions and iconography (Ulbrich 2001). Finally, as Counts (2001: 141–42) has noted, various contemporary documents reveal an air of competition that must have been prevalent among antiquarians in the Mediterranean serving as liaisons to European governments and museums.

This flurry of activity brought to light an enormous corpus of antiquities, including inscriptions, pottery, sculpture, and jewelry, excavated from a wide variety of archaeological contexts, most notably tombs and sanctuaries located around larger well-known sites and smaller, more peripheral sites located in the rural hinterlands (Counts 2001: 130–36). Thus, just as the urban centers of Marion, Paphos, Amathous, Kourion, Kition, Salamis, Tamassos, and Idalion were elucidated, smaller sites such as Amargetti, Malloura, Ayios Photios, Arsos, Akhna, Pyla, and Voni also received attention. Nevertheless, despite the wealth of newly unearthed data, the sporadic nature of discoveries and the inadequate methods of collection and recording meant that no real synthetic, long-term history of the island's archaeological heritage was forthcoming (*pace* attempts by Colonna-Ceccaldi [1882] and Perrot and Chipiez [1885]).

Cypriot Archaeology into the 21st Century

The 20th century AD witnessed the emergence of a systematic, scientific approach to the archaeology of Cyprus. The impact of this moment can perhaps be best observed in the activities of J. L. Myres, who at the turn of the century completed two of the earliest and most significant projects involving the study of Cypriot material culture: (1) the cleaning, organization, and classification of the collections of the Cyprus Museum (Myres and Ohnefalsch-Richter 1899; Karageorghis 1987: 3–5); and (2) the publication of the Cesnola Collection of Cypriot Antiquities at the Metropolitan Museum of Art (Myres 1914; Karageorghis 2000). Both volumes represent a thoughtful attempt to organize and analyze the vast amount of Cypriot material available in the Cyprus Museum, as well as foreign museums in Europe and the United States, including much comparative research. In particular, the cataloguing of the material in the Cyprus Museum not only brought some order to the collection but was preceded by an important "[c]hronicle of excavations undertaken since the British occupation" (i.e., after 1878) (Myres and Ohnefalsch-Richter 1899: 1–12), which remains one of the most complete surveys of archaeological sites on the island at the turn of the 20th century AD.

Undoubtedly, the most influential moment in the history of excavations in Cyprus was the arrival on the island of the Swedish Cyprus Expedition (SCE) in 1927 and their subsequent work on the island until 1931, under the direction of E. Gjerstad. The results of excavations conducted by the SCE, published in four volumes, revolutionized access to each of the principal phases of Cypriot history from prehistoric through Roman times (Gjerstad et al. 1934–1972). Their work encompassed a variety of sites and contexts, from funerary to settlement, and in doing so provided a more synthetic framework within which the material remains uncovered in the previous century could be placed. While the total number of sites and periods covered by the SCE investigations remains unrivaled, the quick pace of their work meant that the interpretation of single sites, or even larger regions, was based primarily on a select few occupational levels. The goal of the SCE was not to study long-term cultural processes within a single site or region, but to produce an island-wide synthetic, historical narrative based on the material remains of a select corpus of settlements, cemeteries, and sanctuaries. Thus, while the Iron Age of ancient Kition receives extensive treatment, there is little mention of the city's post-antique settlement history or even the earliest prehistory of the region (on the SCE and their methodological approach, see especially Reyes 1994; Smith 2009: 220–33).

There is little need to catalogue the fast pace of archaeological activity on the island since the work of the SCE. Under the aegis of the Department of Antiquities (both before and after independence in 1960), Cypriot and foreign archaeologists have conducted significant, long-term projects across the island. In addition to reports and volumes published by the excavators themselves, several studies have set out the more recent history of excavations in Cyprus (Karageorghis 1987; Åström 2000; Pilides 2008); likewise, various annual or occasional surveys in the *Annual Report of the Department of Antiquities, Cyprus, Bulletin de Correspondance Hellénique, American Journal of Archaeology,* and *Archaeological Reports* have provided an important chronicle of work from year to year. The nature and extent of excavations from the late 20th into the 21st century have been impressive. As noted by Kardulias et al. (Ch. 1), however, the focus of work since the SCE has often been on larger settlements associated with urban centers

along the coast and inland (e.g., Marion, Paphos, Amathous, Kourion, Kition, Salamis, Tamassos, Idalion) or single-component sites that offer important snapshots in time (e.g., the focused study of the sanctuary at Polis-*Peristeries* in Smith 1997). In cases where smaller and/or inland rural sites (especially cemeteries and sanctuaries) have been investigated, these have often not been integrated into a larger-scale, long-term regional history, as they frequently come to light through random discovery, salvage excavations, and the publication of museum collections.

Against this backdrop, the AAP's approach to documenting the Malloura landscape through an integrated synthesis of material remains, settlement history, and long-term cultural change provides a significant supplement to the important work that has been done on the island over the last several generations. Through excavation and survey, the project has been able to trace human activity, localized in the Malloura Valley, from prehistoric lithic extraction (see Kardulias and Yerkes, Ch. 8) to modern settlement and displacement within and around the project area (see Counts and Parvis, Ch. 5; Yerkes, Ch. 26). In conjunction with the report on the AAP survey that follows (Kardulias and Yerkes, Ch. 7), this chapter emphasizes the scope and impact of our project's work at Malloura and, more significantly, provides a material context of the lived environment within which the volume's subsequent specialist studies can be placed.

The work of AAP provides the means to examine social dynamics in a rural setting over several millennia. As a critical way of collecting data to evaluate this process, the AAP excavations are focused on Athienou-*Malloura* (Site 1), which covers 260,000 m² (26 ha) at the confluence of two intermittent streams in the center of the Malloura Valley, south of the current regional center of Athienou (see also Yerkes, Ch. 2). Figure 6.1 records the investigated areas discussed in this chapter on a topographical plan of the Malloura Valley. A substantial settlement was established here early in the Roman period (first century BC), and habitation continued through Early Byzantine times. After an interruption between AD 647–1191, Malloura was resettled at the time of Frankish rule

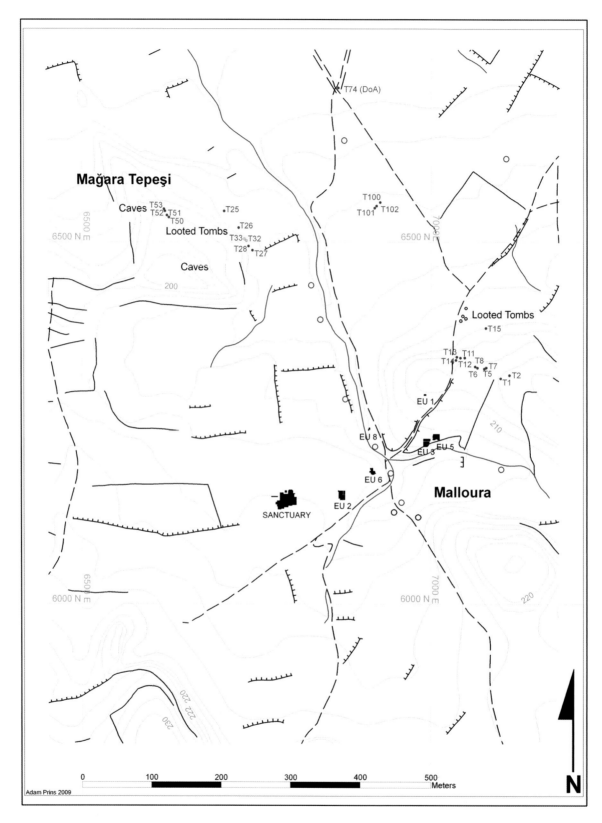

FIG. 6.1   *Topographical map of Malloura Valley showing locations of AAP investigations, 2009 (drawing: A. Prins).*

(1191–1489) and flourished during the Venetian period (1489–1571). During Ottoman rule (1571–1878), the settlement declined and was finally abandoned. A Cypro-Geometric III through Roman sanctuary is located ca. 60 m west of these settlements. A number of rock-cut tombs also dating from the Cypro-Archaic II to Roman periods is found 300 m north of the sanctuary at Mağara Tepeşi ("Hill of Tombs," Site 2). The presence of a large sanctuary and of numerous tombs suggests that a settlement dating to the Cypro-Archaic through Hellenistic periods was located in close proximity, but, to date, we have no archaeological evidence for this. Surface material (including some grave goods) suggests that tombs from later Roman and Early Byzantine periods are located near the settlements at Malloura but have not been excavated.

Excavation Methods

The AAP investigations employ UTM (Universal Transverse Mercator) grid coordinates to record features and artifacts found in the excavations at Athienou-*Malloura*. Natural and cultural features of the landscape were compiled from 1:5,000 topographic maps and cadastral sheets prepared by the Department of Lands and Surveys, geological maps (1:31,680) prepared by I. G. Gass (1960) (for a geological map of the region, see fig. 2.2), and black-and-white Royal Air Force aerial photographs from 1963. During the 1990 and 1991 field seasons, topographical mapping (at 0.5 m contour intervals) of large portions of the site was completed using a total station (Lietz SDM3F). Coordinates and elevations were established with reference to four trigonometric stations set up by the Department of Lands and Surveys.

Because of the large extent of the site (see fig. 6.1) an overall grid plan was not deemed practical. Rather, the various operations at different loci of the site are designated as Excavation Units (EUs) and are usually isolated but may be contiguous — as in the area of the sanctuary. Odd numbers are assigned to EUs east of the intermittent stream that bisects the site, while even ones (save for EU 11, which was inadvertently named) mark those west of the stream. The size of the EUs varies greatly,

depending on the architectural remains encountered and practical considerations. Typically, EUs measure 3 × 5 m, but there is a great deal of variation, ranging, e.g., from 2 × 3 m (EU 1) to as much as 8 × 16 m (EU 10).

The term "Stratigraphic Unit" (SU) is used for distinct strata/layers or deposits; these can be real or arbitrary. Arbitrary SUs, usually 10 or 20 cm in thickness, are used for better stratigraphic control of thick natural strata. Except for the top layer (plowzone), all subsequent SUs are excavated and recorded using "Square Meter Units" (SMUs), i.e., arbitrary 1 × 1 m units for better horizontal control. Each of the SMUs into which an EU is divided is referred to by the coordinates of its southwest corner, e.g., E 546,987/N 3,876,288.

Elevations are taken from the head of an iron stake typically set in concrete 1 m west of the southwest corner of the EU. Aluminum tags fixed by nails into the balks are used to mark the transitions in SUs for rechecking and to help with the drawing of stratigraphic sections. All soil removed during excavation is passed through 7 mm sieves, and soil samples are taken from every SMU. Finds from individual SMUs within a SU are bagged separately. In addition to conventional note-taking during the course of excavation, a variety of forms are filled out recording relevant quantified information (e.g., coordinates, elevations, types of finds, photo and drawing numbers, etc.) for individual SUs, SMUs, pottery lots, and so forth. These are subsequently entered into a large relational database for analysis (originally FoxBase+, currently FileMaker Pro).

In the case of the rock-cut chamber tombs at Mağara Tepeşi, our excavation strategy differed. While it was evident before excavation, from both visual inspection and reports by local informants, that the tombs had already been looted, the excavation followed as much as possible the systematic procedures used for intact deposits described above. Before the excavation of the burial chamber itself, whose *stomion* (entrance) had been left open by the tomb robbers, the *dromos* (passageway, usually stepped) was divided longitudinally into two sections by a string. Subsequently, the southern half of the *dromos* was excavated leaving an intact balk. After completing the excavation of the burial

FIG. 6.2   *Aerial view of the sanctuary of Athienou-Malloura, 2005 (© AAP).*

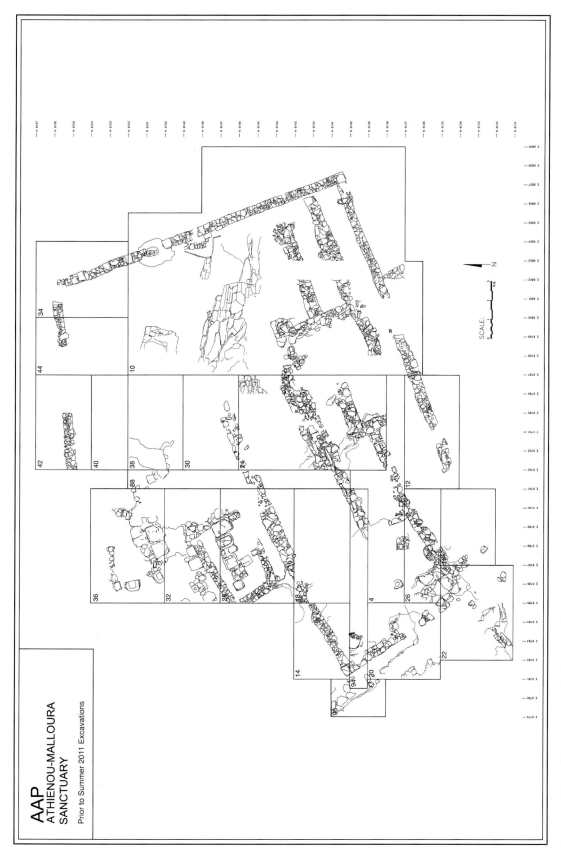

FIG. 6.3 *Plan of the sanctuary of Athienou-Malloura, just prior to summer 2011 excavations (drawing: R. Breuker).*

FIG. 6.4   In situ *sculptures (AAP-AM 1075 and AAP-AM 1076) lying on top of the Hellenistic hard-packed floor layer of the Athienou*-Malloura *sanctuary, 1997 (© AAP).*

FIG. 6.5   *View from north of Hellenistic hard-packed floor and associated southern and eastern walls of the Athienou-* Malloura *sanctuary, 1993 (© AAP).*

chamber and following inspection and drawing of the stratigraphy, the northern half of the *dromos* was excavated. The relatively small size and internal arrangement of the burial chambers, with benches along three sides, prevented us from using SMUs. Nonetheless, because of its large size, the burial chamber of Tomb 27 was excavated using SMUs, with metal pins holding strings secured into the bedrock.

The Sanctuary at Athienou-*Malloura* (Cypro-Geometric through Roman)

The sanctuary on the western edge of Athienou-*Malloura* (figs. 6.2–5) was discovered in 1862 by the French mission led by M. de Vogüé (Counts, Ch. 4). The results of this excavation were never published, although some 70 sculptures in the Louvre have been identified as coming from Malloura (Hermary 1988, 1989). In later years, parts of the sanctuary were looted and hundreds of statues were exported illegally from Cyprus. The sanctuary was relocated during the 1991 AAP field season (Toumazou et al. 1992).

Soils and Deposits

The thickness of the overburden varies in different parts of the site. For example, while a relatively thin plowzone mantle covers those EUs with later materials (e.g., EUs 2, 3, and 5; see fig. 6.1), the deposits directly overlying the sanctuary are as much as 2.5 m deep. Butzer and Harris (2007) have recently published a composite stratigraphic profile from the site of Athienou-*Malloura* (see fig. 2.3), revealing the thick, varied deposits of colluvium covering the built remains (see also Yerkes, Ch. 2).

A brief survey of the various deposits offers a better understanding of the archaeological contexts of both the architecture and the finds. The descriptions that follow pertain primarily to the eastern and central portions of the sanctuary, while to the west the nature of the deposits differs slightly. The uppermost layers overlying the sanctuary have been exposed to repeated wash from rain and, more importantly, the plow. The thickness of the plowzone has varied due to the different types of

plows used by farmers. As recently as 50 years ago, traditional deep plows with iron plowshares were used that penetrated the soil to a depth of 30 cm; in the 1960s, an over-life-size limestone head was turned up by such a plow in the general area of the sanctuary. There is no diagnostic quality to the cultural material found in this zone. Beneath it is a deep layer of a light gray soil with little or no cultural material. This deposit is the product of alluvial washing and varies greatly in thickness. Beneath the alluvial deposit is a thin layer of fine pebbles found in almost all areas of the sanctuary; it is most likely the result of a natural process of heavy rains and flooding following the abandonment of the sanctuary. The pebbly layer signals another sterile alluvial layer consisting of a silty soil with light charcoal-gray marbling, few inclusions, and no cultural material.

This moist layer overlies the surface of a hard-packed floor layer associated with final-phase (Hellenistic–Roman) wall construction. Cultural material resting on the surface of this hard-packed floor is covered by this particular deposit (see fig. 6.4 and also fig. 6.5 for view of hard-packed floor layer with walls). Unfortunately, there are no marked changes in soil deposits when the surface of the hard-packed floor layer is encountered, although it is easily recognized by rocky inclusions and the cultural material that lies on its surface. The floor consists of a construction fill made up of compacted cultural material (e.g., bone, pottery, terracotta, and limestone-statue fragments); this fill may either lie directly on the bedrock or, in some cases, rest on a very fine, sterile brown soil overlying the bedrock. In the southwestern part of the sanctuary, the deposits are much more shallow and thus do not conform to the general nature of deposits described here; this area is also largely void of finds.

Archaeological material is found in several distinct deposits within the stratigraphy discussed above. Countless pits caused by the activities of looters (or possibly the earlier French excavations) are encountered in virtually every EU comprising the sanctuary's limits and yield large amounts of cultural material, including high densities of pottery and many fragments of limestone and terracotta statuary (a typical pit is visible in the center of the balk on the right side of fig. 6.5). These deposits are obviously contaminated and may represent a secondary provenience; pits were often filled in haste with whatever happened to be within shovel's reach. While many pits do not penetrate the pebbly layer, others extend deep to the surface of and within the hard-packed layer. Extensive portions of the Hellenistic *temenos* (sacred precinct) wall have also been robbed out, presumably as part of the same looting episodes. In the eastern portions of the sanctuary, the hard-packed layer yields cultural material both on its surface and within its fill. All cultural material lying on the surface of the hard-packed floor layer is considered, based on stratigraphy, to have been deposited after the late fourth century (the date for the construction of the floor and reorganization of the sanctuary). There are, however, objects encountered on the surface of the packing that are obviously of an earlier date based on style. These pieces should be viewed as survivals of the earlier Cypro-Archaic–Cypro-Classical phase(s) of the sanctuary. Cultural material packed within this layer has a *terminus ante quem* in the late fourth century BC, the date of its construction. This material was utilized to make up the fill of the hard-packed layer and must predate its construction. It is possible that smaller sculptural fragments found in the uppermost parts of this layer are the product of packing and mixing associated with a "use-surface" (a thin layer created by occupation), which may cause intrusions. Finally, the matrix associated with the Hellenistic *temenos* yields a wide variety of cultural material, especially limestone sculptural fragments used as building stones.

Chronological Phases and Architecture

While the vast majority of stratigraphical evidence from the sanctuary places its primary use during the Cypro-Archaic II–Roman periods, the foundation of the sanctuary can be dated to the eighth century, late in the Cypro-Geometric III period (Fourrier, Ch. 9) (see figs. 6.2–3). This phase is represented by a small deposit of pottery (46 fragments belonging to eight different vessels) in the

westernmost SMU of a long exploratory trench, EU 94. To date, no architectural features have been associated with this phase, suggesting that it represents a rather modest level of activity in the open air at this stage or that associated Cypro-Geometric architecture was either destroyed through subsequent building or lies farther to the west in unexcavated areas.

The second phase of the sanctuary is dated to the Cypro-Archaic period. Based on the large amounts of pottery and sculpture (both terracotta and limestone), the Cypro-Archaic II period represents the *floruit* of the site (see Fourrier, Ch. 9; Averett, Ch. 10; Counts, Ch. 11). Cypro-Archaic material is found lying directly on the bedrock in deep deposits in the eastern part of the sanctuary (especially in EU 10) or incorporated as fill into the hard-packed floor associated with the third major phase in the Hellenistic period. Much of the architecture assigned to the second phase has been either destroyed by or incorporated in later constructions. A series of stout walls, constructed in some places directly on bedrock in the southern/eastern part of the excavated area (e.g., EUs 4, 10, 24), belongs to this phase. Better preserved and dating to the same phase — possibly of Cypro-Classical date — is a rectangular structure at the western part of the sanctuary. Oriented east–west, the structure encompasses in its northwest corner a circular feature (hearth or altar) constructed of large upright sherds, enclosed by a low clay rim and showing signs of extensive burning. To the north, in EU 28, a second structure was laid bare. Oriented southwest–northeast, this roughly rectangular structure measures 3 × 5 m and features a clay-lined hearth in its southwestern corner; ceramic evidence suggests this building was used during the Cypro-Archaic II and Cypro-Classical I periods. As noted above, the difficulty in establishing a composite plan of the sanctuary's second, main phase is exacerbated by the significant reorganization of the sanctuary at the end of the fourth century BC and, of course, by many years of indiscriminate looting.

A Hellenistic through Roman construction phase at the sanctuary originated on a hard-packed layer of earth above the Cypro-Archaic and Cypro-Classical levels and is best represented by sections of the sanctuary walls along the southern, eastern, and northern perimeter, enclosing an area that was at least 400 m² (see fig. 6.5). *In-situ* architectural remains from this later phase comprise three long sections of the *peribolos* (enclosing wall) (0.60 m wide) meeting at right angles in the southeast corner of the *temenos* and likely the northeast (damaged) corner. Constructed of field cobbles, the *peribolos* includes in its matrix numerous limestone sculptural fragments (including a headless, life-size votary) of Cypro-Archaic and Cypro-Classical date. As noted above, associated with this early Hellenistic I *peribolos*, which likely served through the end of the sanctuary's use, was a hard-packed layer upon which (and within which) much statuary and other artifacts of earlier date were found. Also associated with the last phase is a series of large worked blocks of limestone in two rows that directly overlays Cypro-Archaic and Cypro-Classical strata in the western part of the sanctuary (EUs 28, 32, 34); several blocks appear to be bases for statues and thus recall similar arrangements found at other sanctuary sites, such as Tamassos, Idalion, Lefkoniko, and Akhna (Ohnefalsch-Richter 1893: 346–47, pl. 10; for comparative plans of several sanctuaries, see Al-Radi 1983).

Despite years of careful systematic excavation, the sanctuary's primary altar had remained elusive until quite recently. Large concentrations of both burnt and unburnt animal bones and elevated phosphate levels (see Beeston, Ch. 24) in the central part of the sanctuary seemed consistent with ritual activity associated with the preparation and use of animals for sacrifice and feasting. In 2007, a large mudbrick platform with extensive burning was partially exposed; in close proximity to the east, a bucranium (worked?) and a limestone statuette were discovered. The altar was in use during the last phase of the sanctuary's occupation; further excavation is required to determine if this represents a continuation of use for the structure from an earlier phase.

In addition to bases for wooden posts, the discovery of an "epistyle" block, worked so as to fit the ends of two wooden roof beams — but used as a building material in the construction of the Hellenistic I *peribolos* — suggests that portions of the *temenos* were roofed. Access to the *temenos* must have been gained through one or more openings in the *peribolos*. A gap in the wall's southern section may represent an entrance, but serious disturbance due to looter activity (with evidence of bulldozer blade claws) makes such a suggestion tentative. In a less-disturbed area, a second gap on the eastern section of the *peribolos* more likely served as an entrance. The discovery of a limestone wall bracket with representations of Bes, an apotropaic deity, in the immediate vicinity lends collaborative evidence to the above suggestion (Counts and Toumazou 2006).

Finds

The major finds include large numbers of limestone statuary ranging in size from a few centimeters to over life-size; Cypro-Archaic and Cypro-Classical terracotta figurines of helmeted warriors, chariots, and animals; large amounts of decorated and plain pottery (mostly Cypro-Archaic); other limestone objects (e.g., incense burners, shovels, circular disks); coins; and a few bronze and iron artifacts. Most of the limestone statuary recovered was badly damaged, sometimes by the looters but also by early Christians in late antiquity. Nonetheless, several pieces are impressive in their dimensions and/or workmanship; many betray Egyptian, Near Eastern, and East Greek influences. A few examples of female figures were found (Counts and Toumazou 2003), but the overwhelming majority of the statues represent male votaries and divinities with iconography traditionally associated with Herakles, Zeus Ammon, Bes, Apollo, and Pan (for divine types from Malloura, especially Zeus Ammon, see Counts 1998: 122–35, 2004, 2009; Counts and Toumazou 2006; see also Cofer, Ch. 12). Several chapters in the volume (e.g., Fourrier, Ch. 9; Averett, Ch. 10; Counts, Ch. 11; Cova, Ch. 13; and Cofer, Ch. 12) detail various objects discovered in the sanctuary.

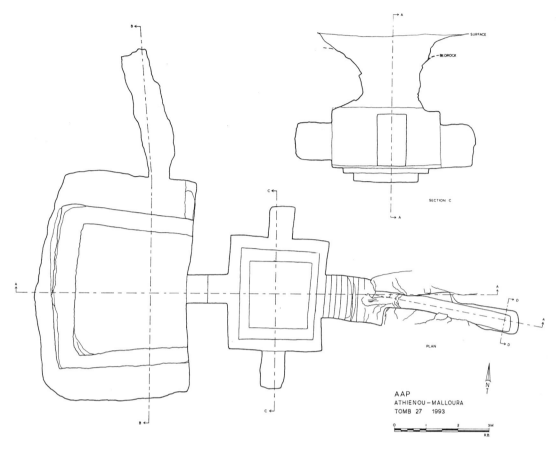

FIG. 6.6   *Plan and section of Tomb 27, 1993 (drawing: R. Breuker).*

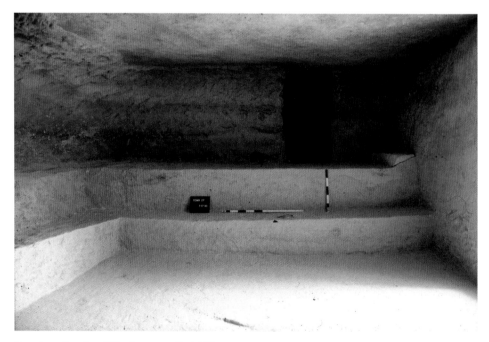

FIG. 6.7   *Interior of Tomb 27, 1993 (© AAP).*

Cypro-Archaic through Roman Tombs

Moderate scatters of Cypro-Archaic, Cypro-Classical, Hellenistic, and Roman material were found around the looted rock-cut tombs northwest of the Malloura site at Mağara Tepeşi (see fig. 6.1). Locals report that as recently as the 1960s, the entire hilltop was dotted with small tombs mostly destroyed by looting, bulldozing, and plowing. Our excavations here focused on two areas, the northwest summit of the hill and the lower northeast slope. Tombs excavated by AAP were numbered in clusters: 20s and 30s (lower northeast slope of Mağara Tepeşi), 50s (northwest summit of the hill), and 100s (in the flat fields east of the hill). At the northwest, a cluster of four small looted chamber tombs was excavated (Tombs 50–53). These consisted of sloping *dromoi* cut through *havara* and conglomerate to a layer of greenish marl, where a roughly circular burial chamber was dug out. Above the entrance to the burial chamber, long narrow cuttings were made in the *havara* for the support of funerary stelai that had been removed prior to our excavations. Two of the tombs (50 and 53) may not have been finished, but fragments of human bone and some Cypro-Archaic ceramics were found in the other two (51 and 52). Excavation of the *dromos* of a larger tomb (59) in 2005 yielded an impressive, albeit fragmentary funerary stele depicting a symposiast holding a drinking cup in his left hand; inexplicably, fragments of as many as three additional stelai of late Cypro-Archaic II/Cypro-Classical I date were found in the same *dromos* as well.

Excavations at the base of the northeast slope of Mağara Tepeşi exposed four large tombs (25–28) cut into the massive white chalk. The typical construction plan included a stepped *dromos* leading down to a single chamber with three benches cut into the rock (figs. 6.6–7, 14.1, and 19.1; for similar tombs at Agia Napa-*Makronisos* see Hadjisavvas 1997). Most impressive from an architectural point of view is Tomb 27, which is by far the largest of the group and includes a stepped sunken forecourt with two small *loculi* as well as a side tunnel and double benches in the burial chamber (see fig. 6.7). The tomb's size and architectural elaboration make

it unique in Cyprus and, in combination with its rich contents, may bespeak of high social status for its occupants (see Harper and Tung, Ch.19). In stark contrast to the sparse finds from Tombs 50–53 of late Cypro-Archaic II/Cypro-Classical I date, located ca. 100 m away on the same hill, large numbers of artifacts overlooked by the looters were recovered during the excavation of this cluster of tombs. They include silver and bronze coins, scraps of metal vessels and nails, gold and silver finger rings and earrings, a gold necklace with carnelian stones, local and imported lamps, and ceramic vessels dating from the Hellenistic period to the second century AD (on the lamps, see Cova, Ch. 13; Gordon, Ch. 14). The quantity and temporal range of the pottery recovered shows that these tombs seem to have been used for generations by extended families. Careful sieving of the fill from Tomb 27, for example, yielded nearly 10,000 pot sherds and skeletal material from no less than 31 individuals (see Harper and Tung, Ch. 19).

Late in the Roman period the eastern end of the *dromos* of Tomb 27 was cut by a water channel that was followed for 6 m of its length (see fig. 6.6). Ground-Penetrating Radar (GPR) survey in this area indicated that the channel continued eastward for nearly 100 m toward the main stream in the valley (see Sarris, Ch. 21). The dimensions of the channel are ca. 0.50 m wide by 1.0 m high, and its roof is corbelled in section. The channel enters the *dromos* of Tomb 27 at a depth nearly 2 m below the surface. Just north of Tomb 28, two essentially identical rock-cut cisterns 5 m apart were excavated (fig. 6.8). No artifacts other than a few non-diagnostic sherds were found in the fill of the cisterns, which are almost certainly contemporary; they may relate to water rituals associated with Hellenistic and Roman funerary practices (Hadjisavvas 1985; see also Kurtz and Boardman 1971: 149–61).

The excavation of a ditch for a water line across the valley in 2001 by the Public Works Department uncovered three small tombs (100–102) in a flat field some 200 m east of Mağara Tepeşi that were subsequently excavated by AAP. At a depth of up to 1.75 m from the surface, these tombs were intact but contained bones and a few artifacts tentatively dated to the Roman period. Moreover, in 2007 an

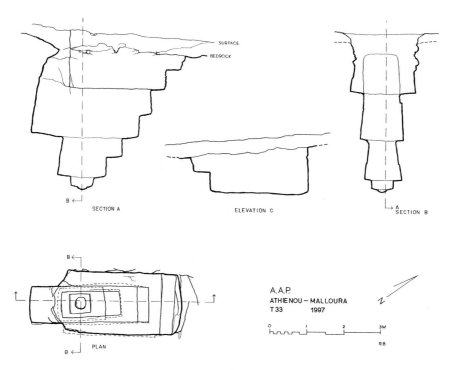

FIG. 6.8 *Plan and section of Cistern T 33, 1997 (© AAP).*

additional tomb of Hellenistic date was discovered ca. 200 m north of Tombs 100–102 in the construction of a paved road leading to the site. The presence of the aforementioned tombs at some distance from the excavated ones in Mağara Tepeşi, in areas previously unsuspected to have contained burials, may suggest that they belong to the same — but much larger than anticipated — cemetery or, possibly, to isolated, more or less contemporary clusters of tombs that reflect distinctions based on social status and/or kinship affiliation.

ROMAN–EARLY BYZANTINE OCCUPATIONS

Several EUs at the Malloura site contain the remains of structures associated with the establishment of a substantial rural settlement at Malloura early in the Roman period (first century BC) that continued through the Early Byzantine era (for recent assessments of these periods see Rautman 2003; Sørensen and Jacobsen 2006). In EU 3, along the southern slope of the knoll overlooking an intermittent stream in the southeast quadrant of

the site, the corner of an Early Byzantine domestic structure was exposed (fig. 6.9). There is evidence to suggest that this structure was burned in the mid-seventh century, early in the period of Arab/Byzantine conflict. Surface materials also suggest that the settlement at Malloura was abandoned at this time. Our efforts to clarify this situation were hampered by the discovery of a Venetian house and associated well overlying the Early Byzantine structure in EU 3.

Approximately 15 m to the east, in EU 5, another structure of similar construction and orientation was discovered that dates to the Roman through Early Byzantine periods (see fig. 6.9). Although damaged by a late medieval pit that robbed out many of its stones, the building is rather well-preserved. Associated pottery included imported African Red Slip, Phocaean Red Slip, and Pompeian Red wares. As in EU 3, the pottery indicates that the settlement was abandoned in the seventh century. EU 6, which has also yielded important material dated to the Early Byzantine period, is discussed below.

FIG. 6.9   *Aerial view of EU 3 (left) and EU 5 (right), 1993; north at top of page (© AAP).*

Frankish–Ottoman-Period Occupations

In EU 2, at the western edge of the settlement (see fig. 6.1), the eastern portion of a well-constructed building, measuring 11.75 × 7.5 m and oriented north–south, was discovered (fig. 6.10; see also fig. 16.1). Excavation of the northern wall showed that the building extends westward, beyond the limits of EU 2. Aside from some fine sgraffito ware and substantial amounts of coarse ware, the most notable finds were a bronze ring and coin, iron nails and knives, a stone weight, and fragments of several terracotta smoking pipes. The pottery indicates the building was constructed during the second half of the 15th century and lasted well into the 16th century, squarely within the Venetian period. In a secondary building phase, the structure was modified by a central north–south wall with a doorway at its southern end. As evidenced by traces of a barely discernible wall running in an entirely different direction than the previous walls, a third phase of use may be ascertained, perhaps reflecting use of the building by squatters. Because of serious disturbance due to plowing, precise dating of the latter two phases is not possible. The discovery of terracotta tobacco pipes in the upper strata indicates the tertiary use must certainly fall

during the (later?) Ottoman period, when the settlement significantly declined and was eventually abandoned.

In its primary use the interior of the building was divided by a series of closely spaced walls (0.40 m wide) traversing its eastern, excavated portion from west to east. The walls formed a series of channels that pass through the outer eastern wall of the building. Fragmentary slabs of gypsum (*marmara*) and countless scraps of decomposed wood were encountered between the cross-walls but never above them. The *marmara* seem to have served as vertical linings of the cross-walls. Interpretation of the function of the structure in EU 2 hinges on the purpose of the east–west walls and channels that seem to have been capped by wooden planks. Were the channels intended for air circulation or, more likely, to carry liquids, probably water? The structure may have been used as a granary (see Spigelman, Ch. 17) or perhaps for the processing of flax (see DeMasi, Ch. 16). Excavation of the western portion of the building, where the cross-walls and channels seem to be absent, and further analysis of the finds will hopefully settle the question of the nature of this unique structure from an important but neglected period in the island's history. Whichever of the two hypotheses concerning the building's function turns out to be correct, it is clear that the structure in EU 2 was a focus of production in the settlement during the Venetian period.

In EU 3, some 180 m northeast of this industrial structure, another building was excavated that also dates to the Venetian period, this time without any Ottoman period overburden (see fig. 6.9). The structure was encountered at depths no more than 30 cm below the surface and overlies the Early Byzantine structure mentioned above. The walls of the Venetian period building are badly preserved because of modern plowing, but its slab-paved floor is largely intact; the floor is traversed by a stone-lined drain running toward the intermittent stream to the south. The impressive dimensions and architectural features of this structure and its associated finds suggest this was the home of a wealthy family. Adjacent to, and likely associated with, the house is an 8.5 m deep well. Its upper part (1.2 m), cut into soil, was stone-lined and plastered with waterproof cement, while the lower part (7.3 m) was cut into bedrock; the well was found capped with a large stone slab held into position by cobbles along its edges.

In EU 6, on a small knoll halfway between these two Venetian period structures, excavations revealed portions of a thick wall that had been severely truncated by plowing and bulldozing operations in the 1960s. The (surface) discovery of a large fragmentary stone cross in close proximity, in addition to excavated *opus sectile* fragments, pieces of painted plaster, and two (gold) *solidi* (minted in Constantinople) of sixth-century-AD date suggest that an Early Byzantine church likely existed in the area that has not been excavated; reportedly,

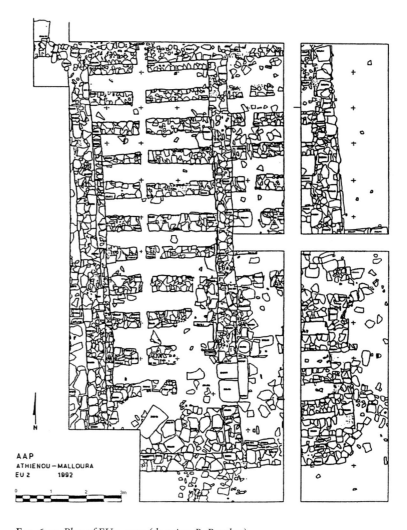

FIG. 6.10 *Plan of EU 2, 1992 (drawing: R. Breuker).*

the bulldozing operations to level the knoll (visible in the 1963 aerial photos) encompassed in EU 6 dislodged a column fragment. Though the settlement — and presumably the church — was abandoned following the earliest Arab raids in the mid-seventh century, the presence of a Christian cemetery in the immediate vicinity of the church is not likely accidental. On either side of the wall, in an area covering approximately 25 m^2, the skeletal remains of at least 57 individuals were excavated (fig. 6.11) (see Harper and Tung, Ch. 19; Harper, Ch. 20; Giacomini 1993). The burials included both adults and infants, and while many were fully articulated, others were badly disturbed by later burials, the plow, or the bulldozer. Most of

FIG. 6.11 *View from east of EU 6 burials, 1992 (© AAP).*

the burials were oriented east–west. Grave goods were sparse, comprising mostly glazed sgraffito ware goblets or bowls, usually placed in the pelvic area of the skeletons. Pieces of a hairnet and burial shroud were found with an adult female. The finds indicate these were Christian burials from the Venetian period (see Rohn et al. 2010: 513–17).

Concluding Remarks

As a result of AAP's excavations at Malloura, a variety of chronological phases and types of occupation (sanctuary, settlement, tombs) spanning more than 2,500 years of the site's utilization (eighth century BC through 19th century AD) has been documented. Prior to the establishment of cultic activity in the area of the sanctuary in the eighth century BC, use of the site seems to have been transient in nature. The sanctuary flourished during the Cypro-Archaic II period, a particularly prosperous era throughout Cyprus, and continued to function under Persian rule. For most of the Cypro-Classical period, the sanctuary was likely controlled by the Kingdom of Kition that annexed the Kingdom of Idalion in the middle of the fifth century (Tatton-Brown 1990: 84; Counts 2004;

see also comments in Fourrier, Ch. 9). The reorganization and eastern expansion of the sanctuary during the last quarter of the fourth century may have been occasioned by destruction caused in the squabbling between Antigonus Monophthalmus and Ptolemy I over control of the island. More specifically, the sanctuary may have been destroyed in 312 BC following the defeat of Kition and the death of its king Poumiathon (Mehr 2000: 630–31). During the long Hellenistic and subsequent Roman periods the sanctuary continued to function, but it was eventually abandoned with the rise of Christianity on the island.

While the presence of a nucleated settlement at Malloura founded early in the Roman period is well established, no evidence for the existence of an earlier settlement in the Malloura Valley has been forthcoming. The presence of the sanctuary in and of itself does not require a corresponding settlement, since rural sanctuaries are well-attested on the island (e.g., Karageorghis 1977). However, the large number of tombs in the valley spanning the Cypro-Archaic II through Hellenistic periods is hard to explain in the absence of a nearby settlement. The nearest attested settlement sites are Golgoi to the north and Idalion to the west, ca.

4.5 and 8.5 km away, respectively, and both sites have their own extensive cemeteries. Therefore, the presence of a nearer settlement to account for the Malloura Valley tombs must be posited. Yet none of the 30 sites identified through survey (see Kardulias and Yerkes, Ch. 7) or excavation 'fits the bill.' Presumably, the elusive settlement of Cypro-Archaic through Hellenistic date is located beyond the AAP survey area or, more likely, lies securely buried in deep alluvial and colluvial deposits in the middle of the valley, not far from its contemporary tombs and sanctuary (Butzer and Harris 2007).

As attested by plentiful imports, such as ceramic wares (from Asia Minor, North Africa, and Italy) and coinage minted at Constantinople, the settlement established at Malloura in the first century BC continued to thrive through the Early Byzantine period. Yet, despite its location 15 km inland and behind the ridges that overlook the Larnaka coast, the settlement suffered destruction and was subsequently abandoned. It may have fallen victim to the first Arab raids on Cyprus in 647/49 and 653/54 by Muawiya, governor of Syria (Runciman 1990: 147–48).

There is no evidence for occupation at Malloura between the seventh and early 14th centuries, spanning the periods of Arab/Byzantine conflict, Late Byzantine renaissance, and early Frankish rule. Settlement at Malloura was resumed sometime in the 14th century—later in the period of Frankish rule. As attested by excavated burials as well as domestic and industrial structures and corroborated by the survey, the settlement flourished during the Venetian period. Reflecting the fortunes of the island in general, during the Ottoman period Malloura gradually declined and was eventually abandoned in the 19th century. By 1878, when the island came into British hands, the rich agricultural land in the Malloura Valley became exclusively the possession of the inhabitants of Petrophani (Turkish Esendagh).

REFERENCES

Al-Radi, S. M. S.
1983   *Phlamoudhi Vounari: A Sanctuary Site in Cyprus.* Göteborg: Åström.

Åström, P.
2000   *A Century of International Cyprological Research.* Nicosia: Bank of Cyprus Cultural Foundation.

Bernhard-Walcher, A.
1999   *Die Sammlung Zyprischer Antiken im Kunsthistorischen Museum.* Vienna: Kunsthistorisches Museum.

Butzer, K. W., and Harris, S. E.
2007   Geoarchaeological Approaches to the Environmental History of Cyprus: Explication and Critical Evaluation. *Journal of Archaeological Science* 34: 1932–52.

Colonna-Ceccaldi, G.
1882   *Monuments antiques de Chypre, de Syrie et d'Egypte.* Paris: Imprimerie Pillet et du Moulin.

Counts, D. B.
1998   Contributions to the Study of Cypriote Sculpture: Limestone Votives from Athienou-Malloura. Unpublished Ph.D. dissertation, Brown University.
2001   Prolegomena to the Study of Cypriote Sculpture. *Cahier du Centre d'Études Chypriotes* 31: 129–81.
2004   Art and Religion in the Cypriote Mesaoria: The View from Athienou-*Malloura. Cahier du Centre d'Études Chypriotes* 34: 173–90.
2009   From Siwa to Cyprus: The Assimilation of Zeus Ammon in the Cypriote Pantheon. Pp. 104–17 in *Egypt and Cyprus in Antiquity,* eds. D. Michaelides, V. Kassianidou, and R. Merrillees. Oxford: Oxbow.

Counts, D. B., and Toumazou, M. K.
2003   Artemis at Malloura? *Cahier du Centre d'Études Chypriotes* 33: 235–50.
2006   New Light on the Iconography of Bes in Archaic Cyprus. Pp. 598–602 in *Common*

Ground: Archaeology, Art, Science, and Humanities. Proceedings of the XVIth International Congress of Classical Archaeology, Boston, August 23–26, 2003, eds. A. Donohue and C. Mattusch. Oxford: Oxbow.

Foucart-Borville, J.
1985   La correspondence chypriote d'Edmond Duthoit (1862 et 1865). *Cahier du Centre d'Études Chypriotes* 4: 3–60.

Gass, I. G.
1960   *The Geology and Mineral Resources of the Dhali Area.* Memoir 4. Nicosia: Geological Survey Department, Cyprus.

Giacomini, B. S.
1993   Byzantine/Medieval Burials on Cyprus. Unpublished M.A. thesis, California State University, Fullerton.

Gjerstad, E.; Lindros, J.; Sjöqvist E.; and Westholm, A.
1934–1972 *The Swedish Cyprus Expedition. Finds and Results of the Excavations in Cyprus, 1927–1931.* Stockholm: The Swedish Cyprus Expedition.

Goring, E. A.
1988   *Mischievous Pastime: Digging in Cyprus in the 19th century.* Edinburgh: National Museums of Scotland.

Hadjisavvas, S.
1985   Excavations at the "Tombs of the Kings"— Kato Paphos. Pp. 262–68 in *Archaeology in Cyprus, 1960–1985*, ed. V. Karageorghis. Nicosia: A. G. Leventis Foundation.
1997   *Agia Napa: Excavations at Makronisos and the Archaeology of the Region.* Nicosia: Agia Napa Municipality and the Cyprus Department of Antiquities.

Hermary, A.
1988   Nouvelles découvertes sur la Mission Vogüé de 1862. *Cahier du Centre d'Études Chypriotes* 12: 15–20.
1989   *Musée du Louvre, Département des antiquités orientales: Catalogue des antiquités de Chypre. Sculptures.* Paris: Editions de la Réunion des Musées Nationaux.

1990   Historie des études sur la sculpture chypriote. *Cahier du Centre d'Études Chypriotes* 14: 7–28.

Karageorghis, V.
1977   *Two Cypriote Sanctuaries of the End of the Cypro-Archaic Period.* Rome: Consiglio Nazionale delle Ricerche.
1987   *The Archaeology of Cyprus: Ninety Years after Myres.* London: Leopard's Head.
2000   *Ancient Art from Cyprus: The Cesnola Collection of the Metropolitan Museum of Art.* New York: Metropolitan Museum of Art and Abrams.

Kurtz, D. C., and Boardman, J.
1971   *Greek Burial Customs.* London: Thames and Hudson.

Mas Latrie, L. de
1862   *Notice sur la construction d'une carte de l'île de Chypre.* Paris: A. Lainé and J. Harvard.

Mehr, A.
2000   Hellenistic Cyprus (in Greek). Pp. 619–761 in *History of Cyprus*, ed. T. Papadopoulos. Nicosia: Archbishop Makarios III Foundation.

Myres, J. L.
1914   *Handbook of the Cesnola Collection of Antiquities from Cyprus, Metropolitan Museum of Art, New York.* New York: The Metropolitan Museum of Art.

Myres, J. L., and Ohnefalsch-Richter, M.
1899   *A Catalogue of the Cyprus Museum.* Oxford: Clarendon.

Ohnefalsch-Richter, M.
1893   *Kypros, the Bible and Homer.* London: Asher.

Perrot G., and Chipiez, C.
1885   *History of Art in Phoenicia and Its Dependencies.* London: Chapman and Hall.

Pilides, D.
2008   An Outline of the History of Archaeological Research in Cyprus. Pp. 15–24 in *Views from Phlamoudhi, Cyprus*, ed. J. S. Smith. Boston: American Schools of Oriental Research.

Rautman, M.
2003   *A Cypriot Village of Late Antiquity. Kalavasos-Kopetra in the Vasilikos Valley.* Journal of Roman Archaeology Supplementary Series 52. Portsmouth, RI: Journal of Roman Archaeology.

Reyes, A. T.
1994   *Archaic Cyprus: A Study of the Textual and Archaeological Evidence.* Oxford: Oxford University.

Rohn, A. H.; Barnes, E.; Sandars, G. D. R.
2010   An Early Ottoman Cemetery at Ancient Corinth. *Hesperia* 78: 501–615.

Runciman, S.
1990   The Byzantine Period. Pp. 136–74 in *Footprints in Cyprus*, ed. D. Hunt. Revised edition. London: Trigraph.

Smith, J. S.
1997   Preliminary Comments on a Rural Cypro-Archaic Sanctuary in Polis-*Peristeries. Bulletin of the American Schools of Oriental Research* 308: 77–98.
2009   *Art and Society in Cyprus from the Bronze Age into the Iron Age.* Cambridge: Cambridge University.

Sørensen, L. W., and Jacobsen, K. W.
2006   *Panayia Ematousa.* Athens: Danish Institute at Athens.

Tatton-Brown, V.
1990   The Classical Period. Pp. 84–97 in *Footprints in Cyprus*, ed. D. Hunt. Revised edition. London: Trigraph.

Tatton-Brown, V. (ed.)
2001   *Cyprus in the Nineteenth Century AD: Fact, Fancy, and Fiction.* Oxford: Oxbow.

Toumazou, M. K.; Kardulias, P. N.; Yerkes, R. W.
1992   Athienou Archaeological Project 1991: The Second Season of Investigations at Athienou-Malloura, Cyprus. *American Journal of Archaeology* 96: 352.

Ulbrich, A.
2001   An Archaeology of Cult? Cypriot Sanctuaries in 19th Century Archaeology. Pp. 93–106 in *Cyprus in the Nineteenth Century AD: Fact, Fancy, and Fiction*, ed. V. Tatton-Brown. Oxford: Oxbow.

Chapter 7

The Malloura Valley Survey

by P. Nick Kardulias and Richard W. Yerkes

Among the first questions that individuals ask archaeologists is, how do you know where to dig? The answer to that query usually includes three typical ways of identifying sites. The first is accidental exposure that results both from natural events, such as erosion, the uncovering of remains by wind, and so forth, and from human activity, including construction and farming. Next is the use of informants who may have a detailed knowledge of local site locations and content. The third is systematic survey undertaken by trained archaeologists. The difference between the first two ways and the third way is that in systematic survey, researchers are able to devise a research design with explicit questions that can be addressed by particular methods of field investigation, rather than the serendipity of the other two forms of data collection. We have adopted a set of theoretical approaches that have guided both our techniques for collecting information in the field and its interpretation. Specifically, systematic survey is a regional approach and thus provides information about settlement distribution (compare, e.g., the approach to similar questions in Counts and Parvis, Ch. 5). Since our survey covers many chronological periods, we can trace the develop-

ment of the human use of a landscape over time as people aggregate, disperse, and shift the locations of their habitations and resource extraction sites. This chapter provides a description of our field methods and their rationale, and then presents some of the main results of our work. A brief history of survey on Cyprus provides context for our work in the Malloura Valley.

While archaeologists have always done some form of locational survey, it is only in the last 60 years that the method has become more systematic. Today survey is recognized as a distinct and valued method of archaeological investigation, but even in the 19th century antiquarians, such as Duthoit and Cesnola (see Counts, Ch. 4), searched for Cypriot antiquities by employing a form of extensive survey. These individuals consulted documents, questioned locals, and examined surface conditions, much as Schliemann explored the Troad to identify the most likely location of the famous Bronze Age city and Layard visited different locales in Mesopotamia. What differentiates these early efforts from later work is that, since the late 1940s, archaeologists incorporate specific questions into research designs to address particular issues and then identify the methods used to obtain relevant data. Willey (1953) was among the first to carve out a niche for survey archaeology with his work in Peru. A host of other Americanists quickly adopted and added to survey methodology in their attempts to understand prehistoric settlement dynamics. A number of archaeologists in western Europe also contributed to this movement, often with the assistance of historical documents for certain periods. All these investigators developed survey into an essential tool of archaeological investigation that complemented, rather than just supplemented, excavation. For classical archaeology of the Greek world, the Minnesota Messenia Expedition (McDonald and Rapp 1972) was the first project to focus on survey as a primary means of data acquisition. The 1970s witnessed a dramatic increase in the number of surveys in the Aegean (Keller and Rupp 1983). This proliferation was accompanied by a significant number of innovations in field methods and analytical techniques that continue to this day (Cherry 1994; Galaty 2005). Among the contributions was the refinement of what has come to be known as the non-site or off-site approach (Dunnell and Dancey 1983; Alcock et al. 1994; Bintliff 2000) in which researchers concentrate on how the total landscape was used in the past through the recording of all artifacts encountered during field walking across an entire survey region, and also through the use of sophisticated sampling techniques (Cherry 1982; Davis et al. 1997). The work of archaeologists in the eastern Mediterranean has also provided thoughtful reflection on another major trend in the discipline, the notion of landscape archaeology (Cherry et al. 1991; Alcock 1993; Ashmore and Knapp 1999; Bintliff 2000; Athanassopoulos and Wandsnider 2004). Furthermore, by its focus on how humans interacted with their surroundings during times of environmental change, survey projects have brought together archaeologists, earth scientists, and other specialists, leading to interdisciplinary work that provided a more comprehensive view of human action in the past (Jameson et al. 1994; Zangger 1998).

Although archaeological work on Cyprus has a long history, systematic survey on the island is a relatively recent phenomenon. The first efforts concentrated on identifying and then compiling inventories of sites (e.g., Megaw 1955; Catling 1963). Beginning in the 1970s, surveys were conducted in the Analiondas region (Stanley-Price 1972), the area around Phlamoudhi (Symeonoglou 1972), the Khrysokhou drainage near Polis (Adovasio et al. 1975), the region around Paphos (Sørensen and Rupp 1993; see Peltenburg et al. 1983 for the Lemba Archaeological Project), the Vasilikos Valley (Todd 1989; Rautman 2003: 22–44), the area around the city-kingdom of Amathous near Limassol (by C. Petit, see Vigne et al. 2000), the region surrounding Agia Napa (Hadjisavvas 1997: 26–42), the Kyrenia District on the north coast (Sevketoglu 2000), the lower slopes of the Troodos Massif (Given and Knapp 2003; Given et al. 2007), and the coastal area around Pyla (Caraher et al. 2007; see also Iacovou 2004 for a summary of survey on Cyprus since the 1980s).

Cyprus is the only large island in the Levantine basin of the Mediterranean Sea. While it lies only about 70 km from Turkey and 100 km from Syria, no land bridge ever connected it to the mainland. The results of systematic survey and excavation projects show that the earliest sites on Cyprus are near the coast. Limited wild food resources on Cyprus may have made it remote and insular to pre-Neolithic groups, but its fertile soils, copper deposits, and strategic location made it accessible and attractive to later seafaring societies. Cyprus' only pre-Neolithic site, Akrotiri-*Aetokremnos* seems to have been occupied during the 10th millennium cal. BC by castaways or explorers who encountered pygmy hippos and dwarf elephants. The first settlements were established by early Aceramic Neolithic groups that may have come from the Levant or Anatolia. These "Cypro-PPNB" settlers imported wild animals (cattle, pig, fallow deer, sheep, goat, dog, cat, and fox), domestic plants, and weeds to the island. The lack of significant morphological modifications in the bones of the hoofed animals suggests that they were part of a Near Eastern pre-domestic husbandry that developed during the PPNB and quickly diffused throughout the eastern Mediterranean. These plants and animals must have been transported across the Mediterranean Sea to Cyprus (Vigne et al. 2000; Peltenburg et al.

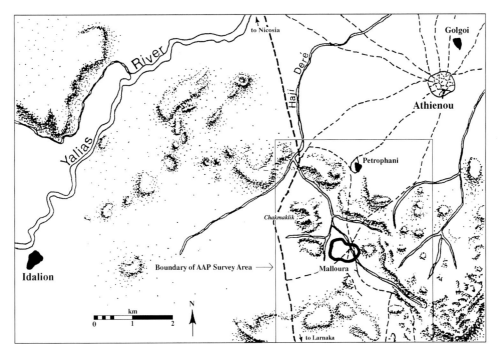

Fig. 7.1 *Map showing the project area in relation to Athienou, Golgoi, and Idalion. Dotted lines indicate roads; thick line in survey zone is outline of artifact distribution at Athienou-Malloura (Site 1) (drawing: R. Yerkes, after Kitchener 1885).*

2001; Guilaine and Le Brun 2003; Peltenburg 2003; Horowitz et al. 2004; Colledge and Conolly 2007). Later colonists of the Khirokitia (Late Aceramic Neolithic), Sotira (Ceramic Neolithic), and Erimi (Chalcolithic) cultures also transported plants and animals to the island. The first inland Neolithic settlements such as Dhali-*Agridhi* I, Ais Yiorkis, and Asprokremnos were established during the end of the Cypro-PPNB stage or during the later Aceramic Neolithic Khirokitian stage (Lehavy 1974, 1989; Peltenburg 2003: Table 11.3), and as the settlements expanded into the interior, there were fewer contacts with the mainland. The AAP Malloura Valley Survey focused on later cultural developments in the interior central part of the island and employed innovative modifications of the non-site concept in these regional investigations.

The Malloura Valley Survey

The surface survey component of the AAP was supervised by the authors. The field crews consisted of students from Ohio State University, Kenyon

College, and other colleges and universities. The main phases of the field investigation took place in 1991 and 1992, when large teams of field walkers covered the majority of the project area, with more targeted fieldwork in 1993–1998 and 2001–2005. The goal of the survey was to document past human use of the landscape in a 20 km² area around the site of Athienou-*Malloura* (fig. 7.1). Specific goals were to determine the extent of Athienou-*Malloura* (Site 1) and to reconstruct the settlement structure in the area from the earliest phase of occupation until the present, with a focus on Malloura (i.e., how does Malloura relate to other sites of the same period located in the project area?). The survey data can be used to construct a regional settlement profile, provide a view of rural occupation in key periods (Cypro-Archaic–Early Byzantine, Late Byzantine–modern) and provide a regional context for the data from the excavation at Malloura.

During the 1991 season (June 7–June 28) the survey team covered 5.5 km² (27.5% of the total project area) and recorded artifact densities that

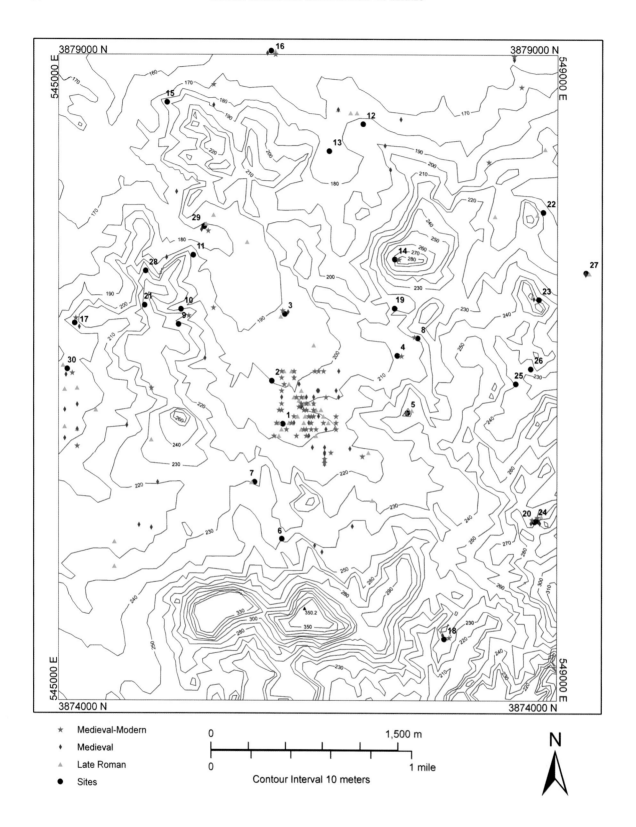

FIG. 7.2   *Map showing site locations and distribution of Roman, medieval, and modern pottery in the project area (map: D. Massey).*

varied from 0.0002 artifacts/m² to 0.06 artifacts/m². In addition, 13 locations with high artifact densities were designated as sites, ranging in date from the Aceramic Neolithic to the Ottoman periods. In 1992 our field teams traversed 8 km², for a combined two-season total of 13.5 km² (67.5% of project area) and identified seven additional sites. In subsequent years, field walking was limited to certain locations thought to be good site candidates based on the information gathered previously, a process through which we located 11 more sites. The latter work also involved revisiting certain sites to gather more artifacts and to record coordinates with GPS units for the creation of a GIS database (see Massey and Kardulias, Ch. 22).

Methods

Field Methods

We used the non-site or off-site method (Dunnell and Dancey 1983), which, instead of recording surface artifacts only in designated sites, dictates recording artifact counts in each transect in the survey region walked by a fieldworker. Transects ran along cardinal directions (east–west and north–south). Survey personnel were spaced at 10–15 m intervals and walked over tracts, recording the quantity of artifacts in their transects on tally counters. A senior staff person recorded the counts every 100 m. Material was gathered in one of two modes: walkover or site sample. In walkover mode, field walkers counted all artifacts (ancient, medieval, modern) and collected diagnostic pieces, such as flaked stone, pottery rims, handles, and bases, terracotta figurines, and coins. The information from walkovers helped us identify high concentrations called sites, where we collected all surface artifacts from either square units (1 × 1 m² or 2 × 2 m²) that were spaced in a systematic manner or radial transects (site sample mode); at each site we would also collect grab samples, which constituted diagnostic artifacts from areas not included in the systematic sample units. The length of walkover transects varied between 250 m and 800 m. This approach contrasts with that followed by a number of other surveys (e.g., Davis

et al. 1997; Given and Knapp 2003; Tartaron et al. 2006) in which researchers used bounded fields as units for field walking. We walked long transects because of the flat nature of the terrain and the often minimal divisions between adjacent fields. From the field counts we determined artifact densities for the various areas and then devised maps showing these artifact concentrations. The distribution map shows that the area at and around Malloura has the densest concentration of artifacts in the entire valley by a substantial degree (fig. 7.2).

We recorded locations of survey units and sites on the 1:5000 contour maps published by the Department of Lands and Surveys. The 20 km² project area covers all of Sheet XXVIII and portions of Sheets IV, V, XXVII, and XXIV. We used the following breakdown of the maps to identify locations of walkovers and sites:

- Area: Roman numeral that identifies the Cyprus map sheet.
- Sector: Arabic numeral 1 to 9 that indicates a 1-km² block on a map sheet.
- Quad: Two-letter compass designation (NW, NE, SE, SW) for a quarter of a Sector (500 × 500 m; indicated by dotted-line blocks on the maps).
- Tract: Arabic numeral for any segment of a Sector walked as a unit.

The Malloura Valley offered ideal conditions for survey. The majority of the project area is in the relatively flat central part of the valley with excellent ground visibility due to mechanical harvesting of large barley fields. The flat zone extends from the twin set of flat-topped Vouyes hills near the southern edge of the project zone north through a landscape of fields nestled between low hills on the east and west. Flat open land continues on the west of the western hills and north of the abandoned Turkish Cypriote village of Petrophani (Turkish Esendagh); the area north of Petrophani now contains a number of cow sheds that have sprung up in the last 20 years as the residents of Athienou turned to raising dairy cattle as a major enterprise. South of the Vouyes, the landscape changes dramatically to a highly dissected terrain with elongated limestone spines descending to the coastal plain near Larnaka

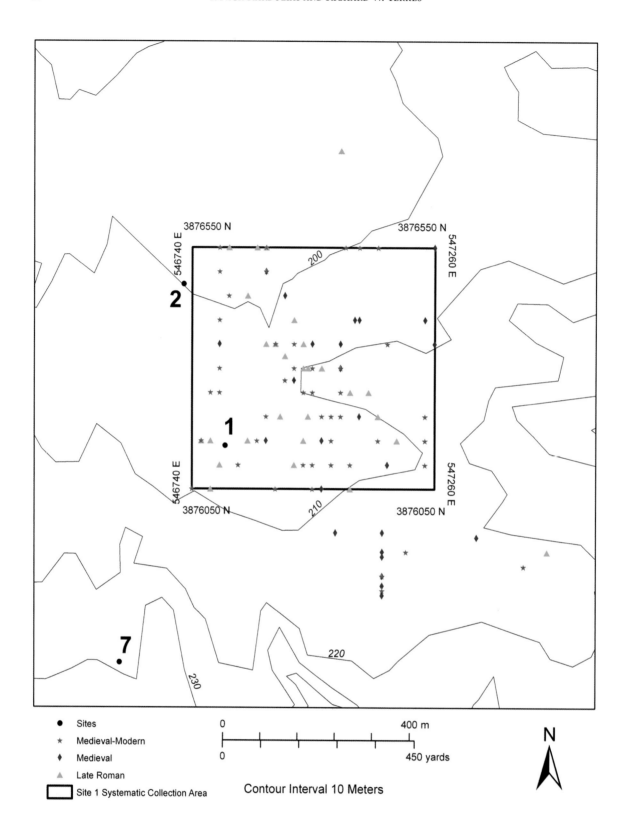

FIG. 7.3 *Ceramics from systematic samples at Athienou-*Malloura *(Site 1) (map: D. Massey).*

(for a more detailed discussion of the physical environment, see Yerkes, Ch. 2).

Sites were sampled in a manner appropriate to their specific locations. For example, on large sites both systematic and grab samples were taken. At Site 1 (Malloura), the systematic collection consisted of a total pickup in a series of 2 × 2 m squares spaced at 50 m intervals north–south along transect lines and separated by 20 m east–west. This spacing was adequate to identify large features in a substantial settlement such as Malloura. At Site 9, a large lithic concentration, the collection unit was a 1 × 1 m square located every 5 m (north–south and east–west); the smaller site size and nature of the material (lithics on a bedrock surface) required a smaller interval to gather a representative sample. At other sites, randomly chosen sample transects sufficed. Crew members would stand at an edge of the site along a randomly selected bearing from the center; the individual collected all artifacts along a 1 m wide swath as he/she walked toward the center. In several other instances, the collections consisted of material inside and outside of structures. Diagnostic items collected outside of either systematic or random units comprised the grab samples.

Ground visibility varied from moderate to excellent over the whole survey area, most of which was covered by barley fields that had been harvested. The terrain consisted of flat valley bottoms surrounded by gently rolling hills. Approximately 5% of the area is inaccessible because of its proximity to the Turkish occupied zone, while another 5% is in sections that have Greek Cypriot military facilities (current military posts, minefields, entrenchments). The good ground visibility combined with intensive survey coverage have produced artifact counts that we believe are representative of the variation across the Malloura Valley.

Analytical Methods

Analysis of the artifacts retrieved from the survey followed techniques that are standard in the eastern Mediterranean and Cyprus. We classified stone tools and ceramics into categories on the basis of morphology, function, and date. Locations

were recorded (as UTM coordinates) and spatial data were collected, using a Brunton compass in the field initially and subsequently, between 2001 and 2003, with a handheld GPS unit. Artifact information and data on the location of field units and sites were stored in electronic files (Excel, Access). The locational data have been analyzed using ArcGIS to address particular questions about the human use of the valley over time (see Massey and Kardulias, Ch. 22).

RESULTS

At the beginning of the first season of field investigation, we conducted a systematic collection at Malloura (Site 1) to gain an understanding of the local artifact assemblage and to study the activities that were performed at various loci of the site. The collection also created a reference point for the rest of the valley in terms of artifact density. To be certain that we covered all potential portions of the site, we laid out a grid over an area 0.52 (east–west) × 0.5 (north–south) km (26 ha) and collected 286 systematic and 8 grab samples (fig. 7.3). The surface material is largely consistent with the evidence from excavation (see Toumazou and Counts, Ch. 6). The concentration of artifacts is heaviest in the area between EU 2 and EU 5 and north of the intermittent streambed (fig. 7.4). The density drops off dramatically ca. 80 m in any direction from the datum point, but there is a consistent background scatter as far as 1 km from the site. This distribution suggests that the settlement proper covers an area of about 7 ha, not all of which was occupied at the same time. The size is comparable to other Roman rural settlements on Cyprus such as Kalavasos-*Kopetra* that covered 4 ha and had an estimated population between 500 and 600 (Rautman 2003: 38). However, the population at Malloura may have been smaller (see Yerkes, Ch. 26). Roman and Late Byzantine forms dominate the identifiable ceramics in all parts of the site (see Moore and Gregory, Ch. 15), but there are also a number of flakes and ground stone pieces. Several large millstones near the streambed that bisects the eastern part of the site suggest a substantial milling operation in late medieval times (fig. 7.5; see also Spigelman, Ch. 17, figs. 17.1a–b). The variety and

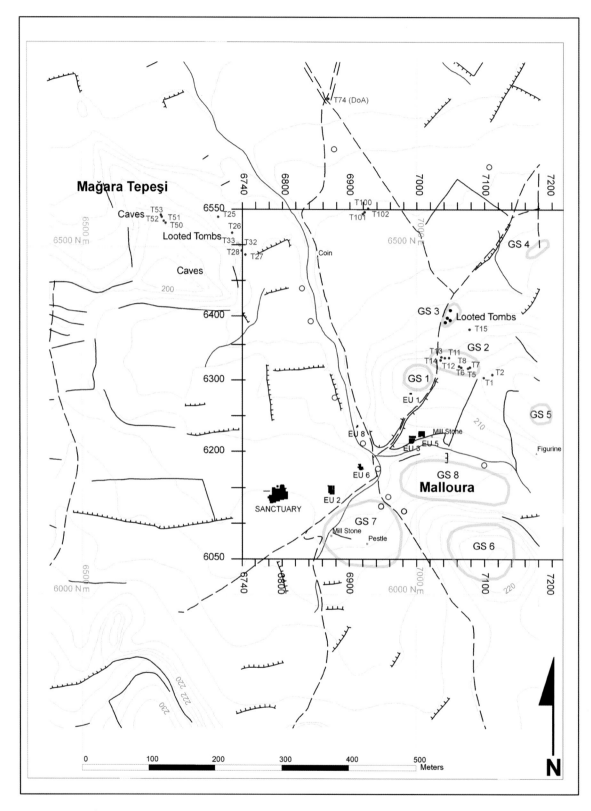

FIG. 7.4   *Map showing distribution of main artifact types, EUs, grab sample areas, and millstones at Athienou-Malloura (Site 1) (drawing: A. Prins and D. Massey).*

FIG. 7.5   *Large millstone (Stone 1) east of EU 5 at Athienou-Malloura. The stone is a mortarium basin for processing olives, with a probable Venetian date. Facing southeast (photo: P. N. Kardulias).*

quality of material retrieved indicate that Malloura was a reasonably prosperous and extensive settlement with Cypro-Archaic to early Roman predecessors. The surface collection revealed a particularly rich assemblage of material in the zone around the Hellenistic–Roman-period tombs in the northeastern part of Malloura (Site 1); artifacts include the corner of a ceramic larnax and several lamps. In the area of the sanctuary at the southwestern corner of the site, the surface collection did not yield any items diagnostic of a religious center (e.g., small votive pots, figurines). There were several pieces of statuary on the surface in the area at the start of our project, and others were reported in the past. The excavation has located the sanctuary at a depth of 1.6 m below ground surface (see Toumazou and Counts, Ch. 6), which most likely accounts for the paucity of surface material related to the religious feature.

The next phase of survey work concentrated on expanding the coverage out from Malloura. We began to the northwest of Malloura in the area of Mağara Tepeşi (Site 2) that lies 300 m northwest of the center of Site 1 and 100 m west of the grid for the systematic samples. Artifact density declined dramatically as we moved westward toward the pre-1974 Larnaka/Nicosia road. In the last part of the first survey season, operations shifted to the north end of the project area. During the second field season in 1992, we linked the central and northern sectors and then examined the hills on the east and west margins of the valley. In subsequent seasons, one or two field walkers investigated additional areas primarily along the eastern and western edges of the project area beyond the main lines of hills.

CHRONOLOGY OF THE SITES

Only six possible prehistoric components were recorded during the survey. Four of these (Sites 9, 11, 21, 28) are lithic processing stations or artifact scatters discovered on the surface of Chakmaklik, the hill on the western edge of the valley; a fifth location (Site 15) is on a low hill north of Chakmaklik. The lithic material processed at these sites was obtained from the chert beds of the Middle Lapithos Formation that outcrop there. Cores, large flakes, and a few blades made of weathered white, pink, and tan chert were concentrated on the exposed bedrock and thin mantle of soil on the crest of Chakmaklik (fig. 7.6; see Kardulias and Yerkes, Ch. 8).

Since prehistoric lithic assemblages from Cyprus are rather nondescript, it is difficult to assign chipped stone artifacts from surface collections to specific cultural periods (Cherry 1990: 154; Knapp 1994: 405). Nonetheless, our analyses

FIG. 7.6   *Lithics from Site 9; scale is in centimeters (photo: P. N. Kardulias).*

revealed that the blades and flakes from the lithic workshops on Chakmaklik resemble the chipped stone artifacts from excavated Neolithic and Chalcolithic sites on Cyprus described by Cauvin (1984), Dikaios (1962), Le Brun (1981, 1994; Le Brun et al. 1987), Lehavy (1974, 1989), Simmons and Corona (1993), Stekelis (1953, 1961), and Waechter (1953). We found no evidence for a prehistoric settlement in the immediate vicinity of these chert work stations. The nearest recorded early prehistoric habitation outside the AAP area is the Aceramic Neolithic site of Dhali-*Agridhi*, which lies 6 km due west of Chakmaklik (Lehavy 1974, 1989).

The sixth possible prehistoric component was recorded at the abandoned Turkish Cypriot village of Petrophani (Site 12), at the northern edge of the valley, where a ground stone bowl fragment and a few chipped stone artifacts were found. Isolated blades and bladelet fragments were also found on the hillslopes and plain near Chakmaklik, and a broken blade was also found on the top of the Mesovounos mesa about 75 m from a small scatter of Late Roman and modern pot sherds. Mesovounos is located more than 3 km southeast of the Chakmaklik chert sources.

No evidence of Bronze Age (2500–1050 BC) or Cypro-Geometric (Early Iron Age, 1050–750 BC) occupations in the Malloura Valley came to light during the survey, although the 1994 excavations

retrieved some Cypro-Geometric pottery from the western edge of the sanctuary (see Fourrier, Ch. 9). It appears that settlement during these periods was limited to an area adjacent to Golgoi, such as the Late Bronze Age site at Athienou-*Pamboulari tis Koukounninas* (Dothan and Ben-Tor 1983; see also Counts, Ch. 4). The prosperity of the Late Bronze Age, the destruction during the era of the "sea peoples" (Drews 1993: 11–12), and the foundation of new cities on the coast (e.g., Salamis, Amathous, Kourion) during the Early Iron Age had very little impact on the more marginal areas of the island like the Malloura Valley. The intensification of copper production under the control of the major centers such as Enkomi and Kition seems to have fragmented into a pattern of local production at smaller regional centers by the end of the Bronze Age (Knapp 1994: 424–28). One of those regional centers may have been at Golgoi (Knapp 1988: 146–48; 2008), but we have no evidence for any contemporary settlements to the south in the Malloura Valley.

Some 2.5 km northeast of the sanctuary at Athienou-*Malloura*, Cypro-Archaic and Cypro-Classical/Hellenistic pottery sherds were found at Site 27 on the east slope of a small hill overlooking the Kryon Neron valley (see fig. 7.2). Survey of tracts located southwest of the Malloura site below the Exovouyes mesa revealed a concentration of Cypro-Classical/Hellenistic sherds near a rock-cut feature (Site 7). Some scatters of Cypro-Classical and Hellenistic pottery were also found west of the Malloura site, along the Larnaka/Nicosia road (Site 30). No other concentrations of Cypro-Archaic or Cypro-Classical/Hellenistic materials were documented between these sites and Athienou-*Malloura*. In fact, artifact density dropped off dramatically in the areas that were surveyed outside the limits of the Malloura site. While there are scores of Cypro-Archaic, Cypro-Classical, and Hellenistic tombs in the Malloura Valley, so far the only evidence for habitation in the region during those periods has come from Athienou-*Malloura*, Site 27 at the northeast corner of the survey area in the Kryon Neron drainage, and Site 30 along the Larnaka/Nicosia road (Table 7.1). Tombs appear in several clusters around the valley. The most notable is the group of tombs at Site 2; three other groups are located within the confines of Site 1. The first of these is on a gentle slope along the northeast edge of the site; a number of artifacts from the surface at these burials were collected as Grab Sample 4. Another cluster of four or five tombs is built into the north face of a small hill on the southeast margin of Malloura; no artifacts were found during the survey walkovers in this section. The third group lies about 200 m north of the sanctuary in a flat area on the northeast side of the site and 100 m south of Site 2, where three tombs were exposed at a depth of 1.5 m when the trench for a waterline was dug across the valley in 2001. These latter tombs (T100, T101, T102) were excavated; while few artifacts and human remains were recovered, the datable pottery from the first two is Cypro-Archaic and Hellenistic in date and Roman for the third. There were few artifacts on the surface above these tombs when it was surveyed in 1991, a fact that may be due to either the meager contents of the small chambers or the subsequent in-filling by alluviation.

Several excavation units at the Malloura site (EU 3, EU 5) contain the remains of structures associated with the establishment of a rural settlement at Malloura during the early Roman period that continued through the Early Byzantine era. Yet, the materials dating to the Roman–Early Byzantine

occupation of the Malloura Valley were not as common as Late Byzantine–Venetian artifacts in the survey tracts (see Moore and Gregory, Ch. 15). Moderate scatters of Roman and Byzantine materials were present in the fields around Petrophani, at Site 16 in the northern portion of the survey area (including a coin [AAP-S 496] of Emperor Phocas dated to AD 606–607), and at Site 30 on the western edge of the valley, but it does not appear that there were substantial late Roman/Early Byzantine settlements at these sites. Rather, it seems that the sites represent farmsteads composed of several households based on the distribution of the surface artifacts. The lack of Middle Byzantine pottery in the survey collections suggests abandonment of the valley beginning in the mid-seventh century, possibly due to the Arab raids, with renewed settlement only some seven centuries later. Surveys in other parts of Cyprus have noted a similar gap (Gregory 2003). During this hiatus, people may have relocated to other settlements outside the valley and exploited the project area only sporadically, as was the case in the prehistoric period.

Sufficient Frankish pottery was found to suggest that a later settlement was established at Malloura in the 14th century (late in the Frankish period). To date, no evidence for activity in this area during the Late Byzantine "renaissance" or the early Frankish period has been found. Later, during the Venetian period (AD 1489–1571), Malloura seems to have flourished. The systematic surface collections at the Malloura site documented a heavy concentration of late medieval materials near these buildings (located in EU 2 and EU 3). The building in EU 2 with an unusual series of cross-walls may have been the location for processing flax into linen (see DeMasi, Ch. 16), and thus part of an economy in the Venetian period that produced items marketed beyond the valley. In addition, several large millstones were found in or near the intermittent streams that cross the site (fig. 7.5) suggesting that there were several mills operating here (see Spigelman, Ch. 17). There are reports of numerous water-driven mills for processing grains in the Ottoman period, and it is reasonable to suggest that such mechanisms existed in the preceding period (Cobham 1908: 247, 288, 350, 373). These features

TABLE 7.1   List of sites in the Malloura Valley.

Site#	Site Name	Area	Sec.	Tract	UTM East	UTM North	Site Type	Cultural Period(s)	Artifacts
1	Malloura	XXXVIII	8	1–4	6740–7260	6050–6550	sanctuary, town	Archaic–Venetian	pottery, tile, glass, lithic, bone, architecture
2	Magara Tepesi	XXXVIII	8	5	6640–6550	6450–6550	tombs	Archaic–Roman	pottery, tile, chipped stone, glass, tombs
3	Diamond Field	XXXVIII	8	8	(54)6820	(387)7000	mudbrick structure	Medieval, Modern	pottery, bone, architecture
4	Sklinikos North	XXXVIII	9	2	(54)7730	(387)6700	stone structure	Classical, Modern	pottery, tile, architecture
5	Sklinikos	XXXVIII	9	1	(54)7800	(387)6225	artifact scatter	Unknown	pottery
6	Jinarotos East	IV	2	1	(54)6840	(387)5320	kiln or furnace?	Classical, Roman	pottery, architecture
7	Khirin Kourats	IV	2	1	(54)6600	(387)5680	tomb/storage pit	Classical, Hellen., Roman	pottery, tile
8	Kokkinokafkallia	XXXVIII	9	2	(54)7825	(387)6875	cut blocks/dump	Modern	cut stone bowl, cut stone blocks
9	Chakmaklik I	XXXVIII	7	3	6060–6230	6860–6975	chert workshop	Early Prehistoric?	chipped stone, some pottery (rare)
10	Chakmaklik II	XXXVIII	4	1	(54)6100	(387)7050	chipping station	Modern	chipped stone, some pottery (rare)
11	Chakmaklik III	XXXVIII	4	1	(54)6125	(387)7425	small chert scatter	Prehistoric?	chipped stone
12	Petrophani	XXXVIII	2	1	7300–7550	8300–8600	village	Prehist? Classical–Modern	pottery, tile, glass, lithic, bone, architecture
13	Petrophani South	XXXVIII	2	3	(54)7175	(387)8260	mudbrick structure	Modern	none
14	Mandra tou Photi	XXXVIII	6	1	(54)7780	(387)7425	artifact scatter	Classical, Modern	pottery, chipped stone
15	Mavri East	XXXVII	3	1	(54)5875	(387)8630	chert workshop	Prehistoric? Modern	chipped stone, some pottery (rare)
16	Mavrous NE	–	–	–	(54)6685	(387)9075	settlement	Classical–Medieval	pottery, some chipped stone, coin (80 m S)
17	Khania East	XXXVII	9	2	5035–5225	6945–6890	settlement	Modern	pottery, tile, architecture
18	Koutsopetrika East	IV	6	1	(54)8085	(387)4565	stone workshop	Classical? Modern	cut stone, some pottery (rare)
19	M.tou Photi South	XXXVIII	6	1	(54)7705	(387)7035	stone hut	Modern?	none
20	Acropolis SE	XXXVIII	8	12	(54)7430	(387)5870	millstone&cistern	Late Roman–Medieval	"millstone", pottery
21	Chakmaklik IV	XXXVII	6	1	5650–5750	6975–7100	chert scatter	Prehistoric?, Modern	chipped stone, some pottery (rare)
22	Asprovounos	XXIX	4	1	(54)8850	(387)7775	artifact scatter	Classical, Roman–Medieval	pottery
23	Dhkyovounon	XXIX	4	2	(54)8850	(387)7110	artifact scatter	Unknown	pottery, statue found in ravine nearby
24	Mesovounos	V	1	1	(54)8920	(387)5490	artifact scatter	Classical,Hellenistic,Mod.	pottery, broken blade
25	Platia Laxia	XXIX	7	1	(54)8685	(387)6450	artifact scatter	Modern	pottery
26	Kryon Neron (W)	XXIX	7	2	(54)8780	(387)6550	artifact scatter	Classical, Hellenistic, Mod.	pottery
27	Kryon Neron (N)	XXIX	5	1	(54)9250	(387)7275	settlement	Classical, Hellen, Medieval	pottery, tile?
28	Chakmaklik V	XXXVIII	6	1	(54)5680	(387)7400	small chert scatter	Unknown	1 pottery, chipped stone
29	Zeitin Tarlasi	XXXVIII	4	1	6165–6220	7665–7715	artifact scatter	Roman,Turkish, Modern	pottery, 1 chipped stone bladelet
30	Trakhonas	XXXVII	9	1	5015–5185	5900–6485	settlement?	Classical–Medieval, Modern	pottery, cut stone, ground stone

FIG. 7.7   *Site 14, one of the hilltop locations used as an observation post. Facing southwest (photo: P. N. Kardulias).*

indicate that Malloura participated in an exchange network that linked this rural area to other regions on the island, and perhaps beyond. A possible millstone cutting and a cistern were found at Site 20, ca. 600 m southeast of the Malloura site, and some late medieval pottery was found nearby. Nearly 1 km south of Site 1, along a track that also runs through Athienou-*Malloura*, the foundation and floor of a circular stone structure were recorded at Site 6 (see fig. 7.2). No diagnostic artifacts were found, but this seems to have been an industrial structure (likely a kiln) and may be associated with the occupation of Athienou-*Malloura* during the Venetian period; two substantial buildings have been uncovered in EU 2 (see DeMasi, Ch. 16) and EU 3, and a Venetian cemetery has been partially revealed in EU 6 (see Harper, Ch. 20).

THE VILLAGE OF PETROPHANI (SITE 12)

Local informants indicated that Petrophani (Turkish Esendagh) was founded late in the period of Ottoman rule. The village appears on an 1873 Ottoman map of Cyprus and on the 1882 map of the island prepared by Lord Kitchener (Kornrumpf and Kornrumpf 1990; see also Counts and Parvis,

Ch. 5). The village structures are all similar in construction. A stone socle supports mudbrick walls, which were plastered inside and out. There are a number of compounds that consist of one- or two-story houses, a large courtyard, and outbuildings for storage and animal pens. According to the 1881 British census, the population of Petrophani was only 18 individuals (Grivaud 1998: 455). During the 19th century, its population likely averaged around 50, but it had grown to 120 by 1960. It reached its maximum recorded population of 171 in 1973 (Goodwin 1984: 1358; Republic of Cyprus 1962: 1973). Since 1974, Greeks from Athienou have used the buildings to shelter sheep and goats. Most of the standing structures in Petrophani date to the recent period, but parts of older buildings from the Ottoman period may have been incorporated into their construction.

HILLTOP SITES

Four sites (5, 14, 23, 24) located atop hills on the eastern edge of the Malloura Valley (fig. 7.7) produced light scatters of pottery sherds dated to the Roman and later periods. Three of these sites (14, 23, 24) are currently being used by the United

Nations troops (UNFICYP) as observation posts and may have been used for similar purposes in antiquity (see Massey and Kardulias, Ch. 22).

Three small ceramic scatters that seem to date to the Roman and later periods have also been found at lower elevations near these outposts, at Sites 22, 25, and 26. Another small scatter of later-period sherds was found at Site 29, near a spring in the central portion of the valley between Malloura and Petrophani. Field walking around Petrophani produced a substantial quantity of late medieval ceramics, even though no settlement is indicated in this locale on the earliest maps of the region. Further investigations are needed to determine if the late medieval and Ottoman occupations at Malloura and Petrophani were contemporary.

Recent Settlements and Undated Sites

Survey teams recorded two abandoned mudbrick structures (Sites 3, 13), two ruined stone structures (Sites 4, 19), and a dump (Site 8) associated with recent trash. Site 13 is a two-room mudbrick structure ca. 200 m south of Petrophani; it probably was an agricultural outbuilding, although there are no artifacts associated with it. One-hundred meters to the south is a small mudbrick structure that served as a well house; the stone-lined shaft outside the west wall is ca. 10 m deep. Among a variety of modern construction debris, Site 8 has parts of modern tombs that were discarded after bodies were moved from the older to the newer part of the Athienou cemetery after 2000 (Womack and Kardulias 2007). The age of two lithic artifact scatters (Sites 10, 21) on Chakmaklik has not been determined. Site 10 contained recent-looking flints that may mark the location where a threshing sledge was prepared (see Yerkes, Ch. 26). The other lithic artifact concentration (Site 21) did not contain any diagnostic materials. Site 15, another lithic workshop, was found on the northern edge of the Petrophani igneous inlier, where an extension of the Middle Lapithos chert lies up against the pillow lavas. The artifacts at Site 15 were not patinated, and we have not been able to determine when the lithic reduction activities took place. The site may also have been a sledge flint workshop.

In the southeast corner of the survey area, Site 22 contains a number of gypsum floor slabs that may have been manufactured there. On a limestone-capped ridge south of the drainage divide, Site 18, a stone-cutting workshop, was found but with no associated diagnostic artifacts. Informants suggest that local stoneworkers produced shallow wash basins and other domestic items here. At Site 17, three stone structures were investigated in a small abandoned Turkish-Cypriot settlement along the Larnaka/Nicosia road that probably is the settlement of Paliochanouta mentioned by Mariti (1769; see Counts and Parvis, Ch. 5). Local informants stated that only three families resided in Site 17 before it was abandoned more than 85 years ago, but Mariti proposes it is a much older settlement. These sites suggest an active rural economy in which local residents utilized local resources for a number of their needs. The sites also point to a level of economic independence from suppliers in major cities and concomitantly indicate the existence of an integrated network of local artisans.

Conclusions

The data from the survey allow us to draw several conclusions about settlement in the Malloura Valley. The only prehistoric components (all possibly Neolithic) exist at Sites 9, 11, 12, 15, 21, and 28, which are primarily lithic processing stations. No surface evidence of Bronze Age, Cypro-Geometric, or Cypro-Archaic settlement came to light in any part of the valley. The lack of evidence for these periods may inform us about the nature of settlement structure in other parts of the island. For example, Knapp (1994: 429) has noted that the end of the Bronze Age witnessed a significant decline in the number and size of regional centers. In this respect, the Malloura Valley may reflect the collapse of Bronze Age complexity. However, the Malloura Valley never contained a Bronze Age site, although the copper production site of Athienou-*Pamboulari tis Koukounninas* lies not too far to the north and it was abandoned in the mid-12th century BC as were many other sites throughout the island (Dothan and Ben-Tor 1983: 139). We suspect that the limited evidence for habitation in the valley in the prehistoric periods indicates extensive use of the land for agricultural production, as is still the case today (Kardulias 2007: 63). Chase-Dunn and Hall (1997:91) call this pattern of land use a "commodified mode of accumulation" in which agricultural products were grown and sold. Their assertion that this activity took place in "capitalist city-states in the semiperipheral interstices of empires dominated by the tributary mode of accumulation" (Chase-Dunn and Hall 1997: 90) provides an appropriate analog for Cyprus.

A pattern of nucleated settlement characterized valley occupation for most of the first millennium AD. Cypro-Classical through modern material is scattered throughout the project area, but concentrations are limited, except for Athienou-*Malloura* (Site 1). Other than very recent material, Late Byzantine artifacts formed the bulk of the diagnostic material collected in walkovers. Current evidence suggests that Malloura was the sole center of occupation during the Roman, Early Byzantine, and Late Byzantine periods, with some scattered homesteads elsewhere. The consistent background artifact scatter, however, indicates widespread use of the area around the site.

The situation was evidently not unlike the modern pattern, that is, a large nucleated rural settlement with access to surrounding fields. In addition to its fertile soil, the drainage system, with the confluence of two intermittent streams, and a series of wells near the site made Malloura a good location for a village. The streams also provided hydraulic power for a series of mills to process grain. The village of Petrophani has several structures whose stone walls exhibit fine workmanship and may be Venetian in date. It is difficult to push back the date of the village much beyond the late medieval period, but analysis of the ceramics is ongoing. In the 17th and 18th centuries, villages or hamlets in the valley included Malloura, Petrophani, and Paliochanouta. The last of these was abandoned by the late 18th century, followed by Malloura in the late 19th century. Petrophani persisted until the 1970s. The valley as a whole has succumbed to political and economic forces, so that for more than 30 years it has been used primarily for agriculture and animal husbandry. In some ways, the valley has gone full cycle, with no permanent residents and serving the surrounding region as an extraction zone for key resources.

References

Adovasio, J. M.; Fry, G. F.; Gunn, J. D.; and Maslowski, R. F.
1975   Prehistoric and Historic Settlement Patterns in Western Cyprus (with a Discussion of Cypriot Neolithic Stone Tool Technology). *World Archaeology* 6: 339–64.

Alcock, S.
1993   *Graecia Capta*. Cambridge: Cambridge University.

Alcock, S. E.; Cherry, J. F.; and Davis, J. L.
1994   Intensive Survey, Agricultural Practice and the Classical Landscape of Greece. Pp. 137–70 in *Classical Greece: Ancient Histories and Modern Archaeologies*, ed. I. Morris. Cambridge: Cambridge University.

Ashmore, W., and Knapp, A. B., (eds.)
1999   *Archaeologies of Landscape: Contemporary Perspectives*. Malden, MA: Blackwell.

Athanassopoulos, E., and Wandsnider, L., (eds.)
2004   *Mediterranean Archaeological Landscapes: Current Issues*. Philadelphia: University of Pennsylvania Museum of Archaeology and Anthropology.

Bintliff, J. L.
2000   The Concepts of "Site" and "Offsite" Archaeology in Surface Artefact Survey. Pp. 200–215 in *Nondestructive Techniques Applied to Landscape Archaeology. The Archaeology of Mediterranean Landscapes 4*, eds. M. Pasquinucii and F. Trément. Oxford: Oxbow.

Caraher, W.; Moore, R. S.; Noller, J.; and Pettegrew, D.
2007   The Pyla-Koutsopetria Archaeological Project: Second Preliminary Report (2005–2006 Seasons). *Report of the Department of Antiquities, Cyprus*: 292–306.

Catling, H. W.
1963   Patterns of Settlement in Bronze Age Cyprus. *Opuscula Atheniensia* 4: 129–69.

Cauvin, M-C.
1984   L'outillage lithique de Khirokitia (Chypre) et le Levant. Pp. 85–87 in *Fouilles récentes à Khirokitia (Chypre), 1977–1981,* ed. A. Le Brun. Récherche sur les grandes civilisations. Mémoire 41 (Etudes Neolithiques). Paris: A. D. P. F.

Chase-Dunn, C., and Hall, T. D.
1997   *Rise and Demise: Comparing World-Systems.* Boulder: Westview.

Cherry, J. F.
1982   A Preliminary Definition of Site Distribution on Melos. Pp. 10–23 in *An Island Polity: The Archaeology of Exploitation in Melos,* eds. C. Renfrew and M. Wagstaff. Cambridge: Cambridge University.
1990   The First Colonization of the Mediterranean Islands: A Review of Recent Research. *Journal of Mediterranean Archaeology* 3: 145–221.
1994   Regional Survey in the Aegean: The "New Wave" (and After). Pp. 91–112 in *Beyond the Site: Regional Studies in the Aegean Area,* ed. P. N. Kardulias. Lanham, MD: University Press of America.

Cherry, J. F.; Davis, J. L.; and Mantzourani, E., (eds.)
1991   *Landscape Archaeology as Long-Term History: Northern Keos in the Cycladic Islands from Earliest Settlement until Modern Times.* Los Angeles: UCLA Institute of Archaeology.

Cobham, C. D.
1908   *Excerpta Cypria. Materials for a History of Cyprus.* Trans. C. D. Cobham. Cambridge: Cambridge University.

Colledge, S., and Conolly, J.
2007   A Review and Synthesis of the Evidence for the Origins of Farming on Cyprus and Crete. Pp. 53–74 in *The Origins and Spread of Domestic Plants in Southwest Asia and Europe,* eds. S. Colledge and J. Conolly. Walnut Creek, CA: Left Coast.

Davis, J. L.; Alcock, S.; Bennet, J.; Lolos, Y.;   and Shelmerdine, C.
1997   The Pylos Regional Archaeological Project. Part 1: Overview and the Archaeological Survey. *Hesperia* 66: 391–494.

Dikaios, P.
1962   The Stone Age. Pp. 1–204 in *Swedish Cyprus Expedition* 4.1A, eds. P. Dikaios and J. R. Stewart. Lund: Swedish Cyprus Expedition.

Dothan, T., and Ben-Tor, A.
1983   *Excavations at Athienou, Cyprus, 1971–1972.* Qedem 16. Jerusalem: Hebrew University.

Drews, R.
1993   *The End of the Bronze Age: Changes in Warfare and the Catastrophe ca. 1200 BC.* Princeton: Princeton University.

Dunnell, R., and Dancey, W.
1983   The Siteless Survey: A Regional Scale Data Collection Strategy. *Advances in Archaeological Method and Theory* 6: 267–87.

Galaty, M.
2005   European Regional Studies: A Coming of Age? *Journal of Archaeological Research* 13(4): 291–336.

Given, M., and Knapp, A. B. (eds.)
2003   *The Sydney Cyprus Survey Project: Social Approaches to Regional Archaeology.* Monumenta Archaeologica 21. Los Angeles: Cotsen Institute.

Given, M.; Corley, H.; and Sollars, L.
2007   Joining the Dots: Continuous Survey, Routine Practice and the Interpretation of a Cypriot Landscape (with Interactive GIS and Integrated Data Archive). *Internet Archaeology* 20: http://intarch.ac.uk/journal/issue20/taesp index.html.

Goodwin, J. C.
1984   *An Historical Toponymy of Cyprus.* London: Goodwin.

Gregory, T. E.
2003   The Byzantine Problem. Pp. 283–84 in *The Sydney Cyprus Survey Project: Social Ap-*

proaches to Regional Archaeology, eds. M. Given and A. B. Knapp. Monumenta Archaeologica 21. Los Angeles: Cotsen Institute.

Grivaud, G.
1998 *Villages désertés à Chypre*. Nicosia: Archbishop Makarios III Foundation.

Guilaine, J., and Le Brun, A.
2003 *Le néolithique de Chypre: Actes du colloque international organisé par le Départment des antiquites de Chypre et l'Ecole française d'Athènes, Nicosie, 17-19 mai 2001*. Bulletin de Correspondance Hellénique. Supplément 43. Athens: Ecole française d'Athènes.

Hadjisavvas, S.
1997 *Agia Napa: Excavations at Makronisos and the Archaeology of the Region*. Nicosia: Agia Napa Municipality and the Cyprus Department of Antiquities.

Horowitz, L. K.; Tchernov, E.; and Hongo, H.
2004 Domestic Status of the early Neolithic Fauna of Cyprus: A View from the Mainland. Pp. 35–48 in *Neolithic Revolution: New Perspectives on Southwest Asia in Light of Recent Discoveries on Cyprus*, eds. E. J. Peltenburg and A. Wasse. Oxford: Oxbow.

Iacovou, M. (ed.)
2004 *Archaeological Field Survey in Cyprus. Past History, Future Potentials*. British School at Athens Studies 2. London: British School at Athens.

Jameson, M.; van Andel, T. H.; and Runnels, C. N.
1994 *A Greek Countryside*. Stanford: Stanford University.

Kardulias, P. N.
2007 Negotiation and Incorporation on the Margins of World-Systems: Examples from Cyprus and North America. *Journal of World-Systems Research* 13(1): 55–82.

Keller, D., and Rupp, D.
1983 *Archaeological Survey in the Mediterranean Region*. British Archaeological Reports, International Series 155. Oxford: British Archaeological Reports.

Knapp, A. B.
1988 Ideology, Archaeology and Polity. *Man* 23: 133–63.
1994 The Prehistory of Cyprus: Problems and Prospects. *Journal of World Prehistory* 8: 377–453.
2008 *Prehistoric and Protohistoric Cyprus: Identity, Insularity, and Connectivity*. Oxford: Oxford University.

Kornrumpf, H.-J., and Kornrumpf, J.
1990 *An Historical Gazetteer of Cyprus (1850–1987) with Notes on Population*. Frankfurt am Main: Peter Lang.

Le Brun, A.
1981 *Un Site néolithique précéramique en Chypre: Cap Andreas-Kastros*. Récherche sur les grandes civilisations. Mémoire 5 (Etudes Neolithiques). Paris: A. D. P. F.
1994 *Fouilles récentes de Khirokitia, Chypre, 1988-1991*. Récherche sur les grandes civilisations. Mémoire 291 (Etudes Neolithiques). Paris: A. D. P. F.

Le Brun, A.; Cluzan, S.; Davis, S. J. M.; Hansen, J.; and Renault-Miskovsky, J.
1987 Le néolithique précéramique de Chypre. *L'Anthropologie* 91: 283, 316.

Lehavy, Y. M.
1974 Excavations at Neolithic Dhali-Agridhi. Pp. 95–118 in *American Expedition to Idalion, Cyprus, First Preliminary Report, Seasons 1971-72*, eds. L. E. Stager, A. Walker, and G. E. Wright. Bulletin of the American Schools of Oriental Research, Supplement 18. Cambridge: Bulletin of the American Schools of Oriental Research.
1989 Dhali-Agridi: The Neolithic by the River. Pp. 203–43 in *American Expedition to Idalion, Cyprus 1973-1980*, eds. L. E. Stager and A. M. Walker. Oriental Institute Communications 24. Chicago: Oriental Institute of the University of Chicago.

Mariti, G.
1769 *Travels in the Island of Cyprus*. Trans. C. D. Cobham, from the Italian. Cambridge: Cambridge University.

McDonald, W. A., and Rapp, G. R., (eds.)
1972   *The Minnesota Messenia Expedition: Reconstructing a Bronze Age Regional Environment.* Minneapolis: University of Minnesota.

Megaw, A. H. S.
1955   Archaeology in Cyprus, 1955. *Archaeological Reports 1955:* 41–46.

Peltenburg, E. J.; Croft, P.; Stewart, J. D.; Woodhead, J.; Elliott, C.; and Philip, G.
1983   The Prehistory of West Cyprus: Ktima Lowlands Investigations 1979–1982. *Report of the Department of Antiquities, Cyprus:* 9–55.

Peltenburg, E., (ed.)
2003   *The Colonisation and Settlement of Cyprus: Investigations at Kissonerga-Mylouthkia, 1976-1996.* Studies in Mediterranean Archaeology LXX:4, Lemba Archaeological Project, Cyprus III.1. Sävedalen, Sweden: Åström.

Peltenburg, E.; Colledge, S.; Croft, P.; Jackson, A.; McCartney, C.; and Murray, M. A.
2001   Neolithic Dispersals from the Levantine Corridor: A Mediterranean Perspective. *Levant* 33: 35–64.

Rautman, M.
2003   *A Cypriot Village of Late Antiquity. Kalavasos-Kopetra in the Vasilikos Valley.* Journal of Roman Archaeology Supplementary Series 52. Portsmouth, RI: Journal of Roman Archaeology.

Republic of Cyprus.
1962   *Census of Population and Agriculture, 1960.* Nicosia: Government Printing Office.
1973   *Census of Population 1973.* Nicosia: Government Printing Office.

Sevketoglu, M.
2000   *Archaeological Field Survey of the Neolithic and Chalcolithic Settlement Sites in Kyrenia District, North Cyprus: Systematic Surface Collection and the Interpretation of Artefact Scatters.* Oxford: Archaeopress.

Simmons, A. H., and Corona, J.
1993   Test Excavations at Kholetria Ortos: A Neolithic Settlement near Paphos. *Report of the Department of Antiquities, Cyprus:* 1–10.

Sørensen, L. W., and Rupp, D. W., (eds.)
1993   *The Land of the Paphian Aphrodite.* Studies in Mediterranean Archaeology 104. Göteborg: Åström.

Stanley-Price, N.
1972   A Prehistoric Survey of the Analiondas Region. *Report of the Department of Antiquities, Cyprus:* 15–21.

Stekelis, M.
1953   Appendix 1: The Flint Implements from Khirokitia. Pp. 409–14 in *Khirokitia,* ed. P. Dikaios. London: Oxford University.
1961   Appendix 2: The Flint Implements. Pp. 230–34 in *Sotira,* ed. P. Dikaios. Museum Monographs. Philadelphia: University Museum, University of Pennsylvania.

Symeonoglou, S.
1972   Archaeological Survey in the Area of Phlamoudhi, Cyprus. *Report of the Department of Antiquities, Cyprus:* 187–98.

Tartaron, T. F.; Gregory, T. E.; Pullen, D. J.; Noller, J. S.; Rothhaus, R. M.; Rife, J. L.; Tzortzopoulou-Gregory, L.; Caraher, W. R.; Pettegrew, D. K.; Nakassis, D.; and Schon, R.
2006   The Eastern Korinthia Archaeological Survey. Integrated Methods for a Dynamic Landscape. *Hesperia* 75: 453–523.

Todd, I.
1989   The 1988 Field Survey in the Vasilikos Valley. *Report of the Department of Antiquities, Cyprus:* 41–50.

Vigne, J-D.; Isabelle Carrère, I. ; Saliége, J. F.; Person, A.; Bocherens, H.; Guilaine, J.; and Briois, J. F.
2000   Predomestic Cattle, Sheep, Goat, and Pig during the Late 9th and the 8th Millennium Cal. BC on Cyprus: Preliminary Results of Shillourokambos (Parekklisha, Limassol). Pp. 83–106 in *Archaeozoology of the Near East IV: Proceedings of the 4th International Symposium on the Archaeology of Southwestern Asia and Adjacent Areas,* eds. H. Buitenhaus, M. Mashkour, and F. Poplin. Gronigen: Center for Archaeological Research.

Waechter, J.
1953   Appendix 1A: A Comparison between the
       Flint Implements of Khirokitia and Erimi. Pp.
       414–15 in *Khirokitia*, ed. P. Dikaios. London:
       Oxford University.

Willey, G. R.
1953   *Prehistoric Settlement Patterns in the Viru
       Valley, Peru.* Bureau of American Ethnology
       Bulletin 155. Washington, D.C.: Smithsonian
       Institution.

Womack, A., and Kardulias, P. N.
2007   The Cemetery of Athienou: A Spatial Analy-
       sis of Mortuary Practices on Cyprus. Paper
       presented at the 72nd Annual Meeting of the
       Society for American Archaeology, April 2007,
       Austin, Texas.

Zangger, E.
1998   The Physical Scientist's Role in Regional Ar-
       chaeology. Pp. 10–13 in *Sandy Pylos*, ed. J. L.
       Davis. Austin: University of Texas.

Chapter 8

Flaked Stone Artifacts from the Malloura Valley Survey and their Cypriot Context

by P. Nick Kardulias and Richard W. Yerkes

In the course of our field investigations in the Malloura Valley, we collected 793 pieces of flaked stone (Table 8.1). While these artifacts constitute a minority of the total survey assemblage, the stone tools are important for at least two reasons: a significant number of the objects are the earliest artifacts found in the project area, and the assemblage includes both finished implements and the residue from tool production, thus providing us with information on most stages of manufacture. Since cultures develop over time through the evolution of technology, the stone tools are part of the founding elements that led to the more complex forms of cultural expression we see represented in the votive offerings in the sanctuary (e.g., Averett, Ch. 10; Fourrier, Ch. 9), the funerary items deposited in the tombs (Gordon, Ch. 14), and the agricultural activities scattered throughout the valley (Kardulias and Yerkes, Ch. 7). Furthermore, the stone tools represent not only the earliest technology in the project area but also one with a continuous presence from antiquity well into the past century. While the artifacts are small, they served as critical parts of the agricultural infrastructure both as individual objects and as parts of large composite tools (e.g., threshing sledges; see Yerkes and Kardulias 1994; Yerkes, Ch. 26). This chapter concentrates on what the survey lithics reveal about the earliest human exploitation of the valley.

Lithic analysis is critical to our understanding of the earliest cultures on Cyprus because the initial colonists did not possess pottery. Recent discoveries have shown that while transient foragers visited the island early in the 10th millennium cal. BC (Simmons 1999), the initial Neolithic colonization of Cyprus may have begun around 8200 cal BC, or 2000 years earlier than the "classic" Aceramic Neolithic (AN) "Khirokitian" stage of ca. 6000 cal BC. The early Aceramic Neolithic stages ("Cypro-PPNB," ca. 8200 to 7000 cal. BC) are associated with different lithic artifact assemblages than the Khirokitian (which is best known for its ground stone industry). The earlier colonists shared technologies, architecture, settlement patterns, and symbols with Aceramic Neolithic groups in the Levant and Anatolia. They seem to be part of a "PPNB interaction sphere" (Bar-Yosef and Belfer-Cohen 1989; Gopher 1989). During the later Aceramic Neolithic Stage (Khirokitian, 7,000–5500 cal. BC) local technologies and styles developed and interactions with the mainland decreased. Flaked and ground stone artifacts are the primary cultural markers that are used to identify these stages on Cyprus (Knapp 1994; Guilaine and Briois 2001; Peltenburg et al. 2001; Guilaine and Le Brun 2003; Peltenburg 2003; Peltenburg and Wasse 2004; Clarke et al. 2007; Flourentzos et al. 2008).

However, one of the problems in using lithics as stage or horizon markers is that the early assemblages are rather nondescript (Knapp 1994: 405), but classification and study of these artifacts can provide insights into the settlement dynamics of prehistoric Cyprus. We also must remember that the manufacture and use of chipped-stone artifacts did not end with the introduction of metal tools (Runnels 1982), and the presence of lithic artifacts in surface collections does not mean that those sites date only to prehistoric times, even if no pottery was found (Sheen 1981: 40).

Cypriot flint knappers were still making chipped-stone blades for threshing sledges in the 1950s (Pearlman 1984; Hayes 1995: 64; Kardulias and Yerkes 1996). Chipped-stone artifacts were used for a long time on Cyprus, and their careful study is required before we can use them to estimate the age of lithic scatters and workshops. There are, however, a number of excavated sites with ¹⁴C dates that do permit one to associate lithic technologies and styles with particular periods and can act as temporal guides for survey material. The problem is twofold: identifying and classifying an Aceramic Neolithic (AN) assemblage, and assigning such an affiliation to surface materials.

EARLY INHABITANTS OF CYPRUS

The colonization of most Mediterranean islands like Cyprus was a relatively late development. Even those islands close to continental shores received only periodic visits prior to the Neolithic, and then usually only for procurement forays (e.g., in the Aegean to obtain obsidian from Melos and perhaps Giali) or as brief layovers during fishing expeditions. Exceptions would be the discoveries of Lower and Middle Paleolithic tools on the southern coast of Crete which suggest that early seafarers from north Africa reached the island (Mortensen 2008; Strasser et al. 2009), the discov-

TABLE 8.1 Breakdown of lithics by site. Material in walkovers constitutes isolated finds.

Site#	n	%
1	89	11.2
2	5	0.6
3	2	0.3
9	398	50.2
10	111	14.0
11	13	1.6
12	14	1.8
14	1	0.1
15	48	6.1
16	3	0.4
21	15	1.9
24	1	0.1
28	8	1.0
29	1	0.1
Walkovers	84	10.6
Total	793	100.0

ery of an Epipaleolithic settlement at the Ouriakos site on Lemnos by Nikos Efstratiou of Thessaloniki Aristotle University (www.ana-mpa.gr/anaweb/user/showplain?maindoc=7735875&maindocimg=7735858&service=144), and Ammerman's claim that people in small boats from the mainland paid seasonal visits to Cyprus possibly as early as 12,000 years ago (Bohannon 2007).

Perhaps the most significant aspect of these early visits, at least in terms of future island developments, was the knowledge gained by the seafarers about navigation and island resources, including cherts and flints, which were relatively abundant on Cyprus. When more permanent settlements were established, they seem to have been the result of well-planned expeditions. Broodbank and Strasser (1991) made a compelling case for the well-planned colonization of Crete in the Early Neolithic; they argue convincingly that the colonists knew precisely where they were going, were aware of the conditions that would greet them, and purposefully bypassed a number of smaller habitable islands for the ecological diversity and areal extent of Crete. Similar arguments have been made for an Early Aceramic Neolithic colonization of Cyprus by PPNB groups from the Levant and Anatolia who transported plants and animals across the sea (Vigne et al. 2000; Peltenburg et al. 2001; Guilaine and Le Brun 2003; Peltenburg 2003; Horowitz et al. 2004; College and Conolly 2007).

Held (1990a, 1993) has delineated concepts particular to insular studies. One key concept is configuration, defined as "the position of an island vis-à-vis neighboring islands and the mainland" (Held 1990a). He places such work in an evolutionary framework. First, he argues that adaptation to island conditions (often quite different from those on the mainland) requires unique adjustments. Second, Held suggests that one must consider the ramifications of the Founder (or Sewall Wright) Effect on island populations after they are established. The primary goal of such analysis is to comprehend the boundary effect, which refers to the impact of resource scarcity on a given population and which varies according to the degree of openness of the system in question. This approach has direct applicability to Cyprus, which, despite its size (9,251 km^2, the third largest in the Mediterranean), experiences constraints on its resources that in turn influenced the trajectory of cultural development. This chapter stresses the role of flaked-stone artifacts as one such resource; these artifacts act as indicators of chronology, resource procurement/trade, and economic function. Here, we concentrate on the chronological aspect.

The site of Akrotiri-*Aetokremnos* has received considerable attention because it offers the best evidence for a pre-Neolithic occupation of Cyprus by transient foragers (Simmons 1991; 1999). However, there also have been claims for human presence on Cyprus during the Pleistocene. Adovasio et al. (1975) suggested a possible Upper Palaeolithic association for several locations examined during an early systematic survey in western Cyprus, but other lithic analysts have serious doubts about these claims. Stockton (1968) also argued for an

Upper Palaeolithic affiliation for lithics collected on the surface near Kyrenia on the north coast. In 1968 Vita-Finzi (1973) found five flaked-stone artifacts on a fossil beach of possible Middle Palaeolithic age on the south coast of the island. While each of these discoveries deserves careful scrutiny, especially in light of the current controversy concerning the emergence of anatomically modern humans and their early presence in the Levant and the recent discovery of Lower Palaeolithic and Middle Palaeolithic tools on Crete (Mortensen 2008; Strasser et al. 2009), the locations of the early stone tools on Cyprus all lack clear stratigraphic and chronological associations. At Akrotiri-*Aetokremnos*, remains of at least 500 extinct pygmy hippopotami (*Phanourios minutus*) and three dwarf elephants (*Elephas Cypriotes*) were found in association with 1,021 chipped-stone artifacts. Substantial remains of marine invertebrates and birds were also found at the site, along with some bones of snakes, turtles, and fish. Land snails and eggshell fragments were also recovered. Akrotiri-*Aetokremnos* has a series of 31 radiocarbon determinations with a weighted average of 10,465 ± 25 BP (9,703 cal BC), which Simmons and Wigand (1994: 248) suggest is the minimum age of the site. This site may represent a Late Pleistocene/Early Holocene cultural adaptation directly associated with the extinction of large mammals (Reese 1989; Simmons 1991; 1999; but see also Bunimovitz and Barkai 1996, with replies by Simmons and Reese). The flaked-stone assemblage from the site has several unique characteristics. First, there is a high percentage of thumbnail scrapers in the collection; second, there are few microliths, items that are ubiquitous in contemporaneous Epipalaeolithic contexts in Anatolia and the Levant. This unusual collection is perhaps an example of the idiosyncratic island development Held discusses. In addition, the description of this early lithic assemblage provides a foundation for the discussion of later collections, including early and later Aceramic Neolithic flaked stone assemblages.

Flaked-Stone Assemblages in The Aceramic Neolithic

At present, the Aetokremnos material is unparalleled on Cyprus. Simmons contends that the subsequent AN Culture stages represent different groups of people who arrived on the island during separate migrations from the mainland. The Late Aceramic Neolithic Khirokitian complex was first identified at the type site of Khirokitia, and by the late 1980s, 20 other sites of this culture had been identified, with perhaps an additional 30 locations recorded by surface surveys (Cherry 1990: 154). One problem was that the Khirokitia material (especially the flaked stone) is considered insufficiently diagnostic to assign AN dates to surface artifacts with any great confidence. The picture has become more complex in the past 15 years as evidence for Cypro-PPNB stages that are older than the Khirokitia complex has been found at several important sites. Excavated sites with the best evidence for the earlier AN stages include the following (earliest date in parentheses): Kissonerga-*Mylouthkia* (9315 ± 60 BP, or 8690–8450 cal. BC), Parekklisha-*Shillourokambos* (9310 ± 80 BP, or 8703–8355 cal BC), Kalavasos-*Tenta* (9240 ± 130 BP, or 8607–8306 cal. BC; Todd 1987: 173–78; Guilaine et al. 1995; Guilaine and Briois 2001; Peltenburg 2003: 83, 86). The sites of Ayia Varvara-*Asprokremnos* and Akanthou-*Arkosyko* have also been included (see Steel 2004: 33–46; McCartney et al. 2007). As noted above, this early Cypro-PPNB stage shares characteristics with the Pre-Pottery Neolithic B of the neighboring Levant (Peltenburg et al. 2001). The assemblages include PPNB artifact types such as naviform cores and arrowheads and exhibit the use of bipolar technique on high-quality chert and small amounts of obsidian to produce blades and flakes that were made into a variety of tools, including notches, scrapers, sickle elements, and points (McCartney 1998; Guilaine and Briois 2001: 45–7; Peltenburg et al. 2001: 78–83; Peltenburg 2003). Other early Cypro-PPNB Aceramic Neolithic stage dates were reported from Khirokitia-*Vounoi* (8850 ± 650 BP, or 9101–7083 cal. BC) and from Akrotiri site 23 (8350 ± 250 BP, or 7648–7043 cal. BC; on shell that

was not corrected for the reservoir effect; see Le Brun and J. Evin 1991: Table 1; Peltenberg 2003: 85). More recently, McCartney et al. (2007: 33–35) have argued for the presence of a PPNA component at Agia Varvara-*Asprokemnos* on the basis of a lithic assemblage in which projectile points made on blades with abbreviated tangs are common, along with burins and some microliths.

Younger Aceramic Neolithic dates reported from Dhali-*Agridhi* (7990 ± 80 BP, or 7049–6778 cal. BC) and Cape Andreas-*Kastros* (7775 ± 125 BP, or 6769–6463 cal. BC; see Peltenburg 2003; Steel 2004: 33–35) would fall within the range for the later Khirokitian Aceramic complex (8000–6500 BP, or 7000/6500–5800/5500 cal. BC; Peltenburg 2003: 99). Several important sites in the southwestern part of the island reported by the Canadian Palaipaphos Survey Project, including Kholetria-*Ortos* (ca. 7600 BP), also date to this later Aceramic Neolithic stage (Rupp et al. 1984; Simmons 1996).

As part of his prescriptive advice for the study of Cypriot prehistory, Held (1990b) suggests that surveys should engage in more systematic analysis of environmental factors, among which is the location of raw materials (e.g., chert sources) used by ancient peoples. Furthermore, he argues for more rigorous analysis of stone tools from newly discovered sites and careful restudy of material from previously known locations. Such studies should attempt to discern the amount of regional variability, methods of production, type of material, types of microwear and functional categories, and distribution patterns on living floors (Held 1990b: 13, 17). We concur with this agenda and wish to extend such treatment of lithics to survey as well as excavation. To provide a comparative foundation for the AAP lithics, we present a somewhat more detailed description of some of the lithics from several important sites. After a discussion of the lithics from Shillourokambos, we focus on material from the later Aceramic Neolithic stage since they are more directly relevant to the assemblage from the Malloura Valley.

Excavation at Shillourokambos has revealed a substantial body of lithic material, the vast majority of which is chert but with many pieces of obsidian. In several of the early phases, residents brought chert blocks to the site, but in subsequent periods the preference was for rough blades and flakes. In addition to blades, the assemblage included grattoirs, becs, and abundant production debris. The excavators identified two Cypro-PPNB Aceramic Neolithic phases, the first (Early A) dated to ca. 9300 BP (ca. 8700–8300 cal. BC) and the second to 7600/7500 BP (ca. 7500–6800 cal. BC) Some of the chipped stone artifacts from the earlier phase share traits with material from period 1A at the Kissonerga-*Mylouthkia* site and from sites in Anatolia and the Levant, including bipolar blade debitage. Other evidence of contact with Anatolia is the Cappadocian origin of the obsidian (Guilaine et al. 1995: 14–15, 29–30).

Definition of the AN at Tenta rests on the basic assumption that there should be a high proportion of blades combined with a lack of ceramics in the assemblage (Hordynsky and Todd 1987: 17). While Tenta is usually associated with the "classic" later Aceramic Neolithic Khirohitian complex, radiocarbon dates from the "Top of Site" area fall within the range for the earlier Cypro-PPNB stage, while many of the dates from lower down the slope were younger (Todd 1987: 173–78; Peltenburg 2003: 86). Of the total 6,217 lithics recorded in the 1976 surface collection, 1,982 (31.8%) were blades, most of which (1,647) were not retouched. The source of virtually all the lithics is the local Lefkara chert. Beds of tan, brown, and green Lefkara chert are found in the chalk and chert member of the Middle Lapithos Group of calcareous rocks (Middle to Lower Eocene) that outcrop near Tenta and all along the southern and eastern flanks of the Troodos Mountains (Gass 1960). It would seem that the emphasis in stone tool production was on self-sufficiency in a local context — especially during the later Aceramic Neolithic stage.

In his classification of the Khirokitia assemblage (which forms the core of the later Aceramic Neolithic Khirokitian complex), Stekelis (1953) noted the following traits: (1) almost exclusive use of chert; (2) the use of soft hammer technique in production; (3) unpatinated surfaces; (4) irregular cores with singular striking platforms; (5) irregular flakes, few of which are retouched; and (6) well-made blades, many of which are retouched

(denticulated, notched, pointed, backed). Blades constitute 28.1% of the assemblage from the early excavations at the site. Later work at the site by the French has not substantially altered the interpretation. Cauvin (1984: 85–6) does add several additional categories, such as burins and grattoirs, and notes the presence of Levallois-like debitage. Microwear analysis of a number of specimens revealed the presence of sickle elements and woodworking implements (Coqueugniot 1984). Chipped stone implements used to engrave stone have also been studied (Austruc 1994).

The lithics from Cape Andreas-*Kastros* present a somewhat different picture (Le Brun 1981: 31–41). Flakes dominate the assemblage (95.8% of the total debitage), but 37.6% of the tools are made on blades. There are more cores and a broader range of tools from Cape Andreas than from most of the other later AN sites. The tools include sickle elements, truncated pieces, picks, perforators, grattoirs, racloirs, burins, and notches. Trace element analysis indicates that the obsidian (n=13) came from Çiftlik in central Anatolia.

One of the largest of the later AN assemblages comes from the site of Kholetria-*Ortos*, where the excavators recovered more than 62,000 lithic artifacts (Simmons 1996). This material attests an efficient mode of reduction in which most of the cores were exhausted despite the fact that much of the chert is local in origin. While blades comprise only 15% of the debitage, almost 50% of the tools were produced on such blanks. After generic retouched pieces, the most abundant tool type (15.9%) is a sickle blade, commonly in a crescent shape. Other tools include various scrapers, tangs, and truncated pieces. The vast quantity of tertiary flakes (76.6% of the assemblage) suggests the final stages of tool production and rejuvenation of edges were more important than primary reduction. Simmons also recovered a very large stone tool assemblage at Ais Yiorkis.

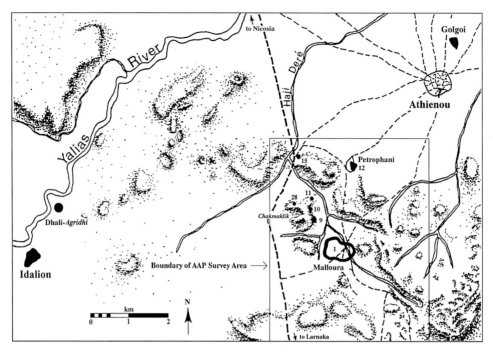

Fig. 8.1   *Map showing lithic sites in the Malloura Valley in relation to Dhali-*Agridhi *(drawing: R. Yerkes, after Kitchener 1885).*

Surveys and Lithic Artifact Analyses on Cyprus

Systematic archaeological survey on Cyprus began in the 1970s with the work of Symeonoglou (1972) in the Phlamoudhi area of northern Cyprus and of Adovasio et al. (1975) in the Khrysokhou drainage (south of Polis in western Cyprus), where 38 prehistoric sites and several chert sources were documented. In 1979, Alun Sheen (1981) extended the exploration of the Khrysokhou drainage eastward through the Paphos forest to the Troodos Mountains with the Stavros tis Psokas Survey that was conducted as part of the Lemba Archaeological Project. The long-term work of Ian Todd in the Vasilikos Valley came to include a survey component that has greatly enhanced knowledge of prehistoric settlement along the southern coast.

Multiperiod surveys became standard in Cyprus during the 1980s. The Canadian Palaipaphos Survey Project (CPSP; Rupp et al. 1984, 1992) concentrated on the southwestern part of the island and covered terrain from the coastal plain to the Troodos Mountains. The CPSP identified many

lithic scatters, including the important later AN site of Kholetria-*Ortos*. The Tremithos Valley Survey also occurred around this time (Baudou et al. 1985).

In the 1990s and in the new century, this momentum continued with work in the Maroni Valley (Manning and Conwell 1992; Manning et al. 1994), along the northern slopes of the Troodos range (Knapp and Given 1996; Given and Knapp 2003), in the Polis region (Maliszewski 1995), the Malloura Valley (Toumazou et al. 1992, 1998), on the coast near Pyla (Caraher et al. 2007), and around Idalion (Margaret Morden and Sally Stewart, personal communication, 1998). In each of these projects, the teams assiduously collected stone tools and have thus expanded our knowledge of prehistoric settlement on the island.

The AAP Sites

In the course of fieldwork in the Malloura Valley, we identified five aceramic lithic scatters that may be prehistoric (fig. 8.1). They were located at the western rim of the Malloura Valley, on the ridge known as Chakmaklik (Hill of Flint). It appears that chert was extracted from outcrops and processed at a series of lithic workshops, which may date to the AN or Chalcolithic. Site 9 was discovered on the surface of one of the low ridges that extend eastward from Chakmaklik. On the exposed bedrock and thin mantle of soil on the crest of the ridge we found a concentration of cores, large flakes, and a few blades made of pink and weathered white and tan chert that was obtained from the Middle Lapithos Formation outcrop on the hill. The heavily patinated condition of the artifacts, the large size of the flakes, and the dearth of ceramics (only two pieces were found, both on a slope a considerable distance from the main lithic concentration) suggest an AN cultural affiliation (see Kingsnorth in Knapp and Given 1996 for similar criteria, although these lithic extraction sites also could have been used during the Ceramic Neolithic and/or Chalcolithic periods). Our preliminary interpretation is that the site served as a workshop where early stages of stone tool production were completed. Formal tools are rare, but elements of both a generalized blade technology and a flake industry are present (cf. Todd 1989: 8). Only 2.5% of the assemblage (10 of 398) were blades (see below). Affinities with the Neolithic industries in western Cyprus described by Adovasio et al. (1975) are not clear, but sufficient similarities exist with other later AN assemblages to suggest the AAP material may date to that period. It should be noted that the lithic artifacts from this lithic extraction site probably do not represent the full range of formal tools and artifacts found at habitation sites. This makes it difficult to compare them to larger assemblages from habitation sites.

A second prehistoric component was recorded at Site 11, a small lithic scatter 300 m north of Site 9; the similarities with the Site 9 assemblage also suggested a later AN affiliation. In the complete collection of 13 pieces from the site, there are no blades. In 1992 another prehistoric component was noted at Site 15. The site is located on a low hill overlooking the plain west of the Malloura Valley. The grainy local gray chert outcrops on the hill and the gentle slopes are littered with the debris of extraction and preliminary tool manufacture. The Site 15 assemblage resembles that from Site 9; there are only two blades (4.2%) among the 48 pieces

picked up in randomly selected samples. A fourth small lithic scatter, Site 28, was found in 1994 on the northwestern edge of Chakmaklik. No blades were recovered, but some large weathered flakes similar to those found at Site 11 were found here. A slightly larger assemblage (n=15) was collected at Site 21 on the west slope of Chakmaklik 400 m south of Site 28; but other than the heavy patination on the flakes, there is nothing particularly distinctive about this group of artifacts.

A possible sixth prehistoric collection appeared at the Turkish village of Petrophani (Site 12), which yielded some flaked-stone artifacts and a ground-stone bowl fragment in the grab samples that were collected around the village and adjacent Turkish cemetery. These artifacts may date to the Aceramic Neolithic.

Historic Lithic Artifacts

Some of the lithic artifacts from Petrophani may date to more recent periods. During the AAP survey of the Malloura Valley, 22 thick, well-worn bladelike flakes were identified as threshing sledge flints. These distinctive artifacts were inserted into the bases of wooden *dhoukanes* (threshing sledges). With microwear analysis, it is possible to identify wear patterns that distinguish threshing sledge flints from similar looking blades that were used as sickles, knives, and scrapers (Kardulias and Yerkes 1996). Eighteen of the 22 threshing sledge flints were found within a 1 km radius of Petrophani and may have been associated with threshing floors that have been used since the Ottoman period (AD 1571–1878). Two other sledge flints were found 2.3 km south of Petrophani on the surface of the late Roman–Early Byzantine and Venetian settlements at Athienou-*Malloura*. One sledge flint was found on the surface of a small late Roman–Early Byzantine site located 2.85 km north of the Malloura site, and another was found near a recently abandoned mudbrick structure located about halfway between Malloura and Petrophani (Kardulias and Yerkes 1996: 660; Toumazou et al. 1998).

No sledge flints were found in the collections from the aceramic lithic scatters on Chakmaklik

(Sites 9, 11, 21, 28), and they were not present in the assemblage from Site 15. None of the lithic artifacts from these sites exhibited the macroscopic or microscopic battering, striations, edge damage, and polish that are found on sledge flints (seven artifacts from Site 9, two from Site 11, and 14 from Site 15 were examined for microwear traces). During the survey, a site was found containing recent-looking flints that may mark the location where a threshing sledge was prepared (although no sledge flints were recovered). This artifact scatter (Site 10) was located only 90 m north of Site 9, but it contained a lithic assemblage that consisted of large flint blocks, amorphous flakes, and shatter. None of the artifacts from Site 10 were patinated, and the characteristic blanks found at Site 9 were absent. A substantial number of lithics (n=89) were found at Site 1, and a few at sites with Cypro-Classical–Hellenistic and Roman pottery, indicating the use of flaked-stone implements in historic periods.

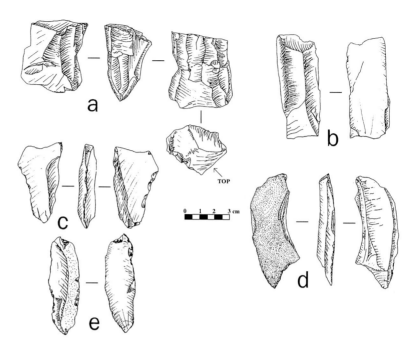

FIG. 8.2 *Lithic artifacts from Malloura Valley Survey Site 9: (a) core; (b) blade; (c) elongated flake; (d) elongated flake; (e) foliate flake (drawing: A. Fuchs).*

Lithics from AAP Site 9

The assemblage from this site is the largest collection of flaked stone from the survey (n=398, 50.2% of the total for the survey) and provides the best basis for comparison with other locations. One feature that is immediately observed is that many pieces in the assemblage have extensive tan to reddish patination. With few exceptions, the material derives from the bedrock that outcrops at the site; the chert is the greenish-gray type prevalent throughout the valley. The original hue is visible on many pieces on which subsequent flaking removed the patination. A process of weathering and dehydration causes this discoloration.

Typology

The Site 9 assemblage consists of various blanks indicative of primary reduction. Many large, irregular flakes, blades, and debris are scattered over the hillside. Examination of the assemblage indicates the presence of certain characteristic types of blanks (see fig. 8.2).

(1) Cores (n=12; fig. 8.2a). Most of the pieces exhibit irregular working, with flakes struck off in a variety of directions from several points on the core surface. Platform preparation is minimal.

(2) Blades (n=10; fig. 8.2b). These pieces have long, parallel to subparallel lateral margins. The pieces tend to be quite large, with plain platforms.

(3) Elongated flakes (n=22; fig. 8.2c, d). These blanks do not have quite the dimensions of blades, nor their configuration. The lateral margins are subparallel to converging in outline but are longer than most other flakes. Perhaps there was an attempt to obtain bladelike dimensions without the expenditure of time necessary to set up the cores properly.

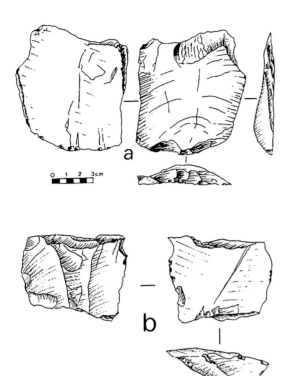

Fig. 8.3   *Tabular flakes from Malloura Valley Survey: (a) Site 9; (b) Site 11 (drawing: A. Fuchs).*

(4) Tabular flakes (n=6; fig. 8.3). These pieces are broad flakes with symmetrical, rectangular outlines. Often the pieces have a regular series of parallel dorsal ridges from prior flake removals.

(5) Foliate flakes (n=4; fig. 8.2e). A number of flakes have a leaf-shaped outline. The configuration is created by a small plain platform and symmetrical margins that widen smoothly to the medial section and then taper to a distal point.

(6) Other flakes (n=300). Cortical and noncortical flakes are present in a variety of shapes and sizes and indicate rapid, expedient reduction of the local chert. The fact that the chert fractures naturally in an angular fashion probably produced pieces from which the variety of flakes derived. There are a number of wide flakes with pronounced bulbs and thick, prominent hinge terminations and concentric force lines.

(7) Debris (n=44). There are a number of highly angular, irregular pieces produced from the initial shattering of core or core fragments; the pieces lack platforms and bulbs.

The density of lithic debitage at Site 9 is moderately high, and the variety in type and size of blanks indicates the flint knappers carried the reduction sequence well into the production trajectory, that is, beyond just the primary level. They did not simply test the material but rather attempted to produce some usable blanks; perhaps elongated flakes or blades were the primary forms desired. Another possibility is that the knappers prepared macrocores at the quarry site and took these to other locations for final reduction of blanks as needed. The small number of cores at Site 9 (and also at Sites 11, 15, 28) provides some negative evidence for this conjecture.

Two general models of lithic raw material procurement are usually presented in discussions of quarry/workshop sites: the "embedded procurement strategy," where stone is collected in the course of basic subsistence activities (Binford 1979: 259); and the "direct procurement strategy," when special trips were made to lithic raw material sources (Torrence 1986: 136). There is no evidence for quarrying or intensive utilization of the Chakmaklik chert source. The lithic raw material seems to have been obtained from the exposed outcrops. The material could have been collected by herders when they took their flocks into the Malloura Valley, employing an embedded procurement strategy similar to the pattern of obsidian acquisition used by Neolithic fishermen (Bintliff 1977; Torrence 1986; Kardulias 1992). However, there was no evidence for "retooling" in the form of heavily utilized, resharpened, or worn-out tools, or any tools made of non-local cherts that were discarded at the Chakmaklik lithic extraction sites. These kinds of artifacts have been found at quarry/ workshops where it is believed that an embedded procurement strategy was practiced (Gramly 1980; Keeley 1982; Yerkes 1993; Lepper et al. 2001). The worn-out tools (sometimes made of exotic raw materials) were discarded and replaced with new tools manufactured at the workshops. There is no evidence of retooling activities at the Malloura Valley workshops. It appears that most of the cores, blanks, and tools produced on Chakmaklik were taken away to be finished and used elsewhere, with only rejected or unfinished tools left behind. Yet there is nothing to suggest that special trips were made to the chert source. At present we have no evidence for a Neolithic settlement in the immediate vicinity of these chert extraction sites, so we must question where the quarried material was taken. The nearest known Neolithic habitation is the later Aceramic Neolithic Dhali-*Agridhi* site (Lehavy 1974, 1989), which lies 6 km due west of Chakmaklik.

DISCUSSION

Preliminary analysis of the flaked artifacts from the three AAP sites with substantial lithic assemblages reveals similarities to the assemblages from some later Aceramic Neolithic sites, but not with the earlier Cypro-PPNB assemblages. The differences between the later Aceramic Neolithic, Ceramic Neolithic, and Chalcolithic industries were first noted by Stekelis (1961), before the earlier Aceramic Neolithic sites had been discovered. He found that the industries of Khirokitia (later Aceramic Neolithic), Sotira (Ceramic Neolithic), and Erimi (Chalocolithic) were distinct. Large irregular blades are common in the later Aceramic Neolithic assemblages, while smaller squarish or pointed blades characterize the Ceramic Neolithic industry. Several forms of scrapers are common in the later Aceramic Neolithic and Chalcolithic collections, while only end scrapers or double end scrapers on blades were usually made by the Ceramic Neolithic groups. Blades are more common in the Ceramic Neolithic assemblages, but the pedunculated blades, gravers, and points that are found in later Aceramic Neolithic collections were absent (Stekelis 1961).

Waechter (1953: 414–15) compared the AN lithic assemblage from Khirokitia with Chalcolithic chipped-stone artifacts from Erimi-*Pamboula*. He concluded that the later AN assemblage is a simple industry of broad blade flakes retouched to produce backed blades, end and side scrapers, simple burins, and some sickles. Points are rare, and the round and discoidal scrapers that characterize the Erimi industry are absent. While broad flakes and blades are present in the Chalcolithic assemblage, most of the blades from Erimi were narrow and exhibited finer retouch.

The assemblages from the AAP sites include some blades but also a substantial number of large, irregular flakes. There is no evidence for specialized production, but this is not uncommon at lithic quarry sites (Torrence 1986). The blades and flakes from the AAP sites both compare favorably to the size and form of blade and flake blanks from some excavated later AN sites on Cyprus. Although there are few formal tools in our AAP assemblages, those we do have exhibit retouch similar to that from the other later AN locations, that is, large, marginal, and mostly irregular. Although Neolithic peoples certainly used lithics for a variety of purposes, there are relatively few distinct tool types in the Aceramic Neolithic assemblages. This suggests that flaked stone blanks served a variety of unspecialized tasks; a number of the unretouched pieces probably also served as ad hoc tools. In addition, the low percentage of blades at Sites 9 and 15, compared with other AN sites, is a function of the nature of these two extractive sites. One would expect to find highly irregular blanks, formed in the process of primary reduction. The large, unstandardized blank dimensions indicate testing or preliminary working of nodules prior to removal from these sites. Thus, we have a sense of some of the variation present on AN sites; there were differences between procurement, settlement, and special function sites, variation the lithic assemblages reflect. Differences with other later AN assemblages, especially as described by Stekelis, center on two issues: contrary to Stekelis's observation concerning the Khirokitia material, the lithics from the Malloura sites have heavy patination — the Khirokitia material he described came from excavated contexts in which the "desert varnish" could not develop; while Stekelis found extensive evidence for the use of soft hammer technique, the flakes and blades in our sample have the large thick bulbs characteristic of hard hammer preparation. In addition, we found virtually no platform preparation, even for blades.

The low percentage of blades from two of the four putative AN sites in the Malloura survey area (n=10, 2.5% at Site 9; n=2, 4.2% at Site 15; no blades were recovered at Sites 11 and 28) compares favorably to the situation at Cape Andreas-*Kastros*. Another similarity is that the Malloura sites, especially Site 9, exhibit considerable variety in the types of retouched implements. The distinct tools from Site 9 fall into eight different categories, including a variety of scrapers, several perforators, and bifaces. There are two burins in the small assemblage from Site 11. Site 15 has only two pieces with some generic retouch.

The site of Kholetria-*Ortos* provides significant comparanda for the proposed Malloura later AN complex (Simmons and Corona 1993; Simmons 1996). Ortos, located in the southwest part of the island, is a single component site with a large flaked-stone assemblage and ^{14}C dates of ca. 7600 BP. The lithics form a generalized collection in which flakes are more abundant than blades and with the whole reduction sequence in evidence. Present in large quantities are distinctive crescent-shaped pieces with steep backing on one edge and sickle sheen on the opposing margin. Simmons (1996) interprets these implements as evidence of the existence of truly diagnostic AN flaked stone tools. In addition, he argues for regional variation as the result of adaptation to specific microenvironments by the different early Neolithic residents of Cyprus. In the Malloura Valley, we see the idiosyncratic development of particular blanks (elongated, foliate, and tabular flakes) rather than a specific retouched form.

Of more direct relevance is the lithic material from the Sydney Cyprus Survey Project (SCSP). The team members identified several possible AN sites on the basis of surface remains alone. One site, Politiko-*Mazovounes*, yielded 60 lithics but no cores, preforms, or identifiable tools. The material reflects manufacture of blades from raw material imported from some other location, where it underwent initial reduction. The stone artifacts, lack of pottery, and topographic setting at an ecotone in an elevated area near a spring are the bases for assigning the site to the AN (Kingsnorth in Knapp and Given 1996: 346). The team identified another AN site in Transects 515–516.5 (Units 1291–93) where they found a collection of chipped stone and raw material and a paucity of ceramics (Kingsnorth in Knapp and Given 1996: 349). The AAP possible AN sites share these general traits in terms of blank type, dearth of pottery, and geographical position.

The typological comparison demonstrates certain patterns that may define the later AN flaked stone assemblages on Cyprus:

(1) There is evidence of extensive use of local chert, perhaps in an effort to be self-sufficient. Since the two key Malloura sites (9, 15) are lithic extraction sites where there is no evidence for "retooling," it is not surprising that there is no exotic obsidian present. The extensive use of the outcrops may indicate the desire to maintain economic autonomy. If the early Neolithic settlements of Cyprus were mutually hostile or at least wary of each other, as some have suggested (Todd 1987: 180), then the use of local chert sources was an important factor of production. Kingsnorth (in Knapp and Given 1996: 346) suggests that blades and bladelets found in some of the SCSP transects and that may be AN in date were locally produced from materials gathered throughout the region; in this area of the Troodos foothills, it seems that during the later AN period, groups utilized stone sources within a relatively small catchment area, although they did not live at these source areas. This is the same pattern we see in the Malloura Valley, where people went to Sites 9 and 15 to collect chert that they then transported elsewhere for final reduction and use.

(2) The later AN assemblages have low percentages of retouched pieces. At Tenta, there were 644 (10.4%) modified implements in a collection of 6,217 from the surface. Malloura Site 9 has 22 (5.5%) retouched artifacts, Site 15 has 2 (4.2%), and Site 11 also has 2 (15.4%). From the earlier excavations at Khirokitia, Stekelis (1953: 413) recorded 213 (17%) retouched items. The somewhat lower percentages for the Malloura Valley sites derive in large part from the fact that they are extraction sites, where one would expect fewer finished tools.

(3) The production of a diversity of blanks, with some emphasis on blades and elongated flakes, which can be readily converted to a variety of tools (e.g., sickle elements, points, scrapers) or used in an ad hoc manner is a common occurrence at the various sites.

(4) The presence of many cortical and noncortical flakes and debris at the Malloura sites and other later AN locations suggests the full range of reduction activities. We interpret this distribution as possible evidence of a lack of specialization among these early inhabitants of the island. Each settlement, if not each household, may have provided its own set of stone implements. Rupp et al. (1992: 301) argue that stone tools were produced independently at the Neolithic and Chalcolithic sites found in the Palaipaphos survey; on sites of the latter period, scrapers and utilized flakes in clustered foci dominate the assemblages.

Connections to the Mainland

While sharing many similarities, in many of its particulars the AN cultural patterns of Cyprus differ from their contemporaries on the neighboring West Asian mainland. Similarities include the use of circular structures, walled enclosures, intramural burial, wall paintings, plastered floors, anthropomorphic figures, and use of the same suite of domesticates (Todd 1987: 183–85; Peltenburg 2003: Table 11.5). Significant differences include the apparent maintenance of traditional architectural styles for a longer period on Cyprus, secondary burial (mainland) vs. primary inhumation (Cyprus), and site location. Lithic artifacts do provide definitive proof of contacts with the mainland (see Karimali 2005 for an overview). Obsidian has been found at Kissonerga-*Mylouthkia*, Parekklisha-*Shillourokambos*, Khirokitia, Cape Andreas-*Kastros*, Troulloi, Tenta, Dhali-*Aghridi* (n=1), Ortos (n=2), and Akanthou-*Arkosyko* (Sevketoglu 2002). The artifacts from the first six sites came from Cappadocian obsidian flows in south-central Anatolia (Gomez et al. 1995; Peltenburg 2003: 34; Todd 1987: 178) and the obsidian artifacts found at the other sites may also have come from there. However, the lithic assemblages from nearby mainland sites (Mersin, Ras Shamra, Hacılar, and Aşıklı Höyük) contrast with those at AN sites on Cyprus. One major difference is the high percentage of obsidian at many Near Eastern sites, especially those in Anatolia

close to major sources. In addition, the number of blades is higher on the mainland (Redman 1978: 160, 164). There also seems to be a greater consistency in retouched types. The insularity of Cyprus during the AN stages may have led to a divergent technological tradition. Typical of the mainland pattern is Abu Hureyra, where the excavators found a preponderance of blades that the Neolithic people transformed into points, knives, scrapers, and sickle elements (Moore 1979; Moore et al. 2000). There are few projectile points at the later Cypriot AN sites, but they do have substantial numbers of sickle elements (Stekelis 1953: 411, 413; 1961: 231, 233).

Microwear Analysis

In the early 1990s, we performed microwear analysis on nine artifacts at Ohio State to determine function; we used the high-power technique pioneered by Semenov (1964) and refined by Keeley (1980). Some scholars argue that surface artifacts are poor candidates for microwear analysis because they are subject to extraneous abrasion unrelated to aboriginal use. Odell (1985), however, has demonstrated that even surface-collected artifacts can maintain traces of wear that an analyst can discern. Most of the lithics we examined exhibited no wear, but two did carry traces of working bone or antler. In 1992 we examined an additional 14 artifacts from Site 15 and several isolated finds by the high-power technique. None of the Site 15 tools exhibits any wear; the only trace on the isolated finds was some possible hafting wear on one blade. The lack of any noticeable wear on the vast majority of the lithics in our sample correlates with our initial assessment of the sites as basic processing stations where raw material was quarried and cores roughed out.

Conclusion

Lithics are seminal for the study of the early occupants of Cyprus. Over the past three decades, archaeological survey has helped to identify many sites with substantial assemblages; some of the sites have been excavated and the lithics have been studied in detail, thus expanding our understanding of how farmers exploited the early agricultural landscape. As such studies continue, the picture of Cypriot AN culture will gain clarity and help resolve certain issues that pertain to the impact humans have on insular ecology and how those environments constrain social evolution. The sites in the Malloura Valley exhibit characteristics of quarries that served as extraction zones for people in neighboring regions. The Malloura sites reflect a concern over the procurement of material vital in the technology that made settled village life possible.

Acknowledgments

We thank William Fraunfelder, James Noone, William Parkinson, and Heather Gayheart Price, who assisted with various aspects of the analysis.

References

Adovasio, J. M.; Fry, G. F.; Gunn, J. D.; and Maslowski, R. F.
1975   Prehistoric and Historic Settlement Patterns in Western Cyprus (with a Discussion of Cypriot Neolithic Stone Tool Technology). *World Archaeology* 6: 339–64.

Austruc, L.
1994   L'outillage en pierre non-taillée et les petits objets. Pp. 215–89 in *Fouilles récentes à Khirokitia (Chypre) 1988–1991*, ed. A. Le Brun. Paris: A. D. P. F.

Bar-Yosef, O., and Belfer-Cohen, A.
1989   The Levantine "PPNB" Interaction Sphere. Pp. 59–72 in *People and Culture in Change*, ed. I. Hershkovitz. BAR International Series 508. Oxford: British Archaeological Reports.

Baudou, E.; Engelmark; R.; Niklasson, K.; and Wennberg, B.
1985   The Tremithos Valley Project. Pp. 369–71 in *Acts of the Second International Congress of Cypriot Studies*, eds. T. Papadopoulos and S. A. Hadjistyllis. Nikosia: Society of Cypriot Studies.

Binford, L. R.
1979   Organization and Formation Processes: Looking at Curated Technologies. *Journal of Anthropological Research* 35: 255–73.

Bintliff, J. L.
1977   *Natural Environment and Human Settlement in Prehistoric Greece.* British Archaeological Reports, Supplementary Series 28. Oxford: British Archaeological Reports.

Bohannon, J.
2007   Exploring the Prehistory of Europe, in a Few Bold Leaps. *Science* 317(5835): 188–89.

Broodbank, C., and Strasser, T.
1991   Migrant Farmers and the Neolithic Colonization of Crete. *Antiquity* 65: 233–45.

Bunimovitz, S., and Barkai, R.
1996   Ancient Bones and Modern Myths: Ninth Millennium BC Hippopotamus Hunters at Akrotiri *Aetokremnos*, Cyprus? *Journal of Mediterranean Archaeology* 9: 85–96.

Caraher, W.; Moore, R. S.; Noller, J.; and Pettegrew, D.
2007   The Pyla-Koutsopetria Archaeological Project: Second Preliminary Report (2005–2006 Seasons). *Report of the Department of Antiquities, Cyprus*: 292–306.

Cauvin, M. C.
1984   L'outillage lithique de Khirokitia (Chypre) et le Levant. Pp. 85–87 in *Fouilles récentes à Khirokitia (Chypre), 1977–1981,* ed. A. Le Brun. Récherche sur les grandes civilisations. Mémoire 41 (Etudes Neolithiques). Paris: A. D. P. F.

Cherry, J. F.
1990   The First Colonization of the Mediterranean Islands: A Review of Recent Research. *Journal of Mediterranean Archaeology* 3: 145–221.

Clarke, J.; McCartney, C.; and Wasse, A.
2007   *On the Margins of Southwest Asia: Cyprus during the 6th to 4th Millennia BC.* Oxford: Oxbow.

Colledge, S., and Conolly, J.
2007 A Review and Synthesis of the Evidence for the Origins of Farming on Cyprus and Crete. Pp. 53–74 in *The Origins and Spread of Domestic Plants in Southwest Asia and Europe*, eds. S. College and J. Conolly. Walnut Creek, CA: Left Coast.

Coqueugniot, E.
1984 Premiers elements concernant l'utilisation des outils de silex de Khirokita (Chypre) campagne de 1981. Pp. 83–93 in *Fouilles récentes à Khirokitia (Chypre) 1977–1981*, by A. Le Brun. Mémoire 41 (Etudes Neolithiques). Paris: A. D. P. F.

Flourentzos, P.; McCartney, C.; Croft, P.; and Reese, D.
2008 *The Neolithic Settlement of Paralimni*. Nicosia: Department of Antiquities of Cyprus.

Gass, I. G.
1960 *The Geology and Mineral Resources of the Dhali Area*. Geological Survey Department, Cyprus, Memoir 4. Nicosia: Geological Survey Department.

Given, M., and Knapp, A. B.
2003 *The Sydney Cyprus Survey Project: Social Approaches to Regional Archaeology*. Monumenta Archaeologica 21. Los Angeles: Cotsen Institute.

Gomez, B.; Glascock, M. D.; Blackman, M. J.; and Todd, I. A.
1995 Neutron Activation Analysis of Obsidian from Kalavasos-*Tenta*. *Journal of Field Archaeology* 22: 503–8.

Gopher, A.
1989 Diffusion Process in the Pre-Pottery Neolithic Levant: The Case of the Helwan Point. Pp. 91–105 in *People and Culture in Change*, ed. I. Hershkovitz. BAR International Series 508. Oxford: British Archaeological Reports.

Gramly, R. M.
1980 Raw Material Sources and "Curated" Tool Assemblages. *American Antiquity* 45: 828–33.

Guilaine, J., and Briois, F.
2001 Parekklisha *Shillourokambos*: An Early Neolithic Site in Cyprus. Pp. 37–53 in *The Earliest Prehistory of Cyprus*, ed. S. Swiny. Cyprus American Archaeological Research Institute Monograph Series 2. Boston: American Schools of Oriental Research.

Guilaine, J.; Briois, F.; Coularou, J.; and Carrere, I.
1995 L'établissement Néolithique de Shillourokambos (Parekklisha, Chypre). Premiers résultats. *Report to the Department of Antiquities, Cyprus*: 11–31.

Guilaine, J., and Le Brun, A.
2003 *Le néolithique de Chypre: Actes du colloque international organisé par le Département des antiquites de Chypre et l'Ecole française d'Athènes, Nicosie, 17–19 mai 2001*. Bulletin de correspondance hellénique. Supplément 43. Athens: Ecole française d'Athènes.

Hayes, P. P.
1995 The Geographical Setting. Pp. 63–72 in *Ancient Akamas I: Settlement and Environment*, ed. Jane Fejfer. Aarhus: Aarhus University.

Held, S.
1990a Sardinia to Samoa: Studying Comparative Insularity and Patterns of Prehistoric Island Colonization. Paper presented at the 89th Annual Meeting of the American Anthropological Association, New Orleans.
1990b Back to What Future? New Directions for Cypriot Early Prehistoric Research in the 1990s. *Report to the Department of Antiquities, Cyprus* 1990: 1–43.
1993 Insularity as a Modifier of Cultural Change: The Case of Prehistoric Cyprus. *Bulletin of the American Schools of Oriental Research* 292: 25–33.

Hordynsky, L., and Todd, I. A.
1987 The Surface Survey of the Site. Pp. 17–20 in *Vasilikos Valley Project 6: Excavations at Kalavasos-*Tenta, Vol. 1, ed. I. A. Todd. Studies in Mediterranean Archaeology 71.6. Göteborg: Åström.

Horowitz, L. K., Tchernov, E., and Hongo, H.

2004 Domestic Status of the Early Neolithic Fauna of Cyprus: A View from the Mainland. Pp. 35–48 in *Neolithic Revolution: New Perspectives on Southwest Asia in Light of Recent Discoveries on Cyprus*, eds. E. J. Peltenburg and A. Wasse. Oxford: Oxbow.

Kardulias, P. N.

1992 The Ecology of Flaked Stone Tool Production in Southern Greece: The Evidence from Agios Stephanos and the Southern Argolid. *American Journal of Archaeology* 96: 421–42.

Kardulias, P. N., and Yerkes, R. W.

1996 Microwear and Metric Analysis of Threshing Sledge Flints from Greece and Cyprus. *Journal of Archaeological Science* 23: 657–66.

Karimali, E.

2005 Lithic Technologies and Use. Pp. 180–214 in *The Archaeology of Mediterranean Prehistory*, eds. E. Blake and A. B. Knapp. London: Blackwell.

Keeley, L.

1980 *Experimental Determination of Stone Tool Uses: A Microwear Analysis*. Chicago: University of Chicago.

1982 Hafting and Retooling: Effects on the Archaeological Record. *American Antiquity* 47: 798–809.

Knapp, A. B.

1994 The Prehistory of Cyprus: Problems and Prospects. *Journal of World Prehistory* 8: 377–453.

Knapp, A. B., and Given, M.

1996 The Sydney Cyprus Survey Project (SCSP): Third Season (1995). *Report to the Department of Antiquities, Cyprus* 1996: 295–366.

Le Brun, A.

1981 *Un Site néolithique précéramique en Chypre: Cap Andreas-Kastros*. Récherche sur les grandes civilisations. Mémoire 5 (Etudes Neolithiques). Paris: A. D. P. F.

Le Brun, A., and Evin, J.

1991 De nouvelles datations ^{14}C pur l'établissement Néolithique Précéramique de Khirokitia. *Report to the Department of Antiquities, Cyprus* 1991: 15–18.

Lehavy, Y.

1974 Excavations at Neolithic Dhali-*Agridhi*. Pp. 95–118 in *American Expedition to Idalion, Cyprus, First Preliminary Report, Seasons 1971–72*, eds. L. E. Stager, A. Walker, and G. E. Wright. Bulletin of the American Schools of Oriental Research Supplement 18. Cambridge: BASOR.

1989 Dhali-*Agridi*: The Neolithic by the River. Pp. 203–43 in *American Expedition to Idalion, Cyprus 1973–1980*, eds. L. E. Stager and A. Walker. Oriental Institute Communications. Chicago: Oriental Institute.

Lepper, B. T.; Yerkes, R. W.; and Pickard, W. H.

2001 Prehistoric Flint Procurement Strategies at Flint Ridge, Licking County, Ohio. *Midcontinental Journal of Archaeology* 26(1): 23–56.

Maliszewski, D.

1995 Polis-Pyrgos Archaeological Project: Second Preliminary Report on the 1994 Survey Season in Northwestern Cyprus. *Report to the Department of Antiquities, Cyprus*: 311–16.

Manning, S. W., and Conwell, D. H.

1992 Maroni Valley Archaeological Survey Project: Preliminary Report on the 1990–1991 Field Seasons. *Report to the Department of Antiquities, Cyprus*: 271–83.

Manning, S. W.; Bolger, W. D.; Swinton, A.; and Ponting, M. J.

1994 Maroni Valley Archaeological Survey Project: Preliminary Report on the 1992–1993 Field Seasons. *Report to the Department of Antiquities, Cyprus*: 345–67.

McCartney, C.

1998 Preliminary Report on the Chipped Stone Assemblage from the Aceramic Neolithic Site of Ayia Varvara Asprokremnos. *Levant* 30: 85–90.

McCartney, C.; Manning, S. W.; Sewell, D.; and Stewart, S. T.

2007 The EENC 2006 Field Season: Excavations at

Agia Varvara-*Asprokremnos* and Survey of the Local Early Holocene Landscape. *Report to the Department of Antiquities, Cyprus*: 27–44.

Moore, A.
1979 A Pre-Neolithic Farmers' Village on the Euphrates. *Scientific American* 241(2): 62–70.

Moore, A. M. T.; Hillman, G.C.; and Legge, A. J.
2000 *Village on the Euphrates: From Foraging to Farming at Abu Hureyra.* Oxford: Oxford University.

Mortensen, P.
2008 Lower to Middle Paleolithic Artefacts from Loutró on the South Coast of Crete. *Antiquity* 82(317): http://www.antiquity.ac.uk/ProjGall/mortensen/index.html.

Odell, G. H.
1985 Small Sites Archaeology and Use Wear on Surface-Collected Artifacts. *Midcontinental Journal of Archaeology* 10: 21–48.

Pearlman, D. A.
1984 Threshing Sledges in the East Mediterranean: Ethnoarchaeology with Chert Knappers and Dhoukanes in Cyprus. Unpublished M. A. thesis, University of Minnesota, Minneapolis.

Peltenburg, E., (ed.)
2003 *The Colonisation and Settlement of Cyprus: Investigations at Kissonerga-Mylouthkia, 1976–1996.* Studies in Mediterranean Archaeology LXX:4, Lemba Archaeological Project, Cyprus III.1. Sävedalen, Sweden: Åström.

Peltenburg, E.; Croft, P.; Jackson, A.; McCartney, C.; and Murray, M. A.
2001 Well-Established Colonists: *Mylouthkia* 1 and the Cypro-Pre-Pottery Neolithic B. Pp. 61–93 in *The Earliest Prehistory of Cyprus*, ed. S. Swiny. Cyprus American Archaeological Research Institute Monograph Series 2. Boston: American Schools of Oriental Research.

Peltenburg, E. J., and Wasse, A., (eds.)
2004 *Neolithic Revolution: New Perspectives on Southwest Asia in Light of Recent Discoveries on Cyprus.* Oxford: Oxbow.

Redman, C. L.
1978 *The Rise of Civilization.* San Francisco: W. F. Freeman.

Reese, D. S.
1989 Tracking the Extinct Pygmy Hippopotamus of Cyprus. *Field Museum of Natural History Bulletin* 30(2): 22–29.

Runnels, C. N.
1982 Flaked Stone Artifacts in Greece during the Historical Period. *Journal of Field Archaeology* 9: 363–74.

Rupp, D. W.; Sørensen, L. W.; King, R. H.; and Fox, W. A.
1984 Canadian Palaipaphos (Cyprus) Survey Project: Second Preliminary Report, 1980–1982. *Journal of Field Archaeology* 11: 133–54.

Rupp, D. W.; Clarke, J. T.; D'Annibale, C.; and Stewart, S. T.
1992 Canadian Palaipaphos Survey Project: 1991 Field Season. *Report to the Department of Antiquities, Cyprus* 1992: 285–317.

Semenov, S. A.
1964 *Prehistoric Technology.* Trans. M. W. Thompson. New York: Barnes and Noble.

Sevketoglu, M.
2002 Akanthou-Arkosyko (Tatlısu-Çiftlikdüzü): The Anatolian Connections in the 9th Millennium B.C. Pp. 98–106 in *World Islands in Prehistory: International Insular Investigations*, eds. W. H. Waldren and J. A. Ensenyat. Oxford: Archaeopress.

Sheen, A.
1981 Stavros tis Psokas Survey, 1979. *Levant* 13: 39–42.

Simmons, A. H.
1991 Humans, Island Colonization and Pleistocene Extinctions in the Mediterranean: The View from Akrotiri *Aetokremnos*, Cyprus. *Antiquity* 65: 857–69.
1996 Preliminary Report on Multidisciplinary Investigations at Neolithic Kholetria-*Ortos*, Paphos District. *Report to the Department of Antiquities, Cyprus*: 29–44.

1999   *Faunal Extinction in an Island Society: Pygmy Hippopotamus Hunters of Cyprus.* New York: Kluwer Academic/Plenum.

Simmons, A. H., and Corona, R. F.
1993   Test Excavations at Kholetria-*Ortos*, a Neolithic Settlement Near Paphos. *Report of the Department of Antiquities of Cyprus*: 1–10.

Simmons, A. H., and Wigand, P. E.
1994   Assessing the Radiocarbon Determinations from Akrotiri Aetokremnos, Cyprus. Pp. 247–64 in *Late Quaternary Chronology and Paleoclimates of the Eastern Mediterranean*, eds. O. Bar-Yosef and R. Kra. Radiocarbon 1994. Cambridge: American School of Prehistoric Research.

Steel, L.
2004   *Cyprus before History. From the Earliest Settlers to the End of the Bronze Age.* London: Duckworth.

Stekelis, M.
1953   The Flint Implements from Khirokitia. Pp. 409–15 in *Khirokitia*, by P. Dikaios. London: Oxford University.
1961   Appendix 2: The Flint Implements. Pp. 230–34 in *Sotira*, by P. Dikaios. University Museum Monographs 4. Philadelphia: University of Pennsylvania.

Stockton, E. D.
1968   Pre-Neolithic Remains at Kyrenia, Cyprus? *Report to the Department of Antiquities, Cyprus*: 16–19.

Strasser, T. F.; Murray, P.; Panagopoulou, E.; Runnels, C. N.; and Thompson, N.
2009   The Results of the Plakias Mesolithic Survey on Crete, 2008. Paper presented at the 110th Annual Meeting of the Archaeological Institute of America, January 2009, Philadelphia.

Symeonoglou, S.
1972   Archaeological Survey in the Area of Phlamoudhi, Cyprus. *Report to the Department of Antiquities, Cyprus* 1972: 187–98.

Todd, I. A.
1987   *Vasilikos Valley Project 6: Excavations at Kalavasos-Tenta.* Studies in Mediterranean Archaeology 41, no. 6. Göteborg: Åström.
1989   Early Prehistoric Society: A View from the Vasilikos Valley. Pp. 2–13 in *Early Society in Cyprus*, ed. E. Peltenburg. Edinburgh: Edinburgh University.

Torrence, R.
1986   *Production and Exchange of Stone Tools.* Cambridge: Cambridge University.

Toumazou, M. K.; Yerkes, R. W.; and Kardulias, P. N.
1992   Excavation and Survey in the Malloura Valley, Central Cyprus: The 1991 Season. *Old World Archaeology Newsletter* 15(3): 18–23.
1998   Athienou Archaeological Project: Interim Report of Investigations in the Malloura Valley, Cyprus, 1990–95. *Journal of Field Archaeology* 25: 163–82.

Vigne, J-D.; Isabelle Carrère, I.; Saliége, J. F.; Person, A.; Bocherens, H.; Guilaine, J.; and Briois, J. F.
2000   Predomestic Cattle, Sheep, Goat, and Pig during the Late 9th and the 8th Millennium Cal. BC on Cyprus: Preliminary Results of Shillourokambos (Parekklisha, Limassol). Pp. 83–106 in *Archaeozoology of the Neat East IV: Proceedings of the 4th International Symposium on the Archaeology of Southwestern Asia and Adjacent Areas*, eds. H. Buitenhaus, M. Mashkour, and F. Poplin. Gronigen: Center for Archaeological Research.

Vita-Finzi, C.
1973   Palaeolithic Finds from Cyprus? *Proceedings of the Prehistoric Society* 39: 453–54.

Waechter, J.
1953   Appendix IA: A Comparison between the Flint Implements of Khirokitia and Erimi. Pp. 414–15 in *Khirokitia*, by P. Dikaios. London: Oxford University.

Yerkes, R. W.
1993   The Ohio State University Investigations at the Flint Ridge State Memorial, Licking County,

Ohio, 1987–1988. *Ohio Archaeological Council Newsletter* 5(3): 8–15.

Yerkes, R. W., and Kardulias, P. N.
1994   Microwear Analysis of Threshing Sledge Flints from Cyprus and Greece: Implications for the Study of Ancient Agriculture. *Helinium* 34(2): 281–93.

Chapter 9

Pots for Goods and for the Gods

The Iron Age Ceramics from the Malloura Sanctuary

by Sabine Fourrier

Since its invention, in the Neolithic period, pottery has played an essential role in every aspect of Cypriot daily life (for carrying, storing, preparing, or consuming goods) as well as in many ritual practices, both funerary and religious (as gifts accompanying the dead and votives for the gods, libations, sacrifices, etc.). Almost indestructible, ceramic sherds are abundant at archaeological sites and thus provide the most secure evidence for comparing and, consequently, dating archaeological levels. Less impressive than limestone sculptures, less directly informative than inscriptions, ceramics nevertheless reflect the cultural background of an ancient society and highlights, through imports and stylistic or morphological borrowing, its relationships with the neighboring cultures (Yon 1976: 1–4).

As is the case with most ancient sites occupied over a long period of time, with no abrupt end sealing the last occupation phase, the ceramics from the Atheniou-*Malloura* sanctuary are very fragmentary (for discussion of the excavated remains, see Toumazou and Counts, Ch. 6). But some morphological elements (e.g., rims, bases, handles) and some decorative features help reconstruct original shapes. A careful numbering of the various ceramic shapes and wares attested in undisturbed archaeological levels enables one to characterize the evolution of ceramic assemblages, and thus to define different chronological phases (Arcelin and Tuffreau-Libre 1998).

The main difficulty in phasing the successive ceramic assemblages results from the long duration of the sanctuary's use; the last phase of occupation is the best-documented and it often obliterates the preceding ones, due to extensive reconstructions. We can catch only glimpses of the earlier periods, be it through some undisturbed layers, buried beneath later buildings, or through sherds reused as filling material (which is then residual, not *in situ*). All conclusions must therefore remain tentative. Only main phases can be distinguished, only broad changes defined, and the ceramic evidence must always be compared with the other archaeological, epigraphic, numismatic evidence and, when they exist, literary documents.

Pots and the Sanctuary's History

Three main phases documented in the ceramic assemblage retrieved from the Malloura sanctuary are Cypro-Geometric III (ca. 900–750 BC), Cypro-Archaic II (ca. 600–480 BC), and Cypro-Classical II–Hellenistic I (fourth–third centuries BC). They represent three successive stages in a continuous history that left differentiated prints in the soil: the first period, the sanctuary's foundation; the second, its first *floruit*; the third, its greatest development and major architectural extension. Of course, the sanctuary was not deserted in the intermediary periods (as Cypro-Archaic I and Cypro-Classical I sherds testify), and Hellenistic II and early Roman material attests its continued, though less important, use after Hellenistic I. But the Cypro-Archaic I and Cypro-Classical I periods are, at least for the moment, not well-documented stratigraphically, due either to chance or to heavy reconstruction on the same spot. Moreover, the three main ceramic phases apparent to the ceramicist's eye may reflect minor topographical shifts in the sanctuary occupation; the major part of the excavated area comprises only levels dating to the last phase, whereas the most ancient layers are confined to the westernmost part of the area, in restricted zones apparently left untouched by later occupation.

The first phase, in Cypro-Geometric III, was evidenced through a small sounding in the westernmost part of the excavation (EU 94, see fig. 6.2). Only 46 sherds were collected, belonging to eight different vases. All are characteristic of the last part of the CG III period, as, for example, the Bichrome III footed bowl with cross decoration (fig. 9.1), which has good parallels in contemporary levels at Amathous (Vandenabeele 1985: 634, fig. 7), Nicosia (Flourentzos 1981: pl. 17:3), Salamis (Dikaios 1963: 175:7), and Stylli (Gjerstad 1948: fig. 11:7). No other sherd dating to the Cypro-Geometric III period

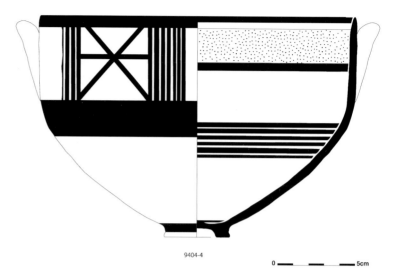

9404-4

0 ———————— 5cm

FIG. 9.1 *Bichrome III footed bowl, sherd inv. no. 9404.4 (drawing: S. Fourrier and A. Flammin).*

has been discovered in other parts of the sanctuary, which raises two hypotheses: either the Cypro-Geometric layers were destroyed by later rebuilding and all was material thrown away in some *bothros* outside the sanctuary limits, which has still to be discovered, or the boundaries of the sacred precinct were moved somehow to the east, leaving some Cypro-Geometric layers to the west undisturbed because they were located outside the limits of the new *temenos*. Another theory, impossible to prove with the present state of documentation, is less convincing: the Cypro-Geometric III layers do not belong to the first phase of the sanctuary occupation but to a small settlement next to which a sanctuary was founded in the following Cypro-Archaic period.

The second phase (Cypro-Archaic II) is better documented, especially through residual material, since most of the Archaic layers have been obliterated by later, generally Cypro-Classical–Hellenistic I rebuilding. Archaic layers were lying directly on the bedrock in the eastern part of the sanctuary (EU 10, see fig. 6.2). There, the ceramic material was included in a rocky layer, associated with numerous fragments of mudbrick, probably belonging to the walls' superstructure, which clearly shows that there were buildings of some kind in the Archaic sanctuary. Other undisturbed Cypro-Archaic II layers (ca. 600–475 BC) were

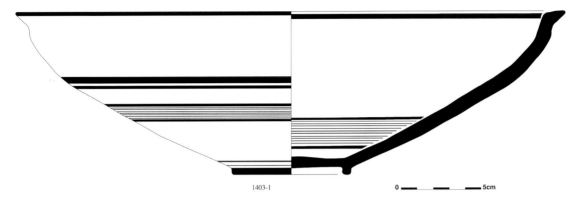

1403-1

0 _____ _____ _____ 5cm

FIG. 9.2   *Black-on-Red II (IV) shallow bowl, sherd inv. no. 1403.1 (drawing: S. Fourrier and A. Flammin).*

located in or near the circular structure laid bare in EU 14 and 94 (see plan, fig. 6.2). This enigmatic structure is probably a ritual hearth/altar of a type known in many Cypriot sanctuaries, mostly of Late Cypriot date (Webb 1977; 1999: 166–69) but also of the Iron Age, as at Kition, Vouni, and Amathous (Petit 2002: 293–94). The layers were full of ash, and many Cypro-Archaic sherds show traces of fire because they were used as building material in the enclosure or because they were deposited in the hearth and burned with their contents. The presence of an altar may explain why the Cypro-Archaic levels were piously preserved in this part of the sanctuary. The uneven distribution of Cypro-Archaic material, which is much more numerous in the western part of the excavated area, inside as well as outside of the Hellenistic *temenos* wall, may also suggest that the limits of the sanctuary were different in the Cypro-Archaic period and that the focus of the cult was displaced farther east at the time of the Hellenistic I reconstruction.

Many ceramic shapes, appearing in the Cypro-Archaic I period, continued to be produced in the sixth century BC, as, for example, the shallow bowls with bevelled rim (fig. 9.2) or the handless cups with purple band decoration (fig. 9.3). Other shapes show clear signs of evolution, such as the amphorae with neatly pending everted rim (fig. 9.4), which are characteristic of the CA II period.

The last ceramic assemblage is exemplary of most of the layers excavated thus far in the sanctuary. It is often very difficult to distinguish between levels of the Cypro-Classical and the following Hellenistic I periods; both are characterized by

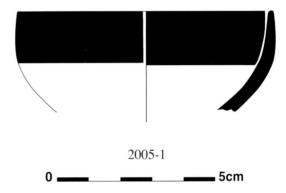

2005-1

0 ▬▬ ▬▬ ▬▬ **5cm**

FIG. 9.3   *White Painted IV bowl, sherd inv. no. 2005.1 (drawing: S. Fourrier and A. Flammin).*

simple shapes in Plain White Ware, such as small bowls with inverted rims (fig. 9.5) and sack-shaped jugs with round mouths (fig. 9.6). The presence of Color-Coated Wares and Hellenistic molded lamps is the only indication that the layer is of the third rather than the fourth century BC. Ceramics of the Cypro-Classical period, repetitive in shape and lacking painted decoration, have attracted less attention than the decorated wares of the Cypro-Geometric and Cypro-Archaic periods and are thus less well-known. The Malloura assemblage, together with material from other recent excavations (e.g., Nicosia-*Agios Georgios*), may shed new light on this crucial phase of the Cypro-Classical kingdoms. The last ceramic assemblage evidently exemplifies the final flowering of the Malloura sanctuary, and it coincides with heavy reconstruction, which obliterated most of the preceding phases of sanctuary activity.

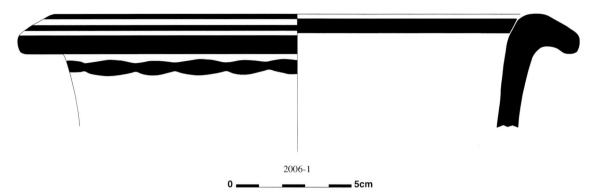

2006-1

0 ▬▬ _ ▬▬ _ ▬▬ 5cm

FIG. 9.4   *Black-on-Red III (V) amphora, sherd inv. no. 2006.1 (drawing: S. Fourrier and A. Flammin).*

The life of the sanctuary, as it can be re-constructed from the pottery, is typical of a Cypriot Iron Age rural sanctuary (Fourrier 2007: 121–24). Founded at the dawn of the Cypro-Archaic period, when Cypriot kingdoms first appear on the international stage, it is frequented without interruption during the whole Iron Age. The abolition of the Cypriot political system (city-kingdoms) at the end of the Cypro-Classical period did not mean the end of the sanctuary's life. On the contrary, this period is marked by an important reshaping of the sacred precinct that points to a renewed vitality.

FIG. 9.5   *Plain White VI bowl with inverted rim, sherd inv. no. 2805.11 (drawing: P. Lanzarote and J. Ravenhurst).*

POTS AND THE SANCTUARY'S EXTERNAL CONTACTS

As is expected for a Cypriot Iron Age sanctuary, the vases used and consecrated at Malloura are not specific of a ritual use; rather, they find good parallels in contemporary tombs and settlements. Here, as at other sites, they were used as votives or implements to cook and consume food and to supply and store goods. The predominance of open and pouring shapes (bowls and jugs) may point to the practice of ritual banquets and libations.

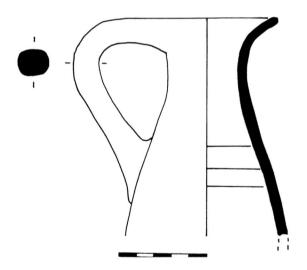

FIG. 9.6   *Plain White VI jug, sherd inv. no. 2805.8 (drawing: P. Lanzarote and J. Ravenhurst).*

With the exception of some torpedo jars, most probably used as transport amphorae for Levantine wine (fig. 9.7), foreign imports are very scarce; only a handful of Aegean imports were found, such as fragments of Attic figured vases and of East Greek amphorae. In fact, Greek imports are not very numerous in Cyprus before the Cypro-Classical period. When present, they seem to have had a social meaning, being displayed by Cypriot elites in tombs and palaces, but very rarely consecrated to the divinity (Gjerstad 1977). Examples are the Attic banquet service deposited in a royal tomb at Salamis (Gjerstad 1979), which is certainly not a sign of the ethnic identity of the dead; the Euboean pedestaled krater, destined to mix wine and water, buried in a rich tomb at Amathous (Coldstream 1987: 24:9); the varieties of Greek imports discovered in the palace and the palatial deposits of Amathous, contrasting with the dozen imports from the rich Cypro-Archaic deposits of the Aphrodite sanctuary (Fourrier 2006: 95). The scarcity of imports is no doubt a matter of choice and not of necessity; in this respect, the rural Malloura sanctuary is similar to the great urban sanctuaries of Zeus at Salamis and of Aphrodite at Amathous, where Iron Age imports are very rare as well. The number

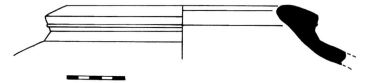

Fig. 9.7 *Torpedo jar, sherd inv. no. 3214.2 (drawing: P. Lanzarote and J. Ravenhurst).*

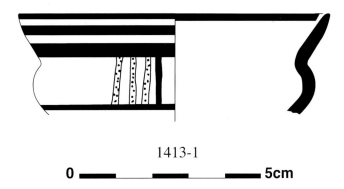

1413-1

0 ▬▬ ▬▬ ▬▬ 5cm

Fig. 9.8 *Bichrome V bowl imitating the Greek skyphos shape, sherd inv. no. 1413.1 (drawing: S. Fourrier and A. Flammin).*

and quality of the limestone sculptures dedicated at Malloura amply demonstrate that the sanctuary was not a remote place. On the other hand, the Greek repertoire was not unknown to local potters (Coldstream 1979). For example, some small Bichrome lip-bowls clearly imitate the shape and decoration of Greek *skyphoi* (drinking cups; *skyphos*, sing.) (fig. 9.8).

The sherds collected during the excavations of the Malloura sanctuary are mostly Cypriot. Whereas Cypriot ceramics of the Geometric period show a remarkable uniformity — local productions being only recognizable by the use of various clays — morphological and stylistic particularities become apparent from the Cypro-Archaic I period onward. This coincides with the first attestation of the existence of Cypriot kingdoms on the stele of the Assyrian king Sargon, erected at the end of the eighth century BC (709/707) at Kition-*Bamboula* (Yon and Malbran-Labat 1995). If the island was already divided into different kingdoms before that time — and there are good reasons to believe it was (Iacovou 2002 and 2008) — the Assyrian domination led to major changes in their organiza-

tion. Officially recognized as kings by the Assyrian sovereign, the Cypriot vassals voluntarily agreed to pay tribute to the empire, which implied a greater control and exploitation of their own territories. Some years later, ten Cypriot kingdoms, assigned to a capital city and a territory of the same name, were listed on a prism of Esarhaddon (673/672 BC). The submission to Assyria thus certainly acted as an impetus to promote and consolidate the Cypriot kingdoms. One aspect of this territorial and political consolidation is the formation of distinct cultural identities, for which ceramics offers ample evidence. Gjerstad already distinguished between an Cypro-Archaic western repertoire, where Cypro-Geometric patterns, especially concentric circles, predominate, and an eastern one, which uses figurative, especially floral and faunal, decoration (Gjerstad 1960: 105–6). More precise distinctions were to be made, he added, by studying ceramics site by site and publishing monographs. Local studies are beginning to fill the gap (Alpe and Fourrier 2003; Fourrier 2006). Some features of the vases discovered at Malloura are typical of the Cypro-Archaic production at Idalion, one of the Cypriot kingdoms listed on Esarhaddon's prism, which lies several kilometers to the west of Malloura. For example, the sanctuary has yielded Cypro-Archaic sherds belonging to small White Painted and Bichrome footed amphorae with vertical handles (fig. 9.9), of a type well-known by the discoveries of the Swedish Cyprus Expedition at Idalion (Gjerstad et al. 1937: pls. 166–67). Broadly speaking, the stylistic tendencies of the Idalion Cypro-Archaic pottery perfectly reflect the geographical location of this inland kingdom; the floral patterns point to Gjerstad's "Oriental Style," whereas the Cypro-Geometric designs are the same as those employed by the western workshops. Toward the end of the Cypro-Archaic period and in the following Cypro-Classical, the local potters often decorated the simple Plain White Ware vases with small clay discs, generally placed on the junction between the handle and the rim of jugs (fig. 9.10). This decorative pattern is not unknown elsewhere in Cyprus, as at Kition or Amathous, but it is especially common at Idalion and at the neighboring site of Athienou-*Golgoi* (Bakalakis 1988: 86, fig. 53; for connections to Golgoi, see also Counts, Ch. 11). The evidence thus suggests that the Malloura sanctuary was in the cultural sphere of influence of the Idalion kingdom and most plausibly located within its territory in the Cypro-Archaic period (see also Averett, Ch. 10, Counts, Ch. 11 and Cova, Ch. 13). The conquest of Idalion by the Phoenician kings of Kition and the abolition of the former kingdom in the first half of the fifth century BC certainly had radical consequences on the political topography of the Mesaoria. But it is still difficult to know if Golgoi was then subordinated to Kition or to Salamis.

In this respect, the Malloura sanctuary is not a rural one, if one understands this as a remote, isolated place, far away from the political, religious, and cultural center, but rather an extra-urban sanctuary, a place located outside the center but closely linked to it as an important and integral part of the kingdom. The exquisite quality and the number of the offerings dedicated at Malloura point to numerous visits by rich devotees, not only by local residents of a neighboring community. For example, the most expensive limestone sculptures may have been consecrated by an elite that gravitated

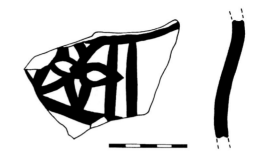

Fig. 9.9 *Sherd belonging to a White Painted IV footed amphora typical of the Idalion repertoire, sherd inv. no. 3211.1 (drawing: P. Lanzarote and J. Ravenhurst).*

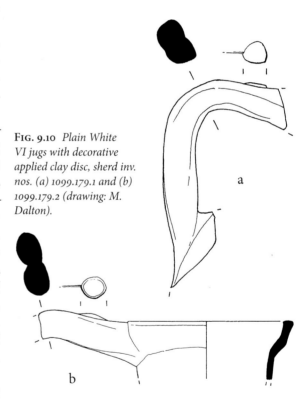

Fig. 9.10 *Plain White VI jugs with decorative applied clay disc, sherd inv. nos. (a) 1099.179.1 and (b) 1099.179.2 (drawing: M. Dalton).*

around the Idalion king's court. It is even possible that processions took place on certain occasions, such as feasts, leading from the political capital city to the sanctuary, as was the case from Paphos to Palaepaphos in the Hellenistic and Roman periods (Strabo 14.6.3; Maier 2004: 27).

Center and periphery were indeed intimately linked in the Iron Age kingdoms' organization. The multiplication of extra-urban sanctuaries from the Cypro-Archaic I period onward reflects an increase in the rural population, but it coincides also with the consolidation of the Cypriot kingdoms. Sanctuaries served as remarkable organizational instruments (Fourrier 2007: 121–24; Ulbrich 2008): they gathered communities around common cults and celebrations, and they may have played a political and economic role also. The Malloura sanctuary, located on a rich agricultural plain, may have marked the transformation of a wild land into an arable territory (de Polignac 1996: 52–60). It is no surprise, then, that the sanctuary was consecrated to the Cypriot Apollo, whose civilizing virtues are well-known (Cayla 2005). Cypriot sanctuaries possessed land, as we know from the Sanctuary of Athena at Idalion thanks to the syllabic inscription of the well-known bronze tablet (Masson 1983: no. 217, 20), and we may presume that, like Greek sanctuaries, they could also possess cattle and collect taxes from their renting. They were thus essential relays in the administration of the highly centralized states that were the Iron Age Cypriot kingdoms.

If the Malloura sanctuary was founded, as it seems, in the Cypro-Geometric III period, it is one of the most ancient Cypriot extra-urban sanctuaries (Al-Radi 1983: 87–8). Its foundation may even be more ancient than the settlement at neighboring Golgoi, which so far has not yielded Geometric material (Bakalakis 1988). Its importance, like that of the Agios Photios sanctuary, may have given impulse to the development of the site of Golgoi, which, from a secondary town in the Cypro-Archaic period, eventually became a city in the Hellenistic era (Hermary 2004).

This last period (Hellenistic I) is best documented in the ceramic assemblages from the Malloura sanctuary. Repetitive and insignificant through the lens of a qualitative analysis, the Plain White Ware that characterizes this chronological horizon, the last flourishing of the sanctuary's activity, acquires historical value through a quantitative analysis. As humble as they are, the Plain White ceramics from Malloura confirm the importance of Golgoi in the Hellenistic period and its probable role as capital of the district (Hermary 2004: 55–57).

Contrary to limestone sculptures and terracotta figurines, the ceramics from the Malloura sanctuary lack iconographic clues that might help in defining the personality of the deity to whom the sanctuary was consecrated; but they give a chronological and cultural frame that helps reconstruct history. Malloura appears not only as a very special sanctuary, where unique votives were dedicated, but also as a typical Cypriot extra-urban sanctuary of the Iron Age.

References

Alpe, L., and Fourrier, S.
2003   Une production originale d'Amathonte. *Cahiers du Centre d'Etudes Chypriotes* 33: 149–67.

Al-Radi, S. M. S.
1983   *Phlamoudhi Vounari: A Sanctuary Site in Cyprus.* Studies in Mediterranean Archaeology 65. Göteborg: Åström.

Arcelin, P., and Tuffreau-Libre, M.
1998   *La quantification des céramiques. Conditions et protocole, Bibracte* 2. Glux-en-Glenne: Centre Archéologique Européen du Mont-Beuvray.

Bakalakis, G.
1988   Ανασκαφή στο Λόφο Γιόρκους ΒΑ της Αθηαίνου, Κύπρος. Athens: Αρχαιολογική Εταιρεία Αθηνών .

Cayla, J.-B.
2005   Apollon ou la vie sauvage: à propos de quelques épiclèses d'Apollon à Chypre. Pp. 227–40 in *Nommer les dieux. Théonymes, épithètes, épiclèses dans l'Antiquité,* eds. N. Belayche, P. Brulé, G. Freyburger, Y. Lehmann, L. Pernot, and Fr. Prost. Recherches sur les rhétoriques religieuses 5. Turnhout: Brepols.

Coldstream, J. N.
1979   Geometric Skyphoi in Cyprus. *Report of the Department of Antiquities, Cyprus*: 255–69.
1987   The Greek Geometric and Archaic Imports. Pp. 21–31 in *La nécropole d'Amathonte, tombes 113–367, II. Céramiques non chypriotes.* Etudes Chypriotes 8, eds. V. Karageorghis and O. Picard. Nicosia: Department of Antiquities, Ecole française d'Athènes, A. G. Leventis Foundation.

de Polignac, F.

1996   *La naissance de la cité grecque,* second revised edition. Paris: La découverte.

Dikaios, P.

1963   A "Royal" Tomb at Salamis, Cyprus. *Archäologischer Anzeiger*: 126–210.

Flourentzos, P.

1981   Four Early Iron Age Tombs from Nicosia Old Municipality. *Report of the Department of Antiquities, Cyprus*: 115–28.

Fourrier, S.

2006   Les deux dépôts archaïques. Pp. 49–126 in *Amathonte VI. Le sanctuaire d'Aphrodite des origines au début de l'époque impériale.* Etudes Chypriotes 17, dir. S. Fourrier and A. Hermary. Athens and Paris: Ecole française d'Athènes and A.G. Leventis Foundation.

2007   *La Coroplastie Chypriote archaïque. Identités culturelles et politiques à l'époque des royaumes.* Travaux de la Maison de l'Orient et de la Méditerranée 46. Lyon: Maison de l'Orient et de la Méditerranée.

Gjerstad, E.

1948   *The Swedish Cyprus Expedition,* IV.2. *The Cypro-Geometric, Cypro-Archaic and Cypro-Classical Periods.* Stockholm: The Swedish Cyprus Expedition.

1960   Pottery Types, Cypro-Geometric to Cypro-Classical. *Opuscula Atheniensia* 3: 105–22.

1977   *Greek Geometric and Archaic Pottery Found in Cyprus. Acta Atheniensia* 26. Stockholm: Åström.

1979   A Cypro-Greek Royal Marriage in the 8th Century BC. Pp. 89–93 in *Studies Presented in Memory of Porphyrios Dikaios,* ed. V. Karageorghis. Nicosia: Lions Club of Nicosia and Zavallis.

Gjerstad, E.; Lindros, J.; Sjöqvist E.; and Westholm, A.

1937   *The Swedish Cyprus Expedition* II. Stockholm: The Swedish Cyprus Expedition.

Hermary, A.

2004   Autour de Golgoi : les cités de la Mesaoria à l'époque hellénistique et sous l'Empire. *Cahiers du Centre d'Etudes Chypriotes* 34: 47–68.

Iacovou, M.

2002   From Ten to Naught. Formation, Consolidation and Abolition of Cyprus' Iron Age Polities. *Cahiers du Centre d'Etudes Chypriotes* 32: 73–87.

2008   Cultural and Political Configurations in Iron Age Cyprus. The Sequel to a Protohistoric Episode. *American Journal of Archaeology* 112: 625–57.

Maier, F. G.

2004   *Guide to Palaipaphos (Kouklia).* Nicosia: Bank of Cyprus Cultural Foundation.

Masson, O.

1983   *Les inscriptions chypriotes syllabiques.* Etudes Chypriotes 1. Second revised edition. Paris: de Boccard.

Petit, T.

2002   Sanctuaires palatiaux d'Amathonte. *Cahiers du Centre d'Etudes Chypriotes* 32: 289–326.

Ulbrich, A.

2008   *Kypris. Heiligtümer und Kulte weiblicher Gottheiten auf Zypern in der kyproarchaischen und kyproklassischen Epoche (Königszeit).* Alter Orient und Altes Testament 44. Münster: Ugarit-Verlag.

Vandenabeele, F.

1985   Un dépôt de céramique archaïque chypriote dans un silo à Amathonte. *Bulletin de Correspondance Hellénique* 109: 629–55.

Webb, J.

1977   Late Cypriote Altars and Offering Structures. *Report of the Department of Antiquities, Cyprus:* 113–32.

1999   *Ritual Architecture, Iconography and Practice in the Late Cypriot Bronze Age.* Studies in Mediterranean Archaeology and Literature Pocket-book 75. Jonsered: Åström.

Yon, M.

1976   *Manuel de céramique chypriote. Collection de la Maison de l'Orient* 1. Lyon: Maison de l'Orient.

Yon, M., and Malbran-Labat, F.

1995   Stèle de Sargon II à Chypre. Pp. 161–79 in *Khorsabad, le palais de Sargon* II, ed. A. Caubet. Paris: La Documentation Française.

Chapter 10

The Ritual Context of the Malloura Terracotta Figurines

by Erin Walcek Averett

Dedicating votive gifts to deities was an integral part of most ancient Mediterranean religious systems (Rouse 1902; van Straten 1981; 1992; 2000; Bergman 1987; Connelly 1989; Snodgrass 1989–1990; Gill et al. 1998). These objects, often displayed in sanctuaries for generations, enhanced the sacred space through the repetition of religious imagery that created and affirmed socio-religious traditions and values (Renfrew 1985: 13–14, 22–24; 1994: 53–54). Votive offerings served as permanent displays of dedicatory gestures and as lasting visual reminders of ephemeral rituals, such as animal sacrifice, feasting, prayer, dance, music, and celebrations (fig. 10.1).

Terracotta figurines were among the most popular votive offerings in the eastern Mediterranean. Crafted of a humble material, clay, figurines are deceptively simple. The coroplasts who produced them, whether by hand, in a mold, or on the potter's wheel, imbued the artifacts with values meaningful to both producers and users. The figurines excavated from the rural sanctuary at Athienou-*Malloura* are a part of the larger Mediterranean and island tradition, but at the same time reflect local cult and society. The popularity and imagery of the figurines are invaluable for reconstructing ancient

cult and ritual behavior, especially when the cult is unattested in the textual and epigraphic record.

Votive figurines were the direct result of a cultic gesture whose primary motivation was communication with the divine. Ancient worshippers invested their gifts to the gods with meaning, though defining the precise significance is challenging. Votives and their dedicants, however, were part of a social structure with culturally determined systems of belief and ways of expressing this belief. Despite the variety of personal motivations for offering, votives followed patterns of standardized types with a repetition of meaningful symbols expressing the desires, hopes, and concerns of the worshippers in a dramatic and visual way. Local and comparative investigation of these symbols brings us closer to reconstructing this ancient Cypriot cult.

The Malloura Figurines in Context

Worshippers offered terracotta figurines throughout the life of the Malloura sanctuary. The rural sanctuary was an open-air *temenos* (sacred precinct) defined by *periboloi* (enclosure walls) that encircled a series of small buildings and an altar. In Cypriot sanctuaries, votive statues were often

FIG. 10.1 *Votive relief with worship and banqueting scene, allegedly from Golgoi, fourth century BC. H: 31.8 cm (photo: © The Metropolitan Museum of Art / Art Resource, NY).*

displayed around the altar or along the walls (Senff 1993; see also Alroth 1988), and it is likely that many of the Malloura figurines were originally deposited in a similar fashion. Unfortunately, most figurines were removed from their original display location.

More than 600 figurines and figurine fragments have been excavated to date. Like many votives, most of the figurines from Malloura were discovered in secondary depositional contexts, which provide little stratigraphic evidence for dating since most of these deposits include a broad range of chronological material. During the late-fourth-century BC reorganization of the sanctuary, most of the earlier votives, including the figurines, were buried as fill for the new floor or built into new walls. Many of the figurines were also found in contaminated contexts, especially in the abundance of 20th-century looters' pits scattered throughout the sanctuary. The lack of closed deposits necessitates dating the figurines broadly based on style.

While there are no inscriptions that identify the deity or deities worshipped at Malloura, the abundance of votive offerings provides insight into the nature of the cult and deity. An analysis of individual votive types as well as a comparative approach to the material remains of the Malloura cult suggest that there was a meaningful pattern of religious iconography. An investigation of the types, quantities, and relation of the figurines to other religious objects from the sanctuary facilitates reconstructing past systems of activities (Hodder 1986: 3, 6; Glassie 1999: 47) and understanding the religious significance of the figurines, their dedicators, and the practice of Cypriot religion in this rural center. As Joyce Marcus (Hamilton et al. 1996: 286) asserts in her study of figurines and women's ritual in ancient Oaxaca, Mexico, we can learn a great deal about ancient rituals by studying the pattern of artifacts in the places where they were performed. Ritual is defined as a religious action repeatedly performed in prescribed ways. Objects involved in ritual, therefore, display patterns of use and discard that coincide with the rites performed (Rappaport 1979: 176). The study of such objects provides evidence for the nature of ritual.

FIG. 10.2 *Bearded face and neck from life-size terracotta statue from Athienou-Malloura, Cypro-Archaic. AAP-AM 3600: Larnaka District Museum, Cyprus (© AAP).*

The Malloura figurine types correspond to assemblages from Cypriot sanctuaries dedicated to male deities throughout the island. Male deities received figurines depicting male worshippers, priests, warriors, and horsemen, while goddesses received figurines of elaborately garbed women, nude females, and pregnant and kourotrophic figures (Ulbrich 2008: 65–102). The sanctuaries of the Mesaoria follow this islandwide pattern; the male votives from the Malloura shrine contrast with the female votives from the nearby goddess sanctuaries at Akhna, Arsos, and Idalion (Ulbrich 2008: 305–6, 313–14, 447–48). Despite regional stylistic and manufacturing preferences, the cultic iconography suggests there was an islandwide visual religious vocabulary.

The Malloura sanctuary functioned as an inland rural shrine, closest to the urban centers of Golgoi and Idalion. Several studies have examined the political implications of artistic styles and workshops on Cyprus, linking stylistic schools with the political boundaries and cultural identities of the royal kingdoms (for figurines, see Monloup 1984; Yon and Caubet 1988; Caubet and Yon 1989; Caubet 1991; 1992; Winter 1991; 1996; Fourrier 1999; 2004; 2007; Nys and Recke 2004). Sabine Fourrier's (2007) study of Archaic figurine production identifies nine distinct coroplastic workshops, whose distribution, she argues, marks the boundaries of the kingdoms. The coroplastic style of Idalion dominates the central region of Cyprus, including the Malloura valley (Fourrier 2007: 39–51, 113, fig. 9), and it is possible that the Malloura sanctuary

was among the religious centers in the territory of the kingdom of Idalion in the Cypro-Archaic and early part of the Cypro-Classical periods (see Fourrier, Ch. 9, and Cova, Ch. 13). The iconography and style of the Malloura figurines suggest that this extra-urban sanctuary, far from being isolated, operated within the general religious traditions of the island, which are found in urban and rural centers, coastal and inland sites.

The coroplastic dedications at Malloura include handmade, wheel-made, and mold-made figures and figurines. Recent excavations have unearthed several fragments of terracotta statues and statuettes, including two slightly under-life-size early Cypro-Archaic heads (fig. 10.2). The Malloura sanctuary has additionally yielded a rich collection of anthropomorphic and grotesque votive masks, which will be the subject of a forthcoming study. This chapter, however, focuses on the small-scale handmade terracotta figurines.

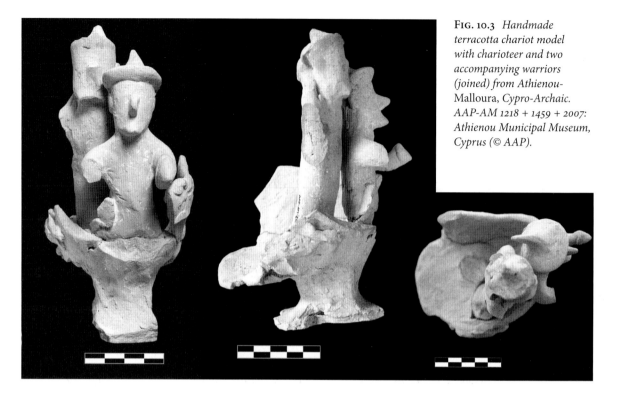

FIG. 10.3 *Handmade terracotta chariot model with charioteer and two accompanying warriors (joined) from Athienou-*Malloura, *Cypro-Archaic.* AAP-AM 1218 + 1459 + 2007: *Athienou Municipal Museum, Cyprus (© AAP).*

CHARIOT GROUPS

Terracotta chariot groups are among the most popular and elaborate of the votive figurines found in Cypriot sanctuaries. Chariot groups have been found at Marion (Serwint 1991), Ayia Irini (Gjerstad et al. 1935: 683, 706–14, 736–48), Kourion (Winter 1996: 100–106, 117–20; Young and Young 1955: 54–169), Meniko (Karageorghis 1977: 26–27, pls. 8, 25), Tamassos (Bossert 1951: no. 137; Masson 1964: 235, fig. 20), and Ayios Therapon-*Silithkia* in the Limassol District (Karageorghis 1995: 111). Although war chariots seem to be used on the island in the Late Bronze Age until the end of the fifth century, terracotta depictions of chariot groups begin in the Cypro-Archaic period and continue through the Hellenistic period. Most date to the seventh and sixth centuries (Littauer and Crouwel 1977: 72–73; Crouwel 1987: 101; Karageorghis 1995: 100–120; see also Herodotos 5.111–13). Chariots also had a funerary symbolism suggested by the presence of model as well as actual chariots in burials. Based on artistic representations and real chariots excavated from the royal necropolis at Salamis, Crouwel (1987:

115) concludes that Cypriot chariots were similar in form and function to those from Assyria, the Levant, and Urartu.

At the Malloura sanctuary, chariot groups are the most common and ambitious of the terracotta dedications, with at least 100 fragments of chariot groups retrieved to date. The groups are small and handmade; no examples of larger chariot groups or wheel-made models, such as those found at the Apollo Hylates sanctuary at Kourion (Young and Young 1955: 54–56, pl. 18, no. 1047), have been found. The Malloura chariot groups, none of which is completely preserved, consist of a handmade base, either a roughly modeled platform or pedestal, the chariot box with two or three occupants (a charioteer, a warrior, and sometimes a third attendant), and two or four draft horses attached by poles. The chariot boxes consist of a single compartment, open at the back, with a charioteer and one or two accompanying warriors (fig. 10.3). One preserved chariot box (fig. 10.4) is more elaborate: a central partition, a distinctly Cypriot element, divides the box into two sections, and is also found on the chariot models from Ayia Irini and on actual chariots unearthed from the Salamis burials

FIG. 10.4 *Handmade terracotta chariot box divided into two sections, with remains of three riders as well as a vertical loop inside from Athienou-Malloura, Cypro-Archaic. AAP-AM 589 + 1193: Larnaka District Museum, Cyprus (© AAP).*

(Karageorghis 1973: 73, pls. 28, 29; Crouwel 1987: 102, 104, 115). The central partition abuts a vertical loop in the center rear of the floor, which would have served as a brace for the front breastwork and additionally would have aided in mounting the chariot, served as support for the occupants while driving, and could have supported a shield (Littauer and Crouwel 1977: 69; Crouwel 1987: 102, 104–5). The remains of two passengers, perhaps both drivers, stand in the front of the box on either side of the central partition, while a lower torso of a third passenger remains next to the rear loop (for a preserved example with two drivers from Meniko, see Karageorghis 1977: 26–27, no. 12, pl. 8). The exterior of the chariot was modeled in detail as well, with a preserved hole for the axle and wheels.

The Malloura chariots contain one to three passengers; the presence of three or sometimes even four occupants is not uncommon in artistic depictions of chariots on Cyprus (Crouwel 1987: 104). The Malloura occupants are often bearded and wear peaked caps that fold over or conical helmets, some with ear caps. The chariots from Ayia Irini often contain three occupants, including a driver and archer or spear bearer in the front (the driver usually on the right), with a shield bearer standing at the rear of the chariot (Crouwel 1987: 112, pls. 37–38). Fragmentary charioteers can be identified as drivers by their arm position, stretched forward with fists clenched to hold the reins (figs. 10.5–6). The bodies of the front occupants are more summarily modeled as cylinders attached directly to the floor or wall of the chariot box. The armed crews of the Malloura chariots indicate that these are war chariots, in keeping with other chariot depictions on Cyprus, and reference the actual use of chariots in warfare in the Cypro-Archaic period (Crouwel 1987: 112–13; Herodotos 5.113). The horses are attached to the chariot by one or two poles joined to yokes (figs. 10.7–8). They wear harnesses, bands, blinkers, and breastplates or dangling tassels (Crouwel 1987: 112–13).

INDIVIDUAL WARRIORS

There are just over twenty excavated fragments of handmade warrior figurines from Malloura

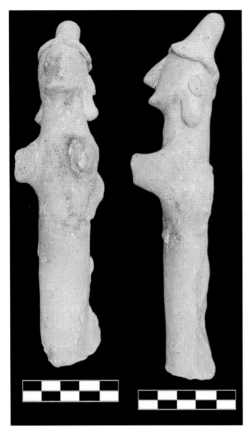

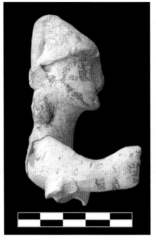

FIG. 10.6 *Handmade terracotta chariteer from Athienou-*Malloura, *Cypro-Archaic. AAP-AM 653: Larnaka District Museum, Cyprus (© AAP).*

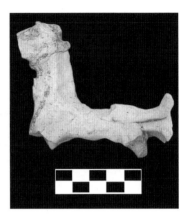

FIG. 10.7 *Terracotta chariot horse with remnants of yoke from Athienou-*Malloura. *Cypro-Archaic. AAP-AM 1690: Larnaka District Museum, Cyprus (© AAP).*

FIG. 10.5 *Handmade terracotta charioteer from Athienou-*Malloura, *Cypro-Archaic. AAP-AM 3535: Larnaka District Museum, Cyprus (© AAP).*

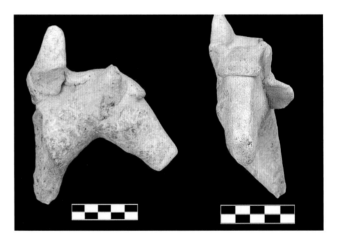

FIG. 10.8 *Terracotta chariot horse with remnants of blinkers and yoke from Athienou-*Malloura, *Cypro-Archaic. AAP-AM 1858: Larnaka District Museum, Cyprus (© AAP).*

(figs. 10.9–10). Handmade warrior figurines were dedicated at other sanctuaries of male deities, including Ayia Irini (Gjerstad et al. 1935: nos. 699, 705, 709, 717, 745, pl. 231:3, 7, 232:7; Karageorghis 1995: 31, nos. 32, 35; 33, no. 42; 34, nos. 1–3; 36, no. 10) and Meniko-*Litharkes* (Karageorghis 1977: 26, 37, pl. V6, no. 9; 1995: 32, no. 40). They were also found in tombs at Kourion-*Kaloriziki* (Young and Young 1955: 27, pl. 61, nos. 404–5, 749–50; Karageorghis 1995: 29–30, nos. 25–29) and Amathous (Karageorghis 1995: 35, no. 5).

At Malloura, the warriors are armed with shields, helmets, and weapons. No complete standing warrior has been found, but the upper bodies and heads of several male figurines are preserved. Like the chariot passengers, the Malloura warriors wear

tall, folded caps or conical helmets. Two torsos (see figs. 10.9–10) preserve warriors with conical helmets wearing shields strapped to their backs. Details of the figurines, including facial features, dress, and shields, are painted in red and black. Because these warriors are fragmentary, it is likely that some of the warriors rode in chariots.

FIG. 10.9 *Handmade terracotta warrior with shield from Athienou-Malloura, Cypro-Archaic. AAP-AM 2100: Larnaka District Museum, Cyprus (© AAP).*

→ FIG. 10.10 *Handmade terracotta warrior with shield from Athienou-Malloura, Cypro-Archaic. AAP-AM 2675: Larnaka District Museum, Cyprus (© AAP).*

Horse-and-Rider Figurines

Horse-and-rider figurines are especially popular in Iron Age Greece (particularly in the Argolid and Boeotia), the Near East, and on Cyprus and appear roughly contemporaneously in all three areas (for transmission of type, see Monloup 1984: 41ff.; Crouwel and Tatton-Brown 1988). The tradition of horse-and-rider figurines on Cyprus dates back to the Cypro-Geometric I period (Monloup 1984: 37–46; Crouwel and Tatton-Brown 1988: 77; Karageorghis 1993a: 65–67, 88–90), but the numbers drastically increase in the eighth and seventh centuries (Crouwel and Tatton-Brown 1988: 77; Karageorghis 1995: 61–93).

Horse-and-rider figurines have been found at Marion (Serwint 1991), Ayia Irini (Törnkvist 1970: nos. 921–22), Idalion, and Salamis, and the nearby Cellarka necropolis (Karageorghis 1970: 230; Monloup 1984: nos. 149–243), but the type was especially abundant at the Apollo Hylates sanctuary at Kourion (Young and Young 1955: 191–233; Monloup 1984: 37–46; Winter 1996). Horse-and-rider groups were also popular as grave goods, and are found in tombs at Amathous and Salamis (Karageorghis 1987: 24–25, 33–34).

There are approximately a dozen horse-and-rider groups from Malloura, and most are not well-preserved. Although many horse-and-rider figurines from Cyprus are armed, the Malloura riders are not overtly militaristic and none are shown in "action" poses, brandishing spears or weapons, as do some of the Kourion riders (Crouwel and Tatton-Brown 1988: 81). One fragment (fig. 10.11) preserves most of the horse with a bridle and harness with tassels hanging at the neck, as well as the saddlecloth and the legs of the rider. Another, smaller example (fig. 10.12) from Malloura depicts a handmade horse with rider pressed onto its back, with no saddlecloth or legs modeled but perhaps originally painted. The horse is short and simple, with a short snout, pointed ears, and forelock of hair; the rider's torso is attached directly to the horse's back, with no legs modeled and hands smoothed to the horse's neck. The rider has a prominent nose, long hair, and pronounced ears.

With the advent and greater skill of equitation in the Archaic period, horses were increasingly used in cavalry units in contemporary warfare. In Assyria, from the ninth century onward, mounted warriors rode alongside chariots, which served primarily as mobile platforms for archers (Littauer and Crouwel 1977: 130–39; Crouwel 1987: 112; Crouwel and Tatton-Brown 1988: 83). Cavalry was superior to chariots because it was cheaper, more mobile in various terrains, and could be used both to protect infantry on the march and as scouts and messengers (Crouwel and Tatton-Brown 1988: 83). The dedication of armed horse riders at other sanctuaries and tombs suggests a link to a contemporary military elite. The simple and seemingly unarmed Malloura riders, however, perhaps suggest ceremonial use.

FEMALE FIGURINES

Female iconography is rare at Malloura. While male imagery dominates both the limestone and terracotta assemblages, a few female figurines have been excavated, including a Cypro-Archaic handmade female head and a Cypro-Classical mold-made female head originally attached to a vase. The only well-preserved figurine from Malloura is a so-called Astarte figurine (fig. 10.13). This female figure stands on a small, rounded base and holds both hands cupped beneath her breasts. The figurine was pressed into a mold, resulting in a flat back with detailed front. The woman depicted wears a Greek-inspired garment and dons a simple conical-shaped headdress and veil. She is bejeweled with a pendant necklace and a longer beaded necklace with a pendant hanging between her breasts. Bracelets adorn both arms. There is another figurine torso from Malloura of a similar bejeweled female that is likely from the same mold as figure 10.13. Mold-made female figurines in this pose are common at goddess sanctuaries and tombs throughout the island, including Kition, Idalion, Tamassos, Arsos, Akhna, and Lapithos, but are most numerous at Amathous (Karageorghis 1999: Type I, 1–67, pls. 1–18; Ulbrich 2008: 70–77, pls. 11–12). They were likely inspired by Near Eastern examples, perhaps imported to

FIG. 10.11 *Handmade terracotta horse and rider from Athienou-Malloura, Cypro-Archaic. AAP-AM 1099: Larnaka District Museum, Cyprus (© AAP).*

FIG. 10.12 *Handmade terracotta horse and rider from Athienou-Malloura, Cypro-Archaic. AAP-AM 1530: Larnaka District Museum, Cyprus (© AAP).*

FIG. 10.14 *Handmade terracotta figurine depicting a man wearing a bull mask and cape from Athienou-*Malloura, *Cypro-Archaic. AAP-AM 1170: Athienou Municipal Museum, Cyprus (© AAP).*

FIG. 10.13 *Mold-made terracotta "Astarte" figurine from Athienou-*Malloura, *late Cypro-Archaic–early Cypro-Classical. AAP-AM 1366 + 1595: Athienou Municipal Museum, Cyprus (© AAP).*

the island by the Phoenicians (Karageorghis 1999: 1–2). The type first appears in the early seventh century and continues into the Cypro-Classical period.

The two mold-made female figurines from Malloura are closest in style and dress to female figurines from a sanctuary in the region of Chytroi and from tombs in Nicosia and Amathous (Karageorghis 1987: 36, pl. 38; 1999: 67, 189–90, nos. 184, 128–30; Ikosi 1993). These figurines are dated to the end of the Cypro-Archaic/beginning of the Cypro-Classical period. The overall rarity of female votive or divine iconography at Malloura suggests there was no official or popular goddess cult at the sanctuary (for Artemis at Athienou-*Malloura*, see Counts and Toumazou 2003). The few female dedications represent rare offerings.

MASKED MEN

Rituals involving a variety of masks were a component of the Malloura cult. In addition to several votive mask fragments, two terracotta figurines depicting masked men have been found at the sanctuary. An especially well-preserved figurine of a man wearing a bull mask, headdress, and cape is one of the best examples of this type from Cyprus (fig. 10.14). Another fragmentary anthropomorphic torso with the head of a ram, perhaps a masked man, was unearthed in 2007.

The tradition of zoomorphic masks on Cyprus, especially bull masks, is well-known and began at least as early as Late Cypriot III, when altered bucrania were displayed at the 12th- and 11th-century sanctuaries at Enkomi and the Late Cypriot III sanctuary at Kition (Karageorghis 1971: 262–63; Caubet and Courtois 1975; Courtois 1982; Karageorghis and Demas 1985: 260; Nobis 1985; Karageorghis 1988; 1993b: 118–22; 1995: 55–57; Belgiorno 1993; Rice 1998: Ch. 15; see also Karageorghis 2006: 160, for a possible earlier example). Not all scholars accept that these bucrania were used as masks (see Nys 1995: 26–27; contra Karageorghis 1996). It is possible that the backs of the bucrania were smoothed to facilitate hanging of the masks on walls, benches, or poles (see Burkert 1983: 2). Nys notes the fire marks and pieces of charcoal associated with the Enkomi skulls, suggesting that they were offered as burnt sacrifice.

The bucrania masking tradition continued or revived in the Iron Age as evidenced by similar worked bull skulls from Toumba tou Skourou (Vermeule 1974: 149–50, fig. 29; Vermeule and Wolsky 1990: 390–91, ill. 9) and from the Iron Age sanctuary of Astarte at Kition (Karageorghis 1993a: 70; Smith 2009: 120–25). These horned bovine skulls were carefully worked, suggesting an important ritual use, likely worn as masks, and/or displayed on sacred architecture (Karageorghis 1971: 161; 1996; Nys 1995; see also O'Bryhim 1999).

Images of animal-masked men and bull masks are not unique to Cyprus. Iron Age bull-skull masks similar to Cypriot examples have been found at Megiddo (May and Engberg 1935: 23, pl. 19), and a seventh-century terracotta figurine of a man wearing a bull mask was found at Sidon (Contenau 1921: 314, fig. 102; for other examples, see Smith 1990: 134–35 n. 47; O'Bryhim 1999: 11). However, Cyprus has produced an abundance of masked figurines. Terracotta figurines clearly depicting men wearing anthropomorphic and zoomorphic masks have been found at the sanctuaries at Ayia Irini, Golgoi, Idalion, Kourion, and Peyia-*Maa*, as well as in tombs at Salamis, Ormidhia, and Amathous dating from the Cypro-Archaic through Cypro-Classical periods (Sjöqvist 1933; Young and Young 1955: 40–41, nos. 814–16, 823, 825–29, pl. 11; Karageorghis 1971; 1987: 16, pl. 2; 1995: 54–57, 136; 1990; Hermary 1979; 2000). A Hellenistic statue of a man holding a bull protome that likely references bull masks, allegedly from the temple at Golgoi, suggests a continuation of this practice into the Hellenistic period (Karageorghis 2000: 249, no. 403). O'Bryhim (1999) controversially proposes that the memory of this masking practice survived even until the Roman period, as evidenced in Ovid's story of the Cerastae from Cyprus. In addition to the masked

bull figurine, the number of incised cattle bones found at the sanctuary suggests a cultic role for this animal at Malloura (see Reese, Ch. 18).

Ethnographic studies demonstrate that masking rites strengthen the relationship between mortals and the divine in a tangible way (Napier 1986; Pernet 1992; Pollock 1995). The physical act of donning a symbol of the deity temporarily blurs the lines between the divine and mortal worlds in a literal and dramatic way. The ritual dramas enacted with masks, whether anthropomorphic, grotesque, or animal, enhanced the sacred aura and heightened religious experience for the participants.

Animal Figurines

Animals are among the most popular terracotta dedications at Mediterranean sanctuaries, and Malloura is no exception. Terracotta rams, bulls, birds, and possibly a lion were dedicated at Malloura. The overwhelming majority of zoomorphic figurines, however, represents horses, with more than 100 horse figurines and fragments from the sanctuary. The preponderance of horses is consistent with the sudden increase in equine and decrease in bovine figurines beginning at the end of the eighth century at Greek and Cypriot sanctuaries (Zimmerman 1989). Almost all Malloura horse figurines are handmade with cylindrical bodies, tapered legs, and long necks; the snouts are either tapered or flare out toward the muzzle, and many have painted facial details in red and black.

Given the high number of chariot group fragments, it is likely that many of the horse figurines originally belonged to chariot groups, and some possibly had riders. Many of the horses have either painted or plastically added reins or harnesses, suggesting that they belong to either chariot or rider groups. Regardless, the prevalence of the horse as a single animal, in chariot groups, and with riders among the coroplastic dedications at Malloura is significant. Despite the agricultural richness of the Mesaoria, agricultural animals are not prominent among the zoomorphic figurines from the Malloura sanctuary.

Figurines and the Malloura Cult

The plethora of votives, especially the figural works in limestone and terracotta, visually defined the Malloura cult. The votives vividly displayed sacred iconography through repetitious symbols. Religious imagery along with monumental architecture and the altar were hallmarks of the sacred space of Malloura. The terracotta and limestone votives were the most abundant and visible offerings there, yet there are interesting differences between the two groups. While the limestone votives depict worshippers and deities (see Counts, Ch. 11, and Cofer, Ch. 12), the terracottas primarily represent worshippers, with some possible exceptions. While the limestone dedications span the Cypro-Archaic through Hellenistic phases of the sanctuary, the terracotta figurines were a distinct part of the Malloura cult only in the Cypro-Archaic period, a pattern typical of Cypriot cults. The dedication of terracotta figurines is drastically reduced at Malloura and other cults in the Cypro-Classical and Hellenistic periods.

The Malloura figurines have a social significance that belies their simple manufacture. The emphasis on the horse and its activities (horse riding, war, and chariots) suggests that the Malloura Valley occupants desired to stress elite military status over agricultural concerns. Regardless of the actual status or occupation of the dedicators, their visible display at a popular sanctuary advertised an elite message. The terracotta warriors and their animal par excellence thus paralleled the message sent by more monumental votives.

Sanctuaries were places where political ideologies and conflicts often played out. In Greece and on Cyprus, the critical period of state development (eighth and seventh centuries) also witnessed a proliferation of sanctuaries (de Polignac 1984; Rupp 1987; Snodgrass 1988; Fourrier 2007; Iacovou 2008, with earlier bibliography). Rural sanctuaries were especially important in demarcating zones of control and political power. Thus, far from functioning as isolated shrines visited only by farmers and shepherds, extra-urban sanctuaries like the one at Malloura could be key players in establishing sociopolitical power structures. Figurines, despite their humble medium and low intrinsic worth, could be active agents in constructing and maintaining social systems and values.

Acknowledgments

This study would not have been possible without the attentive guidance and support of Michael Toumazou and the Athienou Archaeological Project. I would also like to thank Derek Counts and Nick Kardulias for their careful comments and insights. Special thanks go to Adam Prins for preparing the images for publication. All errors remain my own.

References

Alroth, B.
1988   The Positioning of Greek Votive Figurines. Pp. 195–203 in *Early Greek Cult Practice: Proceedings of the Fifth International Symposium at the Swedish Institute at Athens, 26–29 June, 1986*, eds. R. Hägg, N. Marinatos, G. Nordquist. Stockholm: Aström.

Belgiorno, M. R.
1993   Maschere di bovidi e capridi nel rituale religioso egeo-cipriota. *Studi micenei ed egeo-anatolici* 31: 43–54.

Bergman, J.
1987   Religio-Phenomenological Reflections on the Multi-Level Process of Giving to the Gods. Pp. 31–42 in *Gifts to the Gods: Proceedings of the Uppsala Symposium 1985*, eds. T. Linders and G. C. Nordquist. Boreas: Uppsala Studies in Ancient Mediterranean and Near Eastern Civilizations 15. Uppsala: Acta Universitatis Upsaliensis.

Bossert, H. T.
1951   *Altsyrien. Kunst und Handwerk in Cypern, Syrien, Palästina, Transjordan und Arabien in der Griechisch-Römischen Kultur.* Tübingen: Wasmuth.

Burkert, W.
1983   *Homo Necans: The Anthropology of Ancient Greek Sacrificial Ritual and Myth.* Berkeley: University of California.

Caubet, A.
1991   Recherche sur les ateliers de terre cuites de la partie occidentale de Chypre. Pp. 109–14 in *Cypriote Terracottas: Proceedings of the First International Conference of Cypriote Studies. Brussels-Liège-Amsterdam, 29 May–1 June 1989*, eds. F. Vandenabeele and R. Laffineur. Brussels and Liège: A. G. Leventis Foundation.
1992   The Terracotta Workshops of Idalion during the Cypro-Archaic Period. Pp. 128–51 in *Acta Cypria: Acts of an International Congress on Cypriote Archaeology Held in Göteborg on 22–24 August 1991*, vol. 3, ed. P. Åström. Studies in Mediterranean Archaeology and Literature Pocket-book 120. Jonsered: Åström.

Caubet, A., and Courtois, J-C.
1975   Masques chypriotes en terre cuite de XIIe s. av. J.C. *Report of the Department of Antiquities, Cyprus*: 43–49.

Caubet, A., and Yon, M.
1989   Ateliers de figurines à Kition. Pp. 28–43 in *Cyprus and the East Mediterranean in the Iron Age: Proceedings of the Seventh British Museum Classical Colloquium, April 1988*, ed. V. Tatton-Brown. London: British Museum Publications.

Connelly, J. B.
1989   Standing Before One's God: Votive Sculpture and the Cypriot Religious Tradition. *Biblical Archaeologist* 52: 210–18.

Contenau, G.
1921   *Mission archéologique à Sidon (1914).* Paris: Geuthner.

Counts, D. B., and Toumazou, M. K.
2003   Artemis at Malloura? *Cahiers du Centre d'Etudes Chypriotes* 33: 237–51.

Courtois, J.-C.
1982   Un masque en terre cuite d'Enkomi. *Report of the Department of Antiquities, Cyprus*: 69–71.

Crouwel, J.
1987   Chariots in Iron Age Cyprus. *Report of the Department of Antiquities, Cyprus*: 101–18.

Crouwel, J., and Tatton-Brown, V.
1988   Ridden Horses in Iron Age Cyprus. *Report of the Department of Antiquities, Cyprus*: 77–87.

de Polignac, F.
1984   *La naissance de la cité grecque.* Paris: La découverte.

Fourrier, S.
1999   Chypre et la Grèce de l'Est à l'époque archaïque (VIIe–Vie s. av. J.-C.). La plastique chypriote et les échanges en Méditerranée orientale. Unpublished Ph.D. dissertation, Université Lumière-Lyon.
2004   La coroplastie d'Idalion à l'époque archaïque. Ateliers et diffusion. *Cahiers du Centre d'Etudes Chypriotes* 34: 191–209.
2007   *La Coroplastie Chypriote archaïque. Identités culturelles et politiques à l'époque des royaumes.* Travaux de la Maison de l'Orient et de la Méditerranée 46. Lyon: Maison de l'Orient et de la Méditerranée.

Gill, C., Postlethwaite, N., and Seaford, R., eds.
1998   *Reciprocity in Ancient Greece.* Oxford: Oxford University.

Gjerstad, E.; Lindros, J.; Sjöqvist, E.; and Westholm A.
1935   *The Swedish Cyprus Expedition*, vol. 2: *Finds and Results of the Excavations in Cyprus, 1927–1931.* Stockholm: Swedish Cyprus Expedition.

Glassie, H.
1999   *Material Culture.* Bloomington and Indianapolis: Indiana University.

Hamilton, N.; Marcus, J.; Bailey, D.; Haaland, G.; Haaland, R.; and Ucko, P.

1996   Can We Interpret Figurines? *Cambridge Archaeological Journal* 6: 281–307.

Hermary, A.

1979   Statuette d'un "prêtre" masqué. *Bulletin de Correspondance Hellénique* 103: 734–41.

2000   *Amathonte V. Les figurines en terre cuite archaïques et classiques. Les Sculptures en Pierre.* Études Chypriotes 15. Athens: A. G. Leventis Foundation

Hodder, I.

1986   *Reading the Past: Current Approaches to Interpretations in Archaeology.* Cambridge: Cambridge University.

Iacovou, M.

2008   Cultural and Political Configurations in Iron Age Cyprus: The Sequel to a Protohistoric Episode. *American Journal of Archaeology* 112: 625–57.

Ikosi, G.

1993   Kythrea Temenos: Unpublished Material from the Swedish Cyprus Expedition. *Medelhavsmuseet Bulletin* 28: 11–81.

Karageorghis, J.

1999   *The Coroplastic Art of Ancient Cyprus 5. The Cypro-Archaic Period Small Female Figurines. B. Figurines moulées.* Nicosia: A. G. Leventis Foundation.

Karageorghis, V.

1970   *Excavations in the Necropolis of Salamis I.* Nicosia: Department of Antiquities.

1971   Notes on Some Cypriote Priests Wearing Bull-Masks. *Harvard Theological Review* 64: 261–70.

1973   *Excavations in the Necropolis of Salamis III.* Nicosia: Department of Antiquities.

1977   *Two Cypriote Sanctuaries of the End of the Cypro-Archaic Period.* Rome: Consiglio Nazionale delle Ricerche.

1987   The Terracottas. Pp. 1–54 in *La Nécropole d'amathonte tombes 113–367*, vol. 3.1. *The Terracottas.* Etudes Chypriotes 9. Nicosia: A. G. Leventis Foundation.

1988   Some Eleventh-Century BC Clay Masks from Kition. Pp. 65–67 in *Studies in Honour of T. B. L. Webster II*, eds. J. H. Betts, J.T. Hooker, J.R. Green, and T.B.L. Webster. Bristol: Bristol Classical.

1990   Notes on Some Terracotta Masks from Amathus now in the British Museum. *Rivista di studi fenici* 18: 3–5.

1993a   *The Coroplastic Art of Ancient Cyprus 2. Late Cypriote II–Cypro-Geometric III.* Nicosia: A. G. Leventis Foundation.

1993b   *The Coroplastic Art of Ancient Cyprus 3. The Cypro-Archaic Period: Large and Medium Size Sculpture.* Nicosia: A. G. Leventis Foundation.

1995   *The Coroplastic Art of Ancient Cyprus 4. The Cypro-Archaic Period: Small Male Figurines.* Nicosia: A. G. Leventis Foundation.

1996   The Use of Masks Again. *Journal of Prehistoric Religion* 10: 15–16.

2000   *Ancient Art from Cyprus: The Cesnola Collection in the Metropolitan Museum of Art.* New York: Metropolitan Museum of Art.

2006   *Aspects of Everyday Life in Ancient Cyprus: Iconographic Representations.* Nicosia: A. G. Leventis Foundation.

Karageorghis, V., and Demas, M.

1985   *The Pre-Phoenicians Levels. Areas I and II.* Excavations at Kition 5. Nicosia: Department of Antiquities for the Republic of Cyprus.

Littauer, M. A., and Crouwel, J. H.

1977   Terracotta Chariot Model. Pp. 67–73 in *Two Cypriote Sanctuaries of the End of the Cypro-Archaic Period*, by V. Karageorghis. Rome: Consiglio Nazionale delle Ricerche.

Masson, O.

1964   Kypriaka. *Bulletin de Correspondance Hellénique* 88: 199–238.

May, H., and Engberg, R. M.

1935   *Material Remains of the Megiddo Cult.* Chicago: University of Chicago.

Monloup, T.

1984   *Les figurines de terre cuite de tradition archaïque.* Salamis de Chypre 12. Paris: de Boccard.

Napier, A. D.
1986   *Masks, Transformation, and Paradox.*
        Berkeley: University of California.

Nobis, G.
1985   Tierreste aus dem Präphönizischen Kition.
        Pp. 416–33 in *Excavations at Kition 5. The Pre-
        Phoenician Levels. Part 2*, by V. Karageorghis
        and M. Demas. Nicosia: Department of
        Antiquities.

Nys, K.
1995   The Use of Masks in Cyprus during the Late
        Bronze Age. *Journal of Prehistoric Religion* 9:
        19–34.

Nys, K., and Recke, M.
2004   Craftsmanship and the Cultural/Political
        Identity of the Cypriote Kingdoms. *Cahiers du
        Centre d'Etudes Chypriotes* 34: 211–22.

O'Bryhim, S.
1999   The Cerastae and Phoenician Human Sacrifice
        on Cyprus. *Rivista di studi fenici* 27: 3–20.

Pernet, H.
1992   *Deceptions and Revelations.* Trans by L. Grillo.
        Columbia: University of South Carolina.

Pollock, D.
1995   Masks and the Semiotics of Identity. *The
        Journal of the Royal Anthropological Institute* 1:
        581–97.

Rappaport, R. A.
1979   *Ecology, Meaning, and Religion.* Richmond,
        CA: North Atlantic Books.

Renfrew, C.
1985   *The Archaeology of Cult: The Sanctuary at
        Phylakopi.* British School of Archaeology
        at Athens Supplement 18. London: Thames
        and Hudson.
1994   The Archaeology of Religion. Pp. 47–54 in
        *The Ancient Mind: Elements of Cognitive
        Archaeology*, eds. C. Renfrew and E. Zubrow.
        New Directions in Archaeology. Cambridge:
        Cambridge University.

Rice, M.
1998   *The Power of the Bull.* New York: Routledge.

Rouse, W. H. D.
1902   *Greek Votive Offerings: An Essay in the History
        of Greek Religion.* Cambridge: Cambridge
        University.

Rupp, D. W.
1987   Vive le Roi: The Emergence of the State in Iron
        Age Cyprus. Pp. 147–61 in *Western Cyprus
        Connections: An Archaeological Symposium
        held at Brock University, St. Catharines,
        Ontario, Canada, March 21–22, 1986*, eds.
        D. W. Rupp. Studies in Mediterranean
        Archaeology. Göteborg: Åström.

Senff, R.
1993   *Das Apollonheiligtum von Idalion: Architektur
        und Statuenausstattung eines zyprischen Hei-
        ligtums.* Studies in Mediterranean Archaeol-
        ogy 94. Jonsered: Åström.

Serwint, N.
1991   The Terracotta Sculpture from Marion. Pp.
        213–19 in *Cypriote Terracottas: Proceedings of
        the First International Conference of Cypriote
        Studies, Brussels-Liège-Amsterdam, 29 May–1
        June 1989*, eds. F. Vandenabcele and R. Laf-
        fineur. Brussels and Liège: A. G. Leventis
        Foundation.

Sjöqvist, E.
1933   Die Kultgeschichte eines cyprischen Temenos.
        Archiv für Religionswissenschaft 30: 308–59.

Smith, J. S.
2009   *Art and Society in Cyprus from the Bronze
        Age into the Iron Age.* Cambridge: Cambridge
        University.

Smith, M.
1990   *The Early History of God: Yahweh and the
        Other Deities in Ancient Israel.* San Francisco:
        Harper & Row.

Snodgrass, A. M.
1988   *Cyprus and Early Greek History.* Fourth An-
        nual Lecture on History and Archaeology.
        Nicosia: Cultural Foundation of the Bank of
        Cyprus.
1989–90   The Economics of Dedication at Greek
        Sanctuaries. *Scienze dell'Antichità: Storia,
        archeologia, antropologia* 3–4: 287–94.

Törnkvist, S.
1970   Arms, Armour and Dress of the Terracotta
        Figurines from Ayia Irini, Cyprus. Unpub-
        lished Ph.D. dissertation, Lund University.

Ulbrich, A.
2008   *Kypris: Heiligtümer und Kulte weiblicher Gott-
        heiten auf Zypern in der kyproarchaischen und
        kyproklassischen Epoche (Königszeit).* Münster:
        Ugarit-Verlag.

van Straten, F. T.
1981   Gifts for the Gods. Pp. 65–105 in *Faith, Hope,
        and Worship: Aspects of Religious Mentality in
        the Ancient World,* ed. H. S. Versnel. Studies in
        Greek and Roman Religion 2. Leiden: Brill.
2000   Votives and Votaries in Greek Sanctuaries. Pp.
        191–226 in *Oxford Readings in Greek Religion,*
        ed. R. Buxton. Oxford: Oxford University.

Vermeule, E. T.
1974   *Toumba tou Skourou: The Mound of Darkness.
        A Bronze Age Town on Morphou Bay in
        Cyprus.* Boston: Harvard University and
        Museum of Fine Arts.

Vermeule, E. T., and Wolsky, F. Z.
1990   *Toumba tou Skourou, A Bronze Age Potters'
        Quarter on Morphou Bay in Cyprus.*
        Cambridge, MA: Harvard University.

Winter, N.
1991   Terracotta Figurines from Kourion:
        The Workshops. Pp. 221–24 in *Cypriote
        Terracottas. Proceedings of the First
        International Conference of Cypriote Studies.
        Brussels, Liège, and Amsterdam, 29 May–1
        June 1989,* eds. F. Vandenabeele and R.
        Laffineur. Brussels and Liège: A. G. Leventis
        Foundation.
1996   The Terracottas. Pp. 89–137 in *The Sanctuary
        of Apollo Hylates at Kourion: Excavations in
        the Archaic Precinct,* ed. D. Buitron-Oliver.
        Studies in Mediterranean Archaeology 109.
        Jonsered: Åström.

Yon, M., and Caubet, A.
1988   Un culte populaire de la Grande Déesse
        à Lapithos. *Report of the Department of
        Antiquities, Cyprus*: 1–16.

Young, J. M., and Young, S. H.
1955   *Terracotta Figurines from Kourion in Cyprus.*
        Philadelphia: University Museum, University
        of Pennsylvania.

Zimmerman, J-L.
1989   *Les chevaux de bronze dans l'art géométrique
        grec.* Mainz: Philipp von Zabern.

Chapter 11

Local Styles and Regional Trends in Cypriot Limestone Sculpture

The Athienou School

by Derek B. Counts

Since the 1970s, the identification of regional styles within the diverse corpus of Greek sculpture from around the Mediterranean basin has remained a central focus of scholarly debate (for some earlier attempts, see Deonna 1909; Langlotz 1927). Spearheaded by the studies of J. Ducat (1971) and B. Freyer-Schauenburg (1974) and solidified by the monumental volume on Archaic Greek sculpture by B. Ridgway (1977, 1993), the recognition of regional variation in ancient sculpture has had an enormous impact on questions of chronology, provenience, and the social and economic interaction of artists and workshops.

The goals of such studies must be viewed in light of the research of G. Richter, whose volumes on Archaic Greek korai (1968) and kouroi (1970) still influence the study of Greek sculpture today. Richter advocated a linear development of stylistic changes based on the sculptor's constant struggle to create more naturalistic and anatomically accurate representations of the human form. The pitfalls of such an approach are obvious and many; perhaps the most injurious is the idea that sculptors in different parts of the Mediterranean and working under vastly different conditions would embrace a common artistic agenda. As Ridgway notes, Richter's emphasis on chronological, as opposed to geographical/regional, divisions for the kouroi and korai "contributed to obliterating the dividing lines between regional productions" (Ridgway 1993: 10). Since sculptural output is affected by the general conditions within which it was created and used, such as the availability of natural resources and the socio-political environment, it is reasonable to assume that workshops in regions under different rule and subject to different foreign influences will generate an equally diverse product in terms of style and iconography (Ridgway 1993: 10).

In the case of Cypriot sculpture, the rich corpus must be understood and studied within the context of local practice and not as a byproduct of Greek and/or Near Eastern traditions (Counts 2008: 12–15; contra Boardman [1995: 214] where Cypriot sculpture is dismissed as "broadly Greek" and relegated to a section on Levantine sculpture). The island possesses a distinguishable, though admittedly complex, sculptural style and typology. And while it is a relatively easy task to identify the products of Cypriot sculptors or sculptures produced under Cypriot influence found abroad (Sørensen 1978; Fourrier 1999; Counts 2001: 138–40), scholars have often struggled to isolate sculptural workshops within the island itself. Many proponents of classification based on regional variation have wisely cautioned against oversimplification (see, e.g., the discussions in Pedley 1976: 12–17; Ridgway 1977: 7–10; 1993: 10–11), and any attempts to discuss the nature and extent of regionalism in Cypriot limestone sculpture should take note of several important caveats:

(1) Provenience. With some notable exceptions, the bulk of sculpture known from the island was brought to light during late-19th- and early-20th-century explorations and often lacks secure provenience. The uncertainty of these early discoveries and the dearth of proper documentation have meant that exact findspots are often obscure or unknown.

(2) Limestone sources. The only extensive petrographic study of Cypriot sculptures, published by N. Kourou et al. (2002), focuses on limestone statuettes of Cypriot type found abroad. To date, there has been little published work on the sources of limestone used in sculpture within the island beyond simple macroscopic observations. Connelly (1988: 2–3) briefly discusses limestone sources in the region of the eastern Mesaoria; she also cites the important discovery of five unfinished over-life-size Roman statues, which were found alongside several other unfinished pieces at the ancient quarry of Mosphiloudia, 1 km southwest of Xylofagou (published in Vermeule 1979). While it is generally acknowledged that southeast Cyprus possesses the largest quantity of raw material in the foothills skirting the Mesaoria plain, the functioning of these quarries and the location of the actual workshops that exploited them have remained illusive, primarily due to the inaccessibility of sites within the Turkish Occupied area.

(3) Scale and portability. Life-size and over-life-size sculpture in both limestone and terracotta is well-attested in Cyprus. However, most examples are considerably smaller (from statuette to half-life-size) and easily transportable; thus,

even secure findspots do not automatically point to the location of a particular workshop. The fact that patrons would have little trouble transporting votive statuettes purchased in one town to dedicate them at sanctuaries in another only adds to the difficulty in isolating specific schools. Because of the great variations in size, comparisons between large and small statues should be cautiously applied.

(4) Distribution. The use of local stone, combined with a separate and viable market for terracotta statuary, facilitated the emergence of a votive sculptural tradition that favored certain media at certain sanctuaries. Despite the large numbers of statues found on the island, the distribution of limestone sculptures is most densely situated in the central–southeastern part of the island, more specifically in the region of the Mesaoria plain. As a result, an already appreciable degree of artistic insularity becomes even more pronounced since the likelihood of stylistic blending and borrowing between sites and workshops in such close vicinity is greatly increased.

(5) Material. Scholars have often related the flat and rather linear treatment of Cypriot sculpture to the limitations of the limestone itself (e.g., Caubet and Yon 1994). And while it should not be forgotten that Cypriot sculptors had the ability to produce fully rounded and often superbly carved statues, the majority conform to a standard and characteristically shallow form of modeling. Thus, the material itself might blur distinctions between styles as sculptors are offered less opportunity to inject subtle or personal variations into their work; likewise, the surface weathering of the soft Cypriot limestone (vs. marble) tends to obscure such subtleties with time and exposure. Moreover, since the majority of statues is of a smaller scale and seemingly mass-produced, the statues tend to lack many details that might suggest specific hands.

(6) Artists and workshops. Far too little is known about the limestone sculptors' workshops or the chain of production/distribution; the sculptor's initial work would have been completed at the

quarry sites (many of which are now inaccessible); likewise, artist signatures are exceedingly
rare on the island and are difficult to integrate
into a broader, regional analysis.

(7) Religious conservatism and typology. Despite
    individual experimentation recognized in
    Cypriot sculpture, religious conservatism and
    a limited and somewhat predictable typology
    characterize much of the corpus. The reproduc-
    tion of a few types in Cypriot sanctuaries over
    several generations or more often discourages
    the identification of regional traits. This is some-
    what remedied by the presence of numerous
    attributes and accessories, which, although oft
    repeated without much variation, do provide
    the sculptor with an additional means to express
    individualism (Counts 2001: 156–62).

Notwithstanding these obstacles, the classification of Cypriot sculpture has already benefited
from several excellent regional studies. P. Gaber
pioneered this effort through numerous articles
on the subject, as well as in her publication of the
limestone sculpture of Idalion (Gaber-Saletan
1980; 1981; 1986; Gaber 1989; 1992). Gaber rightly
criticized the prevailing assumption that a relative
chronology based on style would be consistent
throughout the island. By examining the sculpture
uncovered by the Swedish Cyprus Expedition in
the Vouni region (sites of Vouni and Mersinaki),
for example, Gaber isolated several traits that
seemed distinct to the area, such as triangular
faces with bowed mouths and a vertical emphasis
(Gaber-Saletan 1981: 45). Likewise, Gaber's work
on the sculpture of Idalion isolated stylistic features that appeared distinct to that site and showed
how the study of regional schools might be used
to elucidate larger historical and social questions,
such as Kition's control over the Dhali region in
the second half of the fifth century BC (Gaber-
Saletan 1986; Gaber 1989). A similar approach
to identifying regional schools was adopted by
J. Connelly (1988), who studied the Hellenistic
votive sculpture from the sites of Arsos, Voni,
Idalion, and Golgoi-*Ayios Photios*. By setting apart
various stylistic traits seen in the sculpture from
these sanctuaries and identifying specific hands,

Connelly (1988: 111–16) was able to refine the
picture of sculptural activity in these regions and
consider larger questions such as the influence of
Hellenistic royal portrait types. Finally, mention
should also be made of V. Tatton-Brown's (1984)
contribution to regional studies in Cyprus. Based
on a close examination of a school of relief sculptors from Golgoi in the fifth century BC, Tatton-
Brown stressed the importance of recognizing
Cypriot stylistic features cast within purely Greek
artistic conventions.

When one considers the density and variety of
archaeological sites located in and around the eastern Mesaoria, the need for a region-based approach
to the material culture of this area becomes readily
apparent (Counts 2004). The Mesaoria represents
a relatively bounded landscape, with the island's
two great mountain ranges to the north (Kyrenia)
and south/southwest (Troodos); the plains ter-
minate to the east/southeast at the coastline (see
map 2 on p. xxii). As a result, there is the potential
for cultural and artistic homogeneity across this
rather self-contained region in antiquity. Equally
significant, with respect to a regional perspective,
is the distribution of cities and sanctuaries within
and around the Mesaoria. The urban centers of
Chytroi to the north, Kition to the south, Salamis
to the east, and Idalion and Tamassos to the west
form a virtual perimeter, while countless secondary sites (especially sanctuaries) are dispersed
throughout the region. While these sites provide
evidence for earlier, prehistoric occupation, the
archaeological record of the Cypro-Geometric
and subsequent Cypro-Archaic periods testifies to
significant expansion. This is especially true in the
case of new sanctuary foundations (Bennett 1980:
694–713; Rupp 1987: 152; Karageorghis 2002: 191–93,
204–11), which occur both in the urban centers and
in the rural peripheries (e.g., Athienou-*Malloura*).

The "Stone of Athienou"

The large volume of sculpture from the region
around modern Athienou—one must only mention the holdings of the Metropolitan Museum of
Art from ancient Golgoi-*Ayios Photios*—points
to a school of sculptors active in the area from the

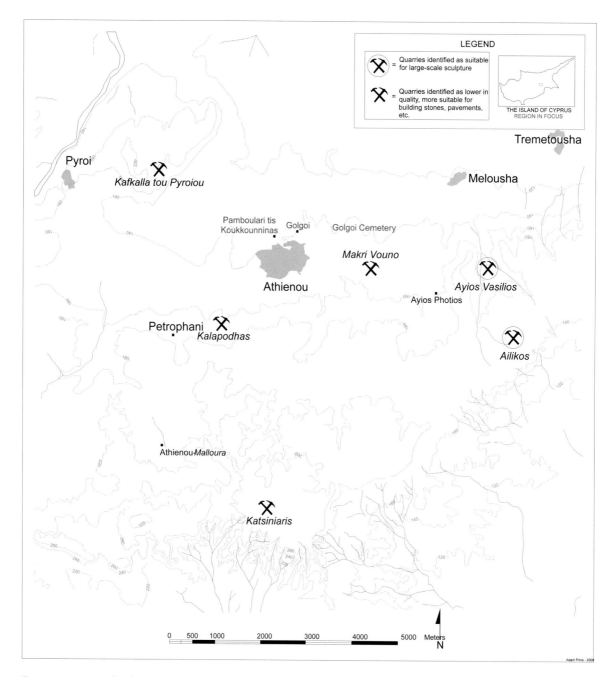

FIG. 11.1 *Topographical map of the Athienou region showing quarries, scale = 1:50 000 (drawing: A. Prins).*

late seventh century BC well into the Hellenistic and even Roman periods (Cesnola 1885; Myres 1914; Karageorghis 2000). This area received much attention in the late 19th century, with visits from a French mission under Melchior de Vogüé as well as L. di Palma Cesnola (see Counts, Ch. 4). The ac-

tivities of Cesnola, who supplied the Metropolitan Museum of Art with its large collection from his excavations at Golgoi, are well-documented. While the likelihood of mixed assemblages from the many sites he excavated is clearly a discouraging factor, scholars have long noted a significant degree of stylistic unity in the collection, especially those objects assigned to areas excavated near the chapel of Ayios Photios. The French mission, which focused its attention on both Ayios Photios and Malloura, seemed particularly interested in museum-quality pieces, often discarding fragments and smaller finds. There is little published record of the French mission's activities; however, contemporary annotated illustrations and the original accession labels listing provenience offer vital clues for many of the finds (Foucart-Bourville 1985: pls. 1–3).

Both Hermary (1981: 10) and Connelly (1988: 3) have highlighted the importance of the Athienou region for its limestone quarries; in fact, this stone is often referred to as the "stone of Athienou" because of the rich deposits of the soft, white stone located in close proximity to the village. Stone of similar texture, consistency, and color was used for statuary dedicated in many sanctuaries throughout the eastern Mesaoria plain.

In the summer of 1997, my colleague Michael Toumazou and I interviewed two local villagers from Athienou who had worked in quarries around the region prior to 1974, when some quarries became inaccessible due to the Turkish Occupation. Figure 11.1 represents a 1:50,000 topographical map of the Athienou region, which includes significant quarries in the area (see also fig. 2.2 for a geological map of the region). The quarrymen interviewed offered key insights into possible sources of stone in the area, while also noting several areas of high concentration, including a red stone characteristic of the flat-topped ridges northwest of the village and a crumbly limestone at the site of Kalapodas, south of modern Petrophani (Turkish Esendagh); both were deemed unsuitable for large-scale sculpture. Two other quarries, Katsouniaris and Makri Vouno (to the south and east, respectively), produced extremely thin sections of limestone, commonly used for pavements and stairs. More significant, both men concurred that the highest quality of limestone (i.e., most suitable for three-dimensional carving) came from two quarries to the east of modern Athienou: Ayios Vasilios and Ailikos. The former is located east and the latter to the southeast of the ancient site of Ayios Photios.

The two quarrymen emphasized the richness and depth of the deposits there, both essential characteristics of stones suitable for larger statuary in the round; moreover, the stone from these quarries shared many qualities with the sculpture they had observed from the area, including Malloura. Ayios Vasilios limestone was described as creamy white and almost dripping with moisture when first quarried (compare the comments by Myres [1914: 130], who describes the stone from the region as "soft as cheese when first quarried," and one of our quarrymen used the same parallel — *halloumi* — to describe the limestone's consistency when first extracted). The stone from Ailikos was characterized as harder, with few inclusions. In several cases, sculptures excavated by AAP were attributed to one of these two quarries based on simple macroscopic inspection (see Counts 1998: 70–71). The location of the quarries of Ayios Vasilios and Ailikos, in close proximity to the sites around Athienou, including Golgoi-*Ayios Photios* (and Golgoi), Arsos, and Athienou-*Malloura*, implies that sculpture from these sites was likely produced from the same quarries. While limestone outcroppings exist in the immediate areas surrounding the sanctuary (see the discussion in Yerkes, Ch. 2), these sources were probably not used in antiquity for sculpture but rather for building materials (Toumazou et al. 1998: 168).

The ongoing excavations in the Malloura Valley by AAP remain critical for a more nuanced understanding of the artistic and even socio-political significance of regional exchange in the area. To date, our excavations have yielded a corpus of more than 2,000 fragments of limestone sculpture, making it one of the largest caches of sculpture unearthed in the last 50 years (Counts 1998). The corpus has clear affinities with other sculptural assemblages from the Athienou region and beyond. As such, it offers a unique opportunity to bring some order to the vast and rather disparate data relative to an "Athienou School" and may provide a starting point for sketching a more complete picture of regional styles in Cypriot sculpture. The preliminary observations that follow are a step in this direction.

The Athienou School

Among the earliest pieces of sculpture found to date at Malloura are two fragments (figs. 11.2a–b [AAP-AM 323], 11.3 [AAP-AM 3250]) from life-size males wearing conical caps. Stylistically, both pieces fit neatly within a tradition of vigorously modeled faces from the region of Athienou dated to the late seventh or early sixth century BC, the masterpiece of which is the colossal head in New York (fig. 11.4) (Cesnola 1885: pl. 39:253; Karageorghis 2000: 108). The full, pursed lips, wide-open eyes, prominent cheeks, and large, fleshy nose are seen on a number of heads from the region, for example another head in the Metropolitan Museum from Golgoi (fig. 11.5) (Cesnola 1885: pl. 49, 289) as well as a head in the Louvre (fig. 11.6) dated by Hermary (1989: 25) to the end of the seventh century BC. These particular facial characteristics—especially the wide-open, staring eyes—predate the appearance of more direct influence from East Greek art later in the century. Hermary (1989: 26–8) has isolated a "transitional" group of male heads—almost exclusively from the Athienou region—with conical caps dating to the first quarter of the sixth century

Fig. 11.2a–b *Photo (a) and drawing (b) of a fragmentary limestone head from Athienou-*Malloura, *late seventh or early sixth century* BC. *AAP-AM 323: Athienou Municipal Museum, Cyprus (© AAP; drawing: J. Ravenhurst).*

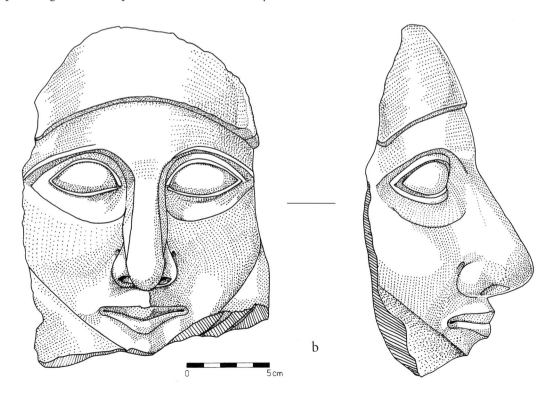

FIG. 11.3 *Fragment of a limestone head from Athienou-Malloura,* late seventh or early sixth century BC. *AAP-AM 3250: Larnaka District Museum, Cyprus (© AAP).*

FIG. 11.4 *Limestone head from Golgoi-*Ayios Photios, *late seventh or early sixth century* BC. *Metropolitan Museum of Art, New York. H: 88.3 cm (© The Metropolitan Museum of Art; Cesnola Collection 74.51.2857).*

FIG, 11.5 *Limestone head from Golgoi-*Ayios Photios. *Metropolitan Museum of Art, New York. H: 42 cm (drawing: A. Cova; after Cesnola 1885, pl. 49:289).*

FIG. 11.6 *Limestone head from Golgoi-*Ayios Photios, *late seventh or early sixth century* BC. *AM 2787: Musée du Louvre. H: 36 cm (drawing: A. Cova, after Hermary 1989: 25).*

FIG. 11.7 *Limestone head fragment from Athienou-Malloura, first quarter of the sixth century* BC. *AAP-AM 833: Larnaka District Museum, Cyprus (© AAP).*

that bridges the gap between these early heads with strong Cypriot characteristics and later ones that betray Greek influence. With their full lips, almond-shaped eyes, and prominent, large noses, our pieces clearly belong to this group and should date to the late seventh or early sixth century BC. A third, extremely fragmentary example of the same type (fig. 11.7 [AAP-AM 833]) discovered at Athienou-*Malloura* exhibits similar facial characteristics to this group—slender eyes and the thin, sharply defined nose bridge—suggesting continued stylistic links between Malloura and Golgoi into the first quarter of the sixth century.

The profusion of sculptures from the area that display a common style in the rendering of the facial features points to the presence of a prominent regional workshop in the area of Athienou during this early period in the history of Cypriot sculpture. A masterpiece such as the Metropolitan head from Golgoi-*Ayios Photios* was the work of a skilled craftsman whose style certainly could have exerted influence on the region. The reach of this regional school beyond its immediate vicinity is illustrated by a head from Amathous now in Brussels (Hermary 1981: 15, pl. 2:1 [inv. no. A 877]), which

FIG. 11.8A–B   *Photo (a) and drawing (b) of limestone head from Athienou-*Malloura*, late sixth or early fifth century BC. AAP-AM 100: Larnaka District Museum, Cyprus. H: 40 cm (© AAP; drawing: J. Ravenhurst).*

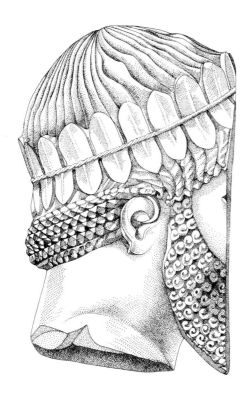

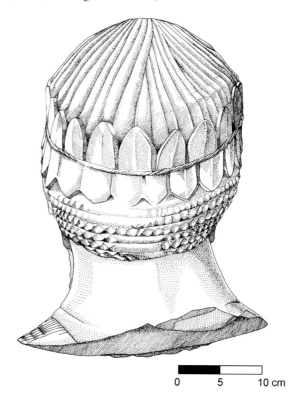

FIG. 11.9 *Limestone head from Golgoi-Ayios Photios, early fifth century* BC. *Metropolitan Museum of Art, New York; Cesnola Collection 74.51.2841. H: 34.3 cm (drawing: A. Cova, after Cesnola 1885: pl. 72:470).*

FIG. 11.10 *Limestone head of unknown provenience, early fifth century* BC. *Inv. no. 419: Ny Carlsberg Glyptotek. H: 17 cm (drawing: A. Cova, after Nielsen 1983: cat. no. 41).*

exhibits the same wide-open eyes, prominent cheeks, and strong nose. The paucity of large-scale limestone statues from Amathous (Hermary 1994) calls into question the existence of a local workshop in that region and suggests that types and styles followed the traditions of more prolific workshops, such as those in the Athienou region.

While questions of style are by nature subjective, it is possible to look at other aspects of sculpture when attempting to identify regional styles and even individual hands. The task of identifying regional schools may be facilitated by a number of attributes and accessories found on statues, a characteristic of Cypriot sculpture less common in contemporary Greek sculpture. The use of flat, stylized leaves set vertically into the wreath as seen on an over-life-size head from Malloura (fig. 11.8 [AAP-AM 100]) illustrates a distinct trait in the representation of male votaries from the region of Athienou during the late sixth and early fifth century BC. Such leaves are paralleled on several other

heads from neighboring Golgoi-*Ayios Photios*. A contemporary bearded head in New York (fig. 11.9) (Cesnola 1885: pl. 72:470; Karageorghis 2000: 120) dated to ca. 500 BC clearly reproduces the low-relief, squarish, vertical leaves, including the leaf's central vein rendered in shallow relief. The representation of the beard curls on the Metropolitan head differs slightly, but the overall modeling of the wreath, as well as the articulation of the hair on the top of the head and along the back, is almost identical.

Two heads in Istanbul that were originally part of the Cesnola collection recall, in an abbreviated form, the basic arrangement of the wreath and the vertical, stylized modeling of the leaves (Ergüleç 1972: C.36, C37). An example in the Ny Carlsberg Glyptotek possesses the same trait (fig. 11.10) (Nielsen 1983: inv. 419). While the provenience of the head is unknown, based on the similarity and the relative paucity of wreathed heads with flat, vertical leaves it is very likely it was the product of the same sculptural workshop active in the

Athienou region during the late sixth and early fifth centuries. Finally, a head in Liverpool of unknown provenience can be added to this list (Droop 1931b: pl. 9:2). The head possesses the same stylized leaves of AAP-AM 100, indicating it was produced in the same workshop in the Athienou region. In fact, Droop (1931a: 7) traces the origins of the collection in Liverpool back to Cesnola.

Perhaps the most enigmatic piece among a group of hand-held attributes excavated by AAP is a fragment from an over-life-size male figure (fig. 11.11 [AAP-AM 254]). Despite its fragmentary nature, its identification as a sword is secure based on comparisons with a fully preserved terracotta warrior figure from Ayia Irini armed with a similar weapon (fig. 11.12) (Gjerstad et al. 1935: pls. 197, 202:1–2 [no. 2102]; Karageorghis 1993: 17, pl. 9). Comparisons with other terracotta warrior figures from Ayia Irini offer comparanda for the particular orientation of the sword cradled in the hand and forearm of the figure (Gjerstad et al. 1935: pls. 194:2, 199:5–6). Karageorghis has published a fragment of a terracotta sword of similar type but of unknown provenience, now in the Cyprus Museum (Karageorghis 1993: 91, fig. 66). The ball-shaped pommel with a series of curved ridges running around it as well as the fluted handle are characteristic of each example. The pommel and forepart of the weapon are extremely large, and as Törnkvist (1972: 40) has pointed out, the heavier pommel was needed to balance out the weight of a longer, presumably larger, weapon.

Karageorghis suggests that the Ayia Irini terracotta warrior mentioned above (no. 2102) was made under the influence of stone sculpture: "this statue is the creation of an able sculptor, who was well aware of the rules of a specific sculptural style. It is likely that by now stone sculpture had appeared"

FIG. 11.11A–B *Limestone arm holding sword from Athienou-Malloura, Cypro-Archaic. AAP-AM 254: Larnaka District Museum, Cyprus. H: 24 cm (© AAP).*

(Karageorghis 1993: 17). Nevertheless, the early date for Ayia Irini 2102 — in the third quarter of the seventh century — and the likelihood that large-scale terracottas preceded their limestone counterparts in the seventh century (Hermary 1991) might suggest that the type was first executed in terracotta and then adapted by a limestone sculptor's workshop. The location of such a workshop is likely to have been in the region of Athienou, because the site of Golgoi-*Ayios Photios* has produced two other analogous fragments in limestone (figs. 11.13a–b) (Cesnola 1885: pl. 28:124–25). Cesnola had originally identified these as "goblets" or "scepters," but they were correctly identified as swords by Myres (1914: 183), who assigned them to Assyrian prototypes and proposed a date of no later than the seventh century BC. In addition to the basic shape of the pommel, the series of crescent-shaped ridges encircling the tip of the pommel are distinctive to the three examples, as well as to the two terracotta objects mentioned above. The arched pattern around the pommel may suggest a misunderstood derivation from, or blending with, the familiar crescent-shaped pommels of the Naue II type (for examples from the East and Greece, see Törnkvist 1972: 39). The spherical pommel is the most salient characteristic of the weapon, and evidence of similarly shaped pommels has been excavated at Salamis (Törnkvist 1972: 39 n. 26). The similarity in style and uniqueness in type leave little doubt that the limestone examples from Malloura and Golgoi-*Ayios Photios* were produced in the same workshop, probably by the same hand. Comparisons to the Ayia Irini statue argue for an early date of production, perhaps the last quarter of the seventh or beginning of the sixth century BC. These fragments represent a rare type of "warrior statue," which, although common in terracotta, is essentially absent in limestone; I know of no other limestone examples from the island (*pace* Cesnola 1885: pl. 73:475, which is equipped with a small dagger, but the figure should not necessarily be interpreted as a warrior).

FROM LOCAL INTERACTIONS TO REGIONAL INTEGRATION

As noted in the introduction to this volume (see pp. xvii–xxii) and discussed more fully in the first chapter (Kardulias et al.), one of the larger research questions that AAP has pursued since its inception is the process through which smaller, potentially marginal landscapes were incorporated into broader exchange systems both within and outside the island. The preceding discussion has highlighted significant parallels between the sculptural assemblages of two sites in the immediate Athienou region, the sanctuaries at Athienou-*Malloura* to the southwest of the modern town and at the site of Ayios Photios near ancient Golgoi. The establishment of this link permits us to move

FIG. 11.12 *Terracotta warrior with sword from Ayia Irini, third quarter of the seventh century BC. Inv. no. 2102: The Cyprus Museum, Nicosia, Cyprus. H: 177 cm (drawing: A. Cova, after Karageorghis 1993: pl. 9).*

FIG. 11.13A–B *Limestone arms holding swords from Golgoi-Ayios Photios, Cypro-Archaic. Metropolitan Museum of Art, New York. L: 16.5 cm (a) and 32 cm (b) (drawing: A. Cova, after Cesnola 1885: pl. 28:124–25).*

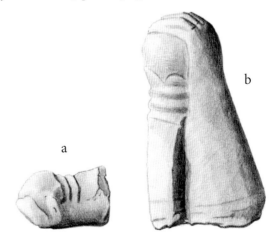

beyond formal, art historical analyses and consider Athienou-*Malloura*'s place within a larger context of regional artistic exchange.

As has been noted (Gordon et al., Ch. 3), the political organization of the island during the Cypro-Archaic and Cypro-Classical periods is defined by the borders of a series of independent city-kingdoms. Although the urban centers of these kingdoms are fairly well-established, the process of incorporation, not to mention control, of smaller, more peripheral sites such as the sanctuaries of Athienou-*Malloura* and Golgoi-*Ayios Photios* is still unclear. In particular, the status of Golgoi within the political landscape of Cyprus during the first millennium BC is difficult to determine. Although initially considered by Six (1883: 305–7) as the possible seat of one of the city-kingdoms based on a series of coins assigned to the site, the reattribution of those coins to the site of Kourion by Kagan (1999) fundamentally calls this earlier interpretation into question. It is more likely that Golgoi functioned as a secondary town to be associated with one of the kingdoms in the area, most likely Idalion only about 13 km to the south-southwest (for similar sentiments, see Fourrier, Ch. 9), thus maintaining a status similar to that of ancient Limassol, which L. Alpe (2006) has convincingly linked to the kingdom of Amathous. The observable connections between Athienou-*Malloura* and Golgoi-*Ayios Photios* illustrated here suggest significant interaction between the two sites and may clarify Malloura's position within this broader regional circuit of artistic exchange. That so many parallels in type and style have been identified is noteworthy; it suggests the presence of a regional center for the production of sculpture, no doubt exploiting the rich quarries to the east and southeast of the village. Complementary evidence from pottery, terracottas, and some sculpture types, as well as evidence for cult, strengthens the case for artistic interaction among Idalion, Golgoi, and Athienou-*Malloura* during this period (Counts 1998, 2004). Furthermore, the archaeological data suggest this pattern of regional activity in the Cypro-Archaic period among the three sites is maintained well into the fifth and fourth centuries BC. While Malloura's status within the geopolitical landscape of Cyprus is discussed more fully by the editors in the volume's conclusion, this chapter illustrates the potential for regional analyses to clarify our understanding of site hierarchies and the complexities of exchange systems within the context of artistic production in southeastern Cyprus.

REFERENCES

Alpe, L.
2006   Les groupes ethniques de Limassol dans l'Antiquité. Pp. 11–35 in *Identités croisées en un milieu méditerranéen: Le cas de Chypre (Antiquité—Moyen Âge)*, eds. S. Fourrier and G. Grivaud. Rouen: Publications des Universités de Rouen et du Havre.

Bennett, C. G.
1980   The Cults of Ancient Greek Cypriots. Unpublished Ph. D. dissertation, University of Pennsylvania.

Boardman J.
1995   *Greek Sculpture. The Late Classical Period.* London: Thames and Hudson.

Caubet, A., and Yon, M.
1994   Ateliers de sculpture de Kition: VIe–IVe s. av. J.-C. Pp. 97–105 in *Cypriote Stone Sculpture*, eds. R. Laffineur and F. Vandenabeele. Brussels and Liège: A. G. Leventis Foundation.

Cesnola, L. P. di
1885   *A Descriptive Atlas of the Cesnola Collection of Cypriote Antiquities in the Metropolitan Museum of Art, New York.* Boston: James R. Osgood.

Connelly, J. B.
1988   *Votive Sculpture of Hellenistic Cyprus.* Nicosia: Department of Antiquities of Cyprus.

Counts, D. B.
1998   Contributions to the Study of Cypriote
        Sculpture: Limestone Votives from Athienou-
        Malloura. Unpublished Ph.D. dissertation,
        Brown University.
2001   Prolegomena to the Study of Cypriote
        Sculpture. *Cahier du Centre d'Etudes
        Chypriotes* 31: 128–81.
2004   Art and Religion in the Cypriote Mesaoria:
        The View from Athienou-*Malloura*. *Cahier du
        Centre d'Etudes Chypriotes* 34: 173–90.
2008   Master of the Lion: Representation and
        Hybridity in Cypriote Sanctuaries.
        American Journal of Archaeology 112: 3–27.

Deonna, W.
1909   Les *"Apollons Archaïques:" Étude sur le type
        masculin de la statuaire grecque au VIme siècle
        avant notre ère.* Geneva: Librairie Georg.

Droop, J. P.
1931a   *Handbook and Guide to the Collection of
        Cypriote Sculpture.* Liverpool: The Museums.
1931b   Some Limestone Heads from Cyprus in
        the Liverpool Public Museums. *Annals of
        Archaeology and Anthropology [Liverpool]* 18:
        29–38.

Ducat, J.
1971   *Les Kouroi du Ptoion: Le sanctuaire d'Apollon
        Ptoieus à l'époque archaïque.* Paris: de Boccard.

Ergüleç, H.
1972   *Large-Sized Cypriot Sculpture in the
        Archaeological Museums of Istanbul.*
        Göteborg: Åström.

Foucart-Borville, J.
1985   La correspondence chypriote d'Edmond
        Duthoit (1862 et 1865). *Cahier du Centre
        d'Études Chypriotes* 4: 3–60.

Fourrier, S.
1999   Petite plastique chypriote de Délos. *Bulletin de
        Correspondance Hellénique* 123: 373–88.

Freyer-Schauenburg, B.
1974   *Bildwerke der archaischen Zeit und des
        strengen Stils.* Bonn: R. Habelt.

Gaber, P.
1989   Regional Styles in Cypriote Limestone
        Sculpture. Pp. 398–401 in *American
        Expedition to Idalion, Cyprus, 1973–1980,* eds.
        L. Stager and A. Walker. Chicago: Oriental
        Institute of the University of Chicago.
1992   Regional Styles and the Chronology of
        Sculpture. Pp. 224–27 in *Acta Cypria,* ed. P.
        Åström. Jonsered: Åström.

Gaber-Saletan, P.
1980   The Limestone Sculpture from Kition.
        Medelhavsmuseet Bulletin 15: 41–49.
1981   The Limestone Sculpture from the Vouni
        Region. *Medelhavsmuseet Bulletin* 16: 39–46.
1986   *Regional Styles in Cypriote Sculpture: The
        Sculpture from Idalion.* New York: Garland.

Gjerstad, E.; Lindros, J.; Sjöqvist, E.; and Westholm, A.
1935   *The Swedish Cyprus Expedition.* Vol. 2, *Finds
        and Results of the Excavations in Cyprus,
        1927–1931.* Stockholm: Swedish Cyprus
        Expedition.

Hermary, A.
1981   *Amathonte. Testimonia 2: La sculpture
        découverte avant 1975.* Paris: A. D. P. F.
1989   *Musée du Louvre, Département des antiquités
        orientales: Catalogue des antiquités de Chypre.
        Sculptures.* Paris: Editions de la Réunion des
        Musées Nationaux.
1991   Les débuts de la grande plastique chypriote en
        terre cuite. Pp. 139–47 in *Cypriote Terracottas,*
        eds. R. Laffineur and F. Vandenabeele. Brussels
        and Liège: A. G. Leventis Foundation.
1994   Sculptures d'Amathonte: Les découvertes de
        la mission française, 1975–1992. Pp. 117–25
        in *Cypriote Stone Sculpture,* eds. R. Laffineur
        and F. Vandenabeele. Brussels and Liège: A. G.
        Leventis Foundation.

Kagan, J.
1999   The Archaic and Early Classical Coinage of
        Kourion. *Cahier du Centre d'Études Chypriotes*
        29: 23–43.

Karageorghis, V.
1993   *The Coroplastic Art of Ancient Cyprus 3. The
        Cypro-Archaic Period: Large and Medium Size
        Sculpture.* Nicosia: A. G. Leventis Foundation.

2000   *Ancient Art from Cyprus: The Cesnola Collection in the Metropolitan Museum of Art.* New York: Metropolitan Museum of Art.

2002   *Early Cyprus: Crossroads of the Mediterranean.* Los Angeles: The J. Paul Getty Museum.

Kourou, N.; Karageorghis, V.; Maniatis, Y.; Polikreti, K.; Bassiakos, Y.; and Xenophontos, C.

2002   *Limestone Statuettes of Cypriote Type Found in the Aegean: Provenance Studies.* Nicosia: A. G. Leventis Foundation.

Langlotz, E.

1927   *Frühgriechische Bildhauerschulen.* Nürnberg: Ernst Fromann & Sohn.

Myres, J. L.

1914   *Handbook of the Cesnola Collection of Antiquities from Cyprus, Metropolitan Museum of Art, New York.* New York: The Metropolitan Museum of Art.

Nielsen. A. M.

1983   *Cypriote Antiquities in the Ny Carlsberg Glyptotek, Copenhagen.* Studies in Mediterranean Archaeology 20.8. Göteborg: Åström.

Pedley, J. G.

1976   *Greek Sculpture of the Archaic Period: The Island Workshops.* Mainz: Philipp von Zabern.

Richter, G. M. A.

1968   *Korai: Archaic Greek Maidens.* London: Phaidon.

1970   *Kouroi: Archaic Greek Youths: A Study of the Development of the Kouros Type in Greek Sculpture.* Second edition. London: Phaidon.

Ridgway, B.

1977   *The Archaic Style in Greek Sculpture.* Princeton: Princeton University.

1993   *The Archaic Style in Greek Sculpture.* Second edition. Chicago: Ares.

Rupp, D. W.

1987   Vive le Roi: The Emergence of the State in Iron Age Cyprus. Pp. 147–61 in *Western Cyprus: Connections*, ed. D. W. Rupp. Göteborg: Åströms.

Six, J. P.

1883   Du classement des series Cypriotes. *Revue Numismatique*: 249–374.

Sørensen, L. W.

1978   Early Archaic Limestone Statuettes in Cypriote Style: A Review of Their Chronology and Place of Manufacture. *Report of the Department of Antiquities, Cyprus*: 111–21.

Tatton-Brown, V.

1984   Sculptors at Golgoi. *Report of the Department of Antiquities, Cyprus*: 169–73.

Törnkvist, S.

1972   Arms, Armour, and Dress of the Terracotta Sculpture from Ayia Irini, Cyprus. *Medelhavsmuseet Bulletin* 6: 7–55.

Toumazou, M. K.; Yerkes, R. W.; and Kardulias, P. N.

1998   Athienou Archaeological Project: Investigations in the Malloura Valley, Cyprus, 1990–1995. *Journal of Field Archaeology* 25: 163–82.

Vermeule, C.

1979   An Imperial Commemorative Monument Never Finished: A Possible Memorial of Trajan's Eastern Conquests. Pp. 188–93 in *Studies Presented in Memory of Porphyrios Dikaios*, ed. V. Karageorghis. Nicosia: Lions Club of Nicosia and Zavallis.

Chapter 12

Cypriot Pan at the Crossroads in Late Classical and Hellenistic Cyprus

The Evidence from Athienou-*Malloura*

by Clay M. Cofer

Large quantities of votive limestone statuettes from Cyprus display attributes that immediately recall the Greek god Pan (fig. 12.1). All of them come from the remains of rural sanctuaries around the Pediaios River valley in the Mesaoria, near the sources of limestone from which they were carved. They do not appear in terracotta or in any other medium other than limestone, and they are not reliably attested in other regions of Cyprus. The god represented by these statuettes is, therefore, one who belongs to the regional landscape, a wide and fertile plain that lies between the foothills of the Troodos Mountains to the south and the steep Kyrenia Mountains to the north. Often regarded as the breadbasket of the island and of the greater southeastern Mediterranean region, the valley has always been valued for its agriculture, pasturing, and livestock farming. The iconographic attributes that group these statuettes together suggest agricultural fertility, herding, and hunting, reflecting both the character of this landscape as well as the needs and concerns of the people of the Mesaoria who dedicated them. These aspects are more or less emphasized through a choice and combination of attributes. Certain combinations repeat in consistent fashion and emerge as distinct types. Of

these types, some are widely popular throughout the Mesaoria, while others are localized to single sanctuaries. Still some seem generic and standardized, while others show carving prowess, originality, and a great degree of individualization.

While these statuettes from the Mesaoria recall images of Pan that are known from the rest of the Mediterranean, and this similarity must surely be significant, exactly which god they actually represent remains unknown. Unfortunately, there is an absence of both epigraphic and other written evidence from Cyprus that would unequivocally associate these statuettes with a specific divinity. Their identification, therefore, is based on their iconography; nevertheless, the god represented may have acquired local names and epithets in the Greek and Phoenician languages that were common in the Mesaoria. For lack of a better alternative then, these statuettes are identified here as Cypriot Pan. While this designation is meant to bring the corpus of statuettes into comparison with the Greek god Pan, the appellation "Cypriot" serves as a reminder that, despite attributes that are familiar to the iconography of Pan, these statuette types are not represented outside the island. Moreover, there is no evidence for the Greek cult of Pan on Cyprus.

FIG. 12.1 *Cypriot Pan statuettes from Athienou-*Malloura. *Larnaka District Museum, Cyprus (© AAP).*

The sanctuary of Athienou-*Malloura* is situated along the low hills that overlook the Mesaoria plain to the north (see map 2 on p. xxii). In many ways, the site is ideal for the study of these statuettes; to date, it is the only sanctuary where they come from stratified contexts. While clearly the sanctuary was not devoted exclusively to a Cypriot Pan, the statuettes far outnumber other representations of divinities recovered from the site; such a large quantity attests to the god's popularity and importance at this sanctuary beginning in the fourth century BC (for the spatial distribution of Cypriot Pans in the sanctuary in the context of other ritual activities, see Blackwell and Johnson, Ch. 23 [especially figs. 23.4–5]). Compared with similar sanctuaries, Athienou-*Malloura* not only shows the greatest variety in the types of Cypriot Pan statuettes but also features several new types.

The study of the Cypriot Pan statuettes at Athienou-*Malloura* is ongoing, and the corpus is continually expanding and new types are still emerging. Not only are the underrepresented and new types becoming more defined and better understood with every new fragment, but systematic excavation is providing a chronology for the statuettes that is based not on style alone. This paper, therefore, is an introduction to the Cypriot Pan statuettes and a preliminary report of those found at Athienou-*Malloura*. The basis of this study was undertaken in an unpublished master's thesis by the same author in 2001, which was directed by A.A. Donohue (Cofer 2001). A grouping of the Cypriot Pan statuettes into categories is suggested and essentially serves to distinguish their variety. The more inclusive term "category" is preferred over the more resolute term "type" at this stage in the study. As more examples emerge from excavation, the distinct types these categories attempt to define will become more refined through revision. Eventually, a definitive typology is planned for a future volume that will include a complete catalogue of the statuettes found from the sanctuary.

The history of the statuettes is fraught with problems concerning their identification and distribution, as well as their relative and absolute chronology (Cofer 2001: 109–39; Donkow 2005: 86–87 n. 31). With the exceptions of P. Flourentzos's 1989 study and grouping of the Cypriot Pan statuettes (Flourentzos 1989) and a thorough analysis of the subject by I. Donkow (Donkow 2005), previous studies are mostly limited to catalogue entries from excavations and the summary analyses that often accompany them. The evidence for a cult related to these statuettes is primarily in the form of sculpture. Since all the pieces lack inscriptions and the majority lacks provenience and an archaeological context, their identification, chronological placement, and any conclusions as to the nature of such a cult tend to derive solely from their iconography and style. While the work at Athienou-*Malloura* has indeed enriched our understanding of the chronology and use of these statuettes within a sanctuary, the identification, nature, and interpretation of cults are still limited to what can be understood from their iconography.

None of the statuettes preserve any ancient inscriptions that might have otherwise clarified the identity of the divinity they represent. If there were inscriptions painted in Greek, Cypro-syllabic, or Phoenician on the small rectilinear bases on which they stood, no trace has since survived. Inscriptions unrelated to the statuettes, which record dedications to Pan or even mention his presence on the island, are equally unattested, and the ancient sources are also silent. This has not discouraged scholars, however, from searching for possible alternative identifications from the known corpus of Cypriot epigraphy. The results of such efforts have been confusing and overwhelmingly misleading.

Throughout the history of their scholarship and even still today, one finds the same statuette types labeled "Opaon Melanthios" (Myres 1914: 178; 1945: 67; Pryce 1928: 93; Karageorghis 1979: 312; Sophocleous 1985: 78; Bakalakis 1988: 126), "Pan Melanthios" (Decaudin 1982: 151, no. 96), "Herakles-Melqart" (Ohnefalsch-Richter 1893: 319, pl. 22, no. 5), and "Pan" (R. H. Lang quoted in Colonna-Ceccaldi 1882: 21; Cesnola 1885: pl. 119; Myres 1914: 178; Pryce

1928: 93; Vessberg and Westholm 1937: 90; Dikaios 1947: 76; Caubet 1976: 173–74; Flourentzos 1989: 121–26; Hermary 1989: 311). Much of the confusion derives from the 19th-century excavation and reconnaissance work of D. G. Hogarth, L. P. di Cesnola, G. Colonna-Ceccaldi, M. Ohnefalsch-Richter, and J. L. Myres. While they all uncovered and handled large quantities of statuettes, some of which were Cypriot Pan statuettes, their limited communication and experience with one another's material led to several misidentifications and various associations (e.g., see discussions in Mitford 1946: 38 n. 38; Cofer 2001: 109–39; Donkow 2005: 86–87 n. 31).

A group of inscriptions, a few of which were inscribed on statuettes, was found at a single sanctuary site near the village of Amargetti in the far western district of Paphos first by M. Aristides and later by D. G. Hogarth between the years 1887 and 1888 (Hogarth et al. 1888: 169–74; Mitford 1946: 37–39). Thirteen inscriptions are dedicated to Opaon Melanthios and one to Apollo Melanthios (Mitford 1946: 38). Of the inscribed statuettes, only one has ever been published with an illustration (fig. 12.2) (Mitford 1946: fig. 16), while the rest have only written descriptions (Hogarth et al. 1888: 171–72; Myres and Ohnefalsch-Richter 1899: 162–63). The published statuette looks little like the Cypriot Pan statuettes that are so common from the sanctuaries of the Mesaoria Valley (fig. 12.3), and even though it is inscribed to *Opaon Melanthios*, Mitford publishes it as "Male Votary" (Mitford 1946: 36). In fact, Mitford's publication of this statuette mentions neither the god Pan nor the Cypriot Pan statuettes found from the sanctuaries in the Mesaoria Valley. Moreover, with the exception of their "phallic character," the written descriptions of the others do not mention any iconographic attributes that might convincingly associate them with the god Pan (Hogarth et al. 1888: 171–72; Myres and Ohnefalsch-Richter 1899: 162–63; Masson 1994: 275). Furthermore, the cult is attested only at this one sanctuary, which is in a different region of Cyprus, far to the west of the Mesaoria (map 2) (Mitford 1946: 38 n. 8). It is indeed dangerous to assume that a cult that is local to Amargetti should imply the participation of the entire island. With the exceptions of the single dedication to Apollo Melanthios and the published statuette (see fig. 12.2), which have both been dated by the style of the inscriptions to the third century BC (Mitford 1946: 37 n. 46; 1961: 143), they are all of a consistently late, Roman date (Mitford 1946: 37–38). Their late date further removes them from the corpus of the Cypriot Pan statuettes from the Mesaoria, which start as early as the mid-fourth century BC.

These serious differences in chronology, distribution, and appearance should disassociate the cults of Apollo Melanthios and Opaon Melanthios at the sanctuary near Amargetti from the types of statuettes found in the Mesaoria that are the subject of this chapter (see Vessberg and Westholm 1937: 90; Bennett 1980: 441–45; Flourentzos 1989: 121; Hermary 1989: 122; Albertson 1991; Masson 1994: 275; Donkow 2005: 86–87 n. 31). Nevertheless, several scholars have associated them on the basis of inquiries into the etymology of "Opaon" and "Melanthios," but this author has not found such arguments convincing in light of the significant differences discussed above (see Brown 1977; Bennett 1980: 442). Moreover, the dedication to Apollo Melanthios started a tradition in scholarship, which began with Hogarth, to understand Opaon and the corpus of statuettes that have subsequently been misleadingly associated with this epithet as just another attribute and manifestation of Apollo in Cyprus (Hogarth et al. 1888: 173; Hill 1940: 81; Masson 1960; Karageorghis 1979: 314, 1981: 83; Bennett 1980: 445; Glover 1981: 148).

While the true name and accompanying epithets of the god to whom these statuettes refer may

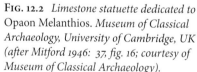

FIG. 12.2 *Limestone statuette dedicated to* Opaon Melanthios. *Museum of Classical Archaeology, University of Cambridge, UK (after Mitford 1946: 37, fig. 16; courtesy of Museum of Classical Archaeology).*

FIG. 12.3 *Limestone statuette of a Category 1 Cypriot Pan. Cyprus Museum E. 58, Nicosia, Cyprus (photo courtesy of the Cyprus Museum).*

never be known, their general appearance associates them easily with the Greek and Roman traditions of representing the god Pan (fig.12.4) (see Marquardt 1995; Boardman 1997: 923–41; Donkow 2005: 75). In these traditions, Pan has a variety of distinctive attributes that identify him. In terms of physiognomy, he shares features from both humans and goats. His head has pointed ears and horns, and he may be bearded. His body can appear completely human (Marquardt 1995: 302;

Boardman 1997: 938, no. 269), or he can have goat legs complete with hoofs (May 1950: 65–68, pl. 3). While his lower body is always naked and may feature a prominent and erect phallus, his shoulders and back may be cloaked with a cape that looks like a *chlamys*. He often carries his *syrinx*, a musical instrument made of reeds, and his *lagobolon*, a long wooden club with a hooked end that is used both in shepherding and in hunting. All these attributes are well-represented in images of Pan from Arcadia (Marquardt 1995: 304; Boardman 1997: 938, nos. 273, 274), Thrace (May 1950: 65–68), and Magna Graecia (Jenkins 1966: 24, pl. 10e) from at least the end of the fifth century BC onward, and with popular combinations that surface at different times and in different regions.

While the Cypriot Pan statuettes share some of these more common attributes, they nevertheless have a distinctive style that is unmistakably Cypriot (see fig. 12.1). This style follows the deeply-rooted local traditions in limestone votive sculpture, which are known for their large-scale production of repetitive votive types, their ability to easily translate new or different elements onto popular local models, and their creative detailing that marks the individuality of each votive (see Connelly 1988; Counts 1998). There is, in other words, a seemingly endless variety in fine detail on otherwise standard and mass-produced forms (see the comments in Counts, this volume, ch. 11).

The abundance and ease with which the finely grained local limestone can be carved afford wide ranges of sizes and quality in production (see discussions of limestone in Westholm 1936: 127–28; Connelly 1988: 2; Counts, this volume, ch. 11). The Cypriot Pan statuettes can be small and with a minimum of carving (fig. 12.5), or they can be as large as small statues with fine modeling (fig. 12.6) and S-curved body profiles (fig. 12.7), and have highly individualized faces with popular hairstyles (figs. 12.8a–b). All of them could be properly described as relief statuettes because below the head they are carved against a background that is flat and roughly hewn at the back. The carvers made good use of relief and painting techniques to maximize their space and minimize unnecessary carving. The relief background is conceived as the back of

FIG. 12.4 *Silver tetradrachm of Antigonos Gonatas showing a bust of the god Pan. Muenzkabinett, Staatliche Museen, Berlin, Germany (© Bildarchiv Preussischer Kulturbesitz / Art Resource, NY).*

Pan's cloak as it falls down from behind his shoulders. The cloak itself is the skin of a goat, which is fastened by tying the hoofs like drawstrings at the chest (Pryce 1928: 93). A wind blows against him from behind, since his cloak clings to his back and billows in the spaces between his arms and legs (figs. 12.5 and 12.9). His arms are usually highly foreshortened with only the forearms carved and the upper arms implied (see fig. 12.6). When he carries his *lagobolon* down at his side, it sometimes shows a similar foreshortening. Even the smaller-scale examples are depicted standing on rectangular statue bases as if they were in fact large statues with monumental bases that were carved separately (see fig. 12.3). These bases are also slightly raised at the back so that his feet rest on a slope and the figure appears more elevated (see fig. 12.6).

Details are often painted instead of carved. When preserved, traces of red, pink, and black paint define what would otherwise be unknown. An exceptional example features the black spotted skin of Cypriot Pan's cape, the woody knobs of his *lagobolon*, and the red laces and straps of boots (see fig. 12.3). When the paint is not preserved, as is more often the case, assumptions based on the carving alone can prove misleading. Most of the figures are shown barefoot, and were it not for the survival of the painted details, the boots on the latter example might be interpreted wrongly as summarily rendered feet. Moreover, without the painted details, some attributes can mistakenly come across as crude and incompetent, and consequently some statuettes have been subject to stylistic chronologies, which are themselves problematic, that assume such characteristics must be indicative of a late date (see, e.g., Myres 1914: 178; Flourentzos 1989: 126).

Many of the small types of statuettes show a preference for painting the features of the face instead of carving them (see fig. 12.3). When the paint is not preserved, these heads can be mistakenly interpreted as crude or even bestial. The latter impression is the single characteristic that distinguishes "Group II" of Flourentzos's typology of the Cypriot Pan statuettes (Flourentzos 1989: 125, pl. 25). The summarily carved faces in this group may have given an impression other than bestial had their painted features survived for analysis. Also, when the painted details do not survive, the heads appear generic and can easily be confused with the heads of Apollo and Artemis that are in a similar state of preservation; they all have comparable hairstyles, and a few cuts of the carver's knife or a single attribute are often all that remain to differentiate between them (see Counts 1998: 186).

Many of the attributes featured on these statuettes are already familiar from other divinities popular in Cypriot votive sculpture. A. Caubet was the first to recognize and seriously discuss these similarities (Caubet 1976, 173–74; Counts 2008). While the cloak worn by Cypriot Pan is a goatskin, it is tied in a "Herakles knot" across the chest in the same manner as the lion skin on votives representing Herakles/Melqart. Also like Herakles/Melqart, Cypriot Pan is armed with a wooden club (Gjerstad et al. 1937: pls. 1–39), which also func-

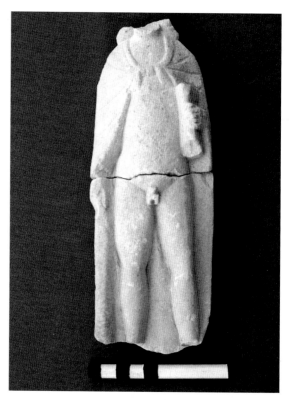

FIG. 12.5 *Fragmentary limestone statuette of a Category 1 Cypriot Pan from Athienou-*Malloura. *AAP-AM 619 + 969: Larnaka District Museum, Cyprus (© AAP).*

FIG. 12.6 *Fragmentary limestone statuette of a Category 5 Cypriot Pan from Athienou-*Malloura. *AAP-AM 1076: Larnaka District Museum, Cyprus (© AAP).*

FIG. 12.7 *Fragmentary limestone statuette of a Category 7 Cypriot Pan from Athienou-*Malloura. *AAP-AM 1230: Larnaka District Museum, Cyprus (© AAP).*

FIG. 12.8A–B *Limestone statuette heads of Cypriot Pan from Athienou-*Malloura. *(a) AAP-AM 2760 and (b) AAP-AM 2740: Larnaka District Museum, Cyprus (© AAP).*

FIG. 12.9 *Fragmentary limestone statuette of a Category 4 Cypriot Pan from Athienou-*Malloura. *AAP-AM 624 + 697: Larnaka District Museum, Cyprus (© AAP).*

tions as a shepherd's *pedum* (crook). His horns are small buds like those seen on statuettes identified as Bes. Bes and Herakles/Melqart can be depicted with their genitalia exposed, as they are on the statuettes of Cypriot Pan (for Bes, see Hermary 1989: 298, no. 596; for Herakles/Melqart, see Sophocleous 1985: 38, pl. 8.2). Moreover, Bes and Cypriot Pan sometimes have comparable hairstyles (cf., fig. 12.8 with Karageorghis 2000: 254, no. 412).

Exceptional examples of Cypriot Pan share more with other divinities than his usual standard attributes. The small lion carried in the left arm of a large Cypriot Pan statuette from Pyla recalls the small lions carried by votives representing Herakles/Melqart (Caubet 1976: 174, pl. 28.6; Hermary 1989: 311, no. 619). An unusual type from Idalion shows a Cypriot Pan dressed in a belted tunic and cloak (Pryce 1928: 93, fig. 152). In addition to his *syrinx*, he supports either a *lagobolon* (Senff 1993: 66) or a horn of abundance (Caubet 1976: 174) against his left arm and shoulder. His costume and possible cornucopia match those of an enthroned Zeus Ammon statuette found at Athienou-*Malloura* by the mission of Vogüé (Hermary 1989: 309, no. 616; Counts 2009).

Besides the statuette from Pyla and the one from Idalion mentioned above, the statuettes of Cypriot Pan conform generally to certain common types. With the exception of two examples that show goat legs, all the Cypriot Pan statuettes stand upright on statue bases, have human legs, and are depicted frontally nude (see fig. 12.6). Some portray him as being ithyphallic, but the majority does not. They also all wear a goatskin cape tied in a Herakles knot in front of the chest. Until now, the study of Flourentzos is the only published attempt to classify these statuettes according to their iconographic features, which he distinguishes into six groups (Flourentzos 1989). Because several new types have emerged since Flourentzos's study, a new grouping is suggested. Nine categories of types are introduced here as a fresh attempt to distinguish the variety of the Cypriot Pan statuettes and will be fully published as a typology together with a catalogue in the future. Three of the categories have correspondences with Flourentzos's groups, and these are noted in their descriptions.

Category 1 Cypriot Pans are by far the most common and most widely-attested in the sanctuaries of the Mesaoria, with seven examples coming from Athienou-*Malloura* and others from Potamia (Karageorghis 1979: pl. 44 nos. 48, 148), Golgoi-*Ayios Photios* (Cesnola 1885: pl. 119, nos. 857, 867, 865), Salamis (Karageorghis 1962: 350), Voni (Ohnefalsch-Richter 1893: pl. 42, no. 5), Lefkoniko (Myres 1945: pl. 41, no. 470), and Pyla (Hermary 1989: 313, no. 622) (see figs. 12.3 and 12.5). Category 1 corresponds with P. Flourentzos's Groups I–II (Flourentzos 1989: 124–25 and pls. XXIV–XXV). Cypriot Pan holds his *lagobolon* down at his side like a shepherd's staff with the hooked end facing forward. His other hand grips his *syrinx* in playing position and holds it closely against the side of his torso. He has a slender body and stands with his weight slightly shifted to the leg next to his *lagobolon*. His head is defined by the wiglike profile of his hair, which curls up from the forehead and falls down onto his shoulders (see fig. 12.3). Small horns bud from the same root at the top of his head, and he has pointed ears that turn out and are in line with the face.

Category 2 Cypriot Pans are many in number but only have secure proveniences at Golgoi-*Ayios Photios* (Cesnola 1885: pl. 119, nos. 856, 858, 859, 866) and Athienou-*Malloura*, where four have been found (fig. 12.10). Category 2 stands out as being ithyphallic, and corresponds with P. Flourentzos's Group III (Flourentzos 1989: 125 and pl. XXVI). Pan does not hold a *lagobolon* but lets his arm and empty hand fall straight down along his side. His other hand holds his *syrinx*, which is in playing position against the front of his chest. His long and oval head has budding horns at the apex and pointed ears that face toward the sides. His hair is pulled back from the forehead and curls around the neck.

Category 3 Cypriot Pans are not attested at Athienou-*Malloura* and have a distribution that is limited to the sanctuary at Lefkoniko (fig. 12.11) (see Myres 1945: 54–68). Category 3 corresponds with P. Flourentzos's Group IV (Flourentzos 1989: 125 and pl. XVII). They hold neither of Pan's favorite attributes, the *lagobolon* and the *syrinx*. He is ithyphallic and has one hand that rests on his hip and the other at his side handling the fringe of his

FIG. 12.10 *Fragmentary limestone statuette of a Category 2 Cypriot Pan from Athienou-*Malloura. *AAP-AM 258: Larnaka District Museum, Cyprus (© AAP).*

FIG. 12.11 *Fragmentary limestone statuette of a Category 3 Cypriot Pan from Lefkoniko. Cyprus Museum E. 423, Nicosia (photo courtesy of the Cyprus Museum).*

cloak. None of the preserved examples has head and feet, so the category has been defined strictly on the basis of the torso and the groin. The abdominal and pectoral muscles are subtly modeled yet well defined, and the hip that supports the hand shifts prominently to the side.

Category 4 refers to a new Cypriot Pan type known only from two examples found at Athienou-*Malloura* (see fig. 12.9). Knowledge of the type is limited to the body, since even the most complete example lacks the head and the feet. With one arm, Category 4 holds his *syrinx* in playing position up against the side of his torso. His other arm falls straight down at his side while he handles the fringe of his cloak. The upper body is robust if not fleshy and appears somewhat squat in comparison with his long and slender legs. His profile curves like an "S" with his weight shifted to one leg.

Category 5 is also a new Cypriot Pan type discovered at Athienou-*Malloura* with three examples attested so far (see fig. 12.6). The manner in which Cypriot Pan holds the *syrinx* distinguishes these statuettes from the other categories. He does not hold the instrument in playing position but sideways, so that the individual pipes are horizontal. He also carries it down and slightly away from the side of his body. With his other hand, he rests his *lagobolon* at his side. The hooked end of the *lagobolon*, however, is turned behind him instead of facing the front as it is in Category 1. All that is known of the head are the curls of hair that rest on his shoulders.

Category 6 is also new and known only at Athienou-*Malloura* (fig. 12.12). The single example is unfortunately fragmentary, with much of the torso and the entire left arm, head, and feet missing. Cypriot Pan holds his *syrinx* sideways and down at his side as in Category 5, but unlike Category 5, this type is ithyphallic.

Category 7 defines yet another new type with most examples coming from Athienou-*Malloura*

FIG. 12.12 *Fragmentary limestone statuette of a Category 6 Cypriot Pan from Athienou-*Malloura. *AAP-AM 300: Larnaka District Museum, Cyprus (© AAP).*

FIG. 12.13 *Fragmentary limestone statuette of a Category 8 Cypriot Pan. Cyprus Museum D. 529, Nicosia, Cyprus (photo courtesy of the Cyprus Museum).*

(see fig. 12.7). His *lagobolon* is held down at his side, and his *syrinx* is held in playing position against the side of his torso as in Category 1. What distinguishes these Pans from Category 1, however, are their accentuated stance and style. Their body profile is more pronounced and makes a prominent S curve with the hips shifted to the side. Three statuettes of this type have been uncovered at Athienou-*Malloura*, with an additional example possibly coming from Pano-Lakatamia-*Drosinospilios* (Flourentzos 1989: 124, no. 39).

Category 8 is attested by only one example, which unfortunately is without provenience (fig. 12.13). Although he carries neither his *lagobolon* nor his *syrinx*, Cypriot Pan is still recognizable because he wears his goatskin cape and is ithyphallic. One arm rests at his side and the other arm rests against the front of his thigh. His body is pear shaped, and, despite being ithyphallic, he has a feminine appearance.

Category 9 includes all the Cypriot Pan statuettes that have the legs of goats (figs. 12.14 and

12.15). These Cypriot Pans are extremely rare, and the two described here may eventually prove to be considered idiosyncratic or exceptional examples. The most impressive is a Cypriot Pan excavated from House 1 at Golgoi (see fig. 12.14) (Bakalakis 1988: 125, no. 1, pl. 80.1). He is shown about to spring forward from his seat on a rock outcropping to catch a sheep that is trying to run away. The head is missing, but what is preserved shows that he bears none of the attributes normally associated with him on Cyprus, such as the *syrinx* and the *lagobolon*. Only his cape is comparable to the other statuettes. While he holds a shield high in a defensive position with his left hand, he reaches forward with his right and grabs the back leg of a sheep trying to escape. It is clear, however, that the sheep will not get away because not only does Cypriot Pan hold its back leg, he also trips the animal from the front with his own goat's leg. At Athienou-*Malloura*, one goat leg was found that likely comes from a standing statuette of Pan (see fig. 12.14). The leg looks anthropomorphic but has a hoof instead of a human foot.

The nine categories described above are variously distributed among the sanctuaries of the Mesaoria. While Category 1 Cypriot Pans are attested at all of them, the remaining have only been attested at three sanctuaries: Golgoi-*Ayios Photios*, Lefkoniko, and Athienou-*Malloura*. Significantly, Lefkoniko has one category (Category 3) and Athienou-*Malloura* has three categories (Categories 4–6) that are distinctively their own. Category 7, moreover, has its highest concentration at Athienou-*Malloura*, and Category 9 shows idiosyncratic examples that are attested only at Athienou-*Malloura* and at Golgoi, which are relatively close geographically. Other exceptional examples of Cypriot Pan are those mentioned above, like the one that carries a baby or miniature lion and comes from the sanctuary at Pyla (Caubet 1976: 174, pl. 28.6; Hermary 1989: 311 no. 619), and the one that is dressed and carries a horn of abundance from the sanctuary at Idalion (Pryce 1928: 93, fig. 152).

A series of finely carved heads of Cypriot Pan has been found disassociated from the bodies but still clearly belonging with the statuette categories above (see figs. 12.8a–b) (see Flourentzos 1989: 125,

FIG. 12.14 *Fragmentary limestone statuette of a Category 9 Cypriot Pan with goat legs from the city of Golgoi. Athienou Municipal Museum Γλ. 1, Cyprus (photo courtesy of the Director of the Department of Antiquities, Cyprus).*

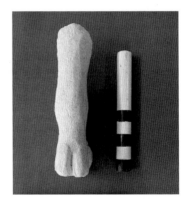

FIG. 12.15 *Limestone hoofed leg of a Category 9 Cypriot Pan from Athienou-Malloura. AAP-AM 2151: Larnaka District Museum, Cyprus (© AAP).*

pls. 28, 29; Donkow 2005). The heads come from larger-scale statuettes, but none are greater than half-life size. The special features and hairstyles are carved in such detail that each face betrays a distinct personality. This apparent attention to individualized heads has been noticed as a characteristic of Cypriot votive sculpture in general, especially in the Hellenistic period (see Connelly 1988). Five such heads have been found so far at Athienou-*Malloura*. Four of them look like elaborated heads of Category 1 Cypriot Pans, while a fifth has a slightly different hairstyle and a more schematic style.

One head has especially deep eye cavities and a prominent brow that are reminiscent of popular styles traditionally associated with representations of Alexander the Great, such as the heads of Herakles on the obverse of coinages minted after his death in 323 BC (see fig. 12.8a) (see Bellinger 1963: 14–21). Still more of the heads show general similarities with the heads of Pan depicted on the Macedonian coinage of Antigonos Gonatas, who ruled most of Greece from ca. 284 to 239 BC (see fig. 12.4) (Panagopoulou 2000). Pan is Antigonos Gonatas's patron deity, and the god's head with budding horns and pointed ears together with a *lagobolon* are featured on the obverse of his coinage (Panagopoulou 2000). At present, the significance of these similarities with respect to the Cypriot Pan statuettes and to the history of Cyprus is not at all clear. It should be known, however, that there has been a tradition in scholarship that understands certain examples of Cypriot votive sculpture to betray the portraiture of Hellenistic kings (Pryce 1928: 93; see also a discussion of Pryce's scholarship in Connelly 1988: 10–11). Although he does not reference Cyprus, H. P. Laubscher believes that many kings of both the Antigonid and Ptolemaic kingdoms were portrayed in the guise of Pan (Laubscher 1985: 333–53, pls. 66–67; Panagopoulou 2000: 88).

These similarities with Hellenistic types and styles have traditionally dated the statuettes of Cypriot Pan to the Hellenistic period (see Pryce 1928: 93; Vessberg and Westholm 1937: 90; Connelly 1988: 10–11; Donkow 2005: 81). With the exception of those from Athienou-*Malloura* and the Cypriot Pan with goat legs from Golgoi (see fig. 12.14), the statuettes have either insecure proveniences or were found deposited together with other statuary in large votive caches called *favissae*. The statuary in these *favissae* was deposited late in the history of these sanctuaries, so they represent a mixed chronological jumble that can only be dated through style (see, e.g., Myres 1945: 58). The excavations at Athienou-*Malloura* have provided a more secure chronology based on examples found from stratified contexts.

The sanctuary at Athienou-*Malloura* went through a major architectural reorganization that has been dated securely to the last quarter of the fourth century BC (see Toumazou and Counts, Chapter 6; Fourrier, Chapter 9). At this time, some of the votives that were standing in the earlier phase were used as building material for the walls of the new *temenos* enclosure and for the packing of the new floor of the sanctuary (Counts 1998: 62–63). Four Cypriot Pan statuettes were found as material for these walls, and one was found in this floor packing. These statuettes must have stood as votives in the sanctuary before the end of the fourth century BC and must, therefore, date from at least the end of the Cypro-Classical period. These early Cypriot Pans include Category 1 and Category 2 examples as well as one of the finely carved heads with individualized features. Seven other statuettes of Cypriot Pan come from secure deposits on the floor of the Hellenistic sanctuary (see figs. 12.6, 12.7, 12.12, and 12.8a). These later Cypriot Pans include examples of Categories 4, 5 (see fig. 12.6), 6 (see fig. 12.12), and 7 (see fig. 12.7). Significantly, these are the same categories known only from Athienou-*Malloura*, which may suggest that an era of local creativity came along with the new Hellenistic-period sanctuary. A finely carved head with individualized features was also found on the Hellenistic floor (see fig. 12.8a), and two more such heads were found in the alluvial layer above (see fig. 12.8b), which is associated with the abandonment of the sanctuary sometime late in the Roman period.

The sanctuary at Athienou-*Malloura* features the largest quantity, the greatest variety of categories of, and the most securely dated statuettes of Cypriot Pan in Cyprus. A total of 47 fragments and fragmentary statuettes of Cypriot Pan have been uncovered, out of which a minimum number of individual statuettes numbers at 22. Cypriot Pan is by far the most conspicuous deity represented at the sanctuary, and his presence endured from

Cypro-Classical times through the reorganization of the sanctuary and into the Hellenistic period.

The differences in categories emphasize the characteristics of Cypriot Pan that specifically concerned the people who dedicated them. The categories that are ithyphallic (Categories 2 [see fig. 12.10], 3 [see fig. 12.11], 6 [fig. 12.12], and 8 [see fig. 12.13]) refer to his role as an agricultural divinity who is fertile and ensures abundance. When he carries his *lagobolon* or is shown wearing boots (Categories 1 [see fig. 12.3] and 5 [see fig. 12.6]), he is not only a shepherd but also a hunter. His shepherding and hunting skills are especially aggressive in the representation of the Cypriot Pan from Golgoi with the legs of a goat (Category 9 [see fig. 12.14]). These various aspects of Cypriot Pan are well-suited to the landscape and character of life in the Mesaoria where he is found. A. Hermary, who was influenced by the study of Laubscher (1985), has gone so far as to suggest that the appearance of these statuettes, especially with their shepherd aspects, is indicative of the rival desires of the Hellenistic kings and rulers to be associated with Pan (Hermary 1989: 311).

From the mid- to later fourth century BC to the first quarter of the third century BC, which is when these Cypriot Pan statuettes are best represented, the Mesaoria was a geopolitical crossroad that witnessed intermittent periods of hardship and prosperity. Since the Mesaoria is the only low and broad plain on the island, it served repeatedly as a landscape for battles and military settlement, as well as for grain and produce exploitation. The valley witnessed substantial ethnic and Diadochic factioning (see Michaelides 1996: 142; Cofer 2001: 5–48). It is clear from the accounts of Diodorus Siculus that the cities of the Mesaoria were divided, sometimes along ethnic Cypriot Greek and Phoenician lines, in their support between the rival Antigonid and Lagid dynasties, which were contending for control of Cyprus (Diodorus Siculus 19.59). Split loyalties in this uncertain time translated into a vacillation of fortune and disaster for many of these cities, since the hegemony of the island changed successively from the Ptolemies (312–306 BC) to the Antigonids (306–294 BC) and then back again to the Ptolemies (after 294

BC). With each new geopolitical turnover, the monetary weight standards changed significantly; consequently, many of the inhabitants must have suffered substantial economic losses (see Bagnall 1976: 240; Mørkholm 1991: 64–67). A coin of Antigonos Monopthalmos, which has been dated ca. 310 BC, was excavated from the sanctuary at Athienou-*Malloura* and is indicative of the geopolitical changes that came at about the same time as the reorganization of the sanctuary (Toumazou and Counts, Chapter 6).

When Demetrios Poliorketes arrived in Cyprus in 306 BC, he brought with him a force of 15,000 infantry and 400 cavalry, and these soldiers battled in the Mesaoria to the west of Salamis (Diodorus Siculus 20.46.4–53.4; Plutarch, *Vit. Dem.* 15.1–17.1). The excavated context of the Cypriot Pan with goat legs from House I at Golgoi provides something of the character of these insecure times (see fig. 12.14). The statuette was found just below a burned layer of material that has been associated with the destruction of the house and settlement about the time of the war between Demetrios Poliorketes and Ptolemy I in 306 BC (Bakalakis 1988: 125–26). The Mesaoria Valley was thus subject to the passing and stationing of various armies, no doubt comprised of multiple nationalities and ethnicities, and the local inhabitants who were recruited would have been exposed to their cultures and vice versa (Mitford 1961: 93–151; Bagnall 1976: appendix B; Młynarczyk 1990: 150 n. 267).

Some scholars think these armies eventually settled in the Mesaoria and managed the land in a system of tax farming, which is well-known from the administration of Ptolemaic Egypt (Bagnall 1976: 6–7; Mitford 1979: 164–65; 1980: 256). The importance of this region and its produce to the Ptolemies must have been considerable, for Ptolemy III Euergetes paid a large sum of money for the grain of Cyprus in 238 BC after the Nile had failed to flood (Michaelides 1996: 142). Some 2,500 inscribed pottery sherds record pleas to a local nymph at a grotto on the dramatic conical hill of Kafizin for help in securing the agricultural production of flax and linseed (Mitford 1979; 1980). The sherds are inscribed in both Cypro-syllabic and Greek scripts and are all securely dated between

225 and 218 BC (Mitford 1979: 164). Most of the dedicants call themselves κοινωνοί, or members of the house of Androclos, so that T. B. Mitford suggests the sanctuary functioned as a sort of "private chapel" for a group or company of flax farmers (Mitford 1979: 165–66; 1980: 256). Some inscriptions indeed reveal an anxiety for agricultural yield, and the nymph is entreated as an intermediary between the company of farmers and the higher deities such as Zeus Olympios (Mitford 1979: 167).

This nymph is worshipped in the same landscape as the Cypriot Pan statuettes, and their dedication in the sanctuaries of the Mesaoria may be the result of similar agricultural concerns and anxieties. Cypriot Pan thus emerges from this environment as a god that secures agricultural and pastoral beneficence while characterizing something of the instability and even the militaristic character of the time. Cypriot Pan dominated a region at the crossroads of Hellenistic armies and loyalties while serving the needs of the local shepherds and farmers.

REFERENCE

Albertson, F.
1991   *Catalogue of Cypriote Sculpture and Terracottas in the Kelsey Museum of Archaeology, University of Michigan.* Studies in Mediterranean Archaeology 20.14. Göteborg: Åström.

Bagnall, R.
1976   *The Administration of the Ptolemaic Possessions Outside Egypt.* Leiden: Brill.

Bakalakis, G.
1988   *Ανασκαφή στο Λόφο Γιόρκους ΒΑ της Αθηαίνου, Κύπρος.* Athens: Αρχαιολογική Εταιρεία Αθηνών.

Bellinger, A. R.
1963   *Essays on the Coinage of Alexander the Great.* Numismatic Studies 11. New York: American Numismatic Society.

Bennett, C.
1980   Cults of the Ancient Greek Cypriots. Unpublished Ph. D. dissertation, University of Pennsylvania.

Boardman, J.
1997   Pan. *Lexicon Iconographicum Mythologiae Classicae* 8: 923–41.

Brown, E. L.
1977   The Divine Name "Pan." *Transactions of the American Philological Association* 107: 57–61.

Caubet, A.
1976   La collection R. Hamilton Lang au Musée du Louvre: Antiquités de Pyla. *Report of the Department of Antiquities, Cyprus*: 168–77.

Cesnola, L. P. di
1885   *A Descriptive Atlas of the Cesnola Collection of Cypriote Antiquities in the Metropolitan Museum of Art, New York.* Boston: J. R. Osgood.

Cofer, C. M.
2001   Relief-Statuettes of Pan from the Mesaoria Valley of Cyprus: Evidence from the Sanctuary of Athienou-*Malloura.* Unpublished M. A. thesis, Bryn Mawr College.

Colonna-Ceccaldi, G.
1882   *Monuments antiques de Chypre, de Syrie et d'Egypte.* Paris: Dedier.

Connelly, J. B.
1988   *Votive Sculpture of Hellenistic Cyprus.* Nicosia and New York: Department of Antiquities of Cyprus and New York University Press with the assistance of the J. Paul Getty Trust.

Counts, D. B.
1998   Contributions to the Study of Cypriote Sculpture: Limestone Votives from Athienou-*Malloura.* Unpublished Ph.D dissertation, Brown University.
2008   Master of the Lion: Representation and Hybridity in Cypriote Sanctuaries. *American Journal of Archaeology* 112: 3–27.

2009   From Siwa to Cyprus: The Assimilation of
        Zeus Ammon in the Cypriote Pantheon. Pp.
        104–17 in *Egypt and Cyprus in Antiquity,*
        eds. D. Michaelides, V. Kassianidou, and R.
        Merrillees. Oxford: Oxbow.

Decaudin, A. J.
1982   *Les antiquités chypriotes dans les collections
        publique françaises.* Paris: A. G. Leventis
        Foundation.

Dikaios, P.
1947   *A Guide to the Cyprus Museum.* Nicosia:
        Cyprus Government Printing Office.

Donkow, I.
2005   Three Cypriote Heads of Pan in the Collection
        of the Museum of Mediterranean and
        Near Eastern Antiquities in Stockholm.
        Medelhavsmuseet. Focus on the Mediterranean
        2: 69–94.

Flourentzos, P.
1989   The Iconography of the God Pan in Cypriot
        Sculpture. *Report of the Department of
        Antiquities, Cyprus*: 121–26.

Gjerstad, E.; Lindros, J.; Sjöqvist, E.; and Westholm, A.
1937   *The Swedish Cyprus Expedition.* Vol. 3.
        Stockholm: The Swedish Cyprus Expedition.

Glover, S. C.
1981   The Cults of Apollo in Cyprus: A Preliminary
        Survey. Pp. 145–51 in *Studies in Cypriote
        Archaeology*, eds. J. C. Biers and D. Soren. Los
        Angeles: Institute of Archaeology, University
        of California.

Hermary, A.
1989   *Musée du Louvre, Département des antiquités
        orientales: Catalogue des antiquités de Chypre.
        Sculptures.* Paris: Editions de la réunion des
        musées nationaux.

Hill, G.
1940   *A History of Cyprus.* Cambridge: Cambridge
        University.

Hogarth, D. G.; James, M. R.; Elsey Smith, R.;
and Gardner, E. A.
1888   Excavations in Cyprus, 1887–1888. Paphos,
        Leontari, Amargetti. *Journal of Hellenic Studies*
        9: 147–271.

Jenkins, K.
1966   *Coins of Greek Sicily.* London: British
        Museum.

Karageorghis, V.
1962   Chronique des Fouilles à Chypre en 1961.
        Bulletin de Correspondance Hellénique 86: 350.
1979   Material from a Sanctuary at Potamia. *Report
        of the Department of Antiquities, Cyprus*:
        289–315.
1981   De l'adaptation et de la transformation de
        la mythologie grecque à Chypre durant les
        périodes archaïque et classique. Pp. 79–82
        in *Mythologie Gréco-Romaine, Mythologies
        Périphériques. Études d'iconographie*, eds. L.
        Kahil and C. Augé. Paris: Centre national de la
        recherche scientifique.
2000   *Ancient Art from Cyprus: The Cesnola
        Collection in the Metropolitan Museum of Art.*
        New York: Metropolitan Museum of Art.

Laubscher, H. P.
1985   Hellenistische Herrscher und Pan. *Mitteilungen
        des Deutschen Archaologischen Instituts.
        Athenische Abteilung* 100: 333–53.

Marquardt, N.
1995   *Pan in der hellenistischen und kaiserzeitlichen
        Plastik.* Bonn: Habelt.

Masson, O.
1960   Cultes indigenes, cultes grecs et cultes
        orientaux à Chypre. Pp. 129–42 in *Eléments
        orientaux dans la religion grecque ancienne*, ed.
        O. Eissfeldt. Paris: Universitaires de France.

May, J. M. F.
1950   *Ainos, Its History and Coinage 471–341 BC.*
        Oxford: Oxford University.

Michaelides, D.
1996   The Economy of Cyprus during the Hellenistic
        and Roman Periods. Pp. 139–52 in *The
        Development of the Cypriot Economy from the*

Prehistoric Period to the Present Day, eds. V. Karageorghis and D. Michaelides. Nicosia: Lithographica.

Mitford, T. B.
1946   Religious Documents from Roman Cyprus. *Journal of Hellenic Studies* 66: 25–32.
1961   Further Contributions to the Epigraphy of Cyprus. *American Journal of Archaeology* 65: 93–151.
1979   The Nymphaeum of Kafizin. Pp. 160–65 in *Studies Presented in Memory of Porphyrios Dikaios*, ed. V. Karageorghis. Nicosia: Lions Club of Nicosia and Zavallis.
1980   *The Nymphaeum of Kafizin: The Inscribed Pottery*. Berlin: W. de Gruyter.

Młynarczyk, J.
1990   *Nea Paphos III: Nea Paphos in the Hellenistic Period*. Warsaw: PWN, Éditions scientifiques de Pologne.

Mørkholm, O.
1991   *Early Hellenistic Coinage: From the Accession of Alexander to the Peace of Apamea (336–188 BC)*, eds. P. Grierson and U. Westermark. Cambridge: Cambridge University.

Myres, J. L.
1914   *Handbook of the Cesnola Collection of Antiquities from Cyprus, Metropolitan Museum of Art, New York*. New York: Metropolitan Museum of Art.
1945   A Sanctuary Site at Lefkoniko. *Annual of the British School at Athens* 41: 54–68.

Myres, J. L., and Ohnefalsch-Richter, M.
1899   *A Catalogue of the Cyprus Museum with a Chronicle of Excavations Undertaken since the British Occupation and Introductory Notes on Cypriote Archaeology*. Oxford: Clarendon.

Ohnefalsch-Richter, M.
1893   *Kypros, the Bible and Homer*. London: Asher.

Panagopoulou, E.
2000   Antigonos Gonatas: Coinage, Money and the Economy. Unpublished Ph.D. dissertation, University College, London.

Pryce, F. N.
1928   *Catalogue of Sculpture in the Department of Greek and Roman Antiquities of the British Museum*. Vol. 1, pt. 2, *Cypriot and Etruscan*. London: Trustees of the British Museum.

Senff, R.
1993   *Das Apollonheiligtum von Idalion: Architektur und Statuenausstattung eines zyprischen Heiligtums*. Studies in Mediterranean Archaeology 94. Jonsered: Åström.

Sophocleous, S.
1985   *Atlas des representations chypro-archaïque des divinités*. Göteborg: Åström.

Vessberg, O., and Westholm, A.
1937   *Swedish Cyprus Expedition*. Vol. 4, pt. 3, *The Hellenistic and Roman Periods in Cyprus*. Stockholm: The Swedish Cyprus Expedition.

Westholm, A.
1936   *The Temples of Soli: Studies on Cypriote Art during the Hellenistic and Roman Periods*. Stockholm: The Swedish Cyprus Expedition.

Chapter 13

Writing from Unknown Hands

A Selection of Inscriptions from Athienou-*Malloura*

by Elisabetta Cova

Since 1990, excavation and survey by the Athienou Archaeological Project at the site of Athienou-*Malloura* have provided a small but interesting corpus of inscribed objects, which are associated primarily with the open-air, rural sanctuary (fig. 13.1; see Toumazou and Counts, Ch. 6). The majority of the inscriptions, like other archaeological finds from the sanctuary, can be dated from the Cypro-Archaic to the Hellenistic period, with few examples ranging from the Roman to the modern period. With the exception of a Roman lamp signed in Latin, Greek appears to be the only language represented, written in both the Cypro-syllabic script and the Greek alphabet. The inscriptions are all incised (vs. painted) and most come from ceramic vessel fragments; one partial inscription is found on a limestone ash shovel. This chapter begins with a brief background on scripts and languages in ancient Cyprus and then presents a selection of inscriptions brought to light by AAP (Table 13.1), offering some preliminary observations regarding their interpretation as well as their contribution to the larger picture of Malloura's place within Iron Age Cyprus.

Writing and Languages on Cyprus

According to the current state of epigraphic evidence, the first script used in Cyprus was the Cypro-Minoan, a syllabic script so named for its similarities to the Minoan Linear A (Masson 1974; Palaima 1989). Cypro-Minoan first appeared toward the end of the 16th century BC and was in use until the 11th century BC; because the script remains undeciphered, the language (or languages) for which it was used is still unknown. During the first millennium BC, the Cypriot syllabary dominates the epigraphic evidence on Cyprus (Masson 1983; Egetmeyer 1992; Bazemore 1998). Considered to have been derived from Cypro-Minoan, the development of the Cypriot syllabary and its relationship to this earlier script are still unclear (Masson 1983: 29–42; Olivier 2008). An *obelos* (skewer) discovered at Palaepaphos inscribed with the Greek name "Opheltas" and dated to the Cypro-Geometric I period (1050–950 BC) had been commonly accepted as the first evidence of the use of the Cypro-syllabic script and the Greek language in the Arcado-Cypriot dialect on Cyprus

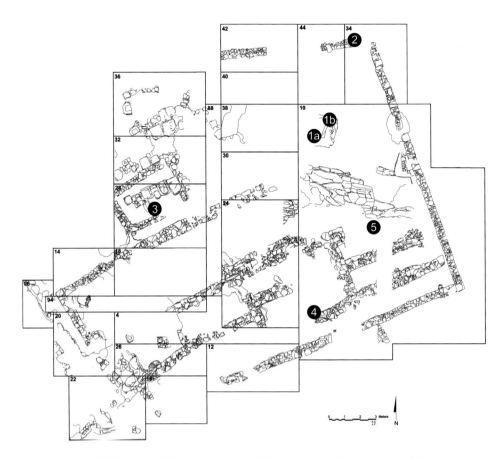

FIG. 13.1 *Plan of Athienou-*Malloura *sanctuary with location of inscriptions presented in the text (drawing: A. Prins).*

TABLE 13.1   Selected inscriptions from Athienou-*Malloura* discussed in the text.

Insc. No.	Accession Number	Dimensions*	Location	Material/Object
1	AAP-AM 1680.1–2	1: L 5.31, W 2.66, Th 0.64 2: L 3.86, W 3.18, Th 0.65	EU 10 (SU 1099.159)	Ceramic vessel
2	AAP-AM 2518	L 6.48, W 7.93, H 4.67	EU 34 (SU 3413)	Limestone ash shovel
3	AAP-AM 2947	L 8.80, W 3.49, Th 0.70	EU 28 (SU 2868)	Ceramic vessel
4	AAP-AM 936	L 2.5, W 1.53, Th 0.25	EU 10 (SU 1099.106)	Ceramic vessel
5	AAP-AM 789	L 11.2, W 7.3, Th 3.5	EU 10 (SU 1099.098)	Ceramic vessel
6	AAP-AM 362	L 6.8, W 5.8, H 1.90	Tomb 27 (SU 2764)	Ceramic lamp

Dimensions are given in cm (L = max. length; W = width; D = depth; Th = thickness; H = height).

(Karageorghis 1983: 60–61; Masson and Masson 1983: 412–14; Palaima 1991: 451–55; Sherratt 2003: 225–27). However, recent paleographic studies have identified the signs of this inscription as Cypro-Minoan, not Cypro-syllabic (Olivier 2008: 608; Panayotou-Triantaphyllopoulou 2008: 653; for other recent discussions of the *obelos,* see Iacovou 2008a: 633; Knapp 2008: 288–89). In light of this new interpretation, the first epigraphic evidence of Cypro-syllabic texts should be dated to the eighth century BC. During the Archaic and Classical periods, the Cypriot syllabary was used on the island to write both the Arcado-Cypriot dialect of Greek and the local, still unknown language (or languages) referred to as Eteocypriot (on the introduction of the Greek language and the Arcado-Cypriot dialect on Cyprus, see Iacovou 2006: 36–39; 2008b: 234–36; for Eteocypriot, see Masson 1983: 85–87; Reyes 1994: 13–17, 22; Given 1998; Petit 1999). Variants within the usage of the Cypriot syllabary can be grouped into two principal categories: the so-called Common syllabary and the Paphian (or Southwestern) syllabary (Masson 1983: 57–67). The Common syllabary is attested across the majority of the island and was used for most of the Eteocypriot inscriptions (mainly from Amathous), while the Paphian syllabary, as the name suggests, was common in Paphos and the southwestern parts of the island. In the majority of the texts the former is sinistroverse (i.e., written right to left) and the latter is dextroverse (left to right). Although the Greek alphabet is attested on the island as early as the late seventh century BC (Mitford 1971: 11–14), the Cypriot syllabary continued to be used widely until the end of the third century BC (for the interaction between the Greek alphabet and the Cypriot syllabary, see Palaima 1991). Its last occurrence is attested in the inscriptions dated to 225–218 BC found at the Nymphaeum of Kafizin north of Idalion (Mitford 1980a), although sealings inscribed with the Cypriot syllabary found at Nea Paphos in the House of Dionysus and dated from the second half of the second century to the end of the first century BC suggest that its use continued after the end of the third century BC (Michaelidou-Nicolaou 1993; Bazemore 2002: 158).

Despite the pro-Hellenic policy of King Evagoras I of Salamis (411–374 BC), it was only from the late fourth or early third century BC, under Ptolemaic rule, that the Greek alphabet became the dominant script on the island (Masson 1983: 78–80; Palaima 1991). Since Greek continued to be the official language of the eastern provinces of the Roman empire, including Cyprus, the evidence for Latin inscriptions is scarce and limited to milestones, dedications of buildings, and epitaphs on gravestones of Roman soldiers (Mitford 1980b: 1355–57).

In addition to Greek and the local Eteocypriot, Phoenician is also attested on the island in the first millennium BC. Although the earliest evidence for Phoenician inscriptions on Cyprus dates to ca. 900 BC (Masson and Sznycer 1972: 15–20, 128–30; Lipinski 2004: 42), the Phoenician alphabet seems to have been "officially" introduced when the Phoenicians first settled at Kition at the end of the ninth century BC (Karageorghis 2002: 144). The Phoenician language and script were widely used in the kingdom of Kition until the beginning of the Hellenistic period (end of the fourth century BC), when Phoenician rule ended and the whole of Cyprus became Ptolemaic territory. An important contribution to the Phoenician epigraphic evidence on the island is represented by the numerous inscriptions dated to the Cypro-Classical period brought to light at the newly discovered administrative complex of Idalion, currently under excavation by Maria Hadjicosti of the Department of Antiquities, Cyprus (Hadjicosti 1997; Sznycer 2004).

THE INSCRIPTIONS FROM ATHIENOU-*MALLOURA*

Cypriot Syllabary

In this section, a selection of Cypro-syllabic inscriptions recovered at the sanctuary of Athienou-*Malloura* is presented. Each is accompanied by a transliteration of the syllabic characters and its Greek alphabetic version, followed by a discussion of possible interpretations, comparable examples, and general observations on their relationship to the archaeological context and ritual practices. The inscriptions' dating relied on their stratigraph-

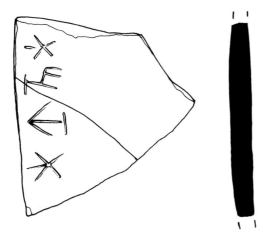

FIG. 13.2 *Cypro-syllabic inscription on two adjoining sherds from Athienou-Malloura. Inscription 1, AAP-AM 1680.1–2: Larnaka District Museum, Cyprus (drawing: M. Dalton).*

ic contexts, since paleographic criteria offer little help when looking at Cypro-syllabic inscriptions. Because most were found on nondiagnostic body sherds of Plain White Ware (a type of ware attested over a long span of time), ceramic ware and style could not provide a more accurate date.

Inscription 1

The inscription that permits the most certain interpretation (1, AAP-AM 1680.1–2) consists of four Cypro-syllabic characters inscribed on two adjoining sherds found in the sanctuary in a Cypro-Classical context (fig. 13.2). The sherds were excavated in the hard-packed deposits underlying the floor associated with the late-fourth-century reorganization of the sanctuary. The inscription, which is sinistroverse and easily legible, reads:

i-tu-ka-i

alph. ἰ(ν) τύχαι

In this formula ἰν = ἐν in the Arcado-Cypriot dialect (ι is used instead of ε before ν) and is followed by the dative ending -αι of the word τύχη. This phrase, translated as "in good fortune," is amply attested in dedications at sanctuaries throughout

the island (for example, see Mitford 1980a: 120–21, no. 156?; 128, no. 168; 128–29, no. 169a; 158–59, no. 216; 187–88, no. 252; Masson 1983: 96, no. 2; 141, no. 85; 142, no. 86; 196, no. 182; 213, no. 204; 216, nos. 209–10; 218, no. 212; 224–26, no. 215; 226–28, no. 216; 246–48, no. 220; 261–62, no. 244; 262, no. 245; 269, no. 252; 286, no. 265; 289, no. 273; 333, no. 335; 336, no. 339; 338, no. 342; 421, no. 352b; 422, nos. 369 [= 339], 343; 1988: 63–68, no. 5). It is usually associated with the name of the god or goddess to whom the dedication is made and often includes the name of the dedicant. In this case, due to the fragmentary condition of the inscription, the names of both the god and dedicant are absent. Nevertheless, the inscription reflects the religious nature of the activities within the sanctuary at Malloura. Like the numerous dedications in terracotta (Averett, Ch. 10) and limestone (Counts, Ch. 11), the dedication of ceramic vessels was an important element in the reciprocal relationships characteristic of votive religion. The dedicant offered the object in good fortune to the god, to give thanks for benefits received or in the hope of future protection and/or munificence.

Inscription 2

The next inscription (2, AAP-AM 2518) is visible on the longer of the two sides of a fragmentary limestone ash shovel (fig. 13.3). It was found in the sanctuary at the beginning of the 2004 season while clearing debris that had fallen into the trench from the northwestern balk of EU 34 and therefore cannot be dated based on stratigraphic context. The inscription consists of four characters written from right to left.

] -?- *u-e-mi*

alph. -?υ ἡμί

The first character, cut off vertically by a break in the limestone, is not sufficiently preserved to allow a definitive reading. The second and third characters, fully preserved, can be transcribed as the vowels -*u*- and -*e*-, while the fourth, although broken off, can be easily identified with the sign for the syllable -*mi*-. The -*u*- could be part of the genitive singular ending -*au*, which is the typical ending for male names with the -α stem in the Cypriot dialect (as in the famous *obelos* of Opheltas). However, the first character (before -*u*-) is too fragmentary to be identified as -*a*- or as a syllable ending in -*a*. Another possible reading for this character could be -*xe*-, but the combination -*xeu* at the end of a word is not previously attested (see Etgemeyer 1992; Hintze 1993). However, an ending in -*u* alone of the genitive is found in the word *pi-lo-ni-u* as the transcription in Cypro-syllabic characters of the Koine ending -ου of the genitive of the male personal name Φιλώνιος or Φιλούνιος (Egetmeyer 1992: 139; Hintze 1993: 61). This form is found in many inscriptions from Kafizin (see Mitford 1980a). The -*e*- character, although roughly inscribed, seems to conform to the Idalion syllabary as described by Masson (1983: 59); similar parallels with the Idalion syllabary are seen in two further inscriptions with the same character (nos. 3 and 4, below). This is one of several inscriptions found at Malloura that present the formula "I am" (ἠμί/εἰμί) followed by what appears to be the genitive of a personal name. This formula, usually found on epitaphs, is also attested on objects or statuary dedicated in sanctuaries or, more generally, in votive contexts where the object itself "speaks," thereby informing us of the owner's/dedicator's name (for examples of dedications from sanctuaries, see Mitford and Masson 1983: 41–42, no. 12; 57, no. 38; Masson and Mitford 1986: 42–43, no. 26; 44–45, no. 33; see Masson 1983: 283, no. 263, on a male votary from Golgoi; see also Karageorghis 2000: 116). In the example from Malloura, the fragmentary state of preservation prevents a clear reading and leaves us no clue to the name of the owner. Although often neglected in publications, ash shovels are common in Cypriot sanctuaries and were used as ritual implements, perhaps to clean the ashes from burnt sacrifices. Many ash shovel fragments have been found in the Malloura sanctuary and at other sites across the island (for two examples from Athienou-*Golgoi*, which are probably associated with a sanctuary within the ancient fortifications, see Bakalakis 1988: 132, nos. 3, 4, pl. 88).

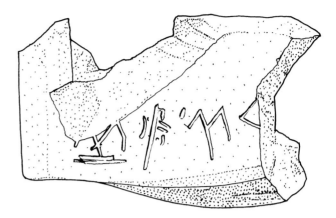

Fig. 13.3 *Cypro-syllabic inscription on a fragmentary limestone ash shovel from Athienou-*Malloura. *Inscription 2, AAP-AM 2518: Larnaka District Museum, Cyprus (drawing: M. Dalton).*

Inscription 3

A third fragmentary Cypro-syllabic inscription (3, AAP-AM 2947) is found on a ceramic sherd broken on all sides discovered at the bottom of a looter's pit. The fact that the sherd was found in a deposit of purely Cypro-Archaic material might suggest that excavators had dug beyond the bottom limits of the pit, penetrating a stratified layer beneath (fig. 13.4). The inscription consists of four fragmentary Cypro-syllabic characters written from right to left. The first of them is not sufficiently preserved to allow even a tentative reading, while the preserved portion of the second character could fit multiple readings, such as -*pi*-, -*o*-, -*so*-, or -*ku*- in both the common and Idalion syllabaries (Masson 1983: 58–59). The third and the fourth characters can be more easily identified as the characteristic -*e*- and -*mi*- (*emi* = I am). The more likely transliteration seems to be:

]-?-*o*/-*ō*-*e*-*mi*

alph. -?ο/ω ἠμί

The character -*o*- could represent the genitive singular of a male personal name, as often attested in this type of inscription with the verb ἠμί (I am of X...). Genitive endings in –*o* are quite common in Cypro-syllabic inscriptions. They have been interpreted either as Greek genitives ending in – ος, where the sigma is missing, or genitives ending in –ω, where ω is the result of the contraction of –οο

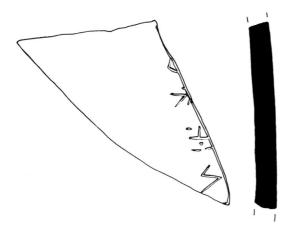

Fig. 13.4 *Cypro-syllabic inscription on ceramic sherd from* Athienou-Malloura. *Inscription 3, AAP-AM 2947: Larnaka District Museum, Cyprus (drawing: M. Dalton).*

Fig. 13.5 *Cypro-syllabic inscription on ceramic sherd from* Athienou-Malloura. *Inscription 4, AAP-AM 936: Larnaka District Museum, Cyprus (drawing: M. Dalton).*

from the original ending -οιο. To cite one example among many, Masson (1983: 144, no. 88a.1/2) reads the name *ti-mo-ke-re-te-o*, found on a funerary stele from Armagetti, as Τιμοκρέτεο(ς), the genitive singular of the male name Τιμοκρέτης (see also Egetmeyer 1992: 189; 2010: 579; Hintze 1993: 82). Masson (1983) also provides many examples of genitives in –ō, such as *pa-si-ti-mo*, which he reads Πασιτίμω, genitive of the male name Πασίτιμος. This form of the name appears on an ex-voto from Rantidhi associated with the verb ἠμί (Masson 1983: 131, no. 57; Egetmeyer 2010: 770, no. 181).

Inscription 4

Another inscribed triangular body fragment of a thin-walled, wheel-made vessel (4, AAP-AM 936) was found in the sanctuary in ancient debris from a collapsed wall that contains mixed pottery from the Cypro-Archaic to Hellenistic periods. The sherd, broken on all sides, is inscribed with three Cypro-syllabic characters (fig. 13.5). The first from the right is partially preserved and can be interpreted as the character -*to*-, the second may be a roughly inscribed -*e*-, while the last is clearly -*mi*-.

]-*to*/-*tō*?-*e*-*mi*

(alph. -το/τω? ἠμί)

As in the previous inscription, here we see the formula "I am of X," but once again the name of the owner/dedicant is not preserved. The character -*to*- is attested as the genitive singular ending of a personal male name in many Cypro-syllabic inscriptions. For example, Masson (1983: 111, no. 15b) reads *o-na-sa-to* as Ὀνάσα(ν)το(ς), genitive of Ὀνάσας found in a dedication on stone from Kouklia. Ὀνάσας seems to be a very common male name, attested several times in the epigraphic record (for other instances of the genitive form of this name, see Masson 1983: 137–38, no. 83; 171–72, no. 154; 316, no. 317; 349, no. 362; 384, no. 444b). Another reading would make the final -o of the genitive long, as in the name *a-ke-se-tō* (alph. Ἀκέστω, genitive of Ἄκεστος, male name; see Masson 1983: 350, no. 364), written on a seal of unknown provenance.

Greek and Latin

The following two examples are part of a very limited corpus of alphabetic inscriptions in Greek and Latin found at Malloura. Significantly, however, they provide important insight to the contacts of Malloura with other areas of the Mediterranean and its place within trade routes inside and outside the island during the Hellenistic and Roman periods.

Inscription 5

The only example of ancient Greek alphabetic inscription discovered in the
sanctuary thus far (with the exception
of coins) appears on a Rhodian stamp
on an amphora handle (5, AAP-AM
789, fig. 13.6) discovered in a stratified
deposit with other Hellenistic material.
The handle is broken just beyond the
curve, but preserves a small portion of
the rim. The shape is characteristic of
Rhodian amphorae (Grace 1976: 203).
The stamp, placed on the top of the
handle, is circular (diameter 2.8 cm)

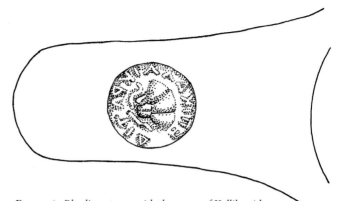

FIG. 13.6 *Rhodian stamp with the name of Kallikratidas
from Athienou-Malloura. Inscription 5, AAP-AM 789:
Larnaka District Museum, Cyprus (drawing: J. Ravenhurst).*

with a rose in relief; Greek letters appear around
the circumference and can be read as follows:

Ἐπί Καλλικρατίδ[α]

Stamps on Rhodian amphorae are mostly circular
(as in our example) or rectangular in shape; they
often depict a rose or, in other cases, the head of
Helios, which are both symbols of Rhodes and
provide clear indication of provenance (Grace
1976: 204). More important, the inscribed stamps
also bear the name of the eponym (the official
who gave his name to the year) in the accusative
after ἐπί (in the term of...) to indicate the date.
Sometimes the date is made more specific by add-
ing the name of a month (absent in our example)
after the name of the eponym. In other cases, the
stamp bears a name alone in the genitive case
("by") indicating the manufacturer. When complete vessels are found, one handle will sometimes
bear the manufacturer's name and the other the
eponym's name (Grace 1976: 204). "Kallikratidas,"
the name on this stamp, is associated with two
different eponyms found on Rhodian amphorae,
Kallikratidas I and II. Stamps of Kallikratidas
I, which are less numerous, can be dated to the
third century BC (the exact chronology is debated; according to Grace [1952: 529], it should
be dated between ca. 300 and 240 BC, while more
recently Nicolaou [2005: 11–14, 288–89] argues for
a later date, between 234 and 220 BC). Stamps of
Kallikratidas II, which are more common, are dated to ca. 188–186 BC by Grace (1985: 8–9; see also

Sztetyłło 1991: 43; Nicolaou 2005: 80–81) and ca.
175/173–169/167 by Finkielsztejn (2001: 196, Table
22.1). Our stamp is very likely of Kallikratidas
II because his stamps are more common on the
island and appear in other examples found in
Nea Paphos, Kition, and Salamis, as both circular
stamps with the rose and rectangular ones without
any additional image (for stamps of Kallikratidas
II found in Cyprus, see Calvet 1972: 30, no. 52; 1978:
226, no. 26; Sztetyłło 1976: 46–47, nos. 101–4; 1983:
368, no. 4; 1991: 43–46, nos. 51–58; Nicolaou 1981:
193, no. 4; 2005: part 1, 80–82, nos. 169–76, part 2,
appendix 1, 289–90, nos. 84–86, appendix 2, 363,
W18). In particular, our stamp finds parallels with
examples from Nea Paphos (Sztetyłło 1991: 43–44,
nos. 51–54; Nicolaou 2005: part 1, 80–81, no. 169),
which are also circular in shape with the rose
and likewise have the month omitted. Our stamp
therefore dates to a period of Rhodian prosperity, characterized by a large number of imports
to many sites on Cyprus (Nicolaou 2005: 9). The
predominance of Rhodian amphorae among imported amphorae on Cyprus reflects more generally the intensity of trade with Rhodes, especially
imports of Rhodian wine during Ptolemaic rule
on Cyprus (third to mid-first century BC). It is
in this period, especially in the third and second
centuries BC, that Rhodes becomes a strong commercial power in the eastern Mediterranean (see
Nicolaou 2005: 5–7). Wine and the amphorae used
to carry it would have been common in sanctuaries, either as dedications or simply as part of the

accoutrements used by priests for various activities, such as the pouring of libations (liquid sacrifices) or ritual feasting in honor of the deity (for an example of ritual feasting and the use of wine in a sanctuary context, see the relief decoration on a plaque from Golgoi; Karageorghis 2000, 221–22, fig. 352). In a rather striking way, the discovery of this amphora handle incorporates the rural sanctuary at Malloura into a larger pan-Mediterranean system. For example, Kallikratidas II stamps from Rhodes, such as the one published here, have also been found in deposits at Pergamon (Schuchhardt 1895: nos. 1063–81) and in the building fill of the Middle Stoa in the Athenian agora (Grace 1985: 9).

Inscription 6

An excellent example of a Latin inscription (6, AAP-AM 362), this time from a funerary context, is found on a mold-made terracotta lamp (fig. 13.7; see also figs. 14.8–9 for a top view and illustration of the inscription) discovered in Tomb 27 at Athienou-*Mağara Tepeşi* (Gordon [Ch. 14] discusses the typology and the dating of the lamp; for a detailed description of the lamp and a general discussion of Romanesis in Cyprus, see Gordon and Cova 2010). The lamp is an example of Vessberg Type 13, which is dated to the mid-first to second century AD but seems to have continued in use for a longer time in Cyprus (Vessberg and Westholm 1956: 189–90). The lamp is circular in shape with an eight-petal rosette decoration in the discus and a leaf wreath on the rim (for a lamp of the same type and decoration, see Vessberg and Westholm 1956, 3, fig. 39, no. 3). On the base, within an impressed circle, is the workshop's name, Romanesis, in Latin letters (see Gordon, Ch. 14, who first identified the signature). It should be noted that the -*n*- in the correct spelling of the word "Romanensis" is dropped (Heres 1968: 204). Other examples of Romanesis lamps present variants in the lettering of the workshop's signature; in some cases Greek letters (Ω and H) are used in place of the Latin O and E (i.e., RΩMANESIS, RΩMANHSIS, ROMANHSIS), and the letter S is often written backward or in a few instances substituted with a Greek lunate sigma C. Occasionally, the signature

Fig. 13.7 *Signed Roman lamp from the Romanesis workshop from Athienou-*Malloura. *Inscription 6, AAP-AM 362: Larnaka District Museum, Cyprus (© AAP).*

is written on two lines (for examples of variants, see Heres 1968: 207–10; see nos. 21, 28 for very similar signatures). Greek slaves or freedmen who inscribed the base of the lamp after molding were probably responsible for the different spellings, but as Heres (1968: 205) explains, these variants should not be necessarily interpreted as evidence of Greek or eastern provenance of the lamps. The signature on our lamp presents the correct spelling, and the letters are well-written on a single line, evenly occupying the available space. This careful execution (especially when compared with other lamps attributed to the same workshop) may indicate a higher level of literacy and expertise on the part of the scribe. According to Heres (1968: 204, 206), the name Romanesis does not indicate the location of the workshop, but the origin of the owner — he was of Italian origin and worked abroad. Heres (1968: 203–4) also suggests that the workshop may have been located in a commercial city of Asia Minor (e.g., Miletos or Knidos) where large numbers of Romanesis lamps have been found. From there they would have easily reached other areas of the central and eastern Mediterranean where similar lamps have been found, such as mainland Greece and the islands, the African coast, Italy, and Dalmatia. In chronological terms, Romanesis lamps seem to range from the last third of the first century to the first half of the second century AD (Heres 1968: 201–3), which would confirm the dating of the lamp based on its type (Vessberg 13). Although other examples of Romanesis lamps have been found on Cyprus (see Gordon, Ch. 14; Gordon and Cova 2010), no signed parallels to our lamp can be identified. However, the presence in Malloura of a lamp from a workshop so strongly established in the Mediterranean provides a glimpse of the wider movement of people and goods within the valley and beyond.

CONCLUSION

The corpus of inscriptions from which this selection is taken is rather small. This is especially evident when considering the large amount of sculpture and pottery excavated at Athienou-*Malloura,* not only in the Cypro-Geometric–Roman sanctuary but also in the Hellenistic–Roman tombs and the Late Roman–Venetian remains. The scarcity of written evidence could be explained as a consequence of the use of paint to mark objects or of perishable materials as writing surfaces (on the use of wood and other perishable materials in the Late Bronze Age and Iron Age Cyprus, see Smith 2002: 7–10). However, it could also be an indication of the limited extent of literacy in the rural Malloura Valley or more simply the result of the randomness of archaeological discoveries.

Although limited, the epigraphic evidence from Malloura provides significant glimpses of the activities within the valley, especially in the sanctuary. In fact, the inscriptions from Malloura and the objects on which they are written clearly reflect their religious context. The Cypro-syllabic formulas "in good fortune" and "I am of X" found on ceramic vessels deposited as offerings bear witness to acts of dedication performed in the sanctuary, while the ash shovel and the amphora remind us of sacrificial and dedicatory rituals connected to the life of the sanctuary. Also the Roman lamp, the only inscribed object found outside the sanctuary, is associated with funerary rites and beliefs (see Gordon, Ch. 14). In other words, the epigraphic record from the Malloura excavations thus far corroborates the evidence for religious and funerary activities within the valley.

In terms of scripts, it should be noted that the Malloura syllabic characters show similarities with the common and Idalion syllabaries as presented by Masson (1983: 58–59). This seems to suggest a connection to the territory of Idalion, which is consistent with additional indications of cultural affinities between the two sites (see Fourrier, Ch. 9 and Averett, Ch. 10). Nevertheless, a linguistic argument defining Malloura as part of Idalion's political circuit would require a larger and more varied corpus of inscriptions. The syllabic epigraphic evidence from Malloura, moreover, indicates a persistence of the local syllabic script (vs. the Greek alphabet) in the Cypro-Archaic and Cypro-Classical periods, which is characteristic of the rest of the island. This can be seen as a sign of pride in local traditions as well as an indication of the relative isolation of the Malloura Valley. For later periods, the alphabetic scripts in Greek and Latin illustrate contact extending even beyond the island's boundaries and reflect the fuller incorporation of local communities into the larger Mediterranean system of the Hellenistic and Roman periods, respectively (see especially the comments in Kardulias et al., Ch. 1). The imported Rhodian stamp is consistent with the picture of Hellenistic Cyprus as a prosperous place with intense trade relationships, where Koine Greek had become the dominant language, while the Latin lamp reveals the "global" connections typical of Rome's large, multicultural empire.

To conclude, while the Cypro-syllabic inscriptions on dedicatory or ritual objects situate Archaic and Classical Malloura as part of a local system of sanctuaries within the island, the Rhodian stamp and the Roman lamp integrate Hellenistic and Roman Malloura into a larger system of commercial exchanges within the Mediterranean. Although modest in size, the corpus reveals important evidence for various forms of ritual activity within the Malloura Valley, in addition to providing an index for tracking broader local and regional connections in Cyprus and the eastern Mediterranean.

References

Bakalakis, G.
1988 *Ανασκαφή στο Λόφο Γιόρκους BA της Αθηαίνου, Κύπρος.* Athens: Αρχαιολογική Εταιρεία Αθηνών.

Bazemore, G. B.
1998 *The Role of Script in Ancient Society.* Unpublished Ph. D. dissertation, University of Chicago.
2002 The Display and Viewing of the Syllabic Inscriptions of Rantidi Sanctuary. Pp. 155–212 in *Script and Seal Use in Cyprus in the Bronze and Iron Age.* Colloquia and Conference Papers 4, ed. J. S. Smith. Boston: Archaeological Institute of America.

Calvet, Y.
1972 *Salamine de Chypre III. Les timbres amphoriques (1965–1970).* Paris: de Boccard.
1978 Timbres amphoriques da Salamine 1971–1974. *Report of the Department of Antiquities, Cyprus*: 222–34.

Egetmeyer, M.
1992 *Wörterbuch zu den Inschriften im Kyprischen Syllabar.* Kadmos Supplement 3. Berlin and New York: de Gruyter.
2010 *Le dialecte grec ancien de Chypre.* Tome I: *Grammaire,* Tome 2: *Répertoire des inscriptions en syllabaire chypro-grec.* Berlin: de Gruyter.

Finkielsztejn, G.
2001 *Chronologie détaillée et révisée des éponymes amphoriques rhodiens, de 270 à 108 av. J.- C. environ. Premier bilan.* British Archaeological Reports, International Series 990. Oxford: Archaeopress.

Given, M.
1998 Inventing the Eteocypriots: Imperialist Archaeology and the Manipulation of Ethnic Identity. *Journal of Mediterranean Archaeology* 11(1): 3–29.

Gordon J. M., and Cova, E.
2010 Romanesis in Cyprus: A Lamp from Athienou-*Malloura. Cahiers du Centre d'Études Chypriotes* 40: 277–94.

Grace, V.
1952 Timbres amphoriques trouvés à Délos. *Bulletin de Correspondance Hellénique* 76: 514–50.
1976 *Stamped Amphora Handles Found in the Athenian Agora 1931–1932.* Chicago: Ares.
1985 The Middle Stoa Dated by Amphora Stamps. *Hesperia* 54: 1–54.

Hadjicosti, M.
1997 The Kingdom of Idalion in the Light of New Evidence. *Bulletin of the American Schools of Oriental Research* 308: 50–63.

Heres, G.
1968 Die Wekstatt des Lampentöpfers Romanensis. *Forschungen und Berichte* 10, *Archäologische Beiträge*: 185–211.

Hintze, A.
1993 *A Lexicon to the Cyprian Syllabic Inscriptions.* Lexicographia Orientalis 2. Hamburg: Helmut Buske.

Iacovou, M.
2006 'Greeks,' 'Phoenicians' and 'Eteocypriots.' Ethnic Identities in the Cypriote Kingdoms. Pp. 27–59 in *"Sweet Land…" Lectures on the History and Culture of Cyprus*, eds. J. Chrysostomides and C. Dendrinos. Camberley: Porphyrogenitus.
2008a Cultural and Political Configurations in Iron Age Cyprus: The Sequel to a Protohistoric Episode. *American Journal of Archaeology* 112: 625–57.
2008b Cyprus: From Migration to Hellenisation. Pp. 219–288 in *Greek Colonisation. An Account of Greek Colonies and Other Settlements Overseas*, ed. G. Tsetskhladze. Mnemosyne Supplement 193, vol. 2. Leiden: Brill.

Karageorghis, V.
1983 *Palaepaphos-Skales: An Iron Age Cemetery in Cyprus.* Konstanz: Universitätsverlag Konstanz.
2000 *Ancient Art from Cyprus: The Cesnola Collection.* New York: Metropolitan Museum of Art.

2002 *Early Cyprus: Crossroads of the Mediterranean.* Los Angeles: The J. Paul Getty Museum.

Knapp, A. B.
2008 *Prehistoric and Protohistoric Cyprus. Identity, Insularity and Connectivity.* Oxford: Oxford University.

Lipinski, E.
2004 *Itineraria Phoenicia.* Studia Phoenicia 18. Orientalia Lovaniensia Analecta. Louvain: Peeters.

Masson, E.
1974 *Cyprominoica: Répertoires, documents de Ras Shamra, essais d'interpretation.* Studies in Mediterranean Archaeology 31:2. Göteborg: Åström.

Masson, O.
1983 *Les inscriptions Chypriotes syllabiques. Recueil critique et commenté. Réimpression augmentée.* Paris: de Boccard.
1988 L'inscription syllabique en paphien récent du village de Tala (Paphos). *Report of the Department of Antiquities, Cyprus* 2: 63–68.

Masson, E., and Masson, O.
1983 Les objects inscrits de Palaepaphos-*Skales.* Pp. 411–15 in *Palaepaphos*-Skales. *An Iron Age Cemetery in Cyprus*, by V. Karageorghis. Konstanz: Universitätsverlag Konstanz.

Masson, E., and Mitford, T. B.
1986 *Les inscriptions syllabiques de Kouklia-Paphos.* Konstanz: Universitätsverlag Konstanz.

Masson, O., and Sznycer, M.
1972 *Recherches sur les Phéniciens à Chypre.* Geneva and Paris: Centre de Recherches d'Historie et de Philologie.

Michaelidou-Nicolaou, I.
1993 Nouveaux documents pour le syllabaire chypriote. *Bulletin de Correspondance Hellénique* 117: 343–47.

Mitford, T. B.
1971 *The Inscriptions of Kourion.* Philadelphia: American Philosophical Society.

1980a *The Nymphaeum of Kafizin. The Inscribed Pottery.* Kadmos Supplement 2. Berlin: de Gruyter.
1980b Roman Cyprus. *Aufstieg und Niedergang der römischen Welt* 2, 7.2: 1285–384.

Mitford, T. B., and Masson, O.
1983 *The Syllabic Inscriptions of Rantidi-Paphos.* Konstanz: Universitätsverlag Konstanz.

Nicolaou, I.
1981 Inscriptiones Cypriae Alphabeticae 10, 1980. *Report of the Department of Antiquities, Cyprus*: 187–204.
2005 *Paphos V. The Stamped Amphora Handles.* Nicosia: Department of Antiquities of Cyprus.

Olivier, J. P.
2008 Les syllabaires chypriotes des deuxième et premier millénaires avant notre ère. État des questions. Pp. 605–20 in *Colloquium Romanum. Atti del XII colloquio internazionale di micenologia, Roma 20-25 febbraio 2006,* eds. A Sacconi, M. Del Freo, L. Godart, M. Negri. Pisa, Rome: Fabrizio Serra.

Palaima, T. G.
1989 Cypro-Minoan Scripts: Problems of Historical Context. Pp. 121–87 in *Problems in Decipherment*, eds. Y. Duhoux, T.G. Palaima, and J. Bennet. Louvain-la-Neuve: Peeters.
1991 The Advent of the Greek Alphabet on Cyprus: A Competition of Scripts. Pp. 449-71 in *Phoinikeia Grammata. Lire et écrire en Méditerranée. Actes du Colloque de Liège, 15-18 novembre 1989,* eds. C. Baurain, C. Bonnet, and V. Krings. Namur: Société de Études Classiques.

Panayoutou-Triantaphyllopoulou, A.
2008 Les écritures chypriotes et la présence mycénienne à Chypre. Pp. 651–58 in *Colloquium Romanum. Atti del XII colloquio internazionale di micenologia, Roma 20–25 febbraio 2006,* eds. A Sacconi, M. Del Freo, L. Godart, M. Negri. Pisa, Rome: Fabrizio Serra.

Petit, T.
1999 Eteocypriot Myth and Amathusian Reality. *Journal of Mediterranean Archaeology* 12(1): 108–20.

Reyes, A. T.
1994   *Archaic Cyprus. A Study of the Textual and Archaeological Evidence.* Oxford: Oxford University.

Schuchhardt, C.
1895   Amphorenstempel. Pp. 423–99 in *Die Inschriften von Pergamon, Altertümer von Pergamon VIII 2,* ed. M. Fränkel. Berlin: Spemann.

Sherratt, S.
2003   Visible Writing: Questions of Script and Identity in Early Iron Age Greece and Cyprus. *Oxford Journal of Archaeology* 22(3): 225–42.

Smith, J. J.
2002   Problems and Prospects in the Study of Script and Seal Use on Cyprus in the Bronze and Iron Ages. Pp. 1–47 in *Script and Seal Use in Cyprus in the Bronze and Iron Age.* Colloquia and Conference Papers 4, ed. J. S. Smith. Boston: Archaeological Institute of America.

Sznycer, M.
2004   Idalion: Capital économique des rois phéniciens de Kition et d'Idalion. *Cahier du Centre d'Études Chypriotes* 34: 85–100.

Sztetyłło, Z.
1976   *Les timbres céramiques (1965–1973), Nea Paphos I.* Warsaw: Editions Scientifiques de Pologne.
1983   *Les timbres céramiques dans les collections du Musée national de Varsovie.* Warsaw: Editions Scientifiques de Pologne.
1991   *Nea Paphos IV. Pottery Stamps (1975–1989).* Warsaw: Centre d'Archéologie Méditerranéenne de l'Académie Polonaise des Sciences.

Vessberg, O., and Westholm, A.
1956   *The Hellenistic and Roman Periods in Cyprus.* The Swedish Cyprus Expedition 4, pt. 3. Stockholm: The Swedish Cyprus Expedition.

Chapter 14

Lux Aeterna

The Terracotta Lamps from the Hellenistic and Roman Tombs at Athienou-*Mağara Tepeşi*

by Jody Michael Gordon

In the Western religious imagination, perhaps the most mysterious, and hence pondered about, metaphorical boundary has been the threshold between life and death (Turner 1993: 1–4; Segal 2004: 1–23). Because humans need to understand the crossing of this boundary and cope with the end of life, people have often constructed visions of the unknown that can be understood according to everyday human experience (Green 1989: 48–50; van Baaren 1989: 98). Thus, imaginings of the afterlife have had to consider not only the natural setting of the "world beyond the grave" but also how this realm is illuminated (van Baaren 1989: 96–101).

For the ancient Greeks and Romans, the afterlife was a dark, subterranean place, the realm of Hades (Long 1989: 164; Turner 1993: 20–39; Segal 2004: 204–47). Yet the advent of Christianity offered an alternative vision. In the Book of John (8:12), Christ himself states, "I am the light of the world [τὸ φῶς τοῦ κόσμου]. Whoever follows me will never walk in darkness [ἐν τῇ σκοτίᾳ] but will have the light of life [τὸ φῶς τῆς ζωῆς]." This spiritual illumination also extended to the Christian setting for the afterlife of the faithful, the brilliantly lit kingdom of heaven (Tober and Lusby 1989: 152–53; Rev. 21–22).

Indeed, the image of a blindingly bright afterlife has become canonical in the Western psyche, and even today the Catholic mass for the dead still includes the words "Lux aeterna luceat eis," or "may eternal light shine upon them" (Kohlenberger III 1993: 186).

With these perspectives on the illumination of the afterlife in mind, this chapter on the Hellenistic and Roman terracotta lamps from the rock-cut chamber tombs at Athienou-*Mağara Tepeşi* highlights yet another type of boundary investigated by the Athienou Archaeological Project: the boundary between life and death. Since terracotta lamps were the primary source of lighting in antiquity, their discovery within a funerary context certainly provides an archaeological insight into ancient perspectives on the afterlife (Green 1989: 45). The lamps from Mağara Tepeşi also emphasize Malloura's position as a site at a crossroads, because lamps are unique ceramic artifacts that can provide information about chronology, trade, settlement patterns, and cultural fashions (Etienne 1987: 13–14; Parks 1999: 356).

This preliminary study of the Mağara Tepeşi lamps will consist of three sections. The first section (*Fiat lux*) briefly touches on how lamps discovered in Cypriot funerary contexts have been interpreted.

The second section (*Lux ex sepulcris*) provides an overview of the main types of lamps found at the necropolis site. A final section (*Lux ex tenebris*) outlines the main observable lamp trends and offers an interpretive discussion of what the lamps, and the site of Mağara Tepeşi in general, can tell us about Hellenistic and Roman Malloura.

FIAT LUX

For many years, Hellenistic and Roman terracotta lamps from Cyprus were not highly regarded as artifacts due to their ubiquity, lack of intrinsic value, and utilitarian nature (Bailey 1975: 206; Parks 1999: 357). By the mid-20th century, however, this situation was remedied by the publication of studies by Olof Vessberg (with Westholm 1956) and Thérèse Oziol (with Pouilloux 1969; 1977), which pioneered a standard typology for ancient Cypriot lamps. These studies were followed by D. M. Bailey's seminal, four-volume *A Catalogue of the Lamps in the British Museum* (1975–1996). In Volume I (Bailey 1975: 205–30; pls. 90–99; pls. 142–43), Bailey catalogued the Cypriot lamps dating from the Bronze Age to the Hellenistic period, while in Volume III (Bailey 1988: 292–318; pls. 63–71) he dealt with those from Roman and Late Roman times.

Most excavations have followed these studies when publishing their Hellenistic and Roman lamps, including two projects located in the Malloura region, Athienou-*Golgoi* (Bakalakis 1988) and Aradhippou-*Panayia Ematousa* (Sørensen and Jacobsen 2006). The Golgoi excavations yielded primarily Early Hellenistic lamps, while the Danish project at Panayia Ematousa uncovered a large corpus encompassing a wide typological and chronological range, making this site the best source of regional comparanda for the Mağara Tepeşi lamps. Nevertheless, besides Bailey's brief analysis of a selection of lamps from tomb assemblages at Kourion (Bailey 1988: 292–93), a broader, holistic study of Cypriot lamps from funerary contexts did not occur until the late 1990s, when Danielle Parks (1999: 356–60) conducted an overview of lamp types and an interpretation of lamp use in Hellenistic and Roman funerary rituals. Parks (1999: 356) observed

that the same locally produced lamp types used in Hellenistic and Roman settlements were also deposited in Cypriot tombs. She further observed that no single design of Roman mold-made lamps with decorated *disci* was more popular than another (Parks 1999: 358). In other words, people seemed to be depositing lamps they used in everyday life, and there were no specific funerary types.

Parks (1999: 356) also noted that the tradition of depositing lamps in Cypriot tombs went back to the Late Bronze Age (see also Vessberg and Westholm 1956: 184) and that the custom had continued through both Hellenistic and Roman times. Furthermore, she classed lamps as "objects linked to funerary ritual" and not as personal possessions of the deceased (Parks 1999: 318). Parks (1999: 283) made this distinction because lamps had a long tradition of use as ritual items in Greco-Roman funerary culture. In addition, she observed that "[f]or the most part, lamps are not associated with a specific burial" (Parks 1999: 356), and so, from an archaeological perspective, it did not seem that they should be classed with personal items such as clothing or jewelry. She therefore proposed that lamps could be ritually used in several ways. First, following the Greco-Roman tradition of a dimly lit afterlife, lamps were deposited "to keep vigil over the dead, lighting their way to the afterworld" (Parks 1999: 356, 392). Second, lamps could be lit to rekindle the spirits of the dead during anniversary tomb feasts such as the *cena novendialis* or the spring festivals of the *rosalia* or *violaria* (Parks 1999: 319–20). Third, lamps could have made their way into the tombs simply as a form of illumination for mourners and morticians (Parks 1999: 357, 392).

The excavations of Sophocles Hadjisavvas (1997) at the necropolis of Agia Napa-*Makronisos* should also be mentioned here due to the archaeological similarities between that site and Mağara Tepeşi. Like Mağara Tepeşi, Makronisos is a necropolis consisting of rock-cut chamber tombs of similar date and architectural design (Hadjisavvas 1997: 33, 39). In addition, several terracotta lamps were recovered that can be effectively compared with those from Mağara Tepeşi to indicate similarities and differences in islandwide lamp use and burial rituals.

FIG. 14.1 *View of the* dromos, forecourt, and stomion *of Tomb 27 at Mağara Tepeşi (photo: J. M. Gordon).*

Lux ex sepulcris

A Preliminary Analysis of the Lamps from Athienou-Mağara Tepeşi

A summary of the excavations and the nature of the discoveries at Mağara Tepeşi have been outlined elsewhere in this volume (see Toumazou and Counts, Ch. 6; Toumazou et al. 1998: 173–74). During the 1992 and 1993 excavation seasons at Mağara Tepeşi (Tombs 25–27), the AAP recovered many Hellenistic and Roman terracotta lamp fragments in various states of preservation (e.g., single fragments, multiple joining fragments, and complete lamps). In 2006 the present author organized and catalogued the remains. In total, 254 lamp sherds were recovered from the tombs. Once all possible joins and sherd fabric groups were correlated, it appeared that 71 distinct (i.e., once complete) lamps, both domestic and imported,

had been deposited throughout the four rock-cut chamber tombs (fig. 14.1). The following analysis of typological, chronological, and production trends is based on this corpus.

Lamp Types and Chronological Phases

AAP Mağara Tepeşi Lamp Type 1:
Wheel-made "Saucer-shaped" Lamps
(Vessberg Type 1; Hellenistic I and II)

The earliest lamps discovered in the tombs were examples of Vessberg Type 1, "saucer-shaped" lamps. These wheel-made lamps were open formed with rounded bases and were shaped like saucers with one section of the thick-walled rim hand-pinched into a wick holder (fig. 14.2; Vessberg and Westholm 1956: 121–22, 184; Oziol and Pouilloux 1969: 15–16). Our best-preserved examples include a full-size, single-wick lamp

(AAP-AM 217) and a miniature lamp (ca. 5 cm wide), both from Tomb 26, as well as a very impressive, large, double-wick version from Tomb 27 (fig. 14.3; AAP-AM 200). In total, 29 of the 254 individual sherds are of this type, or 11% of the assemblage, whereas 22 out of the 71 once complete lamps are of this type, or 31%. Since Type 1 lamps break into much larger sherds than those of other lamp types, however, their percentage within the total of once complete lamps (31%) may provide a better reflection of their original numbers. Fragments of Type 1 lamps were found in all of the tombs.

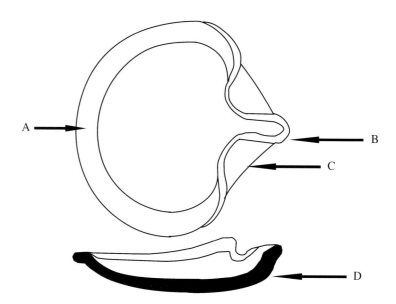

FIG. 14.2 *A typical "saucer-shaped" lamp: (a) rim; (b) wick holder; (c) lip; (d) base (drawing: J. M. Gordon, after Oziol 1969, 17, fig. 6).*

Because these lamps were used for hundreds of years in Cyprus (Bailey 1975: 207), they can be dated most securely by their associated contexts (Wismann 2006: 339). Given the other ceramic and architectural evidence from the tombs, it can be suggested that these examples are Hellenistic versions of a traditional type. One can further surmise that since the best-preserved examples seem akin to recorded Early Hellenistic shapes (e.g., Vessberg and Westholm 1956: fig. 37:1–4), the examples may provide a third-century-BC date for the initial use of these tombs.

Taking into account previous studies of Type 1 lamps from both Cyprus in general and the Malloura region in particular, we can offer the preliminary hypothesis that the Mağara Tepeşi lamps were probably made locally (Oziol 1977: 19; Wismann 2006: 339–40) and that their placement in tombs was a traditional occurrence (Parks 1999: 357). Both pink and pale yellow fabrics, some with small black inclusions, are the most common, but there is variation. In regional terms, similar lamps have been found at both large coastal sites like Salamis (Oziol and Pouilloux 1969: pl. 1) as well as nearby inland settlements such as Panayia Ematousa (Wismann 2006: 339–42). Parks (1999: 357) indicated that these lamps were commonly found in tombs throughout the island (except

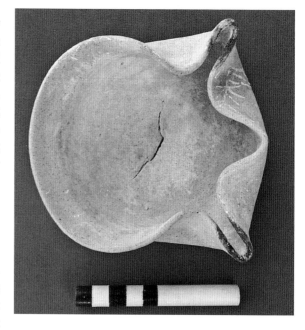

FIG. 14.3 *Double-wick "saucer-shaped" lamp from Tomb 27 at Mağara Tepeşi. AAP-AM 200: Larnaka District Museum, Cyprus (© AAP).*

the Paphos district), yet it does not seem that any complete examples were discovered at the cemetery at Makronisos (Hadjisavvas 1997: *passim*). Most of the saucer-shaped lamps discovered at Mağara Tepeşi show signs of use, and it is probable that this

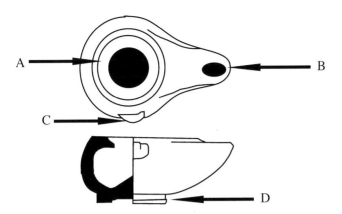

FIG. 14.4 *A typical Vessberg Type 3 "watch-shaped" lamp: (a) rim (surrounding fill-hole); (b) wick hole; (c) side knob; (d) base (drawing: J. M. Gordon, after Oziol 1969, 17, fig. 6).*

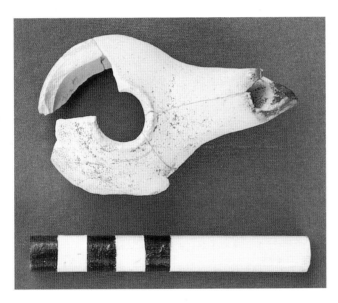

FIG. 14.5 *"Watch-shaped" lamp from Tomb 26 at Mağara Tepeşi. AAP-AM 243: Larnaka District Museum, Cyprus (© AAP).*

date given its fabric, design, and context, perhaps indicates a unique adherence to local lamp designs originally brought to Cyprus following the establishment of Phoenician Kition in the ninth century BC (Coldstream 1990, 53). Furthermore, despite the lamp's novelty, the discovery of AAP-AM 200 in Tomb 27, which had a preponderance of Roman lamps, should not be regarded as unusual. This is because such a lamp could have been deposited either during the first use of the tomb (i.e., during the early to mid-third century BC; this also seems more likely given its intact nature) or could have migrated from one of the other tombs or from the surface at a later date, as the necropolis was frequently looted.

AAP Mağara Tepeşi Lamp Type 2: Wheel-made "Watch-shaped" Lamps (Vessberg Type 3; Hellenistic I)

Another Hellenistic lamp type found at Mağara Tepeşi is the "watch-shaped" type. These lamps were wheel-made, closed vessels with a wick nozzle and a central fill-hole, the latter of which caused them to resemble a watch face (fig. 14.4; Vessberg and Westholm 1956: 121, 184–85; Oziol and Pouilloux 1969: 16; Bailey 1975: 208; Wismann 2006: 342–43). Specifically, the Mağara Tepeşi corpus provides examples corresponding to Vessberg's Types 2 and 3. The only difference between these types is that Type 3 has a side knob and a different style rim, making precise identification difficult but not impossible. At Mağara Tepeşi, most appear to have been Type 3 lamps, and the best-preserved example (AAP-AM 243) from Tomb 26 aptly illustrates this type's appearance (fig. 14.5). Ten sherds of the total corpus of 254, or 4%, were of this type. However, it appears that each sherd also represents the solitary remains of one original lamp. Thus, 14% of the complete lamps from the corpus were probably Vessberg Type 3 lamps. They were found in all of the tombs except Tomb 27, and most of them had signs of use.

occurred either at the time of the funeral or during subsequent ritual occasions.

Although the Type 1 lamps from Mağara Tepeşi generally follow Cypriot trends, it should be noted that double-wick lamps, like AAP-AM 200, are relatively rare in Cyprus (Bailey 1975, 208 and n.1). Instead, double-wick, saucer-shaped lamps are more characteristic of earlier Punic lamps of the Western Mediterranean (Bailey 1975: ibid.). Thus the discovery of such a lamp at Mağara Tepeşi, which should be locally made and Hellenistic in

In terms of date, these lamps are used concurrently with Type 1 lamps, yet they come into fashion only in the third century BC and continue to be used at least until the first century BC (Vessberg and Westholm 1956: 185). Fabrics and slips are of various colors; white, pale yellows, and pale browns are common for fabrics, while slips are mainly varieties of red to dark brown. Type 3 lamps very similar to those from Mağara Tepeşi were found at Panayia Ematousa, and Wismann (2006: 343–46) argues that many of these may be locally made. Furthermore, watch-shaped lamps were found in many of the tombs at Makronisos (Hadjisavvas 1997: 96, pl. 80:2), and Parks (1999: 357) emphasizes that the type has a "wide geographic distribution" in tombs throughout the island. Evidently, the funerary tradition at Mağara Tepeşi was in step with many other sites during the high Hellenistic period.

AAP Mağara Tepeşi Lamp Type 3:
Mold-made "Watch-shaped" Lamps
(Vessberg Type 5a; Hellenistic I and II)

Hellenistic watch-shaped lamps could also be mold-made and feature impressed decoration such as dolphins' or lions' heads (Vessberg and Westholm 1956: 126, 185–86; Bailey 1975: 208–9; Wismann 2006: 346–47). Of the three possible fragments of such lamps discovered at Mağara Tepeşi, only one is preserved sufficiently enough to offer an interpretation. This is a fragment of a Vessberg Type 5a from Tomb 25 (fig. 14.6), which is characterized by its gray fabric, blackish slip, the incised lines radiating from its fill-hole, and the shoulder decoration. The AAP lamp was evidently used, and although it is so poorly preserved that it is difficult to make out the shoulder decoration, a lion's head seems the most probable.

According to Vessberg (and Westholm 1956: 185–86), these lamps have been found throughout the Hellenistic eastern Mediterranean, and most examples seem to date to the second century BC or later. In Cyprus, a lamp from Soloi identified by Vessberg (and Westholm 1956: fig. 37:17) seems comparable to our example, as do some from Salamis (Oziol 1977: pl. 8:118–19) and Akhna (Bailey 1975: 230 no. Q 503; pl. 99). Panayia Ematousa also yielded a

FIG. 14.6 *Mold-made "watch-shaped" lamp with possible relief of a lion's head from Tomb 25 at Mağara Tepeşi (© AAP).*

similar lamp (L8.21) (Wismann 2006: 346, fig. 177, 347). It is believed that the Panayia Ematousa lamp may have been locally produced, due to its beige fabric and reddish yellow to brown slip, while the Mağara Tepeşi lamp, with its gray fabric and blackish slip, seems more characteristic of lamps imported from coastal Phoenicia and Asia Minor (Wismann 2006: 247). The discovery of this lamp indicates that the people at inland Mağara Tepeşi may have had access to imports from nearby regions; yet the paucity of this type within the overall assemblage shows that it may not have been very fashionable or was hard to come by. No examples of Vessberg Type 5a lamps appear to have been found at Makronisos (Hadjisavvas 1997: *passim*), and Parks (1999: 358) confirms that these lamps have been infrequently recovered from Cypriot tombs, a fact that may stress the type's external origins.

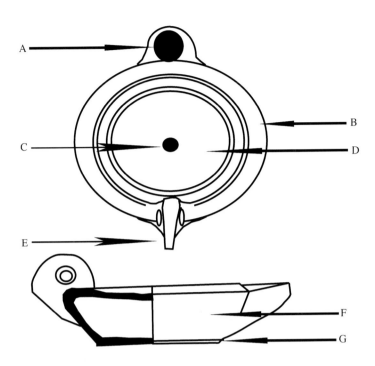

FIG. 14.7 *A typical Roman mold-made lamp: (a) wick hole; (b) rim; (c) fill hole; (d) discus; (e) handle; (f) body; (g) base (drawing: J. M. Gordon, after Oziol 1969, 17, fig. 6).*

AAP Mağara Tepeşi Lamp Type 4: Roman Mold-made Lamps (Vessberg Types 10–14; Roman)

The most common types of lamps found in the tombs at Mağara Tepeşi are mold-made and were produced during Roman times (30 BC–AD 330; Vessberg and Westholm 1956: 123–27, 187–90; Oziol and Pouilloux 1969: 18–21; Bailey 1988: 294–300). In general, these closed form lamps are round, having a rim (sometimes decorated) that surrounds a central, usually relief-decorated, discus with a tiny fill-hole somewhere near the center (fig. 14.7). The nozzles, often decorated with Ionic volutes (a common first-century-AD type; Vessberg Types 10, 10a, 11, 11a, 12), are much closer to the lamp rim and more rounded around the wick hole than in Hellenistic forms. Furthermore, the lamps are extremely thin-walled, some being only a few millimeters thick. Small handles appear on some types (Vessberg Types 11, 11a, 12, 14, 15, 16, and later Types 17–20), while they are absent from others (Vessberg Types 10 and 13). Finally,

shinier red slips as well as a host of relief discus designs (both trends similar to contemporary *sigillata* plate fashions) are typical, particularly for lamps produced in Italy (Vessberg and Westholm 1956: 188).

Both the earlier volute nozzle type (Vessberg Types 10–12) as well as the slightly later non-voluted type (Types 13–14) are represented at Mağara Tepeşi, and lamps of Types 10–14 make up 212 out of the 254 sherds (83.5%). Despite this high percentage, it should be kept in mind that because these thin-walled lamps break into dozens of pieces, this amount may be misleading. Thus, the percentage of once complete lamps may serve as a better indicator concerning the amount of Roman lamps in the corpus in relation to other types. Overall, Roman lamps amount to 38 out of the total 71 (53%) of the once complete lamps from the tombs. These lamps were found in all of the tombs, and, interesting to note, many examples do not appear to have been used.

Type 10 lamps (volute nozzle lamps without a handle) account for the largest number of Roman lamps, with 24 of the 38 (63%) examples. Both slipped and unslipped varieties have been found, and some were decorated with discus designs including lions or griffins, palmettes, and rosettes. A few lamps had lines radiating out from their discus centers. According to the evidence from excavations, these lamps appear to have been the most common in Cyprus during the Roman period, and large numbers have also been discovered at Panayia Ematousa (Wismann 2006: 348–50) and other sites (e.g., Golgoi; Bakalakis 1988: fig. 73:2). They are well-represented in the tombs at Makronisos (Hadjisavvas 1997: *passim*), were found in the tombs at Kourion (Bailey 1988: 292–93, nos. Q 2393, 2424, 2425, 2411), and Parks (1999: 358) identifies them as the most common form of early Roman lamps in her survey. Due to the ubiquity of Type 10 lamps at other sites in the region, the lightly impressed discus images, and the similarity of the AAP lamps with fabrics discovered at Panayia Ematousa, it seems prudent to agree with Wismann's (2006: 349) theory that this type of Roman lamp was locally produced (see also Bailey 1988: 295). Yet the presence of a few lamps with bright slips, clear discus impressions (Vessberg and Westholm 1956: 188), and even one with a signature may also betray a few imports.

Two examples of Type 10a lamps (a volute lamp with a triangular nozzle) as well as a possible Vessberg Type 11 (volute lamps with handles) were also recovered. The latter can be tentatively identified, since its volute nozzle, rim, and discus design (two olive twigs bound into a wreath) are similar to Vessberg's main published example (Vessberg and Westholm 1956: fig. 38:13; for the same discus design on a type 10a volute lamp, see Bailey 1988: pl. 62 no. Q 2363). Although these identifications are merely hypothetical due to the poor preservation of the fragments, they may represent lamp types from Mağara Tepeşi not found at Panayia Ematousa.

Almost all the remaining Roman lamps from the tombs at Mağara Tepeşi are of the Vessberg Type 13 design (mold-made lamps without nozzle volutes or handles; see Bailey's discussion of Loeschke Type VIII lamps, Bailey 1988: 296). Nine of the 38 (24%) Roman lamps from the tombs are of this type, which is longer lived in Cyprus than Types 10–12. Indeed, some seem to be used until the third and fourth centuries AD (Vessberg and Westholm 1956: 190; Parks 1999: 358). Except for one questionable exception from Tomb 26, namely a poorly preserved "scroll-shaped projection" or perhaps "lug handle" similar to a Type 13 lamp published by Vessberg (and Westholm 1956: fig. 39:5; cf. Bailey 1988: pl. 72 Q 2626 who claims the style is from Tarsus), all these lamps were found in Tomb 27, and few of them appear to have been used.

Among these is the best-preserved lamp from the site, AAP-AM 362 (fig. 14.8). This exquisite artifact, found in Tomb 27, is nearly identical to ones discovered at Soloi (Vessberg and Westholm 1956: fig. 39:3) and Tomb 62 at Kourion (Bailey 1988: pl. 67 no. Q 2493; pl. 145). Its discus features

FIG. 14.8 *Roman mold-made lamp from Tomb 27 at Mağara Tepeşi. AAP-AM 362: Larnaka District Museum, Cyprus (© AAP).*

an eight-petal rosette surrounded by what appears to be oak leaves on the rim. It is also unslipped and its fabric is light buff pink, indicating it could have been produced in Cyprus. There is no sign of burning around its wick hole, so it is doubtful that it was ever used.

More important is the fact that this lamp has a fabricant signature on its base (see also Cova, Ch. 13 for a detailed discussion of the epigraphy). Although the writing is difficult to decipher, the most probable interpretation of the name is "Romanesis" in the Latin alphabet (fig. 14.9; see also fig. 13.7 for a photograph). Such a conclusion is quite convincing, as Heres (1968) has identified a massive corpus of lamps produced and signed by Romanesis' workshop (see also Bailey 1988: 99–100; 331–32). These lamps have been found at sites throughout the central and eastern Mediterranean, including Cyprus, as evidenced by many examples from the Cyprus Museum (Oziol 1977: *passim*) and signed versions from Amathous (Petit et al. 1988: 868–69) and Tomb 114 at Kourion (specifically, a Type 10a lamp, purportedly from Knidos, with rosettes similar to AAP-AM 362; see Bailey 1988: pl. 74 no. Q 2659; pl. 145). The location of Romanesis' workshop is uncertain, but Heres believed it may

FIG. 14.9 *Reconstruction of Romanesis's signature on the base of AAP-AM 362 (drawing: J. M. Gordon).*

have been situated in a port city in Asia Minor such as Miletus or, more probably, Knidos (Heres 1968: 203–4). One interpretation then is that this lamp made its way to Mağara Tepeşi from Asia Minor, and Bailey's belief that all lamps from Romanesis' workshop were signed at the main atelier (and thus copies were not signed) supports such a theory (Bailey 1988: 332). Alternatively, it could be a local copy of a Romanesis original, as it is buff in color and lacks the "orange red to red brown glaze" (Williams 1981: 28) that was typically applied to Romanesis' products. Hence, it is also possible that this lamp comes from an unknown Cypriot atelier, as three other lamps from Tomb 27 are of exactly the same type as AAP-AM 362, although they lack the Romanesis trademark.

Whether the AAP Romanesis lamp was a local copy or an imported original, the evidence nevertheless suggests that Vessberg Type 13 lamps with rosette discus decoration were popular both in Cyprus in general and in the Malloura region in particular. In fact, Wismann (2006: 349) states that at nearby Panayia Ematousa "a rosette with eight petals is seen on several pieces." Given the presence of such a popular lamp type at Mağara Tepeşi, it seems that the site was well-integrated into eastern Mediterranean trade routes and that people were

able to either acquire or imitate the most popular ceramic fashions 1. (for an in-depth discussion of AAP-AM 362 and Malloura's trading connections, see Gordon and Cova 2010).

Most of the other Type 13 lamps in the AAP corpus were rather plainly decorated and probably locally made. Some have the seemingly popular ovules on their rims, while one is of a much larger and wider type with an S-shaped design for an "ear" or thumb hold. Parks (1999: 358) cited Type 13 lamps as the second most common type of Roman mold-made lamps found in tombs in Cyprus. So, once again, aside from a few anomalies, the mourners at Mağara Tepeşi seem to have followed similar rituals to those practiced in other areas of Cyprus.

LUX EX TENEBRIS

As this overview of terracotta lamp types recovered from the tombs at Mağara Tepeşi illustrates, placing lamps in tombs was a constant element of local funerary ritual throughout the Hellenistic and Roman periods. Therefore, it is important to offer some preliminary insights into observable lamp trends. In terms of chronology, the lamps corroborate with other evidence to show that the tombs straddle the boundary between the Hellenistic and Roman periods (ca. third century BC to early fourth century AD). At present, it is possible to present a chronological overview of the numbers of lamps recovered from each of the four Mağara Tepeşi tombs with Tomb 25 having the largest percentage of early lamps and the architecturally elaborate Tomb 27 yielding the majority of later lamps (Table 14.1). Based on these chronological statistics, it is tempting to suggest that the necropolis may have been created during the Hellenistic I (ca. 310–150 BC) period and then expanded over time from the northwest to the southeast of the hill (see Toumazou and Counts, Ch. 6 [fig. 6.1] for detailed topographical map). A more holistic analysis of the tombs' architecture, ceramics, and small finds, however, is required to support such a claim. Another chronological question that must be addressed is why the tombs went out of use during the era of Vessberg Type 13 lamps. Again, although more definitive conclusions will

Table 14.1   Overview of chronology, types and distribution of lamps from Mağara Tepeşi (Vessberg Types based on Vessberg and Westholm 1956: 184–93).

Tomb	Hellenistic Lamps divided by Vessberg Type	Total Number of Hellenistic Lamps		Roman Lamps divided by Vessberg Type	Total Number of Roman Lamps	
Tomb 25	Type 1: 5; Type 2: 1; Type 3: 2; Type 5a: 1	9	(75%)	Type 10: 3	3	(25%)
Tomb 26	Type 1: 10; Type 3: 4	14	(67%)	Type 10: 4; Type 10a: 1; Type 12: 1; Type 13 (Possible): 1	7	(23%)
Tomb 27	Type 1: 2	2	(8%)	Type 10: 13; Type 13: 8; Type 14: 1; Unknown Roman Type: 1	23	(92%)
Tomb 28	Type 1: 5; Type 3: 3	8	(62%)	Type 10: 3; Type 10a: 1; Type 11: 1	5	(38%)

await the final publication, practical (such as over-crowding) as well as cultural (the shift from pagan to Christian religion) factors may have played a role in the decline of Mağara Tepeşi as a burial site.

The lamp evidence further indicates that Mağara Tepeşi was a microcosm of the larger forces at play in the region, simultaneously open to outside influences yet bound to long-standing local traditions. For example, the presence of possible imported lamps during both the Hellenistic and Roman periods indicates that the site was not excluded from regional trade routes and fashions. Nevertheless, the site's inland location ensured that age-old customs continued, such as the use of traditional saucer-shaped lamps, including possibly Phoenician-influenced double-wick types, in funerary ritual until they were eventually replaced by mass-produced, mold-made Roman ones.

Finally, it is important to consider whether the Mağara Tepeşi lamps can shed light on how the boundary between life and death was perceived by the people of ancient Malloura. Following Parks' observations concerning lamp use, it appears that similar types of lamps were used in similar ways at Mağara Tepeşi and in Cyprus as a whole. First, lamps seem to have been used simply as a source of illumination within the tombs. This was probably the case especially for the saucer-shaped Hellenistic examples; however, by Roman times, unused lamps seem to have been preferred. Perhaps this preference reflects the second probable use of the Mağara Tepeşi lamps: as offerings intended for use by the deceased during their dark journey to Hades. If the people of early Roman Malloura believed that the deceased required lamps, does the lack of Christian-era (i.e., late Roman) lamps at Mağara Tepeşi indicate a different view on how the afterlife was illuminated? According to Parks' research (1999: 359), the use of lamps (including typical late Roman oval-shaped ones with overt Christian iconography) in Cypriot funerary ritual continued during Christian times. Thus, the lack of these lamps at Mağara Tepeşi may indicate either that the tombs went out of use before then or, more hypothetically, that the Christians of Malloura believed that the dead, who may now have basked in *lux aeterna*, were not in need of terracotta lamps. For them, the Lamb of God himself may have been the only lamp (see Rev. 21:23, "ὁ λύχνος αὐτῆς τὸ ἀρνίον;" *lykhnos* is the New Testament and ancient, Greek word for lamp) required to light their way to the new Jerusalem (Aland et al. 1966: 893).

In conclusion, it seems that an analysis of the funerary lamps from Mağara Tepeşi provides insights not only into the religious beliefs at ancient Malloura but also into the real and metaphorical boundaries of a site situated at the crossroads of Cyprus.

ACKNOWLEDGMENTS

I would like to thank Professor Michael Toumazou for allowing me to study the lamp material from Mağara Tepeşi and for initially inviting me to work with him at Athienou-*Malloura*. In addition, I would like to thank Professor Toumazou, as well as Professors Derek B. Counts and P. Nick Kardulias, for their keen editorial comments on this chapter. Finally, I would like to acknowledge the anonymous reviewers whose editorial suggestions significantly contributed to strengthening this chapter's arguments and observations.

REFERENCES

Aland, K.; Black, M.; Metzger, B.; and Wikgren A. (eds.)
1966   *The Greek New Testament*. Stuttgart: Württemberg Bible Society.

Bailey, D. M.
1975   *Greek, Hellenistic, and Early Roman Pottery Lamps*. A Catalogue of the Lamps in the British Museum I. London: British Museum Publications.
1988   *Roman Provincial Lamps*. A Catalogue of the Lamps in the British Museum III. London: British Museum Publications.

Bakalakis, G.
1988   *Ανασκαφή στο Λόφο Γιόρκους ΒΑ της Αθηαίνου, Κύπρος*. Athens: Αρχαιολογική Εταιρεία Αθηνών.

Coldstream, N.
1990   Early Iron Age (Cypro-Geometric): The Rise of the Ancient Kingdoms c.1100–700 B.C. Pp. 47–64 in *Footprints in Cyprus*, ed. D. Hunt. Revised edition. London: Trigraph.

Etienne, R.
1987   De Lychnis. Pp. 13–15 in *Les Lampes de terre cuite en Méditerranée: Des origines à Justinien: Table ronde du C.N.R.S., tenue à Lyon du 7 au 11 décembre 1981*, eds. T. Oziol and R. Rebuffat. Lyon: Maison de l'Orient.

Gordon, J. M., and Cova E.
2010   Romanesis in Cyprus: A Lamp from Athienou-*Malloura. Cahiers du Centre d'Études Chypriotes* 40: 277–94.

Green, T.
1989   Tombs. Pp. 45–50 in *Death, Afterlife and the Soul*, ed. L. E. Sullivan. New York: Macmillan.

Hadjisavvas, S.
1997   *Agia Napa: Excavations at Makronisos and the Archaeology of the Region*. Nicosia: Cyprus Department of Antiquities.

Heres, G.
1968   Die Werkstatt des Lampentöpfers Romanesis. *Forschungen und Berichte. Staatliche Museen zu Berlin* 10: 185–211.

Kohlenberger III, J. R. (ed.)
1993   *The Greek New Testament: USB4 with NRSV & NIV*. Grand Rapids: Zondervan.

Long, J. B.
1989   The Underworld. Pp. 161–73 in *Death, Afterlife and the Soul*, ed. L. E. Sullivan. New York: Macmillan.

Oziol, T.
1977   *Les lampes du Musée de Chypre*. Salamine de Chypre 7. Paris: de Boccard.

Oziol, T., and Pouilloux, J.
1969   *Les lampes (octobre 1964–mai 1967)*. Salamine de Chypre 1. Paris: de Boccard.

Parks, D. A.
1999   Burial Customs of Roman Cyprus: Origin
        and Development. Unpublished Ph. D.
        dissertation, University of Missouri-Columbia.

Petit, T.; Hermary, A.; and Schmid, M.
1988   Rapport sur les travaux de l'école française à
        Amathonte de Chypre en 1987. *Bulletin de
        Correspondance Hellénique* 112 (2): 857–76.

Segal, A. F.
2004   *Life After Death: A History of the Afterlife
        in the Religions of the West*. New York:
        Doubleday.

Sørensen, L. W., and Jacobsen, K. W. (eds.)
2006   *Panayia Ematousa I: A Rural Site in South-
        eastern Cyprus*. Monographs of the Danish
        Institute at Athens 6.1. Aarhus: Aarhus
        University.

Tober, L. M., and Lusby, F. S.
1989   Heaven and Hell. Pp. 151–60 in *Death,
        Afterlife and the Soul*, ed. L. E. Sullivan. New
        York: Macmillan.

Toumazou, M. K.; Yerkes, R. W.; and Kardulias, P. N.
1998   Athienou Archaeological Project:
        Investigations in the Malloura Valley, Cyprus,
        1990–1995. *Journal of Field Archaeology* 25:
        163–82.

Turner, A.
1993   *The History of Hell*. New York: Harcourt Brace.

van Baaren, T. P.
1989   Geographies of Death. Pp. 96–101 in *Death,
        Afterlife and the Soul*, ed. L. E. Sullivan. New
        York: Macmillan.

Vessberg, O., and Westholm, A.
1956   *The Hellenistic and Roman Periods in Cyprus*.
        The Swedish Cyprus Expedition 4, pt. 3.
        Stockholm: The Swedish Cyprus Expedition.

Williams, H.
1981   *The Lamps*. Kenchreai, Eastern Port of
        Corinth: Results of Investigations by the
        University of Chicago and Indiana University
        for the American School of Classical Studies
        at Athens 5. Leiden: Brill.

Wismann, T.
2006   The Lamps. Pp. 338–54 in *Panayia Ematousa
        I: A Rural Site in South-eastern Cyprus*.
        Monographs of the Danish Institute at Athens
        6.1, eds. L. W. Sørensen and K. W. Jacobsen.
        Aarhus: Aarhus University.

Chapter 15

Athienou Archaeological Project Survey Pottery

by R. Scott Moore and Timothy E. Gregory

OVERVIEW OF THE CERAMIC COLLECTION

Ceramics are the most common artifact found in archaeological excavations and by surveys in the Mediterranean region. The durability of ceramics ensures that a ceramic vessel's broken pieces, or sherds, survive for thousands of years. Several factors contribute to the value in analyzing pottery collected by archaeological investigation, such as survey. First, ceramics were common objects of their time and every household possessed some type of pottery, and concentrated collections of pottery in one location can indicate the presence of a house, village, or town. Second, since different sites have differing collections of sherds, the type of pottery (storage, cooking ware, or fine ware) at a particular site can help reveal the location's function. Third, since ceramics were owned by people from all levels of society, the analysis of the pottery from a location can help determine the wealth or social status of the inhabitants. Fourth, the design or decoration of the pottery can be used to establish the date and place of manufacture, which can then be used to illustrate lines of communication and trading routes.

The surface pottery gathered during the course of the AAP survey and analyzed in this chapter included 2,741 ceramic artifacts collected by field walkers while investigating a 13.5 km² area. The AAP fieldworkers were instructed to collect all diagnostic pieces (rims, handles, bases, and decorated); therefore, body sherds are probably underrepresented in the sample when compared with the number of such artifacts field walkers would have encountered. This practice is common in most surveys, so it does not invalidate comparisons with the results of other such projects. The survey also employed two different collection strategies at designated sites. At Malloura (Site 1), the fieldworkers performed a total collection of all artifacts in 2-m² sample units spaced evenly over the entire site (see Kardulias and Yerkes, Ch. 7). At the other sites, the field walkers measured out four radial transects from a central point to the edge of the concentration and then collected all artifacts in a 1-m-wide swath along each transect. Field walkers also collected artifacts in the walkover mode outside of sites. These transects were walked in cardinal directions (east–west and north–south) with field walkers separated by 10–15 m, recording

TABLE 15.1   Breakdown of survey ceramics by period.

Site	Total Sherds	Undiagnostic	Archaic	Classical	Hellenistic	Roman	Medieval	Modern
Unassigned	327	119		14	16	84	59	35
1	1476	772	6	39	35	323	239	62
2	27	23			2	2		
3	37	25		2	2	3	2	3
4	16			2				14
5	37			1		2		34
6	3	2			1			
7	15	12			2	1		
8	10	5						5
9	1	1						
10	7	7						
11	0							
12	185	27		2	3	13	65	75
13	0							
14	23	19		3				1
15	13	13						
16	323	215		5	5	35	43	20
17	21						10	11
18	17	3					10	4
19	0							
20	8					2	6	
21	0							
22	1					1		
23	12	11					1	
24	14	10		1		1	1	1
25	6	6						
26	5	4		1				
27	12	3		4	2	3		
28	1	1						
29	27	12					6	9
30	117	61			2	17	31	6
Total	2741	1351	6	74	70	487	473	280

the quantity of artifacts in their tracts and collecting diagnostic pieces, such as rims, handles, and bases.

The assemblage of pottery and other artifacts collected by the survey represents many of the characteristics that are typical of archaeological survey, with several significant differences. As would be expected, and despite the practice of discouraging the collection of body sherds, the initial breakdown of the sherds revealed that, in fact, the most frequently collected ceramic parts were body sherds (73.6%), followed by rims (12%), handles (8.25%), bases (5.75%), and toes (0.4%). When the sherds were then separated into categories based on their fabric types, which presumably have strong correlations with function, the largest category consisted of coarse wares (71.9%), then kitchen or cooking wares (14.2%), and finally fine wares (13.65%). While this functional breakdown mirrors that of other survey projects, it is interesting to note that unlike other projects along the southern coast of Cyprus, such as Kalavasos-*Kopetra* (Rautman 2003), Maroni (Manning 2002), Aradhippou-*Panagia Ematousa* (Sørensen and Jacobsen 2000), and the Pyla-Koutsopetria Archaeological Project (Caraher et al. 2007), AAP field walkers found very few amphora sherds. In fact, amphora sherds accounted for only 1.8% of the total discovered during the course of the survey. This can be partially explained as a bias in the collection strategy, which favored diagnostic parts of the vessels and the tendency of amphorae to produce a relatively small number of diagnostic sherds in relation to their total size.

The lack of amphorae in the survey area, however, raises questions concerning the usage of the land and could perhaps indicate that the majority of the land was undeveloped. This hypothesis is perhaps supported by the lack of roof tiles (less than 2%) discovered in the survey area. In fact, if the tiles from the modern era are discounted, only 20 roof tile fragments were discovered in the survey area, or less than 1% of the total sherds collected. These premodern roof tiles were discovered at only four sites (1, 4, 16, 24) and would seem to indicate a lack of substantial urban development in the AAP survey region. The bias against body sherds in the collection strategy, however, should temper making too much of this observation.

In examining the geographical distribution of the sherds, the majority, more than half the total AAP ceramic collection (54%), were collected at a single location, Site 1 (Malloura). This is to be expected because the more intensive collection strategy was employed at this site: total collection of all sherds vs. sampling in other areas. The sherds from Malloura included artifacts from all the periods present in the larger survey, Cypro-Archaic through modern. Examination of the sherd collections from all the sites within the broader AAP survey area shows the same chronological profile, with the oldest sherds dating to the Classical or Hellenistic period, and then a significant portion of the remaining sherds dating to the Roman, medieval, and modern periods. The only exceptions to this pattern are a few sites at which the AAP field walkers collected fewer than five sherds and which appear to be single-period sites (Table 15.1).

Coarse wares were present at most sites in the survey area and were spread fairly evenly throughout the region. The kitchenwares, however, show a different distributional pattern. While they are present at about half the sites (1, 2, 3, 6, 7, 9, 10, 12, 16, 20, 23, 24, 25, 27, 29, 30), almost all the sites that contained kitchenwares are clustered together in two main areas, one in the middle of the survey area (sites 1, 2, 3, 6, 7, 9, 10, 29) and the other at the western edge (sites 20, 23, 24, 25, 27). The fine wares also reveal a slightly different geographical distributional pattern, mainly occurring at sites in the south-central half of the survey area (sites 1, 2, 3, 5, 6, 7, 12, 16, 17, 18, 20, 24, 27, 29, 30; Table. 15.2). Eleven sites (sites 1, 2, 3, 6, 7, 16, 20, 24, 27, 29, 30) had both cooking wares and fine wares present, indicating they are the most likely sites for habitation (Table 15.2).

Chronologically, as would be expected of survey pottery that is often small, broken, and difficult to identify, the largest category of sherds consisted of pieces that could only be dated to the very broad and undiagnostic "ceramic age" (49.3%). The largest category of sherds that could be dated to a specific chronological period was from the Roman period (17.8%), followed by medieval (17.3%), modern/early modern (10.2%), Cypro-Classical (2.7%), Hellenistic (2.6%), and Cypro-Archaic (less than 1%) (fig. 15.1).

Cypro-Archaic to Hellenistic (Eighth to First Century bc)

The oldest datable sherds discovered during the survey, only six in number, are from the Cypro-Archaic period. All the Cypro-Archaic sherds are from Site 1 (Malloura) and are mainly undecorated coarse wares. The majority of the Cypro-Classical sherds (n=74) are course ware (74.62%), cooking wares (14.92%), and fine wares (10.44%). Body sherds accounted for 47.76% of the Cypro-Classical collection, handles 22.39%, bases 16.41%, rims 10.45%, and toes 2.9%. While the majority of these sherds come from Site 1 (52.94%), Cypro-Classical sherds were found at sites throughout the survey area (3, 4, 5, 7, 12, 14, 16, 24, 26, 27). The majority of these sherds are locally produced (80%), and the largest fabric type was coarse ware (40%).

As with the Cypro-Classical sherds, the majority of the Hellenistic sherds (n=70) were discovered at Site 1, with the rest being discovered at sites 2, 3, 6, 7, 12, 16, 24, 27, and 30. While all functional classes are present, the two most common ceramic types for this period were Hellenistic Black Glaze (21.28%) and Hellenistic Color Coated Wares (15.96%). The majority of the sherds in these two fine ware categories were locally produced, with only a few sherds (9%) imported from outside Cyprus.

Roman–Early Byzantine (First Century bc to Seventh Century ad)

The majority of the sherds (n=487) from the Roman period were coarse wares (55%), followed by fine wares (35%) and kitchenwares (9%). These ceramics show a marked increase from earlier periods in the number of imports (Eastern Sigillata A, Eastern Sigillata B, and Koan-type amphora), with imports totaling nearly 19% of the sherds from these periods. In particular, Eastern Sigillata A accounted for three-quarters of the imported wares. The other fine wares consisted of Cypriot Sigillata and locally produced Roman Red Slips. In addition to the ceramic artifacts, there was a substantial number of glass fragments from the Roman period present in the survey area, all from Site 1.

Table 15.2   Breakdown by fabric type.

Site	Coarse Wares	Kitchen/ Cooking	Fine Wares
1	1,030	231	192
2	17	3	6
3	21	11	5
4	10		1
5	34		3
6	1	1	1
7	7	6	2
8	7		
9		1	
10	6	1	
11			
12	147	1	35
13			
14	22		
15	13		
16	251	36	29
17	12		2
18	7		10
19			
20	4	1	3
21			
22			
23		12	
24	7	5	1
25	5	1	
26	5		
27	6	3	3
28	1		
29	14	5	6
30	90	17	9
Total	1717	335	308

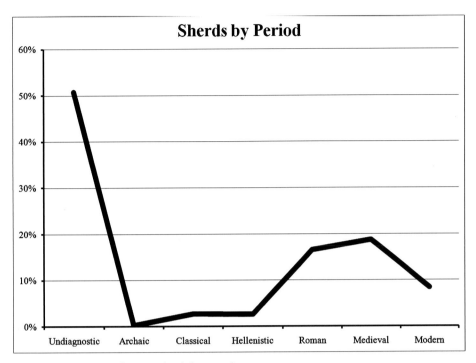

FIG. 15.1 *Percentage of Survey Sherds by Period.*

In looking at the late Roman fine wares, the locally produced Cypriot Red Slip, as at most sites on Cyprus, is the most prevalent fine ware, accounting for 47.45% of the late Roman fine wares, followed by Phocaean Red Slip Ware (37.28%) and African Red Slip Ware (10.16%). It is clear that there were few fine ware imports in this period reaching the area and that the inhabitants of the region in the late Roman period relied on the locally produced Cypriot Red Slip and locally produced imitation Red Slip Wares, such as Imitation Phocaean Red Slip Ware.

The range of late Roman fine ware forms collected during the survey helps to illustrate the continuity of settlement in the AAP survey area during the late Roman period, particularly for the fourth to seventh centuries. The two identifiable African Red Slip forms include an ARS rim form 59, which dates to the fourth century AD, and an ARS rim form 93A, from the late fifth/early sixth century AD. The Phocaean Red Slip Ware rim sherds belong to only two forms, PHW 3 and PHW 10, the two most common of this ware. The PHW 3 sherds include the subcategories 3B and 3C, which date to AD 450–550, while the PHW 10

forms include the subcategories 10A and 10B and date to AD 575–675 (Hayes 1972: 96–100, 145–48, 329–38, 343–46; Table 15.3).

The identifiable Cypriot Red Slip sherds are from only four forms. They include the fairly uncommon CRS form 1 (dating to the mid-fifth century AD) and a CRS form 10 sherd from the middle of the seventh century AD. While CRS form 2 (AD 450–550) is a relatively common find on Cyprus, only two examples were found in the AAP survey area. The most common CRS type retrieved during the survey was CRS form 9, which dates to the seventh century AD and accounted for more than half the identifiable CRS forms collected during the survey (Hayes 1972: 371–86).

This reliance on locally produced ceramics in the late Roman period is also supported by the amphora collected by the AAP field walkers. Overall, there was a relative scarcity of late Roman amphora sherds, with only 14 examples collected. Compared with other Cypriot sites where late Roman amphora sherds account for a sizable portion of the entire ceramic collection, the AAP late Roman amphora collection is very small. In addition to the overall paucity of late Roman amphora sherds, there was

Table 15.3　Late Roman Fine Wares.

Ware	Number	Forms	Sites
African Red Slip	6	59, 93A	1, 2
Cypriot Red Slip	28	1, 2, 9, 10	1, 2, 7, 12, 16
Phocaean Red Slip	22	3B, 3C, 10A, 10B	1, 5, 7, 12, 16
Total	56		

little variety among the sherds, with only two types — Late Roman 1 and Palestinian — identified. Several amphora types that are relatively common at other Cypriot sites are not present in the AAP area, such as Late Roman 2, Late Roman 4, or any North African amphorae. While Late Roman 1 amphora sherds account for nearly half the late Roman amphora sherds (42.85%) and would indicate a reliance on locally produced amphorae, the small size of the collection suggests caution in making generalizations from these data.

Medieval Pottery (8th–19th Centuries)

Turning from the ancient to the medieval and modern periods, we see a significant decrease in the quantity of identifiable pottery, consistent with what has been noted elsewhere throughout Cyprus and most of the Mediterranean area (cf. the useful comments of von Wartburg 2007). Indeed, from the whole of the medieval period, only 473 sherds could be assigned to this 1,000-year period, representing 17.26% of the total. The survey project has subdivided this long era into three subperiods, called the early Medieval (8th–12th centuries), the late Medieval (13th–15th centuries), and the Venetian–Ottoman (16th–late 19th centuries; a period that might not be thought to be medieval but that does not, in Cyprus, easily fall into the modern period either). This periodization is notably imprecise and is determined more by changes in ceramic traditions than by political change. The key events in this period, of course, were the seizure of Cyprus by Richard Lionheart in 1191, the beginning of Venetian rule in 1491, the fall of Nicosia to the Ottomans in 1570, and the begin-

ning of British control of the island in 1878 (as the terminus of what we are here calling "Medieval"). As mentioned, this periodization is based primarily on changes in pottery manufacture, including surface treatment (types and colors of glaze and ways of making designs, different places of manufacture using different sources of clay, and changes in the shapes and sizes of vessels). Details on the numbers of finds from these periods from the study area are shown in Table 15.4.

The medieval pottery identified was overwhelmingly glazed fine ware, in part because this brightly colored pottery is easily recognized, especially compared with the poorly-known other types of medieval pottery found on Cyprus (Sanders 2004: 165–66). Notable, of course, is the paucity of material from the Early Medieval period; in addition, all three examples are from the very end of this period and all appear to have been imported from elsewhere, probably from the Aegean or Asia Minor. The three examples were found at Malloura (Site 1). In the late Medieval (or Frankish) period, the numbers rise significantly, and pottery is found at eight sites throughout the survey area. Glazed fine ware continues to make up the totality of the assemblage, but most of the pieces were now manufactured in Cyprus, an indication that the island had become a major supplier of pottery for the whole of the eastern Mediterranean (cf. Boas 1999: 143–50). Only a single piece of Zeuxippos Ware, one fragment of Port St. Symeon Ware (from al-Mina, the port of Antioch), and a couple of other sgraffito pieces could be identified as imports. In the Venetian–Ottoman period the numbers drop somewhat, perhaps partly a reflection of the effects of the Ottoman attack and conquest of the island

Table 15.4 Details of medieval pottery.

	No. of Artifacts	% of Total	Types of Material	Sites
Early Medieval	3	0.11%	glazed fineware, 11th–12th centuries	1
Late Medieval	53	1.93%	all glazed fineware	1,2,3,12,16,18,20,30
Venetian/Ottoman	31	1.13%	all glazed fineware except for 3 coarse and 1 Turkish pipe	1,12,18,20
Medieval (uncertain subperiod)	386	14.08%	glazed fineware, plus 362 coarse, 1 medium coarse, 3 kitchen ware	1,12,16,30
Total	473	17.26%		

in the late 16th century. Nonetheless, the number of artifacts from this period is nearly the same as that of the previous two centuries, although the distribution is significantly less, down from eight to four sites. Likewise, imports rise significantly, especially from Italy, and these make up nearly half the identified artifacts. Fine ware continues to dominate, with only four examples of coarse ware in the material from the survey.

Medieval Cypriot glazed pottery has traditionally been divided typologically and chronologically into a series of groups (du Plat Taylor 1933; du Plat Taylor and Megaw 1937–1939; Dikigoropoulos and Megaw 1940–1948). More recent studies, especially by Papanikola-Bakirzis (1993), have refined this chronology significantly and have pointed to local centers of production, especially at Lemba, Lapithos, and Famagusta (Ammochostos). The identification of pottery from survey is always somewhat imprecise, given the condition of the objects and their normally fragmentary nature. This is especially true of medieval fine wares (not to speak of other medieval wares, which are frequently of local manufacture and rarely identified and/or published from excavated contexts). Although it is relatively easy to determine if a given sherd is decorated with vitreous glaze (and therefore datable to the medieval or modern period), it is

commonly impossible to place the piece in a finer category because the defining parts of the vessel (both shape and details of decoration) may be missing. Nonetheless, it is worth noting the appearance of fine ware within the AAP collection that can be assigned to specific categories and/or chronologies. Thus, using the standard Cypriot groups as a guide, we can see the numbers in Table 15.5.

The figures, small as they are, conform generally with information from other survey projects in Cyprus (Gregory 1993, 2003), except that other projects have encountered proportionally larger quantities of Lemba Ware, Group VI, and Group VIII. It is also significant that the earlier medieval material (i.e., prior to the 15th century) collected by AAP was confined exclusively to Site 1. Although the evidence is (again) small in number, it may indicate that major earlier medieval activity in the survey area was restricted to that site.

Rather surprisingly, AAP discovered only one fragment of the well-known vessels (cones and pots) used for the manufacture of sugar in Cyprus (von Wartburg 1995). This pottery is relatively easy to identify and present in enormous quantities in many parts of Cyprus, so it is hard to be certain whether the ware was simply not collected by the field walkers (as we have seen, not a single example of coarse or medium coarse pottery has been as-

Table 15.5 Medieval Cypriot glazed pottery from the survey.

	Number	Period	Sites
Lemba Ware	1	13th century	1
Group VI	5	14th century	1
Group VIIIB	1	15th–16th century	1
Group IX	12	16th century	1, 3, 16, 18, 30
Cypriot Glazed, uncertain group	16	13th–16th century	1, 2, 12, 20
Total	35		

signed to the later Medieval period (a cone rim from Malloura) and only three coarseware sherds from the Venetian–Ottoman period; cf. Gabrieli 2009). Undoubtedly, had recent ceramic studies (Gabrieli 2004, 2006, 2009) been available at the time of the survey, it would have been possible to collect and identify more material from the medieval period and this, in turn, would have allowed a much more sophisticated analysis of the survey evidence from this time. Of course, this is a characteristic of survey evidence and why many more recent surveys have sought to describe and collect a much more representative sample of wares, moving away from the quite subjective practice of "diagnostic" collection (Gregory 2004).

Modern Pottery
(Late 19th–20th Centuries)

Material from the modern period (roughly 1878 onward) is, unfortunately, not systematically collected or studied by survey projects in the Mediterranean area (but cf. Diacopoulos 2004). The AAP survey seems generally to have followed in that tradition; only thus can we explain the relatively low numbers of artifacts from the past century and a half, since the surface of the ground in Cyprus is literally covered with such objects. Indeed, one reason this material is consciously not collected by many projects is simply because to do so, using the same process to collect material

from the more distant past, would lead to an overwhelming burden both on those studying the pottery and in the facilities necessary for its storage.

From the modern period the AAP collected 280 artifacts, representing 10.22% of all the items collected. Of these, 121 artifacts were assigned to the Early Modern period (1878 to 1959), or 4.41% of the whole; 37 artifacts to the Modern Present period (1960 and after), or 1.35% of the whole; and 122 artifacts to the modern period, without finer distinction, or 4.45% of the whole.

Table 15.6 provides details about the modern material collected by the project. Clear conclusions are difficult to reach about these finds, in part because of the manner in which they were collected; a quick look at the artifacts suggests that many may have been gathered because the field walkers suspected they were, in fact, premodern in date. Interestingly, glazed fine ware made up a significant proportion of the Early Modern and broader modern classifications, but coarse ware sherds were significantly larger in number, a striking difference with what we observed in the medieval periods. Fragments of building material (broken tiles, bricks, etc.) made up the majority of the Modern Present artifacts, a certain indication that the field walkers were selecting them for collection, again, probably because they considered the possibility they were ancient or medieval in date.

Beyond the material we have just quickly examined, there is another class of pottery that should

TABLE 15.6 Details of modern artifacts.

	No. of Artifacts	% of Total	Types of Material	Sites
Early Modern	121	4.41%	34 glazed fineware, 73 pithos/coarse ware, 4 kitchen ware	1, 3, 4, 12, 16, 17, 24, 29, 30
Modern Present	37	1.35%	3 coins, 2 glazed fineware, 1 coarseware, 7 glass fragments, 24 building materials	1, 2, 8, 12, 14, 16, 29
Modern	122	4.45%	38 glazed fineware, 2 medium coarse, 48 coarse, 3 kitchen ware, 12 glass fragments, 3 metal	1, 3, 4, 8, 12, 16, 18, 29, 30
Total	280	10.22%		

be mentioned. This is a medium-coarse ware in a variety of medium to dark brown fabrics used to make several types of utilitarian vessels: medium-size globular water jars, pithoi, milk containers, and so forth, many with stamped, incised, or molded decoration. The fabrics are similar to or the same as those used by potters in the 19th–20th centuries at Kornos, in central Cyprus, one of the centers that continued to carry out traditional ceramic manufacture into the mid–late 20th century (Ionas 2000; cf. Gabrieli 2004, 2006, 2009). The AAP collected some 334 examples of this pottery, in seven slightly different fabrics, and it was found at 11 sites (1, 4, 5, 12, 16, 17, 18, 24, 27, 29, 30). Clearly some of the vessels in this category are modern, and some are still being manufactured today (mainly for tourist consumption); at the same time, some of the artifacts are clearly older, and one of the fabrics has tentatively been dated to the late Medieval period (without clear identification in excavation contexts elsewhere). This specific fabric was found in large numbers (n=251) and at 10 of the 11 sites at which the more general ware was found. It is difficult, therefore, to assign this material, or even specific items, to a particular date or one of the narrow periods used by the project. Clearly, all this material is to be dated somewhere between the late

Medieval period and the present, but it is difficult to be more precise than this.

The analysis of the surface material from the AAP survey allows several conclusions to be drawn. First, the range of ceramic material is fairly uniform within each period with only a limited number of wares present. Second, some of the more common wares discovered at other sites on Cyprus were not found during the survey. Third, relatively few sherds that could be identified as imported wares were identified, suggesting that the survey area was relatively isolated from the main trade routes of the Mediterranean, even in some of the periods (Cypro-Classical, late Roman, late Medieval) when survey material in other projects often provides evidence of significant exchange of goods. Finally, the site of Malloura (Site 1) appears to have been continually inhabited from antiquity to the present, but its overwhelming presence in the ceramic record is due in part to the differing collection strategies employed in surveying the site.

References

Boas, A. J.
1999 *Crusader Archaeology. The Material Culture of the Latin East.* London: Routledge.

Caraher, W.; Moore, R. S.; and Pettegrew, D.
2007 The Pyla-*Koutsopetria* Archaeological Project: Second Preliminary Report (2005–2006 Seasons). *Report of the Department of Antiquities, Cyprus*: 293–306.

Diacopoulos, L.
2004 The Archaeology of Modern Greece. Pp. 183–98 in *Mediterranean Archaeological Landscapes: Current Issues,* eds. E. Athanassopoulos and L. Wandsnider. Philadelphia: University of Pennsylvania Museum of Archaeology and Anthropology.

Dikigoropoulos, A. I., and Megaw, A. H. S.
1940–1948 Early Glazed Pottery from Polis. *Report of the Department of Antiquities, Cyprus*: 77–95.

du Plat Taylor, J.
1933 Some Notes on Byzantine Glazed Ware in Cyprus. *Report of the Department of Antiquities, Cyprus*: 24–25.

du Plat Taylor, J., and Megaw, A. H. S.
1937–1939 Cypriot Medieval Glazed Pottery: Notes for a Preliminary Classification. *Report of the Department of Antiquities, Cyprus*: 1–13.

Gabrieli, R. S.
2004 Under the Surface: Decoration and Shape in the Coarse Ware of Medieval and Post-Medieval Cyprus. *Mediterranean Archaeology* 17: 287–98.
2006 Silent Witnesses: The Evidence of Domestic Wares of the 13th–19th Centuries in Paphos, Cyprus, for Local Economy and Social Organisation. Unpublished Ph. D. dissertation, University of Sydney.
2009 Stability and Change in Ottoman Coarse Wares in Cyprus. Pp. 67–77, 154–63 in *Reflections of Empire: Archaeological and Ethnographic Studies on the Pottery of the Ottoman Levant,* ed. B. Walker. Annual of the American Schools of Oriental Research, Vol. 64. American Schools of Oriental Research: Boston.

Gregory, T. E.
1993 Byzantine and Medieval Pottery. Pp. 157–76 in *The Land of Paphian Aphrodite,* part 2, ed. Lone Wriedt Sørensen. Studies in Mediterranean Archaeology 104. Göteborg: Åström.
2003 The Byzantine Problem and Medieval to Modern Pottery. Pp. 283–94 in *The Sydney Cyprus Survey Project: Social Approaches to Regional Archaeological Survey,* eds. M. Given and A. B. Knapp. Monumenta Archaeologica 21. Los Angeles: Cotsen Institute.
2004 Less is Better: The Quality of Ceramic Evidence from Archaeological Survey and Practical Proposals for Low-Impact Survey in a Mediterranean Context. Pp. 32–69 in *Mediterranean Archaeological Landscapes: Current Issues,* eds. E. Athanassopoulos and L. Wandsnider. Philadelphia: University of Pennsylvania.

Hayes, J. W.
1972 *Late Roman Pottery*. London: The British School at Rome.

Ionas, I.
2000 *Traditional Pottery and Potters in Cyprus. The Disappearance of an Ancient Craft Industry in the 19th and 20th Centuries.* Birmingham Byzantine and Ottoman Monographs 6. Aldershot: Ashgate.

Manning, S. W.
2002 *The Late Roman Church at Maroni Petrera.* Nicosia: The A.G. Leventis Foundation.

Papanikola-Bakirtzis, D.
1993 Cypriot Medieval Glazed Pottery. Answers and Questions. Pp. 115–30 in *"The Sweet Land of Cyprus." Papers Given at the 25th Jubilee Spring Symposium of Byzantine Studies,* eds. A. Breyer and G. Georghallides. Nicosia: Cyprus Research Centre.

Rautman, M.

2003   *A Cypriot Village of Late Antiquity: Kalavasos-Kopetra in the Vasilikos Valley.* Journal of Roman Archaeology Supplementary Series 52. Portsmouth, RI: Journal of Roman Archaeology.

Sanders, G. D. R.

2004   Problems in Interpreting Rural and Urban Settlement in Southern Greece, AD 365–700. Pp. 163–93 in *Landscapes of Change: Rural Evolutions in Late Antiquity and the Early Middle Ages,* eds. N. Christie and S. Scott. Aldershot: Ashgate.

Sørensen, L. W., and Jacobsen, K. W.

2000   *Panayia Ematousa: Approaches to Regional Studies.* Aarhus: Aarhus University.

von Wartburg, M-L.

1995   Design and Technology of the Medieval Cane Sugar Refineries in Cyprus. A Case Study in Industrial Archaeology. Pp. 81–116 in *Paisages del azúcar. Actas del quinto seminario internacional sobre la caña de azúcar,* ed. A. Malpica. Motril: Diputación provincial de Granada.

2007   *Chronology and Stratigraphy of the Medieval Pottery of Cyprus: A Critical Review.* Pp. 419–40 in *Çanak: Late Antique and Medieval Pottery and Tiles in Mediterranean Archaeological Contexts,* eds. B. Böhlendorf-Arslan, A. O. Uysal, and J. Witte-Orr. Istanbul: Ege Yayınları.

Chapter 16

Textile Production at Athienou-*Malloura*?

The Case for the Processing of Flax in the Venetian Period

by Mercedes A. DeMasi

This chapter explores the enigmatic nature of the large building in EU 2, an unusual structure dating to the Venetian period located at the southwest corner of Athienou-*Malloura*. As noted by Toumazou and Counts (Ch. 6), the site has evidence of occupation stretching from the Cypro-Archaic period to the Ottoman period, despite abandonment following the Arab raids of the seventh century. Occupation of Malloura had resumed during the Frankish period, and the settlement flourished during the late Frankish–Venetian period before its eventual abandonment by the end of the Ottoman period. In the Venetian period Malloura was a thriving rural community with evidence of large-scale milling of grain (see Spigelman, Ch. 17) and strong indication of some industrial activity, including textile production (see below and Harper, Ch. 20).

Excavation of the large building in EU 2 began upon its discovery by the Athienou Archaeological Project during its 1990 inaugural season and continued in the 1991 to 1993 field seasons. Sgrafitto pottery found in the interior of the building dates the structure to ca. the mid-15th or 16th century. The size and construction of the large building in EU 2 have led to the conclusion that its primary function was industrial rather than domestic; however, archaeological remains from the 17th and 18th centuries recovered from the excavation of the building suggest that domestic activities, such as squatting, may have occurred after the structure was no longer utilized for its original purpose (Toumazou et al. 1998: 176; Toumazou and Counts, Ch. 6).

Late-period archaeological excavations on Cyprus often overlook domestic structures in favor of churches, fortifications, and other monumental architecture, resulting in a dearth of information on domestic life and operations. This unfortunate situation has made it difficult to speak with any authority concerning the conditions that prevailed in some critical transitional periods, such as the times of the Arab raids of the seventh century AD and the initial phases of western domination under the Franks and Venetians, when the status of Cyprus in the Mediterranean world-system shifted (see the comments in Gordon et al., Ch. 3). The void of archaeological studies on medieval and early modern domestic structures contributes to the problem of determining the function of the large building in EU 2. Several possible uses have been suggested for this enigmatic structure (see,

FIG. 16.1   *Aerial view of EU 2 at Athienou-*Malloura, *1993; north at top of page (© AAP).*

for example, Spigelman, Ch. 17), although its archaeological significance in EU 2 has yet to be fully ascertained as the analysis of its architecture and ceramic contents continues. This chapter examines the history of flax textiles in relation to Cyprus and argues that the industrial processing and production of fiber flax (*Linum usitatissimum*) may have been the original purpose of the large building in EU 2 at Athienou-*Malloura* (see also Spigelman, Ch. 17, where an alternative interpretation for the building in EU 2 as a granary is presented). Flax was an important commodity in ancient and medieval economies. Linen is the most popular fiber-flax product; here, "linen" and "flax" are used interchangeably to describe textiles woven from the bast fibers of *Linum usitatissimum*. The building in EU 2 is discussed first, followed by an overview of flax processing in order to build an argument for linen production at Malloura.

The Structure in EU 2

The large building at Athienou-*Malloura* located within EU 2 has been dated to the Venetian period by sgraffito pottery sherds dating to the mid-15th to 16th century found in the vicinity (Toumazou et al. 1998; Toumazou and Counts, Ch. 6). Slight architectural modifications and some later artifacts, such as pipe fragments from the Ottoman period (17th or 18th century), suggest that the structure was used for several centuries, eventually changing functions from an industrial processing center during the Venetian period to a shelter for squatters or shepherds during Ottoman times (Toumazou et al. 1998: 176; Toumazou and Counts, Ch. 6). The structure covers 54 m² and consists of 22 walls constructed of limestone cobbles and boulders surrounded by soil and pebbles; there are one northeast–southwest wall, four north–south walls, and 17 east–west walls (fig. 16.1; see also fig. 6.10). The east–west cross-walls (ca. 0.40 m wide) are parallel and evenly spaced, with short breaks or channels connecting the areas between the walls. The channels between the east–west cross-walls were seemingly lined with thin, flat, upright gypsum slabs and hydraulic plaster (plaster mixed with small black pebbles), suggesting that the purpose of these channels required waterproofing. Toumazou et al. (1998: 176) note that "countless scraps of decomposed wood were encountered between the cross-walls, but never above them, suggesting the presence of planks or boards in the original arrangement" and speculate that the purpose of these channels was to move an unknown element through the structure, such as air or liquid, and that the wooden boards laid on top of the gypsum slabs lining the east–west trenches

allowed for circulation. Two breaks in the north–south exterior walls referred to as "windows" in field notes are on the same elevation as breaks in the east–west walls and parallel to the channel connecting the trenches.

A History of Flax

It has been proposed that flax was the first plant cultivated for purposes other than human consumption (Kampp 1939: 165). The Latin term for flax is *linum*, which is used for the many commodities derived from flax but not for the plant *Linum usitatissimum* itself. Likewise, the Greek λίνον (τό) is representative of a wide variety of products made from flax, such as cloth, thread, string, hunting line, and lamp wick (Mayerson 1997: 203). The cultivation of *Linum usitatissimum* is believed to have started in the eastern Mediterranean zone in prehistoric times. J. M. Renfrew (1969: 168) suggests that flax was cultivated in the Middle East as early as the first half of the 8th millennium BC. E. J. W. Barber (1991: 12) describes a cache of textile artifacts radiocarbon-dated to the 7th millennium BC utilizing flax recovered from a PPNB (Pre-Pottery Neolithic B) context in a cave in Israel (Nahal Hemar in the Judean desert, west of the southern end of the Dead Sea), but it is unknown whether the flax used in the production of these textiles was sourced from wild or domesticated stock. The widespread use of flax in the eastern Mediterranean is evident in Anatolian linens that predate the earliest definitive archaeological evidence for the domestication of flax found in Iraq in the form of imported flax remains (ca. 5500 BC) and improvements in seed quality (ca. 5000 BC). Between 5000 and 3000 BC, flax spread as far west as Syria and Egypt and as far north as Switzerland and Germany, diversifying its stock to adapt to varied environments (Barber 1991: 12). Linear B tablets (ca. 1200 BC) found during Blegen's excavations of the Mycenaean palace at Pylos suggest the presence of a significant linen industry (Robkin 1979: 469). Moreover, "frequent allusions" to flax and linen in the Bible provide epigraphic evidence for the industrial cultivation and processing of *Linum usitatissimum* during antiquity (Tanner 1922: 174).

The Processing of Flax

Linum usitatissimum has many valuable nutritional, medicinal, industrial, and household uses. There are two main reasons for cultivating flax: fiber and seed. The cultivation of *Linum usitatissimum* for fiber occurred thousands of years ago, and the cultivation of flax for seed commodity began in 14th-century Europe. The recognition of the usefulness of linseed oil, a by-product of flax seeds, provided an important technological advance for artists during this time, facilitating the rise in popularity of oil painting during the Renaissance period. Flax is an economic crop, producing a high yield of raw material per acre, and its fibers, also known as "bast," are long, flexible, strong, durable, and versatile (Kampp 1939: 165). Flax cultivated for fiber is generally harvested before the oil in the stems redistributes to the flowers and the seeds; Barber (1991: 12) writes, "the flax stem yields the nicest fiber … before the seed develops." Robkin (1979: 470) notes that flax seeds continue to ripen on harvested stalks being dried in preparation for retting, allowing flax cultivated for high-quality fiber to also produce a secondary seed crop. As flax ripens, the bast fibers become coarse and tough; the youngest plants have the finest, supplest fibers, and harvesting flax before it flowers ensures the malleability of the bast fibers and increases the potential for creating higher quality textiles (Barber 1991: 12–13). Flax grown for seed does not require the careful cultivation, handling, and production necessary for the growth of fiber flax and is sown sparsely to encourage branching and seed production. The seeds of the flax plant can be used as animal feed or processed for their oil, commonly referred to as linseed oil (Barker 1917: 501–3).

The growth and processing of *Linum usitatissimum* are labor intensive and have experienced few changes during several thousand years of cultivation. Flax plants are carefully pulled up by their roots, preferably before they have gone to seed, then bound together by their stalks and left to dry. After being dried, flax must be retted before it is processed further. The word "ret" is an old causative form of the verb "rot;" therefore, to ret flax means to rot away the binding plant material (called pectin) in the stem in order to free the valuable cellulose bast fibers. There are two types of retting, dew retting and water retting, and both make use of microbial fermentation to disintegrate the pectin binding bast to stem. Dew retting is a slow process requiring a moist climate and makes the resulting bast fibers brittle and silvery gray. In dew retting, bundles of flax are placed outdoors, allowing fungus and atmospheric dew to gradually rot away the pectin in the stalk. Water retting is a technological improvement over dew retting, requiring less time and producing finer, more supple bast fibers that result in higher quality cloth. Barber (1991: 13) notes that the fine, golden appearance of water-retted flax is the origin for the term "flaxen hair." Water retting involves the submersion of dried flax in ponds, basins, or slow-moving streams and weighting down the bundles of flax with stones or boards to encourage the microbial fermentation of pectin. The fermentation of pectin produces offensive odors and releases large amounts of rotting organic materials (phosphates) into the water; thus, the retting of flax in bodies of water results in putrefaction, limiting the human use and consumption of water from these areas. Temperature is an important factor in the successful retting of flax, and nonoptimal conditions during the retting process may result in the retardation or undesired increase of the microbial processes that facilitate retting. The optimal temperature for retting is 30° C (Tanner 1922: 174–77). After retting, flax is dried, broken up to remove unwanted stem material, and beaten with implements in a process called scutching, which separates the woody fibers of the flax stem from the bast fibers. Ground stone beaters were found in the southern part of EU 2, perhaps intended for use in the scutching of flax fibers. Long, valuable fibers of bast are known as "line," and short broken pieces of flax are referred to as "tow." The length of bast fibers after scutching may be 75–100 cm, a suitable length for spinning. Scutched flax is then hackled (combed) to remove the last pieces of fiber from stem (Barber 1991: 13).

Flax is easiest to spin while wet, transforming from brittle fibers to supple linen yarn. There are several ways of keeping flax moist: through spinning bowls filled with water, spinning in a damp

Fig. 16.2 *Detail of Attic red-figure vase depicting mouth spinning, early fifth century* BC *(drawing: J. Ravenhurst, after Blümner 1877: pl. 6).*

place such as a cellar, or saliva. Catullus describes the Fates of Greek mythology as spinning thread by drawing it through their mouths. Barber documents several cultures that utilized saliva as an aid in spinning flax and speculates that saliva may have allowed Egyptian linen to be spliced without knots:

> Eventually I learned that flax has the peculiar property that when wet with saliva it partially disintegrates into a gluey substance. … Saliva is thus preferable to plain water in working with flax. Possibly the Egyptians induced their splices to stick together without knots by using saliva; the splicers do not appear to have bowls of water. (Barber 1991: 49)

Hungarian flax spinners sucked on plum pits while spinning to increase saliva production for their work. Barber (1991: 46) also cites ethnographic evidence from early-20th-century Egypt (Crowfoot 1974) of women "spinning flax 'through the mouth'" and provides a photograph of a Classical Greek red-figure vase from the fifth century BC, in which a young female spinning with a distaff pulls the fiber through her mouth (fig. 16.2), although Barber speculates that this depiction illustrates the spinning of wool rather than flax due to the short length of the woman's distaff.

EVIDENCE FOR FLAX PRODUCTION ON CYPRUS AND AT ATHIENOU-*MALLOURA*

The Venetian levels at Athienou-*Malloura* have yielded some evidence that the processing of flax occurred at the site. The information is basically of two types: (1) indications of peculiar dental wear patterns from osteological analysis; and (2) the unique architecture of the large Venetian structure in EU 2. There are 45 burials at Malloura (in EU 6) that have a Venetian context, only 15 of which have preserved dental material. Five of these 15 burials exhibit dental wear consisting of notches and/or grooves, patterns of wear consistent with textile work or production. Harper (2005, 2006, Ch. 20) argues that wear patterns on the teeth of these individuals, in conjunction with historical knowledge of the Venetian economy, suggests the existence of textile production such as spinning or weaving at Malloura during this time. Harper (2005), citing Arbel (2000), interprets this dental wear as indicative of the repeated pulling of cotton or flax fibers through the mouth and notes Malloura's history of flax and cotton production during medieval times. Individuals engaged in textile production at Malloura may have done so from a young age, indicated by the amount of wear on the teeth of a girl aged 15–18 years (fig. 16.3). A medieval burial of a seamstress at Polis shows the same patterns of dental wear as the individuals at Malloura whose occupations are indeterminate (Baker et al. 2007).

Definitive information on flax cultivation and production during any time period on Cyprus is difficult to locate. J. Smith's research on Late Bronze Age textiles in Cyprus identifies flax and wool as the two primary fibers in woven textiles during this period. Epigraphic evidence from the Late Bronze Age suggests that Cyprus produced woolen and linen textiles for export to the west and east, and Linear B and other tablets found in the eastern Mediterranean region (including Anatolia, Syria, the Levant) list Alashiya (an ancient name for Cyprus) as an exporter of linen (Smith 2002:

290). Fragments of cloth wrapped around a bronze dagger and knife in the Cyprus Museum provide archaeological evidence for the use of linen on the island during the Early and Middle Cypriot periods (Conroy 2000: 227–28). The preservation of ancient textiles relies on extraordinary conditions; fragments of linen cloth from antiquity that survive disintegration often do so by absorbing mineral deposits (metal salts) during burial. Sulphides leached into fabric from metal combine with moisture in the soil and preserve the cloth fibers. Conroy (2000: 227) writes of fragments of linen cloth found on a skeleton dating to the early Roman period at the House of Dionysos in Paphos: "this piece of cloth provides invaluable evidence for an everyday fabric of the second century, a linen garment or bag preserved by chance rather than as carefully chosen grave goods or as a dedicatory offering to a deity." These fragments of cloth were preserved by coins whose copper oxide leached into the fabric, preserving it. Conroy speculates that the fragments of linen recovered from Paphos came from Cyprus rather than Egypt, as Egyptian linen was much finer in quality and the number of threads per centimeter in the Paphos example matches a scrap of everyday linen found preserved in wax on a Cypro-Archaic II vessel. The size and weight (7–15 g) of stone loom weights and spindle whorls found in domestic contexts at Paphos indicate that fine fibers such as linen and cotton were being spun for everyday use. Coarser flax is hard and would require heavier whorls (up to 150 g), while short fibers such as cotton, wool, and tow (flax) require less weight (8–33 g) to be spun. Conroy (2000: 224–28) also notes that in addition to "providing the main occupation of women in the household, making textiles was a vital component in satisfying ritual needs." At Salamis, needles, bone bobbins, and small whorls from the late Roman period provide further evidence of the production of very fine textiles such as cotton, silk, and linen in Cyprus during antiquity.

Flax was an important commodity for domestic and commercial economies. In addition to high-quality fine textiles for personal use, products made from coarser fiber flax such as rope, twine, netting, bagging, lamp wicking, and sailcloth were valuable

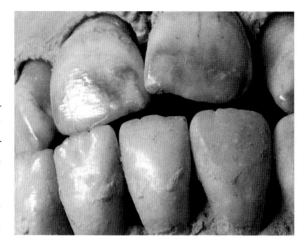

FIG. 16.3 *Detail of teeth from a Venetian-period burial (EU 6) showing dental wear consistent with textile production (photo: N. Harper).*

commodities for international trade and became a source of economic power for locales involved in flax production and processing (Barker 1917: 501). The Geniza documents from 11th–13th-century Egypt are records of "an extensive business operation in which exceptionally large amounts of flax were exported and sold to communities throughout the Mediterranean" (Mayerson 1997: 201). Through correspondence, bills, and other business documents, these texts preserved in the Cairo Geniza give evidence of the major role of linen textiles in the economy during medieval times. The main industrial crop in Egypt at the time was flax, which was exported to other parts of North Africa, the Near East, and Europe. The Arab occupation of Egypt in the seventh century marked a shift in the domestic economy away from the cultivation and export of grain, allowing the "burgeoning textile industry [to create] a demand for flax" and flax to supplant grain as the main product for export (Mayerson 1997: 205–7). The ecological stresses of focusing on industrial crops for export rather than grain for domestic use led to famines in the 11th century.

Harper (2006) notes that during the medieval period, the eastern Mediterranean (specifically Egypt and Syria, both of which have histories of contact and trade with Cyprus dating back to the Bronze Age) was a center for the production of textiles such as cotton and linen. When these areas became inaccessible after the Crusades, Cyprus was an important producer of light textiles because of its similar climate and convenient location for trade. Through the Byzantine and Venetian periods, Cypriot silk, wool, cotton, and linen were well-known from traveler accounts (Jennings 1993; Arbel 2000). During the Byzantine and Ottoman periods, silk production on Cyprus was tightly regulated by these governments. Flax in particular "was one of the most prevalent fibers used to produce thread in the eastern Mediterranean and was used to provide fine textiles for households and clothing" (Harper 2006). Research on Cypriot textiles from the Byzantine through Ottoman periods appears to eschew everyday textiles such as linen and cotton in favor of silk.

The textile trade flourished in the eastern Mediterranean during the Venetian period (AD 1489–1571), and in 1558 the trading center of the region was relocated from Syria to Cyprus. Textile production and export were an important part of the economy of Cyprus during the 16th century, as Portuguese cultivation of cane sugar in the New World undermined sugar production on Cyprus. Cotton became the cash crop in Cyprus, and the textile industry thrived (Lane 1933: 232). More than 36 cargo ships sailed from Venice to Cyprus over a 30-month period between 1558 and 1560, and Cypriot textiles were a sought-after product of export (Lane 1933: 232). The importance of textiles in relation to international trade continued through the Ottoman period and played an important part in the Cypriot economy (Panzac 1992).

The site of Malloura is located in the Mesaoria, the fertile central plain of Cyprus known as the island's breadbasket. *Linum usitatissimum* is capable of adapting to widely different environments and its optimal growing conditions would have been met at Malloura. Flax prefers light clay, slightly alkaline, sandy soil with well-drained subsoil so that the roots of the plant remain above the water table; tests conducted during the summer 2007 field season on soil samples previously collected from EU 2 indicate alkaline soil with a pH level of 8 (see Beeston, Ch. 24). Flax thrives in moist, temperate climates, requiring about 12 cm of rainfall evenly dispersed over its growing period

of 70–150 days and night temperatures no lower than 3–4° C (Kampp 1939: 165). Robkin (1979: 471) states that the growing season for flax in the eastern Mediterranean is winter, when cool, moist conditions favor the growth of the most valuable type of fiber. If *Linum usitatissimum* were grown at Malloura during the winter, temperature requirements would be within the optimal range and additional moisture requirements could be supplemented by irrigation redirected from the two seasonal streams in the vicinity of EU 2. Malloura has the correct soil structure, pH, sun, water, and nutrient conditions to promote the cultivation of flax as an industrial crop.

I suggest that the building within EU 2 at Malloura was used for the retting and processing of flax and that the evenly spaced cross-walls with short breaks or channels connecting them are architecturally congruent with the conditions needed to ret flax in a controlled environment. Tanner (1922: 185) describes water retting as preferable to dew retting because "the retting process can be shortened and a better quality of fiber produced by carrying it out under controlled conditions where the optimum environment may be maintained." The channels in the large building within EU 2 would perhaps allow for a slow, constant flow of water through the structure in a temperature-controlled environment and prevent the pollution of potable-water supplies. The wood presumed to be planks or boards was placed on top of bundles of flax immersed in water in the channels and weighted down with stones to expedite fermentation and therefore the retting process. The use of boards weighted with stones is attested in ethnographic research of the retting of flax (Barker 1917: 509). Soil samples from EU 2 analyzed during the 2007 field season reveal high phosphate levels, suggesting human activities involving organic matter in this area (see Beeston, Ch. 24); the decomposition of plant matter through the retting of flax could serve as one explanation for the elevated phosphate levels in this structure. The upright gypsum slabs that line the trenches between the east–west walls may have provided the ideal surface for hackling flax.

Archaeological evidence from other locales identified as textile processing sites on Cyprus is congruent with data collected from the excava-tion of the large building in EU 2. Buxton's (1921: 19) ethnographic study of Cypriot textiles at the beginning of the 20th century found that peasant women had a preference for using hare bones to counterweight the pulleys on their looms. A cache of small animal bones found in the southern half of the large building in EU 2 may have been used as tools during weaving. A textile workshop for dye-ing fabrics from Bronze Age Kition is a structure with channels connecting a series of pits and vats similar to the arrangements in the large building in EU 2 at Malloura. Ashes, bones, and fragments of gypsum are present in and around the large building in EU 2, as well as at the known textile workshop at Kition. Early field reports for EU 2 speculated that the burnt layer and soil surround-ing EU 2 came from secondary occupation during the Ottoman period; but Smith (2002: 302–3) de-tails the use of ash for dyeing and washing textiles. In addition to an intact limestone trough or basin, three fragments of a worked limestone basin esti-mated to measure 50 cm in diameter were located in EU 2 in 1992. Perhaps these basins were used for washing, dyeing, or rinsing textiles.

CONCLUSION

The participation of Cyprus in the international textile trade during the Venetian period along with osteological evidence from Malloura (see Harper, Ch. 20) can lead us to assume that the peo-ple of Malloura were in some way connected with the industrial processing or production of textiles. Malloura presents the ideal climate and location for the cultivation of flax. The large building in EU 2 was an industrial structure, and the amount of dental wear from skeletons exhumed in EU 6 suggests a high occupational frequency of thread being drawn through the teeth. These individu-als were involved in the production of fiber-flax textiles, as human saliva contains the optimal en-zymatic properties that promote the disintegration of the pectin in flax that binds the bast fibers to the stem (Barber 1991: 72). Archaeological evidence from elsewhere on the island, as well as modern ethnographic observations correlate an extensive, significant relationship between Cyprus and linen and suggest that the large building in EU 2 may have been used for flax production, specifically the retting of flax. Preliminary soil tests done during the summer 2007 field season confirm high pH and phosphate levels in EU 2, congruent with an area where flax would be retted or where textiles would be processed and dyed. The hypothesis of the production and processing of flax in the EU 2 structure merits further examination by conduct-ing extensive flotation on soil in and around EU 2 in search of preserved flax remains and chemical soil analysis. In this way, the work at Malloura could contribute to a clearer understanding of the medieval domestic economy on Cyprus.

ACKNOWLEDGMENTS

The author would like to thank Professors Michael Toumazou and P. Nick Kardulias for their help in preparing this chapter and Janie Ravenhurst for her drawing of the Attic red-figure vase detail (fig. 16.2).

REFERENCES

Arbel, B.
2000   *Cyprus, the Franks and Venice, 13th–16th Centuries*. Variorum Collected Studies Series. Burlington, VT: Ashgate.

Baker, B. J.; Terhune, C. E.; and Papalexandrou, A.
2007   Sew Long: A Seamstress Buried at Medieval Polis, Cyprus. Poster presented at the 76th Annual Meeting of the American Association of Physical Anthropologists, Philadelphia, Pennsylvania, March 2007.

Barber, E. J. W.
1991   *Prehistoric Textiles*. Princeton: Princeton University.

Barker, W. S.
1917   Flax: The Fiber and Seed. A Study in Agricultural Contrasts. *The Quarterly Journal of Economics* 31(3): 500–29.

Blümner, H.
1877   Denkmäler-Nachlese zur Technologie. *Archäologische Zeitung* 35: 51–55.

Buxton, L. H. D.
1921   Notes on Cypriot Textiles. *Man* 21: 17–19.

Conroy, D. W.
2000   Textile Artefacts and a Fragment of Cloth from Paphos, Cyprus. *Report of the Department of Antiquities, Cyprus*: 221–32.

Crowfoot, G. M.
1974   *Methods of Handspinning in Egypt and the Sudan.* McMinnville, OR: Robin and Russ Handweavers.

Harper, N. K.
2005   Specialized Dental Wear from Venetian Period Cyprus. Poster presented at the 70th Annual Meeting of the Society of American Archaeology, Salt Lake City, Utah, March–April, 2005.
2006   Industrial Dental Wear from Venetian Period Cyprus. Poster presented at the 16th European Meeting of the Paleopathology Association, Santorini, Greece, August 29, 2006.

Jennings, R. C.
1993   *Christians and Muslims in Ottoman Cyprus and the Mediterranean World, 1571–1640.* New York: New York University.

Kampp, A. H.
1939   Geography of the Fiber-Flax Industry. *Economic Geography* 15(2): 165–68.

Lane, F. C.
1933   Venetian Shipping during the Commercial Revolution. *The American Historical Review* 38(2): 219–32.

Mayerson, P.
1997   The Role of Flax in Roman and Fatimid Egypt. *Journal of Near Eastern Studies* 56(3): 201–7.

Panzac, D.
1992   International and Domestic Maritime Trade in the Ottoman Empire during the 18th Century. *International Journal of Middle East Studies* 24(2): 189–206.

Renfrew, J. M.
1969   The Archaeological Evidence for the Domestication of Plants: Methods and Problems. Pp. 149–72 in *The Domestication and Exploitation of Plants and Animals*, eds. P. J. Ucko and G. W. Dimbleby. Chicago: Aldine.

Robkin, A. L. H.
1979   The Agricultural Year, the Commodity SA and the Linen Industry of Mycenean Pylos. *American Journal of Archaeology* 83(4): 469–74.

Smith, J. S.
2002   Changes in the Workplace: Women and Textile Production on Late Bronze Age Cyprus. Pp. 281–312 in *Engendering Aphrodite: Women and Society in Ancient Cyprus*, eds. D. Bolger and N. Serwint. Boston: American Schools of Oriental Research.

Tanner, F. W.
1922   Microbiology of Flax Retting. *Botanical Gazette* 74(2): 174–85.

Toumazou, M.K.; Yerkes, R.W.; and Kardulias, P.N.
1998   Athienou Archaeological Project: Investigations in the Malloura Valley Cyprus 1990-1995. *Journal of Field Archaeology* 25(2): 163–82.

Chapter 17

Agroindustrial Installations
in the Malloura Valley

by Matthew Spigelman

This chapter investigates five worked stones found in the Malloura Valley in the course of survey and excavation (Toumazou et al. 1998). These stones are reconstructed as having functioned in agroindustrial installations, for the milling of grain, the extraction of olive oil, and possibly the production of wine. Dating these installations is difficult because most of the worked stones were found as surface finds; however, each object can be placed within a broad chronological scheme, based on technological developments and the chronological and spatial development of settlement in the valley as a whole (Toumazou et al. 1998). The study of these installations provides a better understanding of the process by which marginal areas, such as the Malloura Valley, were inhabited and exploited (see Kardulias et al., Ch. 1).

The Athienou Archaeological Project's diachronic study of land use in the Malloura Valley has demonstrated that settlement and agricultural use of the valley peaked twice, during the periods of Roman and Venetian rule, when the island saw high population density and increased international trade (Toumazou et al. 1998). These developments have been interpreted in previous publications of the AAP (Kardulias 2007) within the framework of world-systems analysis (e.g., Chase-Dunn and Hall 1993), building upon the view of the modern world proposed by world-systems theory (Wallerstein 1976). These models give primacy to long-distance trade and large-scale political forces, thereby downplaying the role of urban development and the demands it places upon rural agriculture (e.g., Wright and Johnson 1975; for a less centralized view, see Crumley 1987). This technological study of agricultural processing equipment presents evidence for the scale and organization of rural development, providing an avenue to investigate the social, political, and economic mechanisms behind the creation of agricultural surplus.

DISTRIBUTION OF FINDS

The worked stones investigated in this study were found in and around the two streambeds of the Malloura Valley (map 2 on p. xxii); some were at the edges of fields flanking the streams, others in the beds themselves. Presumably those at the edges of fields were brought to the surface through plowing, while those found within the streambeds were exposed by erosion. Surface survey and excavation have shown that both the Roman and medieval-period settlements were nucleated in this location (Toumazou and Counts, Ch. 6, and Kardulias and Yerkes, Ch. 7).

CATALOGUE

Stone 1

Stone 1 (figs. 17.1a–b; see also fig. 7.6) is reconstructed as a rotary crushing basin for preparing olives prior to pressing (fig. 17.2). It is roughly cylindrical in shape, with a maximum diameter of 1.03 m and a maximum thickness of 0.58 m. One face is slightly larger than the other; this larger face contains a circular trough, preserved to a depth of 10 cm. At the center of the trough is a raised column, broken on its upper surface, with a square socket. A similar square socket is located at the center of its flat bottom surface. It is carved from a hard, gray metamorphic stone, which is likely from the Kantara region of the Pentadaktylos range (Stuart Swiny, personal communication to Michael Toumazou, 1991).

Stone 1 was found in the course of surface survey, at the edge of a plowed field, overlooking the streambed, sitting in a vertical position. It is preserved in two pieces, both of which are standing up on end and are partially buried. The orientation and location of the stone suggest that it is not *in situ* but was probably uncovered in the course of modern agricultural plowing and dragged to the edge of the field. Its great size, however, suggests that it was not moved very far, so too does the close proximity of its two pieces to each other.

FIG. 17.1A–B   *(a) flat underside and (b) trough of rotary crushing basin from Athienou*-Malloura. *Stone 1 (photos: M. Spigelman).*

FIG. 17.2   *Rotary crushing basin (modern) from Kykko Monastery, Cyprus (photo: M. Spigelman).*

FIG. 17.3 *Weight stone for lever and screw olive press from Athienou-Malloura. Stone 2 (photo: M. Spigelman).*

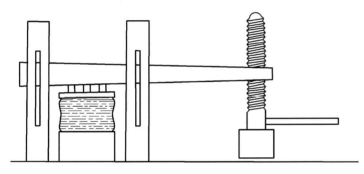

FIG. 17.4 *Reconstruction of a lever and screw olive press (drawing: M. Spigelman, after Drachmann 1932).*

of metal. Based on this morphology, Stone 1 is a Hadjisavvas Type 2(a) crushing basin (Hadjisavvas 1992: 14).

The chronology of Stone 1 can only be roughly presented. The rotary crushing basin was known to the Roman author Columella (*De re rustica* 12.52.6–7) in the first century AD (Humphrey et al. 1998: 160) but is attested to archaeologically earlier, beginning on Cyprus during the Hellenistic period, with the earliest known example found at Kalavasos-*Kopetra* (Hadjisavvas 1988, where the site is referred to as Mari-*Kopetra*). The technology remained in use and largely unchanged until the turn of the 20th century, and many examples can still be observed in rural villages. This long period of use, more than 2,000 years, makes a precise dating of Stone 1 impossible on typological grounds. That the piece, made of nonlocal stone, was preserved rather than refashioned into another stone implement suggests that it was in use until a relatively late date, likely in the Venetian or Ottoman period.

Stone 1 is reconstructed, based on its morphological characteristics, as the lower portion of a rotary crushing basin (*mortarium*) (fig. 17.2). This device was used in the crushing of olives, prior to pressing for the actual oil extraction (White 1984: 71–72; Hadjisavvas 1992: 7–11). Olives were placed in the trough, after washing, and were crushed by a circular millstone rolled over them. This millstone was supported by a horizontal axle, the end of which was connected to a vertical post. In some arrangements this post rotated and therefore was set in a circular socket; in others, the post remained stationary and the axle rotated on a pivot, in which case the post was set in a square socket. Stone 1 preserves a square socket, therefore it would have held a stationary post topped by a pivot, probably made

Stone 2

Stone 2 (fig. 17.3) is reconstructed as the weight stone for a lever-and-screw olive press (fig. 17.4). It is disk shaped, with a preserved diameter of 1.05 m (reconstructed to 1.1 m) and thickness of 0.35 m and is made of a white limestone. At the center of its upper face is a circular cutting, which has a maximum diameter of 0.24 m and a depth of 0.19–0.21 m. This cutting does not pass through the full thickness of the stone. The central cutting is flanked by two rectangular cuttings of indeterminate size due to partial preservation. Stone 2 was found sitting on the side of a dirt road, with a collection of other large rocks. This road overlooks the stream junction and sits at the heart of the ancient settlement. The location of the weight stone close to the streambed, though clearly not *in situ*, conforms to expectations. The pressing stage of oil extraction utilized large amounts of boiling water to prepare olives for their second and third pressings, drawing out remaining oil that had not been removed by the first "cold" pressing (Hadjisavvas 1992: 81).

Stone 2 is reconstructed, based on morphological characteristics, as the weight stone of a lever-and-screw olive press (see fig. 17.4) or, alternatively, a wine press. In a lever-and-screw press, the large wooden screw sits in the central cutting of the weight stone and is held fast to the stone by crosspieces secured in rectangular mortises. The lever is a long wooden log, which is fixed at one end. Bags of crushed olives are placed beneath it, close to the fixed end; they serve as the fulcrum for the lever. The free end of the lever is threaded by the large wooden screw. When the screw is turned, it draws the free end of the lever down, pressing the bags of olives, thereby extracting the oil (White 1984: 69). Pliny the Elder (*HN* 18.317) mentions the lever-and-screw press, and it was introduced to Cyprus during the late Roman period, when it quickly replaced the lever-and-weight press (Hadjisavvas 1992: 45–54, 117–20). As with the rotary crushing basin, the lever-and-screw press was a successful technological solution and was utilized up through the advent of metal presses in the 19th century. Stone 2 is an example of a Hadjisavvas Type 2(e) weight stone (Hadjisavvas 1992: 62); it is similar to examples found at Komi-Kebir–Strogylia, a Late Roman–Early Byzantine settlement (Hadjisavvas 1991: 43–44), which suggests a similar date for our stone.

Stone 3

Stone 3 (fig. 17.5) is reconstructed as the bearing stone of a horizontal water wheel (fig. 17.6), used in the grinding of cereal grains. It is a large, roughly circular block of limestone, over 1 m in diameter, with a flattened top. It is firmly planted at the base of the streambed, with a level orientation that appears deliberate, suggesting it remains *in situ*. Its

FIG. 17.5 *Bearing stone for horizontal water wheel (note: central socket) from Athienou-Malloura. Stone 3 (photo: M. Spigelman).*

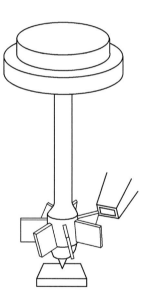

FIG. 17.6
Reconstruction of a horizontal water wheel (drawing: M. Spigelman, after Reynolds 1984).

defining feature is a small conical socket at the center. This socket is approximately 10 cm deep, tapering from a width of 5 cm at the top to 2 cm at the bottom. The smooth interior of the socket suggests that it once held a vertical axle. Stone 3 was found a short distance beyond the point where the valley's two streams merge.

Based on its morphology and *in situ* location, Stone 3 can be reconstructed as the bearing stone for a horizontal water wheel (see fig. 17.6). The horizontal blades of the water wheel would have been attached to this vertical axle and rotated by means of a jet of water directed at them. In such a setup,

FIG. 17.7 *In situ millstone (note: rind cutting at center) from Athienou-Malloura. Stone 4 (© AAP).*

FIG. 17.8 *Quarter millstone of vesicular volcanic rock from Athienou-Malloura. Stone 5 (photo: M. Spigelman).*

wheel was developed first, in the eastern Mediterranean during the later centuries BC; it alone is mentioned in the works of Vitruvius (*De architectura* 10.5.2) and Strabo (12.3.10) (White 1984: 55; Wikander 2000: 394–97). The horizontal wheel, while a simpler technology, was developed later, with the earliest known example found in seventh-century AD Ireland (Wikander 2000: 373–76). Although it is unclear when or where the horizontal water wheel was first developed, it is well-documented archaeologically and historically in Italy beginning in the 13th century AD (Muendel 1974) and in Anatolia during the Ottoman period (Donners et al. 2002). Given the abandonment of the Malloura Valley from the mid-seventh to the 13th century (Toumazou et al. 1998), Stone 3 must date to the later Frankish, Venetian, or Ottoman period of rule.

Stones 4 and 5

Stone 4 and Stone 5 (figs. 17.7–8) are both reconstructed as millstones for grinding grain. Stone 4 was uncovered in controlled excavations by the AAP in the 1992 season; it was left in place and has since been either reburied or lost. Based on notes and pictures, Stone 4 was disk shaped, with a circular hole at its center. The circular hole was accompanied by a rynd cutting (Runnels 1981: fig. 15), which accepted the crosspiece that allowed the axle to provide torque on the millstone. The date of Stone 4 can be restricted to the Frankish, Venetian, or Ottoman periods of habitation in the valley based on its reconstructed use within a water-powered mill. The small and intermittent streams of the Malloura Valley necessitated the use of a horizontal water wheel and would have not been able to support the vertical wheels of the Hellenistic or Roman period.

the water directed against the horizontal wheel was constantly washing over the bearing block, requiring that it be quite large to resist being undermined. The horizontal water wheel is well-suited to smaller streams in hilly or mountainous terrain, as opposed to the more complicated vertical wheel, which is designed for rivers with larger volumes (Wikander 2000: 375–78; Donners et al. 2002). The vertical

Stone 5 is a quarter of a cylinder, found in the streambed, exposed by the winter rains. The reconstructed stone is 0.7 m in diameter and 0.35 m thick, with a center hole 18 cm in diameter. The stone is volcanic in origin, with many vesicles (air pockets), and light yellow, almost white, in color. The material and morphology of Stone 5 suggest a possible production date and provenience based on parallels with published descriptions of millstones from the Rema quarry on the island of Melos. Millstones from Rema were produced as composite millstones, constructed of constituent pieces held together with iron hoops (Runnels 1981: 235–36). The regular shape of Stone 5 (it forms a perfect quarter of a circle) suggests that it was deliberately cut to be a piece of a composite millstone. Runnels reports that the quarries at Rema were exploited during the medieval period, beginning possibly as early as the 10th century but certainly by the 14th century. The millstone industry at Rema grew to become the main source for the Mediterranean region and was worked until the middle of the 20th century, when new technology supplanted millstones for the grinding of grain (Runnels 1990). The dating of Stone 5 to the Frankish, Venetian, or Ottoman period of rule falls in line with the dating proposed for Stones 3 and 4.

SOCIAL AND ECONOMIC ORGANIZATION

The archaeological evidence from survey and excavation in the Malloura Valley conforms to more generalized observations of recent land use in Cyprus, during the Ottoman period, as nucleated in villages, with a widespread avoidance of isolated rural farmsteads (Christodoulou 1959: 86–87; Given 2000: 215). The worked stones presented here were all found within the area of the Malloura settlement cluster, suggesting that the processing of agricultural products (e.g., cereals, olives, possibly grapes) was nucleated as well. The social and economic reasons driving this patterning are considered here. Ancient literary and archaeological evidence, as well as modern ethnographic accounts, shows that agroindustrial installations, such as the ones reconstructed here, require a

great deal of material and specialized labor to construct and maintain (Humphrey et al. 1998: 148–49, 160–61; Wikander 2000: 393–95). At times, independent entrepreneurs were able to marshal sufficient resources to finance their construction (Donners et al. 2002); however, far more often the archaeological and historical records show that an economic, social, or religious institution of some sort was responsible (Hadjisavvas 1992: 82–84).

In his diachronic study of olive oil production on Cyprus, Hadjisavvas reconstructs a connection between religious authority and control of economic activities, such as agricultural processing and copper production, dating back to the Late Bronze Age (Hadjisavvas 1992; see also Knapp 1986). In this model, a portion of the product served as both payment for the use of the processing equipment and a tithe to the religious body (Hadjisavvas 1992: 82–83). This view is confirmed by the documentary and archaeological research of Given, which shows that church-sponsored oil production existed in the Ottoman period and continued through the 1920s (Given 2000: 216–17). The archaeological remains at Malloura reveal the consistent presence of religious institutions at the site, with a rural sanctuary dating to the Cypro-Geometric through Roman periods, some evidence for an Early Christian basilica, and two churches during the late medieval and Ottoman periods (Toumazou et al. 1998).

In his historical studies of Cyprus under Venetian control, Arbel (1996, 2000) reconstructs an economic structure that is both heavily rural and centrally controlled. Venice sought to extract agricultural surplus from the island through taxation of the general populace and the direct control of agricultural production on estates run by appointment of the crown (Arbel 2000: 183–214). Under Venetian rule, Cypriot farmers would have had the option to bring their products for processing to either church-owned installations or those on the crown estates (Arbel 2000: 175–76).

Venetian archaeological remains have been excavated by AAP, revealing a diverse range of household, industrial, and burial activities within the nucleated settlement at Malloura (Toumazou et al. 1998). As noted by Counts and Parvis (Ch.

5), Frankish-period land grant documents of the mid-15th century suggest the (re)founding of the settlement during this period, with continued reference to the toponym in Venetian-period maps and tax records. The remains of a large Venetian-period building uncovered at Malloura in EU 2 (Toumazou et al. 1998: 175–76; see also Toumazou and Counts, Ch. 6) suggest that some form of institutional control over agricultural storage or processing was in operation during the Venetian period. While DeMasi (Ch. 16) suggests that the building served as an industrial complex for flax production, the building's extensive system of subfloor channels finds close parallels in granary designs (see figs. 6.10 and 16.1). The use of subfloor channels to promote drainage and airflow is a cross-culturally known strategy of grain storage. It was developed along with the first exploitation of cereals in the Near East (Kuijt and Finlayson 2009) and was in use during the third-millennium-BC urbanization of Mesopotamia (Hole 1999) and later at sites throughout the Greco-Roman world (Rickman 1971; Bell and Holloway 1988). The nature of institutional control over the EU 2 building during the Venetian period is unknown; however, it seems to have not continued into the Ottoman period, when the building was divided by a cross-wall and, at least partially, fell out of use (Toumazou et al. 1998).

The Venetian-period house uncovered at Malloura in EU 3, with its courtyard and private well (Toumazou et al. 1998: 176), suggests the presence of wealthy families at Malloura during this time. Excavations in EU 3 revealed the remains of a large, paved courtyard, presumably with adjoining household structures (Toumazou and Counts, Ch. 6; see also fig. 6.9). It is currently unknown if these structures contained agricultural processing and/or storage facilities apart from those seemingly preserved in EU 2. It is assumed that this wealthy house fell out of use in the Ottoman period or took on a diminished function; however, the ceramics have not yet been analyzed in detail.

The presence at Malloura, during the Venetian period, of wealthy families, institutionalized storage, and multiple churches indicates that a rich network of kin-based, religious, and political institutions was in operation at that time. The evidence for agroindustrial installations presented here suggests that the processing of agricultural products occurred at the supra-household level, embedded within this formal and informal institutional structure. The large number of agroindustrial implements recovered through survey and excavations lends support to the argument that the valley was exploited, at least during the Venetian period, to produce an agricultural surplus. This study does not, however, speak to the extent to which this economy was centrally controlled by, or oriented toward, the Venetian administrative apparatus and its demands for agricultural produce for export.

References

Arbel, B.

1996   The Economy of Cyprus during the Venetian Period (1473–1571). Pp. 185–92 in *The Development of the Cypriot Economy from the Prehistoric Period to the Present*, eds. V. Karageorghis and D. Michaelides. Nicosia: The University of Cyprus and the Bank of Cyprus.

2000   *Cyprus, the Franks and Venice, 13th–16th Centuries.* Variorum Collected Studies Series. Burlington, VT: Ashgate.

Bell III, M., and Holloway, R. R.

1988   Excavations at Morgantina, 1980–1985: Preliminary Report XII. *American Journal of Archaeology* 92(3):313–42.

Chase-Dunn, C. K., and Hall, T. D.

1993   Comparing World-Systems: Concepts and Working Hypotheses. *Social Forces* 71(4): 851–86.

Christodoulou, D.

1959   *The Evolution of the Rural Land Use Pattern in Cyprus.* The World Land Use Survey, Regional Monograph 2. Cornwall: Geographical Publications.

Crumley, C. L.
1987   Historical Ecology. Pp. 237–64 in *Regional Dynamics: Burgundian Landscapes in Historical Perspective*, eds. C. L. Crumley and W. H. Marquardt. San Diego: Academic.

Donners, K., Waelkens, M., and Deckers, J.
2002   Water Mills in the Area of Sagalassos: A Disappearing Ancient Technology. *Anatolian Studies* 52: 1–17.

Drachmann, A. G.
1932   *Ancient Oil Mills and Presses.* Copenhagen: Bianco Lunos Bogtrykkeri.

Given, M.
2000   Agriculture, Settlement and Landscape in Ottoman Cyprus. *Levant* 32: 209–30.

Hadjisavvas, S.
1988   Olive Oil Production in Ancient Cyprus. *Report of the Department of Antiquities, Cyprus (Part 2)*: 111–20.
1991   *KATABOLES 1.* Nicosia: Department of Antiquities.
1992   *Olive Oil Processing in Cyprus: From the Bronze Age to the Byzantine Period.* Studies in Mediterranean Archaeology and Literature Pocket-book 99. Göteborg: Åström.

Hole, F.
1999   Economic Implications of Possible Storage Structures at Tell Ziyadeh, NE Syria. *Journal of Field Archaeology* 26(3): 267–83.

Humphrey, J. W., Oleson, J. P., and Sherwood, A. N.
1998   *Greek and Roman Technology: A Sourcebook.* London: Routledge.

Kardulias, P. N.
2007   Negotiation and Incorporation on the Margins of World-Systems: Examples from Cyprus and North America. *Journal of World-Systems Research* 13(1): 55-82.

Knapp, A. B.
1986   *Copper Production and Divine Protection: Archaeology, Ideology and Social Complexity on Bronze Age Cyprus.* vol. 42, *Studies in Mediterranean Archaeology, Pocketbook.* Göteborg: Åström.

Kuijt, I., and Finlayson, B.
2009   Evidence for Food Storage and Predomestication Granaries 11,000 Years Ago in the Jordan Valley. *Proceedings of the National Academy of Sciences* 106(27): 10966–970.

Muendel, J.
1974   The Horizontal Mills of Medieval Pistoia. *Technology and Culture* 15(2): 194–225.

Reynolds, T. S.
1984   Medieval Roots of the Industrial Revolution. *Scientific American* 251: 122–30.

Rickman, G. E.
1971   *Roman Granaries and Store Buildings.* Cambridge: Cambridge University.

Runnels, C. N.
1981   A Diachronic Study and Economic Analysis of Millstones from the Argolid, Greece. Unpublished Ph. D. dissertation, Program in Classical Archaeology, Indiana University, Bloomington.
1990   Rotary Querns in Greece. *Journal of Roman Archaeology* 3: 147–54.

Toumazou, M. K.; Yerkes, R. W.; and Kardulias, P. N.
1998   Athienou Archaeological Project: Investigations in the Malloura Valley, Cyprus, 1990–1995. *Journal of Field Archaeology* 25(2): 163–82.

Wallerstein, I.
1976   A World-System Perspective on the Social Sciences. *The British Journal of Sociology* 27(3): 343–52.

White, K. D.
1984   *Greek and Roman Technology.* Ithaca, NY: Cornell University.

Wikander, Ö.
2000   The Water-Mill. Pp. 371–400 in *Handbook of Ancient Water Technology*, ed. Ö. Wikander. Leiden: Brill.

Wright, H. T., and Johnson, G. A.
1975   Population, Exchange, and Early State Formation in Southwestern Iran. *American Anthropologist* 77(2): 267–89.

Chapter 18

Faunal Remains from Athienou

by David S. Reese

As early as the 1870s, animal bones were mentioned as present in Cypriot tombs (Reese 2007). However, these were not scientifically identified. Swedish excavations on the island in the late 1920s and early 1930s saved animal bones, but most were never studied. About 1934, a Swedish zoologist identified a few animal bones from the 1927 excavation of a Lapithos tomb. The first study by a zoologist was published in 1950 on material excavated in the late 1930s at a Bellapais cemetery (Reese 2007).

By the 1950s, animal bones and shells were more systematically saved. However, sieving was not generally performed, so smaller and younger animals were not typically recovered. Today most excavations have someone to study the animal bones and shells, with dry-sieving very common and wet-sieving or flotation frequently practiced (Reese 2007). A faunal (or zooarchaeological or archaeozoological) analysis is primarily conducted to determine the animals consumed as food or kept for traction or as pets, as well as the animals naturally present in the environment. We are concerned with the species present, their ages, sex, and how humans exploited them (body part selection, cut bones, burnt bones, worked bones). In the case

of a sanctuary site, we are also interested in the animals (or their specific body parts) that were burnt as offerings.

The Malloura fauna discussed here comes from the 1991–1995, 1997–1999, 2001–2002, and 2004–2005 excavation seasons in the Cypro-Geometric (CG) III to Roman rural sanctuary, the Hellenistic to Roman tombs, and from late Roman and Venetian structures. Dates and contexts of the sanctuary deposits are based on the pottery studies of S. Fourrier (Ch. 9), but not all the excavated ceramics have been studied. Specific contexts of the stratified Hellenistic and earlier material have yet to be finalized.

The Sanctuary Fauna

The majority of the Malloura excavation effort has been devoted to the sanctuary area, and the faunal remains come largely from this area.

Animal Bones

The faunal remains are grouped by their archaeological contexts and dating: surface/cleaning, looters' pits, undated, and the stratified deposits

TABLE 18.1   Animal bones from Athienou-*Malloura*.

a) Surface/Cleaning/Looters' Pits/Alluvial Deposits/Undated
(2,378 Bones [272 Burnt], 180 Stratigraphic Units [SU]; Minimum Number of Individuals [MNI] based on SU occurrence, a quantification of the bone sample based on the number of SU samples and the presence of one or more MNI in each SU).

	Ovis/Capra	*Bos*	Other
EU 4	8	4	1 *Canis*
EU 10	26	10	1 *Canis*, 1 *Equus* sp., 1 *Dama*
EU 11	3	2	
EU 12	1	0	2 *E. caballus*
EU 14	1	0	
EU 18	10	2	
EU 20	3	1	
EU 22	2	0	
EU 24	24	10	2 *Canis*, 1 *E. caballus*, 1 *Equus* sp.
EU 28	33	10	1 rodent
EU 30	15	4	1 *Sus*, 1 rodent, 3 bird, 5 lizard/snake, 1 frog
EU 32	14	6	1 *Canis*
EU 34	9	2	
EU 36	6	1	
EU 88	3	2	

b) Hellenistic (3,139 bones [337 burnt], 107 SUs; MNI based on SU occurrence).

	Ovis/Capra	*Bos*	Other
EU 4	7	2	1 *Canis*
EU 10	24	11	1 *Sus*, 1 *Canis*, 1 *E. caballus*, 1 *E. asinus*, 1 bird
EU 11	3	0	
EU 12	2	0	
EU 18	7	4	
EU 22	1	0	
EU 24	23	9	2 *Dama*
EU 26	1	0	
EU 28	10	4	
EU 30	7	3	1 *Sus*, 2 *Canis*, 1 *Dama*, 4 rodent, 4 bird, 7 lizard/snake
EU 32	17	5	1 *Dama*, 1 *Vulpes*, 1 *Hemiechinus*

c) "Pre-Hellenistic" (928 bones [23 burnt], 37 SUs; MNI based on SU occurrence).

	Ovis/Capra	*Bos*	Other
EU 4	1	1	
EU 10	21	12	2 *Canis*, 1 *E. asinus*, 2 *Dama*, 1 *Lepus*
EU 22	1	1	
EU 24	3	2	1 *Canis*
EU 28	6	1	

(Hellenistic, Cypro-Classical [CC], Cypro-Archaic [CA], and Cypro-Geometric [CG] III). Details on the animal bones are provided in the appendix at the end of this chapter.

Most of the animals present are sheep (*Ovis aries*) and goat (*Capra hircus*), considered together here as *Ovis/Capra*, followed by cattle (*Bos taurus*). There are much smaller numbers of pig (*Sus scrofa*), dog (*Canis familiaris*), horse (*Equus caballus*), donkey or ass (*Equus asinus*), Persian fallow deer (*Dama mesopotamica*), hare (*Lepus europaeus cyprius*), red fox (*Vulpes vulpes indutus*), hedgehog (*Hemiechinus auritus dorotheae*), rodents, birds (mainly chicken [*Gallus gallus*]), lizard/snake, and frog. Table 18.1 shows where the bone material comes from.

As the table indicates, 36.9% of the material is surface/cleaning/looters' pits/alluvial deposits/undated, of which 11.4% are burnt. From the Hellenistic period come 48.7% of the bones with 10.7% burnt, and from the "pre-Hellenistic" (CG III, CA, CC) are 14.4% of the bones, with 2.5% burnt. Most of the burnt bones are *Ovis/Capra* and *Bos* fragments, with no clear patterning in the bone elements represented. This burning could be from food preparation/consumption rather than burnt sacrifice. A few of the larger samples of burnt bones are worth noting in an attempt to understand burnt animal sacrifice at Malloura.

The Hellenistic SU 2471 produced 125 bone fragments, with 81 burnt, or 64.8% of the sample (68 *Ovis/Capra*, 13 *Bos*). Most of the bones are not specifically identifiable, but one *Ovis/Capra* proximal femur head and one *Bos* distal tibia (unfused [UF]) are noteworthy. Of the 17 bones within the Hellenistic SU 2813, 4 are burnt, including an *Ovis/Capra* proximal femur (?UF). The Hellenistic SU 3208 produced 61 bones, including 44 *Ovis/Capra* burnt shaft fragments, or 72% of this sample. The Hellenistic SU 3227 produced 19 bones, with 5 burnt *Ovis/Capra* bones, including a proximal femur fragment, 3 distal femora fragments, and 1 unidentifiable fragment. The Hellenistic SU 3228 produced 18 bones, with 12 *Ovis/Capra* bones burnt including a distal femur fragment (UF).

SU 2802, a looters' pit with CA to Hellenistic material, produced 12 burnt *Ovis/Capra* bones

of 36 bones, including an *Ovis/Capra* femur head (fused [F]) and patella. The surface level SU 2817, with CA to Hellenistic material, produced 2 burnt *Ovis/Capra* bones of 4 bones found, including a proximal femur head (UF).

While the burnt bone samples are generally small, the presence of a number of hind limb bones suggests that this section of the animal might have been specifically chosen for burnt sacrifice, as known from other votive deposits in Greece and Cyprus (Reese 1989, 2000, 2005b; Davis 1996; Gebhard and Reese 2005).

The rarity of *Sus* in the sanctuary is remarkable, with only 4 unburnt bones seen (1 ?CA, 2 Hellenistic, 1 undated). *Sus* are quite rare at the primarily Late Cypriot [LC] II–IIIA site of Athienou-*Pamboulari tis Koukounninas* nearby and not found at all in the few Iron Age samples there (Reese 2005a: 88, 98) or in Venetian (AD 1489–1571) Malloura (EU 2 and EU 3). Pigs are common, however, in Late Roman–Early Byzantine Malloura (EU 5).

Also worth remarking on are the *Dama* remains. Except for one series of adult upper teeth (from SU 3209, Hellenistic), all the remains are antler fragments (SU 1099.201, Hellenistic; 1099.202, ?CA II; 1099.204, ?CA II; 2481, Hellenistic; 3017, Hellenistic with some CA; 3209, Hellenistic). *Dama* remains are rare at *Pamboulari tis Koukounninas* (Reese 2005a: 88–9) and not present in Malloura EU 5, EU 2, or EU 3 contexts.

Marine Shells

The sanctuary produced 24 Mediterranean shells, coming 16 km from the coast (as the crow flies). These include 3 holed basket shells (*Arcularia gibbosulus*) and 1 naturally holed dentalium (*Dentalium dentalis*), all probably used as ornaments.

Osteological Comparanda: Sanctuary Sites

Malloura is not the only Iron Age Cypriot sanctuary with fauna analyzed. Here the other sites are surveyed as a means of interpreting the Malloura sanctuary collection.

Tamassos

The 1970–1973 excavations produced fauna from four major areas (Nobis 1976–1977). The mainly seventh–fourth centuries BC altar area of the Temple of Astarte-Aphrodite produced 305 remains in 22 excavation units: 170 *Ovis/Capra* bones (21 units), 59 *Bos* (16 units), 41 *Sus* (15 units), 9 *Canis* (6 units), 4 *E. caballus* (2 units), 6 *E. asinus* (5 units), 4 *E. caballus x asinus* (4 units), 1 *Dama*, 3 *Lepus* (3 units), and 8 birds (6 units). A few of these bones were partly burnt (H.-G. Buchholz, excavation director, personal communication, June 20, 1996).

The sixth century to ca. 300 BC workshop area of the temple produced 91 bones in 27 excavation units: 46 *Ovis/Capra* bones (18 units), 15 *Bos* (10 units), 5 *Sus* (4 units), 1 *Canis*, 7 *E. caballus* (3 units), 7 *E. asinus* (6 units), 2 *Dama* (1 unit), 5 *Lepus* (2 units), and 3 birds (2 units). From mainly sixth–third centuries BC bothroi east of the temple come 53 bones in 13 units: 37 *Ovis/Capra* bones (11 units), 9 *Bos* (6 units), 2 *Sus* (1 unit), 2 *Canis* (2 units), 2 *E. asinus* (1 unit), and 1 bird. Finally, the fifth–third/second centuries BC city-wall ditch produced 24 bones from 5 units: 15 *Ovis/Capra* bones (4 units), 5 *Bos* (3 units), 1 *E. asinus*, 2 *Dama* (1 unit), and 1 *Lepus*.

Kourion

Animal bones from three CA areas at the Sanctuary of Apollo Hylates have been published (Davis 1996) with a total of 585 bones and teeth identified. The late eighth to sixth centuries BC Archaic Altar (Trench Jg) produced 456 identified bone fragments, all burnt, and mainly *Ovis/Capra*: 12 teeth, 2 distal humeri epiphses (2 UF), 1 proximal radius epiphysis (UF, R), 3 distal radii (3 UF, 2 R, 1 L), 5 pelves/ischium fragments (3 R, 2 L), 15 femora heads (15 UF), 38 distal femora condyle fragments, 40 patellae, 4 proximal tibiae epiphyses (4 UF), 71 distal tibiae (60 UF [57 R, 2 L, 1 unknown], 11 F [9 R, 2 L]), 142 calcanei fragments (89 UF [76 R, 7 L, 6 unknown], 11 F [9 R, 2 L], 45 central fragments [44 R, 1 L]), 70 astragali (68 R, 2 L), 1 proximal metacarpus, 1 proximal metatarsus, 10 distal meta-

podials (10 UF), 7 phalanx 1 fragments, 8 phalanx 2, 2 phalanx 3, 7 vertebrae fragments, and 6 rib heads. There are also 8 *Bos* bones: 2 teeth fragments, 2 distal tibiae (2 UF, 2 R), 2 astragali (2 R), 2 calcanei (2 UF, 2 R); 2 ?*Sus* bones: 1 calcaneus (UF), 1 metapodial (UF); and 1 ?*E. asinus* tooth fragment.

For *Ovis/Capra*, based on the 85 right proximal calcanei, there are at least 85 and as many as 91 right hind limbs in the sample. At least two of the much rarer forelimbs are under ten months old based on the epiphyseal fusion of the distal radius, distal humerus, and proximal radius. For the hind limb, based on the 67 right distal tibiae, 57 are under 1.5–2 years old, while using the right calcaneus there are 76 under 2.5–3 yrs. and 9 over this age. So, there are remains of 2 right and 1 left forelimbs, at least 85 right hind limbs, and at least 9 left hind limbs. For *Bos*, based on the 2 right tibiae, and single astragalus and calcaneus, these 2 limbs are under 2–2.5 yrs.

The partially excavated Semicircular Altar produced 56 remains with 44 burnt (78.6%). The burnt bones, all *Ovis/Capra*, include: 1 scapula (L), 2 femorae heads (2 UF), 6 distal femorae fragments, 2 patellae, 2 proximal tibiae epiphyses (2 UF), 8 distal tibiae (7 UF [6 R, 1 L], 1 F R), 17 calcanei fragments (11 UF [9 R, 1 L, 1 unknown], 3 F R, 3 R fragments), 4 astragali (3 R, 1 unknown), 1 metapodial (UF), and 1 phalanx 1. Based on the 7 right distal tibiae, 6 are under 1.5–2 yrs. and 1 is over this age. Based on the 12 right calcanei there are 9 under 2.5–3 yrs. and 3 over this age. So, there are remains of 1 left forelimb, 12 right hind limbs, and 1 left hind limb. The unburnt bones include 9 *Ovis/Capra* (8 teeth) and 3 *Bos* remains (2 teeth).

The Votive Area produced 73 remains with only 1 burnt. The burnt bone is a *Bos* astragalus, but "several bones" are said to be slightly charred (Davis 1996: 181). The unburnt remains are 70 *Ovis/Capra* (34 teeth), 1 *Bos* phalanx, and 1 *Vulpes* humerus.

It must be noted, however, that there is much more fauna than suggested by the 585 bones published by Davis. He did not note the number of unidentified bones he examined and probably saw only a few of the excavated samples. It appears that the Tr. Jg sample published by Davis with 456 identifiable bones is Jg Locus 013, excavated in 1980 and sorted and photographed in 1984, with over 5000 bone fragments.

After ten days of study in 2009, I estimate the total Buitron-Oliver-excavated fauna collection at about 60,000 burnt fragments and 500 unburnt pieces. No *Sus* or *Equus* bones were seen, and most of the *Bos* remains were unburnt. There are also several samples of unburnt bird bones. Most of the burnt *Ovis/Capra* bones were femur, tibia, calcaneus, and astagalus. So the burning here includes many lower hind limb elements not usually found at the other sanctuary sites where there is specific preference for burning hind limbs. At this point I cannot confirm the right side hind limb preference noted by Davis. A detailed study of the full collection will be published in the near future.

Kition

The fauna found during the 1967–1976 excavations at the Iron Age sanctuary complex was published by Nobis in 2000. He recorded 1,325 bones: 969 *Ovis/Capra* bones (121 MNI), 290 *Bos*, 1 *Sus* humerus (CC I-Hellenistic Bothros 18), 30 *E. asinus* (11 MNI), 2 *E. caballus* (CG III–CA II), 1 *Canis* atlas (CA I–early CA II), 12 *Dama* (with 5 antler), 2 *Lepus*, 8 bird, and 10 fish. However, it is clear from a reanalysis of the fauna conducted by the author that Nobis did not examine all the available remains and also recorded many of the contexts incorrectly.

Here details are noted for a few reanalyzed samples. The mainly CG III Bothros 10 (foundation deposit) in Temple 1 produced 1,967 bones with 1,850 *Ovis/Capra* bones (10 MNI, 23 bones burnt), 57 *Bos* (1 MNI, 4 burnt), and 60 fish (10 MNI of 8 species, 6 burnt). The mainly CG III Bothros 9 (second layer) in Temenos B produced 174 unburnt bones, with 111 *Ovis/Capra* bones (4 MNI), 62 *Bos* (2 MNI), 1 bird, and 1 fish bone. The CA I–early CA II Bothros 17 in Courtyard A produced 38 bones, with 29 *Ovis/Capra* bones (3 MNI) and 9 *Bos* (1 MNI, 1 burnt). The CC I to Hellenistic Bothros 2 produced 137 unburnt bones with 107 *Ovis/Capra* bones (3 MNI), 11 *Bos* (1 MNI), and 1 *Gallus*. It is striking how rare *Sus* is in these Kition Iron Age levels, but it should also be noted that pigs are similarly rare in LC Kition deposits (9 bones from

2 MNI; Nobis 1985 and personal analysis). This is in contrast to other Iron Age sites where pig is much more common.

Amathous

At the Sanctuary of Aphrodite a CA *bothros* produced 190 bone fragments, with 147 identifiable, including 124 *Ovis/Capra* bones (10 MNI, 4 bones burnt), 19 *Bos* (3 MNI, 3 burnt), 1 *Canis*, 1 bird, and 2 fish (1 MNI) (Columeau 2006: 167, 169). The CA *grotte* produced 1,301 identifiable bone fragments: 1,005 *Ovis/Capra* bones (about 200 MNI), 293 *Bos* (42 MNI), 1 *Sus*, and 2 bird (2 MNI) (Columeau 2006: 170). The general CC–Roman deposits here (with 80% CC) produced 2,801 identifiable bone fragments: 1,770 *Ovis/Capra* bones (about 350 MNI), 1,017 *Bos* (42 MNI), 1 *E. caballus*, 1 *E. asinus*, 2 deer, 1 *Lepus*, 8 *Oryctolagus cuniculus* (rabbit, 6 MNI), and 1 bird (Columeau 2006: 174). Once again, *Sus* is extremely rare.

Idalion

From recent excavations at the Iron Age "Lang's Temple" at Idalion it was noted that

> One room contained the key to the site: In it we found numerous bone fragments — all radii (leg bones) of sheep or goats, the traditional body part used in making burnt offerings. The structure was not a temple, but it was a sacred space, a kind of *temenos* — an outdoor sacred precinct…. [I]n the sanctuary excavators found … numerous leg bones of sheep and goats, used to make burnt offerings to a deity. In one room they found numerous fragments of leg bones from sheep and goats; these are traditionally the animal parts used to make burnt offerings to a deity (Gaber and Dever 1998: 50–51, 53).

While Lang's Temple may have many radii, it is unclear if these were burnt or unburnt. Also, radii are forelimb bones, while the bone elements burnt as offerings are from hind limbs (particularly the femur and tibia) (Reese 1989, 2000, 2005b; Gebhard and Reese 2005).

OSTEOLOGICAL COMPARANDA: NON-SANCTUARY SITES

Three other Cypriot Iron Age sites studied produced fauna. Cypriot excavations of 1992–2004 and 2007 at Idalion produced 3,458 bone fragments from 283 units studied by the author. These are *Ovis/Capra* (220 units; 234 MNI), *Bos* (127 units), *Sus* (1 unit), *Canis* (10 units), *E. caballus* (14 units), *E. asinus* (9 units), *Equus* sp. (8 units), *Dama* (10 units), *Lepus* (13 units), *Vulpes* (1 unit), rodent (3 units), bird (15 units), and fish (8 units). *Sus* were not found at all during 1970s American excavations at CA and Hellenistic–Early Roman Idalion (Schwartz 1973: 216) and they are extremely rare in all Iron Age levels at recent American excavations there (E. Lax, personal communication, October 17, 2006).

The CC (fifth–fourth centuries BC) Palace at Amathous produced 6,673 identified animal remains: 5,222 *Ovis/Capra* (including 327 *Ovis* and 66 *Capra*; 87 MNI), 677 *Bos* (18 MNI), 184 *Sus* (8 MNI), 34 *Canis*, 9 *Equus*, 7 *Dama*, 265 *Lepus*, 18 *Vulpes*, 1 *Mustela*, 95 *Gallus*, 43 *Anser anser* (domestic goose), 76 other bird bones (10 species), and 42 fish bones (10 species) (Lignereux et al. 2003: 599, 601, 613).

A Hellenistic sample from Basin 417 at Kition-*Bamboula* produced 110 bone fragments: 25 *Ovis/Capra*, 23 *Bos*, 5 *Sus*, 21 *Equus*, 22 *Oryctolagus*, 2 *Mustela*, 8 bird, and 4 fish (Desse 1993; Reese 2008a: 194).

The Incised Scapulae

Incised *Bos* scapulae, with a few *Ovis/Capra*, are known from LC and Iron Age Cyprus, with the first examples published more than 30 years ago (Reese 2002). Recently, Early Cypriot Sotira-*Kaminoudhia* produced a unique incised *Dama* scapula. This is the oldest from the island and the only made on a deer scapula. The Sotira example was probably used as a tool and is actually quite different from the LC and later Cypriot examples.

Nine years ago I surveyed the examples of incised scapulae then known from Cyprus and elsewhere in the Mediterranean and Near East (Reese 2002). Additional examples have been found since then on Cyprus (several more from Malloura, one more from LC Enkomi, Amathous [Fourrier 2004–2005]), in Syria (Tell al-Raqā'i, Tell 'Atij, Umm el-Marra [4 Late Bronze Age, 1 unstratified]), at Iron Age IB Tel Kinrot in Israel (Marom et al. 2006), and at Iron Age IIA Tell eṣ-Ṣâfî/Gath in Israel (Zukerman et al. 2007). These are all surveyed in a recent paper (Reese 2009).

From LC III Cyprus incised *Bos* scapulae are known from Kition (n=5) and Enkomi (n=5). From Iron Age Cyprus examples are known from six sites. All of these are *Bos* except for two or three *Ovis/Capra* examples from Malloura (fig. 18.1). Most examples were found at Kition (10; from CG I [2], CG II, CG III–CA I [2], CG III–CA I–II, CA I–II, CC I–II [2], and ?CC), the CA II Limassol-*Komissariato* sanctuary, Tomb 104 mixed fill (with CA) at Palaipaphos-*Teratsoudhia* (possibly dump from a sanctuary), CA Polis (Marion)–A.H9 sanctuary (at least 3 fragments), and the CA Polis (Marion)-*Peristeries* (B.D7) sanctuary (more than 6 fragments), Amathous, and Athienou-*Malloura* (1 EU 4, 12 EU 10 fragments [1 *Ovis/Capra*], 3 EU 18 fragments, 1 EU 24, 1 EU 30 [*Ovis/Capra*], 1 EU 32, 3 EU 36 fragments, and 1 EU 94).

Incised scapulae have been variously interpreted as rasping or scraping musical instruments (Dunand 1973: 75; Courtois in Webb 1977: 78; von den Driesch and Boessneck 1981: pl. 3; 1985; Otte et al. 1982; Nobis 1985: 424; 2000: 125; Caubet 1987: 735; 1996: 12, 26; Becker 1988: 381–83; Karageorghis 1990a: 67; 1990b; Dunham 1994; Dothan 1998: 155; Ayalon and Sorek 1999: 47; Stager 2000; Kolotourou 2005: 187–88; Stern 2006: 394), the bridge of a musical instrument (Marom et al. 2006: 39), tallies for record keeping (du Plat Taylor 1957: 78), counting bones or musical instruments (Redman 1973: 258), tools or musical instruments (Watson and LeBlanc 1990: 93), tools (Starr 1939: 488), or possibly items used in divination or prophecy (scapulomancy or omoplatoscopy; Webb 1977: 79–80; 1985: 325–27; Stern 1994: 6; 2006: 394), or part of a loom (Zukerman et al. 2007: 71). For Cyprus, all the examples with context are from sanctuaries or, in the case of *Teratsoudhia*, probable dump from a sanctuary. This suggests to the present author that they were used in a religious rite, probably divination.

Fig. 18.1 *Incised* Ovis/Capra *scapula (24 total incisions) from the sanctuary at Athienou*-Malloura (EU 30, SU 3016). *AAP-AM 2396: Larnaka District Museum, Cyprus.*

Fauna from Funerary Contexts

The four Hellenistic to Roman chamber tombs excavated by AAP at the locality Mağara Tepeşi (Site 2), ca. 300 m north of the sanctuary, produced a large number of animal bones. Due to extensive looting, however, it is unclear if these bones, or a portion thereof, were part of the burial assemblage or later intrusions. Tomb 25 produced 50 animal bones (*Ovis/Capra, Sus, Bos/Equus, Gallus* [2 MNI]). Tomb 26 produced 60 bones (*Ovis/Capra, Sus, Gallus* [5 MNI]). Tomb 27 produced 140 bones (*Ovis/Capra, Sus, Gallus* [4 MNI], small bird, rodent, frog). Tomb 28 produced 225 bones (*Ovis/Capra, E. caballus, E. asinus, Gallus* [6 MNI]).

The Venetian cemetery in EU 6 produced 35 animal bone fragments from 21 SUs, including *Ovis/Capra, Bos, Sus, E. asinus*, bird eggshells (SU 619), and even a fossil shark tooth (SU 620). It is unclear if any of these remains are to be considered part of the burial assemblages. Shark teeth or vertebrae (either fossil or Recent) are items found at several other Cypriot sites (Reese 1984).

There are a number of purposeful equid burials from Iron Age Cyprus, from Salamis, Larnaka, Amathous, and Palaepaphos (Kouklia; several tombs, including *Kato Alonia*) (Reese 1995; Hermary 2005). These are all rather complete skeletons, unlike the few scattered bones from Mağara Tepeşi Tomb 28. *Ovis/Capra* bones (uncut but clearly animal joints) are known from several locations in an unlooted Hellenistic (third–late second centuries) tomb at Pegeia-*Pappara* (Croft 2002).

It is unclear if the bird bones and Venetian eggshells are tomb offerings. Bird bones were found in late CG III–CA I Salamis Tomb 79 (Tring Museum 1973), and *Gallus* bones were found in 1930s excavations in Classical to Hellenistic Tsambres and Aphenrika (Dray and du Plat Taylor 1951). *Gallus* bones (cut into joints) and eggshells are also known from the Pegeia tomb. Eggshells have been found in tombs at Iron Age Salamis (Tyler 1970; Tyler and Talbot 1973) and CG Palaipaphos-*Skales* (King 1983). Imported ostrich eggshells, often decorated, are known from several LC tombs (Reese 2008a: 194–95).

Tomb 25 at Mağara Tepeşi produced undecorated fragments of a bivalve from the Red Sea, *Pinctada margaritifera*. These were probably used as platters or plates for trinkets. Other examples, often with incised decoration on the shell interior, are known from contemporary graves on

Cyprus (Salamis, Kourion-*Ermoyenis*, Amathous, Palaepaphos, Paphos; Reese 1991: 168–69; 1992: 125, pl. 26:2 and unpublished additions; Michaelides 1995: pls. 4–15). They are also known from sites in Greece, Italy, and the Near East (Reese 1991: 171, 173–74, fig. 21; 2008b: 458–59, figs. 273–74).

Pinctada is not the only Red Sea shell known from Iron Age Cyprus. Red Sea cowries (*Cypraea annulus* and *C. moneta*), holed as personal ornaments, are known from two CA II and one CC II tombs at Salamis (Demetropoulos 1970: 301, fig. 2, pls. 49, 205), five Iron Age tombs at Larnaka-*Ayios Giorgios* (Reese, in press), 16 Iron Age tombs at Amathous (Reese 1992: 123–24, pl. 24:4 and unpublished additions), and one Iron Age child's grave at Polis (Marion) (Reese 2008a: 196). There are also holed Red Sea shells from the Iron Age Kition sanctuary. There is 1 CC *C. annulus* and from the CA to CC I there are 25 *C. annulus*, 2 *Tectus dentatus*, and 1 *Nerita* (Reese 2003: 414, 418–19, 427, pls. 34:6–8, 35:1–2).

CONCLUSIONS

The Malloura sanctuary fauna is similar to the other Iron Age sites noted, dominated by *Ovis/Capra* followed by *Bos* and with the other mammals found in small numbers. *Sus* is very rare at these sites. Most of the Cypriot Iron Age sanctuary sites have very few burnt bones, the exception being the Kourion sanctuary, where there is a clear preference for the burning of *Ovis/Capra* hind limbs. Some of the burnt bones from the Malloura sanctuary follow this burning pattern, but the sample is too small to be certain.

The incised scapulae are definite offerings, but their precise use remains unclear (for their distribution within the sanctuary, see Blackwell and Johnson, Ch. 24). Since almost all the Cypriot Iron Age examples are found in sanctuaries, their function within some religious rite seems likely, although the numerous other suggestions for their use cannot be ruled out. It is unclear if the animal bones from the Mağara Tepeşi tombs should be considered as offerings. Animal remains are definite offerings at several other burials. The imported *Pinctada* shell does seem to be part of the funerary equipment, as also at several other Cypriot tombs. When the Malloura final phasing and contexts become available it is hoped that the faunal analysis conclusions can be refined and clarified.

APPENDIX: CATALOGUE OF MALLOURA SANCTUARY ANIMAL BONES

EU 4. 153 bones with 5 burnt (19 SUs)
Surface (4 SUs, 26 bones [2 burnt])
   3 *Ovis/Capra* MNI, 2 *Bos* MNI, 1 *Canis* MNI.
Looters' pits (5 SUs, 7 bones)
   3 *Ovis/Capra*, 2 *Bos*.
Undated (2 SUs, 6 bones)
   2 *Ovis/Capra*.
Hellenistic (7 SUs, 98 bones [3 burnt])
   7 *Ovis/Capra*, 2 *Bos*, 1 *Canis*.
CA–CC (1 SU, 16 bones)
   1 *Ovis/Capra*, 1 *Bos*.

EU 10. 2,329 bones with 29 burnt (87 SUs)
Surface/Cleaning/Alluvial deposits
(9 SUs, 78 bones)
   5 *Ovis/Capra*, 5 *Bos*.
Looters' pits (13 SUs, 107 bones)
   12 *Ovis/Capra*, 3 *Bos*, 1 *Equus* sp.

Undated (10 SUs, 233 bones [4 burnt])
   9 *Ovis/Capra*, 2 *Bos*, 1 *Dama* (antler in SU 1099.201).
Hellenistic (28 SUs, 1,134 bones [17 burnt]):
387 in SU 1099.155 (6 burnt), 208 in SU 1099.158, 140 in SU 1099.179 (2 burnt)
   24 *Ovis/Capra*, 11 *Bos*, 1 *Sus*, 1 *Canis*, 1 *E. caballus*, 1 *E. asinus*, 1 bird.
CC + ?CC (6 SUs, 412 bones [8 burnt]): 153 in SU 1099.159, 138 in SU 1099.158
   5 *Ovis/Capra*, 3 *Bos*, 2 *Canis*, 1 *E. asinus*, 1 *Lepus*.
CA + ?CA (21 SUs, 365 bones)
   16 *Ovis/Capra*, 9 *Bos*, 2 *Dama* (antler in SU 1099.202 + 204).

EU 11. 44 bones (6 SUs)
Looters' pits (2 SUs, 19 bones)
   2 *Ovis/Capra*, 2 *Bos*.

Undated (1 SU, 5 bones)
  1 *Ovis/Capra.*
Hellenistic (3 SUs, 20 bones)
  3 *Ovis/Capra.*

EU 12. 29 bones (6 SUs)
Surface (2 SUs, 2 bones)
  1 *E. caballus.*
Looters' pits (2 SUs, 2 bones)
  1 *Ovis/Capra,* 1 *E. caballus.*
Hellenistic (2 SUs, 23 bones)
  2 *Ovis/Capra.*

EU 14 (Circular clay-lined feature [?kiln])
2 bones with 2 burnt (1 SU)
Undated (1 SU, 2 bones [2 burnt])
  1 *Ovis/Capra.*

EU 18. 390 bones with 53 burnt (19 SUs)
Undated (12 SUs, 121 bones [13 burnt in 7 SUs])
  10 *Ovis/Capra,* 2 *Bos.*
Hellenistic (7 SUs, 269 bones [40 burnt in 6 SUs])
  7 *Ovis/Capra,* 4 *Bos.*

EU 20. 16 bones (3 SUs)
Surface/Cleaning (3 SUs, 16 bones)
  3 *Ovis/Capra,* 1 *Bos.*

EU 22. 26 bones (6 SUs)
Undated (6 SUs, 26 bones)
  5 *Ovis/Capra,* 1 *Bos.*

EU 24. 1,413 bones with 188 burnt (13.3%) (50 SUs)
Surface/Cleaning (11 SUs, 162 bones [7 burnt])
  11 *Ovis/Capra,* 4 *Bos,* 1 *Canis,* 1 *E. caballus.*
Looters' pits (9 SUs, 374 bones [40 burnt]):
172 in SU 2424 (22 burnt), 72 in SU 2408
  9 *Ovis/Capra,* 6 *Bos,* 1 *Canis,* 1 *Equus* sp.
Undated (4 SUs, 30 bones [4 burnt])
  4 *Ovis/Capra.*
Hellenistic (23 SUs, 761 bones [136 burnt—17.9%]):
135 in SU 2477, 125 in SU 2471 (81 burnt—64.8%),
99 in SU 2458
  23 *Ovis/Capra,* 9 *Bos,* 1 *Dama* (mainly antler).
?pre-Hellenistic (3 SUs, 86 bones [1 burnt])
  3 *Ovis/Capra,* 2 *Bos,* 1 *Canis.*

EU 26. 2 bones (1 SU)
Hellenistic (1 SU, 2 bones)
  1 *Ovis/Capra.*

EU 28. 747 bones with 189 burnt (25.3%) (52 SUs)
Surface/Cleaning (15 SUs, 126 bones [53 burnt
—43.1%])
  14 *Ovis/Capra,* 4 *Bos.*
Looters' pits (19 SUs, 347 bones [87 burnt—25.1%])
  18 *Ovis/Capra,* 6 *Bos,* 1 rodent.
Undated (1 SU, 1 bone)
  1 *Ovis/Capra.*
Hellenistic (11 SUs, 179 bones [35 burnt—19.6%])
  10 *Ovis/Capra,* 4 *Bos.*
CC II (5 SUs, 82 bones [8 burnt])
  5 *Ovis/Capra,* 1 *Bos.*
CA (1 SU, 12 bones [6 burnt])
  1 *Ovis/Capra.*

EU 30. 667 bones with 26 burnt (23 SUs)
Surface/Cleaning (8 SUs, 20 bones [2 burnt])
  8 *Ovis/Capra.*
Looters' pits (7 SUs, 124 bones [2 burnt])
  7 *Ovis/Capra,* 3 *Bos,* 1 *Sus,* 2 rodent, 3 bird,
  5 lizard/snake.
Undated (1 SU, 5 bones [1 burnt])
  1 *Bos,* 1 frog.
Hellenistic (7 SUs, 517 bones [21 burnt]): 295 bones
in SU 3017, 159 bones in SU 3016
  7 *Ovis/Capra,* 3 *Bos,* 1 *Sus,* 2 *Canis,* 1 *Dama*
  (antler only), 4 rodent, 4 bird (2 *Gallus*), 7 lizard/
  snake.

EU 32. 435 bones with 115 burnt (26.4%) (23 SUs)
Surface (8 SUs, 63 bones [6 burnt])
  8 *Ovis/Capra,* 3 *Bos.*
Looters' pits (5 SUs, 141 bones [20 burnt])
  5 *Ovis/Capra,* 3 *Bos,* 1 *Canis.*
Undated (1 SU, 6 bones [2 burnt])
  1 *Ovis/Capra.*
Hellenistic (17 SUs, 225 bones [87 burnt, with 44
of 61 bones in SU 3208])
  17 *Ovis/Capra,* 5 *Bos,* 1 *Dama,* 1 *Vulpes,*
  1 *Hemiechinus.*

EU 34. 176 bones with 3 burnt (10 SUs)
Surface/Cleaning (6 SUs, 36 bones [2 burnt])
   5 *Ovis/Capra*, 1 *Bos*.
Looters' pits (4 SUs, 140 bones [1 burnt])
   4 *Ovis/Capra*, 1 *Bos*.

EU 36. 168 bones with 9 burnt (5 SUs)
Surface (3 SUs, 56 bones [1 burnt])
   3 *Ovis/Capra*.
Looters' pits (2 SUs, 112 bones [8 burnt])
   3 *Ovis/Capra*, 1 *Bos*.

EU 88. 31 bones with 3 burnt (3 SUs)
Cleaning (2 SUs, 17 bones [2 burnt])
   2 *Ovis/Capra*, 2 *Bos*.
Undated (1 SU, 14 bones [1 burnt])
   1 *Ovis/Capra*.

EU 90. 2 bones (1 SU)
Cleaning (1 SU, 2 bones)
   1 *E. caballus*.

EU 92. 1 bone (1 SU)
Cleaning (1 SU, 1 bone)
   1 *Ovis/Capra*.

EU 94. 165 bones with 6 burnt (10 SUs)
Surface/Cleaning (3 SUs, 19 bones [1 burnt])
   3 *Ovis/Capra*, 1 *Bos*.
Looters' pits (2 SUs, 10 bones [1 burnt])
   2 *Ovis/Capra*, 1 *Bos*.
Hellenistic (2 SUs, 53 bones [3 burnt])
   1 *Ovis/Capra*, 1 *Bos*.
?CA (2 SUs, 28 bones)
   2 *Ovis/Capra*, 1 *Bos*, 1 *Sus*.
Late CG III (1 SU, 55 bones [1 burnt])
   1 *Ovis/Capra*, 1 *Bos*.

REFERENCES

Ayalon, E., and Sorek, C.
1999   *Bare Bones: Ancient Artifacts from Animal Bones*. Tel-Aviv: Eretz Israel Museum.

Becker, C.
1988   Die Tierknochenfunde vom Tell Bdēri 1985. *Damaszener Mitteilungen* 3: 379–86.

Caubet, A.
1987   La musique à Ougarit. *Comptes Rendues des Séances de l'Académie des Inscriptions et Belles-lettres*: 731–54.
1996   La musique à Ougarit: Nouveaux témoignages matériels. Pp. 9–31 in *Ugarit, Religion and Culture. Proceedings of the International Colloquium on Ugarit, Religion and Culture. Edinburgh, July 1994. Essays Presented in Honour of Professor John C. L. Gibson*, eds. N. Wyatt, W. G. E. Watson, and J. B. Lloyd. Ugaritisch-Biblische Literatur 12. Münster: Ugarit-Verlag.

Columeau, P.
2006   Les restes de faune et la consommation des animaux sacrifiés. Pp. 166–81 in *Amathonte VI. Le Sanctuaire d'Aphrodite des origines au début de l'Epoque Impériale,* by S. Fourrier

and A. Hermary. Etudes Chypriotes 17. Paris: École française d'Athenes.

Croft, P.
2002   Animal Bones from the Hellenistic Tomb at Pegeia. Pp. 228–33 in A Hellenistic Tomb in Pegea (P.M. 3534) by E. Raptou, E. Stylianov, and E. Vassiliou. *Report of the Department of Antiquities, Cyprus*.

Davis, S. J. M.
1996   Animal Sacrifices. Pp. 181–82 in *The Sanctuary of Apollo at Kourion: Excavations in the Archaic Precinct,* by D. Buitron-Oliver. Studies in Mediterranean Archaeology 109. Göteborg: Åström.

Demetropoulos, A.
1970   Marine Molluscs, Land Snails, etc. Pp. 299–305 in *Excavations in the Necropolis of Salamis 2/4,* by V. Karageorghis. Nicosia: Department of Antiquities.

Desse, J.
1993   Les vestiges osseux du bassin 417. Pp. 103–5 in *Les Niveaux Hellenistiques,* by F. Salles. Kition-Bamboula 4. Paris: A.D.P.F.

Dothan, T.
1998   Initial Philistine Settlement: From Migration to Coexistence. Pp. 148–61 in *Mediterranean Peoples in Transition: Thirteenth to Early Tenth Centuries BCE*, eds. S. Gitin, A. Mazar, and E. Stern. Jerusalem: Israel Exploration Society.

Dray, E., and du Plat Taylor, J.
1951   Tsambres and Aphendrika, Two Classical and Hellenistic Cemeteries in Cyprus. *Report of the Department of Antiquities, Cyprus (1937–1939)*: 24–123.

Dunand, M.
1973   *Fouilles de Byblos* 5. Paris: Librairie d'Amérique et d'Orient Adrien Maisonneuve.

Dunham, S.
1994   An Early Percussion Instrument from Tell al-Raqā'i, North Syria. *Source Notes in the History of Art* 13(4): 36–43.

du Plat Taylor, J.
1957   *Myrtou-Pigadhes, a Late Bronze Age Sanctuary in Cyprus*. Oxford: Ashmolean Museum.

Fourrier, S.
2004–2005   Les *scapulae* gravées. Pp. 95–97 in Le dépot archaïque du rempart Nord d'Amathonte III. Les petits objets, by S. Fourrier, E. Louca, D. Meeks, J. P. Olivier, and M. Sznycer. *Bulletin de Correspondance Hellénique* 128–29: 67–118.

Gaber, P., and Dever, W. G.
1998   The Birth of Adonis?: Cyprus Excavation Suggests a Connection Between the Greek God and Hebrew *Adon. Archaeology Odyssey* 1(2): 48–55, 61.

Gebhard, E. R., and Reese, D. S.
2005   Sacrifices for Poseidon and Melikertes-Palaimon at Isthmia. Pp. 125–53 in *Greek Sacrificial Ritual, Olympian and Chthonian: Proceedings of the Sixth International Seminar on Ancient Greek Cult, Organized by the Department of Classical Archaeology and Ancient History, Göteborg University, 25–27 April 1997*, eds. R. Hägg and B. Alroth. Skrifter utgivna av Svenska institutet i Athen, 8°, 18. Stockholm: Svenska institutet i Athen.

Hermary A.
2005   Les équidés à Chypre à l'époque des royaumes. Pp. 183–95 in *Les Equidés dans le Monde Méditerranéen Antique. Actes du colloque organisé par l'École française d'Athènes, le Centre Camille Jullian, et l'UMR 5140 du CNRS, Athènes, 26–28 Novembre 2003*, ed. A. Gardeisen. Lattes: Édition de l'Association pour le Développement de l'Archéologie en Languedoc-Roussillon.

Karageorghis, V.
1990a   *Tombs at Palaepaphos: 1. Teratsoudhia, 2. Eliomylia*. Nicosia: A. G. Leventis Foundation.
1990b   Miscellanea from Late Bronze Age Cyprus II. A Late Bronze Age Musical Instrument? *Levant* 22: 159.

King, A.
1983   Report on Some Eggshell from Tomb 66. P. 453 in *Palaepaphos-Skales, An Iron Age Cemetery in Cyprus*, by V. Karageorghis. Deutsches Archäologisches Institut 3. Konstanz: Universitätsverlag.

Kolotourou, K.
2005   Music and Cult: The Significance of Percussion and the Cypriote Connection. Pp. 183–204 in *Cyprus: Religion and Society from the Late Bronze Age to the End of the Archaic Periods*, eds. V. Karageorghis, H. Matthäus, and S. Rogge. Möhnesee-Wamel: Bibliopolis.

Lignereux, Y.;. Obermaier, H.; and Schneider, S.
2008   Les Restes Animaux du Palais d'Amathonte à Chypre, à l'Époque Classique (Ve-IVe S. av. J.-C.). Pp. 507–628 in *Archaeolozoology of the Near East 8. Proceedings of the Eighth International Symposium on the Archaeozoology of Southwestern Asia and Adjacent Areas* 2, eds. E. Vila, L. Gourichon, A. M. Choyke, and H. Buitenhuis. TMO 49. Lyon: Maison de l'Orient et de la Méditerranée.

Marom, N.; Bar-Oz, G.; and Münger, S.
2006   A New Incised Scapula from Tel Kinrot. *Near Eastern Archaeology* 69(1): 37–40.

Michaelides, D.

1995   Cyprus and the Persian Gulf in the Hellenistic and Roman Periods: The Case of *Pinctada margaritifera*. Pp. 211–26 in *Proceedings of the International Symposium, Cyprus and the Sea, Nicosia, 25–26 September, 1993,* eds. D. Michaelides and V. Karageorghis. Nicosia: Department of Antiquities.

Nobis, G.

1976–1977 Tierreste aus Tamassos auf Zypern. *Acta Praehistorica et Archaeologica* 7–8: 271–300.

1985   Tierreste aus dem Präphönizischen Kition. Pp. 416–33 in *Excavations at Kition 5. The Pre-Phoenician Levels. Part 2,* by V. Karageorghis and M. Demas. Nicosia: Department of Antiquities.

2000   Tierreste aus dem phönizischen Kition. Pp. 121–34 in *PERIPLUS: Festschrift für Hans-Günter Buchholz zu seinem achtzigsten Geburtstag am 24.Dezember 1999,* eds. P. Åström and D. Sürenhagen. Studies in Mediterranean Archaeology 127. Jonsered: Åström.

Otte, M.; Gautier, A.; and Bibuyck, P.

1982   Interprétation d'un ossement encoché de la préhistoire syrienne. *Paléorient* 8(1): 85–86.

Redman, C. L.

1973   Early Village Technology: A View through the Microscope. *Paléorient* 1(2): 249–61.

Reese, D. S.

1984   Shark and Ray Remains in Aegean and Cypriote Archaeology. *Opuscula Atheniensia* 15: l88–92.

1989   Faunal Remains from the Altar of Aphrodite Ourania, Athens. *Hesperia* 58(1): 63–70.

1991   The Trade of Indo-Pacific Shells into the Mediterranean Basin and Europe. *Oxford Journal of Archaeology* 10(2): 159–96.

1992   Shells and Animal Bones. Pp. 123–44 in *La Nécropole d'Amathonte Tombes 113–367, 6,* eds. V. Karageorghis, O. Picard, and C. Tytgat. Études Chypriotes 14. Nicosia: A. G. Leventis Foundation.

1995   Equid Sacrifices/Burials in Greece and Cyprus: An Addendum. *Journal of Prehistoric Religion* 9: 35–42.

2000   The Iron Age Fauna (Introduction and Methodology; The Mammal Remains; The Bird Remains; The Marine Invertebrates; The Insects). Pp. 398–407, 415–95, 560–646 in *Kommos 4, the Greek Sanctuary,* eds. J. W. Shaw and M. C. Shaw. Princeton: Princeton University.

2002   On the Incised Cattle Scapulae from the East Mediterranean and Near East. *Bonner zoologische Beiträge* 50(3): 183–98.

2003   The Shells, Astragali and Fish. Pp. 413–28 in *Excavations at Kition 6. The Phoenician and Later Levels* 2, by V. Karageorghis. Nicosia: Department of Antiquities.

2005a   Faunal Remains from Israeli Excavations at Athienou-*Pampoulari tis Koukkouninas. Report of the Department of Antiquities, Cyprus*: 87–108.

2005b   Faunal Remains from Greek Sanctuaries: A Survey (Abstract). Pp. 121–23 in *Greek Sacrificial Ritual, Olympian and Chthonian: Proceedings of the Sixth International Seminar on Ancient Greek Cult, Organized by the Department of Classical Archaeology and Ancient History, Göteborg University, 25–27 April 1997,* eds. R. Hägg and B. Alroth. Skrifter utgivna av Svenska institutet i Athen, 8°, 18. Stockholm: Svenska institutet i Athen.

2007   Zooarchaeology on Cyprus. *Report of the Department of Antiquities, Cyprus*: 469–84.

2008a   Organic Imports from Late Bronze Age Cyprus (with Special Reference to Hala Sultan Tekke). *Opuscula Atheniensia* 31–32 (2006–2007): 191–209.

2008b   Shells from Jerusalem: Sites B, D, E, J, S and V. Pp. 455–66 in *Excavations by K. M. Kenyon in Jerusalem 1961–1967, 5. Discoveries in Hellenistic to Ottoman Jerusalem. Centenary Volume: Kathleen M. Kenyon 1906–1978,* by K. Prag. Levant Supplementary Series 7. Oxford: Council for British Research in the Levant and Oxbow.

2009   On Incised Scapulae and *Tridacna*. Pp. 188*–93* in *Eretz-Israel: Archaeological, Historical and Geographic Studies* 29 (Ephraim Stern Volume), eds. J. Aviram, A. Ben-Tor, I. Ephal, S. Gitin, R. Reich. Jerusalem: Israel Exploration Society.

In press   Shells and Astragali from the Larnaka-
            Ayios Giorgios Necropolis. In *The Larnaka-
            Ayios Giorgios Necropolis*, ed. S. Hadjisavvas.
            Nicosia: Department of Antiquities.

Schwartz, J. H.
1973   The Palaeozoology of Cyprus: A Preliminary
        Report on Recently Analyzed Sites. *World
        Archaeology* 5(2): 215–20.

Stager, L. E.
2000   *Ashkelon Excavations, The Leon Levy
        Expedition, 2000.* Cambridge, MA: Harvard
        University (brochure).

Starr, R. F. S.
1939   *Nuzi, Excavations at Yorgan Tepe Near Kirkuk
        (1927–1931).* Cambridge: Harvard University.

Stern, E.
1994   A Phoenician-Cypriote Votive Scapula from
        Tel Dor: A Maritime Scene. *Israel Exploration
        Journal* 44(1–2): 1–12.
2006   The Sea Peoples Cult in Philistia and Northern
        Israel. Pp. 385–98 in *"I Will Speak the Riddles
        of Times:" Archaeological and Historical Studies
        in Honor of Amihai Mazar on the Occasion of
        His Sixtieth Birthday*, vol. 1, eds. A. M. Maier
        and P. de Miroschedji. Winona Lake, IN:
        Eisenbrauns.

Tring Museum.
1973   Bird Bones. P. 269 in *Excavations in the Ne-
        cropolis of Salamis* 3(5), by V. Karageorghis.
        Nicosia: Department of Antiquities.

Tyler, C.
1970   Egg Shells from Salamis. Pp. 313–17 in
        Excavations in the Necropolis of Salamis 2(4),
        by V. Karageorghis. Nicosia: Department of
        Antiquities.

Tyler, C., and Talbot, C. J.
1973   Egg Shells from Salamis. Pp. 256–58 in
        Excavations in the Necropolis of Salamis 3(5),
        by V. Karageorghis. Nicosia: Department of
        Antiquities.

von den Driesch, A., and Boessneck, J.
1981   Über drei gekerbte Schulterblätter im archäol-
        ogischen Fundgut von Norşuntepe/Ostanato-
        lien. *Archäologie und Naturwissenschaften* 2:
        72–75.
1985   Osteologische Besonderheiten vom Morro de
        Mezquitilla/Malága. *Madrider Mitteilungen*
        26: 45–48.

Watson, P. J., and LeBlanc, S. A.
1990   *Girikihaciyan, a Halafian Site in Southeastern
        Turkey.* Monograph 33. Los Angeles: Institute
        of Archaeology, University of California at Los
        Angeles.

Webb, J. M.
1977   A Scapula from Limassol-"Komissariato" No.
        176. Pp. 74–80 in The Limassol Sanctuary.
        Part 2 in *Two Cypriote Sanctuaries of the End
        of the Cypro-Archaic Period*, by V. Kara-
        georghis. Rome: Consiglio Nazionale delle
        Ricerche.
1985   The Incised Scapulae. Pp. 317–28 in *Excava-
        tions at Kition* 5(2), by V. Karageorghis. Nico-
        sia: Department of Antiquities.

Zukerman, A.; Kolska-Horwitz, L.; Lev-Tov, J.;
and Maier, A.
2007   A Bone of Contention? Iron Age IIA Notched
        Scapulae from Tell es-Sâfi/Gath, Israel.
        *Bulletin of the American Schools of Oriental
        Research* 347: 57–81.

Chapter 19

Burial Treatment Based on Kinship?

The Hellenistic–Roman and Venetian-Period Tombs in the Malloura Valley

by Nathan K. Harper and Tiffiny A. Tung

Kinship is one of the primary structuring forces in human social organization. Kinship can structure marriage patterns, dictating who is acceptable as a marriage partner, and it can define who inherits land, naming rights, and a variety of resources. It can also affect where, and with whom and what, you are buried; conversely, where and with whom you are buried can redefine your kinship status and that of your descendents (both biological and fictive). In this way, burial practices are a vivid and powerful way to express kinship affiliation (and other kinds of social relationships) and highlight the kinds of benefits (and responsibilities) that those affiliations foster, such as inheritance of land or animals and the obligation to care properly for them. Death and the rituals surrounding it provide a profound moment for mourners to both create and express the deceased individual's identity and that of the group or wider community. Burial rites are used to accentuate or construct the persona of both the dead and the living (Barrett 1990), reinforce social and political continuity, and highlight social and economic connections with the deceased (Saxe 1970; Binford 1971; Goldstein 1980; Charles and Buikstra 1983; Brown 1995; Buikstra 1995).

Studies in bioarchaeology and archaeology have addressed many questions concerning kinship networks (Alt and Vach 1995, 1998), intracemetery variation (Stojanowski and Schillaci 2006; Stojanowski et al. 2007), social identity (Knudson and Stojanowski 2008), and burial practices (Corrucini and Shimada 2002). Underlying these analyses is the idea that an understanding of social organization — as revealed in how a community organizes the burial of their dead — can help clarify the social identity, social divisions, and the internal and external relationships of the people who populated the landscape.

The question of kinship and burial practices at Malloura is addressed here from a bioarchaeological perspective that examines dental nonmetric traits as a proxy for biological relatedness. These data are situated within a framework that accounts for the complex social negotiation that occurs when mourners transform the landscape by placing formal (and often prominent) tombs or cemeteries in a particular zone, both to construct community memory and claim rights to land and its resources (Saxe 1970: 119; Goldstein 1980; Buikstra 1995; Knapp and Ashmore 1999).

This study uses dental morphological traits to investigate how burial location was shaped by kin affiliation among the individuals buried in the Hellenistic–Roman (310 BC–AD 150) cemetery at Mağara Tepeşi in central Cyprus (Toumazou and Counts, Ch. 6; Gordon, Ch. 14). Their relationship to the later Frankish–Venetian-period (AD 1191–1571) groups from Athienou-*Malloura* are also examined (Toumazou and Counts, Ch. 6; Harper, Ch. 20). If biological kinship was a significant structuring force in mortuary placement in ancient Malloura, then we expect to see distinct groups in each tomb. If any of the groups from Mağara Tepeşi were successful in maintaining control over land and resources, then we might observe a significant biological relationship with the later Venetian-period cemetery population. Although 1,000 years is a long time span, during which major population movements may have led to the introduction of a new biological group to the region, long-term continuity within regional populations is the norm (e.g., central Illinois, Steadman 1998; highland Peru, Kemp et al. 2009; South Africa, Stynder et al. 2007; Egypt, Irish 2005; Zakrzewski 2007).

The following presents an overview of Hellenistic and Roman-period burial practices and kinship in Cyprus. Kin and corporate group burial practices from the Hellenistic and Roman tombs are assessed statistically via dental morphological traits comparing these individuals to burials from the later Venetian-period cemetery at Malloura. By addressing questions of kin group continuity, land use, and land claims, we might better understand the social strategies employed by corporate groups in ancient Cyprus.

ARCHAEOLOGICAL MODELS OF KINSHIP AND BURIAL IN CYPRUS

Mortuary analysis in Cyprus has only recently come of age with several large studies focusing on the burial practices in the Neolithic through Iron Age (Toumazou 1987; Niklasson 1991; Steel 1995; Parks 1999; Keswani 2004; Janes 2008). Keswani (2004: 54), in particular, documented collective secondary burials apparently structured by large extended kin groupings in the Early and Middle Cypriot periods. By the Late Cypriot period, Keswani sees a shift, as larger "urban" centers drew people from across the region. She argues that unlike the earlier large, collective, kin-based mortuary groups, such as those seen at Ayios Iakovos-*Melia*, the new urban immigrants attempted to keep their ancestors close to their households, such as at Enkomi and Kalavasos-*Ayios Dhimitrios* (Keswani 2004: 140). To date, bioarchaeological testing of these hypotheses has been limited (Harper 2010).

Parks (1999) suggests that burial rites in Cyprus remained stable through the Hellenistic and Roman periods. Burial rites, especially in an island environment, can be conservative depending on external contact and internal acceptance of changing practices (Renfrew 1984). Cypriot rites remained relatively unchanged from earlier periods, absorbing some foreign elements (peristyle tombs) while rejecting others (cremation). Inhumation in family-maintained, rock-cut chamber tombs, surrounded by personal possessions, offerings of food and drink, and other ritual elements (see Gordon, Ch. 14), is the norm on the island before Hellenistic times. Notably, aspects of these rituals, such as the lighting of lamps, libations, and exhumation, are still visible in burial rites in modern Cyprus.

There are several shared traits between the various Hellenistic–Roman cemeteries in Cyprus. Tombs were closely packed together in marginal areas alongside ancient roads on the edge of towns. It appears that tracts of land or cemetery plots were measured out and sold by landowners to family groups or other organizations, including burial clubs or *collegia*. These plots may have been delineated by walled enclosures, as seen in Nea Paphos (Hadjisavvas 1985). Cippi, plaques, and burial stelai marking Hellenistic and Roman-period tombs and graves are found throughout Cyprus, and the epitaphs upon them often identified the decedent in terms of family relationships (i.e., "Sogenes, son of Sokrates, son of … ") (Parks 1999: 181, 482). Parks (1999: 182) does, however, identify one set of epitaphs from Chytroi that appears to represent three families located in one tomb. To clarify further relationships between spatial burial organization and kinship, the first author is also analyzing human

TABLE 19.1   Age profiles from each tomb at Mağara Tepeşi and the Venetian cemetery at Athienou-*Malloura*.

	Infant	Child	Juvenile	Adult	Total
Tomb 25	2	1	–	22	25
Tomb 26	–	4	1	31	36
Tomb 27	–	3	1	27	31
Tomb 28	1	2	3	36	42
Venetian	11	7	8	31	57

remains from Kourion's Amathous Gate Cemetery (Harper, in press).

Beginning in the Late Roman period there is a distinct movement away from the use of chamber tombs and more individuals are buried in association with basilicas (Fox 1997; Parks 1999: 385). The quantity of grave goods is reduced, though the use of lamps and coins remains common (see Gordon, Ch. 14). This reorganization is largely attributed to the introduction of Christianity, when more and more individuals were being interred in churches and churchyards. This new mortuary practice that began around the Late Roman period continues into the medieval and Venetian periods, as evidenced by the excavation of PA.SY.D.Y Hill and the Palaion Demarcheion areas of Nicosia (Pilides 2003; Violaris 2004; Fox et al. 2008). Early church burials have also been recorded at the Church of Archangelos Michael (ca. 16th–17th centuries AD), in the AAP area.

Grave goods for the medieval and Venetian periods are rather sparse. Often the only offerings were sgraffito bowls or footed bowls (see Toumazou and Counts, Ch. 6). These bowls or cups may have been used to pour oil or other libations onto the corpse, as is practiced today in modern Cyprus: "During the funeral service the priest uses a vessel out of which he pours oil onto the body of the deceased, and then throws this vessel into the grave, which usually breaks. The present-day custom requires a common household vessel, often used, and this must also have been practiced in Medieval times" (Papanicola-Bakirtzis and Iacovou 1998: 133). Other medieval grave goods include bone hairpins or bone clothing pins that may have been used to pin shrouds (Baker et al. 2007).

THE PEOPLE FROM MAĞARA TEPEŞI AND MEDIEVAL MALLOURA

A series of tombs is located approximately 300 m north–northeast of a rural sanctuary (see Toumazou and Counts, Ch. 6) in a part of the valley known as Mağara Tepeşi, "Hill of Tombs." A series of looted Cypro-Archaic- to Cypro-Classical-period tombs (Tombs 50–53) is located at the north end of the small hill (see fig. 6.1). Clearing of these tombs revealed very few grave goods and little skeletal material. Four tombs (Tombs 25–28) on the northeast slope of Mağara Tepeşi were excavated during the 1991–1993 field seasons (Toumazou et al. 1998; Toumazou and Counts, Ch. 6). Tombs 25, 26, and 28 were standard tombs of Hellenistic and Roman Cyprus style with stepped dromoi leading to a chamber with three benches bounding its walls (fig. 19.1). Tomb 27 was larger and more elaborate, with a long, stepped *dromos* and a sunken forecourt with small loculi flanking the entrance (see fig. 6.6). The chamber was large (7 × 4 m), consisting of two stepped benches and a side chamber (see fig. 6.7).

Preliminary analyses of the recovered skeletal remains estimated the total minimum number of individuals (MNI) at 132: Tomb 25 MNI = 25; Tomb 26 MNI = 34; Tomb 27 MNI = 31; and Tomb 28 MNI = 42 (Table 19.1) (Agelarakis 1997; Tung 2000). Most of these individuals were fragmentary and commingled, though one from Tomb 26 was recovered as a complete burial. Looting contributed to much of this disturbance, but tomb reuse also must have played a role in the fragmentation and mixing of the remains. In many chamber tombs, the previous interments were collected and

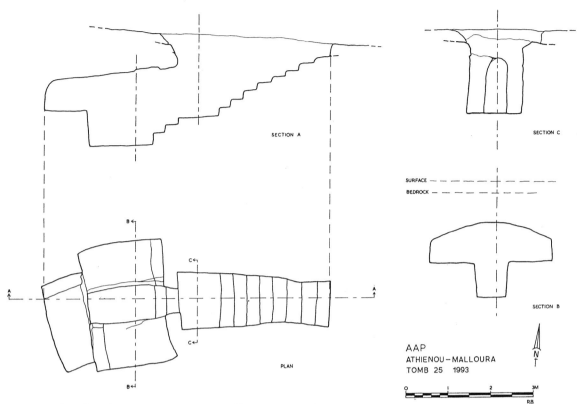

FIG. 19.1 *Plan of Tomb 25 at Mağara Tepeşi, 1993 (drawing: R. Breuker).*

stacked, pushed to the sides of the benches, or in some cases swept into the center of the chamber (Parks 1999: 231–37).

The Venetian-period burials are located in EU 6 on a small knoll between EU 2 and EU 3 (see fig. 6.1). Bulldozing and plowing disturbed a stone wall and burials, but later excavations in 1991 and 1992 uncovered at least 57 intact individuals (Agelarakis 1997). Most of the burials were oriented east–west, with individuals in stone-lined cist graves and, in one case, multiple successive interments. Grave goods were sparse but included glazed, sgraffito-ware footed bowls and preserved textiles, perhaps from a hairnet or shroud (Toumazou et al. 1998: 176). The wall in the area has not been investigated, but its association with a church would not be out of the question. At the nearby Archangelos monastery, dating to at least the 16th century, burials possessing sgraffito wares can still be seen eroding from the churchyard.

In comparing the two localities, the burials from the Venetian-period cemetery were in much better condition than those from Mağara Tepeşi. Discrete burials, such as those found in the Venetian cemetery, enable a more thorough analysis of an individual's and a population's overall health by clearly assigning pathologies to a single person. The status of the individuals buried in the Venetian-period cemetery is difficult to evaluate. High-status individuals from Christian burials tended to be buried inside the church. The location of these individuals in relation to a church is unknown, though burial in consecrated ground was preferred. These individuals may represent the *paroikoi* (serfs) or *francomati* (freedmen) of the area rather than high-status landholders.

TEETH AND KINSHIP

Teeth are some of the most commonly preserved human remains, especially in Cyprus, where tomb conditions and persistent reuse have damaged and commingled the skeletal material. Teeth are also some of the most genetically conservative portions of the human skeleton; that is, a set number of genes controls tooth development, and environmental and developmental factors have less impact (Scott and Turner 1997; but see Stojanowski et al. 2007). Teeth, then, are an excellent source of information concerning biological relationships of individuals and groups and are well-preserved enough for population and tomb-level analyses in Cyprus. Dental nonmetric analyses have been conducted on Chalcolithic populations of Cyprus (Parras 2004, 2006), and Fox (1997: 454), in her study of the paleopathology of Roman Paphos, noted several dental and osseous traits she considered to be related to "family" tombs.

For this study, dental nonmetric traits, which include such characteristics as small variations in the number of cusps, roots, or other minor morphological features of the tooth, were scored using the Arizona State University Dental Anthropology System (ASUDAS) (Turner et al. 1991; Scott and Turner 1997). Traits observed on the sample teeth are compared to a set of standardized plaques that are accompanied with textual descriptions. The tooth under consideration is then given a score for each observable nonmetric trait; these scores can range from 1 to 3 or 1 to 8, depending on the trait being observed. After dental nonmetric scores are collected, they are later collapsed into binary categories of present or absent for a particular trait. A total of 127 traits can be recorded from the permanent dentition.

Harper scored the material from the Venetian cemetery, and Tung scored traits for Mağara Tepeşi (Tung 2000). To account for inter-observer error, one sample (Tomb 26) was recorded by both authors. Chi-square tests showed significant observer differences in the scoring of the size of Cusp 5 of the mandibular molars. These traits were excluded from further analysis. After culling of traits that showed complete expression (0%) or no expression (100%), 22 traits were subjected to further analysis (Table 19.2). Statistical analysis of the traits requires the rank-scale variables be dichotomized into "present" and "absent" scores. The cut-off points for determining presence or absence are listed under the trait names in Table 19.2.

The percentages of trait expression were analyzed using principal components analysis (PCA) (Irish and Guatelli-Steinberg 2003). PCA reduces the original number of correlated data into several uncorrelated components. Correlations between the original data and the derived components indicate which traits are the most responsible for intersample variation. Component scores for each group can then be plotted in two- or three-dimensional space allowing for a visual representation of variation. All statistical analyses were undertaken using SPSS 17.0 (SPSS 2008).

Relationships among the Dead

The PCA analysis produced three components that account for 95% of the variation. The component loading, eigenvalues, and proportion of variation are given in Table 19.3. The first component accounts for 50% of the variation, and the traits with high loadings (>0.5) are distributed throughout the dental arcade. No standardized patterning of dental variation is seen in the total sample. The first PC separates the Venetian sample from the other tombs and is based on the presence of shoveled incisors, *tuberculum dentale*, and M^2 root number (fig. 19.2). The second PC accounts for 26% of the total variation and separates Tomb 27 — the most elaborate tomb — from the other groups. The traits responsible for this separation are the double shoveling of the maxillary incisors and enamel extension on the M^2. The third PC accounts for a little more than 18% of the total variation of the sample and separates Tomb 26 from the other groups based on the interruption groove of the I^2 and M_2 root number. When the PCs are plotted together in a three-dimensional space, Tombs 25 and 28 occupy a central position, while Tombs 26, 27, and the Venetian samples are at the extremities of the first three PCs (fig. 19.3).

These results match those of the univariate analyses provided by Tung (2000). In her analysis, teeth from Tomb 27 exhibited three traits that significantly deviated from the population norms: double shoveling of the upper incisors, M_1 cusp number, and M_1 protostylid (Tung 2000: 47). Tomb 26 shows three significantly different traits includ-

TABLE 19.2 Dental traits, cut-off points and frequencies under analysis.

Trait		Tomb 25	Tomb 26	Tomb 27	Tomb 28	Venetian
I² Shovel	%	67	0	10	0	12
(+ = ASU 1-6)	N	9	23	10	3	26
I¹ Shovel	%	0	0	0	0	4
(+ = ASU 3-6)	N	9	23	10	3	26
I² Double Shovel	%	0	0	33	0	4
(+ = ASU 2-6)	N	6	23	12	3	26
I¹ Double Shovel	%	0	3	36	20	21
(+ = ASU 2-6)	N	7	30	25	10	33
I² Interrupt Groove	%	11	57	36	0	21
(+ = ASU Present)	N	9	23	11	3	24
I¹ Interrupt Groove	%	13	7	28	10	9
(+ = ASU Present)	N	8	30	25	10	33
I² Tuberculum Dentale	%	0	91	0	0	81
(+ = ASU 2-6)	N	9	23	35	2	26
I¹ Tuberculum Dentale	%	38	53	33	56	70
(+ = ASU 2-6)	N	8	30	24	9	33
C Mesial Distal Accessory Ridge	%	46	36	25	100	3
(+ = ASU 2-5)	N	13	14	12	5	31
M² Hypocone	%	83	95	76	89	83
(+ = ASU 2-5)	N	6	19	17	9	24
M² Carabelli's Trait	%	11	15	11	13	29
(+ = ASU 2-7)	N	9	20	19	8	24
M¹ Carabelli's Trait	%	50	56	59	37	41
(+ = ASU 2-7)	N	14	39	17	19	41
M³ Parastyle	%	0	0	0	11	17
(+ = ASU 2-6)	N	5	0	4	9	18
M² Enamel Extension	%	0	0	21	0	5
(+ = ASU 2-3)	N	7	20	14	6	21
M¹ Enamel Extension	%	0	21	0	0	3
(+ = ASU 2-3)	N	14	39	11	21	36
M² Root Number	%	11	89	0	0	94
(+ = ASU 3)	N	9	9	14	7	17
M₂ Groove Pattern	%	13	53	36	12	52
(+ = ASU "+")	N	23	15	33	17	27
M₁ Groove Pattern	%	9	13	0	7	27
(+ = ASU "+")	N	11	23	17	14	26
M₁ Cusp Number	%	18	0	10	6	25
(+ = ASU 6+)	N	17	23	21	16	32
M₁ Deflecting Wrinkle	%	0	4	17	0	5
(+ = ASU 2-3)	N	1	25	6	1	22
M₁ Protostylid	%	75	40	26	44	67
(+ = ASU 1-6)	N	12	25	19	16	33
M₂ Root Number	%	8	13	0	13	4
(+ = ASU 1)	N	12	16	20	15	26

Table 19.3 The first three components and the loading for traits. Large (> 0.5) loading are in bold and italics. Large negative loadings (<-0.5) are underlined. Eigenvalues and percentage of variance are shown at the bottom of the table.

Trait	Component 1	Component 2	Component 3
I² Shovel	-.087	-.021	_-.674_
I¹ Shovel	*.867*	.011	-.495
I² Double Shovel	.167	_-.948_	.271
I¹ Double Shovel	*.543*	_-.817_	.041
I² Interrupt Groove	.492	.366	*.759*
I¹ Interrupt Groove	.280	_-.882_	.378
I² Tuberculum Dentale	*.836*	.492	.230
I¹ Tuberculum Dentale	*.975*	.198	.091
C Mesial Ridge	_-.864_	.431	.168
M² Hypocone	*.927*	.074	.359
M² Carabelli's Trait	*.981*	.059	-.185
M¹ Carabelli's Trait	*.729*	.418	*.528*
M³ Parastyle	*.734*	.076	_-.581_
M² Enamel Extension	.241	_-.943_	.228
M¹ Enamel Extension	.271	*.607*	*.732*
M² Root Number	*.934*	.322	-.138
M₂ Groove Pattern	*.867*	-.454	.179
M₁ Groove Pattern	*.892*	.347	-.289
M₁ Cusp Number	*.696*	-.169	-.685
M₁ Deflecting Wrinkle	*.791*	-.260	*.545*
M₁ Protostylid	*.845*	.271	-.456
M₂ Root Number	-.134	*.910*	.096
Eigenvalues	11.085	5.821	4.067
Percent Variance	50.386	26.458	18.487
Cumulative Variance	50.386	76.844	95.331

ing double shovel of the I¹, the M₁ protostylid, and the M² root number.

Relationships among the Living

Results of the dental analysis suggest that kinship played a role in the organization of burials in the Hellenistic and Roman periods in the Malloura Valley. The individuals in Tombs 26 and 27 were distinct from one another, while the individuals from Tombs 25 and 28 showed more common-

alities. This suggests that individuals interred in Tombs 25 and 28 may have been more biologically related to one another than to those buried in Tombs 26 and 27. In terms of temporal differences, the Venetian-period burial population was significantly different from the Hellenistic–Roman-era individuals. This suggests that the Venetian-period population may not be biological descendents of the Hellenistic–Roman-era communities that occupied the lands some 1,000 years earlier.

Mortuary rituals and burial can be used as social strategies to promote many different ideas, among them claims on land and other critical resources (Saxe 1970: 119; Buikstra 1995). The biological relationships between the dead in the Malloura Valley are now better understood, but how do these results inform us about the social strategies and social structure of the people living in the valley in the past?

The placement of the tombs stretching from the southeast ridge to the northwest slope of Mağara Tepeşi is informative. Tombs 25, 26, and 28 constructed during the Hellenistic era are closer to the earlier Cypro-Archaic and Cypro-Classical tombs, indicating, perhaps, continuity with those earlier populations. The location of Tomb 27 in particular fits with its elaborate construction and rich grave goods. Tomb 27 occupies a preferred position on the hill. When standing at the top of the stepped *dromos*, one can view the agricultural fields to the north, the early Roman and Byzantine structures, and the sanctuary proper.

Other tombs across the valley may have been placed in specific fields or on the outskirts of the settlement, as with Tombs 101 and 102. Mağara Tepeşi could have bounded a road or track running along the intermittent stream that courses through the settlement and sanctuary area. The display of mortuary architecture along roads entering towns and cities is well-documented (Parks 1999: 117–18). Tomb 27, with its apparently preferred location at the southeast slope of the hill, in addition to its later construction date, represents a break from the earlier line of tombs; these characteristics may also suggest the establishment of a high-status kin group within Malloura. If Tomb 27 is actually earlier than the others, then this might reflect an older, higher-status corporate group in the Malloura Valley.

The excavated portion of the later Venetian-period cemetery could represent lower-status individuals from the settlement, perhaps the *paroikoi* or *francomati*. If indeed this cemetery is associated with a church, then higher-status individuals should be located in the church, as

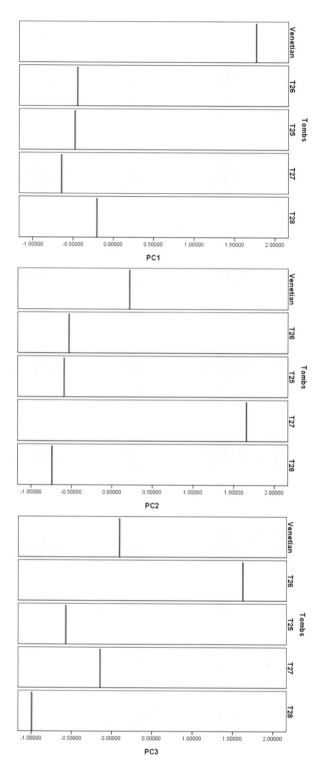

FIG. 19.2 *This figure shows the three principal components and the scores for each group. On PC1 at the top of the figure, the Venetian group is seen separated to the right. PC2 shows the separation of Tomb 27 to the right of the graph. PC3 at the bottom shows the position of Tomb 26.*

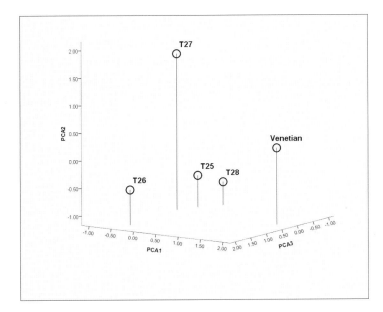

Fig. 19.3. *A three-dimensional plot of all three principal components. The placement of Tomb 27, Tomb 26 and the Venetian sample are clear. Tombs 25 and 26 occupy a position at the center of the plot.*

is seen at PA.SY.D.Y. and the Palaion Demarcheion in Nicosia. Future investigations of this area should pursue the possibility that this cemetery is more extensive and may include a church. With a larger sample of individuals from both inside and outside the church area, questions of long-term continuity in corporate groups can be examined.

Conclusion

The tombs from Mağara Tepeşi in the Malloura Valley of central Cyprus provide a unique example of well-excavated Hellenistic–Roman tombs. This study of dental nonmetric traits from the individuals in the tombs at Malloura shows that burial treatment (i.e., placement) may be strongly linked to kin or corporate group identity. This apparent emphasis on placing related individuals in specific tombs — tombs that would have been highly visible to others — in an environment where access to ownership of agricultural land was limited and closely monitored provides a picture of mortuary practices that were key components for constructing beliefs about the legitimacy of ownership and access to lands. Tomb architecture and grave goods have led the excavators to suggest that the

larger and more elaborate of these tombs may have housed the dead of a high-status corporate or kin group. To test this hypothesis, nonmetric dental traits, a reliable indicator of genetic relatedness, were analyzed to document the biological relationships between those buried in the Hellenistic–Roman tombs to evaluate whether particular kin groups used specific tombs. This study also compared the Hellenistic–Roman population to the later Venetian-period burial population at Malloura to evaluate whether there was population continuity or whether a distinct biological group migrated into the region centuries later. Results indicate that Tombs 27 and 26 likely housed separate kin or corporate groups, while Tombs 25 and 28 show a close relationship suggesting that together they may represent another kin group. Nonetheless, all four tomb populations exhibit a high level of biological relatedness that likely had a significant impact on corporate group claims to land and critical resources.

No continuity between the burials of Mağara Tepeşi and those of Venetian Malloura is indicated in the dental data, but this is not surprising in light of the long temporal span and the history of Cyprus as a crossroads. By the Venetian period, the burial program that had previously been a symbol of prestige and a marker of land ownership was replaced by austere burial in Christian churchyards. This change may in part reflect the different character of Malloura in the two periods. During the time when the tombs were being used, the sanctuary served as a location where elites could dedicate elaborate statues and other offerings (see Counts, Ch. 11). By the Venetian period, Malloura was the location of an agricultural settlement, which, while it had some expensive structures, also clearly contained a rural population of common farmers. If these changes in the biological profile are not related to those expected from natural selection and genetic drift, then the data suggest a distinct population migrated into the area sometime after the collapse of the Roman Empire or just prior to the Venetian-era occupation of this region. As the study of these several populations continues, we hope to discern more clearly the health and social status of valley residents, qualities that are in part reflected in their skeletal remains. The bioarchaeological approach to burial and the construction of identity has much to offer future research within Malloura, Cyprus, and the eastern Mediterranean.

REFERENCES

Agelarakis, A.
1997   Paleopathology and Its Contributions to the Decipherment of the Human Condition in Antiquity: The Case of Two Populations from *Malloura* in Cyprus. *Report of the Department of Antiquities, Cyprus*: 239–50.

Alt, K. W., and Vach, W.
1995   Odontological Kinship Analysis in Skeletal Remains. *Forensic Science International* 74: 99–113
1998   Kinship Studies in Skeletal Remains: Concepts and Examples. Pp. 537–54 in *Dental Anthropology*, eds. K. W. Alt, F. W. Rösing, and M. Teschler-Nicola. Vienna: Springer.

Baker, B.; Terhune, C.; and Papalexandrou, A.
2007   Sew Long: A Seamstress Buried at Medieval Polis, Cyprus. Poster presented at the Annual Meeting of the American Association of Physical Anthropologists, Philadelphia, Pennsylvania, March 2007.

Barrett, J.
1990   The Monumentality of Death: The Character of Early Bronze Age Mortuary Mounds in Southern Britain. *World Archaeology* 22: 179–89.

Binford, L.
1971   Mortuary Practices: Their Study and Potential. Pp. 6–29 in *Approaches to the Social Dimensions of Mortuary Practices*, ed. J. Brown. Society for American Archaeology Memoir 25. Washington, DC: Society for American Archaeology.

Brown, J.
1995   On Mortuary Analysis, with Special Reference to the Saxe-Binford Research Program. Pp. 3–26 in *Regional Approaches to Mortuary Analysis*, ed. Lane Beck. New York: Plenum.

Buikstra, J. E.
1995   Tombs for the Living … or … for the Dead: The Osmore Ancestors. Pp. 229–79 in *Tombs for the Living: Andean Mortuary Practices*, ed. T. D. Dillehay. Washington, D.C.: Dumbarton Oaks.

Charles, D. R., and Buikstra, J. E.
1983   Archaeology in the Central Mississippi Drainage: Distribution, Structure, and Behavioral Implications. Pp. 117–45 in *Archaic Hunters and Gatherers in the American Midwest*, eds. J. L. Phillips and J. A. Brown. New York: Academic.

Corruccini, R.S., and Shimada, I.
2002   Dental Relatedness Corresponding to Mortuary Patterning at Huaca Loro, Peru. *American Journal of Physical Anthropology* 117: 113–21.

Fox, S. C.
1997   Comparative Health from Paleopathological Analysis of the Human Skeletal Remains Dating to the Hellenistic and Roman Periods, from Paphos, Cyprus and Corinth, Greece. Unpublished Ph. D. dissertation, University of Arizona.

Fox, S. C.; Moutafi, I.; Prevedorou, E. A.; and Pilides, D.
2008   Trauma Patterns in Early Christian Cyprus. Paper presented at "Medicine in the Ancient Mediterranean World," September 28, 2008, Nicosia, Cyprus.

Goldstein, L.
1980   *Mississippian Mortuary Practices: A Case Study of Two Cemeteries in the Lower Illinois Valley*. Evanston: Northwestern University Archaeological Program.

Hadjisavvas, S.
1985   Excavations at the "Tombs of the Kings"—
        Kato Paphos. Pp. 262–68 in *Archaeology in
        Cyprus, 1960–1985,* ed. V. Karageorghis.
        Nicosia: A. G. Leventis Foundation.

Harper, N. K.
2010   From Typology to Population Genetics:
        Biodistance in Cypriot Archaeology. Pp. 1–38
        in *Proceedings of the 7th Annual Meetings of
        Postgraduate Cypriot Archaeology (POCA),*
        eds. S. Christodoulou and A. Satraki.
        Newcastle upon Tyne: Cambridge Scholars.
In press   People of the Kouris Valley: The Univer-
        sity Museum and its Contribution to Cypriot
        Physical Anthropology. In *The Ancient
        Kourion Area: Penn Museum's Legacy and
        Recent Research in Cyprus,* ed. E. Herscher.
        Philadelphia: University of Pennsylvania.

Irish, J. D.
2005   Population Continuity vs. Discontinuity
        Revisited: Dental Affinities among Late
        Paleolithic through Christian-Era Nubians.
        American Journal of Physical Anthropology
        128: 520–35.

Irish, J. D., and Guatelli-Steinberg, D.
2003   Ancient Teeth and Modern Human Origins:
        An Expanded Comparison of African Plio-
        Pleistocene and Recent World Dental Samples.
        Journal of Human Evolution 45: 113–44.

Janes, S.
2008   The Cypro-Geometric Horizon, a View from
        Below: Identity and Social Change in the
        Mortuary Record. Unpublished Ph. D.
        dissertation, University of Glasgow.

Kemp, B.; Tung, T. A.; and Summar, M. L.
2009   Genetic Continuity after the Collapse of the
        Wari Empire: Mitochondrial DNA Profiles
        from Wari and Post-Wari Populations in the
        Ancient Andes. *American Journal of Physical
        Anthropology* 140: 80–91.

Keswani, P.
2004   *Mortuary Ritual and Society in Bronze Age
        Cyprus.* Monographs in Mediterranean
        Archaeology. London: Equinox.

Knapp, A. B., and Ashmore, W.
1999   Archaeological Landscapes: Constructed,
        Conceptualized, Ideational. Pp. 1-32, in
        Archaeologies of Landscape, eds. W. Ashmore
        and A. B. Knapp. Oxford: Blackwell.

Knudson, K. J., and Stojanowski, C. M.
2008   New Directions in Bioarchaeology: Recent
        Contributions to the Study of Human Social
        Identities. *Journal of Archaeological Research*
        16: 397–432.

Niklasson, K.
1991   *Early Prehistoric Burials in Cyprus.* Studies
        in Mediterranean Archaeology 46. Jonsered:
        Åström.

Papanicola-Bakirtzis, D., and Iacovou, M.
1998   *Byzantine Medieval Cyprus.* Nicosia: Bank of
        Cyprus Cultural Foundation.

Parks, D. A.
1999   Burial Customs of Roman Cyprus: Origin and
        Development. Unpublished Ph. D. disserta-
        tion, University of Missouri-Columbia.

Parras, Z.
2004   *The Biological Affinities of the Eastern
        Mediterranean in the Chalcolithic and Bronze
        Age: A Regional Dental Non-Metric Approach.*
        Oxford: Archaeopress.
2006   Looking for Immigrants at Kissonerga-
        Mosphilia in the Late Chalcolithic: A
        Dental Non-Metric Perspective of Chalcolithic
        and Early Bronze Age Southwest Cyprus. Pp.
        63–74 in *Island Dialogues: Cyprus in the Medi-
        terranean Network,* ed. A. P. McCarthy. Uni-
        versity of Edinburgh Archaeology Occasional
        Paper 21. Edinburgh: University of Edinburgh.

Pilides, D.
2003   Excavations at the Hill of Agios Georgios (PA.
        SY.D.Y.), Nicosia, 2002 Season —Preliminary
        Report. *Report of the Department of
        Antiquities, Cyprus:* 181–238.

Renfrew, C.
1984   Islands out of Time. Pp. 200-224 in
        Approaches to Social Archaeology, ed.
        C. Renfrew. Cambridge: Harvard University.

Saxe, A.
1970   *Social Dimensions of Mortuary Practice.*
        Unpublished Ph. D. dissertation. Ann Arbor:
        University Microfilms International.

Scott, G. R., and Turner III, C. G.
1997   *The Anthropology of Modern Human Teeth:*
        Dental Morphology and Its Variation in Recent
        Human Populations. Cambridge: Cambridge
        University.

SPSS Inc.
2008   *SPSS Statistics Base 17.0 User's Guide.* Chicago:
        SPSS

Steadman, D. W.
1998   The Population Shuffle in Central Illinois: A
        Diachronic Model of Mississippian Biocultur-
        al Interactions. *World Archaeology* 30: 306–26.

Steel, L. F.
1995   Differential Burial Practices in Cyprus at the
        Transition from the Bronze Age to the Iron
        Age. Pp. 199–205 in *Death in the Ancient Near*
        East, eds. S. Campbell and A. Green. Oxford:
        Oxbow.

Stojanowski, C. M., and Schillaci, M. A.
2006   Phenotypic Approaches for Understanding
        Patterns of Intracemetery Biological Variation.
        Yearbook of Physical Anthropology 131: 49–88.

Stojanowski, C. M.; Larsen, C. S.; Tung, T. A.;
and McEwan, B. G.
2007   Biological Structure and Health Implica-
        tions from Tooth Size at Mission San Luis
        de Apalachee. *American Journal of Physical*
        Anthropology 132: 207–22.

Stynder, D. D.; Ackermann, R. R.; and Sealy, J. C.
2007   Craniofacial Variation and Population Con-
        tinuity during the South African Holocene.
        American Journal of Physical Anthropology
        134: 489–500.

Toumazou, M. K.
1987   Aspects of Burial Practices in Early Prehistoric
        Cypriote Sites, c. 7,000–2,500/2,300 B.C.
        Unpublished Ph. D. dissertation, Bryn Mawr
        College.

Toumazou, M. K.; Yerkes, R. W.; and Kardulias, P. N.
1998   Athienou Archaeological Project: Investiga-
        tions in the Malloura Valley, Cyprus, 1990–
        1995. *Journal of Field Archaeology* 25: 163–82.

Tung, T. A.
2000   Kin-Based Burial Groups in Hellenistic–
        Early Roman (325 BC–AD 150) Cyprus:
        A Biodistance Analysis of Mortuary
        Organization. Unpublished M. A. thesis,
        University of North Carolina, Chapel Hill.

Turner II, C. G.; Nichol, C. R.; and Scott, R. G.
1991   Scoring Procedures for Key Morphological
        Traits of the Permanent Dentition: The
        Arizona State University Dental Anthropology
        System. Pp. 13–31 in *Advances in Dental*
        Anthropology, eds. M. A. Kelley and C. S.
        Larsen. New York: Willey.

Violaris, I.
2004   Excavations at the Site of Palaion
        Demarcheion, Lefkosia. *Cahier du Centre*
        d'Études Chypriotes 34: 69–80.

Zakrzewski, S.
2007   Population Continuity or Population Change:
        Formation of the Ancient Egyptian State.
        American Journal of Physical Anthropology
        132: 501–9.

Chapter 20

Trade or Trousseau

Skeletal Evidence for Spinning and Weaving in Medieval Athienou-*Malloura*

by Nathan K. Harper

As highlighted in the other chapters of this volume, Cyprus's geographic position between the East and the West and Athienou's location within this Mediterranean crossroads provide a compelling example of the response of indigenous practices to external influence. This volume also offers examples of the role of local production and consumption and trade of various materials from an archaeological perspective. Ceramic figurines (Averett, Ch. 10), lamps (Gordon, Ch. 14), and even millstones (Spigelman, Ch. 17) inform the social environment of the past, providing a richer characterization of the lives of the people in the Malloura Valley.

This chapter investigates the production and control of fiber plants, the spinning of these fibers into thread, and the possible manufacture of these resources into textiles sold on the wider European markets through analyses of the skeletal remains of the people who would have undertaken the labor. Cyprus has a detailed history of cotton and flax production for export to western Europe, and the production of textiles was tightly controlled under Latin, Venetian, and Ottoman rule (Arbel 2000). By investigating a suite of dental wear patterns that includes notches, grooves, and lingual surface at-trition of the maxillary anterior teeth (LSAMAT) in a sample of 35 adults from Venetian-period Athienou-*Malloura* (AD 1489–1571), the role of local Cypriots in the wider textile trade of the eastern Mediterranean can be better interpreted.

THE MEDIEVAL CEMETERY OF ATHIENOU-*MALLOURA*

Toumazou and Counts (Ch. 6) discuss the excavation and recovery of the human skeletal remains from EU 6 at Athienou-*Malloura* (see also Harper and Tung, Ch. 19). In brief, from 1991 to 1993, a cemetery was excavated from an area that included a wall, plaster, and *opus sectile* fragments. The burials were in simple earth-cut pit or rock-built cist graves. Plowing and recent bulldozing in the area caused serious disturbance to many of the burials (Toumazou et al. 1998). Generally, these were discrete burials, but in some cases previous burials were disturbed, perhaps by the subsequent use of plots by family groups. Grave goods were minimal, limited to sgraffito pottery (mostly), metal eyelets, and tiny fragments of preserved textile.

ANALYSIS

Anthropological analysis of the excavated remains brought to light a minimum number of 57 individuals, of which 45 were discrete burials. While some cists were used successively, in some cases bodies may have been exhumed with little regard. The age and sex profiles of the Venetian cemetery are not out of the ordinary for archaeological populations in Cyprus (Harper and Fox 2008; Harper, in press), with the exception of a larger proportion of identified females (figs. 20.1–2). The disturbed and fragmentary burials elevate the numbers of indeterminate ages and sexes. A full paleopathological analysis recognized porotic hyperostosis, degenerative joint disease, dental disease, and other common health stress markers. Of particular interest was the discovery of significant nonalimentary notches or grooves in the anterior dentition (incisors and canines) of eight individuals (Harper 2005, 2006).

Most dental wear is the result of tooth-on-tooth contact (attrition) or tooth on external materials, such as food (abrasion). Attrition is generally identifiable and it leaves predictable patterns in groups that share similar diets. Other common patterns of dental wear are due to the use of teeth as tools or as a "third hand" (Lukacs and Pastor 1988). The splitting of cane for basketry (Larsen 1985), the chewing of hides (Merbs 1983), and the use of the mouth in the spinning of yarns (Mellink and Angel 1968: 262; Erdal 2008) have all been documented ethnographically and in archaeological contexts. Of particular interest is the study of 32 individuals from Byzantine-period Sinop in northern Anatolia (Erdal 2008). There, five females were identified as possessing mesiodistal (along the length of the crown) occlusal grooves. Erdal (2008) uses ethnographic correlates to make a convincing argument that the grooving is the result of the use

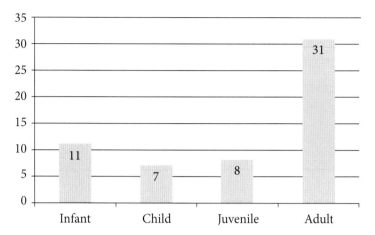

FIG. 20.1 *Age profile of individuals in the Venetian cemetery (EU 6) at* Athienou-*Malloura.*

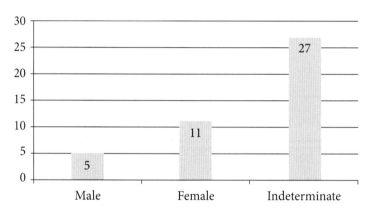

FIG. 20.2 *Sex profile of individuals in the Venetian cemetery (EU 6) at* Athienou-*Malloura.*

of the mouth to wet yarn or thread during spinning or the making of cord. Other dental markers such as linear enamel hypoplasias (LEH) leave a very different pattern on teeth unrelated to attrition or abrasion.

A total of 63 incisors (maxillary 33/63 [52%], mandibular 30/63 [48%]) from Malloura were investigated macroscopically for evidence of grooves, notches, chipping, and other nonalimentary dental wear. Grooves are defined as the abraded loss of enamel material in a linear pattern along either the occlusal or nonocclusal surface. Notches are defined as the chipped or abraded loss of tooth enamel on the occlusal surface of the anterior teeth, isolated to a small (<25%) area of the occlusal surface. Chipping is defined as the loss of enamel

TABLE 20.1   Table showing which individuals possess what types of non-alimentary tooth wear and temporo-mandibular joint alterations.

Individual	Sex	Grooves	Notches	Chipping	TMJ
6.1.2	Ind.	√			
6.4.1	Ind.	√			√
6.11.2	Ind.	√	√	√	
6.14	F?	√	√		
6.16	F	√	√		√
6.17	F	√	√		√
6.19.3	Ind.		√	√	
6.23	Ind.	√			
6.30	Ind.	√			
6.31	Ind.	√			

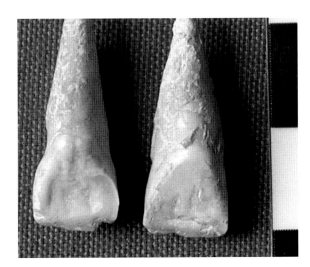

FIG. 20.3 *Central maxillary incisors of Individual 6.11.2 viewed from the labial side. This individual exhibits threadwear grooving, notches and chipping.*

through spalling of the labial or buccal surfaces of the anterior teeth. Of the total 63 incisors, 29 (46%) had nonalimentary dental wear including grooves (7/63 [11%]), notches (6/63 [10%]), or chipping (16/63 [25%]) (Table 20.1). Grooves and notches were found predominantly on the maxillary incisors (grooves 6/7, notches 5/6) (fig. 20.3).

Grooves are oriented mesiodistally and located mainly on the distal interproximal surfaces. In cases where the dentition is complete, paired grooves are seen with one groove located on the

lower portion of the distal angle of the incisor and a paired groove found on the ipsilateral incisor (same tooth on the opposite side of the mouth) but at a higher location along the crown in the interproximal space between either the I¹ and I² or I² and C¹. The grooves are no more than 1 mm in width. Notches measured between 1 and 3 mm in diameter and are located mainly on the mesial edge of the upper central incisors (fig. 20.4). Chipping is more prevalent and was found across the labial and lingual surfaces of crowns adjacent to the occlusal surface. No marker was found to be mutually exclusive of the others, and in many cases all three markers could be found on the same tooth.

Is it possible that the observed grooves occurred naturally? There are several developmental disturbances that occur in teeth that might manifest as a line or groove, particularly linear enamel hypoplasias (LEH). LEHs are a disturbance in enamel formation in childhood, often from illness or simply a slight fever. LEHs appear as transverse lines, pits, or discolorations in the enamel of a tooth crown (Goodman and Armelagos 1985; Condon and Rose 1992). These are different from the perikymata, which are the natural transverse grooves or ridges from sequential enamel formation (Hillson 2005: 168). To understand better the etiology of these dental markers, the anterior teeth were molded and cast using high-viscosity polyvinylsiloxane

(President's Jet light body) and epoxy (3M). The casts were then analyzed under high magnification using a scanning electron microscope (SEM) at the electron microanalysis and imaging laboratory, in the Department of Geosciences at the University of Nevada, Las Vegas.

Images derived from the SEM analysis showed that grooves are distinct from hypoplasias in several ways. Hypoplasias show a series of reduced perikymata that disturb the profile of the crown as shown in figure 20.5 (Hillson 1992). On this same tooth we have an example of an abraded groove with delineated edges; perikymata do not seem to be involved. In closer examination of grooves in other specimens, transverse striations are apparent in the groove (fig. 20.6). This suggests that material was pulled in a transverse motion through the groove leading to the abraded loss of enamel material. Microscopic examination also revealed two other examples of grooves that were not visible macroscopically. These grooves were very shallow and were often found in pairs, indicating that placement of the fiber on the tooth surface was variable until a dominant groove was formed (fig. 20.7).

Other markers associated with the use of the teeth or mouth as a third hand or tool include degenerative changes in the mandible. The mandibular condyles of at least four individuals show remodeling, and in one case a pseudarthrosis is developed on the zygomatic process of the temporal bone (fig. 20.8). While the causes of condylar pits and deformation are multiple (Angel 1948; Oxenham and Whitworth 2006), repetitive use and the anterior projection of the mandible can also cause changes in the shape of the condyle (fig. 20.9). Three of the four individuals with changes in the mandibular condyle also show grooves or notches in the anterior dentition.

Close analyses of the dental and skeletal markers suggest long-term use of the teeth as tools throughout the life course. While the ultimate cause of these markers is unclear, the pattern closely resembles grooves and notches seen in other archaeological populations that have been related to such diverse activities as hide chewing, reed splitting for basketry, and spinning of yarn.

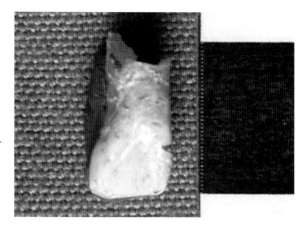

FIG. 20.4 *Right lateral maxillary incisor of Individual 6.14 exhibiting threadwear groove on the mesiodistal surface.*

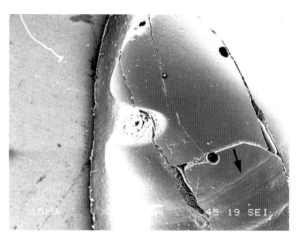

FIG. 20.5 *Scanning electron image of the left maxillary canine of Individual 6.31. The arrow points to a linear enamel hypolasia (LEH). This individual also possesses a threadwear groove. The occlusal surface is to the top.*

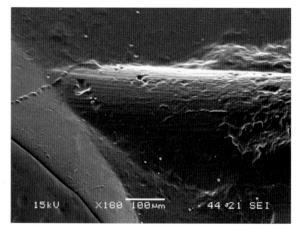

FIG. 20.6 *SEM image of threadwear groove on the left lateral maxillary incisor of Individual 6.30 showing parallel striations.*

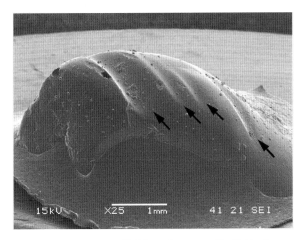

FIG. 20.7 *SEM image of left lateral incisor of Individual 6.14 showing multiple threadwear grooves. Macroscopic examination detected one groove. Occlusal surface is to the left.*

For Trade?

The Malloura Valley lies in a significant location between the capital city of Nicosia and the major ports of Famagusta and Larnaka. The most direct route between the seat of government at Nicosia and the coastal centers was through the Malloura Valley. With its rich agricultural lands, this rural hinterland of Cyprus was not buffered from the geopolitical and economic changes occurring in the 13th- and 14th-century eastern Mediterranean (see also DeMasi, Ch. 16; Spigelman, Ch. 17; Beeston, Ch. 24).

When Acre fell to Mamluk forces in AD 1291, there was a significant influx of aristocratic Latins into Cyprus (Edbury 1999; 2005; Coureas 2005). Cyprus became the de facto Kingdom of Jerusalem and was divided among the Latin aristocracy that had lost significant holdings in Syria and Palestine. Following the Papal Embargo of 1291 (which lasted until 1344), Cyprus in general and Famagusta in particular became the center of western European trade with the Muslim Near East. These two factors led to a significant increase in the production of commodities on Cyprus and their trade to western Europe from the Lusignan through the Ottoman periods.

Sugar, salt, grain, silk, and cotton all saw significant increase in production following the loss of the Latin holdings in the Holy Land. Sugar plantations and skilled workers in Syria were transported to Cyprus virtually *in toto* after 1291. Major sugar plantations were founded along the south coast at Kolossi, Episkopi, and Kouklia, locations with access to stands of sugar cane and consistent water supplies. Sugar production in Cyprus declined in the late 16th century, with many of the lands

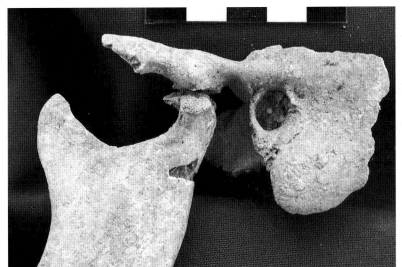

FIG. 20.8 *Left mandibular condyle and temporal bone of Individual 6.17 showing altered mandibular condyle and pseudoarthropothy on zygomatic process.*

FIG. 20.9 *Pit on surface of mandibular condyle of Individual 6.16, a 16–18 year old female.*

previously given over to sugar replaced by cotton fields. Salt was already a major portion of Cypriot trade from Larnaka, and the salt pans there were the exclusive holding of the Royal House (Coureas 2005). Large amounts of grain were exported to locations all over western Europe but mainly to the Hospitallers in Rhodes, Cilician Armenia, and later to the Venetians (Coureas 2005).

The first accounts of cotton on the island come from notarial deeds dating from 1301 (Coureas 2005: 109), though there is no indication of high levels of local production until 1370, when the Genoese ceased the importation of Egyptian cottons. Production of cotton increased from that point, rising to its highest levels in the Venetian and Ottoman periods. In most areas, the cultivation of cotton was associated with sugar production due to the large amount of land and irrigation required. Cotton cultivation was both capital and labor intensive, and only aristocratic families with means undertook production. Estates in the south and southwest at Kolossi, Episkopi, and Kouklia were particularly important (Mazzaoui 1981). Cotton exports to Venice increased greatly during this period, often in the form of raw, baled cotton, though textiles of various forms and qualities were also exported. Camlets (textiles woven mainly with a wool warp and a silk or cotton weft), fustian (cotton with linen), and samites (heavy silk) were the main textiles exported to Europe (Arbel 2000; Coureas 2005).

The limitations of labor, land, and water ensured that cotton production was mainly undertaken by manors and estates. Control of water sources for irrigation was especially important for estates in the Mesaoria. Recent work on water installations at the royal manor house at Potamia, a little more than 6 km from Malloura, have shown a highly sophisticated chain of wells, water wheels, canals, and water-driven mills (Lecuyer et al. 2002; Amouric 2004). The *terminus ante quem* for these wells is AD 1348 (Lecuyer et al. 2002). Though sugar production is historically recorded from Potamia, to date no archaeological examples of ceramics associated with sugar production, such as jars or molds, have been found.

Textiles, particularly cotton, were too valuable a commodity for there not to be any seigniorial management. In the late 13th and early 14th centuries, many items, such as drapes and camlets, were under direct royal supervision, and certain textiles required a royal stamp (Coureas 2005: 118). There were several options to acquire the necessary labor for cultivation, harvesting, and production of textiles. Slave trade and labor are known from Cyprus and persisted through the Ottoman period (Arbel 1993), but these individuals largely would have worked in households. The other two major labor divisions consisted of the *paroikoi* (serfs) and *francomati* (freemen). The *paroikoi* were tied to their lord's land, gave over one-third of their field production to the lord, and performed two to three days of corvée labor service to the estate (Nicolaou-Konnari 2005). *Paroikoi* did not have freedom of movement and could not take part in any commerce. The *francomati* leased land for cultivation, had freedom of movement, and did not have to take part in corvée. Taxes on their production were only one-fourth or one-fifth of the yearly total. The cultivation, spinning, and weaving of cotton were under tight control, and it is possible the corvées demanded of the *paroikoi* were related to these activities. The household may have been the main production outlet during this period.

Household production was generally a female task, undertaken when other domestic tasks were finished, and spinning and weaving were integral parts of female identity in Cyprus (Smith 2002; Bolger 2003). Hand spinning is represented by spindle whorls (Crewe 1998), which constitute a significant portion of the ancient remains of all periods from Cyprus. Beyond the production of yarn or thread, many households would have had their own loom. Ethnographic reports indicate that personal looms are often located in inner rooms of the house such as the bedroom (Christodoulou 1959: 65). Some historic village houses still exhibit pegs in roof beams for the vertical runners of thread. The types of looms used would have been variable, but the pit loom with the treadles sunk in a pit in the floor is seen as late as 1948 at Episkopi (Photo, Angel Archives, National Anthropological Archives). Christodoulou (1959: 138) estimated that as late as 1946 there were 22,000 handlooms — but only 4,553 practicing weavers — on the island.

While household spinning and weaving were dominated by females, when textile production is centralized or commercialized there is a shift toward strict sexual division of labor and male primacy in the control of fiber preparation and weaving. This is well-documented in Central and South America (Brumfiel 1991; Costin 1996) as well as Mesopotamia (Wright 1996). In Flanders, during the same period as the increase in cotton production in Cyprus, males became the main force of labor and many women were excluded from commercial textile guilds (Howell 1986; Karras 2004). Raw or cleaned cotton was shipped to the workshops in Flanders, where the material was prepared and woven in a male-dominated commercial environment (Mazzaoui 1981).

For Trousseau?

Even with the intensification of a commercial and export textile industry, women remained important at many levels of production. In cities, women were used mainly as finishers of fine cloth, in contrast to women in rural hinterlands such as Malloura, who may have undertaken the entire process of fiber and textile production. The role of women in textile production in rural areas would have been tied to both the necessity of textile production for the clothing of the family and to the long connection of fiber and textile production with female identity.

Spinning and weaving played significant roles in the construction of female identity in medieval and Venetian Cyprus. The protection of female and family honor was closely associated with a potential bride's industriousness and skill, and these ideals are reinforced in the folklore of the period (Schneider 1989). As part of proving that she would be a hard-working and competent wife, a young girl was expected to produce a significant trousseau (Karras 2004). Females were obligated to provide clothing, tablecloths, sheets, and other "linens" for the household. The traditional trousseau consisted of cotton or linen textiles, sheets, tablecloths, runners, laces, and undergarments, all produced by the prospective bride or her family. These goods were brought to the marriage as part of the dowry,

and in the case of an unsuccessful marriage, the trousseau remained with the wife. The custom of the dowry in Cyprus persists today, with handmade linens replaced by mass-produced goods.

A girl was required to participate in household spinning and weaving activities from a young age. By watching the older household females, young girls learned how to prepare, spin, and weave fibers. Younger daughters helped in the making of the oldest daughter's trousseau, some of which was saved for their own future dowry. The materials of the trousseau would have been enhanced through embroidery and edging with lace. As each piece was completed, it was placed in a wooden wedding chest, similar to modern hope chests (Cobham 1908: 443).

Rizopoulou-Egoumenidou (2004) describes traditional Cypriot wedding customs from the early 20th century (see also Ohnefalsch-Richter 2006). In the days leading up to a wedding, the trousseau served as an important representation of the bride's identity. Women went to the bride's home, where the contents of her wedding chest were displayed in a practice known as *manassa* or *prasto* (Rizopoulou-Egoumenidou 2004: 122). The trousseau was inspected for quantity and quality, with the number and intricacy of the pieces serving as signs of industriousness and prestige. The sheets were used for the marriage bed, and a special sheet (*mesalin*) was used to prove that the marriage had been consummated. This sheet was saved the next day to be inspected by the families as a final estimation of the purity and industriousness of the bride.

Conclusion

An investigation of the distinct markers on the bodies of the people from the medieval/Venetian cemetery at Malloura indicates that they used their teeth in the processing and production of yarn or thread. Though we cannot identify exactly what fibers were being processed, textual evidence from the time period indicates that the production of cotton increased after AD 1291. Are the markers on the bodies of these people an example of increased local production of extraregional commodities or a reflection of the construction and maintenance of the Cypriot female identity?

By looking at the economic and social milieu of the period, it could be argued that the increase in cotton production and the assumed increase in the production of cotton yarn, thread, and textiles were the result of local practice (spinning and weaving for personal use or putting-out) being exploited for commercial reasons (export). Rural Malloura, located between cosmopolitan Nicosia, with its dye houses, and the commercial port of Larnaka, with its access to foreign markets, sat in a fortuitous position in which locals could exploit the financial gain of commercial enterprise while maintaining their local cultural practices of trousseau.

ACKNOWLEDGMENTS

The author would like to thank the editors for allowing the presentation of this work, the Electron Microanalysis and Imaging Laboratory at University of Nevada, Las Vegas, and the AAP παρέα.

REFERENCES

Amouric, H.
2004   Administration de l'eau et structures hydrauliques sur le territoire d' Agios Sozomenos. *Cahier du Centre d'Études Chypriotes* 34: 81–82.

Angel, J. L.
1948   Factors in Temporomandibular Joint Form. *The American Journal of Anatomy* 83(2): 223–46.

Arbel, B.
1993   Slave Trade and Slave Labour in Frankish Cyprus (1191–1571). *Studies in Medieval and Renaissance History* 14: 149–90.
2000   *Cyprus, the Franks and Venice, 13th–16th Centuries.* Variorum Collected Studies Series. Burlington, VT: Ashgate.

Bolger, D.
2003   *Gender in Ancient Cyprus: Narratives of Social Change on a Mediterranean Island.* Walnut Creek: Altamira.

Brumfiel, E.
1991   Weaving and Cooking: Women's Production in Aztec Mexico. Pp. 224–51 in *Engendering Archaeology: Women and Prehistory,* eds. J. Gero and M. Conkey. Oxford: Blackwell.

Christodoulou, D.
1959   *The Evolution of the Rural Land Use Pattern in Cyprus.* The World Land Use Survey, Regional Monograph 2. Cornwall: Geographical Publications.

Cobham, C.D.
1908   *Excerpta Cypria: Materials for a History of Cyprus.* Cambridge: Cambridge University.

Condon, K., and Rose, J. C.
1992   Intertooth and Intratooth Variability in the Occurrence of Developmental Enamel Defects. Pp. 61–77 in *Recent Contributions to the Study of Enamel Developmental Defects,* eds. A. H. Goodman and L. L. Capasso. Monographic Publication 2. Chieti, Italy: Journal of Paleopathology.

Costin, C.
1996   Exploring the Relationship between Gender and Craft in Complex Societies: Methodological and Theoretical Issues of Gender Attribution. Pp. 111–40 in *Gender and Archaeology.* ed. R. Wright. Philadelphia: University of Pennsylvania.

Coureas, N.
2005   Economy. Pp. 103–56 in *Cyprus Society and Culture 1191–1374,* eds. A. Nicolaou-Konnari and C. Schabel. Leiden: Brill.

Crewe, L.
1998   *Spindle Whorls. A Study of Form, Function and Decoration in Prehistoric Bronze Age Cyprus.* Studies in Mediterranean Archaeology and Literature Pocket-book 149. Jonsered: Åström.

Edbury, P.
1999   The State of Research: Cyprus under the Lusignans and Venetians, 1991–1998. *Journal of Medieval History* 25: 57–65.

2005   Franks. Pp. 63–102 in *Cyprus Society and Culture 1191–1374*, eds. A. Nicolaou-Konnari and C. Schabel. Leiden: Brill.

Erdal, Y. S.
2008   Occlusal Grooves in Anterior Dentition among Kovuklukaya Inhabitants (Sinop, Northern Anatolia, 10th Century AD). *International Journal of Osteoarchaeology* 18(2): 152–66.

Goodman, A. H., and Armelagos, G. J.
1985   Factors Affecting the Distribution of Enamel Hypoplasias within the Human Permanent Dentition. *American Journal of Physical Anthropology* 68: 479–93.

Harper, N. K.
2005   Specialized Dental Wear from Venetian Period Cyprus. Poster presented at the 70th Annual Meeting of the Society of American Archaeology, Salt Lake City, Utah, March–April, 2005.
2006   Industrial Dental Wear from Venetian Period Cyprus. Poster presentation at the 16th European meeting of the Paleopathology Association, Santorini, Greece, August 28–September 1, 2006.
In press Ancient Cypriots in the Kouris River Valley: The University Museum's Contribution to Physical Anthropology. In *The Ancient Kourion Area: Penn Museum's Legacy and Recent Research in Cyprus*, ed. E. Herscher. Philadelphia: University of Pennsylvania.

Harper, N. K., and Fox, S.
2008   Recent Research in Cypriot Bioarchaeology. *Bioarchaeology of the Near East* 2: 1–38.

Hillson S. W.
1992   Studies of Growth in Dental Tissues. *Journal of Human Ecology, Special Issue* 2: 7–23.
2005   *Teeth*. Cambridge: Cambridge University.

Howell, M.
1986   *Women, Production and Patriarchy in Late Medieval Cities*. Chicago: University of Chicago.

Karras, R.
2004   "This Skill in a Woman Is by No Means To Be Despised:" Weaving and the Gender Division of Labor in the Middle Ages. Pp. 89–104 in *Medieval Fabrications: Dress, Textiles, and Other Cultural Imaginings*, ed. E. J. Burns. New York: MacMillan

Larsen, C. S.
1985   Dental Modifications and Tool Use in the Western Great Basin. *American Journal of Physical Anthropology* 67: 393–402.

Lecuyer, N.; Decock, L.; Devillers, B.; François, V.; Grivaud, G.; Michaelides, D.; Nicolaides, A.; Saulner, J-M.; Simon, B.; Thernot, R.; Vallauri, L.; and C. Vanderheyde
2002   Potamia-Agios Sozomenos (Chypre). La constitution des paysages dans l'Orient médiéval 2001. *Bulletin de Correspondance Hellénique* 125(2): 655–78.

Lukacs, J. R., and Pastor, R. F.
1988   Activity-Induced Patterns of Dental Abrasion in Prehistoric Pakistan: Evidence from Mehrgarh and Harappa. *American Journal of Physical Anthropology* 76(3): 377–98.

Mazzaoui, M.
1981   *The Italian Cotton Industry in the Later Middle Ages, 1100–1600*. Cambridge: Cambridge University.

Mellink, M., and Angel, J.
1968   Excavations at Karataş-Semayük in Lycia, 1967. *American Journal of Archaeology* 72(3): 243–63.

Merbs, C. F.
1983   *Patterns of Activity-Induced Pathology in a Canadian Inuit Population*. Archaeological Survey of Canada, Paper No. 119. Ottawa: National Museum of Man.

Nicolaou-Konnari, A.
2005   Greeks Pp. 13–62 in *Cyprus Society and Culture 1191–1374*. eds. A. Nicolaou-Konnari and C. Schabel. Leiden:Brill.

Ohnefalsch-Richter, M.
2006   *Greek Customs and Mores in Cyprus*. Nicosia: Laiki Group Cultural Centre.

Oxenham, M. F., and Whitworth, J.
2006   Frequency, Location, Morphology and
        Aetiology of Osseous Mandibular Condylar
        Concavities. *International Journal of
        Osteoarchaeology* 16(6): 517–27.

Rizopoulou-Egoumenidou, E.
2004   The Traditional Wedding of the Greek
        Cypriots. *Archiv für Völkerkunde* 54: 113–28.

Schneider, J.
1989   Rumpelstiltskin's Bargain: Folklore and
        the Merchant Capitalist Intensification
        of Linen Manufacture in Early Modern
        Europe. Pp. 177–213 in *Cloth and the Human
        Experience,* eds. A. B. Weiner and J. Schneider.
        Washington, DC: Smithsonian Institution.

Smith, J.
2002   Changes in the Workplace: Women and
        Textile Production in Late Bronze Age Cyprus.
        Pp. 281–312 in *Engendering Aphrodite:
        Women and Society in Ancient Cyprus,* eds.
        D. Bolger and N. Serwint. Boston: American
        Schools of Oriental Research.

Toumazou, M. K.; Yerkes, R. W.; and Kardulias, P. N.
1998   Athienou Archaeological Project: Investiga-
        tions in the Malloura Valley, Cyprus, 1990–
        1995. *Journal of Field Archaeology* 25: 163–82.

Wright, R.
1996   Technology, Gender and Class: Worlds of
        Difference in Ur III Mesopotamia. Pp. 79–110
        in *Gender and Archaeology,* ed. R. Wright.
        Philadelphia: University of Pennsylvania.

Chapter 21

Geophysical Prospection at Malloura

by Apostolos Sarris

The use of geophysical techniques has become commonplace in Mediterranean archaeology (Sarris and Jones 2000). These methods examine the subsurface in a noninvasive or minimally intrusive manner to define anomalies that indicate archaeological features (e.g., walls, hearths, pits, collections of artifacts) (Sarris 2008). By taking readings at the surface, geophysical methods provide a rapid way of identifying areas of interest, making excavation more targeted and efficient. On Cyprus, the first major use of these techniques was at Hala Sultan Tekke (Fischer 1980a, 1980b). Since that time, geophysical methods have been used on many projects, including the Athienou Archaeological Project.

Geophysical survey was carried out on three different occasions at Malloura. In 1990, a team from the University of Patras and the University of Nebraska-Lincoln employed total magnetic field intensity and soil resistance techniques for the survey of a limited area close to the Cypro-Geometric III–Roman sanctuary, on the hilltop near EU 1, and about halfway between the sanctuary and Mağara Tepeşi (fig. 21.1; see also fig. 6.1) (Papamarinopoulos et al. 1991, 1992). This preliminary geophysical survey provided information related to the geological

background of the region and indicated a strong geological trend existing in the vicinity of the site. In 1994 and 1995, a small team from the Institute for Mediterranean Studies (IMS-FORTH) took measurements of the soil resistance and the vertical magnetic gradient and used ground-penetrating radar (GPR) in various sections of the site, focusing in the area around the sanctuary and the tombs at Mağara Tepeşi (on excavations, see Toumazou and Counts, Ch. 6), located about 300 m to the north of the ritual enclosure.

GEOPHYSICAL TECHNIQUES: METHODOLOGY

During the 1990 survey season, primarily two methods were employed for the geophysical prospection of the site: soil electrical resistance using the RM4 Twin probe array and proton magnetometry using two ELSEC 820 units to evaluate the total magnetic field intensity in an effort to identify the location of the sanctuary (fig. 21.2). Four 20 × 20 m blocks, located about 30 m west of EU 2, which had yielded portions of architectural remains (see Toumazou and Counts, Ch. 6; DeMasi, Ch. 16; Spigelman, Ch. 17), were covered by both methods (see fig. 21.1). Soil samples were

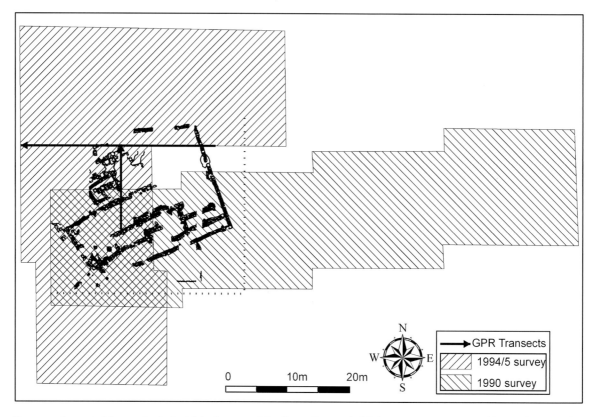

FIG. 21.1 *Layout of the geophysical grids in the area of the Cypro-Geometric III–Roman sanctuary at Malloura. The 2007 plan of the excavated architectural relics is also superimposed on the map.*

collected from a depth of 30 cm below the surface at the edges of the four adjacent blocks for measuring the soil's magnetic susceptibility. Soil samples were also collected from the south balk of EU 3, at 5 cm intervals, from the surface down to a depth of 60 cm for further analysis of the magnetic susceptibility and the measurement of the "Le Borgne Contrast." Several more areas on the nearby hill and in the area of the tombs east of it were investigated using magnetic methods (see fig. 6.1). A high-resolution search (0.25 m sampling interval) was carried out inside a rock-cut, looted tomb (T 15), located about 110 m northeast of the top of the hill at the center of the settlement (location of EU 1).

The proton magnetometers were employed in a differential mode, and the simultaneous measurements of the total magnetic field intensity insured an accurate correction of the magnetic data from the diurnal variations of the magnetic field. Sensor height was set at 30 cm above the ground, and

readings were acquired every meter along parallel traverses 1 m apart. The raw magnetic data suffered a strong geological trend with increasing values toward the east. Data were processed with a removal of trend filter and a series of high-pass filters to emphasize the weak magnetic anomalies. The statistical analysis of the common lines of adjacent grids through a method of regression interpolation improved the mosaic of the geophysical data. The mapping process was achieved through cubic spline or kriging interpolation algorithms, while frequency-enhancement filters and despiking of noise signals were used for the better presentation of the geophysical anomalies (Sarris 1992).

A Twin probe array with 0.5 m spacing between the mobile probes was used for the measurements of the soil resistance. The hardness of the soil did not allow the use of the portable frame that carries the probes and reading unit; instead, all electrodes had to be inserted into the ground through hammering (see fig. 21.2). The removal of trend and

FIG. 21.2 *Details from the geophysical survey project in the Malloura Valley: Magnetic survey using the proton magnetometers (top) and soil resistance equipment (center) in the sanctuary (1990), and the employment of the GPR above Tomb 25 at Mağara Tepeşi (bottom) (1995).*

the application of Hanning filter were capable of improving the image of the soil resistance map.

In 1994 and 1995, a Geoscan Research FM36 and an RM15 were employed to measure the vertical magnetic gradient and the soil's electrical resistance. The area of investigation was in the vicinity of the Malloura sanctuary and had a partial overlap with the geophysical grids of the 1990 survey season (see fig. 21.1). Different heights (30 cm, 50 cm, and 70 cm above the surface) of the FM36 sensor were tried, using a polyester vertical base to hold the instrument. Since the instrument measures simultaneously the vertical component of the magnetic field at two sensors, measurements were free of the diurnal variations of the magnetic field. Still, a strong trend was noticed, mainly due to the large temperature variations during the course of the day. Thus, data had to be processed through the use of several high-pass filters. Similar processing was carried out on the soil resistance measurements. A small area in the northern part of the grid system was investigated using a Twin probe with a 120 cm electrode spacing in an effort to penetrate deeper into the subsurface.

The GPR (see fig. 21.2) was employed in selected areas (at Mağara Tepeşi, between T 25 and T 26 and southwest of T 27) to identify architecture and additional tombs. The underlying principle of GPR is that an electromagnetic pulse of radio frequency (~50–1,000 MHz) is passed into the ground. When this pulse reaches a layer with different electrical properties, some of the energy will be reflected back to the surface while the remainder will be transmitted farther into the ground. As transmitter and receiver are towed along the surface (profiling method), images are built up that show the time elapsed between wave transmission and reflection. Knowing the electrical conductivity and the magnetic permeability of the subsurface layers, a time-section record is obtained, allowing an estimation of their depth to be made. In the survey at Mağara Tepeşi, the Sensors & Software EKKO 1000 GPR system was used, employing two antennae at 450 MHz and 225 MHz. An initial examination of the GPR readings in the field indicated specific regions of interest that were later examined by both antennae and with a finer sampling interval (5 cm).

Different processing procedures were used to determine the optimum way to represent the GPR data, including high-pass filters for minimizing the low frequencies (wow effect), DC level removal, gain functions to compensate for the weaker signals, spatial filters in the horizontal (spatial) direction of the collected data (trace to trace averaging), compression or stretching of the dynamic range of the data, and time-slicing techniques.

Discussion of Results

The 1990 Survey Season

The 1990 survey season was mainly exploratory. Soil resistance measurements in the area of the sanctuary identified a number of high- and medium-resistance anomalies. The electrical resistance background was 18.64 ohms, and the histogram of the resistance values was unimodal in nature with a trend toward large values of resistance reaching a maximum of 55 ohms. It was clear from the geophysical survey, and confirmed by later excavation in the area, that the compactness of the soil would not permit good discrimination of the architectural remains. Most of the soil resistance anomalies were attributed to fluctuations of the shallow bedrock or to pockets of disturbed earth created either by looters or by past excavations of the French team that initially investigated the site (see Counts, Ch. 4).

The initial magnetic measurements of the total magnetic field intensity were quite disappointing, since the geological background created a strong regional trend, increasing toward the east, that masked almost all the anomalous features of the map. Only the very strong anomalies appeared in the original data. Even the application of the removal of trend and a Hanning smoothing filter were not able to recover the strong masking of the archaeological features. Just a few anomalies were suggested by both magnetic and soil resistance measurements, and most of them were attributed to the existence of wall remains.

Magnetic Susceptibility Study

High-frequency (4.6 kHz) and low-frequency (0.46 kHz) measurements of the magnetic susceptibility were conducted for soil samples collected above the surface and from the south balk of EU 3. Nineteen samples were collected over the area of the four 20 × 20 m grids of the 1990 survey season in the area later identified as the location of the sanctuary. The susceptibility values ranged from 19 to 50 × 10^{-6} cgs/gr. The readings indicated two areas of interest, diametrically opposite from each other. One was the area around EU 3, where the 1990 excavations revealed significant architectural remains in deeply stratified deposits; the other was located at the western extremity of the site, where excavations brought to light the abundant remains of the sanctuary (see fig. 6.1; Toumazou and Counts, Ch. 6).

The unimodal nature of the histograms of the low-frequency magnetic susceptibility and frequency-dependent susceptibility (fig. 21.3) suggested an absence of surface concentrations of anthropogenic material, which can be explained by the suspected erosion episodes in the wider area of interest. However, the Le Borgne Contrast (LBC, the vertical variation of susceptibility), which varies with the grain-size distribution and the dilution factor, proved to be a valuable tool for confirming the occupation layers in the area of EU 3 (settlement) where samples were collected. The susceptibility values of the collected samples ranged from 15 to 82 × 10^{-6} cgs/gr, showing a peak at 30 cm below the surface (see fig. 21.3). This depth was identified as the main occupation level at this area of the settlement and corresponds to the Frankish–Venetian

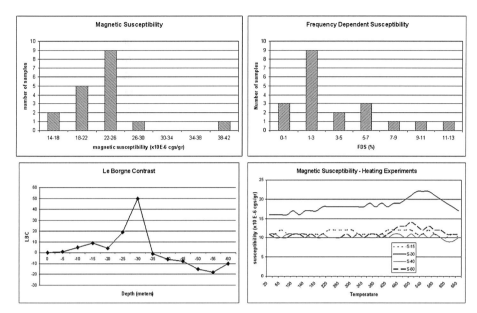

Fig. 21.3 *Histogram of the low-frequency magnetic susceptibility (top left) and of the frequency dependent susceptibility (top right). Variation of the Le Borgne Contrast (magnetic susceptibity vs. depth) (bottom left) and of the surface magnetic susceptibility vs. temperature (heating process under normal environmental conditions) for a limited number of samples (bottom right). Surface susceptibility samples were collected in 1990 in the area of the sanctuary; samples referring to the vertical variation of the susceptibility were collected in the area of the settlement (EU 3).*

period. Upon reaching the maximum value, the susceptibility starts to decline until the last 5 cm (55 cm below the surface), where a second occupation level was identified, consisting of burned soil, black in color, which likely corresponds to the abandonment of the site in the mid-seventh century AD (Toumazou et al. 1998: 175; Toumazou and Counts, Ch. 6). Thus, the low susceptibility values correlate with the gap in occupation during the period of the Arab raids.

The absolute value of the normalized LBC becomes larger than 0.5 at the two "occupation" levels, which implies that the site would be worth prospecting with magnetic methods, even if there is a strong geological magnetic gradient. However, viscosity and frequency dependent susceptibility increased slowly with depth in a quite unstable way. Neither of them indicated any irregularity at 30 cm, suggesting no significant differences in the magnetic domain particle size of the soil samples. Nonetheless, both of them show a substantial increase at the "destruction" level, 55–60 cm below surface.

Similar conclusions were suggested by the heating experiments of the soil samples and the corresponding behavior of the magnetic susceptibility with respect to the increase in temperature (see fig. 21.3). The heating curve of the 30 cm depth sample occurs at a steeper rate than the rest. Together with the 60 cm sample, it indicated a behavior characteristic for single domain particles, increasing to 530° C, after which they decay. The other two samples selected (15 and 40 cm below the surface) remained constant probably due to their paramagnetic nature. In general, single domain behavior of soils suggests anthropogenic activity, indicative of the occupation layers of a site. In contrast, soil samples of paramagnetic character signal geological/natural processes probably associated with the abandonment of the site.

Fast Fourier Transform of the Magnetic Measurements

The Fast Fourier transformation (FFT) of the magnetic data verified the results of the measure-

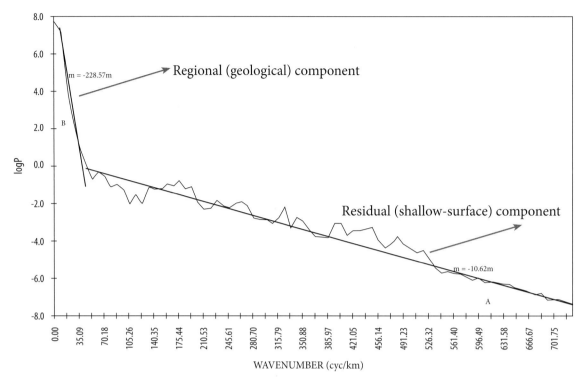

FIG. 21.4 *Results of the power spectrum estimation from the Fast Fourier Transform of the measurements of the total magnetic field intensity. Two different sections of the power spectrum have been identified corresponding to the lower (regional-geological) and the higher (residual-shallower) components. The slope (m) of each segment of the power spectrum is used to calculate the depth of each of the above components (strata).*

ments of the magnetic susceptibility of the soil (Sarris 1992, 1993). As the total magnetic field anomaly can be considered to consist of a regional and a residual (near-surface) component, the graph showing the logarithm of the energy spectrum *vs.* the radial component can be used to estimate the different slopes of the spectrum curve's two parts that are a consequence of the difference in depths between regional and near-surface sources (Spector and Bhattacharyya 1966; Spector and Grand 1970; Spector 1975). The deep geological features are characterized by wave number components that are lower than those resulting from shallower features, and the best-fit straight lines to the spectra (in the least squares sense) have a slope (m) directly proportional to the depth of the features (from the sensor's level). The examination of the power spectrum of the FFT of the magnetic potential field data revealed

two main depths of interest: one from the deep regional geological trends, with a depth of 17.89 m below the surface; and one from the shallow (residual) features, at a depth of 0.55 m below the surface (fig. 21.4). The great depth of the geological trend is not in agreement with the depth of the bedrock (d=0.60–3 m below the surface) found in the excavations of the area, even though in most cases the regional geological trend corresponds to the bedrock. The discrepancy between the two values cannot be easily explained, because there are no detailed records or reports regarding the geological background of the area. A possible explanation for this discrepancy is that the bedrock thickness is quite large, and the power spectrum cannot easily resolve the depth of the geological layer due to its strong, natural magnetic trend (even after the smoothing of the data). Moreover, the roughness of the power spectrum in the average wave number range (30<k<520 cyc/km) is an indication that the upper subsurface level varies in thickness. In contrast, in the very low and very high wave number range (k<30 and >520 cyc/km), the graph of the logarithm of the power spectrum is smooth, without many variations. It may be that there is a deeper, much more magnetic geological formation that influences the values of the slope at this range. So, it is as if we are identifying three layers: one for the upper anthropogenic horizons, another for the usual bedrock, and a third much deeper (and probably much more magnetically influenced) geological formation.

The above results were also confirmed by the experiments conducted in part of the surveyed region using different sensor heights (10 cm, 35 cm, and 70 cm above the ground surface). The rejection of the regional portion of the spectrum (0<k<0.05 cyc/m) eliminated the long range geological trend; but still the non-uniformity of the upper soil layer obscured the surface features of the site. Similar results were exhibited by the application of a Butterworth smoothing filter (rejection of data with a central wave number of 0.05 or 0.5 cyc/m). The strong magnetic geological trend was also responsible for reducing the effect of the downward continuation (to depths of 10 cm, 30 cm, 50 cm, and 90 cm below the surface). However, the difference between the adjacent levels was computed so that the archaeological layer could be established within the range of +/- 20 cm. It was thus indicated that in the area of the sanctuary, the lesser trend existed in the layer at a depth of 50 to 70 cm below the surface (Sarris 1992). In other words, the strong regional magnetic signal masked some of the archaeological anomalies that constitute features of the buried sanctuary.

Magnetic Survey in the Area of the Cemetery

Similar results were drawn from the magnetic survey of a 30 × 20 m region in the area of chamber tombs located northeast and east of the settlement. One of the tombs, Tomb 15, was located directly below the surveyed area, and signs of others were noted at the time of the survey (see fig. 6.1). In this particular sector, the power spectrum of the

FFT suggested that the geological layer (0<k<0.1 cyc/m) lies 6.33 m below the surface, whereas most of the magnetic influence of the upper layer originates from a depth of 1.05 m below the surface, approximately equal to the depth to the top or the center of the looted tombs. Two anomalous magnetic features were recognized and correlated to differences (in color) of the ground vegetation, which is, in some cases, indicative of the existence of tombs.

For experimental reasons, a magnetic survey was also carried out in the interior of Tomb 15, which had been looted. The tomb was located about 1 m below the rocky surface, and its entrance was clear and easily accessible. The shape of the chamber was almost circular, with an average diameter of 4 m (3.10–4.8 m) and its height ranged from 1.10 to 1.50 m. A smaller side chamber (1.90 × 0.85 × 1.10 m) is located in the western part of the tomb. The floor of the tomb consisted of a thin sand layer (20–30 cm below current surface), probably as a result of the heavy erosion of the tomb's walls. It was decided to conduct a detailed survey inside the tomb to recognize any patterns related to remnants left by the looters or any evidence of burial remains.

The magnetic survey was adapted to the constraints of the tomb's dimensions. A grid of 25 cm step interval was laid out inside the tomb prior to the survey. The survey was conducted at midday, in order to have sufficient daylight inside the tomb and to avoid using artificial light, the power source of which could interfere with our measurements. The moving sensor's height was set at 15–20 cm above the tomb's floor, whereas the base station magnetometer was placed outside the tomb at a height of 30 cm, measuring the geomagnetic field simultaneously with the moving magnetometer. The electronics case of the moving magnetometer was placed at the top of the tomb's entrance, to avoid any interference with the sensor inside the tomb.

Two areas of interest in the center of the tomb, characterized by high total magnetic field intensity, were identified through FFT processing of the magnetic potential data: one within the range of 0–0.5 cyc/m corresponding to the deep-lying features (d=1 m below the sensor) and another in the range of 0.5–3 cyc/m corresponding to the shallower features (d=0.3 m below the sensor). A band-pass filter that included the lower portion of the spectrum (o<k<0.5 cyc/m) isolated the regional trends. A high-pass filter passing very high wave numbers (k>2 cyc/m) was successful in recognizing small anomalies and resolving subtle details of the magnetic data. The resemblance between the extra-high-pass (k>2 cyc/m) filtered data and the 30 cm downward continued data suggested that the origin of the small subsurface magnetic variations was located just a few centimeters below the thin layer of the sandy floor. Examination of the high-frequency anomalies of the above maps revealed a few linear features of small width (10–20 cm), aligned in a south–north direction, which are probably caused by metal features. The particular anomalies could have been caused either by funeral votives or by residues of past illegal excavations. Generally, the particular experiment manifested the potential of the magnetic techniques for exploring the interior of the tombs and pinpointing specific features that can be correlated with the location of the graves or later interventions by looters.

The 1994–1995 Survey Seasons

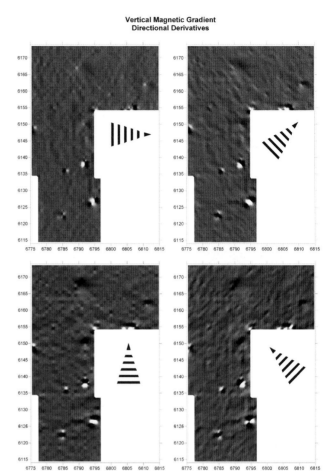

FIG. 21.5　Application of first order directional derivatives to the vertical magnetic gradient measurements. The derivatives were calculated for directions of 0°, 45°, 90°, and 135°.

Having the experience of the 1990 survey season to draw from, in summer 1994, the IMS-FORTH team carried out complementary research using a fluxgate gradiometer (Geoscan Research FM36) and a resistivity meter (Geoscan Research RM15) using the Twin probe array with 1 m separation between the mobile probes. Both data sets were manipulated in a similar way to those obtained in the 1990 survey season. The application of directional derivatives was particularly successful in identifying linear features close to the sanctuary, which were masked by the original drift of the magnetic measurements (due to the temperature variations in the course of the day) (fig. 21.5) and the high range of both magnetic and soil resistance data. The survey provided an enhanced image of

the site suggesting a number of anomalies, some of which are in close correlation to the excavated features of the site (fig. 21.6). A few more linear anomalies were identified to the west and south of that part of the sanctuary exposed at the time, suggesting the continuation of the complex in those directions. In particular, a large number of high-resistance values in the area within and around the sanctuary provided evidence for its extent. Subsequent excavation in part corroborated these findings.

Several experiments employing the GPR were conducted above excavated tombs and cisterns in order to specify the velocity of propagation of the electromagnetic signals (fig. 21.7). Experiments under controlled conditions proved that the GPR

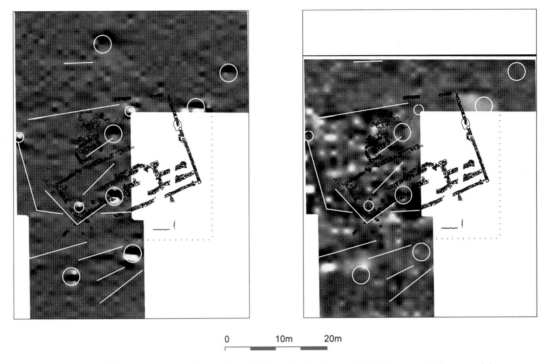

0   10m   20m

FIG. 21.6 *Results of the vertical magnetic gradient (left) and soil resistance (right) surveys in the area of the Malloura sanctuary. The diagrammatic interpretation of the geophysical anomalies and the plan of the excavated sanctuary are overlaid on the corresponding maps. Probable wall extensions are indicated by straight lines; isolated anomalies are represented by circles. Both data sets indicate the extension of the sanctuary to the west and south.*

was able to distinguish — although with some difficulty — pits dug by looters. For example, this kind of measurement right next to Tomb 88 produced satisfactory results, and these data were used for the laboratory processing and the final interpretation of the radar results. Two transects were scanned in the area of the sanctuary (see fig. 21.1), whereas the remaining 15 transects were laid out in the area of the cemetery in the northeastern part of the site.

Similar experiments were performed in the area of the tombs at Mağara Tepeşi (Site 2), where a rock-cut cistern water channel (*laoumi*) had been excavated 2 m below the surface (Toumazou and Counts, Ch. 6). The channel was 30 cm wide and 70 cm high, extending for at least 5 m in a northeast direction toward a small stream 100 m away. It is possible that the channel was part of an irrigation system dated to the Hellenistic–Roman era. The GPR proved successful in detecting the location of the tunnel and traced it for a distance of about 10 m from the east side of Tomb 27 (see figs. 6.6–7).

The radar prospection survey was extended to the flat summit of Mağara Tepeşi. The survey was justified by the findings of the excavations that took place in several rock-cut tombs, such as Tomb 26 (see plan, fig. 19.1). The radar survey was conducted in the vicinity of Tombs 26 and 27, as well as in a few other areas defined as possible tombs either by their closeness to other burial spots or by the vegetation differences that appeared in specific locations. A number of probable archaeological candidates were recognized by the radar data halfway between Tomb 25 and Tomb 26, but subsequent excavation revealed no tomb.

FINAL REMARKS

The archaeological site of Athienou-*Malloura,* with its difficult environmental conditions, constituted a real challenge for the effective application of geophysical prospection techniques. The original total intensity magnetometer and electrical resistance surveys were of limited success in identifying the

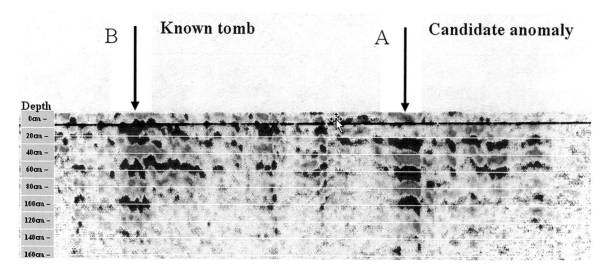

remnants of walls of superimposed buildings and floors. Fragmentary stone and gypsum slabs and concentrations of pottery could not be located. The slab-paved floors of the Venetian building in EU 3 could not create a strong magnetic or resistance contrast with the shallow bedrock, and for this reason their signature was lost within the strong resistance and magnetic regional trend. Processing of magnetic data in both spatial and spectral domains provided some assistance in interpreting the information.

However, the surface maps and their corresponding three-dimensional projection of the low-frequency susceptibility and frequency dependent susceptibility indicated two main areas of interest in close correlation to the maps of the total magnetic field intensity measurements. In the area of the sanctuary, the magnetic susceptibility identified two occupation layers at depths of 30 cm and 60 cm below the surface.

A magnetic survey in the area of the cemetery at the northeast edge of the site yielded several anomalies that showed a partial correlation with the rock-cut tombs. A detailed survey (0.25 m step interval) inside a large looted chamber tomb (Tomb 15) located some interesting areas, probably containing a number of artifacts that were either of archaeological interest or residues left by the looters. Excavation in the interior of Tomb 26, similar to Tomb 15 but in the Mağara Tepeşi section of Malloura, resulted in the discovery of

FIG. 21.7A–B *Controlled experiments above excavated tombs and channels provided an estimate of the EM propagation velocity within the ground. The reflectance signature of an irrigation channel feeding into the dromos of Tomb 27 at Mağara Tepeşi helped trace its projection for at least 10 m within the ground (below). In the area of the northeast cemetery, several reflectors (candidate tombs) have been suggested based on the signature of known looted tombs (above).*

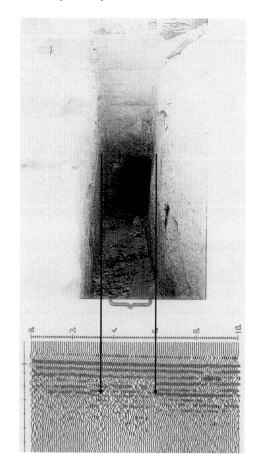

20 silver and bronze coins, scraps of metal vessels and nails, Roman lamps, nearly 1,000 human teeth (corresponding to about 35 individuals), and other smaller artifacts (see Gordon, Ch. 14; Harper and Tung, Ch. 19). It is obvious that geophysical investigations in the interior of the tombs could be very fruitful. Although the GPR had some difficulties in recognizing older pits, it was valuable in recognizing parts of the wall structure of the cemetery and provided some information on the location of possible tombs and the mapping of an irrigation channel's extension at Mağara Tepeşi.

As a nondestructive methodology, geophysical survey offers archaeologists a relatively rapid way of investigating the subsurface to identify features. At Malloura, a suite of techniques was employed in the effort to identify walls associated with the sanctuary and additional tombs at Mağara Tepeşi and the northeast cemetery. In general, the magnetic and electrical methods proved marginally successful in this endeavor, although soil and other conditions limited the effectiveness of certain equipment. Overall, the effort was also important because it created another link between disciplines (archaeology and geophysics). The crossroads theme of this book is thus reflected in professional interaction in the present as well as cultural contacts in the past.

References

Fischer, P.
1980a   Geophysical Prospecting at Hala Sultan Tekke, Cyprus. *Journal of Field Archaeology* 7(4): 479–84.
1980b   The Use of a Metal Detector in Archaeology. *Opuscula Atheniensia* 13(9): 151–53.

Papamarinopoulos, S.; Sarris, A.; and Toumazou, M.
1991   Geophysical Investigations in the Green Belt in Cyprus. Paper presented at the First Conference for the Geosciences and the Environment, Department of Geology, University of Patras, Patras, Greece.
1992   Geomagnetic and Geoelectric Investigations in Athienou-*Malloura*, Cyprus. Paper presented at the International Symposium on Archaeometry (Archaeometry 92), Los Angeles, CA.

Sarris, A.
1992   Shallow Depth Geophysical Investigations Through the Use of Magnetic and Electric Resistance Techniques. Unpublished Ph. D. dissertation, University of Nebraska–Lincoln.
1993   The Importance of the Power Spectrum Analysis in the Study of Shallow Geomagnetic Prospection Data. Paper presented at the Sixth Symposium of Greek Physicists, Komotini.
2008   Remote Sensing Approaches/Geophysical. Pp. 1912–21 in *Encyclopedia of Archaeology*, vol. 3, ed. D. M. Rearsall. New York: Academic.

Sarris, A., and Jones, R. E.
2000   Geophysical and Related Techniques Applied to Archaeological Survey in the Mediterranean: A Review. *Journal of Mediterranean Archaeology* 13: 3–75.

Spector, A.
1975   Application of Aeromagnetic Data for Porphyry Copper Exploration in Areas of Volcanic Cover. Paper presented at the 45th Annual International Meeting of the Society of Exploration Geophysicists, Denver, Colorado.

Spector, A., and Bhattacharyya, B. K.
1966   Energy Density Spectrum and Autocorrelation Function of Anomalies due to Simple Magnetic Models. *Geophysical Prospection* 14: 242–72.

Spector, A., and Grant, F. S.
1970   Statistical Models for Interpreting Aeromagnetic Data. *Geophysics* 35: 293–302.

Toumazou, M. K.; Yerkes, R. W.; and Kardulias, P. N.
1998   Athienou Archaeological Project: Investigations in the Malloura Valley, Cyprus, 1990–95. *Journal of Field Archaeology* 25: 163–82.

Chapter 22

Viewing the Digital Landscape

The Use of GIS in the Malloura Valley Survey

by David P. Massey and P. Nick Kardulias

The central goals of archaeological survey are to determine where people did things in the past and why. Consequently, developing archaeological models that acknowledge and incorporate dynamic environmental and cognitive variables is integral to the interpretation of past landscapes (Renfrew 1994; Doran 1999; Church et al. 2000; Gimblett 2002; Kvamme 2006; Kohler et al. 2007; Wilkinson et al. 2007). Within archaeology, many models developed through Geographic Information Systems (GIS) focus on "site prediction" and often rely exclusively on environmental (quantitative) variables (Judge and Sebastian 1988; for a recent example, see Ford et al. 2009). Although predictive models have been used effectively, particularly in the western United States for the management of large areas of land, they do not necessarily elucidate all the decisions people make about settlement location (Brown 2008). Understanding past landscapes may require archaeologists to consider other forms of modeling, simulating, and visualizing the relationships between spatio-temporal data (Llobera 2003; Christiansen and Altaweel 2006; Andrienko et al. 2007; Kohler et al. 2007; Wilkinson et al. 2007; Huisman et al. 2009).

A goal of the ongoing investigations by the Athienou Archaeological Project (AAP) is to build models that explore the degree to which peripheral landscapes, like the Malloura Valley, were integrated into regional and interregional networks through which people exchanged material resources and information (Toumazou et al. 1998; Kardulias and Yerkes 2004; Kardulias et al., Ch. 1). For example, the sanctuary at Malloura provides evidence for religious syncretism during the period of Phoenician influence and again at the transition from paganism to Christianity. In addition, the archaeological record from the valley, in the form of imported ceramics (see Moore and Gregory, Ch. 15), demonstrates clear connections between the rural sites and the interregional and international economic systems that linked ancient and medieval polities. Supporting this ambitious goal involves many steps, and AAP engaged some of these issues from the outset. Since 1990, the excavation has utilized electronic databases to store critical information recorded in the field as well as inventories of catalogued objects, photographs, and drawings. More recently, we have begun to digitally manage the archaeological knowledge recorded from the AAP survey to examine the settlement dynamics of the Malloura Valley within the context of GIS. This chapter provides a brief discussion of the use of GIS and archaeology, AAP's GIS database and survey, some specific GIS applications that help us interpret site distribution and use, and a guideline for future research.

GIS AND ARCHAEOLOGY

Kenneth Kvamme, one of the first proponents of the use of GIS in archaeology (Kvamme 1980), describes GIS as

> Tools for handling and processing spatially referenced information … allowing easy access to vast amounts of information, new ways of data visualization that promote insight through pattern recognition, and unique methodologies that allow entirely new approaches to study the past (Kvamme 1999: 153).

Today, the use of GIS in archaeology is ubiquitous. Nearly all the data recovered by archaeologists have a spatial component, and the ability of GIS to store, analyze, model, and display spatial data makes it an important tool (Wheatley and Gillings 2002). Some of the earliest adopters of GIS were cultural resource management (CRM) firms analyzing large areas of land to predict and manage archaeological sites in the western part of the United States (Kohler and Parker 1986). As archaeologists became increasingly aware of GIS as an important tool in the 1990s, some post-processualists claimed that the method reintroduced environmental determinism because of its emphasis on features of the physical terrain to the exclusion of cultural factors. Some further argue that the landscapes that humans inhabit are as much ideational as they are natural (Knapp and Ashmore 1999). The resulting debate has led to a bifurcation of the concept of landscape; we reserve discussion of this matter for another publication.

Over the past 15 years, the use of GIS has become standard practice on many archaeological projects throughout the Mediterranean (Foss and Schindler 2005). On Cyprus, researchers have used GIS on the Sydney Cyprus Survey Project (Given

and Knapp 2003), the Troodos Archaeological and Environmental Survey Project (Given et al. 2002), and the Pyla-Koutsopetria Archaeological Project (Caraher et al. 2007). AAP's initial foray into GIS in the mid-1990s utilized the Map II software that had limited ability, but we have adopted the more robust ESRI GIS software since 2001. Most of the GIS applications on Cyprus, as elsewhere, examine regional site and artifact distributions. However, increasingly archaeologists are using GIS to analyze artifact and feature distributions within sites (W. Caraher, personal communication, 2009; see also Blackwell and Johnson, Ch. 23).

AAP GIS DATABASE AND SURVEY METHODS

Due to the Malloura Valley's sensitive location in the United Nations Buffer Zone, it has not been possible to obtain high-resolution geospatial data for this region from the Cyprus Department of Lands and Surveys. As a result, much of AAP's geospatial data were created through the digitization of maps. Our GIS database conceptualizes the Malloura Valley in raster and vector data. Raster data (continuous/field) are made of cells, whereas vector data (discrete/object) consist of points, lines, and polygons. The initial survey data include survey boundaries, tracts, transects, sites, artifact densities, and isolated finds. Other data include rivers, soil, and local roads. Data from the excavation exist in a separate database currently, and we hope to incorporate it into the GIS soon. Our digital elevation model (DEM) was created by digitizing a mosaic of seven georeferenced topographic maps purchased from the Cyprus Department of Lands and Surveys. The contour interval of these maps is 4 m. The DEM permits us to create a three-dimensional image of the project area and to create viewsheds (see below). In addition, several declassified images taken by the United States military CORONA satellite were acquired from the United States Geological Survey as base maps for the investigation.

During the major phase of survey work in the Malloura Valley between 1991 and 1998, locational data about tracts, transects, sites, and isolated finds were recorded by hand on 1:5000

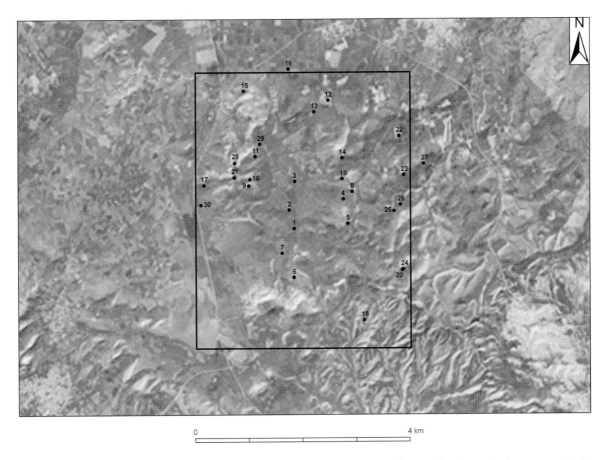

0   4 km

FIG. 22.1 *Map of the Athienou region showing location of sites identified by the Malloura Valley Survey. Project area outlined in black.*

maps. Coordinates were determined in the field by use of a Brunton compass (see Kardulias and Yerkes, Ch. 7). To create digital databases for use with ESRI GIS software programs (initially ArcView, subsequently ArcGIS), teams revisited all the sites between 2001 and 2004 and recorded coordinates with a handheld GPS unit. In addition, the tract and transect data stored in Excel files were imported into ArcView for storage and analysis. Furthermore, project personnel converted the Map II files for use in ArcView and ArcGIS. The conversion process encountered several problems, primary of which was that an improper projection had been used in the initial work. Thus, when we began to generate distribution maps, site locations were offset by about 500 m. This problem required extensive reworking of the databases. To refine the data, many of the 30 sites were visited again to confirm coordinates.

GIS ANALYSIS

To date, AAP has recorded 30 sites in the project area (see Kardulias and Yerkes, Ch. 7). The GIS gives us the ability to portray the distribution of these sites in ways that emphasize several different dimensions of the landscape and can thus assist in determining the factors that informed the selection of locales for particular activities in the past. This process can involve combining several features on one map, which GIS facilitates by creating discrete layers of data that can be combined or examined separately. For example, we can display site location on a base plan of the project area (fig. 22.1), and then combine it with one that shows the distribution of ceramics by time period, thus providing a rapid view of valley use over time (see fig. 7.2). An environmental feature that can have a significant impact on site location is topo-

FIG. 22.2 *Distribution of sites in Malloura Valley shown in ArcScene using the digital elevation model (DEM). View facing southeast from northwest corner of project area.*

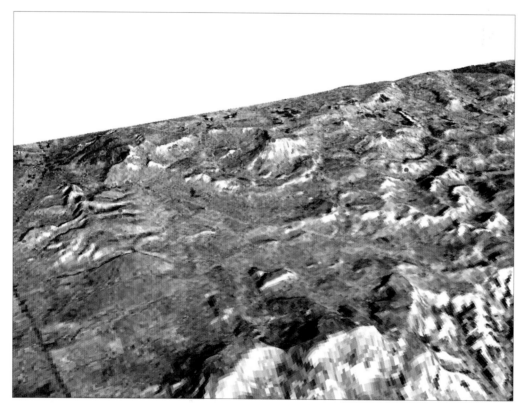

FIG. 22.3 *Distribution of sites in Malloura Valley shown in ArcScene using the DEM. View facing north–northeast from southern edge of project area.*

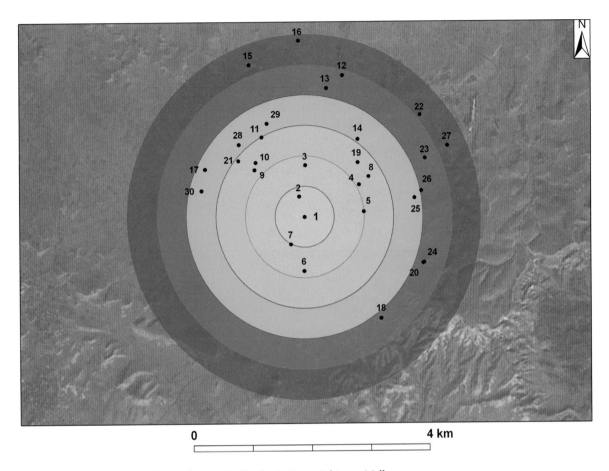

Fig. 22.4 *Site proximity analysis with 500 m buffers beginning at Athienou-Malloura.*

graphic relief. While conventional contour maps offer a way to assess the importance of elevation in site location, a DEM generated by GIS simulates a three-dimensional image that highlights the topographic variability in a settlement system. Not only do such images provide graphical clarity, they also contain detailed elevational data that can give precise quantitative measures of topographic zoning. Furthermore, one can rotate the images to see what the configuration of sites looks like from different angles (figs. 22.2–3).

In addition to their general distribution over a landscape, the proximity of sites to one another is also a critical feature in a settlement system. Based on the fieldwork, an initial hypothesis was that the settlement pattern in the valley was consistently a nucleated one from the Cypro-Archaic period down to the late nineteenth century (Moore and Gregory [Ch. 15] provide a precise breakdown of

site chronology based on ceramics). By placing a series of buffers at 500 m intervals (fig. 22.4) around Malloura, we can demonstrate visually the proximity of all other sites to the main settlement. The buffer map shows Athienou-*Malloura* (Site 1) as a distinct settlement, with the tombs at Mağara Tepeşi (Site 2) and a light scatter of ancient material (Site 7) the only other ancient sites within 1 km. Other substantial concentrations of Roman material are found at Sites 16 and 30, between 2 and 2.5 km distant. Two distinct clusters of sites can be found at a distance of 1–1.5 km to the northeast and northwest. The northeast cluster consists of three modern sites (4, 8, 19) and two ancient to medieval sites (5, 14; see below) on hilltops with good views of the valley. The sites in the northwest cluster (9, 10, 11, 21, 28) are located on Chakmaklik and contain scatters of chert from the local outcrops; they range in date from early prehistoric to modern (see

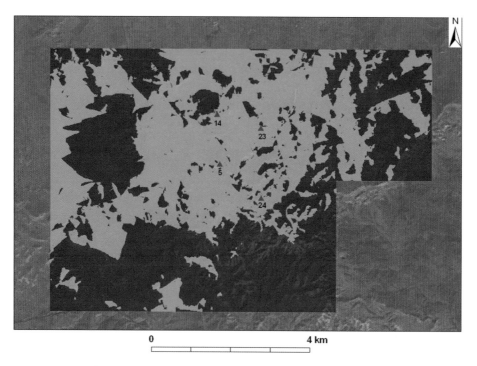

FIG. 22.5 *Cumulative viewshed analysis showing total area visible from Sites 5, 14, 23, and 24.*

Kardulias and Yerkes, Ch. 7). But as extraction or quarry sites with no permanent residents, their close proximity had minimal impact on local settlements other than to act as a source of usable stone.

Knowledge of the precise connections between the archaeological site locations unfortunately existed only in the minds of those who created them. However, several studies (Gaffney et al. 1995; Maschner 1996; Wheatley 1996; Belcher et al. 1999) have suggested that examining the visibility and intervisibility of sites can provide cognitive and perceptual insight into settlement locations. One way of studying visibility is through viewshed analysis, which calculates the raster cells in a DEM that can be seen by an uninterrupted line of sight from a specific point. During the systematic survey we noted that small scatters of ceramics were found on high hills with panoramic views. Between 1993 and 1996, individuals visited several similar topographic settings that were not systematically surveyed and recorded several more such sites. Our primary concern in this work has been to investigate four sites (5, 14, 23, 24) located on hilltops along the eastern edge of the Malloura Valley.

These locations have scatters of late Roman–Early Byzantine and/or late Medieval–Ottoman-period ceramics (Moore and Gregory, Ch. 15); three of the sites also have UN sentry posts. Based on our current DEM (54.4 km², much larger than our survey area) the cumulative viewsheds from these sites show that 46% of the valley is visible from these four locations (fig. 22.5). An offset of 1 m was used.

We have suggested (Toumazou et al. 1998) that the ancient and medieval inhabitants of the valley may have used the sites also to observe activities in surrounding areas, since each site offers a panoramic view of the project area and even as far away as Nicosia. We suspect that in the troubled periods of the Arab raids (seventh century AD) and Ottoman invasion (16th century AD), and perhaps at other times, these vantage points may have served to warn residents of potential danger. The analyses clearly demonstrate the commanding view each of the positions enjoyed and provide strong support for our initial hypothesis concerning the function of these sites. These locales may have operated both in isolation as watch stations and also in conjunction with one another as an integrated system for observation of surrounding areas. While each site has a good to excellent view of the surrounding region, by mutual communication, observers at the sites working as part of an interactive network would have had access to the enhanced view range depicted in figure 22.5. The viewshed and other analyses thus force us to think about how the sites in the Malloura Valley worked as a system, with areas for primary occupation, fields where agricultural activities occurred, and observation posts to provide security for the valley community.

It is important to note that viewsheds do have several limitations. First, they are models, abstractions, and we have not yet accounted for geologic, vegetation, or atmospheric changes over time. Also, these results only apply to the particular area we have chosen, and with the extension of the DEM, the visibility would change. Although this viewshed can calculate the visibility from a location, we plan on expanding this analysis to determine whether the visibility is meaningful by examining the horizontal visual angle from site locations as suggested by Higuchi (1983) and adapted by Llobera (2007).

The GIS can also present the locations of certain artifact classes in the project area. While these artifacts may not be part of clusters that we identified as sites, they may still reflect important use of the landscape in the past. For example, one of our foci is on the agricultural component that was the central activity of valley residents throughout the millennia. The locations of threshing sledge flints (Yerkes and Kardulias 1994; Kardulias and Yerkes 1996) indicate the possible loci of a vital agricultural activity that did not occur at or immediately adjacent to residences or other large installations identifiable as sites (fig. 22.6). We do see, however, a cluster of threshing sledge flints at the northern edge of the project area, in fields near Petrophani. This distribution of the flints primarily to the north and east of the village suggests two things: (1) the use of a traditional implement by the Turkish residents of Petrophani well into the 20th century, and (2) the locations of threshing floors in a slightly elevated location to assist in subsequent

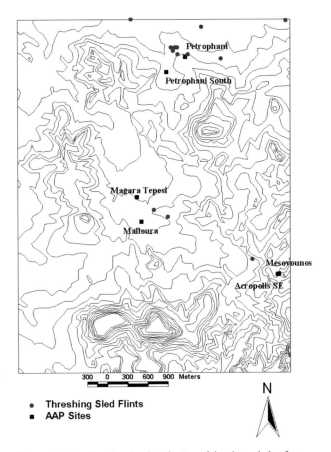

FIG. 22.6 *Map showing the distribution of threshing sledge flints in the project area.*

winnowing. Residents of Athienou have informed us that in the first half of the twentieth century, before mechanical combines replaced the wooden sledges, threshing also took place at the north end of the town because of the prevailing winds in that district. Figure 22.6 also shows the presence of two threshing sledge flints near Malloura and another near the east-central part of the project area. The former pair are to the north and east of Malloura, outside the confines of the settlement but in a location open to the north wind; the isolated piece is in a hilly zone that flanks the valley on the east and may indicate the need to have several locations for threshing when the harvested fields are too distant from where the processed grain would be stored and consumed. In the near future, we will be able to display the distribution of many other classes of artifacts (e.g., ground stone tools [Kardulias 1996], milling stones [see Spigelman, Ch. 17], Late

Roman fine wares, etc.) that will provide insights into how past occupants divided their landscape into identifiable parts based on economic activity, burials or other ritual practices, and ethnic divides (e.g., between Turkish- and Greek-owned land).

CONCLUSION

The work reported here and in the next chapter by Blackwell and Johnson demonstrates how archaeologists are becoming increasingly reliant on spatial technologies to record, store, analyze, and visualize digital information. Today, these approaches include GPS, GIS, Laser Scanning, LiDAR, Remote Sensing (e.g., ground-penetrating radar, magnetometry, and electrical resistivity; see Sarris, Ch. 21), and a wide range of software packages. We need to be careful, however, to use these powerful tools in ways that help us address archaeological questions, and to avoid having the method overpower the basic thrust of the investigation. When used judiciously, the various tools for spatial analysis can facilitate the exploration of what Binford (1982) has called an archaeology of place. By being sensitive to variation and change in our findings, we can assemble more nuanced explanations of how Cypriots have used their landscape over time.

Excavation and survey in the Malloura Valley over the past 20 years have revealed a sequence of occupation from the Aceramic Neolithic to the modern era. Unlike many of the surrounding regions, the Malloura area experienced a consistent system of nucleated settlement, especially in the periods for which there is the best evidence — the Hellenistic, Roman, and late medieval (Frankish) periods. The reasons for this pattern seem to include physiographic, political, economic, and social factors. To sort out the complex web of human-land interaction over a period of 8,000 years, we employed GIS to identify the elements of the various overlapping landscapes that have defined site parameters. Using data from the main site of Malloura in the center of the valley, where excavation and systematic surface collection have demonstrated the presence of the sanctuary dating from the Cypro-Geometric III to Roman period, and a Roman–late medieval village, and from an intensive survey in an area of 20 km², the GIS analysis has generated a settlement model that stresses the role of the area as an extraction zone for raw materials in various periods (see Chase-Dunn and Hall 1997). By examining site proximity, elevation, and viewsheds in the present study (and with future work on hydrology and location of ceremonial sites [the sanctuary and tombs]), we demonstrate how past inhabitants of the valley divided and used space for multiple purposes but always within the constraints of resource availability.

ACKNOWLEDGMENTS

We thank Aaron Fuleki for his work in collecting GPS readings, for converting the Map II files to a form usable in ArcView, and for other tasks associated with creating the GIS databases. We appreciate the advice of Jon Vanderplough who served as a consultant on several GIS issues.

REFERENCES

Andrienko, G.; Andrienko, N.; Jankowski, P.; Keim, D.; Kraak, M.-J.; Maceachren, A.; and Wrobel, S.
2007   Geovisual Analytics for Spatial Decision Support: Setting the Research Agenda. *International Journal of Geographical Information Science* 21(8): 839–57.

Belcher, M.; Harrison, A.; and Stoddart, S.
1999   Analysing Rome's Hinterland. Pp. 95–102 in *Geographical Information Systems and Landscape Archaeology*, eds. M. Gillings, D. Mattingly, and J. van Dalen. Oxford: Oxbow.

Binford, L. R.
1982   The Archaeology of Place. *Journal of Anthropological Archaeology* 1: 5–31.

Brown, A.
2008   Geoarchaeology, the Four Dimensional (4D) Fluvial Matrix and Climatic Causality. *Geomorphology* 101(1–2): 278–97.

Caraher, W.; Moore, R.; Noller, J.; and Pettegrew, D.
2007   The Pyla-Koutsopetria Archaeological Project: Second Preliminary Report (2005–2006 Seasons). *Report of the Department of Antiquities, Cyprus*: 292–306.

Chase-Dunn, C., and Hall, T. D.
1997   *Rise and Demise: Comparing World-Systems.* Boulder: Westview.

Christiansen, J., and Altaweel, M.
2006   Simulation of Natural and Social Process Interactions: An Example from Bronze Age Mesopotamia. *Social Science Computer Review* 24(2): 209–26.

Church, T.; Brandon, R.; and Burgett, G.
2000   GIS Applications in Archaeology, Method in Search of Theory. Pp. 135–55 in *Practical Applications of GIS for Archaeologists, a Predictive Modeling Kit*, eds. K. Westcott and R. Brandon. London: Taylor and Francis.

Doran, J.
1999   Prospects for Agent-Based Modelling in Archaeology. *Archeologia e Calcolatori* 10: 33–44.

Ford, A.; Clarke, K.; and Raines, G.
2009   Modeling Settlement Patterns of the Late Classic Maya Civilization with Bayesian Methods and Geographic Information Systems. *Annals of the Association of American Geographers* 99(3): 496–520.

Foss, P., and Schindler, R.
2005   CGMA: The Collaboratory for GIS and Mediterranean Archaeology, an Undergraduate Teaching and Research Program. Paper presented at the Theoretical Roman Archaeology Conference, Birmingham, England, 2005. http://cgma.depauw.edu/.

Gaffney, V.; Stancic, Z.; and Watson, H.
1995   Moving from Catchments to Cognition: Tentative Steps Towards a Larger Archaeological Context for GIS. *Scottish Archaeological Review* 9/10: 41–64.

Gimblett, H.
2002   Integrating Geographic Information Systems and Agent-Based Technologies for Modeling and Simulating Social and Ecological Phenomena. Pp. 1–20 in *Integrating Geographic Information Systems and Agent-Based Modeling Techniques*, ed. H. Gimblett. Santa Fe Institute Studies in the Science of Complexity. New York: Oxford University.

Given, M., and Knapp, A. B.
2003   *The Sydney Cyprus Survey Project: Social Approaches to Regional Archaeological Survey.* Los Angeles: Cotsen Institute.

Given, M.; Kassianidou, V.; Knapp, A. B.; and Noller, J.
2002   Troodos Archaeological and Environmental Survey Project, Cyprus: Report on the 2001 Season. *Levant* 34: 25–38.

Higuchi, T.
1983   *The Visual and Spatial Structure of Landscapes.* Cambridge: Massachusetts Institute of Technology.

Huisman, O.; Santiago, I.; Kraak, M.-J.; and Retsios, B.
2009   Developing a Geovisual Analytics Environment for Investigating Archaeological Events: Extending the Space–Time Cube. *Cartography and Geographic Information Science* 36(3): 225–36.

Judge, W. J., and Sebastian, L. (eds.)
1988   *Quantifying the Present and Predicting the Past: Theory, Method and Application of Archaeological Predictive Modeling.* Washington, DC: US Government Printing Office.

Kardulias, P. N.
1996   Lithic Implements, Domestic Economy, and Interregional Exchange: The AAP Stone Tools. Paper presented at the 98th Annual Meeting of the Archaeological Institute of America, New York, New York, December 30, 1996.

Kardulias, P. N., and Yerkes, R. W.
1996   Microwear and Metric Analysis of Threshing Sledge Flints from Greece and Cyprus. *Journal of Archaeological Science* 23: 657–66.
2004   World-Systems Theory and Regional Survey: The Malloura Valley Survey on Cyprus. Pp. 143–64 in *Mediterranean Archaeological Landscapes: Current Issues,* eds. E. Athanassopoulos

and L. Wandsnider. Philadelphia: University of Pennsylvania Museum of Archaeology and Anthropology.

Knapp, A. B., and Ashmore, W.
1999   Archaeological Landscapes: Constructed, Conceptualized, Ideational. Pp. 1–32 in *Archaeologies of Landscape: Contemporary Perspectives,* eds. W. Ashmore and A. B. Knapp. Malden, MA: Blackwell.

Kohler, T.; Johnson, C.; Varien, M.; Ortman, S.; Reynolds, R.; Kobti, Z.; Cowan, J.; Kolm, K.; Smith, S.; and Yap, L.
2007   Settlement Ecodynamics in the Prehispanic Central Mesa Verde Region. Pp. 61–104 in *The Model-Based Archaeology of Socionatural Systems,* eds. T. Kohler and S. van der Leeuw. Santa Fe: School for Advanced Research.

Kohler, T. A., and Parker, S.
1986   Predictive Models for Archaeological Resource Location. *Advances in Archaeological Method and Theory* 9: 397–452.

Kvamme, K.
1980   Predictive Model of Site Location in the Glenwood Springs Resource Area. In *A Class II Cultural Resource Inventory of the Bureau of Land Management's Glenwood Springs Resource Area.* Report submitted to U.S. Department of Interior, Bureau of Land Management, Grand Junction District, Colorado. Montrose, CO: Nickens and Associates.
1999   Recent Directions and Developments in Geographical Information Systems. *Journal of Archaeological Research* 7(2): 153–201.
2006   There and Back Again: Revisiting Archaeological Locational Modeling. Pp. 4–62 in *GIS and Archaeological Site Location Modeling,* eds. M. Mehrer and K. Wescott. New York: Taylor and Francis.

Llobera, M.
2003   Extending Visual Analysis: The Concept of *Visualscapes. International Journal of Geographical Information Science* 17(2): 25–48.
2007   Reconstructing Visual Landscapes. *World Archaeology* 39(1): 51–69.

Maschner, H. D. G.
1996   Theory, Technology, and the Future of Geographic Information Systems in Archaeology. Pp. 301–8 in *New Methods, Old Problems: Geographic Information Systems in Modern Archaeological Research*, ed. H. D. G. Maschner. Occasional Paper 23. Center for Archaeological Investigations, Southern Illinois University, Carbondale. Carbondale: Southern Illinois University.

Renfrew, C.
1994   Towards a Cognitive Archaeology. Pp. 3–12 in *The Ancient Mind: Elements of Cognitive Archaeology*, eds. C. Renfrew and E. Zubrow. Cambridge: Cambridge University.

Toumazou, M. K.; Yerkes, R. W.; and Kardulias, P. N.
1998   Athienou Archaeological Project: Investigations in the Malloura Valley, Cyprus, 1990–1995. *Journal of Field Archaeology* 25: 163–82.

Wheatley, D.
1996   The Use of GIS to Understand Regional Variation in Earlier Neolithic Wessex. Pp. 75–103 in *New Methods, Old Problems: Geographic Information Systems in Modern Archaeological Research*, ed. H. D. G. Maschner. Occasional Paper 23. Center for Archaeological Investigations, Southern Illinois University, Carbondale. Carbondale: Southern Illinois University.

Wheatley, D., and Gillings, M.
2002   *Spatial Technology and Archaeology: The Archaeological Applications of GIS.* London: Taylor and Francis.

Wilkinson, T.; Christiansen, J.; Ur, J.; Widell, M.; and Altaweel, M.
2007   Urbanization within a Dynamic Environment: Modeling Bronze Age Communities in Upper Mesopotamia. *American Anthropologist* 109: 52–69.

Yerkes, R. W., and Kardulias, P. N.
1994   Microwear Analysis of Threshing Sledge Flints from Cyprus and Greece: Implications for the Study of Ancient Agriculture. *Helinium* 34(2): 281–93.

Chapter 23

Exploring Sacred Space

GIS Applications for Analyzing the Athienou-*Malloura* Sanctuary

by Nicholas G. Blackwell and James A. Johnson

The production of sacred space has often been considered at the regional and inter-regional levels, most often under the guise of landscapes. This is likely due to the entangled nature of sacred spaces with the emergence of regional socio-political and economic systems. For instance, François de Polignac (1984; 1994: 11) has noted that sacred spaces in the form of rural sanctuaries were produced by and subsequently acted as loci for ritualized social competition visible through dedicatory offerings of prestige goods characteristic of elite relations. He argues that such actions would have concretized social and political networks, strengthened economic ties between smaller regional polities, and served as efficient means of marking territory (de Polignac 1994: 12–13). Alternatively, Katherine Spielmann (2002) has noted among a variety of ethnographically documented societies that strong connections between ritual-based modes of production, value transformation, and economic intensification are intrinsic to the development of communities in small-scale societies; such connections shift the focus from emergent leaders to the strengthening of social bonds between local community members through material practices. This chapter

suggests that the space in between these models (regional, elite-oriented ritual competition and local, ritual-based material practices as the basis for community development) remains largely underexplored and undertheorized. It investigates how small-scale, ritual-based communities were materialized through an analysis of the rural Cypro-Geometric III through Roman sanctuary of Athienou-*Malloura* (Toumazou and Counts, Ch. 6). Utilizing Geographic Information Systems (GIS)-based analyses, depositional patterns of specific object categories within the sanctuary are presented to identify ritual activities and their functional spaces. It is hoped that understanding sanctuary use will elucidate the link between the production of both the sanctuary and its communities.

RITUAL MODES OF PRODUCTION AND COMMUNITIES

Discussions of ritual are often convoluted and contradictory, and one solution, proposed by Catherine Bell (1992: 74), is to refer to the contingencies and strategies that generate and differentiate activities. Spielmann (2002: 195) also argues that many studies of ritual, especially those examining prehistoric ritual activities, have focused predominantly on the emergence of elites and resultant (or causal) economic intensification. She suggests that individual and communal participation in ritual and ceremonial activities has been omitted, and, consequently, we have a poor understanding of how and why communities may intensify their economic activities in response to ceremonial or ritual obligations. Furthermore, A. B. Knapp (2003: 271) has suggested that communities are produced through material conditions constantly reworked according to necessity and localized material realities. Knapp (2003) and others (see Canuto and Yaeger 2000) have indicated that everyday practices can act as centripetal forces for the production of communities.

Drawing upon Benedict Anderson's (1991) notion of "imagined communities," many archaeologists have begun to examine how communities are formed and maintained through socially and historically contingent material practices. This is especially pertinent to the investigation of rural sanctuaries and their place as foci for ritual activities in marginal or peripheral areas, such as votive depositions and sacrifice in the production and reproduction of Cypriot social and political life. Ritual is one of the primary forces in the construction of communities as close-knit, localized social entities or as loose, dispersed groupings. Either manifestation of community would occur at different tempos and scales and through various forms of media. Consequently, we should not be looking for specific patterns of everyday practices alone but rather instances of variation in the spatial distribution of objects in relation to one another to better determine how rural (and other) sanctuaries were utilized by a spectrum of social groups, possibly forming ritual-based communities.

COMMUNITY AND SANCTUARIES IN CYPRUS

The potential complexity between community development and sanctuaries on Cyprus is underscored by a range of economic, socio-political, ideological and/or religious, and demographic elements. For example, the Late Cypriot period witnessed a proliferation of constructed sanc-

tuaries that are often associated with industrial activities. A coexistence of cult and metallurgy is substantiated by two bronze statuettes, each standing upon a miniature oxhide copper ingot, that may have served as protective deities overseeing the island's metallurgical industry (Schaeffer 1965: 56–57; 1971; Knapp 1986; Kassianidou 2005). Kition-*Kathari* (Karageorghis and Demas 1985: 81), Athienou-*Pamboulari tis Koukounninas* (Dothan and Ben-Tor 1983: 140; see also Counts, Ch. 4), Kalopsidha-*Koufos* (Webb 1999: 113–16), and possibly Enkomi (Webb 1999: 113) confirm a metallurgical relationship with prehistoric cults. The broad communities linked to these sanctuaries were complex, representing a blend of individuals probably from various regions with divergent statuses (worshippers, industrial workers, and elites potentially controlling industry and religion).

We should consider the various participants in ritual activities, including specialists or practitioners, as well as different types of visitors to sanctuaries. A range of audiences would have participated in, and formed, different types of social communities, each with an associated locality. Each community member helped produce a sanctuary as a distinct locality, symbolically charged with meaning and imbued with memory and tradition generating a sense of belonging. The following sections examine the spatial distributions and functions of ritual objects through a series of GIS-based analyses to ascertain whether the Athienou-*Malloura* rural sanctuary was a geographic and social destination (and a crossroad) for a multifaceted, ritually-based community.

GIS-BASED ANALYSES
AND ATHIENOU-*MALLOURA*

GIS has become an increasingly important tool for analysis of archaeological phenomena, in particular at the regional level (see Kardulias and Massey, Ch. 22). For example, Wheatley and Gillings (2002: 19–20) have traced the development of the partnership between GIS studies and archaeology, demonstrating the almost exclusive relationship between regional levels of analysis and the use of GIS in archaeological research. GIS can be an equally powerful tool for intrasite analyses (see Hietala and Larson 1984; Kroll and Price 1991); the present study, however, is the first attempt to employ GIS for interpretations of the sanctuary. At its basic level, GIS provides database management that enables the plotting of all artifacts upon the site plan. For instance, spatial clustering of artifacts near architecture (or not) may indicate the functionality of particular sanctuary spaces.

In applying GIS analyses to the Malloura sanctuary, the widespread disruption at the site must be emphasized. The sanctuary experienced pervasive looting in the late 19th and early 20th centuries. Modern excavations have rediscovered fragmentary artifacts that looters threw back into the clandestine pits that were created. Both fragments and whole objects were treated as a count of one so as to determine spatial patterning by object rather than comparing counts of objects or proportions by location within the sanctuary. We have attempted to exclude those objects from the study that were not found in stratified contexts. The results of the distributions, therefore, would be enhanced with a larger, contextually-stratified sample of artifacts.

Because of the disturbed nature of the sanctuary, the refined site chronology is still being worked out in terms of architecture and ceramic phases. The sanctuary spanned the Cypro-Geometric III through Roman periods and had at least three well-defined phases, two of which are separated by a period of reorganization and expansion at the end of the fourth century BC (Toumazou et al. 1998; Toumazou and Counts, Ch. 6; Fourrier, Ch. 9). The sanctuary's mudbrick altar (shown in all figures as a light red polygon) is located in the north-central part of the sanctuary and dates to the Hellenistic period. The earlier altar (or altars) has not been positively identified, although a circular feature with extensive burning located in the western part of the sanctuary may have served that purpose during the Cypro-Archaic period (Toumazou and Counts, Ch. 6; Fourrier, Ch. 9). It is important to note that some of our plot distributions include material from multiple phases, yet we still believe that general patterns of activity and deviances from patterning are discernible. Our distributions examine multiple object types within the sanctuary,

yet the two most prominent object types, terracotta and limestone votaries, are excluded from this analysis. The quantity of these objects necessitates a detailed spatial and chronological investigation beyond the scope of this chapter. Our present analyses indicate that different patterns of ritual activity are visible within the sanctuary through selected groups of artifacts and/or individual artifacts, and these conclusions can be checked by future analysis of the terracotta and limestone dedications. Cultic objects may have been moved throughout the sanctuary at any point, yet the current artifact distributions, regardless of whether in primary or secondary depositional locations, still offer important information regarding particular spaces for ritual activity. Although our study employs GIS (ArcGIS 9.3—ArcMap) merely as a tool for point-distribution plotting, the paper demonstrates the utility of GIS for intrasite analyses and for the spatial interpretation of a heavily looted site. There are more sophisticated capabilities of GIS, and we hope to apply density maps and statistical analyses to our data in the future.

Hypotheses and the Athienou-*Malloura* Artifact Distributions

To help focus and strengthen our analyses, hypotheses were generated to allow us to produce specific queries of the Athienou Archaeological Project database.

Hypothesis 1

If ritual specialists (priests, priestesses, etc.) performed specific activities on a regular basis (daily, weekly, etc.), then we should expect to find areas in sanctuaries that exhibit similarities in the clustered distributions of objects.

Groupings of certain object types are suggestive of standardized locations of ritual activity within the sanctuary. The distribution of *thymiateria* (n=33), or incense burners, incised bones (n=20), and limestone disks (n=70) relates an interesting picture when the objects are compared to one another (fig. 23.1). *Thymiateria* are typical of sanctuaries, and their ritual association is evident. Incised

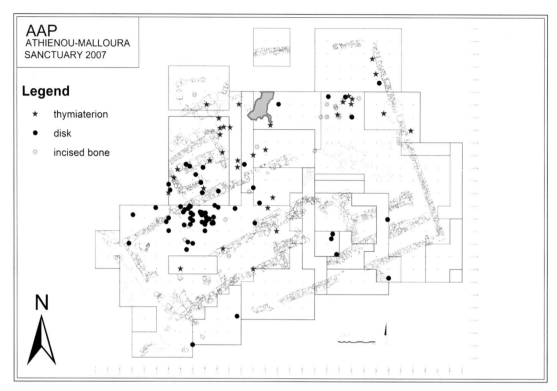

FIG. 23.1 *Plan of Athienou-*Malloura *sanctuary. Spatial distribution of* thymiateria, *incised bone, and limestone disks.*

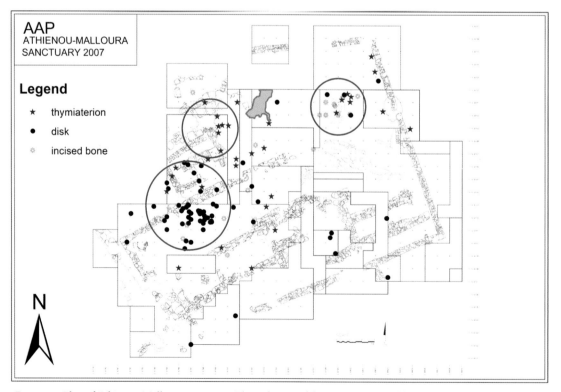

FIG. 23.2 *Plan of Athienou-*Malloura *sanctuary. Three clusters of* thymiateria, *incised bone, and limestone disks highlighted in circles.*

bones, usually scapulae, may have served as para-phernalia in divination rituals (Webb 1985: 325–27; Reese 2002: 184–85; Smith 2009: 159–60) or as musical instruments through rubbing (Karageorghis 1990a: 67, 1990b). Smith (2009: 160) notes that notched scapulae are likely oracular devices used in "apyromatic scapulamancy," as suggested by a Cypro-Archaic scapula from Polis-*Peristeries*. On this bone, a partial Cypro-syllabic inscription preserved the words "asking that," which appears to be formulaic and intended for divination use. Regardless of the purpose of notched scapulae, *thymiateria* and incised bones are ritual objects that are associated spatially at Malloura (for a report on the incised bones from the sanctuary, see Reese, Ch. 18). Moreover, these cultic items reveal clustered patterns with numerous, roughly circular stone objects. These limestone disks are the most enigmatic object type recovered at Malloura. Their function is elusive; they could be either utilitarian or cultic in purpose. The placement of the *thymiateria* and incised bones in relation to the limestone disks sheds light on the nature of the ambiguous items.

The materials mentioned above do not occur in the southwestern or southeastern part of the sanctuary, suggesting a dearth of ritual activity. Yet, three major concentrations of artifacts with potential cultic associations are evident in other areas of the sanctuary (fig. 23.2). The first cluster is in the northeastern open area, with a tight concentration of incised bones (primary object), *thymiateria,* and limestone disks. Another, albeit looser, cluster in proximity to the altar's southwestern side includes *thymiateria* and incised bones but no limestone disks. The most conspicuous artifact cluster appears within an apparent open space in the southwest, with limestone disks (primary object) and incised bones. The latter group may or may not have a cultic affiliation, depending on the interpretation of the limestone disks. The comparable assemblages and localities (e.g., both in open space) between the northeast and southwest clusters suggest a ritual association for both artifact concentrations. These distributions begin to answer our first hypothesis, as "standardized" object clusters are apparent, although some variation is evident.

Deviation from the patterned deposition of items such as the limestone disks, incised bones, and *thymiateria* provide evidence of different types of participation in the ritual activities at Malloura. For example, the distribution of the jugs and juglets warrants further consideration. These objects occur throughout the sanctuary, with a few jugs and juglets found in the artifact concentrations identified above, while the majority is found near walls and possibly in rooms (fig. 23.3). The items are prominent in the southern part of the sanctuary as well as the northwestern section of the site, as currently exposed. Thus, these vessels may have been used in cultic activities, such as libations, in open spaces, while other containers were placed in more restricted areas.

Hypothesis 2

If rural sanctuaries acted as loci for the production of an imagined community, we can expect to find a higher degree of variation in the location of certain types of material assemblages, as the sanctuary itself was the important place (locality) for visitors, not necessarily a specific space within the sanctuary.

While a range of divine iconographic types have been identified among the statuary discovered at Malloura, including those types commonly referred to as Zeus Ammon or Baal-Hammon, Herakles, Apollo, Artemis, Bes (dating primarily to the Cypro-Archaic and Cypro-Classical periods), large concentrations of fragmentary statuettes displaying the iconography of the Greek god Pan (n=38) are associated with the Hellenistic phase of the sanctuary (fig. 23.4) (Cofer, Ch. 12, refers to the type as "Cypriot Pan"). The distribution of these divine images indicates an especially strong association with the Hellenistic *temenos* and the east-central area of the sanctuary. The deposition of Hellenistic temple boys, however, is much more dispersed. Comparatively, the clustering of the "Cypriot Pans" near the eastern *temenos* wall is conspicuous. While the iconography of Pan becomes popular within the sanctuary sometime during or immediately before the Hellenistic period (Cofer 2001), the spatial disjunction between Pans and temple boys alone seems incongruous

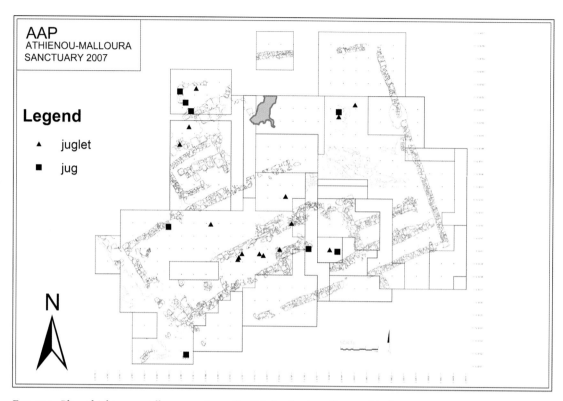

FIG. 23.3 *Plan of Athienou-*Malloura *sanctuary. Spatial distribution of jugs and juglets.*

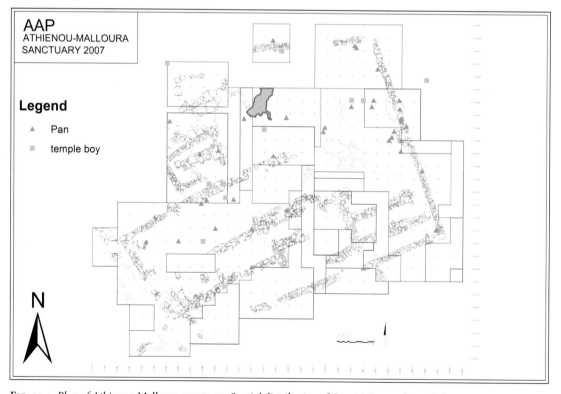

FIG. 23.4 *Plan of Athienou-*Malloura *sanctuary. Spatial distribution of Cypriot Pan and temple boys.*

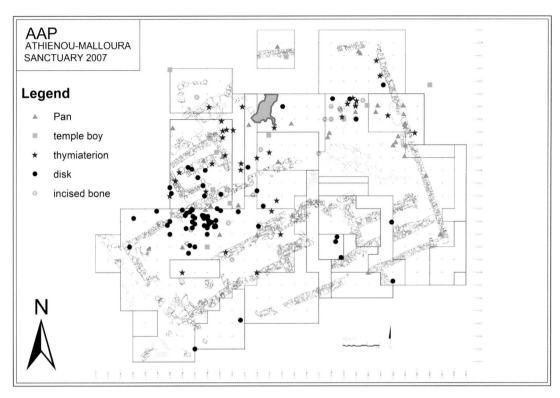

FIG. 23.5 *Plan of Athienou-*Malloura *sanctuary. Spatial distribution of Cypriot Pan, temple boys,* thymiateria, *incised bones, and limestone disks.*

with the notion of ideologically or symbolically linked community members.

When the spatial patterning of the Cypriot Pan statuettes and temple boys is combined with other artifact distributions, three distinct artifact clusters appear (fig. 23.5; these object clusters were first highlighted in fig. 23.2). The inclusion of Pan and temple boys within the clusters further validates these spaces as localities of ritualized activity. Although variation exists in the concentrations, there are three to five items that are grouped (tightly or loosely) in three different spaces. Pans, temple boys, and incised bones occur in all three cluster areas. Limestone disks occur in the southwestern and northeastern groupings, while *thymiateria* appear in the northeastern and altar clusters. It is unclear what type of ritual activity occurred, but it is significant that at least two of these clusters (southwest and northeast) are affiliated with open space. Since we have similar material assemblages in divergent locations, the evidence appears to support our stated hypothesis. Clearly

there is a certain degree of variation in the location of ritual performances. This flexibility may have resulted from multiple open spaces, which would allow groups to assemble and participate in cultic activities collectively.

Hypothesis 3

Given the range of audiences utilizing the sanctuary as a mode of communication and loci for ritual activity, we should expect to find more heterogeneity in the material assemblages away from areas where ritual specialists performed, such as altars.

Some of our distributions hint at a greater heterogeneity away from areas of ritual performances, yet we would be better equipped to address this statement with different object distributions. Despite some relatively clear patterns developing, this hypothesis was difficult to test. It assumes that objects remained in the locations where visitors deposited them, and it fails to account for sanctuary regulations. An example of general maintenance is evident from the fact that objects from the sanctuary's earlier phases were moved during the period of reorganization. Although there is general heterogeneity throughout the sanctuary, a detailed study of the distributions of the limestone and terracotta votaries could better address this hypothesis (for general discussions of terracotta and limestone sculpture from the sanctuary, see Averett, Ch. 10, and Counts, Ch. 11, respectively).

Spatial Analysis of the Athienou-*Malloura* Sanctuary

Standard or normative views of archaeological analysis and interpretation suggest that it is through the identification and analysis of patterned depositions of artifacts that we can begin to understand past human behavior. Yet, for social and ritual phenomena such as religious activities at rural sanctuaries, patterned deposits may not be the only thing for which we should be looking, and the possibility (and value) of singular actions by individuals and small groups needs to be taken into account. In other words, social processes such as ritual are multiscalar activities that should be investigated from various perspectives, including individual/group and synchronic/diachronic. With this in mind, the GIS-based analysis of our selected artifact distributions revealed some intriguing aspects of the use of sanctuary space and possibilities for the interpretation of community participation. The distribution of materials at Athienou-*Malloura* indicates that multiple areas might have been used for ritual performances. Perhaps more important is that some spaces were not directly affiliated with the altar, the assumed focal point of ritual activities within the rural sanctuary. Three general areas of the sanctuary, which are summarized below, were highlighted by our analysis.

Nonritual Spaces

The *temenos* wall most likely delineates the sacred from the profane, marking a boundary between interior and exterior space. Therefore, it is surprising that there is a lower concentration of artifacts in the southwestern and southeastern corners of the sanctuary. Although these spaces are within the *temenos* walls, the lack of examined objects from these areas reveals a dearth of ritual activities. There is clearly a functional difference in the southern corners of the sanctuary compared to the northern sections.

Open Areas with Ritual Object Clusters

There are two distinctive open spaces within the sanctuary, located in the southwestern and northeastern areas of the site. Object clusters are found in both localities, which appear to be spaces for ritual performances and possibly audience participation. These clusters include incised bones, limestone disks, Cypriot Pan and temple boy statuettes or fragments, and *thymiateria* (only in the northeast cluster). The exact nature of the limestone disks is uncertain, and the ritual affiliation of the northeastern cluster is stronger than the southwestern, as the latter is primarily composed of limestone disks. The combination of the incised bones, Pans, and temple boys may demonstrate that the limestone disks in the southwestern concentration were also sacred in nature. Although the principal deity of the sanctuary is unknown, it is intriguing that Pans appear in both open-space clusters. It is noteworthy that these two loci for ritual performances occurred in locations other than the altar itself. This is not to say that the northeast cluster was not associated with the altar; the northeastern open space in fact had unimpeded access to the altar. Yet it is possible that rituals were practiced in this locality due to the open space rather than because of the altar's proximity. The location of incised bones, utilized for divination and/or music, in these exposed areas may suggest oracular activities or other ritual performances such as dance.

Object Cluster near Altar

A third, rather loose bunch of artifacts occurs directly southwest of the altar, and these objects are significant for their proximity to the mudbrick altar. This grouping is represented by *thymiateria,* incised bones, temple boys, and Pans. The cluster resembles the other two artifact concentrations identified, except that the altar area grouping lacks limestone disks. The four object types represented in this cluster are all ritual objects whose function is only strengthened by the altar's propinquity.

RURAL SANCTUARIES AND THE PRODUCTION OF SACRED SPACE

Rural sanctuaries have been framed primarily as responses to developments of urban centers or cores, including territorial markers (de Polignac 1994). Such interpretations, however, omit explanations for the actions that can help define sanctuaries in terms of social and ritual interaction among local populations, visitors (pilgrims), and ritual specialists. To what extent did individual and group rituals at sanctuaries strengthen social bonds for community development? Were rural sanctuaries marginal loci in comparison to the surrounding social and political landscapes, or were rural sanctuary locations deliberate, meaning to induce acts of pilgrimage and attrition through ritual acts of sacrifice and votive deposition? Such questions may be addressed when artifact assemblages are considered not only within their contexts but also in terms of general patterns and instances of deviation from those patterns.

Detailed knowledge of spatially delineated ritual activities within Cypriot sanctuaries is surprisingly limited. Cultic behavior must have been more complex than simply depositing a dedicatory object near an altar. It is unclear whether worship at shrines was intended for individual or group experiences. Religious spaces are often locations of performance such as sacrifices, feasts, dances, or even role-playing activities with masks. Yet, it is difficult for us (as archaeologists) to identify distinct sensory experiences for both performers and audiences. The distribution of *thymiateria* in the Malloura sanctuary, however, indicates one potential avenue for exploring such sensory experiences. Lamps, which were not covered in this analysis, would also have altered or enhanced visibility, while *thymiateria* may have manipulated the sanctuary's smell and character. Lamps could

also reveal distinctions between open spaces and areas near walls, leading to questions of use of closed vs. open spaces and whether nocturnal activities occurred at Malloura. The incense burners were found more frequently near the altar, possibly indicative of smell as an important aspect of worship. Assessing the various sensory experiences represents an excellent arena for future research.

CONCLUSION

This study attempted to determine whether materials deposited at the Athienou-*Malloura* rural sanctuary were the result of participation in either a regional socio-ideological polity, as suggested by de Polignac (1984,) or smaller-scale, ritual-based communities, as suggested by Spielmann (2002). If visitors were coming from farther away and less frequently, items would be deposited in a more random fashion, as those visitors would most likely not have developed preferences for where to place objects. Visitors from the local area, however, would be expected to be more intimately aware of the sanctuary, to visit more often, and possibly even to have developed traditions for where to place their dedicatory offerings. Perhaps one of the most persistent issues is the geographic origin of the objects. If items were produced locally and used by either local or nonlocal visitors to the sanctuary, they would fit very neatly into Spielmann's model of ritual production that leads to local economic intensification. This scenario would suggest that rural sanctuaries were not necessarily subject to larger socio-political units, such as the Cypriot city-kingdoms, but rather may have functioned independently. But, if items were produced nonlocally and were carried by visitors travelling from varying distances, this would indicate that rural sanctuaries (and rural populations in general) were most likely parts of broader socio-political systems. In either case, rural sanctuaries became specific localities that evoked notions of belonging and tradition, which in turn would have led to the production of imagined communities substantiated in the geographic and social periphery.

The distribution of materials from Athienou-*Malloura* conforms to some of our expectations.

Unfortunately, our analyses did not discern whether regional elites, pilgrims, locals, or some combination of these formed the audience base for the Malloura ritual community. Variety in object value (bronze objects vs. simple limestone disks, as well as quality of workmanship for votaries) reflects one future method for evaluating the mix of individuals that utilized the site. Despite being unable to differentiate locals from pilgrims, we believe that the Malloura sanctuary was a focal point for various populations and exhibits the possibility for community-based ritual activities. Such practices at Malloura are highlighted by the dispersed nature of both material clusters and individual finds. For example, by the Hellenistic period, clusters of Pan objects appear near the eastern *temenos,* yet temple boys lack a strong spatial association with Pan-related artifacts despite their possible contemporaneity. When combined with other artifact groupings (limestone disks, *thymiateria,* incised bones), Pans and temple boys can be distinguished as components of distinct clusters of symbolically charged materials. For instance, three clusters indicating ritual activity have been identified through this analysis. Two of these clusters are found in open areas, indicating possible group ritual activities, while the third cluster is located around the altar. The northeastern space of the Malloura sanctuary, following the late fourth century BC, consisted of a ritually charged, hard-packed floor composed of outdated Cypro-Archaic and Cypro-Classical limestone and terracotta votaries reused as construction fill (see Toumazou and Counts, Ch. 6). The sanctuary's reorganization and expansion during this phase seem to have created a larger space for groups to gather and participate in ritual activities. If this is the case, we have an excellent example of the production and elabora-tion of sacred space for a potentially diverse and, as of yet, undefined community.

Based on the results of this preliminary analysis, current models for the nature and role of rural sanctuaries need to be amended. Recent work has indicated that variation in assemblages highlights the influences on the production and deposition of certain categories of materials, which in turn leads to the production of hybrid identities subject to space-time relational contexts (Counts 2008). Rural sanctuaries and their material assemblages need to be examined before testing regional models espousing domination of peripheries by urban centers. Kardulias (2007; Kardulias and Hall 2008) has noted that peripheries often negotiate the terms in which these areas interact with cores or urban centers. Thus, without investigating intrasite phenomena, we omit crucial lines of evidence when trying to better understand societal change on Cyprus and other geographical areas where similar developments occur.

ACKNOWLEDGMENTS

We would like to thank Michael Toumazou, Nick Kardulias, and Derek Counts for all the support and encouragement offered to both of us over the years , including reading several drafts of this chapter. Our participation in the Athienou Archaeological Project at Athienou-*Malloura* has been productive and formative to our budding careers. We gratefully used the Athienou-*Malloura* site plans created by Remko Breuker when forming our GIS images. In addition, we thank Brian Nicholls (University of Wisconsin-Milwaukee), for offering much needed guidance during the completion of the analysis.

REFERENCES

Anderson, B.
1991   *Imagined Communities: Reflections on the Origin and Spread of Nationalism.* Revised edition. London: Verso.

Bell, C.
1992   *Ritual Theory, Ritual Practice.* Oxford: Oxford University.

Canuto, M., and Yaeger, J. (eds.)
2000   *The Archaeology of Communities: A New World Perspective.* London: Routledge.

Cofer, C.
2001   Relief-Statuettes of Pan from the Mesaoria Valley of Cyprus: Evidence from the Sanctuary of Athienou-Malloura. M.A. thesis, Bryn Mawr College.

Counts, D. B.
2008   Master of the Lion: Representation and Hybridity in Cypriote Sanctuaries. *American Journal of Archaeology* 112: 3–27.

de Polignac, F.
1984   *Cults, Territory and the Origins of the Greek City-State.* Chicago: University of Chicago.
1994   Mediation, Competition, and Sovereignty: The Evolution of Rural Sanctuaries in Geometric Greece. Pp. 3–18 in *Placing the Gods: Sanctuaries and Sacred Space in Ancient Greece,* eds. S. Alcock and R. Osborne. Oxford: Clarendon.

Dothan, T., and Ben-Tor, A.
1983   *Excavations at Athienou, Cyprus, 1971–1972.* Jerusalem: Institute of Archaeology, Hebrew University of Jerusalem.

Hietala, H., and Larson, P.
1984   *Intrasite Spatial Analysis in Archaeology.* Cambridge: Cambridge University.

Karageorghis, V.
1990a   *Tombs at Palaepaphos.* Nicosia: A. G. Leventis Foundation.
1990b   Miscellanea from Late Bronze Age Cyprus II. A Late Bronze Age Musical Instrument? *Levant* 22: 159.

Karageorghis, V., and Demas, M.
1985   *Excavations at Kition V: The Pre-Phoenician Levels. Areas I and II.* Part 1. Nicosia: Department of Antiquities, Cyprus.

Kardulias, P. N.
2007   Negotiation and Incorporation on the Margins of World-Systems: Examples from Cyprus and North America. *Journal of World Systems Research* 13(1): 55–82.

Kardulias, P. N., and Hall, T.
2008   Archaeology and World-Systems Analysis. *World Archaeology* 40(4): 572–83.

Kassianidou, V.
2005   Was Copper Production under Divine Protection in Late Bronze Age Cyprus? Some Thoughts on an Old Question. Pp. 127–41 in *Cyprus: Religion and Society from the Late Bronze Age to the End of the Archaic Period. Proceedings of an International Symposium on Cypriote Archaeology, Erlangen, 23–24 July 2004,* eds. V. Karageorghis, H. Matthäus, and S. Rogge. Möhnesee-Wamel: Bibliopolis.

Knapp, A. B.
1986   *Copper Production and Divine Protection: Archaeology, Ideology and Social Complexity on Bronze Age Cyprus.* Göteborg: Åström.
2003   The Archaeology of Community on Bronze Age Cyprus: Politiko *Phorades* in Context. *American Journal of Archaeology* 107: 559–80.

Kroll, E., and Price, T. D.
1991   *The Interpretation of Archaeological Spatial Patterning.* New York: Plenum.

Reese, D. S.
2002   On the Incised Cattle Scapulae from the East Mediterranean and Near East. *Bonner Zoologische Beiträge* 50(3): 183–98.

Schaeffer, C. F. A.
1965   An Ingot God from Cyprus. *Antiquity* 39: 56–57.
1971   *Alasia I: Première série.* Paris: Mission archéologique d'Alasia.

Smith, J. S.
2009   *Art and Society in Cyprus from the Bronze Age into the Iron Age.* New York: Cambridge University.

Spielmann, K.
2002   Feasting, Craft Specialization, and the Ritual Mode of Production in Small-Scale Societies. *American Anthropologist* 104(1): 195–207.

Toumazou, M. K.; Yerkes, R. W.; and Kardulias, P. N.
1998   Athienou Archaeological Project: Investiga-
        tions in the Malloura Valley, Cyprus, 1990–
        1995. *Journal of Field Archaeology* 25: 163–82.

Webb, J. M.
1985   The Incised Scapulae—Appendix VI. Pp.
        317–28 in *Excavations at Kition V. The Pre-
        Phoenician Levels, Areas I and II,* Part 2, ed.
        V. Karageorghis. Nicosia: Department of
        Antiquities, Cyprus.

1999   *Ritual Architecture: Iconography and Practice
        in the Late Cypriot Bronze Age.* Studies in
        Mediterranean Archaeology and Literature
        Pocket-Book 75. Jonsered: Åström.

Wheatley, D., and Gillings, M.
2002   *Spatial Technology and Archaeology: The
        Archaeological Applications of GIS.* London:
        Taylor and Francis.

Chapter 24

The Chemistry of Malloura

Adventures in Anthrosol Analysis

by Ruth F. Beeston

Because excavation is one large, unrepeatable experiment, archaeologists routinely and systematically collect samples of soil retrieved from each excavated layer. Samples are carefully bagged, labeled, sorted, and stored. But for what purpose? What possible value might there be in these bags of sediment from the past? Clues in the soil—changes in color, texture, porosity, dampness, or other properties—help differentiate stratigraphic layers. In addition, soil is the matrix that surrounds the features and artifacts being uncovered. The characteristics of the soil determine the burial environment and therefore the fate or condition of the objects it encases. The processes by which various materials decompose, and therefore the extent to which they are preserved, depend on factors such as temperature, moisture, acidity (pH), oxygen, and the activity of organisms—from rodents and insects to mold and bacteria. Soil chemistry, therefore, plays a role in protecting against or accelerating deterioration of material remains, and understanding that role is important. But an even more fundamental reason to save these samples for further study is that the soil is itself an artifact. A soil sample may contain evidence in the form of alterations in soil chemistry that are a direct result of past human activity.

The term "anthrosols" has been coined to describe soil and sediment samples that have been modified by the presence of humans. The ability of certain particles within soil to attract and hold ions means that these particles can retain evidence of substances with which they came in contact, an ability that is referred to as "soil memory" (Wells 2006: 126). Some soil types are better than others at preserving this information. Furthermore, different activities (e.g., food preparation and consumption, disposal of refuse, burial of remains, burning of fuel, agricultural and craft practices, the deposition of human and animal excrement) will result in different sorts of soil chemistry changes. Since the extent of the changes (the concentrations of adsorbed ions) depends on the intensity of human activity at the site, the soil can provide a link, through chemical analysis, to patterns of occupation, land use, and function.

The scientific analysis of anthrosols is gaining increased attention in archaeological studies, but it is not a new method; the use of soil chemistry as a means of archaeological "prospecting" dates back to the 1930s (Bethell and Máté 1989: 1–2). The most commonly studied, human-derived soil additives are phosphates, compounds containing the PO_4^{3-} ion. Phosphates are derived from both mineral and biological sources; phosphorus is a component of all living cells and is an important ingredient in bones and teeth, nucleic acids, and numerous other biomolecules. Along with carbon and nitrogen, phosphorus is added to soil when biological material — plant, animal, or human — is discarded or buried and then decays. Natural cycles exist in which carbon and nitrogen are depleted from the soil, but phosphorus is incorporated into the soil in the form of insoluble phosphate compounds that build up and then remain at elevated levels for long periods of time. The relative amounts of phosphate in the soil can therefore act as an "indicator of the extent, duration, and nature of past human habitation" (Goffer 2007: 227).

It is quite likely, for example, that the soil has already been altered in the area under and around the "lunch hut," where AAP students and personnel gather each day during the excavation season for a simple meal of village bread, cheese, salami, cucumber, tomato, and, best of all, dripping slices of *karpouzi* (watermelon). If one were to compare the chemistry of the soil that received the drippings and droppings on a daily basis, it would differ perceptibly from that of the hillside behind it. The soil phosphate is undoubtedly increasing from year to year, although perhaps not as fast as it would in a grave or under an outhouse, trash heap, or fire pit. But some day, long after the tin roof has blown away and the flies have given up hope, the chemical imprint of those gatherings will remain in that spot.

In addition to indicating past cultural activity, phosphates can be present in or introduced into soil by a variety of other sources, such as the weathering of phosphate minerals in nearby geological formations. For that reason it is important to obtain samples from surrounding areas that are removed from the archaeological features in order to assess "background" levels. Phosphate may also be introduced via agriculture (fertilizer) and wastewater runoff. Many detergents and pesticides contain significant amounts of phosphate, and the possibility of contamination of samples by these modern sources must be considered in interpreting analytical results.

OVERVIEW OF STUDIES AT MALLOURA

The earliest uses of soil phosphate analysis in archaeology involved the location and delineation of sites by defining areas where phosphate levels were enriched relative to surrounding areas. And, in fact, at Malloura the initial goal of this collaboration was to look for a missing settlement, a village contemporary with the sanctuary, in which the individuals who were buried in the chamber tombs at Magara Tepeşi spent their better days. But over the course of five seasons (1999, 2001, 2004, 2005, 2007) the scope of this study of the chemistry of Malloura widened. The individual projects conducted during these seasons involved the following:

1) Exploration of phosphate analysis methodology, including the comparison of results from quantitative spectrophotometric analyses conducted in the chemistry labs at Davidson College to observations from simple "spot tests" conducted in the field and to phosphorus levels determined by ICP-AES (inductively coupled plasma atomic emission spectroscopy).

2) Verification that a correlation exists between phosphate levels and other indicators of human activity in the soil at Malloura. Phosphate levels in samples obtained from tombs and from vertical profiles above and within cultural levels of the sanctuary were compared.

3) Sampling and analysis of soil from a hillside near the sanctuary as well as along a portion of a trench dug by the town for a water-line installation. High levels of phosphate were sought as possible evidence for the existence of a settlement at that location.

4) Investigation of several small tombs revealed along the water-line trench. Some of these tombs were empty (no evidence of human remains), yielding only small ceramic vessels.

5) Use of soil chemistry to predict the location of the altar in the sanctuary, by measuring and mapping phosphate levels from the hard-packed layer corresponding to the sanctuary floor.

6) Phosphate and multi-elemental analyses of the unusual industrial structure (EU 2) in an attempt to discern the possible function of this building. Multi-elemental analyses by ICP-AES of extracts from EU 2 samples were conducted at the University of South Florida in collaboration with Christian Wells.

A further goal of this collaboration from the beginning has been the education of undergraduate students and other project participants. Field school students were exposed to the important role of chemistry in archaeology through both an evening lecture each season and participation in soil chemistry workshops. Several of the students conducted independent projects on topics related to archaeological chemistry. At Davidson, students enrolled in an advanced laboratory methods course participated in the analysis of soil samples from Malloura in 2001. And in 2007, a Davidson College chemistry major joined the AAP team for several weeks and had the opportunity to participate in the sanctuary excavation as well as the ongoing study of the chemistry of Malloura, both in the field and in the research lab at Davidson.

Methods

The analysis of phosphate in soil requires a series of steps, including sampling, drying, sieving, and treatment of the powdered sample with an extractant solution (usually an acid) that dissolves some portion of the phosphorus compounds in the soil. The resulting soil extract is then treated chemically with a reagent or series of reagents that react with phosphate to produce a colored complex. The intensity of the solution color depends on the phosphate concentration in the extract and can be assessed qualitatively (e.g., light, medium, dark) or quantitatively, by measuring with a spectrophotometer the amount of light absorbed at some characteristic wavelength. The results are compared to those obtained for standard solutions, containing known quantities of phosphate, in order to convert absorbance values into phosphate concentrations in the extract and, ultimately, to determine the amount of phosphate in the soil in parts per million (mg PO_4^{3-}/kg soil).

Unfortunately, a vast number of variations on the above theme have been reported in the literature (e.g., Bethell and Máté 1989: 10–13). The chemistry of soil is exceedingly complex, and phosphorus can be tied up in various compounds with other elements and in different forms within the heterogeneous mixture making up the soil. Depending on the procedure chosen, one may measure available phosphate (that which is made soluble by a weak acid extractant and is available for uptake by plants), inorganic phosphate (or some portion thereof), organic phosphate, or total phosphate. Because soil composition varies considerably, it is not clear which of the published methods is most appropriate in terms of obtaining archaeologically significant results in general, or with Cypriot soil in particular. At Malloura we were primarily interested in comparison of samples within the site, rather than precise determination of total phosphate or discrimination between organic and inorganic phosphates. We were interested in demonstrating a correlation between measured phosphate levels and other indicators of human activity, and in exploiting that correlation to gain insights regarding the nature of the cultural activity at Malloura. Most important to this study was the development of a quantitative spectrophotometric method that could be consistently applied to all samples and used to correlate the results of other methods (such as the spot test and ICP-AES). Experimental procedures for the methods we chose are described below.

Sampling and Preparation

Soil samples were collected from the field using a soil auger and metal spoon. Other samples were obtained during excavation or from bags stored from previous seasons. All samples were placed in plastic bags (Whirl Pak®) and carefully labeled. A portion of each sample was transferred to a small porcelain crucible and oven-dried overnight at 100°C (for quantitative method) or air dried (spot test). After drying, the soil was crushed lightly with the end of a glass stirring rod, then screened using a #60 soil sieve. All glassware used for the analytical procedures was washed with phosphate-free detergent and rinsed with deionized water, which was used for preparation of all solutions.

Extraction and Analysis: Quantitative Method

The quantitative method was derived from a literature method (Sánchez et al. 1996: 152–55). It relies on 2.00 M HCl as the extractant and Murphy Riley reagent for the spectrophotometric determination. Murphy Riley reagent was made fresh each day by mixing 100 mL 2.5 M sulfuric acid, 30 mL ammonium molybdate solution (40.0 g/L), 10 mL potassium antimonyl tartrate solution (2.27 g/L), and 60 mL ascorbic acid solution (1.67 g/L). The standard phosphate stock solution contained 0.105 g ammonium biphosphate (NH_4HPO_4) in 500 mL 2.00 M HCl.

For each soil sample, a 0.100 g portion was transferred into a 17 × 100 mm disposable polystyrene test tube; 5.00 mL of 2.00 M HCl was added slowly by pipette (a vigorous neutralization reaction occurs, causing effervescence as CO_2 is released from the calcium carbonate in the soil). The tube was covered with parafilm, shaken gently, then placed in a beaker of water in an ultrasonic bath for 15 minutes. After centrifugation for five minutes, a 1.00 mL portion of the clear extract was transferred to a 50 mL volumetric flask. Murphy Riley reagent (10.0 mL) was added by pipette, and the flask was filled to the mark with deionized water. Exactly 30 minutes after addition of Murphy Riley reagent, the solution was transferred to a 1.00 cm cuvette, and its absorbance was measured at 605 and 885 nm using a Cary 300 BIO UV-visible spectrophotometer. During the 30-minute interval, a blue color develops in the solution as a polymolybdophosphate complex is formed (a time- and temperature-dependent process). The intensity of the blue color, as measured by absorbance at these wavelengths, is directly proportional to the phosphate concentration in the extract.

Typically, 14 samples were processed at the same time. After the 1.00 mL portions of each extract were transferred into volumetric flasks, the Murphy Riley reagent was added to consecutive flasks at two-minute intervals. Absorbance measurements were also timed such that a constant interval of 30 minutes passed between addition of reagent and measurement of absorbance for each extract.

Because of a variety of factors, it was necessary to analyze a "blank" and a series of four phosphate standards on the same day as the analysis. This involved transferring 0, 0.200, 0.400, 0.600, or 0.800 mL of the phosphate stock solution along with 1.00, 0.800, 0.600, 0.400, or 0.200 mL, respectively, of 2.00 M HCl to additional 50 mL volumetric flasks. These flasks were then processed in the same way as the flasks containing soil extracts. Calibration curves were prepared from the absorbance results of the standards at each wavelength and the known mass of PO_4^{3-} in each standard (0 mg, 0.030 mg, 0.060 mg, 0.090 mg, and 0.120 mg, respectively). Linear regression analysis was utilized in the determination of the mass (mg) of phosphate in each of the soil extracts. The phosphate concentration (ppm) in each soil sample was calculated by multiplying the mg phosphate in the extract by 5, dividing by the mass of soil extracted (~0.100 g), and multiplying by 1,000.

Qualitative Phosphate Spot Test

The spot-test procedure used on-site was a modification of a previously described method (Eidt 1977: 1329). For each test, a small amount of soil was placed on a sheet of ashless filter paper, and two drops of a solution containing the extractant (1.5 M HCl) and ammonium molybdate (50.0 g/L) were added. After 30 seconds, two drops of a freshly prepared ascorbic acid solution (5.0 g/L) were added. The intensity of the blue color that developed in two minutes was described on a scale from 1 (light) to 6 (very dark).

Multi-Elemental Analysis

Each soil sample to be analyzed by ICP-AES was air dried and sieved through a 2 mm² screen. A 2.00 g portion of each sample was crushed using a mortar and pestle and placed in a clean polyethylene vial (40 mL). To each sample 15.0 mL of acid extractant (1.2 M in HCl and 0.32 M in HNO_3) was

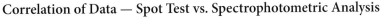

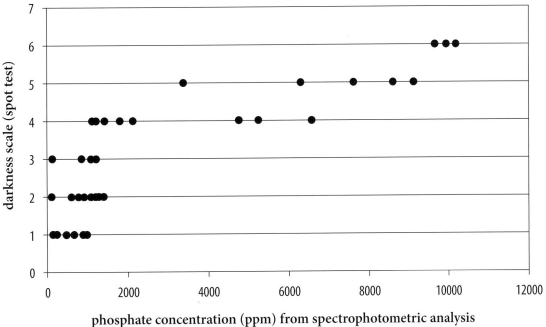

FIG. 24.1 *Actual concentrations as determined by spectrophotometric analysis for samples from various contexts analyzed by the qualitative spot test method.*

added 5.0 mL at a time, with at least an hour between additions to allow the effervescence to slow. After a final addition of 5.0 mL of deionized water, the extract/soil mixtures were allowed to sit overnight and were then filtered through Whatman #42 ashless filter paper. The extracts were diluted 1:10 with deionized water prior to analysis with a Perkin Elmer Optical Emission Spectrometer (Optima 4300 DV). Samples were analyzed for Co, Fe, K, Mg, Mn, Na, Ni, P, Al, Ba, Ca, Cu, and Pb.

RESULTS

Spot-Test Results

One of the goals of this work was to evaluate the reliability of the spot-test method, which enables one to very quickly test a soil sample in the field. A total of 53 samples collected in 2001 from various contexts were analyzed by both methods. In figure 24.1, spot-test results (color intensity from 1–6) are plotted against concentration (in ppm) as measured by the quantitative spectrophotometric

analysis method. Along each horizontal line can be seen the range of actual concentrations determined for soils producing a particular color intensity. It is clear that there is a great deal of overlap and a wide range of actual concentrations within one color rating. The limits of the spot test are obvious. However, a spot test can readily distinguish those samples with very low and very high phosphate levels. Those samples giving dark and very dark (5 and 6) spot-test results were all found to have greatly enriched amounts of phosphate. However, to study more subtle trends in phosphate concentration over an area, the quantitative method is clearly required.

Horizontal Survey: Prospecting

One of the initial projects involved an attempt to use soil chemistry to delineate the northern boundary of the Roman–Ottoman settlement — as ascertained through surface survey (see Kardulias and Yerkes, Ch. 7) — to correlate chemical analysis results with the distribution of surface artifacts.

The ground in the chosen area was penetrated at 4 m intervals along a line due north from the top of the hillside under study. The hand-powered auger was no match for the parched, rocky soil, but sampling depths of 28 cm were achieved in most cases. The 54 samples obtained and analyzed revealed levels between 1,000 and 2,000 ppm, with a few exceptions. Somewhat higher levels were recorded for some samples obtained at shallower depths (6–15 cm), where rocks prevented a deeper core. In addition, a few samples obtained from the top of the hill were found to be enriched relative to the others (2,000–4,000 ppm phosphate). A conversation with a local farmer revealed that the hillside is typically planted with barley in the fall, a process that involves the application of fertilizer. Most likely, the phosphate levels in our samples were influenced more by this recent activity than by archaeological sources, and so we were unable to verify the extent to which phosphate levels and survey results correspond.

Recognizing that consistent sampling at depths beneath the plow zone was not feasible without a mechanically driven auger, we determined that additional prospecting activities — including the search for a missing Cypro-Archaic settlement — were unlikely to be fruitful. However, two years later a trench was dug through the Malloura Valley for the purpose of installing a water pipe. Fortunately, the installation coincided with the excavation season, and we were able to obtain samples along a two-mile stretch of this still-open trench at variable intervals and with positions recorded via GPS. Sampling depths of 30–50 cm from the surface were achievable using just a pick and a spoon. These soil samples were analyzed by both the spot-test procedure in the field and the quantitative method described above. Low levels of phosphate were observed, with most values under 1,000 ppm, a result that was consistent with the very low frequency of cultural finds (only a few pottery sherds were seen along the trench).

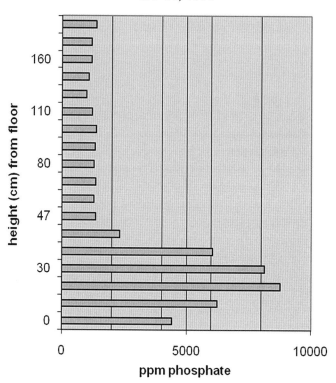

FIG. 24.2 *Vertical study of phosphate concentrations in the Athienou-Malloura sanctuary. High levels of phosphate correspond to cultural layers.*

The location of a Cypro-Archaic-period settlement at Malloura remains elusive.

Vertical Sampling: Sanctuary

Two sets of samples were collected vertically along the baulks of two different excavation units within the sanctuary, EU 10 and EU 24, and these were analyzed for phosphate using the quantitative method. A bar graph showing phosphate levels (ppm) vs. sample depth from the EU 10 baulk is shown in figure 24.2; similar results were observed with the samples from EU 24. The phosphate levels in the alluvial soil above the excavated sanctuary are low and relatively constant. But nearer to the "hard-packed" levels corresponding to the floor of the sanctuary, the phosphate content begins to increase, and at floor level is enriched by a factor of six or so. These data indicate that phosphate levels do vary predictably with intensity of human activity, as evidenced by the presence of pottery, figurines, sculpture, and other artifacts in the hard-packed layer.

Tombs

The digging of the water-line trench in 2001 revealed the presence of three small tombs whose openings or capstones were apparent in the vertical faces of the trench. These were excavated by AAP personnel and students. Two of these tombs (T100 and T101) consisted of very small chambers with no evidence of human remains; each contained only one small pottery vessel. We examined the soil from the tomb floor and inside the pots and found very low phosphate levels, consistent with the absence of bones and teeth. These tombs remain a mystery; even an infant burial should have yielded material and chemical evidence. The third tomb (T102) contained the remains of two individuals. Soil tests from within this tomb showed very high phosphate levels (6,000–10,000 ppm) in the tomb floor, as expected. Soil from stratigraphic levels containing the bones, and those just under those levels, were more highly enriched than soil above the remains.

As part of the soil survey, we also analyzed soil samples from the excavation of a large chamber tomb (T28) containing the skeletal remains of approximately 30 individuals. These samples yielded the highest values for phosphate of any samples retrieved from Malloura (5,000–15,000 ppm).

Mapping Phosphates on the Sanctuary Floor

In 2004, 116 samples from the sanctuary (EU 10, EU 11, EU 24, EU 30, EU 34, EU 88), collected during previous excavation seasons (1991–2003), were obtained for analysis. The purpose of this study was to obtain samples from the floor of the Hellenistic phase of the sanctuary to "map" the phosphate content in a way that could shed light on the location of the as-yet-uncovered altar. Field reports were consulted to identify which stratigraphic units encompassed the "hard-packed layer," a stratum consisting of compact soil con-taining a high density of artifacts, limestone inclusions, and cobbles. Where soil from these SUs could be identified and located in the storeroom, a sample was obtained from each available square meter unit and was analyzed using the quantitative spectrophotometric method. Results were recorded along with the easting and northing of the SU from each sample. Values ranged from about 1,000 ppm to more than 9,000 ppm, with most of the samples showing greatest enrichment originating from EU 30 and the northern segment of EU 10. Figure 24.3 shows the sanctuary plan with superimposed symbols representing ranges of phosphate levels. This "map" indicated that the most likely location for the altar, where one would expect to find higher concentrations of both artifacts and soil phosphate originating from ritual activities, was north of EU 30 and northwest of EU 10. During the 2007 excavation season, the altar was indeed uncovered in this vicinity.

Multi-Elemental Analysis and the Industrial Structure, EU 2

While it has been shown that phosphate levels in anthrosols can provide a reliable indication of the intensity of human activity, phosphate enrichment by itself does not provide clues about the nature of the activities that led to elevated levels. However, other elements in the soil would be expected to increase in concentration as a result of specific endeavors (Wells 2004: 71), such as cooking (sodium and potassium from ash; calcium from processing or disposal of bone/shell), pottery production (aluminum and iron from clay), metal smelting or working, processing or use of pigments, dyes, and mordants, tanning, and so forth. In 2007, 65 samples were obtained from EU 2, a medieval industrial structure of unknown function. Of these, 44 samples had been collected during the 1991 and 1993 excavation seasons, 6 were control samples procured in 2007 from locations outside the structure, and 15 were obtained at different depths from two cores dug within the structure in 2007. Each sample was analyzed for phosphate using the spectrophotometric method and was also subjected to multi-elemental analysis by ICP-

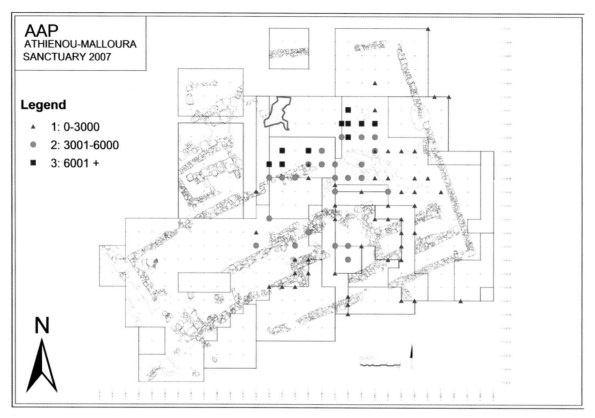

FIG. 24.3 *Soil phosphate results for hard-packed layer of the Athienou-*Malloura *sanctuary, superimposed on sanctuary plan. Altar area shown in pale yellow, center top (drawing: J. Johnson).*

AES to reveal any unusual chemical signature that could perhaps shed some light on the function of this enigmatic structure. The system of parallel walls and channels, along with the discovery that some spaces between the walls were lined with "Cypriot marble," suggested that the structure was designed to control the flow of liquids. But what liquid, and for what purpose?

The phosphate results indicated that most samples contain between 1,500 and 3,000 ppm phosphate, consistent with other anthrosols at Malloura. However, one of the control samples and several samples on the east side of the structure and the southeast corner just outside the structure (where an ash layer indicated that some activity involving burning took place) showed significant phosphate enrichment. A reasonable correlation was observed between the spectrophotometric phosphate analysis results and the elemental phosphorus (P) results obtained by ICP-AES in the soil extracts.

Other elements that appear to be significantly enriched within the walls of EU 2, as compared with the control samples, include cobalt, magnesium, manganese, and in some locations nickel and copper. No enrichment of lead or iron was observed (with the exception of one sample that was found in proximity to an iron nail and the core samples obtained using the auger). Samples associated with the ash layer/firepit were dramatically enriched in aluminum, barium, potassium, and sodium, as well as phosphorus.

The interpretation of these results does not easily lead to a conclusion regarding the function of EU 2. If used for soaking organic materials (e.g., the retting of flax, as has been proposed [DeMasi, Ch. 16]), then phosphate enrichment would be expected. But to determine the effect of this activity on other elements would require ethnographic or experimental archaeology studies. And without a detailed understanding of the composition of the rocks and other building materials, as well as various site formation processes (Schiffer 1987), it is not possible to extrapolate what was going on in this uniquely designed structure.

CONCLUSIONS

Collaborating with a diverse group of archaeologists and specialists in an ongoing effort to understand the past has been an enormously satisfying undertaking. We have demonstrated that soil studies can reveal significant information about the intensity of human activity in the Malloura Valley, but the limitations of doing analytical chemistry at a remote location are also readily apparent. While a phosphate spot-test procedure can be used to prescreen soil samples on-site, the acquisition of reliable data requires the use of instrumentation, equipment, and chemicals in a well-equipped chemistry laboratory. However, carrying out the analyses in a home laboratory means choosing carefully which samples to bring (and waiting until the next season for another opportunity). The importance of proper storage and labeling of soil/sediments collected from archaeological excavations is also quite clear. Samples should be air dried and stored in plastic bags that are clearly and permanently labeled on the outside (we encountered some bags of moist soil containing a paper label that had decomposed — sacrificing both soil chemistry and legibility).

We were most encouraged by our studies within the sanctuary, demonstrating archaeologically significant changes in phosphate concentration with both vertical and horizontal sampling. The results obtained in the lab were entirely consistent with the artifactual evidence. While we initially envisioned a chemical prospecting method that would allow us to locate unexcavated features at Malloura, the scale of such a project would be prohibitive, requiring large-scale sampling with a mechanical auger that could potentially damage underlying structures or artifacts.

The application of multi-elemental analysis in archaeology is likely to steadily increase. The ability to study elemental soil "signatures" as they relate to human activity and craft practices will greatly extend the role of soil analysis in understanding the past.

ACKNOWLEDGMENTS

Many Davidson students, most notably Brent Wilson, Joe Palatinus, and Halley Brantley, participated in the development of extraction and analysis methods appropriate for Malloura soil samples and assisted in the collection of data and organization of results. The phosphate map shown in fig. 24.3 was generated from the phosphate data and superimposed on the sanctuary plan by James Johnson. The work was funded through summer Faculty Study and Research grants generously provided by Davidson College as well as a Davidson Research Initiative grant in 2007. On-site expenses were provided by the Athienou Archaeological Project, and supplies and chemicals were provided by the Davidson College chemistry department. Access to the ICP-AES instrument housed at the paleoclimatology, paleoceanography, and biogeochemistry laboratory in the College of Marine Science, University of South Florida, was made possible by a collaboration with Christian Wells. I am grateful to each of these individuals and organizations for the effort and support that made this work possible.

REFERENCES

Bethell, P., and Máté, I.
1989   The Use of Soil Phosphate Analysis in Archaeology: A Critique. Pp. 1–29 in *Scientific Analysis in Archaeology,* ed. J. Henderson. Monograph 19. Oxford: Oxford School of Archaeology Publications.

Eidt, R. C.
1977   Detection and Examination of Anthrosols by Phosphate Analysis. *Science* 197: 1327–32.

Goffer, Z.
2007   *Archaeological Chemistry.* Second edition. Hoboken: Wiley-Interscience.

Sánchez, A; Cañabate, M. L.; and Lizcano, R.
1996   Phosphorus Analysis at Archaeological Sites: An Optimization of the Method and Interpretation of the Results. *Archaeometry* 38(1): 151–64.

Schiffer, M. B.
1987   *Formation Processes of the Archaeological Record.* Albuquerque: University of New Mexico.

Wells, E. C.
2004   Investigating Activity Patterns in Prehispanic Plazas: Weak Acid-Extraction ICP-AES Analysis of Anthrosols at Classic Period El Coyote, Northwestern Honduras. *Archaeometry* 46(1): 67–84.
2006   Cultural Soilscapes. Pp. 125–32 in *Function of Soils for Human Societies and the Environment,* eds. E. Frossard, W. E. H. Blum, and B. P. Warkentin. London: The Geological Society of London.

Chapter 25

Site Conservation and Planning at Malloura

by Margaret Breuker and Remko Breuker

As discussed elsewhere in this volume (see especially Toumazou and Counts, Ch. 6), the Athienou Archaeological Project has brought to light a wide range of architectural features, including limestone foundation walls associated with the sanctuary and later settlements, as well as rock-cut chamber tombs and cisterns. In 1995, the AAP director (Toumazou) began to explore possible conservation options for the site. As a result, a Conservation Site Plan was developed that presented practical conservation alternatives for protecting and maintaining the excavated remains of Athienou-*Malloura*, in addition to planning the future of the site as a potential tourist park. A Site Condition Survey Form was used for each EU, developed to assess the significance of existing and potential threats, inherent problems, and the condition of the existing materials or fabric of the site. To understand more fully the degradation mechanisms, during 1997–2000 chemical, geological, and biological analyses were conducted on the limestone from the tomb area of the site. Based on these surveys and scientific analyses, various site-preservation methods have been performed thus far, including wall consolidation of architectural features, the construction

of shelter over five separate tomb structures to prevent further degradation, and the integration of a self-supporting, wooden staircase within the *dromos* of the largest tomb (T 27) that has enabled safe public access while also protecting the fragile architectural fabric. Most of the construction was performed in conjunction with, and through the financial support of, the town of Athienou. This chapter provides an overview of these various activities and the rationale behind them.

METHODOLOGY OF SITE CONSERVATION AT ATHIENOU-MALLOURA

Professional archaeological site conservation is a relatively new field. However, archaeologists have been practicing various conservation methods for some time. Indeed, in the last few years, there has been a greater consciousness on the part of archaeologists of the need to preserve their sites. Three leading professional organizations for archaeologists in the United States (the Society for American Archaeology [SAA], the Archaeological Institute of America [AIA], and the American Schools for Oriental Research [ASOR]) have established ethical codes regarding site preservation, and each has formally recognized site preservation in its professional guidelines. Guidelines for archaeological site conservation have been discussed by scholars, and two of the resulting charters that have been written, namely the Venice Charter adopted in 1966 and the Burra Charter in 1979 (revised in 1992 and 1999), provide useful strategies for the conservation of archaeological sites (Marquis-Kyle and Walker 1999).

We chose to base our approach to the conservation of Athienou-*Malloura* on the methodology described in the Australia ICOMOS Burra Charter, 1999 (*http://australia.icomos.org/wp-content/uploads/BURRA_CHARTER.pdf*) due to its wide acceptance and use. The Burra Charter states that one must establish the significance of a site to understand clearly what is to be preserved and why. The significance of a site is determined by the "aesthetic, historic, scientific, social, or spiritual value for past, present, or future generations" (Burra Charter Article 1.2; see also Marquis-Kyle and Walker 1999). These values are not rigid descriptions but rather categories that allow for more insightful consideration of the meanings that a site holds for society. Assessing the archaeological remains in this way allows a greater understanding of the resources that a site possesses. For example, not only is the physical evidence assessed but aesthetic values are also considered, such as the surrounding landscape and local vegetation, which may be a significant feature of the site and a necessity to preserve. The significance of Athienou-*Malloura* was evaluated and documented to create a "statement of significance." This statement served as a beginning point for a more detailed condition assessment of the architectural features in each excavation area. It should be understood that the significance of a site may change as excavations progress and should therefore be regularly reevaluated. A statement of significance may also result in the construction of an overall conservation and site management plan, which discusses future development of the site such as designation as a tourist park or reburial. Site management plans are primarily created by governmental bodies (e.g., the Department of Antiquities of the Republic of Cyprus), the project director, a site conservator, other experts, and various local authorities.

THE IMPLEMENTATION OF A CONDITION SURVEY

After the significance of the site had been established through the discovery of the sanctuary and domestic structures, as well as cisterns and tombs, a survey into the condition of the individual units and the architectural features was conducted. We created a survey form for Athienou-*Malloura* relevant to our needs and specific to the excavated units of the site. The survey allowed for prioritization of individual units or features on both the macro and micro levels. Using the survey forms, we were able to identify problems common to most archaeological sites, such as uncontrolled vegetation growth and the rapid deterioration of the exposed limestone architectural features. In the case of the tombs and cisterns, we observed substantial cracking and exfoliation of the stone (fig. 25.1); the reasons for these conditions can be quite complex and therefore necessitated prompt, detailed analysis of the deteriorating limestone.

ASSESSMENT OF THE CONDITIONS OBSERVED AT MAĞARA TEPEŞI

An examination of physical fabric can be achieved by both visual analysis and analytical techniques. At Athienou-*Malloura*, a better understanding of the limestone's performance was gained through the examination of its petrology, specifically mineralogy, porosity, and permeability, as well as chemical factors such as the effects of salts. We conducted salt content tests to establish whether or not various cracks found on the walls of the rock-cut tombs and cisterns were due to expansion and contraction of salt crystals. Microchemical spot tests were performed to identify the anions present for the most common soluble salts found on sites, namely sulfates, chlorides, nitrates, and phosphates. Microchemical spot tests consist of various reagents that qualitatively identify the presence of salts through precipitous reactions. Quantitative tests for these same salts were performed by use of EM Quant® strips. These are commercially produced paper strips that colormetrically identify levels of salt ions (EM Quant®Test Strips,

Fig. 25.1 *Cracks apparent in the doorway of Tomb 27 (photo: M. Breuker).*

EMD Chemicals. Sulfate test 10019-1, chloride test 10079-1, nitrate test 10020-1, and phosphate test 10428-1). These tests were chosen because they can be conducted in the field and are easy to interpret.

After testing both soil and limestone samples from the tomb area, we found nondetectable levels of sulfates and chlorides, but nitrates in all areas and phosphates in various areas. Salt levels of sulfates, chlorides, nitrates, and phosphates were measured at mg/l on limestone samples taken from the tombs. Phosphate levels ranged from 10 to 250 mg/l, and nitrate levels 10 to 100 mg/l; sulfate and chloride levels were negligible in most areas. The lack of significant levels of chlorides and sulfates is surprising given that the site is composed of sedimentary stone of marine origin (on the physical environment, see Yerkes, Ch. 2). The higher presence of nitrates and phosphates, however, is

not surprising given the agricultural history of the site, as well as the presence of burials (see also the discussion of soil chemistry in Sarris, Ch. 21 and Beeston, Ch. 24). Moreover, the lack of recurring and extreme wetting and drying cycles prevents salts from being the exclusive cause for the exfoliation and cracking of the stone.

We then examined the physical characteristics of the limestone itself to determine if the cracking could be caused by an inherent property of the stone, such as poor cohesion of the individual grains. Petrological analysis revealed the structure of the grains, the grain contact characteristics, the interparticle surface area, as well as the overall composition of the stone. In summary, the stone can be characterized as a fine-grained, chalky limestone, consisting mainly (ca. 95%) of calcium carbonate. Classified as Biomicritic, it can be called a kind of "calcareous mud," a very weak material highly vulnerable to water erosion, especially acid rain (fig. 25.2).

The inherent characteristics of the limestone, as understood through the petrographic analysis, are major factors in the present appearance of the tombs and cisterns. Chemical means of decay, such as the effects of water, combined with the large amount of calcium carbonate and the inherent soft and porous nature of the stone result in cracking, exfoliation, and loss. However, this is not the only possible cause for the conditions observed. Fungi, bacteria, algae, moss, or lichens, which colonize stone surfaces as a natural consequence of exposure, have various effects on the stone such as change to the appearance of the surface and chemical and mechanical damage from the directed growth of hyphae into cracks and fissures (Honeyborne 1990: 168). In addition, microbial populations growing on limestone surfaces can lead to enhanced physical weathering (Papida and Murphy 2000: 305–17). The microbiological causes for deterioration were investigated at the laboratory of applied microbiology in the division of engineering and applied sciences at Harvard University. The bacterium *Bacillus cereus* was isolated from water cistern T 31 excavated in 1995. This organism, as well as organisms collected from Tomb 25, was capable of dissolving calcium carbonate, the primary element in the limestone,

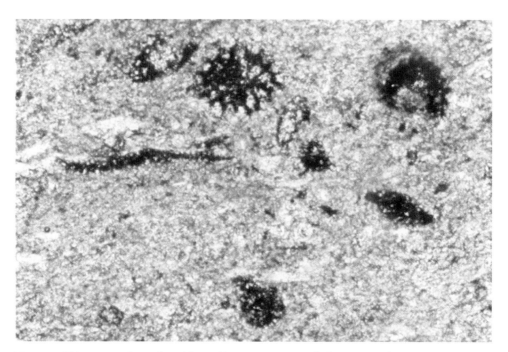

FIG. 25.2 *Thin section of stone from Mağara Tepeşi at 15 microns thickness, magnification 25×, PPL (Plane Polarized Light), impregnated with blue epoxy.*

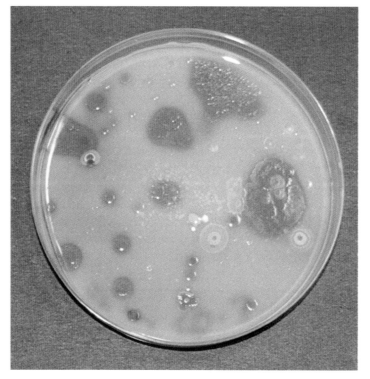

FIG. 25.3 *Mixed inoculum plated on EM medium containing precipitated calcium carbonate. Cleared areas of plate indicate areas where chemicals excreted by microorganisms have solubilized calcium carbonate.*

FIG. 25.4 *Scanning electron micrograph of a biofilm growing on the limestone surface, magnification 1,000×.*

on medium plates (Perry et al. 2004) (fig. 25.3). Chemically, organisms can excrete organic acids (oxalic, etc.) and mineral acids (nitric or sulphuric), which dissolve minerals from the stone, thereby rendering it weak and highly vulnerable to weathering (Perry et al. 2003: 176). Additionally, microorganisms can form biofilms on the stone surface that aid in the ingress and retention of water, itself causing fragmentation of the stone (Perry et al. 2003: 176) (fig. 25.4). These biological processes have been the subject of study in recent years, and the research performed with the microorganisms from Athienou-*Malloura* have contributed unique findings to this area of preservation research.

CONSERVATION OPTIONS

To slow the deterioration of the limestone, we explored conservation techniques that would be practical, relatively inexpensive, and effective for all stages of the excavation (i.e., for immediate stabilization, between-season efforts, and finally after the excavation has ceased). The most significant preservation measures used for the protection of the tombs and cisterns were the erection of permanent shelters and the construction of a noninvasive, stable staircase in the *dromos* of T 27 (see figs. 6.6–7). Protective shelters were built over all excavated tombs, as well as over a pair of cisterns situated along the same ridge (fig. 25.5). Postexcavation exposure has caused the soft and fissured limestone to become extremely vulnerable to exfoliation. In addition, rainwater was collecting at the bottom of the stepped *dromoi* and within the tomb chambers. The combination of the intense Cypriot sun, wind, and seasonal rainfall had resulted in visible signs of erosion on the limestone even in one year's time. In consultation with the Cypriot Department of Antiquities and the municipality of Athienou, it was decided that the tombs and cisterns remain exposed for visitors. Consequently, the construction of protective shelters was commissioned. Since 1994, a total of five shelters have been erected: four over Tombs

Fig. 25.5 *Shelter erected above Tomb 27 showing structural pillars and vernacular roof (photo: R. Breuker).*

26, 27, 28, and 29, and a larger one over the two cisterns. Because of the rapid deterioration of the two adjacent — and visually identical — cisterns, it was decided to back-fill one for better preservation. The degree of limestone deterioration among the features determined priorities in the sequence of construction.

All preservation charters state that conservation treatments on ancient monuments must maintain the authenticity of the original fabric. In other words, the least possible intervention should occur to the existing material, not altering or distorting evidence provided by the original fabric. Any stabilization or construction measures undertaken on a site should therefore do the following: (1) allow the maximum amount of existing historical material to be retained; (2) ensure harmony with the original design and workmanship of the archaeological feature; and (3) not allow any new additions, such as protective shelters, to dominate the original material and structure. Correspondingly, an appropriate shelter should fulfill several conditions. Most important, it should protect the archaeological remains from the elements. Moreover, the shelter should be large enough to completely cover the unit, ensuring that its structural members not rest directly on any

archaeological remains. The shelter must also have appropriate drainage, and water should be directed a safe distance away from the remains below. Finally, the materials employed in the shelter's design must be compatible with the site, both aesthetically and practically; if a shelter is built with materials that are difficult to obtain or maintain (such as particular types of wood, metal, or paint) instead of materials in common use in a specific region, it may be difficult to sustain or never be built in the first place. The use of local materials usually ensures readily available building material and a higher number of local skilled contractors, resulting in a structure that is easier and more likely to be repaired as required. In turn, these factors result in lower overall construction costs, ease of maintenance, and increased longevity of the shelter structure.

In the case of Athienou-*Malloura*, construction of the shelters was performed by local building contractors under AAP's direct supervision. The Athienou municipality assumed the cost of materials and labor. Almost all the materials were either recycled building elements removed from older houses in Athienou or found in the vicinity of the site. In terms of design, simple stone perimeter walls (ca. 40 cm thick and 60 cm in height) sur-

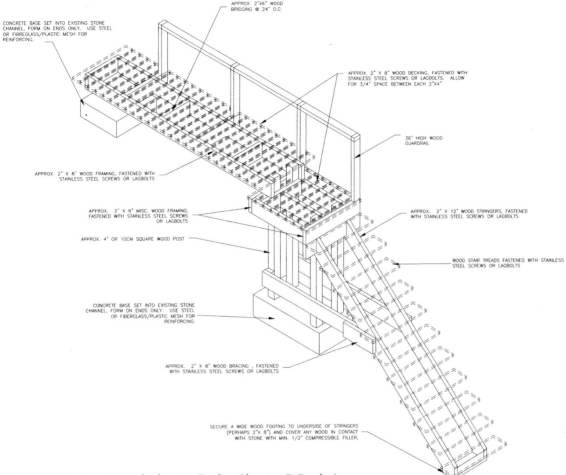

APPROX. 2"x6" WOOD
BRIDGING @ 24" O.C.

CONCRETE BASE SET INTO EXISTING STONE
CHANNEL, FORM ON ENDS ONLY. USE STEEL
OR FIBREGLASS/PLASTIC MESH FOR
REINFORCING.

APPROX. 2" X 8" WOOD DECKING, FASTENED WITH
STAINLESS STEEL SCREWS OR LAGBOLTS. ALLOW
FOR 3/4" SPACE BETWEEN EACH 2"x4"

36" HIGH WOOD
GUARDRAIL

APPROX. 2" X 8" WOOD FRAMING, FASTENED WITH
STAINLESS STEEL SCREWS OR LAGBOLTS

APPROX. 2" X 6" MISC. WOOD FRAMING,
FASTENED WITH STAINLESS STEEL SCREWS
OR LAGBOLTS

APPROX. 2" X 12" WOOD STRINGERS, FASTENED
WITH STAINLESS STEEL SCREWS OR LAGBOLTS

APPROX. 4" OR 10CM SQUARE WOOD POST

WOOD STAIR TREADS FASTENED WITH STAINLESS
STEEL SCREWS OR LAGBOLTS

CONCRETE BASE SET INTO EXISTING STONE
CHANNEL, FORM ON ENDS ONLY. USE STEEL
OR FIBERGLASS/PLASTIC MESH FOR
REINFORCING.

APPROX. 2" X 8" WOOD BRACING , FASTENED
WITH STAINLESS STEEL SCREWS OR LAGBOLTS

SECURE A WIDE WOOD FOOTING TO UNDERSIDE OF STRINGERS
(PERHAPS 2"x 8") AND COVER ANY WOOD IN CONTACT
WITH STONE WITH MIN. 1/2" COMPRESSIBLE FILLER,

FIG. 25.6 *Protective stairway leading into Tomb 27 (drawing: R. Breuker).*

round three sides of the *dromos* in a π-shape, and steel pipes encased in stone masonry support the roof. Reused wood beams form the structure of the roof and are secured with metal straps to steel pipes. The roof is then finished in typical Cypriot vernacular style, with a bamboo ceiling and roof tiles set in a bed of mud mortar. For additional protection, tar paper was placed between the mud mortar and the bamboo ceiling.

ACCESS STAIRS TO TOMB 27

Another element constructed in our site-conservation efforts is a stairway into the largest of the tombs (Tomb 27; fig. 25.6). Access to the burial chamber was difficult because the original steps in the *dromos* had been destroyed by the subsequent (still ancient) construction of an aquifer leading water from a small stream into the tomb (see Toumazou and Counts, Ch. 6; see also discussion in Sarris, Ch. 21). Moreover, the few steps that had been spared were rapidly deteriorating due to heavy foot traffic and weathering. It was decided to construct a stairway over the original ancient steps that would both facilitate safe entry into the tomb for visitors and AAP staff as well as protect the tomb fabric. Many of the same design principles implemented in the shelter structures were also used for the new stair. It had to be minimal in its composition and independent of both the tomb and the protective shelter. Also, its method of construction and choice of materials had to ensure the least impact on the ancient remains as well as the surrounding bedrock. Design details were incorporated so that the stairs' various components could be easily maintained and, when necessary, replaced.

In fact, its entirety could be completely removed, leaving essentially no trace of its existence.

To slow the deterioration of the excavated architecture at the site, we began to point the stone walls of EU 5 in 1999, followed by the walls in EU 10 the following year. There was evidence of original mortar on the northern side of Wall 1 in EU 5. This was sampled and kept with other conservation site samples in the *apotheke*. Because the stone at the site contains large amounts of calcium carbonate, a lime mortar was chosen. Lime mortars in particular show a relatively high rate of deformability; that is, they are able to accommodate differential movement. They are also likely to have a large pore-size distribution favoring moisture transmission and evaporation. Pointing in between stones not only helped secure the sides of the walls but also prevented vegetation growth.

Conclusion and Comments on Current Efforts in Conservation and Site Maintenance

All preservation treatments of the archaeological remains of Athienou-*Malloura* must be maintained and reevaluated seasonally to insure proper protection. Archaeological site preservation is an interdisciplinary effort, a collaboration between professionals from various backgrounds and areas of expertise. Thus, all conditions can be properly assessed, appropriate options can be considered, and a common solution attained. The development and implementation of a site conservation plan for Athienou-*Malloura* have required successive years of funding, labor, and maintenance; nevertheless, the value of preserving the cultural heritage of the region remains a significant part of AAP's research design. Further work has continued to the present in an effort to complement the work described above. In the area of the sanctuary, a more formidable, protective fence was erected around the principal excavation units, with steel pipes set into a stone base at regular intervals. Trees have also been planted around the sanctuary to provide shade and aesthetic appeal. In the area of the tombs at Mağara Tepeşi, bronze placards have been affixed to each tomb shelter that provide basic information regarding the architectural plan and chronology of each tomb; trees have also been planted. In the future, a pebble pathway leading the visitor through the tomb area will offer a more directed tour of these monuments; a bathroom will also be included. Finally, in 2007 brown signs marking the direction to Malloura were erected to lead visitors from the main road into Athienou; these were complemented by a paved road to facilitate unimpeded and safe (and relatively dust-free) travel to the site.

References

Honeyborne, D. B.
1990   Weathering and Decay of Masonry. Chapter 7. Pp. 153–78 in *Conservation of Building and Decorative Stone,* vol. 1, London: Butterworth-Heinemann.

Marquis-Kyle, P., and Walker, M.
1999   *The Illustrated Burra Charter.* Brisbane, Victoria: Australia International Council on Monuments and Sites.

Papida, S. W., and Murphy, E. May.
2000   Enhancement of Physical Weathering of Building Stone by Microbial Populations. *International Biodeterioration and Biodegradation* 46(4): 305–17.

Perry, T. D., Breuker, M.; Hernandez-Duqué, G.; and Mitchell, R.
2003   Interaction of Microorganisms with Maya Archaeological Materials. Pp. 175–92 in *The Lowland Maya Area: Three Millennia at the Human-Wildland Interface,* eds. A. Gomez-Pompa, M.F.Allen, S.L. Fedick, J.J. Jimenez-Osornio. Binghamton: Hayworth.

Perry, T. D.; Duckworth, O. W.; McNamara, C. J.; Martin, S. T.; Breuker, M.; and Mitchell, R.
2004   Biologically Produced Polymers Affect Calcite Dissolution. Pp.1367–70 in *Proceedings of the 11th International Symposium on Water-Rock Interaction,* eds. R. B. Wanty and R. R. Seal. Saratoga Springs, NY: A.A. Blakeman.

Chapter 26

Viewing the Past through the Present

Ethnoarchaeological Studies of Population and Ancient Agriculture

by Richard W. Yerkes

The Athienou Archaeological Project has employed a multidisciplinary approach in its investigations over the past two decades to answer key questions about ancient life in the Malloura Valley. This perspective facilitates the study of changes in the environment, economy, and population that occurred away from the ancient political and cultural centers on the coast of Cyprus such as Salamis, Kition, Amathous, and Paphos. It has been suggested that rural areas like the Malloura Valley are less stable than the population centers, and that responses to cultural and environmental changes in the hinterlands are more dramatic (Alcock 1993; Fejfer 1995; Fejfer and Hayes 1995: 63). If this is the case, then we may get a clearer picture of the rich and diverse cultural history of Cyprus if we view it from the periphery (see Kardulias et al., Ch. 1). As other chapters in this volume attest, AAP personnel have examined many different aspects of ancient and modern life, including studies of the biological diversity of ancient and modern populations, environmental changes, and political, economic, and ritual activities. Methods employed in these studies include geophysical prospecting, the identification and analysis of floral and faunal remains, and techno-logical, stylistic, and functional studies of ancient pottery, lithic artifacts, statuary, and architecture.

Ethnoarchaeology is another key component of the multidisciplinary studies by the AAP. The residents of Athienou have provided our staff and students with a wealth of information about traditional life in Cyprus. Ethnoarchaeological investigations have been conducted at the nearby villages of Alambra (Sallade 1989) and Dhali (Allen 1989), and several studies of rural land use (Surridge 1930; Christodoulou 1959; Allan 1965: 13, 275–76, 436; Karouzis 1977; Thirgood 1987), domestic architecture (Sinos 1986), and other aspects of Cypriot history and culture have provided a context for our own studies (Beckingham 1957; Attalides 1976; Markides et al. 1978; Solsten 1993; Wallace 1995; Karageorghis and Michaelides 1996). Our research on contemporary life has helped us understand the ancient inhabitants of the Malloura Valley. In this chapter, two ethnographic case studies employ information from informants and studies of modern rural settlements and material data, respectively, to (1) examine the relationship among population, household size, and settlement area in the past (Murphy and Yerkes 1998; Yerkes 2000) and (2) learn how observations of traditional

TABLE 26.1 Methods used to estimate population size.

1. Site Area

		Area(m²)	Max. Population	Area per Person(m²)
Petrophani	*Total Area*	43,478	171 (in 1973)*	254
	Inhabited Area	38,578	171	226
Alambra**	*Total Area*	43,240	600 (in 1976)	72
	Inhabited Area	38,920	600	65
Athienou-Malloura	*Total Area*	49,833 divided by 254 = 196 (if Petrophani area is used)		
		49,833 divided by 72 = 692 (if Alambra area is used)		
	Inhabited Area	*Roman settlement*	16,988 divided by 226 = 75 (if Petrophani area is used)	
			16,988 divided by 65 = 261 (if Alambra area is used)	
		Medieval settlement	39,866 divided by 226 = 176 (if Petrophani area is used)	
			39,866 divided by 65 = 613 (if Alambra area is used)	

2. Residential Floor Area

Petrophani	3,126 m²	divided by 10 (Narroll) = 313 persons
	3,126 m²	divided by 18.3 (actual) = 171 persons

3. Number of Household Compounds

Settlement	# of Households	Max. Population***	Ave. Size(m²)	# per Household
Petrophani	35	171	1100	5.0
Alambra	108	600	360	5.5

Athienou-Malloura

1. If the average compound size is 1100 m² (based on Petrophani)

Roman estimate   15 × 4 = 60; 15 × 5 = 75; 15 × 5.5 = 82
Medieval estimate   36 × 4 = 144; 36 × 5 = 180; 36 × 5.5 = 198

2. If the average compound size is 360 m² (based on Alambra)

Roman estimate   47 × 4 = 188; 47 × 5 = 235; 47 × 5.5 = 258
Medieval estimate   111 × 4 = 444; 111 × 5 = 555; 111 × 5.5 = 610

* Republic of Cyprus 1973.
** Sallade 1989.
*** Christodoulou 1959: 64; Republic of Cyprus 1962.

agricultural practices can be used to provide insights about past behavior (Yerkes and Kardulias 1994; Kardulias and Yerkes 1996).

ETHNOGRAPHIC CASE STUDY I: SITE SIZE AND ANCIENT POPULATION

This study was initiated during the first field season of the AAP survey in 1991 (Kardulias and Yerkes, Ch. 7). Additional data were collected in later seasons, with a substantial contribution from an undergraduate research project conducted by John Murphy under Yerkes's supervision during the 1997 AAP summer field school (Murphy and Yerkes 1998). An intensive program of undergraduate training in field and laboratory methods and Mediterranean and Near Eastern archaeological research has been offered through the AAP since 1991 (see Kardulias et al., Ch. 1), and ethnoarchaeology has been a key component of the program.

After Cyprus gained independence from the British in 1960, ethnic and political conflicts between Greek and Turkish Cypriots led to rebellion, a Greek coup, and the partitioning of the island after the Turkish invasion in 1974. The village of Athienou and the Malloura Valley became part of the United Nations-controlled buffer zone south of the area occupied by Turkish forces (Solsten 1993: 43; Kapsos 1995). Many refugees were settled in Athienou after the invasion. The Greek Cypriot population in the Larnaka district where Athienou is located increased by 75% between 1973 and 1976 (St. John-Jones 1983: Table 18). The village farmers lost 65% of their fields in the Mesaoria, north of the village, and had to change their farming practices and reorganize their economy. Through hard work, innovation, and cooperation, Athienou has become one of the most prosperous communities on the island.

The Village of Petrophani

While Athienou was adjusting to the challenges of post-1974 Cyprus, the nearby Turkish Cypriot village of Petrophani (Turkish Esendagh) became a ghost town when its residents were forced to move to the Turkish-occupied areas in north-

ern Cyprus. Since the preinvasion population of Petrophani was known from census records (Republic of Cyprus 1962, 1973; Goodwin 1984: 1358; Kornrumpf and Kornrumpf 1990), the relationship between population size and the organization of rural agricultural villages could be studied by measuring the buildings and compounds in Petrophani and determining the area covered by the village. Methods that archaeologists use to estimate ancient population levels from the size of settlements and buildings were applied in our study of Petrophani (Narroll 1962; Cook and Heizer 1968; Casselberry 1974; Wiessner 1974; De Roche 1983; Kolb 1985; Sumner 1989; Kardulias 1992; Schreiber and Kintigh 1996). The results were compared with available census figures and used to refine some of these methods. Then, the refined methods were used to estimate the population of the Roman and medieval settlements at Athienou-*Malloura*, where no census figures were available (Table 26.1).

Already a village during the Venetian period (see Counts and Parvis, Ch. 5), Petrophani was apparently abandoned and then reoccupied during the period of Ottoman rule. The village appears on an 1873 Ottoman map of Cyprus and on the 1882 map of the island prepared by Lord Kitchener (Kornrumpf and Kornrumpf 1990; see Counts and Parvis, Ch. 5). According to the 1881 British census, the population of Petrophani was 18 (Grivaud 1998: 455); during the 19th century, its population likely averaged about 50, but it had grown to 120 by 1960 (Goodwin 1984: 1358). It reached its maximum recorded population of 171 in 1973, one year before the Turkish invasion (Republic of Cyprus 1973). After it was abandoned, farmers from Athienou began using the buildings in the village to shelter sheep, goats, and cattle. Most of the standing structures in Petrophani date to the recent period, but parts of older buildings from the Ottoman period may have been incorporated into their construction.

Petrophani is a typical, nucleated Cypriot village. Such villages have been described as living museums and repositories of traditional culture (Christodoulou 1959: 64; Allen 1989: 426). There are some modern houses made of reinforced concrete in Petrophani, but the style of architecture found in most of the buildings (where a stone socle supports mudbrick walls covered with plaster on the interior and exterior) shows remarkable conservatism and continuity with ancient dwellings (Gjerstad 1926; Christodoulou 1959: 61–64; Allen 1989: 426).

Measurements and Population Estimates

There are a number of different ways that the population of an ancient settlement can be estimated (see Table 26.1; also see Narroll 1962; Wiessner 1974; Hassan 1976; Kolb 1985; Sumner 1989). The total area covered by a site can be determined and used to estimate the number of people that lived there (Cook and Treganza 1950; Cook and Heizer 1968; Wiessner 1974; De Roche 1983; Sumner 1989; Schreiber and Kintigh 1996). The sum of the amount of floor space in all the dwellings can be calculated and divided by the average space needed by each resident to determine how many people lived in the settlement (Narroll 1962; Cook and Heizer 1968; LeBlanc 1971; Casselberry 1974; Hassan 1976; Kardulias 1992). If the number of households in a settlement can be determined, this figure can be multiplied by the average number of people per household to obtain a population estimate (Christodoulou 1959; Culbert and Rice 1990).

To use these three methods in Petrophani, it was necessary to determine the area of the village and to count and measure the buildings. Using the 1:5000 topographic map published by the Cyprus Division of Lands and Surveys (map # DLS 31/XXVIII), John Murphy superimposed a 1 m grid on the village and counted the number of grid squares covered by Petrophani. By this method, the total site area for Petrophani is 43,478 m². If the area of the roads and the space in the center of Petrophani where the school (which was also used as the village mosque) was located is subtracted, the inhabited area of the village is 38,578 m². If the maximum population figure of 171 is used, then there are 254 m² of total site area per person in the village, or 226 m² of inhabited area per person (see Table 26.1).

Do these figures represent the "normal" relationship between settlement size and population levels in rural Cyprus? There is significant variation in the structure and organization of traditional rural farming villages on the Island (Christodoulou 1959). The buildings in Petrophani are "loosely packed" — there are open spaces between some of the household compounds — and the compounds are large. Other villages have smaller household compounds that are tightly packed together. To illustrate the range of variation between loosely packed and tightly packed settlements, some data from the tightly packed Greek Cypriot village of Alambra are included in table 26.1. When Jane K. Sallade (1989: fig. 2) conducted ethnoarchaeological research there in 1976, she found that there were 108 household compounds. If we superimpose a grid over her map of Alambra, we find that the 108 households were contained within an area of about 43,240 m². Alambra and Petrophani are about the same size, but Alambra has almost three times as many household compounds tightly packed together within the same area.

If the area in Alambra covered by the churchyard and roads is subtracted, we are left with an inhabited area of 38,920 m². The population of Alambra was 600 in 1976 (Sallade 1989: 408), and that would mean there is only 72 m² of total village area per resident and 65 m² of inhabited space. This shows that the packing or density of households in a settlement can have a major effect on the relationship between population and site area. Alambra and Petrophani are about the same size, but Alambra has a population that is three-and-a-half times greater.

There are no detailed census records for Athienou-*Malloura* because it was abandoned before the first organized census of Cyprus was taken in 1881 (Papadopoullos 1965; see also Counts and Parvis, Ch. 5). The only indication comes from Venetian records of 1565, which record 81 adult freedmen (*francomates*) at Malloura (Grivaud 1998: 457), which does not reflect the total population. For our estimate of the population of Athienou-*Malloura*, we used data from reconnaissance and surface collections to compute the total area of the Roman and medieval settlements (Toumazou et al. 1998). The area to the north and east of the streams at Malloura contained sherds from both the Roman and medieval periods, while only medieval sherds were found to the south and west of the streams (fig. 26.1). The boundaries of these two settlements were estimated by mapping the extent of the building foundation stones found on the surface (there is no standing architecture at the site today).

Murphy calculated the total area of the Malloura settlements at 49,833 m², slightly larger than Petrophani. If the households at Malloura were loosely packed, we can divide the total area by 254 (the average area per person for Petrophani in m²) and get an estimated population of 196 persons. If the households were tightly packed, we can divide the total area by the smaller average area per person for Alambra (72) and obtain an estimate of 692 for the maximum population (see Table 26.1).

At Petrophani and Alambra, about 90% of the total site area was classified as inhabited. At medieval Malloura, the inhabited area may have been smaller, since streams flow through the site. If only 80% of the total area of the settlement was inhabited (the other 20% being covered by perhaps two churches, a cemetery [e.g., EU 6; see Harper, Ch. 20], at least one industrial building [e.g., EU 2; see DeMasi, Ch. 16 and Spigelman, Ch. 17], and streams; see Toumazou et al. 1998; Toumazou and Counts, Ch. 6), we would have 39,866 m² of inhabited area. If we divide by the inhabited area per person for Petrophani (226), we would get a maximum population of 176 for the later (medieval) settlement if it were loosely packed; and if we divide by 65 (the inhabited area per person from Alambra), the estimated population of a densely packed settlement would be 613.

The distribution of ceramics on the surface suggests that the earlier Roman settlement at Malloura was smaller. Murphy estimated that the inhabited area was only 16,988 m². Dividing by 226, we would have a population of 75 for a loosely packed Roman village, and dividing by 65, the estimate would be 261 for a densely packed settlement (see Table 26.1). The estimates based on site area, therefore, produce a substantial range of variation; to obtain a more precise estimate of population from site area, we must determine how densely packed the settlements at Malloura were. This is difficult to establish from the distribution of artifacts on the surface,

although the impression is that the households were loosely packed. To date, excavations have exposed parts of only two of the earlier Roman houses and one medieval dwelling (Toumazou et al. 1998; Toumazou and Counts, Ch. 6).

Population Estimates Based on Floor Area

In 1991 and 1996 we measured a sample of buildings in Petrophani and compared their dimensions indicated on the 1:5000 topographical map. We found that the calculations of house size taken from the map were in agreement with the actual measurements. Murphy was thus able to use the map to calculate the total floor space of the buildings in Petrophani as 6,229 m². If the floor area of the two-story buildings in the settlement is added, the revised total floor space would be 7,634 m². In the field, we classified the buildings as residential if they had framed doors and windows, stairways, and so on. Using this classification, Murphy estimated there were 3,126 m² of residential floor space in the village. Narroll (1962) proposed that the population of a settlement would be one-tenth of the residential floor area. If we apply this to Petrophani, there is a maximum population of 313 people in the village. However, the 1973 census figure (171 persons) is less than half that number. We would have to divide the floor area by 18.3 instead of 10 to obtain an accurate estimate. Even if we revised Narroll's coefficient, we do not have data on residential floor space from the Athienou-*Malloura* site, so we cannot obtain a population estimate with this method.

Population Estimates Based on the Number of Households

During our survey, we tried to determine the number of household compounds in Petrophani. The typical compound was enclosed by a mud-brick wall and included several buildings. The compounds are arranged in a "beehive" or "pueblo" fashion, with adjacent compounds often sharing common walls (also see Sallade 1989: fig. 2). Our best estimate was a total of 35 households for Petrophani. If the maximum population of 171 is

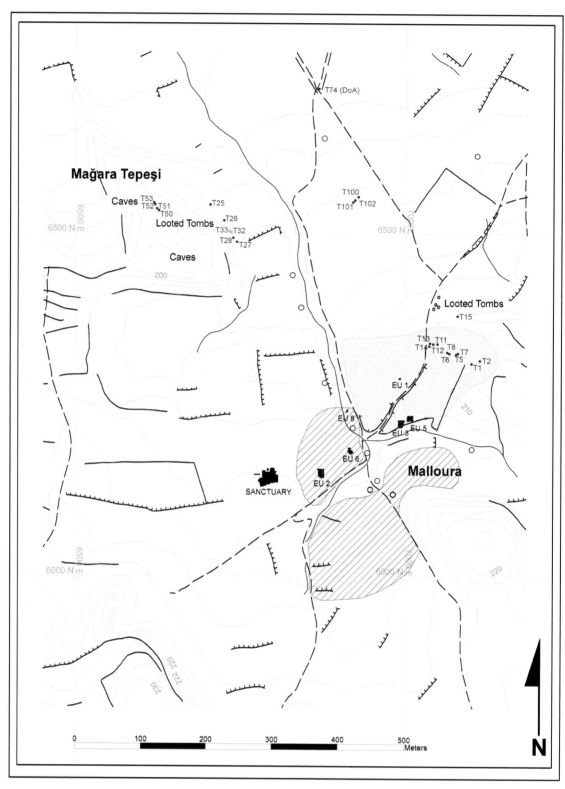

Fig. 26.1 *Map of the extent of the Roman and medieval settlements at Athienou-Malloura. Blue dotted area is where Roman and medieval sherds were found. Gray hatched area is where only medieval sherds were present. Black rectangles are EUs, red dots are tombs (drawing: A. Prins and D. Massey).*

divided by 35, there is an average of five persons per household. This is slightly larger than the median size of rural households reported in the 1946 census for Cyprus, which was 3.69 (Christodoulou 1959: 64). By the 1960 census, the average was 3.93 persons per household (Republic of Cyprus 1963).

The 108 household compounds in Alambra had an estimated population of 600 in 1976, or an average of 5.5 persons per household. It is possible that the higher average for Alambra is the result of refugees from occupied Cyprus moving to the village after 1974. However, St. John-Jones (1983: Table 18) shows that the non-Turkish population of the Nicosia district where Alambra is located only increased 0.5% between 1973 and 1976. The range of variation in the size of a rural household between 1946 and 1976 is small, and if we could determine the number of households at an ancient site, we could multiply by four, five, or 5.5 and get a reasonable population estimate. Unfortunately, we cannot identify individual household compounds at Malloura from surface debris. To estimate how many households there may have been in the Roman and medieval villages, we have to determine the average size of a household compound at the sites where we have population figures (see Table 26.1).

There were 108 households at Alambra (Sallade 1989), and the inhabited site area was 38,920 m², so the average size of a household compound was 360 m². We could fit 47 "Alambra" compounds into the inhabited area of 16,988 m² at the Roman settlement at Malloura. Multiplying by the average numbers of four, five, and 5.5 people per household, population estimates range from 188 to 258 if the Roman settlement was tightly packed.

We identified 35 households at Petrophani. The average size of these loosely packed compounds is 1,100 m². If we divide the inhabited area of the Roman village by this larger number, we find that we could fit 15 "Petrophani" households in the settlement. Multiplying by the average numbers of people per household, we find that a loosely packed Roman village would hold between 60 and 82 people. If we follow the same procedure for the medieval settlement, we would estimate that between 144 and 198 people lived in a loosely

packed town, while there would have been between 444 and 610 in a tightly packed settlement.

Site Size, Floor Area, Household Size, and Estimated Population Levels

Our ethnoarchaeological studies at Petrophani and the work of Sallade at Alambra provided us with some baseline data on the relationship among site size, floor area, number of households, and population levels in rural villages in central Cyprus. It was found that if we employed Narroll's coefficient (population = $0.10 \times$ residential floor area), we would not obtain an accurate estimate of the population of these nucleated villages. It appears that the best estimates are derived by multiplying the number of households in a settlement by four, five, or 5.5 (the average number of persons per household). If it is difficult to determine the number of households, population can be estimated from site area. However, the way the households are packed into the settlement can vary, and there can be substantial differences in the population of loosely packed sites and densely packed sites with the same total area.

Based on what we know about the settlements at Athienou-*Malloura* from our surface surveys, it seems to have been a loosely packed settlement during the Roman and medieval periods. The density and extent of building stones and domestic artifacts on the surface and the excavations to date do not suggest that there were tightly packed compounds. The maximum population of the medieval settlement would probably be about the same as the maximum population of Petrophani — about 170 to 180 people. The smaller Roman village probably had a population of between 60 and 75 people. Further excavations at Athienou-*Malloura* are needed to refine these estimates, but the ethnoarchaeological studies have allowed us to establish some parameters. Without these studies, we would have had to use universal coefficients like Narroll's, and they would have led to very inflated population estimates.

FIG. 26.2 *(a) Threshing on a packed-dirt threshing floor* (aloni) *at Athienou in 1895. The bottom of a threshing sledge* (dhoukani) *can be seen on the left, while two other sledges are in use on the right. One thresher is standing on the* dhoukani, *the other is sitting on a chair and breast-feeding her child; (b) Winnowing near the* aloni *at Athienou in 1895 (Ohnefalsch-Richter 1994, figs. 65a–b; © Marfin Popular Bank Cultural Foundation).*

ETHNOGRAPHIC CASE STUDY II:
TRADITIONAL AGRICULTURE
AND THE USE OF THE THRESHING SLEDGE
IN ANCIENT AND MODERN TIMES

Large quantities of grain were exported from Cyprus in antiquity, and by the Bronze Age, Cypriot farmers had developed an effective system of draft plow grain cultivation (Christodoulou 1959: 123; Allen 1989: 430; Knapp 1990: 155–59; Grishin 1996: 102). A grain farming system of growing wheat or barley crops in fields after one to three fallow years seemed to have changed very little until the middle of the 20th century. Fields were prepared with the ard, or scratch plow. Sowing and weeding were done by hand, and cereals were harvested with sickles and scythes. Threshing was done on a threshing floor (*aloni*) with threshing sledges (*dhoukanes*), while wooden shovels and pitchforks were used in the winnowing (fig. 26.2a–b). Traditional farming tools also show little change since prehistoric times (Allan 1965: 275, Allen 1989; Whittaker 1996, 1999, 2000, 2003; Given 2004). Ethnoarchaeological studies of traditional agricultural techniques in places like Cyprus, where there has been a great deal of continuity, can be used to help us study the origin and evolution of agriculture in the eastern Mediterranean.

An important part of traditional agricultural technology was the threshing sledge, or *dhoukani*, which was used in Cyprus until the 1950s when it was replaced by modern farm machinery (Pearlman 1984; Given 2004). Many scholars believed that the threshing sledge was a Roman invention (Isager and Skydsgaard 1992), but several recent studies have shown that sledges were used in Turkey, Syria, and the Balkans during the Late Neolithic, Chalcolithic/Copper Age, and Bronze Age (Skakun 1993, 1994; 1999; Anderson 1994, 1998, 1999, 2003; Anderson and Inizan 1994; Ataman 1999; Anderson and Chabot 2004; Anderson et al. 2004, 2006; Chabot and Eid 2007; Gurova and Chabot 2007). The initial use of the threshing sledge is associated with farming systems that included domesticated cattle; oxen may have been used to pull the sledges (and plows). Ethnoarchaeological

studies of *dhoukani* manufacture and use in Cyprus may provide us with a view of how ancient agricultural systems operated.

Threshing sledges consist of a platform of wooden boards that have offset rows of slots chiseled into their bases (see fig. 26.2a). A chipped-stone insert of chert, flint, or basalt is hammered into each slot. Sometimes pitch or bitumen is used to bond the stones to the sledge (Yerkes and Kardulias 1994; Whittaker 1996, 1999, 2000, 2003; Anderson 1998, 2003; Chabot and Eid 2007). Sledges were harnessed to draft animals, stones or children were added for extra weight, and a driver stood (or sat in a chair) and drove the sledge in a circle over heaps of harvested grain on a threshing floor (see fig. 26.2a; Young 1956: 124; Gjerstad 1980: 79; Isager and Skydsgaard 1992: pl. 3.5; Lohmann 1992: fig. 23; Whittaker 1996, 1999, 2000, 2003; Given 2004: 126–29). The flint "teeth" in the base of the sledge separated the grain from the chaff and stalk and also chopped up the straw, which was used as fodder or as temper for mudbricks (Anderson 1994, 1998, 2003; Anderson et al. 2006).

A few decades ago, sledges were still used by farmers throughout most of southern Europe and Southwest Asia. This widespread use of the threshing sledge in the 20th century shows that the device was more than just an antique used by "unsophisticated" farmers. The sledge is an efficient tool for the vital task of threshing grain. The grains of cereals and grasses are tightly bound in the glumes and must be parched, beat, and ground to be freed from the chaff and become edible (Anderson 1998, 1999, 2003; Anderson et al. 2006; Chabot and Eid 2007). Even with the domestication of free-threshing varieties of wheat and barley, separating the grain from the chaff remained a tedious and time-consuming chore. Preindustrial methods of threshing include beating grain with handheld flails, trampling stalks beneath the hooves of animals, or employing the threshing sledge. Ethnoarchaeological studies have shown that the sledge is more efficient than flailing or animal hooves for threshing grain (White 1967; Cheetham 1982; Anderson 1998, 1999, 2003; Anderson et al. 2006; Chabot and Eid 2007). The device would be needed to process large quantities of grain.

Threshing Sledge Flints

The hundreds of flint or chert teeth that stud the bottom of threshing sledges can be used to document the ancient use of threshing devices long after the wooden parts of the sledge have disintegrated. The sledge inserts may look like sickles, bifaces, or other chipped-stone tools (Hornell 1930; Stanley-Price 1972: 21), but on close inspection, it is found that they have a very distinctive form (Skakun 1993, 1994, 1999; Yerkes and Kardulias 1994; Kardulias and Yerkes 1996; Anderson et al. 2006; Chabot and Eid 2007; Gurova and Chabot 2007). Sledge flints are made from blade segments, or elongated flakes, with a desired length of ca. 4.5 cm. The lateral margins of sledge flints are parallel or subparallel; they exhibit minimal retouch. Edges and bulbs of percussion are thinned to facilitate insertion in the sledges. Some of the "retouch" on the exposed working edge is the result of hammering them into the slots in the sledge.

The wear traces on sledge flints are also distinctive. Macroscopic traces on sledge inserts show the initial battering, severe edge rounding, and, finally, the accumulation of gloss on their edges. Microscopic examination is needed to distinguish threshing traces from similar wear traces on sickles or plant knives that result from reaping or plant cutting. Whallon (1978: 320) noted that the wear on sledge flints differs from sickles in the polished and rounded character of the working edges and surfaces. Examination at higher magnifications (50×–300×) with an incident light microscope revealed other distinctive wear traces that result from threshing. The distribution of the microwear polish or gloss on sledge flints and the orientation and characteristics of abrasion tracks and striations on their working edges are different than the microwear observed on sickles. While sickles develop tiny dotted striae during use (presumably caused by soil grains on plant stems rolling over the flint surface when sickles are used to harvest grains), these microscopic features do not develop on sledge flints. Instead, randomly oriented striations and wide comet-shaped grooves form that give the impression that parts of the flint surface may have been torn away during the threshing.

Striations on sledge inserts run parallel to the edge, while striae on sickles and plant knives are usually oriented at an oblique (or even perpendicular) angle, since reaping is done with a sweeping motion that forces the sickle to glide along the plant stem and then through the stem at an acute angle (Juel Jensen 1989; van Gijn 1999). Threshing with the sledge causes the flints to be dragged through the grain, and stalks and the sledge inserts develop parallel wear traces. The intensity and distribution of the gloss on sledge flints are different from that observed on sickles. Usually, one face of the utilized edge of a sledge insert has well-developed wear traces and gloss, while the opposite face has spotty and less intensive wear (Runnels 1982; Skakun 1993, 1994, 1999; Anderson 1994; Anderson and Inizan 1994; Yerkes and Kardulias 1994; Kardulias and Yerkes 1996; Anderson et al. 2006; Chabot and Eid 2007; Gurova and Chabot 2007). A chronology of the introduction and diffusion of the threshing sledge may be obtained through the study of sledge flints in the archaeological record, and careful study of their form and wear traces can provide evidence for the use of sledges and threshing floors in ancient times.

Ethnographic and Archaeological Evidence for the Production and Use of Threshing Sledges

Jaques Bordaz (1965, 1969) described a five-stage lithic production system for sledge inserts in Turkey. Flint knappers living near quarries (1) obtained raw material, (2) prepared cores, (3) produced large blade blanks and manufactured sledge inserts. Next they (4) distributed preform blades to regional markets and distant sledge makers, who (5) reduced preform blades to blade segments and mounted them in sledges. Turkish preform blades are trapezoidal, 8 to 13 cm long with small bulbs of percussion. The exhausted cores are conical and 10–13 cm in length. An iron anvil and a rectangular iron bar are used to retouch the blade preforms. The retouched sledge inserts are ellipsoidal in outline. Hammers are used to mount them in the slots of the threshing sledge (Bordaz 1969; Pearlman 1984; Ataman 1992; Givens 2004). The Turkish system is similar to the blade-production trajectory that Skakun (1993, 1994, 1999) described for the Chalcolithic (or Eneolithic, 6000 BC) of Bulgaria, where large, standardized blades were produced to serve as blanks for threshing sledge flints (and also for sickle inserts). Pearlman (1984) noted that the Turkish production system is designed to produce large quantities of blade segments that are redistributed to sledge makers and then are retouched and used as sledge inserts. This system would serve consumers who do not have access to suitable flint or chert sources or know how to produce large blades.

The *dhoukani* makers of Cyprus employed a different production system (Fox 1984; Pearlman 1984; Whittaker 1996, 1999, 2000, 2003). The entire process, from chert acquisition to the final retouching and mounting of the flake blades in the sledges, is carried out by carpenters who became known as *athkiakádhes* when they mastered the art of flint knapping. In contrast to the Turkish system, a single Cypriot craftsman was responsible for making the entire threshing sledge.

Use of the *dhoukani* was widespread in Cyprus, and most villages had large threshing floors (*alonia*) located on the edge of town. However, only a few villages specialized in *dhoukani* manufacturing, and itinerant *athkiakádhes* would travel to distant farming villages to make sledges for local farmers. Pearlman (1984) outlined four stages in the system employed by Cypriot *athkiakádhes*: (1) raw material acquisition; (2) cobble testing, nodule reduction, and core preparation; (3) knapping flake-blade sledge inserts from cores; and (4) retouching the flake blades and inserting them into the sledges. *Athkiakádhes* did not go to established lithic quarries to obtain their chert like the Turkish knappers. Instead, they traveled to outcrops, streambeds, or fields where chert nodules, cobbles, or tabular blocks could be obtained at or near the ground surface. The initial reduction of the raw material usually took place at a shady area near the source. Amorphous flake cores that exhibited little or no core preparation were produced from cobble fragments or large flakes. The initial striking platforms were usually on the fresh fracture faces of split cobbles or blocks. Flake blanks were collected and taken to the *dhoukani*. The final retouching of the

flake blanks was done with a small metal knapping hammer (similar to the type used by the Turkish knappers) near the sledge, either in the *dhoukani* workshops or at a repair site.

Morphological characteristics of Cypriot sledge inserts and the debitage associated with flake-blade production enabled Fox to identify *dhoukani* production activities at 113 sites in southwestern Cyprus. The activity occurred at nearly two-thirds of the sites with lithic artifacts that were located by the Palaepaphos survey teams (Rupp et al. 1984: 139–40).

Ethnographic and Archaeological Sledge Flints from the Malloura Valley

Athienou and Petrophani were not among the villages in Cyprus that specialized in *dhoukani* manufacturing (personal communications with local informants, see also Pearlman 1984; Whittaker 1996, 1999, 2000, 2003). Moreover, there were no surviving *athkiakádhes* at either village. However, sledges were used in these villages before mechanical threshing machines were introduced. There is even a story recorded in an interview by Pearlman (1984: 214–16) of several *athkiakádhes* from Kazaphani (in the Kyrenia District) making a "double-wide" *dhoukani* in 1926 that was to be pulled by a tractor in Athienou. Four boards, instead of two, were used to make this sledge, which was 160 cm wide. It may have been pulled by the only tractor in Cyprus at that time, signaling an interesting union of older, traditional technology with the latest innovations in machine-driven farm equipment.

We found several sledges in storage in Athienou, and during our survey of Petrophani, we found a sledge that had been recycled and used as a door lintel. We collected flints from several of these sledges in Athienou and Petrophani and studied their morphology and microwear traces. We also examined 23 flints collected during our systematic survey of the Malloura Valley (fig. 26.3). Three of the historic sledge flints from Athienou and Petrophani and six of the flints from the survey were examined for microwear traces. We employed an incident light metallurgical microscope in the analysis (Yerkes and Kardulias 1993; Kardulias and Yerkes, Ch. 8), and found that five of the six sledge flints from our survey had the same distinctive wear traces that we saw on the flints we removed from sledges stored in and around Athienou (fig. 26.4). The sixth implement had microwear traces that indicated it had been used to scrape hide or some other soft material (Kardulias and Yerkes 1996: 660). The use wear traces we observed on the five sledge flints in our sample from the Malloura Valley were identical to the microwear traces that other researchers identified on prehistoric and historic sledge flints (Whallon 1978; Skakun 1993, 1994, 1999; Anderson 1994, 1998, 1999, 2003; Anderson and Inizan 1994; Yerkes and Kardulias 1994; Kardulias and Yerkes 1996; Yerkes 2000; Anderson et al. 2004, 2006; Chabot and Eid 2007; Gurova and Chabot 2007).

Eighteen of the 22 sledge flints (82%) recovered during the AAP survey were found within a 1 km radius of the village of Petrophani. These sledge flints may be associated with threshing floors lying outside of Petrophani that had been used since the Ottoman period, or even earlier. Two sledge flints were recovered on the surface of the Athienou-*Malloura* site, in the area of the Roman and medieval settlements. A single sledge flint was found on the surface of a small Late Roman–Byzantine site located 2.85 km north of the Malloura site and 1.25 km northwest of Petrophani, and another was found near a recently abandoned mudbrick structure that lies about halfway between Malloura and Petrophani (see fig. 26.3). The 22 sledge inserts from the Malloura survey were all made on elongated flakes; four were cortical, 18 were noncortical flakes. They are moderately thick pieces with minimal retouch. Their average length is 4 cm, slightly smaller that the standard length of the Cypriot flake-blade blanks described by Fox (1984) and Pearlman (1984). The flints in our Malloura sample exhibited heavy, rounded edges near their proximal ends. This indicates that they were extensively utilized, but secondary retouch was minimal. All five of the sledge flints in the microwear sample have continuous and invasive polish extending more than 8 mm in from the edge all along one lateral margin. The wear traces include well-developed plant polish,

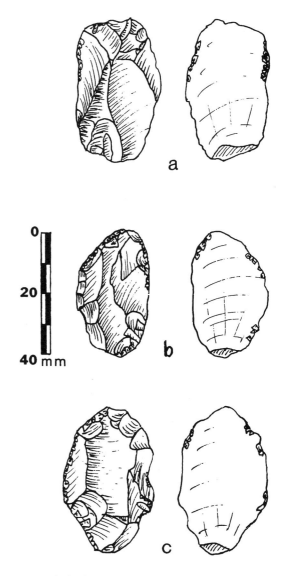

FIG. 26.3 *Sledge flints: (a) from Petrophani; (b) found near an isolated mudbrick structure in the Malloura Valley; (c) found on the surface in a barley field in the southeastern portion of the project area in the Malloura Valley (after Yerkes and Kardulias 1994: fig. 2j, k, l).*

linear striations, and extensive edge damage and rounding. Comet-shaped pits were common, but there was little or no stone-on-stone polish, suggesting that the Malloura sledges may have been used on earthen, rather than stone, threshing floors. In a sample of 13 sledge flints collected in Greece by Curtis Runnels and Nick Kardulias, two of the flint inserts had stone-on-stone microwear traces that may have developed when they were used on paved stone threshing floors (Kardulias and Yerkes 1996:

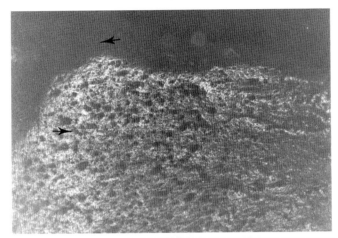

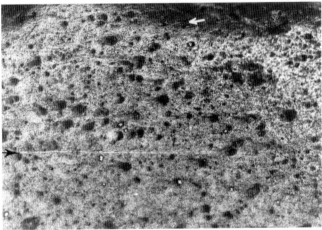

FIG. 26.4 *(a) Microwear traces on sledge flint from the base of a* dhoukani *stored in the village of Athienou. Wear on the ventral face of the exposed edge is shown. Some edge rounding can be seen at the top of the photo. Plant microwear polish, striations, and comet-shaped pits extend well back from the edge of the sledge flint (100×). (b) Top portion of same sledge flint at 150×, just to the left, showing many comet-shaped pits and a long striation parallel to the edge (after* Yerkes 2000).

662). However, threshing experiments conducted by Patty Anderson and her team on grass, beaten clay, and paved threshing floors did not produce noticeable differences in the microwear traces on the experimental sledge flints (Anderson et al. 2004). It should be noted that the wear on these modern experimental sledge inserts is not as well-developed as the visible microwear on prehistoric and historic implements, where stone-on-stone polish has been observed on some specimens. A long-term program of threshing experiments would have to be completed before different types of threshing floors can be identified from the microwear traces on the sledge flints.

Conclusions

Recent studies have shown that threshing sledges may have been used as early as 6700 BC (Late Neolithic) in the Near East and were present during the Chalcolithic period (6000 BC) in the Balkans (Skakun 1993, 1994, 1999; Anderson 1994, 1998, 1999, 2003). Bordaz (1965) proposed that the sledge came into use when cattle were domesticated, and Whallon (1978) argued sledges would have appeared when free-threshing wheat became common (also see Anderson 1998, 2003). The introduction of the device corresponds to the onset of intensive farming. It is not clear when the threshing sledge was introduced on Cyprus. It may not have been adopted until the time of the transitional Chalcolithic–Early Bronze Age Philia culture. Sledges may have been part of the cattle-plow complex that came to Cyprus during the "secondary products revolution," or second generation of agricultural innovations (Sherratt 1981; Knapp 1990: 155–59, 1994: 418, 2008: 71–73). Age profiles for Early Bronze Age cattle on Cyprus suggest they may have been producing milk, and plowing scenes are depicted in terracotta models dated to ca. 1900 BC from the cemetery at Vounous on the north coast (Dikaios 1940: pls. 9, 18; Karageorghis 1981: 30; Knapp 1990, 1994, 2008). There is no empirical evidence for the use of threshing sledges during the Bronze Age on Cyprus, but it is possible that they were part of the complex of new tools developed as cereal cultivation and agricultural production intensified.

In the Malloura Valley, the oldest sledge flints date to the early Roman period (first century BC; Toumazou et al. 1998). The distribution of sledge flints supports the view that the prehistoric use of the valley was limited and that the rural sanctuary and tombs in the center of the valley were established before there were any adjacent farming settlements. The earlier (Roman) settlement at Athienou-*Malloura* was the first nucleated farming village in the valley. It was established in the first century BC at the time when Cyprus became a Roman possession (Vermeule 1976; St. John-Jones 1983: 26). Malloura was abandoned during the epoch of Arab-Byzantine conflict (AD 647–965), but it was resettled during the period of Frankish (Lusignan) rule (St. John-Jones 1983: 26–27). Survey data suggest that the use of the valley was similar to the modern pattern, where the residents of nucleated rural settlements had vineyards, orchards, and cereal field dispersed throughout the surrounding countryside. A mixed economy of cultivation and herding was probably practiced in the settlements at Athienou-*Malloura*. The confluence of the intermittent streams and the series of wells that were dug there provided fresh water and hydraulic power for the residents.

Why did the Roman and medieval groups that came to the Malloura Valley choose to live together in a village and travel out to their fields and grazing lands rather than live on their land in dispersed farmsteads? Christodoulou (1959: 63) remarked that the reasons for nucleated settlements on Cyprus are security, water supply, and sociability. His explanation seems to be confirmed by these ethnoarchaeological investigations. Water availability drew the settlers to the center of the Malloura Valley, but the small scatters of Roman and medieval ceramics at lookout sites on the high mesas along the eastern edge of the valley (where U.N. observation posts are located) show that security was also a major concern. The results of use-wear studies, experimental archaeology programs, and ethnographic and historical research have helped us understand the cultural dynamics of rural Cyprus, but we still have so much to learn from the local residents. Their vast knowledge and their interest in the past make them an invaluable source of cultural information.

ACKNOWLEDGMENTS

This chapter represents an updated and slightly expanded version of an article that appeared in a special issue of *Near Eastern Archaeology* edited by Gloria London (Yerkes 2000). The author would like to take this opportunity to thank the editors of *NEA* for permission to reproduce, in part, that article. The author would also like to thank the Marfin Popular Bank Cultural Foundation and its director, Ms. Marina Vryonidou-Yiangou, for providing high-resolution images for figures 26.2a–b and for kindly granting permission to republish them here.

REFERENCES

Alcock, S.
1993   *Graecia Capta. The Landscapes of Roman Greece.* Cambridge: Cambridge University.

Allan, W.
1965   *The African Husbandman.* New York: Barnes and Noble.

Allen, P. S.
1989   Dhali: A Traditional Community in Transition. Pp. 425–46 in *American Expedition to Idalion, Cyprus 1973–1980,* eds. L. E. Stager and A. M. Walker. Oriental Institute Communications 24. Chicago: Oriental Institute of the University of Chicago.

Anderson, P. C.
1994   Interpreting Traces of Near Eastern Neolithic Craft Activities: An Ancestor of the Threshing Sledge for Processing Domestic Crops? *Helinium* 34(2): 306–21.
1998   History of Harvesting and Threshing Techniques for Cereals in the Prehistoric Near East. Pp. 145–59 in *The Origins of Agriculture and Crop Domestication, the Harlan Symposium,* eds. A. B. Damania, J. Valkoun, G. Wilcox, and C. O. Qualset. Aleppo: ICARDA.
1999   Experimental Cultivation, Harvest and Threshing of Wild Cereals. Pp. 104–18 in *Prehistory of Agriculture: New Experimental and Ethnographic Approaches,* ed. P. C. Anderson.

UCLA Institute of Archaeology, Monograph 40. Los Angeles: Cotsen Institute.

2003 Observations on the Threshing Sledge and Its Products in Ancient and Present-day Mesopotamia. Pp. 417–38 in *Le Traitement des Récoltes: Un Regard sur la diversité du Néolithique au Présent*, eds. P. C. Anderson, L. S. Cummings, T. K. Schippers, and B. Simonel. Antibes: ADPCA.

Anderson, P. C., and Chabot, J.
2004 Les lames cananéennes et la première machine agricole. *Les Dossiers de l'Archéologie* 290: 44–51.

Anderson, P. C., and Inizan, M.-L.
1994 Utilisation du Tribulum au Début du IIIe Millénaire: Des Lames "Cananéennes" Lustrées à Kutan (Ninive V) dans la Région de Mossoul, Iraq. *Paléorient* 20(2): 85–103.

Anderson, P. C.; Chabot, J.; and van Gijn, A.
2004 The Functional Riddle of "Glossy" Canaanean Blades and Near Eastern Threshing Sledges. *Journal of Mediterranean Archaeology* 17(1): 87–130.

Anderson, P. C.; Georges, J.-M.; Vargiolu, R.; and Zahouani, H.
2006 Insights from a Tribological Analysis of the Tribulum. *Journal of Archaeological Science* 33: 1559–68.

Ataman, K.
1999 *Prehistory of Agriculture: New Experimental and Ethnographic Approaches*, ed. P. C. Anderson. UCLA Institute of Archaeology, Monograph 40. Los Angeles: Cotsen Institute.

Attalides, M.
1976 Forms of Peasant Incorporation in Cyprus during the Last Century. Pp. 363–78 in *Regional Variations in Modern Greece and Cyprus: Towards a Perspective on the Ethnography of Greece*, eds. M. Dimen and E. Friedl. New York: Annals of the New York Academy of Science.

Beckingham, C. F.
1957 The Turks of Cyprus. *Journal of the Royal Anthropological Institute of Great Britain and Ireland* 87(2): 165–74.

Bordaz, J.
1965 The Threshing Sledge. *Natural History* 74(4): 26–29.
1969 Flint Flaking in Turkey. *Natural History* 78(2): 73–77.

Casselberry, S. E.
1974 Further Refinement of Formulae for Determining Population from Floor Area. *World Archaeology* 6: 117–22.

Chabot, J., and Eid, P.
2007 Stone Tools from a Bronze Age Village (Tell Nusstell, Syria) in Their Wider Context. *Berytus* 50: 7–36.

Cheetham, L.
1982 Threshing and Winnowing: An Ethnographic Study. *Antiquity* 56(1): 127–30.

Christodoulou, D.
1959 *The Evolution of the Rural Land Use Pattern in Cyprus*. World Land Use Survey Monograph 2. Cornwall: Geographical Publications Unlimited.

Cook, S. F., and Heizer, R. F.
1968 Relationships among Houses, Settlement Areas, and Population in Aboriginal California. Pp. 79–116 in *Settlement Archaeology*, ed. K. C. Chang. Palo Alto: National Press Books.

Cook, S. F., and Treganza, A. E.
1950 The Quantitative Investigation of Indian Mounds. *University of California Publications in American Archaeology and Ethnology* 40: 223–61.

Culbert, T. P., and Rice, D. S., (eds.)
1990 *Precolumbian Population History in the Maya Lowlands*. Albuquerque: University of New Mexico.

De Roche, C. D.
1983   Population Estimates from Settlement Area and Number of Residences. *Journal of Field Archaeology* 10(1): 187–92.

Dikaios, P.
1940   The Excavations at Vounous-Bellapais in Cyprus, 1931–32. *Archaeologia* 88. Oxford: London Society of Antiquities.

Fejfer, J., (ed.)
1995   *Ancient Akamas I: Settlement and Environment*. Aarhus: Aarhus University.

Fejfer, J., and Hayes, P.
1995   Ancient Akamas and the Abandonment of Sites in 7th Century AD Cyprus. Pp. 62–69 in *Visitors, Immigrants, and Invaders in Cyprus*, ed. P. W. Wallace. Albany: Institute of Cypriot Studies, SUNY Albany.

Fox, W. A.
1984   Dhoukani Flake Blade Production in Cyprus. *Lithic Technology* 13(1): 62–67.

Given, M.
2004   *The Archaeology of the Colonized*. London: Routledge

Gjerstad, E.
1926   *Studies on Prehistoric Cyprus*. Uppsala: Universitets Årsskrift.
1980   *Ages and Days in Cyprus*. Göteborg: Åström.

Goodwin, J. C.
1984   *An Historical Toponymy of Cyprus I, II*. London: Goodwin.

Grishin, A. D.
1996   *A Pilgrim's Account of Cyprus: Bars'kyj's Travels in Cyprus*. Sources for the History of Cyprus 3. Altamont, NY: Greece and Cyprus Research Center.

Grivaud, G.
1998   *Villages désertés à Chypre*. Nicosia: Archbishop Makarios III Foundation.

Gurova, M., and Chabot, J.
2007   Typologie, fonction, traces d'usure et contexte: Où est le juste milieu? Exemples de Bulgarie, de Troie et de Mésopotamie septentrionale.

Pp. 75–87 in *La mesure du passé: Contributions à la recherche en archéométrie (2000–2006)*, eds. A. Bain, J. Chabot, and M. Moussette. Série archéométrie numéro 5, CELAT, Université Laval Québec. British Archaeological Reports, International Series 1700. Oxford: Archeopress.

Hassan, F. A.
1976   Demographic Archaeology. Pp. 49–103 in *Advances in Archaeological Method and Theory*, vol. 1, ed. M. B. Schiffer. San Diego: Academic.

Hornell, J.
1930   The Cypriote Threshing Sledge. *Man* 30(1): 135–39.

Isager, S., and Skydsgaard, J. E.
1992   *Ancient Greek Agriculture, an Introduction*. London: Routledge.

Juel Jensen, H.
1989   Plant Harvesting and Processing with Flint Implements in the Danish Stone Age, a View from the Microscope. *Acta Archaeologica* 59: 131–42.

Kapsos, C.
1995   Modern Invaders in Cyprus. Pp. 184–89 in *Visitors, Immigrants, and Invaders in Cyprus*, ed. P. Wallace. Albany: Institute of Cypriot Studies, SUNY Albany.

Karageorghis, V.
1981   *Ancient Cyprus*. Baton Rouge: Louisiana State University.

Karageorghis, V., and Michaelides, D., (eds.)
1996   *The Development of the Cypriot Economy from the Prehistoric Period to the Present Day*. Nicosia: University of Cyprus and the Bank of Cyprus.

Kardulias, P. N.
1992   Estimating Population at Ancient Military Sites: The Use of Historical and Contemporary Analogy. *American Antiquity* 57(2): 276–87.

Kardulias, P. N., and Yerkes, R. W.

1996   Microwear and Metric Analysis of Threshing Sledge Flints from Greece and Cyprus. *Journal of Archaeological Science* 23: 657–66.

Karouzis, G.

1977   *Land Ownership in Cyprus, Past and Present.* London: Zeno Booksellers.

Knapp, A. B.

1990   Production, Location, and Integration in Bronze Age Cyprus. *Current Anthropology* 31(1): 147–76.

1994   The Prehistory of Cyprus: Problems and Prospects. *Journal of World Prehistory* 8(4): 377–453.

2008   *Prehistoric and Protohistoric Cyprus: Identity, Insularity, and Connectivity.* Oxford: Oxford University.

Kolb, C. C.

1985   Demographic Estimates in Archaeology: Contributions from Ethnoarchaeology of Mesoamerican Peasants. *Current Anthropology* 26: 581–99.

Kornrumpf, H.-J., and Kornrumpf, J.

1990   *An Historical Gazetteer of Cyprus (1850–1987) with Notes on Population.* Frankfurt am Main: Peter Lang.

LeBlanc, S.

1971   An Addition to Narroll's Suggested Floor Area and Settlement Population Relationship. *American Antiquity* 36(2): 210–11.

Lohmann, H.

1992   Agriculture and Country Life in Classical Attica. Pp. 29–57 in *Agriculture in Ancient Greece*, eds. B. Wells. Göteborg: Åström.

Markides, K. C.; Nikita, E. S.; and Rangou, E.

1978   *Lysi: Social Change in a Cypriot Village.* Nicosia: Social Research Centre.

Murphy, J. T., and Yerkes, R. W.

1998   Exploring the Relationship between Site Size and Population: A Test Case from Cyprus. Paper presented at the 63rd Annual Meeting of the Society for American Archaeology, Seattle.

Narroll, R.

1962   Floor Area and Settlement Population. *American Antiquity* 27(4): 587–89.

Ohnefalsch-Richter, M.

1994   Photographic album in *Studies in Cyprus,* eds. A. Marangou and A. Malecos. Nicosia: Cultural Centre Cyprus Popular Bank.

Papadopoullos, T.

1965   *Social and Historical Data on Population (1570–1881).* Cyprus Research Centre, Texts and Studies of the History of Cyprus 1. Nicosia: Zavallis.

Pearlman, D. A.

1984   Threshing Sledges in the Eastern Mediterranean: Ethnoarchaeology with Chert Knappers and Dhoukanes in Cyprus. M.A. thesis, University of Minnesota.

Republic of Cyprus.

1962   *Census of Population and Agriculture, 1960.* Nicosia: Government Printing Office.

1973   *Census of Population 1973.* Nicosia: Government Printing Office.

Runnels, C. N.

1982   Flaked Stone Artifacts in Greece during the Historical Period. *Journal of Field Archaeology* 9(3): 363–73.

Rupp, D. W.; Sorensen, L. W.; King, R. H.; and Fox, W. A.

1984   Canadian Paliapaphos (Cyprus) Survey Project: Second Preliminary Report, 1980–1982. *Journal of Field Archaeology* 11(2): 135–54.

Sallade, J. K.

1989   Ethnoarchaeological Investigations, 1976. Pp. 407–24 in *American Expedition to Idalion, Cyprus 1973–1980*, eds. L. E. Stager and A. M. Walker. Oriental Institute Communications 24. Chicago: Oriental Institute.

Schreiber, K. J., and Kintigh, K. W.

1996   A Test of the Relationship between Site Size and Population. *American Antiquity* 61(3): 573–79.

Sherratt, A. G.
1981   Plough and Pastoralism: Aspects of the Secondary Products Revolution. Pp. 261–305 in *Pattern of the Past: Studies in Honour of David Clarke,* eds. I. Hodder, G. Isaac, and N. Hammond. Cambridge: Cambridge University.

Sinos, S
1986   Types of Rural Dwellings in Cyprus. Pp. 520–33 in *Acts of the International Archaeological Symposium "Cyprus between the Orient and the Occident,"* ed. V. Karageorghis. Nicosia: Department of Antiquities, Republic of Cyprus.

Skakun, N.
1993   Agricultural Implements in the Neolithic and Eneolithic Cultures of Bulgaria. Pp. 361–68 in *Traces et Fonction: Les Gestes Retrouves,* eds. P. C. Anderson, S. Beyries, M. Otte, and H. Plisson. Liège: Etudes et Recherches Archéologiques de l'Université de Liège 50.
1994   Agricultural Implements and the Problem of Spreading of Agriculture in Southeastern Europe. *Helinium* 2: 294–305.
1999   Evolution of Agricultural Techniques in Eneolithic (Chalcolithic) Bulgaria: Data from Use-Wear Analysis. Pp. 199–210 in *Prehistory of Agriculture: New Experimental and Ethnographic Approaches,* ed. P. Anderson. Monograph 40. Los Angeles: Cotsen Institute of Archaeology, UCLA.

Solsten, Eric, (ed.)
1993   *Cyprus: A Country Study.* Fourth edition. Washington: U.S. Information Service, Area Handbook Series.

Stanley-Price, N.
1972   A Prehistoric Survey of the Analiondas Region. *Report of the Department of Antiquities, Cyprus* (1972): 15–21.

St. John-Jones, L. W.
1983   *The Population of Cyprus: Demographic Trends and Socio-Economic Influences.* University of London Institute of Commonwealth Studies, Commonwealth Papers 23. London: Temple Smith.

Sumner, W. M.
1989   Population and Settlement Area: An Example from Iran. *American Anthropologist* 91(4): 631–41.

Surridge, B. J.
1930   *A Survey of Rural Life in Cyprus.* Nicosia: Government Printing Office.

Thirgood, J. K.
1987   *Cyprus: A Chronicle of Its Forests, Land, and People.* Vancouver: University of British Columbia.

Toumazou, M. K.; Yerkes, R. W.; and Kardulias, P. N.
1998   Athienou Archaeological Project: Investigations in the Malloura Valley, Cyprus, 1990–1995. *Journal of Field Archaeology* 25(2): 163–82.

van Gijn, A. L.
1999   The Interpretation of Sickles: A Cautionary Tale. Pp. 254–59 in *Prehistory of Agriculture: New Experimental and Ethnographic Approaches,* ed. P. C. Anderson. Monograph 40. Los Angeles: Cotsen Institute.

Vermeule, C. C.
1976   *Greek and Roman Cyprus: Art from Classical Through Late Antique Times.* Boston: Museum of Fine Arts.

Wallace, P. W., (ed.)
1995   *Visitors, Immigrants, and Invaders in Cyprus.* Albany: Institute of Cypriot Studies, SUNY Albany.

Whallon, R. J.
1978   Threshing Sledge Flints: A Distinctive Pattern of Wear. *Paléorient* 4(4): 319–24.

White, K. D.
1967   *Agricultural Implements of the Roman World.* London: Cambridge University.

Whittaker, J.
1996   *Ahkiajas*: A Cypriote Flintknapper and the Threshing Sledge Industry. *Lithic Technology* 21(2): 108–20.
1999   *Alonia*: The Ethnoarchaeology of Cypriot Threshing Floors. *Journal of Mediterranean Archaeology* 12: 7–25.

2000 *Alonia* and *Dhoukanes*: The Ethnoarchaeology of Threshing in Cyprus. *Near Eastern Archaeology* 63(2): 62–69.

2003 Threshing Sledges and Threshing Floors in Cyprus. Pp. 375–88 in *Le Traitement des Récoltes: Un Regard sur la diversité du Néolithique au Présent*, eds. P. C. Anderson, L. S. Cummings, T. K. Schippers, and B. Simonel. Antibes: International Center for Agricultural Research in the Dry Areas (ICARDA).

Wiessner, P.
1974 A Functional Estimator of Population from Floor Area. *American Antiquity* 39(3): 343–50.

Yerkes, R. W.
2000 Ethnoarchaeology in Central Cyprus: Interdisciplinary Studies of Ancient Population and Agriculture by the Athienou Archaeological Project. *Near Eastern Archaeology* 63(1): 20–34.

Yerkes, R. W., and Kardulias, P. N.
1993 Recent Developments in the Analysis of Lithic Artifacts. *Journal of Archaeological Research* 1(2): 89–119.

1994 Microwear Analysis of Threshing Sledge Flints from Cyprus and Greece: Implications for the Study of Ancient Agriculture. *Helinium* 34(2): 281–93.

Young, J. H.
1956 Studies in South Attica: Country Estates at Sounion. *Hesperia* 25: 122–46.

Chapter 27

Archaeology and the Structure
of Community Relations in Athienou

by P. Nick Kardulias, Michael K. Toumazou, and Derek B. Counts

Archaeologists often live rather anonymously in communities during field projects. In the case of the Athienou Archaeological Project, a mutually supportive relationship exists between the project and the town of Athienou. The local government and various businesses have provided an unprecedented level of logistical support, as have many individuals. In turn, the archaeologists have made sustained efforts in historical and archaeological preservation, salvage excavations, and public presentations to the community concerning the various phases of work; the project also contributes to the local economy through various expenditures. In many ways, the project has become well-integrated with the local community. This chapter documents the extent of this cooperation and the effects on both the people of Athienou and the visiting archaeologists.

THEORY: ARCHAEOLOGY AND COMMUNITY

As archaeologists, how we think about our work is critical to the archaeological endeavor itself. The debate centers on which approach best allows us to deal faithfully with the issues. In anthropology, the struggle centers on the applicability of a scientific perspective. A generalizing scientific perspective offers a more complete explanation for a variety of phenomena, including the topic of this chapter. In particular, the cultural materialist perspective of Marvin Harris provides a useful model for understanding the social relations discussed here. The cultural materialist approach can link economic concerns, social relations, and ideology within a comprehensive framework.

Harris leaves no doubt as to what he perceives to be the ultimate motivating factors behind human behavior:

> The essence of cultural materialism is that it directs attention to the interaction between behavior and environment as mediated by the human organism and its cultural apparatus. It does so as an order of priority in conformity with the prediction that group structure and ideology are responsive to these classes of material conditions. (Harris 1968: 659)

Thus, cultural materialism provides a programmatic statement that allows one to pinpoint the crucial components underlying social life. This perspective is based on "the premise that human social life is a response to the practical problems of earthly existence" (Harris 1979: ix). Humans are seen as engaged in an ongoing attempt to ameliorate their environment or to deal with demographic pressure by expanding the potential of the environment through the process of intensification, that is, increased exploitation of available resources in response to ecological shifts (both natural and cultural). In the Athienou region, we see multiple examples of this flexibility in human response to changed conditions. For example, after the establishment of the political

FIG. 27.1 *Enclosed dairy cattle in area north of Petrophani (photo: P. N. Kardulias).*

cal barrier between the two parts of Cyprus in 1974, and the subsequent exchange of populations, the people of Athienou who lost access to the rich farmland north of the town focused their attention on the Malloura Valley to the south and initiated extensive crop alteration, accompanied by the introduction of dairy cattle of northern European type (fig. 27.1).

Harris lays out the theoretical principles of cultural materialism. These principles deal with understanding the relationships among the parts of sociocultural systems and with the evolution of these systems. He calls the recurrent aspects of such systems the universal pattern, which has three major subdivisions: (1) infrastructure, comprised of the activities by which every society meets its basic subsistence requirements (mode of production) and by which every society controls population size (mode of reproduction); (2) structure, comprised of economic and political activities by which every society forms groups to allocate, regulate, and exchange labor and goods (domestic economy refers to the organization of basic production and reproduction, exchange and consumption within camps, houses, or other domestic settings; political economy refers to the organization of these same

activities within and between bands, villages, chiefdoms, states, and empires); (3) superstructure, comprised of thought and behavior concerned with artistic, playful, religious, and intellectual efforts, plus the mental aspects of infrastructure and structure (Harris 1987: 17). These are the basic aspects of an anthropological research strategy that provides causal explanations for the similarities and differences in thought and behavior exhibited by various human societies. This task is best conducted by examining the material constraints that delimit human activity (Harris 1987: 421).

Cultural materialism is especially well-suited to archaeology because archaeologists deal directly with the material record as the primary source of data. This perspective asserts the strategic priority of infrastructural over structural and superstructural conditions and processes. However, it does not deny the possibility that superstructural and structural components may achieve a degree of independence from infrastructure. There is an attempt to build a theory of culture that incorporates the lawful regularities occurring in nature. There are two entrenched laws humans must face. First, people must expend energy to obtain energy. Second, the human ability to produce children exceeds the ability to obtain energy for them. Harris suggests that the best humans can do is to seek a balance between reproduction, on the one hand, and the production and consumption of energy, on the other. He then argues that cultural evolution, like biological evolution, has occurred through opportunistic alterations that increase benefits and lower costs to individuals. Success of a group depends on the success of its individuals (Harris 1979: 56, 60). The implications of this thesis for the understanding of past human societies center on the notion that most people engage in activities they believe will enhance their material position in the world. Ideology is also part of such a survival strategy. Those individuals who adopt strategies yielding the greatest returns can be termed successful because of the advantages they garner for themselves, their kin, and their followers.

The types of community relations that are the focus of this chapter lie in the structure, while expressions of cultural value are elements of the superstructure (see Kardulias et al., Ch. 1). What the cultural materialist approach makes possible is an understanding of the dynamic relationship between these aspects of social behavior. Social identity is inextricably linked to local subsistence patterns, which in turn are reflected in the ties that members of social groups share with each other and with outsiders. The main community values for the people of Athienou have to do with their lives as farmers and in associated vocations, and archaeology helps to confirm the long-standing nature of these values in this particular area. Furthermore, a materialist approach helps us comprehend how the sense of local identity is maintained as the economy becomes increasingly integrated into regional, national, and international networks (i.e., globalization). Fundamental elements of production still occur at the local level, and family structures are crucial in the new economic systems that arise by providing important capital outlay and a committed pool of labor; by maintaining a sense of self and place, the people of Athienou do well to take advantage of opportunities as they arise.

Scholars with other perspectives have weighed in on the issue of the formation and maintenance of local identity, and it is important to mention

some of their points. Taking their cue from works such as David Lowenthal's *The Past Is a Foreign Country* (1985), some have argued that depictions of the past are constructed to serve various contemporary purposes and may, as a result, bear little resemblance to what actually happened historically. Herzfeld (1982, 1987) has argued that western scholars who discuss ancient Greece engage, to some extent at least, in a hegemonic discourse that has disenfranchised the modern inhabitants of the country. Since the 19th century AD, however, Greeks have sought actively to reclaim that heritage for their own purposes, including the development of a nationalist ideology to unite the fledgling Greek state. Herzfeld (1991: 5) has also dealt with the issue of historical preservation in Rethymno, Crete, where he argues there occurred a "battle over the future of the past." In this case, it was a struggle between the Greek governmental bureaucracy and local residents whose efforts to control their own property were constrained by the government's designation of the old part of the city as historically unique and thus not open to renovation outside certain guidelines. He also posits the existence of "monumental time" as something that is "extremely vulnerable to creative reuse by the same social forces that it seeks to control" (Herzfeld 1991: 15). The use of time is thus an element of power that different groups manipulate in developing a notion of place. In such circumstances, archaeologists can be viewed as members of the bureaucracy that seeks to establish a certain approach to the past by maintaining old structures against the desires of the owners.

Fotiadis (1995) has also addressed the relationship between archaeologists and the people whom they study. In discussing the development of regional studies in Greece, he asserts that a modernist approach emerged. A key element of the perspective is "a sharp distinction between researchers and researched" (Fotiadis 1995: 74). Here is a matter of general concern for those of us who work in the Mediterranean. As Trigger has noted, "While archaeologists generally are caricatured as embodiments of the myopic, the unworldly and the inconsequential, the findings of archaeology have always been sources of public controversy"

(Trigger 1984: 357). To what extent do archaeologists distance themselves from the modern people in whose communities they reside while they study the region's past inhabitants? While this question is certainly a matter of considerable importance, we suggest that a materialist perspective can make significant contributions to understanding the role of archaeology in modern society. Perhaps the most significant aspect of this study, in contrast to the others mentioned above, is that we argue for a more fully comparative, scientific approach. Just as Harris (1974) made sense of "riddles of culture" through cultural materialism, we suggest there is a role for this theoretical framework in understanding the relationship between our project and the local community.

Fitting In: Archaeology in Athienou

The AAP has enjoyed exceptional local support from its inception. There are various reasons for this positive relationship, and below we explore some of the dimensions of that cordial dialogue. Among these are the political climate in Cyprus and Athienou, the support provided by local civic institutions and private individuals, financial assistance from expatriate Athienites, the interactive economic effects between the project and the town, and the educational/cultural impact of the project (for both Athienou and AAP).

One of the major advantages of AAP is that its director (Toumazou) is a native Cypriot, with many relatives in Athienou. The locals take pride in the fact that "one of their own" is a professor at an American university and has undertaken a major research project in their backyard. This is a symbiotic relationship. Toumazou was looking for an area to conduct an excavation in the late 1980s, and certain Athienites were anxious to revitalize interest in their town, which since August 1974 had become peripheral and largely cut-off from the rest of the free parts of the Republic. While much was known about the history of the region because of historical references and the earlier work of archaeologists (Cesnola 1878; Dothan and Ben-Tor 1983; Bakalakis 1988; see also Counts, Ch. 4), in the view of many residents, Athienou received far less atten-

tion than its historical position merited. In addition, the townspeople speak proudly about the economic prosperity that Athienou has generated and the accomplishments of its residents in many fields, much of which occurred after the 1974 war and the resulting loss of access to ca. 80–85% of their agricultural land to the east, west, and, primarily, north of town. Local community leaders saw the AAP as the ideal way to convey a message to the outside world; by putting Athienou more firmly on the archaeological map, the town would be able to showcase its other accomplishments. Civic pride is a powerful economic and political motivator. Here we see a mutual feedback between infrastructure and superstructure, in which the ideational component strongly reinforces the economic strides that the community has made, especially since 1974. The town of Athienou has in many ways redefined itself and gained a high level of economic well-being, often described as nothing less than an "economic miracle." Making a show of the local archaeology is one way to demonstrate that fact. The possibility of drawing Cypriot as well as foreign tourists to the town certainly plays into some of the plans as well. Beyond the local level of support, AAP has benefited equally from the receptive attitude of the Department of Antiquities to foreign projects. In sharp contrast to the situation in Greece, where increasing restrictions create significant obstacles for foreign archaeological missions (see Kardulias 1994), the Republic of Cyprus has retained a more open posture. Certainly, the fact that Toumazou, a native Cypriot, leads the project is significant, and AAP has benefited from official sanction and support for the project at the national level, which complements the local enthusiasm.

Like most other Cypriot towns, Athienou has vocal political factions, the members of which frequent their respective social clubs. There are two points of interest here. First, several of the clubs bear the names of historical or literary places or individuals (e.g., Golgoi, Othello), the former with a local flavor (fig. 27.2). Second, despite the sometimes acrimonious disputes that can occur between members of opposing political parties, there is general agreement on the value of the AAP. In other words, archaeology serves as a mechanism

FIG. 27.2   *View of the Golgoi Athletic Club building in Athienou (photo: P. N. Kardulias).*

a   b

FIG. 27.3A–B   *Logos for the (a) town of Athienou and (b) the Athienou Archaeological Project (AAP logo design: Daniel Coslett).*

to crosscut social and political divisions, much like sodalities do in various cultures. As proof of this role, AAP has received consistently excellent treatment by successive mayoral administrations of different political persuasions (fig. 27.3). Beginning with Kostas Sakkalos in 1990, and continuing under the administrations of Panayiotis Koumis, Gavriel Kazazis, and Spyros Papouis, the municipality has provided the following assistance to the project:

1. Vehicles. The town council authorizes our use of a municipal four-wheel-drive truck during the field season and has co-purchased a multiseat

minibus, which it maintains and licenses. The municipality also pays for all our fuel and drivers' insurance.

2. Housing. The town administration has provided between one and four buildings to house project personnel each year. In some instances, these are public facilities (e.g., new preschool, municipal gym) or private homes or structures for which the town pays the rent. Between 1995 and 2008, the Kostas Lambaskis family generously made available to us at no charge their magnificent old home (called "the Palace" by project members) on a year-round basis and it served as project headquarters; the municipality paid for water, electricity, and telephone service. Senior project members and specialists studying project material who came to Cyprus at other times stayed in this house (fig. 27.4–5). The municipality also supplied us with a building to serve as our archaeological laboratory each year. When a new municipal building, the Kallinikeion Megaron, was completed in 2006, it included

FIG. 27.4 *Project members and local people. Left to right: James Acton (project volunteer), Father Kallinikos (native of Athienou and renowned icon painter), Kostas Sakkalos (former mayor of Athienou), Susan Toumazou, Michael Toumazou (AAP Director). Photo taken outside the workshop of Father Kallinikos at Stavrovouni (photo: G. Sakkalos).*

FIG. 27.5 *The Lambaskis house in Athienou, AAP headquarters from 1995 to 2008 (photo: M. K. Toumazou).*

FIG. 27.6 *The archaeology laboratory in the new municipal building (photo: M. K. Toumazou).*

the Athienou Municipal Museum. In addition to ethnographic exhibits and an important collection of icons painted by the renowned native son Father Kallinikos, this impressive facility includes archaeological artifacts from systematic and salvage excavations in the Athienou area and showcases AAP artifacts and images. Moreover, the Kallinikeion Megaron includes a permanent state-of-the-art archaeological laboratory, with ample storage areas, designed with AAP's needs in mind (fig. 27.6). Plans are underway to renovate an old building in the town to replace the old "Palace" and serve as the permanent project headquarters.

3. Payment of electric and water bills. The municipal administration also pays for maintenance of the buildings used by project personnel.

4. End-of-the-season banquet for the whole project staff, to coincide with the village lecture given by the director in Greek; additionally, subvention is provided for food prepared by the cook at the municipal retirement home.

5. Logistical support. The mayors and town secretaries have provided information, advice, and other services, including access to the photocopy machine and fax, and now internet service, in the municipal building. Moreover, during the early years of the project when the town's water supply was rationed the municipality made sure that "the archaeologists" got more than their share of water supplies!

The AAP is engaged directly with the "Cyprus problem" because the town is located in the buffer or 'dead zone' along the green line between the occupied part of the island to the north and the Republic of Cyprus to the south. The U.N. has a military base at the north end of Athienou and patrols the entire project area. To conduct our investigations, we require permission from the government of Cyprus, but need cooperation of the U.N. command as well. The nationality of the U.N. troops and police officers in Athienou has changed several times since the inception of the project. We have dealt with Australian and Irish police, as well

FIG. 27.7   *Austrian U. N. troops at Malloura (photo: P. N. Kardulias).*

FIG. 27.8   *Visit by United States Ambassador to the Republic of Cyprus Donald K. Bandler to Athienou-Malloura (photo: D. B. Counts).*

as Austrian, British, and Hungarian troops who have demonstrated varying degrees of interest in our work. In some seasons U.N. patrols passed by the main excavation site at Athienou-*Malloura* on a daily basis, and in some years even maintained regular watch over our field activities (fig. 27.7). By and large, the project has enjoyed good relations with the U.N. An almost annual event, however, is the initial unfriendly contact with the U.N. when the troops first notice our presence in the field. At the inception of several field seasons we were informed that we do not have the right to engage in any activity in the buffer zone. After discussions between the project director, the local U.N. commander, and the ranking U.N. officials in Nicosia, the situation is always rectified, but it demonstrates a breakdown in the military chain of communication, as U.N. personnel change frequently and new troops often are unaware of the permission granted for our fieldwork at the inception of the project. The local Cypriot officials also intercede on our behalf, an action that cements our relationship. We must note that our relations with the U.N. are generally good and have in some years been excellent. Several times when there was an Austrian contingent in Athienou, the local U.N. commander invited all project members to their camp for dinner. The mere presence of the U.N. in the town, of course, is a constant reminder to the locals that they have lost part of their patrimony; it is also something the project members come to understand as part of the larger political and economic context within which AAP exists, a fact that often elicits considerable sympathy for our hosts. As directors, we remind our students regularly of the geopolitical situation, and they come to understand quickly that archaeology does not take place in a cultural or historical void.

At the invitation of the project director, successive U.S. ambassadors to Cyprus have visited the project on many occasions. These visits are important cultural and political events for both the people of Athienou and the members of the project (fig. 27.8). Typically, the ambassador arrives with an entourage that includes officials from the embassy and the U.N. After an official greeting at the city hall, the group takes a tour of the excavation and then returns to Athienou to inspect the latest finds; a luncheon sponsored by the municipality follows. It is a singular honor for the town to have the ambassador present, and the visit receives national media coverage, placing the small town on the political landscape.

In addition to the assistance from the municipality, the Athienou Cooperative [Bank] or CO-OP has provided a number of important services. Since 1991, during seasons when we have field school students, the bank has paid for a bus and driver on weekends to transport AAP students and staff on excursions to historic, archaeological, and natural sites throughout the island. These day-long trips have become a regular part of the AAP educational program. The bank has also assisted AAP with a variety of financial matters, such as partial funding for vehicle purchase and printing of T-shirts during field seasons. Moreover, along with the municipality, the Athienou CO-OP has supported our efforts at site preservation. Of course, there are additional issues that are part of this benefit. For example, the trips are an opportunity for bus drivers to earn supplemental income. The project director must be aware of this issue, and occasionally gets involved in the negotiations concerning a particular trip and competing drivers. On our end, the project conducts its financial transactions through the CO-OP, and, in the days before ATM machines, project members exchanged money and travelers' checks there.

Our project touches the deep-seated sense of civic pride of individual Athienites as well as officials. People in town constantly ask us about what we have found. They commonly stop by the excavation to see firsthand the work and finds. Since its inception, the project has employed four to five local youth from Athienou yearly as excavators that serve as natural bridges between our students and the village. As a consequence of their experience with AAP, several went on to study in the US or to pursue careers in archaeology. Others go on to become prominent citizens in the town with a well-founded understanding and support of our work. What has been particularly fascinating for us is the level of interest that expatriate Athienites exhibit about the project. For example, Nikos Mouyiaris, an Athienou native and successful New York City businessman, has made generous cash donations to the project that made possible the initial seasons of work. In addition, groups of Athienou natives in New York City and Australia have given money to the project on several occasions.

We have also received other material support. Kostas Zorbas, owner of the famous "Zorbas Bakeries" in Athienou and other towns, has directed the employees in his local establishment to provide us with as much bread as we need to feed the project members; as a result, we have not paid for a loaf of bread in nearly 20 years. In addition, through an arrangement with the Athienou Cattle Owners Association, various individuals provide us with unlimited supplies of cheese (Cypriot halloumi) at no charge; one even permitted us to use his large walk-in refrigerator to cool water containers and the prepared lunch food that goes out to the field team each day during excavation seasons. Since 1994, we have also been supplied with free eggs by the Hadjiyannakou Brothers Farm. While we gain financial and in-kind support for our endeavors, the contributors reinforce their social identities as members of a specific Cypriot community.

As noted above, the relationship between the project and the town is symbiotic. The municipality, CO-OP, and various individuals all provide financial support and/or services without which AAP would require a much larger budget, charge students far more for attending, and so on. The project, however, also gives to the community in a number of ways. First, there is the financial component. While contributions of money have been very important, several funding agencies (primarily the National Science Foundation Research Experience for Undergraduates program) have provided the major monetary support for the project since 1995. The money from those sources pays for meals, equipment, and various supplies purchased from local businesses. The single largest component of these expenditures is food. To feed 40 to 50 project members during field seasons over a period of seven to eight weeks, we have frequented a number of local restaurants and on occasion hired a cook. In addition, we purchase large quantities of food for group lunches. As with the bus drivers, the local

restaurants compete for our business; the director handles these negotiations, the results of which have a significant impact on particular businesses. In addition to this large-scale infusion of cash by the AAP into the local economy, individual project members purchase food, drink, and other items on their own. Faculty and students have also used the services of a local travel agent to book excursions to Egypt and Israel. Collectively, these activities increase the cash flow in the town.

Second, the locals and project members have developed personal relationships. At a general level, the welcome we have received over the years reflects the traditional Cypriot hospitality. From the purchase of rounds of drinks at local cafes to the plate of pastries that appears on a table in a project house to invitations to visit homes and attend weddings (as many as two per week), we have repeatedly witnessed the extraordinary generosity of the people of Athienou. These acts are part, of course, of a reciprocal gift-exchange complex that has deep roots in Cypriot and Mediterranean culture. Nonetheless, our hosts are under no obligation to us, especially the contingent of students that changes on an annual basis. The community has certainly embraced the project and its members. Numerous friendships have blossomed over the years between the locals and project members, and when given the opportunity, the Americans have acted to repay the generosity we have received. At the personal level, the daughter of the former mayor Sakkalos attended Davidson College, and various members of the project, including senior staff and students, treated her as the friend that she, her family, and town have been to AAP. In addition, our yearly presence serves as a diversion from the routine of daily life in the town.

Another reason for this happy coexistence is the important role the project has come to play in reinforcing the cultural identity of the town's residents. For two decades, Athienou, considered a rural backwater by many, has had its own excavation and so, to some extent, is on a par with more renowned locations such as Idalion, Amathous, or even Paphos. The construction of a museum in the town has enhanced this standing, especially because important finds from past work are being returned

Fig. 27.9 *Grade school students from Athienou visiting the tombs at Mağara Tepeşi (Site 2) during a tour of Malloura (photo: M. K. Toumazou).*

from other museums, such as that in Larnaka. The work of the project has been featured prominently in several publications about Athienou produced by the residents. For example, images from the excavation can be found in a brochure about the town. In a book about Athienou, 13 pages are devoted to the AAP. The chapter ends: "The people of Athienou hope that this knight of Malloura [Toumazou] with the characteristic cowboy hat, which he never removes even at night, will come for many more summers with his beloved team and each time throw yet more light on the history and culture of Cyprus in general and of Athienou in particular" (Lambrou 2001: 177). Toumazou has made it a key goal of the project to inform the residents about what we are doing and finding. Each summer he presents a public lecture in Greek to a full house of local residents followed by visual inspection of noteworthy finds (and, as mentioned above, the entire project is invited to be guests at a celebratory dinner); in many years, the town has given project members gifts (including desk clocks, mouse pads, duffle bags, T-shirts, hats, souvenir medallions), often with the Athienou logo, so that we take a

part of Athienou back to our various states. In addition, grade- and junior high-school students visit Malloura on a regular basis, and Toumazou gives them a guided tour of the site. Recently, elementary school teachers created a unit on the project and made it a regular part of the curriculum (fig. 27.9). Students write essays about the excavation and post these on a board for public display. The teachers use the project as a way to instill pride in local history and build a sense of community. The effort has been so successful that on a visit to the school a few years ago, Toumazou received spontaneous cheers from students; in accordance with this celebrity status, the students asked for his autograph. To our knowledge, not even luminaries such as Lewis Binford or Patty Jo Watson have received such accolades in the United States.

Preservation of some of the key remains at Malloura has become an important matter for the municipal government. Together with the Athienou CO-OP, it donated materials and the cost of labor to build protective covers over the rock-cut chamber tombs at Mağara Tepeşi (Site 2) as well as fence and plant with trees some of the excavated

FIG. 27.10 *Sign for archaeological site at Malloura (photo: M. K. Toumazou).*

areas. Members of AAP also offered labor and technical expertise in this effort, beginning with the evaluation phase and continuing with the construction of a stairway into the largest of the tombs (see Breuker and Breuker, Ch. 25). Along with the stabilization of walls in the Cypro-Geometric III–Roman sanctuary undertaken by our conservator (Breuker and Breuker, Ch. 25), we have begun the process of site preservation in concert with the local officials and the Department of Antiquities. The ultimate goal is to create an archaeological park where future visitors may gain a fuller appreciation of the site. The municipality will have something tangible to show for its support of the project, both to the tourists and dignitaries who visit the site and, perhaps more importantly, to the people of Athienou and other Cypriots. In 2008 major strides were made in this direction with the paving of the road from Athienou to Malloura and the installation of the characteristic brown road signs reserved for historical and archaeological monuments (fig. 27.10). The following year, a parking area large enough to accommodate several buses was built next to the covered tombs at Mağara Tepeşi

(Site 2), and a group of Cypriot tour guides visited Malloura to learn about the remains in preparation for bringing tourists to the site.

We conclude this section and the chapter with a final example of how deeply to heart the people of Athienou have taken the project. A group of interested Athienou citizens formed a civic cultural club in 2001 named the Malloura Club. Among its various activities, the organization sponsors public events at which traditional Cypriot dances and music are performed (significantly, in front of a large wooden stage set elaborately painted with a landscape of the Malloura Valley and its antiquities). Two members of the Malloura Club, Kostas Mavrou and Mihalis Agapiou have, respectively, written the lyrics, and performed and recorded a song titled *Archaia Malloura Mou* (*My Ancient Malloura*) in the Cypriot Greek dialect accompanied by traditional Cypriot music which makes specific reference to AAP. Agapiou has performed the song at several public events in Athienou (fig. 27.11) and recorded a version for members of the AAP. Below are the lyrics by Mavrou:

FIG. 27.11 *Mihalis Agapiou singing* My Ancient Malloura *at an event in Athienou sponsored by the Malloura Club (photo: M. K. Toumazou).*

Mesaoria's jewel,
the golden one of the fields,
you linger in my heart.

You are for me, from now on,
an ornament in all the world,
that beautifies Creation.

And my heart delights
that they came and resurrected you,
like a bride they adorned you,
my ancient Malloura.

And my soul delights,
my mind, my body,
you are my dreams,
my ancient Malloura.

You beautify the "Two-hill" [mount]
and shine, and flaunt yourself
so that all are envious.

All the villages want
to have such beauty,
and everybody praises you.

And my heart delights
that they came and resurrected you,

like a bride they adorned you
my ancient Malloura

And my soul delights,
my mind, my body,
you are my dreams,
my ancient Malloura

In the summertime evenings,
as the sun dips,
you lie down, finally rest.

And with the mounts as company
and the Archangel's church
you resurrect memories.

And my heart delights
that they came and resurrected you,
like a bride they adorned you
my ancient Malloura

And my soul delights,
my mind, my body
you are my dreams
my ancient Malloura
my ancient Malloura.

Conclusion

The AAP has enjoyed an unparalleled degree of cooperation from the people of Athienou. The project could not operate as productively and efficiently as it does without the support of the various constituencies identified above. The benefits do not come without effort, of course. Toumazou and other members of the staff spend a considerable amount of time cultivating the relationships with individuals and institutions that facilitate the archaeological work. By acknowledging the need and desire of Athienites to know about their past, we treat our hosts as active agents in the creation of knowledge and open a dialogue that works to the benefit of all concerned. In this way, there are clear and dynamic links between the practical aspects of infrastructure and the ideational elements of superstructure. The work of AAP offers the people of Athienou an opportunity to reinforce their local identity, a vital element in creating and maintaining a sense of place that facilitates the integration of social, economic, political, and religious networks in a community. The project simultaneously serves our academic needs and the ideological and practical concerns of the people of Athienou. The result has been an unusually strong bond between the local people and the archaeologists as their respective interests coincide.

References

Bakalakis, G.
1988   Ανασκαφή στο Λόφο Γιόρκους ΒΑ της Αθηαίνου, Κύπρος. Athens: Αρχαιολογική Εταιρεία Αθηνών.

Cesnola, L. P. di
1878   *Cyprus: Its Ancient Cities, Tombs, and Temples.* New York: Harper. Reprint 1991.

Dothan, T., and, Ben-Tor, A.
1983   *Excavations at Athienou, Cyprus, 1971/1972.* Qedem 16. Jerusalem: Hebrew University.

Fotiadis, M.
1995   Modernity and the Past-Still-Present: Politics of Time in the Birth of Regional Archaeological Projects in Greece. *American Journal of Archaeology* 99: 59–78.

Harris, M.
1968   *The Rise of Anthropological Theory.* New York: Thomas Y. Crowell.
1974   *Cows, Pigs, Wars, and Witches: The Riddles of Culture.* New York: Random House.
1979   *Cultural Materialism.* New York: Random House.
1987   *Cultural Anthropology.* Second edition. New York: Harper and Row.

Herzfeld, M.
1982   *Ours Once More: Folklore, Idology, and the Making of Modern Greece.* Austin: University of Texas.
1987   *Anthropology through the Looking-Glass: Critical Ethnography in the Margins of Europe.* Cambridge: Cambridge University.
1991   *A Place in History: Social and Monumental Time in a Cretan Town.* Princeton: Princeton University.

Kardulias, P. N.
1994   Archaeology in Modern Greece: Bureaucracy, Politics, and Science. Pp. 373-87 in *Beyond the Site: Regional Studies in the Aegean Area,* ed. P. N. Kardulias. Lanham, MD: University Press of America.

Lambrou, G. K.
2001   Ο Μιχάλης Τουμάζου καί οί Ανασκαφές στή Μάλλουρα. Pp. 165–77 in *Αθηένου,* ed. M. Mallouris, D. Zannettidou-Bougerasi, B. Trachilou, and R. Ierodiakonou. Αθηένου: Δήμος Αθηένου.

Lowenthal, D.
1985   *The Past Is a Foreign Country.* Cambridge: Cambridge University.

Trigger, B.
1984   Alternative Archaeologies: Nationalist, Colonialist, Imperialist. *Man* 19: 355–70.

Conclusion

by P. Nick Kardulias, Derek B. Counts, and Michael K. Toumazou

The preceding chapters have presented a range of specific studies on the various aspects of our project. The individual contributors comprise a large group who have all worked directly with either the excavation or survey in the field and, in some cases, taking part in both parts of our investigations. This intimate familiarity with the project, the region, and the material culture provides important insights to the ways in which objects, architecture, and land use changed over time. To access this rich store of data, the investigators had recourse to various methods. The techniques they employ range from quantitative analyses (e.g., magnetometry and soil chemistry) to qualitative assessments (e.g., object typology and artistic style). However, encompassing all of this work are several central concerns. Among these are how and why ancient Cypriots chose to utilize various parts of the Malloura region differently over time, and the degree to which the factors that drove those actions were local or external. To help us explain these processes, we adopted the approaches outlined in Chapter 1, including cultural ecology, materialism, world-systems analysis, and traditional interpretive methods, which all share a concern with how people define themselves, their surroundings, and their relationships with others. It is from this emphasis that we draw our understanding of the complex ways in which the Malloura Valley has been both a crossroad and a boundary region over its long history.

Through the recognition of complex and overlapping socio-economic, political, and religious linkages, the studies that comprise this volume explore the specific ways in which people in this part of Cyprus have managed their lives. For example, through the examination of pottery, statuary, flaked stone, and millstones, as well as sacred architecture and tombs, we get a sense of how past people in the region utilized the available resources to address immediate needs for subsistence, tool production, and shelter, and to express their individual and collective identities through ritual activities such as votive deposition and interment. From this collection of studies we also obtain an understanding of how the past residents of the valley were tied to this place. We do not suggest that our investigations have provided a final, definitive picture of life in central Cyprus in the past, but the evidence at hand does indicate some strong trends. Perhaps most significantly, the data presented here support the broader theme of negotiation — that

355

is, the active participation of the residents in shaping and reshaping the particular circumstances of life, at times in a proactive fashion, and in some periods as a reaction to other events. Through their individual studies, the contributors show how this decision-making process occurred at a variety of levels over time.

To demonstrate more clearly how the individual chapters reflect the general approaches laid out in Chapter 1, we outline some of the themes that run through the volume. Cultural processes lead to material products, the residue of which constitutes the archaeological record; that material reflects human behavior that it is the goal of archaeology to reconstruct, given its fragmentary nature. We see several distinct themes that stem from this fundamental precept. First is that our work reveals multiple tiers of interaction. At the local level, we examine things that are restricted in distribution. Within the confines of the sites we identified, we attempt to determine what the proximity of artifacts and features means in terms of human action both at one time and over a period of years. In the excavated material, a key concern is what the spread of material tells us about site function. The system for recording provenience in the excavation (Ch. 6) provides the necessary context for determining key spatial relationships and is the basis for interpreting particular activities, from ritual events (dedications of votive items such as inscribed objects [Ch. 13], terracotta figurines [Ch. 10], limestone statuary [Chs. 11, 12]); burials (Chs. 19, 20), subsistence activities (placement of millstones [Ch. 17] and faunal remains [Ch. 18]), to craft activities (production of textiles [Chs. 16, 20], and manufacture of stone tools [Chs. 8, 26]). Some objects clearly served both ritual and more utilitarian functions; these materials include pottery from the sanctuary (Ch. 9) and lamps from the tombs (Ch. 14), and their distribution is also critical to piecing together the chronology of the Malloura site. Several of the chapters deal explicitly with the issue of intra-site and inter-site distribution in an attempt to explain human presence and activity. Chapters 21, 23, and 24 present data from a suite of techniques (geophysics, GIS, and soil analysis, respectively) to determine both the presence of

certain features and the loci of specialized activities at the Malloura sanctuary. The archaeological survey (Ch. 7) identified a number of sites in the valley; analysis of the pottery from those sites (Ch. 15) demonstrates where people were at what times, with a distinctly nucleated pattern of settlement in most periods. GIS analysis of the survey data (Ch. 22) suggests how the sites related to one another (e.g., hilltop posts served as lookouts for the small residential areas in the valley).

The second tier of interaction is regional in scale and bears witness to Malloura's role within local systems of exchange, extending north and east of Athienou into the Mesaoria proper, west to Dhali/*Idalion*, and south to Larnaka/*Kition*, Pyla and the coast. Our primary concern here is how Malloura fit into the political, economic, and religious networks of the area. Several chapters pursue this theme to varying degrees. For example, Chapters 9 and 11 both seek to place Malloura within the socio-political framework of the Iron age city-kingdoms in the Cypro-Geometric, Cypro-Archaic, and Cypro-Classical periods through its relationship to the ancient city of Golgoi (itself an important regional town). Evidence from a variety of artifact types (including sculpture [Chs. 10, 11], inscriptions [Ch. 13], and pottery [Ch. 9]), but also evidence for ritual activities [Chs. 6, 12], situates Malloura more directly within a circuit of exchange during the Cypro-Archaic, Cypro-Classical and Hellenistic periods that included not only Golgoi, but also the city-kingdom of Idalion to the west. Widening this view, therefore, it is reasonable to assume that the fate of both Athienou-*Malloura* and Golgoi mirrored that of Idalion in the middle of the fifth century BC, with all three sites enveloped by the northern expansion of Kition. While such conclusions are necessarily speculative at this stage, our evidence does suggest that Malloura was a periphery on the border between several competing mini-states. The nature of the material from the valley betrays a complex mixing of styles and types at various times that indicates how residents negotiated various facets of their culture not only by adopting and adapting outside influences selectively, but also transforming these forces into uniquely local products.

A third tier of interaction witnesses Malloura's repeated incorporation into various larger and much more expansive Mediterranean systems. As early as the Cypro-Archaic and Cypro-Classical periods, evidence from the sanctuary reveals direct links to east Greece and the Levant (Chs. 9, 10, 11); by the Hellenistic period, however, evidence for imported pottery (including a stamped Rhodian amphora handle [Ch. 13]) and images related to the Greek god Pan (Ch. 12) place the site squarely within the cultural milieu of the Hellenistic kingdoms of the eastern Mediterranean. Pottery from the survey (Ch. 15) and lamps from the tombs (Ch. 14) include Cypriot versions of well-known Roman wares but also imports from elsewhere in the Mediterranean, demonstrating that the rings of exchange reached across the island and well beyond. Likewise, through both excavation and survey we have uncovered Malloura's distant but nonetheless documented life in the midst of historical watersheds such as the reign of Constantine and the spread of Christianity, the expansion of the Byzantine world and its clash with Islam, the Crusades, as well as Venetian hegemony in the Mediterranean and the eventual conflict with the Ottoman empire. The transfer of Cyprus from Ottoman to British control in the 19th century reflects the continuing incorporation of Cyprus into imperial systems. The political and economic links with the broader Mediterranean world have persisted and in many ways grown since independence in 1960. The admission of Cyprus into the European Union is the most recent manifestation of the long-term process of globalization — just another term for incorporation into a world-system — that the island has experienced since at least the Bronze Age.

A second major theme, and linked to the first, deals with the movement of people. Because our project area is an interior valley, we are interested in the relationship between coastal and inland zones and communication between the two. The Malloura Valley can also be considered a transitional space between the Mesaoria (and the mountains to the west) and the sea, not only in terms of its location, but also its climate, geology, and physical topography (Ch. 2). The survey revealed limited use of the valley in the prehistoric period, and then only for extraction of chert in the Neolithic (Ch. 8). Beginning in the Cypro-Geometric, and then much more so in the Cypro-Archaic period, the pace of cultural activity in the valley increased substantially (Chs. 3, 6, 7). From where these initial inhabitants came is a question we cannot answer at present. However, as noted above, the presence of both imported goods, such as pottery, and of styles seen on objects, such as statuary, indicate that the residents of the valley maintained strong connections with neighboring regions and areas outside the island. We also assume that some of the agricultural crops grown and processed in the valley were transported to other parts of the island, especially in the later periods where evidence of industrial activity in the valley is clear (Chs. 16, 17, 20). In the 19th century, Athienou was known for its muleteers who transported materials throughout Cyprus, and a caravanserai built ca. 1900 hosted traveling merchants regularly (Ch. 5); we suspect that this pattern goes back at least to the late medieval period, given the quantity and variety of material from that period found in the valley (Chs. 6, 15).

A third theme deals with archaeology as a contemporary enterprise. There are two concerns in this respect. The first is a general one that all archaeologists confront — the responsibility to preserve the material that they uncover in the process of conducting field work. It is axiomatic by now to acknowledge the necessity to conserve individual objects that are brought in for analysis and storage, and to stabilize and properly protect the various features that remain in the field. AAP's approach to some of these issues was outlined in Chapter 25 and includes both steps taken to preserve exposed, above-ground remains, but also to prevent further damage from the environment. A second concern is to understand how our project fits into the local community. We explore this element as both a historical phenomenon of the last 150 years, with the discussion of the early archaeological work in the area around Athienou (Ch. 4), and as a current matter that entails many kinds of interactions between the local residents and project personnel (Ch. 27). What has emerged is a sense that despite the long and eventful history of archaeological work in the area, our project remains quite unique both for the longevity of our stay, and for the level of integration into the fabric of the local community.

A final theme that is at least implicit in some of the chapters and explicit in others is the presence of gaps in the material record for our project area during certain chronological phases. Some of these gaps are consistent with lacunae found in other parts of Cyprus, while some are seemingly local phenomena. Our initial gap, of the latter type, is the largest, from the Aceramic Neolithic to the Cypro-Geometric (i.e., 5000+ years). The Malloura Valley has yielded no evidence of later Neolithic, Chalcolithic, or Bronze Age occupation (and even the Cypro-Geometric material is very limited), despite the presence of important prehistoric sites in the surrounding region (Ch. 3). World-systems analysis is helpful in explaining this hiatus by suggesting the Malloura Valley was an extraction zone rather than a residential zone in those periods. As an extraction zone, the Malloura Valley has provided stone (chert, limestone, gypsum) for various purposes, pasturage for domesticated animals, and arable land for food crops while the people who exploited these resources resided elsewhere in many periods (Ch. 7).

The second major gap, from the middle of the seventh century AD to sometime in the 14th century, is one that other projects on Cyprus have noted (especially the first half of that time stretch). It seems that the valley resorted to the status of an extraction zone following substantial use from the Cypro-Archaic to Early Byzantine eras; from the seventh to the ninth centuries, the abandonment seems to have been complete, perhaps without even the peripheral use as an extraction zone. A gap of a somewhat different kind is the lack of a recognized settlement in the valley during the long period (Cypro-Archaic to Hellenistic) when the sanctuary was in operation and the residents interred many people in the tombs with substantial offerings. We hope to address this latter problem in the future, perhaps by means of systematic coring to see if there is a hitherto undetected, buried settlement that corresponds temporally with the sanctuary and the many tombs in the valley.

What we strive for is a holistic archaeology, one that considers the multiple facets of an investigation. This volume represents a step in that direction by providing an up-to-date, comprehensive view of our investigations from the perspective of specialist studies. While many chapters might be read as interim or even preliminary reports, each contributor has also sought to place the analysis and presentation of data into a proper context from which some broader conclusions have been drawn. Still, *Crossroads and Boundaries* is not meant to be a stopping point; individual authors and the project itself recognize the importance of continued work and the possibility of revising our thinking as more data become available. Thus the book serves as a precursor to a more synthetic, final publication of the site. In pursuit of that goal, we plan a series of final reports that will follow the present publication. Individual volumes will deal with four major topics: the survey, the sanctuary, the settlement, and the tombs. Each of these subsequent books will build on and expand the treatment of the respective material presented in this volume. While the contributors to those future volumes will provide more detailed descriptions of the material, and some may come up with alternative interpretations to some specific questions, a central theme will again be a focus on individuals deciding and acting in a social matrix laid over the physical environment.

About the Editors

MICHAEL K. TOUMAZOU, a native of Cyprus, is Director of the Athienou Archaeological Project and Professor and former chair of Classics at Davidson College. He received his B.A. in physics and classics from Franklin and Marshall College, a M.A. in classics from Loyola University of Chicago, and a M.A. and Ph.D. in classical and near eastern archaeology from Bryn Mawr College. His publications include articles in *Old World Archaeology Newsletter, Journal of Field Archaeology, Annual Report to the Department of Antiquities, Cyprus, Cahier du Centre d'Études Chypriotes*, and translations of several works from Greek to English. Toumazou's research, which has been funded by grants from Dumbarton Oaks, the National Endowment for the Humanities, and the National Science Foundation, centers on the history and prehistory of Cyprus, Greece, and the Levant, mortuary practices, and ancient Greek art. In 2003, he was awarded Davidson College's prestigious Hunter-Hamilton Love of Teaching Award for excellence in teaching.

P. NICK KARDULIAS is Associate Director of the Athienou Archaeological Project and Professor of Anthropology and Archaeology at the College of Wooster (Ohio). He also serves as lithic analyst for the Eastern Korinthia Archaeological Survey in Greece and Co-Director of the Ashland/Wooster/Columbus Archaeological and Geological Consortium. He received his B.A. (anthropology and history) and a M.A. (history) from Youngstown State University, a M.A. (anthropology) from SUNY-Binghamton, and a Ph.D. in anthropology from the Ohio State University. He has edited four books and authored a monograph, *From Classical to Byzantine: Social Evolution in Late Antiquity and the Fortress at Isthmia, Greece* (2005). He has written more than 40 articles in edited collections and professional journals. His research interests include the archaeology and ethnography of the Mediterranean region, the archaeology of North America, world-systems theory, and stone tools in historic and prehistoric periods. Kardulias serves as first Vice President of the Central States Anthropological Society and President of the Oberlin-Wooster Chapter of the Archeological Institute of America (AIA). In 2002, he received the AIA National Award for Excellence in Undergraduate Teaching. He serves on the editorial boards of *Ethnoarchaeology* and *Reviews in Anthropology*.

DEREK B. COUNTS is Associate Director of the Athienou Archaeological Project and Associate Professor of Classical Art and Archaeology in the Department of Art History at the University of Wisconsin-Milwaukee. He received his Ph.D. in old world archaeology and art from Brown University; he holds additional degrees in classics from Davidson College (A.B.) and the University of Georgia (M.A.). He recently published two co-edited volumes: *Koine: Mediterranean Studies in Honor of R. Ross Holloway* (Oxbow Books: Oxford, 2009) and *The Master of Animals in Old World Iconography* (Archaeolingua: Budapest, 2010). He has published extensively on the archaeology of Iron Age Cyprus, with a particular emphasis on Cypriot religion, as well as limestone votive sculpture and its associated iconography. His current research explores divine representation in Cypriot sanctuaries; he is preparing a monograph (for *Monographs in Mediterranean Archaeology*, Equinox) that explores the intersection of cult and cultural identity in the formation of communities using a broad theoretical model largely informed by postcolonial critiques of culture contact. Counts serves on the editorial boards of the *Bulletin of the American Schools of Oriental Research* and the *Cahier du Centre d'Études Chypriotes*; he also serves as Co-Editor of Book Reviews for the *American Journal of Archaeology*.

List of Contributors

ERIN WALCEK AVERETT is Resident Assistant Professor of Art History in the Department of Fine and Performing Arts at Creighton University. She earned her Ph.D. in classical archaeology at the University of Missouri-Columbia in the Department of Art History and Archaeology in 2007. Her research interests include the art and archaeology of Geometric and Archaic Greece and Cyprus, Greek and Cypriot religion and cult, and constructions of gender in the ancient Mediterranean. She is the Assistant Director of the Athienou Archaeological Project (after first joining the project in 1997 as an NSF-REU recipient) and is currently working on the final publication of the coroplastic dedications from the sanctuary. Averett was the Brunilde Ridgway and the Homer and Dorothy Thompson fellow of the American School of Classical Studies at Athens from 2002–2004.

RUTH F. BEESTON is Professor of Chemistry at Davidson College, where she has taught advanced laboratory methods, general chemistry, and courses on the interface between chemistry, art, and archaeology since 1984. She has a B.S. in chemistry from Bucknell University and a Ph.D. in inorganic chemistry from the University of North Carolina at Chapel Hill. Her association with the Athienou Archaeological Project and her research interests in anthrosol analysis and organic residue analysis of pottery have been ongoing since 1999. Her other research interests and professional activities include synthetic chemistry and educational outreach activities, seminars, and workshops for public school K–12 teachers.

NICHOLAS G. BLACKWELL received his Ph.D. in Classical and Near Eastern Archaeology in 2011 from Bryn Mawr College with a dissertation titled "Middle and Late Bronze Age Metal Tools from the Aegean, Eastern Mediterranean, and Anatolia: Im-plications for Cultural/Regional Interaction and Craftsmanship." He has worked on the Athienou Archaeological Project since 2000, and has served in various capacities, including the Basic Field School Director, for the Mitrou Archaeological Project in Greece. Currently, he is pursuing postdoctoral research on 1) the tool marks (e.g., drill holes and saw cuts) on the Mycenae Lion Gate relief, as a recipient of the Archaeological Institute of America's Harriet and Leon Pomerance Fellowship, and on 2) Levantine metallurgy and metal implements, as an Educational and Cultural Affairs (ECA) Junior Research Fellow at the W. F. Albright Institute of Archaeological Research in Jerusalem.

MARGARET D. BREUKER is currently Objects Conservator for the Collections Conservation Branch, Northeast Museum Services Center, National Park Service, and a Professional Associate of the American Institute for Conservation of Historic and Artistic Works (AIC). Breuker earned a M.S. in architectural conservation from Columbia University in 1999, where her main focus concerned archaeological site conservation. As a Samuel H. Kress Conservation Research Fellow at the Laboratory of Applied Microbial Ecology at Harvard University, Breuker conducted research on the biodeterioration of calcareous stone. She has been the Site and Objects Conservator for the Athienou Archaeological Project in Cyprus since 1992.

REMKO BREUKER is Principal of Breuker Design in Manchester, Massachusetts. Prior to earning a postgraduate degree in architecture from the University of British Columbia, Vancouver, in 1994, Breuker studied classical archaeology and conducted archaeological fieldwork in Greece, Serbia, and the United Kingdom. In addition to recording, interpreting, and researching architectural evidence, other interests include site design and management for preservation and cultural tourism. Breuker has been the Site Architect of the Athienou Archaeological Project since 1992.

CLAY M. COFER is Assistant Director of the Athienou Archaeological Project; he first joined AAP as a Field School student and an NSF-REU recipient in 1997 and in subsequent years served as a trench supervisor. He graduated from Davidson College with an A.B. in classics. He is currently A.B.D. at Bryn Mawr College in the Classical and Near Eastern Archaeology Department. He completed his M.A. in 2001 at Bryn Mawr with a thesis on the Cypriot manifestation of the Greek god Pan in Cyprus, which featured a study and catalogue of the relief statuettes of Pan from Athienou-*Malloura*. Cofer was a student member of the American School of Classical Studies in Athens in 2004–2005 and served as a Samuel H. Kress Fellow in 2005–2006.

ELISABETTA COVA is Assistant Professor of Classics in the Department of Foreign Languages and Literature at the University of Wisconsin-Milwaukee. She graduated in *Lettere Classiche* from the University of Bologna (Italy) and received her M.Phil. in archaeology at the University of Cambridge (United Kingdom). Her research interests include Roman Cyprus, Roman domestic architecture, and the archaeology of Pompeii and the Bay of Naples; she also maintains an interest in museum studies. She is a senior staff member of Athienou Archaeological Project and is charged with the publication of the Late Roman/ Early Byzantine settlement as well as the corpus of inscriptions excavated by the project. She currently serves as Co-Editor of Book Review for the *American Journal of Archaeology.*

MERCEDES A. DEMASI is an undergraduate student at Western Connecticut State University pursuing a degree in cultural anthropology. She was a student participant in the Athienou Archaeological Project's summer 2007 field season and has also worked for a cultural resource management firm in New England. Her research interests include domestic and economic archaeology, symbolism, conflict studies, and popular culture.

SABINE FOURRIER is a Research Fellow at the Centre National de la Recherche Scientifique in Lyon. She received her Ph.D. from the University of Lyon in 1999. She previously served as Director of the French Archaeological Mission at Amathous; since 2008, she has been Director of the French Archaeological Mission of Kition and Salamis. She is a former member of the Ecole Normale Supérieure and the French Archaeological School at Athens. Her research interests include the history and archaeology of Cyprus in the Iron Age, particularly the study of Cypriote ceramic and coroplastic productions. Recent publications include *La coroplastie chypriote archaïque: Identités culturelles et politiques à l'époque des royaumes* (Lyon: Maison de l'Orient et de la Méditerranée, 2007) and *Amathonte VI: Le sanctuaire d'Aphrodite des origines au début de l'époque impérial* (Athens: Ecole française d'Athènes, 2006), with Antoine Hermary.

JODY MICHAEL GORDON is Assistant Director of the Athienou Archaeological Project and is currently a Ph.D. candidate in classical archaeology at the University of Cincinnati. His dissertation involves a study of the effect of the Ptolemaic and Roman empires on the construction of local identities in ancient Cyprus. Aside from his work with the Athienou Archaeological Project, Jody has also worked with the Nissi Beach pre-Aceramic Neolithic excavations, was a resident at CAARI in Nicosia, and was Site Director of the 2008 Roman area excavations at Episkopi-*Bamboula*. Previous archaeological work includes Tunisia (Leptiminus), Greece (Pylos; Athenian Agora), and Italy (Monte Polizzo; American Academy in Rome). During 2008–2009, he served as the Crake Doctoral Fellow in Classical Studies at Mount Allison University, and in the spring of 2009 he was awarded the Danielle Parks Memorial Fellowship to pursue his doctoral research at CAARI.

TIMOTHY E. GREGORY is Professor of History at the Ohio State University. Gregory's areas of specialization are Byzantine history and classical archaeology. He is currently Director of the Ohio State University Excavations at Isthmia and served as the Codirector of the Eastern Korinthia Archaeological Survey. Gregory's primary interest is the use of archaeological evidence for historical reconstruction. He is working on a landscape approach to the history of the eastern Mediterranean area, especially in late antiquity and the Middle Ages. His publications include books and articles on the archaeology of Greece and the history of early Christianity. He teaches courses on classical archaeology and Byzantine history.

NATHAN K. HARPER is completing his Ph.D. in the Department of Anthropology at the University of Nevada, Las Vegas. He has conducted museum and fieldwork in Cyprus, Mexico, Greece, Jordan, and at the National Museum of Natural History in Washington D.C. and the American Museum of Natural History in New York. His published research has appeared in the *Report of the Department of Antiquities, Cyprus* and *Near Eastern Archaeology*. His dissertation investigates the phenomenon of intermarriage between migrants and local communities in Late Bronze Age Cyprus.

JAMES A. JOHNSON received his M.S. in anthropology from the University of Wisconsin-Milwaukee and is a doctoral candidate in the Department of Anthropology at the University of Pittsburgh. He has worked with the Athienou Archaeological Project since 2004. His primary research interests include ritual, performance, community, identity, spatial analysis, and Geographical Information Systems (GIS) applications in anthropology. He is currently finishing his dissertation, which is a spatial analysis of diachronic changes to community organization and demography in Bronze Age southern Russia.

DAVID P. MASSEY began working with the Athienou Archaeological Project in 2002 as an undergraduate Field School student. He received his B.A. in archaeology from the College of Wooster and is currently a graduate student in the Department of Geography at the Ohio State University. His research interests include GIScience, emergence, participatory modeling, crowdsourcing, visualiz-

ing spatio-temporal data, and modeling human–environmental interactions.

R. SCOTT MOORE is Professor of History at Indiana University of Pennsylvania and teaches courses on ancient Greek, Roman, Byzantine, and medieval history. His research focuses on trade and communication in the eastern Mediterranean from the Hellenistic period through the end of the Late Roman period. Moore has participated in archeological projects in Cyprus and Greece and is the Codirector of the Pyla-Koutsopetria Archaeological Project (PKAP). This is a diachronic, intensive archaeological investigation of the region around the modern village of Pyla, Cyprus, along the southern coast to the east of the city of Larnaka.

JOSEPH A. PARVIS holds a M.A. in anthropology and history from the University of Michigan. He worked with the Athienou Archaeological Project from 1990 through 1999, serving as volunteer, Area Supervisor, and Assistant Field Director. During the course of his time in Athienou, he lectured in medieval and modern history for the AAP Field School (1998–1999) and also worked as liaison with local municipal and community authorities in the initial development of the Athienou Archaeological Park at the Athienou-*Malloura* site. In 1996–1997 he was awarded a Fulbright scholarship and worked with the Leventis Municipal Museum of Nicosia in the initial digitization of their photographic archive.

DAVID S. REESE has an A.B. in anthropology from Harvard College and a Ph.D. in archaeology from the University of Cambridge (England). He has studied the animal bones and shells from numerous excavations in the Mediterranean basin and Near East, including remains from many sites on Cyprus. His particular research interests are the extinct Pleistocene animals of Mediterranean islands, Neolithic and Bronze Age faunas from the Mediterranean, the trade of organic remains, the analysis of archaeological shells, and sacrificed fauna from circum-Mediterranean religious sites. For 16 years he worked out of the Field Museum in Chicago. During the past 10 years he has been with the Peabody Museum of Natural History at Yale University.

Apostolos Sarris is Director of Research of the Laboratory of Geophysical and Satellite Remote Sensing and Archaeo-environment at the Institute for Mediterranean Studies-FORTH and a contracted Lecturer of Archaeometry at the Aristotelian University of Thessaloniki. He received a B.A. in astronomy and physics (1985) and a M.A. in physics (1988) from Boston University and subsequently earned a M.S. (1990) and a Ph.D. in physics (1992) from the University of Nebraska-Lincoln. He has organized, planned, and participated in more than 110 geophysical/satellite remote sensing/GIS/GPS projects in various parts of the world and organized and/or participated in more than 50 Greek and international large-scale projects. He is an Associate Editor of the *Society for Archaeological Sciences Bulletin* and *Archaeological Prospection*. He has been an Assistant Greek Representative in the scientific committee for Peace and Security of NATO and since 2007 and is a Vice-Chair of the International Society for Archaeological Prospection (ISAP).

Matthew Spigelman is Assistant Director of the Athienou Archaeological Project. He began working with AAP as a Field School student in 2002, returning in subsequent summers as a trench supervisor and ceramic analyst. He received his B.A. from Haverford College and is currently a graduate student in the Department of Anthropology at New York University, researching his Ph.D. dissertation on the production and exchange of Cypriote Red-on-Black–style ceramics during the Middle Bronze Age. The final version of this chapter was prepared while in residence at CAARI as a 2009–2010 Fulbright fellow.

Tiffiny A. Tung is Associate Professor of Anthropology at Vanderbilt University. She is an anthropological bioarchaeologist, and her main research investigates how ancient forms of imperialism affect community health status, lived experience, and the prevalence of warfare and other forms of violence. She examines these issues primarily in the context of the Peruvian Andes, where she studies the impact of Wari imperial rule (AD 600–1000), findings published in her book, "Violence, Ritual, and the Wari Empire: A Social Bioarchaeology of Imperialism in the Ancient Andes" (Univ. Press of Florida). She has also conducted bioarchaeological research in the Mediterranean, North America, and Europe.

Richard W. Yerkes, Professor of Anthropology at Ohio State University, received his B.A. from Beloit College and his M.A. and Ph.D. in anthropology from the University of Wisconsin-Madison. He has been involved in archaeological research in Cyprus, Egypt, Greece, Hungary, Israel, and the United States for more than 30 years, with major grants from the National Science Foundation and Wenner-Gren. He has authored more than 60 publications on the transition to food production, ancient land use and settlement patterns, lithic artifact analysis and microwear, craft specialization and social complexity, GIS applications in archaeology, and zooarchaeology. He has directed or codirected several multidisciplinary field schools in the United States, Cyprus, and Hungary. He is Codirector of the Körös Regional Archaeological Project, southeastern Hungary, with William A. Parkinson and Attila Gyucha.

Index

chipped stone blades (*see* lithics)

chlamys 167

Christian(-ity) 33–36, 50, 77, 82–83, 191, 200, 230, 249–50, 255, 281, 357, 363

chronology xix, xxiii, 25–39, 95–99, 109, 149, 151, 164–66, 173, 185, 191, 199–200, 209, 227, 285, 293, 320, 330, 356

    Aceramic Neolithic xviii, xxiii, 13, 26–27, 88–89, 91, 96, 107–11, 113, 116, 288, 358, 362

    Akrotiri Phase xxiii, 25–26

    Archaic (*see* Cypro-Archaic)

    Bronze Age xvii, 1, 7, 15, 27–29, 50, 55, 87, 96, 100, 136, 187, 192, 219–20, 222, 230, 238, 329, 333, 357–58

    Byzantine xxiii, 19–20, 33–36, 69, 71, 80, 82, 84, 89, 93, 97, 101, 113, 206, 221, 228, 235, 254, 260, 286, 332, 357–58

    Ceramic Neolithic xxiii, 15, 89, 116

    Chalcolithic xxiii, 27–28, 89, 96, 113, 116, 118, 251, 329, 331, 333, 358

    Classical (*see* Cypro-Classical)

    Cretaceous 14–15

    Cypro-Archaic xxiii, 20, 28–31, 39, 50, 55, 67, 71, 76–77, 79, 83–84, 89, 95–98, 100, 126–31, 135–43, 151, 158–60, 179, 181, 183–84, 187, 204–6, 215, 220, 235–36, 249, 254, 285, 293, 295, 300, 308, 356–58

    Cypro-Classical xxiii, 30–33, 50, 55, 76–77, 79, 83, 96–98, 101, 114, 126–28, 130, 135, 140–43, 160, 173–74, 181–82, 187, 204–6, 211, 235, 249, 254, 295, 300, 356–57

    Cypro-Geometric xviii, xxiii, 28–29, 71, 75–76, 96, 100, 126–27, 129–31, 139, 151, 179, 187, 230, 233, 235, 269–70, 288, 291, 293, 352, 356–58

    Early Cypriot xxiii, 27, 173, 238, 248

    Early Modern 55–64, 205, 210–11, 215

    Epipaleolithic 25, 109

    Frankish xxiii, 35–38, 56, 59, 69, 81–84, 97, 208, 215, 229–31, 248, 272, 288, 334

    Geometric (*see* Cypro-Geometric)

    Hellenistic xix, xxiii, 18, 20, 32–33, 50, 71, 74–80, 83–84, 95–98, 114, 126–27, 130–31, 136, 142–43, 151–52, 163, 173–75, 179, 181, 184–85, 187, 191–97, 199–200, 204–6, 227, 229, 233–35, 237–42, 247–49, 253–55, 277, 288, 293, 295, 300, 309, 356–58

    Iron Age xviii, 3, 7, 20, 50–51, 55, 69, 96, 125–31, 139, 142, 179, 187, 235, 237–40, 248, 356

    Khirokitian stage 89, 107, 110–11, 116

    Late Antiquity 77

    Late Cypriot xxiii, 27, 127, 141, 235, 248, 292

    Late Medieval xviii, xix, 80, 93, 97, 99–101, 208–9, 211, 230, 286, 288, 357

    Late Roman 19, 96–98, 113, 166, 187, 192, 200, 207–8, 211, 220, 228, 233, 235, 249, 286, 332

    Medieval xviii, 4, 8, 19, 36, 38, 56, 90–91, 98, 204–5, 208–11, 215, 217, 219–20, 222, 226, 230, 249, 259, 265, 281, 285–86, 309, 322–27, 332, 334, 357

    Middle Cypriot xxiii, 220, 248

    Miocene 1, 13–14, 17

    Ottoman xxiii, 18, 20–21, 37–39, 56, 59–61, 63, 71, 81–82, 84, 91, 97, 99, 100, 113, 208–10, 215, 217, 221–22, 227, 229–31, 259, 263–64, 286, 307, 323, 332, 357

    Palaeolithic 108

    Pleistocene 14, 21, 109

    Pre-Pottery Neolithic B (PPNB) 26, 110, 217

    Prehistoric xxiii, 1, 2, 6, 18, 20, 25–27, 29, 55, 69, 88, 95–98, 100–101, 108, 112–13, 151, 217, 285, 292, 329, 332–33, 357–58

    Roman xviii–xix, xxiii, 18–19, 32–35, 39, 48, 50, 55–57, 69, 71, 75–76, 79–80, 83, 90, 93, 95–101, 11314, 126, 130, 142, 152, 166, 173, 179, 181, 184, 187, 191–201, 204–8, 211, 220, 225–31, 233, 235, 237–39, 247–49, 251, 253–55, 269–70, 277, 285–86, 288, 291, 293, 307, 322–27, 332–34, 352

    Venetian xvii, xix, xxiii, 18, 20–21, 35–39, 56–59, 68, 71, 80–84, 95, 97–99, 101, 113, 187, 208–10, 215–22, 225, 227, 229–31, 233, 235, 239, 247–56, 259–60, 264–65, 272, 278, 323–24, 357

church (*see also* Archangelos, church of; Christian(it)y; religion)

    Byzantine 82

    of Cyprus 34

    Latin 36

    Orthodox 33

Chytroi 28, 55, 141, 151, 248

cippus(i) 248

cist grave (*see* burial)

cistern (*see* burial; water)

Classical (*see* chronology)

climate xvii–xviii, 3, 15, 18–19, 218, 221–22, 344, 357

    drought 19

    precipitation 18

    temperature, local 18, 218, 221, 271, 273, 276, 303, 306

coarse ware (*see* pottery)

cognitive approach (*see* theory)

coin(s) xv, xviii, 31–34, 77, 79, 81–82, 91, 97–98, 160, 173–74, 185, 211, 220, 249, 279

    solidus(i) 82

collegia 248

Colonna-Ceccaldi, G. 49, 68, 165

Color-Coated Ware (*see* pottery)

Columella 227

Comocio, G. 56, 59

conical cap/helmet (*see* attribute)

conservation xv, xix, 47, 313–20 (*see also* Burra Charter)

    acid dissolution 305, 317

    bacteria 303, 315

    biofilm 317

Conservation Site Plan 313

Constantine 19, 357

Constantinople 33, 36, 82, 84

cooking ware (*see* pottery)

core/periphery (*see* periphery)

core states 4, 6

cornucopia/horn of abundance (*see* attribute)

Coronelli, V. 59

coroplastic 135, 142